MULTICULTURALISM IN THE UNITED STATES

A Comparative Guide to Acculturation and Ethnicity

Revised and Expanded Edition

**Edited by
John D. Buenker and Lorman A. Ratner**

GREENWOOD PRESS
Westport, Connecticut • London

Library of Congress Cataloging-in-Publication Data

Multiculturalism in the United States : a comparative guide to acculturation
and ethnicity / edited by John D. Buenker and Lorman A. Ratner.—Rev. and
expanded ed.
     p.   cm.
   Includes bibliographical references and index.
   ISBN 0–313–32404–2 (alk. paper)
  1. Minorities—United States.   2. Multiculturalism—United States.
3. Pluralism (Social sciences)—United States.   4. Acculturation—United
States.   5. Ethnicity—United States.   6. United States—Ethnic relations.
7. United States—Race relations.   I. Buenker, John D.   II. Ratner, Lorman.
   E184.A1M85   2005
    305.8'00973—dc22   2004022473

British Library Cataloguing in Publication Data is available.

Library of Congress Catalog Card Number: 2004022473
ISBN: 0–313–32404–2

First published in 2005

Greenwood Press, 88 Post Road West, Westport, CT 06881
An imprint of Greenwood Publishing Group, Inc.
www.greenwood.com

Printed in the United States of America

The paper used in this book complies with the
Permanent Paper Standard issued by the National
Information Standards Organization (Z39.48–1984).

10 9 8 7 6 5 4 3 2 1

In memory of Matt S. Meier, 1917–2003.
A true pioneer of the multicultural borderlands.

During the course of producing this volume, we lost a great soul. Matt Meier expired on August 11, 2003, at age eighty-six, after a long and courageous battle with leukemia. Those who knew Matt will not be surprised to know that one of his greatest concerns was to finish the essay on Mexican Americans that graces this volume before he succumbed to the inevitable. We would even like to think that his determination to finish his work kept him going a while longer. Like the whole of his life, the last few months were an exemplar of dedication, courage, and integrity. We are especially grateful to Matt's son, Professor G. Patrick Meier of Washington State University, and his colleague Professor Nancy C. Unger of the Santa Clara University history department, for their help in making sure that the final version of Matt's essay was worthy of its author. We respectfully dedicate this book to Matt Meier, who was the personification of multiculturalism.

CONTENTS

ACKNOWLEDGMENTS

We are grateful to Cynthia Harris at Greenwood Press for encouraging us to take on the challenges that come with undertaking a project with many contributors. Sarah Colwell at Greenwood Press has kept the appropriate amount of pressure on us to see this project through to completion.

We thank Dianne Vecchio and James Bergquist for suggesting possible authors of essays to be added to this expanded edition.

We are especially grateful to our spouses, Paula Kaufman and Beverly Kastman Buenker for their encouragement and for their editorial assistance. Paula's computer skills have been essential to the completion of the manuscript.

Finally, we thank all those in the growing community of ethnic studies scholarship whose acceptance of our first effort to put all this together led us to believe a new, expanded volume would be useful.

INTRODUCTION

John D. Buenker and Lorman A. Ratner

In the twelve years since the publication of the first edition of *Multiculturalism in the United States*, interest in ethnic studies has grown exponentially. Awareness of the variety and complexity of reasons motivating individual and group migration in and to the United States has been heightened tremendously, as has our understanding of the forces governing interaction among ethnic groups and with the host society. The perspectives gained from intensive study of more established ethnic groups have better prepared us to appreciate the similarities and differences between their experiences and those of more recent arrivals from Asia, Latin America, the Caribbean, the Middle East, and Africa. It is for that reason we decided to edit an updated and expanded second edition.

Readers will find essays on seven ethnic groups not included in the first edition: Arab Americans, Asian Indian Americans, and Dominican Americans, Filipino Americans, Haitian Americans, Korean Americans, Vietnamese Americans. In addition, there are totally new essays—by different authors—on three groups covered in the first edition: Irish Americans, Chinese Americans, and Mexican Americans. Moreover, the authors of the essays on African Americans, American Indians, German Americans, Italian Americans, Jewish Americans, Polish Americans, and Scandinavian Americans have substantially revised and updated their contributions from the first edition.

The authors of the chapters in this volume have provided all manner of fact and reflection regarding the complex question of how American culture—by which we mean a widely accepted collection of values, attitudes, institutions, and beliefs—was shaped from the cultures of Europe, much of Asia, Africa, pre-Columbian America, and, in more recent times, Latin America. The contributions to American culture by people of these diverse origins, which, taken individually, reflect differences dependent on class, occupation, and religion, are duly noted. So, too, are the conflicts and tensions between the traditions of newly arrived immigrants and what came to be mainstream American culture. Finally, the contributors note the changes over time both of the cultures brought to America and of the culture that received them.

In order to enhance the value of this work as a comparative handbook or reference tool, each author has addressed a number of common topics that helped determine the pace and degree of acculturation for every ethnic group. What kind of voluntary self-help institutions served as conduits between the ethnic group and mainstream culture? What was the impact of the modernizing forces in mainstream America on group identity and culture? What strategies, political and socioeconomic, were developed by each group to gain tangible benefits, recognition, and protection of its cultural heritage? What internal divisions arose over those who wished to become Americanized and those who wished to remain traditionalists, and how did these conflicts affect acculturation? What effect did residential and social mobility and exogamous marriage patterns have on group cohesion? What role did formal education play in the acculturation process, and to what extent did it contribute to intergenerational conflict and estrangement? Was the group's adaptation a straight path toward acculturation, or did it ebb and flow over time and across generations? How did the group respond to the efforts of mainstream "Americanizers?" What strategies did the group develop for language maintenance and religious orthodoxy? In short, what were the specific variables that determined the course and velocity of each group's adaptation to American life?

At the same time, however, the authors were instructed that our list was meant to be suggestive, not prescriptive. They were free to organize their chapters in whatever manner seemed most appropriate, to stress the themes that each deemed more significant, and to incorporate whatever additional themes or dimensions seemed appropriate. Generally speaking, our goal was to produce chapters that addressed universal questions in a framework that permitted each scholar sufficient latitude in which to present the unique perspective gained from specializing in the history and culture of a specific ethnic group.

A glance at the table of contents might prompt the reader to question why certain cultural groups are omitted or combined in a single essay. From the outset, we recognized that any attempt or claim to be comprehensive in our coverage was foredoomed to failure and frustration and would lay us open to justifiable criticism from scholars and from ethnic groups that felt unfairly neglected. Our major goal was to provide a sample of ethnic groups large enough to be reasonably representative of the various waves of settlement that have, over time, populated the United States and from which we could make valid generalizations concerning patterns of acculturation and adaptation. We also wanted a sample that would provide a meaningful comparison between the experiences of European-derived ethnic groups and those from Africa, Asia, and Latin America, in order to allow our readers to weigh adequately the factor of racial distinctiveness. Within those various time periods and geographical/ethnic origins, we generally tried to present the best scholarship available on the specific ethnic groups that comprised the largest numerical portions of the different waves of settlement. Thus, we decided on a lineup that included the only indigenous ethnic group (American Indians); several groups that were representative of the migration waves of either the colonial period or of the great immigration wave, 1840–1890 (African Americans, Chinese Americans, German Americans, Irish Americans, and Scandinavian Americans); several that arrived in significant numbers mostly in the twentieth century (Italian Americans, Jewish Americans, Mexican Americans, and Polish Americans); and several that are representative of the post-1945 immigration that continues to enrich our culture (Arab Americans, Asian Indian Americans, Dominican Americans, Filipino Americans, Haitian Americans, Korean Americans, and Vietnamese Americans). While we seriously considered the inclusion of other eastern European, Latin American, African, or Asian peoples, such as Japanese Americans and Puerto Rican Americans, our inability to match up the scholars we wanted within the time sequence involved caused us to abandon such notions. While we recognize that the differences between the experiences of Japanese and Chinese Americans or Mexican and Puerto Rican Americans, for example, are every bit as important and instructive as the similarities between them, we believe our selective sample is as representative as circumstances permitted and is large and varied enough to enable readers to make valid comparisons across time and ethnicity, to discern the major variables that condition the acculturation process, and to formulate at least a tentative hypothesis regarding the essentials of that phenomenon.

These same considerations underlay our decisions about the focus and scope of the seventeen chapters that eventually comprised the bulk of this volume. Germans, Poles, Irish, Italians, and Chinese are examined separately, but Norwegians, Swedes, and Danes are all subsumed in the chapter on Scandinavian Americans, because their process of acculturation was similar enough to justify doing so, at least in the opinion of the experts we consulted. Similarly, the emphasis in the essay on Jewish Americans is on the experiences of eastern European immigrants and their descendants, but those of the larger resident Sephardic and German Jews are not neglected. The essay on Arab Americans focuses on the shared experiences of all those who have immigrated from the Middle East and North Africa, while trying to give proper attention to the significant ethnic and religious diversity that exists within their ranks. American Indians and African Americans are both included, even though their experiences deviate so greatly from the varieties of the immigrant experience represented in the other essays as to be considered differences of kind rather than degree. However, our primary interest is in the process of interaction between minority cultures and mainstream America, and the experiences of both American Indians and African Americans shed much valuable light on that phenomenon. While the uniqueness of the experience in America of each of the seventeen cultural groups considered is readily apparent and while diversity rather than unity characterizes the totality of what follows, we firmly believe that there are enough common elements in the overall process to allow the reader to draw meaningful generalizations regarding how cultural interaction leads to mutual cultural change. Our purpose in this introduction is to observe the commonalities of the cultural process and to offer some tentative generalizations.

Since the eighteenth century, observers of the American scene have been convinced that the American was "a new man." But just how people of diverse cultures, from many lands, occupations, environments, and religions could be melded together into one culture, one nationality, has been in dispute. What does seem evident from the collective efforts of the authors of these chapters is that such metaphors as a melting pot or a coat of many colors cloud more than clarify our understanding of what has happened. Having noted the complexity of the process by which people of widely differing cultures interact with one another and with a host culture, some generalizations may be drawn from the experiences of the seventeen ethnic groups considered. Our sample includes Native Americans, African Americans whose ancestry dates back almost four centuries, three immigrant groups from northern and western Europe in the nineteenth century, three from southern and eastern Europe in the early twentieth century, five ethnic groups of Asian ancestry, four of Latin-American/Caribbean origins, and one of Middle Eastern/North African derivation. Of the last ten groups, eight are primarily the product of the phenomenal shift in the origins of immigration to the United States triggered by the Immigration and Naturalization (Hart-Celler) Act of 1965 and by dramatic changes in the push-pull dynamic that characterizes global migration patterns. The other two—Mexicans and Chinese—are of much longer residence in the United States than are several of the European groups.

First, it is clear that, at least for the first generation of most immigrant groups, it is inaccurate to assume that the culture they brought with them was defined by their nationality. Poles, Norwegians, Italians, and Germans defined themselves by characteristics drawn from region, class, religion, and locale rather than nationality. In the same way, but not in the same time span, the diverse cultures among the various tribes of Native Americans came to accept a common label, *Indian*. Only as time and generations in America passed did a hyphenated nationality label come to be accepted. Hence, it is probable that the phenomenon that the historian Marcus Lee Hansen described as first-generation immigrants holding to an old identity, second-generation immigrants rejecting their origins and accepting an American one, and third-generation immigrants seeking to rediscover their roots is really a process in which the first generation held to a culture defined by factors other than nationality, the second generation identified with the culture of the host country, and the third generation developed a new "hyphenated" identity consisting of elements of both the old country and the new. Whether currently arriving immigrant groups will display that same general pattern of adaptation is still an open question.

Second, to the degree that ethnic identification has persisted and in some cases become stronger decades after the end of any significant immigration of a particular ethnic group, we might theorize that the phenomenon is largely the result of certain forces at work in American society. Given a society so open and fluid and a people so geographically mobile, Americans seek to identify themselves by membership in a variety of organizations and groups. Hence, we might suppose that the third generation's search for ethnic identity occurs for the same reason that most Americans identify with a church, a political party, a civic club, or other mediating institution. If that is true, then the search for ethnic identity is primarily a manifestation of the universal desire for social and personal location in modem mass society.

Third, the situation with regard to "racial groups," other than African Americans, is similar to that of immigrant-derived peoples. Local, regional, and even national differences in origin have given way, and new identities such as "Asian Americans" or "Hispanics" have appeared. Such identifications have evolved over time and have served social, political, and cultural functions for the groups involved.

Fourth, this process of identification by racial and ethnic groups, both with the mainstream culture and some subset of it, takes place at different rates of speed depending on the degree to which those already in the host society find newcomers acceptable and to which their traditions can be merged with that of the host culture without obliterating its key features. So it seems that Jews held many cultural values, attitudes, and beliefs that could be connected with those of the host society. Many, though not all, Jews were willing and able to compromise in order to accomplish that melding. Only antagonism, more evident at some times in American history than at others, has prevented that process of a new Jewish American culture from proceeding even further. In the case of Native Americans, the process of forming a new Indian American culture has proceeded much more slowly as a result of cultures that are not completely compatible, and of antagonisms, laws, and practices of the host society that have held Indians apart. In the case of Chinese Americans, we see a dissimilarity of cultural values as well as host-society antagonism preventing the development of a new hyphenated culture until just after World War II. Since that time, the change in attitude of the host society has allowed for the rapid development of a new culture.

Fifth, while the process of identification has resulted in the development of new hyphenated cultures among all these ten groups, we should recognize that key factors (such as geographic and economic mobility) that break down group loyalties are the same forces that promote the search for group identification. What might appear to be nostalgia in the search for one's roots might in fact be a natural human response on the part of people who can only identify with massive mainstream culture through the prism of familiar subcultures. Ethnic festivals and interest in genealogy and regional history seem to go hand in hand with the loss of place, alternation in social mores, and change of religious affiliation. The influence of the national mass-communications media in establishing a standardized mode of dress, taste in music, and blurring of distinctions in manner of speech all give reason to regain a form of complex cultural identity. The hyphenated American may well be the result of the process by which original identification was lost and a new identification found. In effect, at the same time that Americans become more like one another, they develop a sense of being a part of a subgroup that marks them as different from one other. The more we are alike, the more we are different.

The chapters that follow give us good material from which to attempt to understand and generalize about a highly complex and critical subject. In spite of our effort to find and outline a common pattern of cultural change of ethnic groups over time, there are many differences among each ethnic group's experience in the United States. In his chapter on Germans in the United States, James M. Bergquist makes clear that, as the first large group of non-English-speaking settlers, Germans were considered by their neighbors to be "aggressively resistant to adaptation to mainstream American society." He says that the creation of German American institutions served both to preserve Old World ways and to prepare German newcomers to accept new ways. His description of the role of foreign language newspapers and social and political clubs as a bridge between old and new is applicable to all other ethnic groups. The great degree to which German Americans, over generations, and lacking any influx of new immigrants from the old country, lost contact with their past seems more pronounced than was the case with other ethnic groups described in this volume.

While German immigrants professed a diversity of religions, the later arriving Poles were almost uniformly Roman Catholic. German newcomers consisted of nearly every possible social class, many of whom embraced farming as an occupation in both the Old World and the New, but Polish immigrants were primarily peasants, most of whom lacked the inclination or the capital to work the land. They also valued a more communal life than would have been possible if they farmed in the United States, according to Edward R. Kantowicz. Success for the Poles was measured by the establishment of community, the ownership of property, primarily a home, the opportunity to work hard and steadily and to avoid any reliance on the state or on any other entity beyond immediate family, church, and community.

The experiences of Italian immigrants in many ways mirrored that of Poles. The majority of southern Italians also came from a peasant background, but the need to travel around Europe in search of seasonal employment caused Italians to be less tied to community, and their views on religion made them less committed to a militant form of Roman Catholicism. Like the Poles, Italians valued hard work and property ownership, eschewing education and movement into the professions. For both groups, the latter two attitudes have markedly changed since World War II, as Dominic Candeloro makes clear. Italians, like Poles, created fraternal and benevolent societies as both a bridge to Americanizing new immigrants and a means of preserving some Old World identity.

The Irish experience in America has more in common with that of the Germans than with either the Poles or Italians, despite some important differences.

Like the Germans, the Irish were geographically mobile but, since they spoke English and had no strong cultural base, they could integrate more readily into mainstream American society. While most Germans lacked any strong sense of old-country nationalism, Irish Americans did and do have such a sense. More than any other immigrant group, the Irish created organizations that held them together, despite their dispersal in the United States. Determined to avoid the rural, agricultural existence that had proven so disastrous in their native land, according to Lawrence J. McCaffrey, Irish immigrants became "pioneers of urban-ethnic ghettos in the United States." Although their ethnicity and Catholicism helped them to achieve incredible social mobility over the generations, the author concludes that the "Irish American experience is more of a case study in assimilation and acculturation than in ethnic preservation."

Even more dramatically than the Germans and the Irish, Jews who came to America left behind the Old World and adopted the New. To the degree that U.S. society was open to them, Jews took advantage of the opportunity to become part of their new society. At the same time, Jews have struggled to define and resolve any contradiction between being both a Jew and an American. Indeed, in his essay on Jewish Americans, Edward Shapiro argues that "no other ethnic group has been as concerned with defining their relationship to America." For many American Jews, the hope for and ultimately the creation of a nation, Israel, served as a common bond. Paradoxically, Zionism was reconciled with a sense of integration into American life by regarding that ideology as a humanitarian approach toward people in need rather than as a form of Jewish nationalism in the United States. Over time, increasing interreligious marriage has further weakened the identity of Jews in America.

As described by John Robert Christianson, Scandinavians generally lacked any tie to an Old World nation, a common Old World religion, or a single economic class or occupation, much like their German counterparts. Also as with the Germans, geographic mobility and economic mobility worked against a sense of Norwegian, Swedish, or Danish nationalism, hyphenated or otherwise. It only arose after 1900 and began to disappear after World War I.

The importance of the culture that immigrants brought with them and how that culture was influenced by their place in the United States is perhaps most clear in the case of the Chinese. For nearly a century, George Anthony Peffer demonstrates, the Chinese who arrived in America came as laborers intending to acquire wealth and return to their home country. They felt strong ties to their homeland, its culture, and the families they left behind. Faced with virulent discrimination and hostile legislation, they were forced into forming pocket communities that were culturally, if not geographically, isolated from the rest of America. During the twentieth century, however, a small but growing group of American-born Chinese transformed themselves into "studious, intellectually gifted examples of a 'model minority,'" and "increasingly were found in the economy's most lucrative and prestigious professions." With the barriers to their immigration and citizenship finally removed by 1965, the rapidly increasing population of Chinese Americans have adopted a strategy of liminality, a concept denoting "life in between cultures, sometimes uncomfortable but often valuable as a means of navigating the gaps between ethnic and mainstream identities."

As varied as the experiences of the ethnic groups already noted are, that of the American Indian provides still different sets of conditions and responses to American culture. As Vine Deloria, Jr., points out in describing American Indians, "Their ethnicity is a product of historical process and political ideology rather than racial and cultural homogeneity. Indeed 'Indian' is a generic term akin to 'Asian' or 'European' in the sense that it refers to a large grouping of diverse peoples who occupy a continental land mass rather than a nationalistic entity with similar historic homogeneous roots."

The American culture might have created a mythic counterculture, the Indian culture, as a way of defining itself. In short, Indian culture as described by Americans provided them with a cultural contrast that in part, by its differences, defined the American culture. Indians were described as a cultural entity when in fact no single, Indian culture existed. If they had not been set up as a separate nation and a distinct racial group, Indians, as Deloria notes, might have been assimilated a century ago. As with the Chinese since World War II, changes both in law and attitude, as well as economic conditions and geographic mobility, have finally given impetus to such assimilation. Whether Indian culture in the form that Deloria describes as "traditionalism" will take hold and preserve some of the essentials remains to be seen. In that sense, the Indian experience in the United States might come to resemble that of the Jews who seek to be both Americans and Jews.

The degree of ambiguity that characterized the relationship between these various groups and mainstream culture is apparent most dramatically in the historical interaction between Americans and Mexicans. Conflict between often-hostile national neighbors, land hunger, and religious differences served to keep apart people who, in many other respects, shared a common history. Mexican Americans, as Matt S. Meier describes them, were at times a labor force, a tool in the economic development of lands taken from Mexico. At other times, they were a barrier to American economic development and geographic expansion. With the tremendous increase in Mexican immigration to the United States since 1965, Meier sees what he calls a "reconquest of the borderlands" taken from Mexico in 1848, "not with force or warfare, but slowly and surely with the enduring and long-suffering patience of farm workers, gardeners, sweatshop workers, housemaids, waiters, barbers, and shopkeepers," and with the "leadership of congressmen, businessmen, lawyers, diplomats, writers, poets, artists and others who have become a highly visible part of American culture by mere numbers."

In many ways, the acculturation process of African Americans is the most complex of all the groups considered in this collection. Numerically, they constitute the largest single group, while the time span of their interaction with Euro-America is far longer than any other, except for the American Indians. No other single group of ethnic Americans has pursued acculturation and assimilation with more determination over such a long period of time, only to experience recurring rejection and frustration. Cynthia Greggs Fleming, quoting Bernard Makhosezwe Magubane, contends that an African American is fundamentally "an American who is not accepted as an American, hence a kind of negative American." One hundred years of striving for acculturation and assimilation by the late 1960s left many African American leaders wondering if conformity to Anglo-American values and cultural norms was not too high a price to pay for the integration they had so steadfastly and vainly pursued. With W.E.B. Du Bois, modern African Americans sought a way to be both American and Negro without having to "bleach his Negro soul in a flood of white Americanism." Fleming shows that this creative tension between African roots and American experience, similar and yet different from that felt by Euro-Americans, has persisted throughout African American history from early colonial times to the present day. Unlike most Euro-American groups, however, African Americans have been plagued with an unsettling ambivalence about their ancestral continent that has compounded the ambivalent attitude that America has consistently displayed toward all ethnic minorities. Uncertain about both their place in American society and their relationship to a rapidly changing Africa, at the end of the twentieth century African Americans remained uneasily conscious of their "twoness," still "marginal, negative Americans."

While all of the ethnic groups just named have had a substantial presence in the United States for at least a century and have experienced the process of adaptation to mainstream American life over several generations, the remaining seven peoples examined in this book (Dominicans, Haitians, Filipinos, Koreans, Asian Indians, Vietnamese, and Arabs) are largely the product of large-scale, post-1965 immigration to this country and have generally undergone the adaptive process over just one or two generations. Moreover, they are all "nonwhite" immigrants from countries outside Europe, a circumstance that differentiates their situations drastically from all of the above groups save African Americans and American Indians. Even so, it is valuable to compare their experiences to those of the ten groups covered in the first edition of this book and to make a careful and thoughtful inventory of the similarities and differences among all seventeen peoples.

Although Filipinos began coming to United States as soon as their country became a U.S. territory in 1899, there were less than 40,000 on the mainland and 55,000 in Hawaii by 1931. Apart from a few thousand students, most were agricultural laborers or held menial jobs in hotels and restaurants. They suffered intense discrimination and frequent persecution, especially on the West Coast. In the 1934 Tydings-McDuffie Act that gave the Philippines commonwealth status, Filipino immigrants received a quota of 50 per year. The Repatriation Act of the following year provided free transportation to Filipinos who wished to return to the homeland—in exchange for an agreement not to return to the United States. Since 1965, however, more than 1.5 million Filipinos have immigrated, a total exceeded only by Mexican immigrants, and they are the second largest Asian

American group, second only to Chinese Americans. As they continue to grow in numbers and socioeconomic status, according to Augusto Espiritu, Filipino Americans face "a moment of insecurity . . . as they reach a critical mass in the population and look at their relative powerlessness in American society." It is essential, he asserts, for them to view contemporary challenges grounded in the experience of their forebearers and "take a hold of the opportunity for self-assertion that this historical moment provides."

As early as 1902, Koreans also began to immigrate to Hawaii and the West Coast, although in significantly fewer numbers than Filipinos. As prejudice and discrimination against Koreans escalated, their immigration was virtually eliminated by the Oriental Exclusion Act of 1924. By 1930, only slightly more than 1,000 Koreans lived in California, where they were frequently mistaken for Japanese. Large-scale immigration began with the arrival of war brides just after the Korean War and accelerated rapidly with the passage of the landmark Immigration and Naturalization Act of 1965. During the next three decades, Korean immigration approached one million, the fifth largest total among components of the newest wave of newcomers. In a paper based largely on interviews with recent immigrants, anthropologist Kyeyoung Park argues that "the making of Korean American culture is a creative and critical process drawing from Korean, American, and other cultures," which the interviewees view in terms of "tree grafting." Park concludes that the emerging culture of Korean Americans will have only its origins in the homeland and that its "development and elaboration will be in America."

Just behind Koreans in terms of numbers of immigrants over the past three decades are Asian Indians, the largest component of what Karen I. Leonard defines as "South Asians," a constructed category including peoples from India, Pakistan, Bangladesh, Sri Lanka, Nepal, Bhutan, the Maldive Islands, and Afghanistan and differentiated from a similar category of Southeast Asians. Focusing on Asian Indians, Leonard contends that "the more striking differences are between those who came before and after 1965." The "old" immigrants began coming to the United States at the end of the nineteenth century, but their numbers were severely curtailed by the quota of 105 a year, as allocated by the 1924 National Origins Quota Act. They were predominantly male, rural, uneducated, mostly from Punjab, commonly called Hindus, and declared "non-white" by the Supreme Court in 1923. Post-1965 immigrants, Leonard declares are "strikingly diverse" in origin and culture, "predominantly urban, highly educated professionals," and migrate in family units. Together, the descendants of the "old" immigrants and the newer arrivals are striving to produce new concepts of identity and community.

Even more diverse in origins and culture, according to Gregory Orfalea, are Arab Americans, whose ranks include dozens of nationalities and a sizeable minority of Christians in the midst of a Muslim majority. The first wave, according to Orfalea, came between 1878 and 1924, and was almost exclusively from Syria, Lebanon, and Palestine. It was 90 percent Christian. The second wave, which came between 1948 and 1967, was half Christian and half Muslim and came primarily from Egypt, Iraq, Syria, and Lebanon. The third wave—post 1968—is about 60 percent Muslim and consists largely of refugees from war and repression in Yemen, Lebanon, Morocco, Syria, Algeria, Israel, and Iraq. Mixing scholarly analysis with personal and family experiences, Orfalea describes how the disaster of September 11, 2001, and the escalating War on Terror has adversely affected all Arab Americans, Muslim and Christian alike, and severely handicapped their efforts to be perceived as loyal and productive Americans. For many Arab Americans, Orfalea laments quoting a favorite expression of his maternal grandmother, the situation "can't be no worse."

Much more hopeful, according to Silvio Torres-Saillant, are the prospects for newcomers from the Dominican Republic, who constitute the largest single component of post-1965 immigration from the Caribbean area. With over a million compatriots residing in the United States as of 2004, Dominican Americans have adapted rapidly and are able to exercise their ethnic and cultural differences as workers, parents, students, and consumers. Their greatest asset, Torres-Saillant concludes, is their propensity to embrace diversity, a quality that enables Dominican Americans to harmonize elements of African, Iberian, Latino, and mainstream American culture.

Considerably more bleak have been the experiences and prospects of those immigrants who resided on the other side of the Island of Santo Domingo. To begin with, as Marc Prou demonstrates, Haitians have had a much more difficult time getting out of Haiti and into the United States. By 1968, there were an estimated 75,000 Haitians in the United States, most of them part of the "brain drain" that deprived their homeland of 80 percent of its doctors, lawyers, engineers, teachers, and other professionals. Most had to enter the United States as undocumented aliens and "were forced to live a meager and precarious existence without the benefits of work permits, welfare, educational assistance, and legal protection." Since then, thousands of Haitians each year have tried to enter the country as refugees, including the highly publicized waves of "boat people," and most have been denied asylum. By 1993, there were almost 300,000 legal immigrants from Haiti, and at least that many illegal ones. Torres-Saillant judiciously explores not only the reasons behind American rejection of Haitian immigrants but also the strides that the latter have made over the past three decades in maintaining their "transnational" identity while becoming more involved in their new country's political and public life. Haitian Americans, he concludes "no longer perceive the United States as a safe haven; rather, it is a place for them to achieve their aspirations, to live the American Dream."

By any measure, the Vietnamese people are among the newest of the new, so far as immigration to the United States is concerned. Prior to American involvement in the Vietnam War, immigration from Southeast Asia was almost nonexistent. Unlike Haitians fleeing the right-wing dictatorship of the Duvaliers and their successors, the Vietnamese generally had little or no difficulty entering the United States as refugees, a distinction that they held with Castro-era Cubans, among others. Between 1975 and 1993, more than one million Indochinese entered the United States, of whom nearly three-fourths were Vietnamese. According to Hien Duc Do, they arrived to a mixed reception that reflected internal American divisions over the war, combined with the country's perpetual ambivalence toward immigration, particularly when it involves people of color. While their initial focus was on economic survival and adaptation to life in the United States, he contends, Vietnamese Americans have increasingly turned their attention to claiming a voice in America, participation in social, political, economic, and educational institutions, and the formation of ethnic communities.

It is our hope that the reader of this book will gain some insight into just how diverse, and how much alike, were the experiences of a number of ethnic groups who came to America. The process of interaction between and among these cultures was complex and always important in the shaping of what today is that welter of commonly held values, attitudes, and beliefs that is American culture.

AFRICAN AMERICANS

Cynthia Griggs Fleming

The African American is the only American in America who says, "I want to be an American." More or less, all other Americans are born Americans and take their Americanness for granted. Hence the African American's effort to be an American is a self-conscious thing. America is something outside of him, and he wishes to become part of that America. But, since color easily marks him off from being an ordinary American, and since he lives amid social conditions pregnant with racism, he becomes an American who is not accepted as an American, hence a kind of negative American.[1]

A generation has passed since the civil rights movement of the 1960s. In recent years, it has become increasingly fashionable to hold reunions, forums, and all manner of meetings that attempt to assess the movement's importance. At the same time, a large number of scholarly studies have been published that examine the movement's history and the issues it raised. A major focus of most who seek to evaluate the civil rights movement is the question of whether, in fact, it changed anything for Americans of African descent. Have they stopped being negative Americans?

Most agree that at least some changes have occurred, because prior to the activism of the 1960s, African Americans all over the country suffered from the effects of segregation. In the North it was de facto, while in the South it was de jure. Because of the blatant and public nature of southern segregation, much of the early movement activity and national outrage was directed against racist conditions facing black southerners. Yet, while northern racism was much quieter, it was every bit as effective in relegating black citizens to society's fringes. Thus, throughout the country, African Americans were faced with segregated and often substandard housing, medical care, and occupational and educational opportunities.

From the late nineteenth century, after black people were freed by the Civil War, and on through the twentieth century, African Americans have fought against attempts to segregate them in all areas of American life. Sometimes these fights have been waged by individuals, and sometimes they have been collective struggles. During the twentieth century, one group that expended an enormous amount of energy in the fight against legal segregation was the National Association for the Advancement of Colored People (NAACP). The strategy of this interracial organization, which was founded in 1909, was to use the court system to put segregation on trial. Indeed, the vast majority of the civil rights cases tried in the first part of the twentieth century were conducted with the support and often the direct participation of the NAACP and its legal staff.

A number of the most celebrated cases involved the issue of segregated education. For example, in 1947, with NAACP support, Heman Sweatt, a black Texas resident, sued the University of Texas Law School for refusing him admission because of his race. The case of *Sweatt v. Painter* went all the way to the U.S. Supreme Court. The Court ordered that either Sweatt should be admitted to the law school or the state should provide equal facilities for African Americans. Such a strategy did not challenge the constitutionality of segregation. Rather, segregation was still considered legal as long as equal facilities were provided for black residents. In an effort to keep Sweatt out of the University of Texas Law School, the state established a separate law school just for black residents.[2]

This tactic did not work, however, because the Supreme Court later found that the new law school was not equal to the University of Texas. The court's decision, which was written by Chief Justice Vinson, carefully addressed this issue. "What is more important [than the disparity in physical facilities] the University of Texas Law School possesses to a far greater degree those qualities which are incapable of objective measurement, but which make for greatness in a law school. Such qualities, to name but a few, include reputation of the faculty, experience of the administration, position and influence of the alumni, standing in the community, traditions and prestige."[3]

Sweatt was admitted to the university's law school. The Texas reaction in this case clearly illustrates the lengths to which the white South was willing to go to preserve its segregated system. Yet, this reaction would prove to be mild in comparison to the firestorm created by the 1954 case of *Brown v. the Board of Education of Topeka*. In this case the NAACP legal staff challenged the constitutionality of segregation: they challenged it and won. The Supreme Court ruled that separate could never be equal, and so legal segregation was finally dead.

However, even as certain judicial decisions began to support black rights, world events also began to affect black aspirations. From the late 1940s through the 1950s, developments like the advent of the cold war, the emergence of many Third World nations, and the American ascendancy to a position of global leadership worked in concert to heighten U.S. sensitivity to criticism from abroad. Government officials soon realized that the United States was particularly vulnerable to criticism in the area of race relations. This realization prompted increasing concern among many about racial justice. Such postwar developments helped fuel a cautious but persistent black optimism that would lay the foundation for the activism of the 1950s and 1960s.

While black hope was nourished by government concern, white resistance was encouraged by government ambivalence. Despite the existence of a number of Supreme Court decisions favoring black rights, little changed because the federal government routinely demonstrated a reluctance to enforce these decisions. Federal action on the *Smith v. Allwright* case provides a graphic illustration of such government reluctance. This case, decided in 1944, outlawed the white primary, a device that had been used to reinforce black disenfranchisement. The law establishing the white primary had designated the Democratic Party in most Southern states as a "private club." Because this club did not accept black members, registered black voters were barred from voting in the Democratic primary. In the solidly Democratic South of this era, selection as a Democratic candidate was tantamount to election to office. After *Smith v. Allwright*, black voters who had been denied the right to participate in Democratic primaries expected the federal government to aid their attempts to extend the franchise. They were disappointed. Rather, federal officials refused to become involved: they left this responsibility to the states.[4]

Thus, the Supreme Court ruled in favor of black rights. The legislative branch passed laws in support of black rights. The executive branch created commissions and issued executive orders supporting black rights. Yet only half-hearted attempts were made toward enforcement and implementation. These realities, juxtaposed against each other, sent mixed signals to the white South. Many staunch supporters of segregation felt the beginnings of an assault on their cherished way of life. At the same time, they were comforted by federal reluctance to provide too much support for black rights.

In this unsettled atmosphere, southern white violence against African Americans continued, but by this time it began to receive increased publicity. One of the most dramatic incidents of such violence occurred just one year after the landmark *Brown* decision. In the summer of 1955 Emmett Till, a black youth from Chicago visiting relatives in Mississippi, was brutally beaten and murdered. Till was beaten so badly that only the right side of his head was intact, one eye dangled from its socket, and his tongue was swollen to eight times its normal size.[5] Two white defendants were tried for Till's murder, but it took an "all-white jury just one hour and seven minutes to acquit them. One juror explained, 'If we hadn't stopped to drink pop . . . it wouldn't have taken that long.'"[6]

Against this backdrop of white violence and government ambivalence, black resistance to segregation continued to strengthen. It is important to recognize that all those cases leading up to and including the *Brown* decision came to the Supreme Court because of black instigation and NAACP legal support. At the same time, however, black resistance to segregation was expressed in many other ways too. Countless African Americans became fed up with sitting in the back of buses, drinking out of dingy little "colored" water fountains, and using dirty "colored" restrooms. And so, many simply refused. In 1955 a movement coalesced around one of those who refused: Mrs. Rosa Parks, a black Montgomery, Alabama, resident. When Parks was arrested for refusing to give up her seat to a white man on a Montgomery, Alabama, bus, the city's black residents boycotted the buses for over a year. As a result of their action, Montgomery's buses were desegregated, and one of their local black leaders, Dr. Martin Luther King, Jr., became famous.

On February 1, 1960, four black college students at North Carolina Agricultural and Technical College in Greensboro sat in at a downtown lunch counter. This action launched an intense period of nonviolent direct demonstrations by black college students all over the South against segregated facilities. By the spring of that year student activists had met and established the Student Nonviolent Coordinating Committee (SNCC). With nothing but their faith in themselves and their courage to protect them, these students confronted segregation head on. One former SNCC member, Zohara Simmons, vividly recalls the difficulties inherent in such a challenge:

> Once you actually go and have white folk come out of a restaurant and spit on you and call you nigger, and [tell you to] go back to Africa you coons, baboons, you know, the kinds of things. Then of course you're probably going to have one of two reactions. Either you're going to be so afraid that you say "Oh, I can't expose myself to that." Or you're going to be so mad that you know it's like, "I'll be back, come hell or high water."[7]

Students were not the only ones demonstrating. Many people from various backgrounds became involved in this assault on segregation. As these activists picketed, boycotted, sat in, and participated in freedom rides, the walls of segregation began to crumble. Oddly enough, however, many African Americans who were veterans of the civil rights battles that changed the South and the country still did not feel like full-fledged Americans. At the beginning, integration had been their goal. Soon, many began to ask themselves, Integration on whose terms, and at what cost? The answers they found were more than a little disturbing. By 1964 and 1965, many began to recognize that the integration they had so desperately desired demanded a very high price: conformity to Anglo-American values and cultural norms. Their realization prompted many to echo the words of W.E.B. Du Bois in his 1903 classic *The Souls of Black Folk*:

> One ever feels his twoness—an American, a Negro; two souls, two thoughts, two unreconciled strivings; two warring ideals in one dark body, whose dogged strength alone keeps it from being torn asunder. The history of the American Negro is the history of this strife—this longing to attain selfconscious manhood, to merge his double self into a better and truer self. In this merging he wishes neither of the older selves to be lost. He would not Africanize America, for America has too much to teach the world and Africa. He would not bleach his Negro

soul in a flood of white Americanism, for he knows that Negro blood has a message for the world. He simply wishes to make it possible for a man to be both a Negro and an American.[8]

At this point, increasing numbers of activists who had been jailed, beaten, and brutalized in the name of civil rights began to question their identity as Americans, and they began a serious exploration of their connection with the African continent. They began to understand that black was, after all, more than just a color. It is important to note, however, that this was not the first time that Americans of African descent in this country had felt the need to understand their connection to the land of their ancestors.

In fact, that interest in Africa had first surfaced as early as the colonial period, and from that very early time on, exploration of that connection has been difficult and emotional. Much of the difficulty has been based on the negative views of Africa and Africans that have been popularized in this country since its infancy. Indeed, even before the English established their first permanent settlement in the New World, they had a negative view of the concept of blackness. Before the sixteenth century, the *Oxford English Dictionary*'s definition of the color black included, "Deeply stained with dirt; soiled, dirty, foul. . . . Having dark or deadly purposes, malignant; pertaining to or involving death, deadly; baneful, disastrous, sinister. . . . Foul, iniquitous, atrocious, horrible, wicked."[9]

Furthermore, the British regularly juxtaposed the "negative" color black against the "positive" color white. "White and black connoted purity and filthiness, virginity and sin, virtue and baseness, beauty and ugliness, beneficence and evil, God and the devil."[10] When the English saw their first African people, they automatically projected their feelings about the color black onto these dark-skinned people.

Later on, English settlers carried their negative views of Africans and their descendants with them when they colonized America. These views were embellished and popularized by succeeding generations of white Americans who ascribed such characteristics as laziness, stupidity, immorality, and sexual excess to Africans and African Americans. One nineteenth-century Baltimore physician clearly echoed these sentiments:

> It is this sexual question that is the barrier which keeps the philanthropist and moralist from realizing that the phylogenies of the Caucasian and African races are divergent, almost antithetical, and that it is gross folly to attempt to educate both on the same basis. When education will reduce the large size of the negro's penis as well as bring about the sensitiveness of the terminal fibers which exist in the Caucasian, then will it also be able to prevent the African's birthright to sexual madness and excess.[11]

Predictably, apologists for the institution of slavery eagerly embraced these negative notions. However, even white liberals who were sympathetic to the black plight subscribed to certain stereotypical notions of black character. For example, a number of white abolitionists, including Harriet Beecher Stowe, Hollis Read, Theodore Parker, and Lydia Maria Child, believed that African Americans were "predisposed toward 'feminine' languidity and softness."[12]

Given the widespread and enduring nature of such negative stereotypes, it is hardly surprising that African Americans would be affected by them. The effects were quite varied and often unpredictable. Some became ashamed of Africa, its inhabitants, and anything that connected them to such a "barbaric" background. Others refused to accept such negative images of themselves and the continent of their ancestors, and they frequently articulated their pride in their African background. Because the negative images were so pervasive, however, even those African descendants who championed the race's cause were unable to ignore these stereotypes completely. Consider the reasoning of Edward Wilmot Blyden, one of the foremost black intellectuals of the late nineteenth century. Blyden, who was a Pan-Africanist, did not totally repudiate nineteenth-century racial stereotypes. Rather, he rearranged them. "The Northern races will take the raw material from Africa and bring them back in such forms as will contribute to the comfort and even elegance of life in that country, while the African in the simplicity and purity of rural enterprises will be able to cultivate those spiritual elements in humanity which are suppressed, silent and inactive under the pressure and exigencies of material progress."[13]

Blyden's message in this passage is quite clear: Africans are different after all. There are admirable things about them, but they are different. Blyden, who was born in St. Thomas, Virgin Islands, struggled with the issue of African identity and his own relationship to it throughout his life. While he admired many things about African culture, he still measured that culture with a Western yardstick. He was a descendant of Africa, but a westernized descendant of Africa after all. Thus, despite his admiration for African culture, Blyden's Western viewpoint prompted him to write:

> To those who have lived any time in West Africa, three things are indisputably clear—first, that it was absolutely necessary that large numbers of the people should be taken into exile for discipline and training under a more advanced race; second, that they should be kept separate from the dominant race; third, that chosen spirits from among the exiles should in course of time return and settle among their brethren in the fatherland to guide them into the path of civilization.[14]

Edward Blyden's views clearly indicate the complexity of the dilemma that he faced. Although his ancestry was African, his views were Western, Blyden was not the first, nor would he be the last, African descendant in the New World to face this uncertainty. In fact, as early as the late eighteenth century, Americans of African descent began to make attempts to explore their relationship and their responsibility to the continent of their ancestors. One of the by-products of this exploration of identity was the establishment of a number of separate black institutions that incorporated the label *Africa* in their titles. At the same time, though, African Americans were not the only ones groping toward a new identity, and so the drama of their search must be examined in the broader context of American attempts to define the national character. In the aftermath of the American Revolution, black and white Americans sought to understand just what it meant to be an American. While both shared a number of common experiences, the definitions of their Americanness were quite different.

Descendants of Africans had participated in all of the important early American milestones, including the Revolutionary War. African Americans, both slave and free, fought in the Revolutionary War in substantial numbers. On the eve of the war, slavery existed in all thirteen colonies, but by the time the war ended most northern states had made provisions for the gradual emancipation of their slaves. In the South, however, legislation designed to eliminate slavery was considered but defeated, and so slavery continued. In such an atmosphere, the status of African Americans remained uncertain. Some were slaves and some were free, and those who were legally free were not sure what their status as free people meant. The question of what citizenship rights they could exercise was determined by the policies of the state where they resided.

Amid this extreme and unsettling uncertainty, many African Americans began tentatively exploring their relationship with the land of their ancestors. The African Institution of Boston, the Free African Society of Philadelphia, the African Methodist Episcopal Church, and the African Lodge are just a few of the separate institutions organized by African Americans in the late eighteenth and early nineteenth centuries.[15] The tendency to include the word *African* in the title of these organizations is indicative of how these early African Americans identified with their African ancestry and the sympathy they felt for the African plight. That sympathy was tempered by a large amount of ambivalence, however.

The words of Prince Hall, founder of the African Lodge, clearly illustrate his sympathetic feelings for his enslaved African brethren: "Let us see our friends and brethren; and first let us see them dragged from their native country, by the iron hand of tyranny and oppression, from their dear friends and connections, with weeping eyes and aching hearts, to a strange land, and among a strange people, whose tender mercies are cruel—and there to bear the iron yoke of slavery and cruelty."[16] Just a few years after Prince Hall's address, officers of the African Institution of Boston wrote to Paul Cuffe, a prosperous free black entrepreneur who transported a number of free African Americans to the land of their ancestors at his own expense. "I received yours of the 10th last month in due season & think we ought most cheerfully to sacrifice ease & many other privileges & comforts, for the purpose of diffusing light & civilization & knowledge in Africa."[17]

These men were not the only contemporaries of Cuffe who felt that Africa needed to be uplifted. Peter Williams, a black Episcopal priest, echoed the sentiments of African Institution officials when he described Cuffe's efforts in these terms: "He [Cuffe] could not think of enjoying repose while he reflected that he might, in any degree, administer to the relief of the multitudes of his brethren, who were groaning under the yoke of bondage, or groping in the dark and horrible night of heathenish superstition and ignorance."[18]

Paul Cuffe, born in 1759, built his fortune on his oceangoing ventures. By 1806, his personal wealth included a number of ships, houses, and land holdings. Because of his prosperity, Cuffe was required to pay Massachusetts property taxes, but since he was not allowed to vote in his home state, he refused to pay the taxes. Cuffe's action eventually led to a change in Massachusetts law, allowing free black property owners to vote. Sometime later, Cuffe converted to the Quaker religion, and it was at this point that he became interested in using part of his fortune to help improve conditions among his African American brethren. His plan for improvement was built on his conviction that emigration to Africa would improve the lot of African Americans even as it brought the blessings of civilization and Christianity to the land of his ancestors. Accordingly, in 1815, Cuffe transported thirty-eight free African Americans to Africa at his own expense. His assessment of Africa as a place that needed to be civilized was entirely consistent with the views of his nineteenth-century contemporaries in the United States, both black and white.[19]

African Americans living in these years—from the end of the Revolution to about 1820—clearly felt sympathy for the land of their ancestors and the fate of its inhabitants. At the same time, however, they filtered their views of Africa through the prism of their adopted Western perceptions. Obviously, this prism distorted their view and prompted them to measure African culture with a Western yardstick. By such a measurement, these African Americans judged the culture of their ancestors to be barbaric, primitive, and in need of civilizing influences. Thus, at a time when African Americans were not fully accepted as equals by their white contemporaries, these same African Americans did not fully accept the integrity and equality of the culture of their ancestors. This reality meant that in many ways black Americans were people without a country.

Later in the nineteenth century, as sectional lines widened, slavery was debated and the fate of free African Americans was questioned. At that time, black people all over the country began to reassess their views of Africa and African culture. This reassessment took place in the midst of some crucial developments that affected black thinking. One of those developments was the establishment of the American Colonization Society. The society, which was founded in December 1816, was particularly interested in colonizing free black Americans.[20] This group was considered quite troublesome by their white contemporaries because their status was so unclear. One white North Carolinian succinctly expressed white concern: "It is impossible for us to be happy, if, after manumission they are to remain among us."[21]

Acting on such concerns, a number of prominent white Americans, including Judge Bushrod Washington, who was George Washington's nephew, Henry Clay, and John Randolph, organized the American Colonization Society (ACS). One of the society's major goals was the establishment of a West African colony for the resettlement of free black Americans.[22] The ACS and its aims proved to be enormously popular among large numbers of white Americans at the time. In fact, enthusiastic agreement with the society's aims prompted individuals and even state legislatures to donate money to the society's coffers.[23] Increasing numbers of white Americans, desperate for a solution to their "Negro problem," began to see colonization as that solution. The editor of the *Virginia Argus* expressed the enthusiasm that many felt for the colonization strategy. "If 12,520 Negroes of the right age and sex were sent to Africa each year, Virginia would be clear of Negroes in twenty years at an annual cost of only £103,620 which might be obtained by a tax on slave ownership; exportation of 30,000 annually would in twenty years empty the entire nation of Negroes whose places could be filled by White Europeans."[24]

This grand plan had no chance of success if the society could not convince free black Americans that they should leave America. However, the arguments that white colonization advocates proposed were so offensive to African Americans that few wanted to have anything at all to do with the ACS. An example of one such argument was published in an 1825 edition of the *African Repository*, the organ of the ACS. The *Repository* insisted that African Americans should emigrate because their situation in American society was so unfavorable: "Introduced among us by violence, notoriously ignorant, degraded and miserable, mentally diseased, brokenspirited, acted upon by no motive to honourable exertions, scarcely reached in their debasement by the heavenly light."[25] Thus, to improve this condition, they should emigrate to Africa, reasoned the proponents of colonization.

While many African Americans were incensed and insulted by such a characterization, there were still some who wanted to emigrate to Africa badly enough to work with the ACS. For example, one group of free black Cincinnati, Ohio, residents wrote to the *African Repository* expressing their favorable view of colonization: "Resolved, that we believe that Liberia offers to the oppressed children of Africa a home where they may be free: and that it is the only place where we can establish a nationality, and be acknowledged as men by the nations of the earth."[26]

Whether they were willing to work with the ACS or not, an increasingly vocal group of African Americans in antebellum America began to support the notion of emigration to Africa. This rising tide of support came at a time when free black status was deteriorating steadily and precipitously. By the 1830s and 1840s, black political rights that had existed for some time were being curtailed, and black freedom of movement was being threatened. Even though free black people were supposed to be Americans, a number of northern and border states passed legislation that made it exceedingly difficult for them to move into a new state and establish residence.[27] This trend toward the restriction of black rights culminated in the *Dred Scott* decision of 1857. In that case, the Supreme Court decided that in the century prior to the adoption of the U.S. Constitution, African Americans had "been regarded as beings of an inferior order, and altogether unfit to associate with the white race, either in social or political relations and so far inferior, that they had no rights which the white man was bound to respect."[28]

This decision dealt a crushing blow to the hopes of free black people for inclusion into American society. Against this backdrop, increasing numbers of African Americans continued to reevaluate Africa and their relationship to it. In fact, by this time, many of them began to extol the virtues of their ancestral homeland. For example, Henry Highland Gamet, a black Presbyterian minister, insisted that Africans had been famous in the ancient world because of their many accomplishments. These accomplishments generated "a frame, which arose from every virtue, and talent, that renders mortals pre-eminently great. From the conquests of love and beauty, from the prowess of their arms, and their architecture, poetry, mathematics, generosity, and piety."[29] Furthermore, this generation of antebellum African Americans also began to see a direct and powerful link between their fate and that of other descendants of Africa: "The elevation of the colored man can only be completed by the elevation of the pure descendants of Africa."[30]

Yet, even though this generation of African Americans began to support and popularize positive views of their ancestral homeland, they were still haunted by the negative African images that plagued the views of their predecessors. The words of Alexander Crummell, a black Episcopal priest, clearly illustrated the persistence of continued negative views of Africa among African Americans. Speaking in 1852, Crummell characterized Africa as a continent badly in need of uplift: "For ages hath she lain beneath the incubus of the 'demon of her idolatry.' For ages hath she suffered the ravages of vice, corruption, iniquity, and guilt. For ages hath she been 'stricken and smitten' by the deadly thrusts of murder and hate, revenge and slaughter."[31] Thus, on the eve of the Civil War, Americans of African descent were still ambivalent about their identification with America and their views of Africa.

Just as things appeared darkest, the Civil War erupted, slavery ended, and the American definition of black citizenship rights changed—at least legally. Such dramatic developments nourished black hopes, at least for a while, that things might finally be different. The death of Reconstruction just a few years after the war, however, made it quite clear that white Americans were no more willing to accept African Americans as fellow citizens after the war than they had been before. In this atmosphere, the freed men felt compelled to evaluate their relationship to Africa and America once again. Their evaluation in the postwar era led many to believe that they were, in fact, more African than American.

At this point, the ACS, which had been virtually dormant during the Civil War, was besieged by letters from enthusiastic freedmen seeking aid to emigrate. Moreover, a large number of African Americans who were unwilling to wait for ACS support established their own joint stock companies to transport emigrants to Africa. A letter from the president of the Liberian Joint Stock Steamship Company in South Carolina clearly indicates the recognition of a positive connection between African Americans and their ancestral homeland. "Dear Sir, This will inform you that the colored people of America and especially of the Southern

States desire to return to their fatherland."[32] Not only were these people interested in emigrating to improve their situation, they also wanted to "aid in building up a nationality of Africans."[33]

Postbellum black emigration advocate Henry M. Turner even insisted that while they embraced Africa, African Americans should reject American society and culture. While few were willing to go this far, most African Americans through the end of the nineteenth century continued to wrestle with their feelings about Africa and America. As they deliberated, many tempered their praise for the fatherland with criticism engendered by their Western viewpoints. Edward Wilmot Blyden's previously reported negative judgment of African culture is indicative of this reality.

In fact, those negative views of Africa harbored by black Americans were further reinforced by events of the late nineteenth century. For example, at the 1884 Berlin Conference, Europeans divided up Africa as they made plans to colonize the continent. At the same time, on the other side of the world, America annexed Hawaii, dispatched troops to the Philippines, and fully subscribed to the notion of the White Man's Burden. Widespread Western imperialism directed at the world's darker peoples only served to strengthen the old stereotypes based on a deeply rooted belief in black inferiority. Thus, African Americans exploring their relationship to Africa still had to contend with those familiar stereotypes that had colored the perceptions of their ancestors.

By the early twentieth century, despite the colonial abuse suffered by the land of their ancestors, many African Americans began to express an unequivocal and enthusiastic desire to identify with their African ancestry. Into this twentieth-century black enthusiasm stepped Marcus Josiah Garvey. Garvey, a native of Jamaica, was an admirer of Booker T. Washington and a student of conditions in America. After traveling around and observing conditions in the Western Hemisphere, Garvey was prompted to ask, " 'Where is the black man's Government?' 'Where is his king and his kingdom?' 'Where is his President, his country and his ambassador, his army, his navy, his men of big affairs?' I could not find them, and then I declared, 'I will help to make them.' "[34]

Acting on his concerns, Garvey founded the Universal Negro Improvement Association (UNIA). The UNIA attracted a large following among people of African descent in various parts of the world. Yet, the UNIA's stronghold proved to be Harlem. Here, Garvey's message of race purity, race pride, and Africa for the Africans appealed to large numbers of African Americans. During the movement's heyday in the mid-1920s, Garvey had more than a million followers. In addition to his emphasis on the glorious African past, however, Garvey also preached a message of African uplift that implied his belief in at least a certain amount of African backwardness. Garvey's advice to his followers clearly illustrated this belief:

> It strikes me that with all the civilization this Western Hemisphere affords, Negroes ought to take better advantage of the cause of higher education. We could

make of ourselves better mechanics and scientists, and in cases where we can help our brothers in Africa by making use of the knowledge we possess, it would be but our duty. If Africa is to be redeemed, the Western Negro will have to make a valuable contribution along technical and scientific lines.[35]

Thus, although Garvey saw an important link between the destinies of Africans and African Americans, he saw Westernized black people as leaders and Africans on the continent as followers.

Those who joined the UNIA were attracted to the sense of importance and confidence it gave them. Finally, here was a movement that told them their ancestral homeland was glorious and that they had a great destiny to fulfill. Garvey was able to sustain this sense of excitement and importance by involving his followers in a variety of UNIA activities that ranged from participation in the Black Cross Nurses to involvement in the Royal African Motor Corps or the African Orthodox Church. Then there were the parades—grand parades—that wound through Harlem and gave UNIA members the chance to wear the splendid uniforms that indicated their position in the organization.[36]

Yet, even as many African Americans in the early part of the twentieth century gloried in their African heritage, the pernicious stereotypes about the continent and its inhabitants continued to endure. With the beginning of the motion picture industry during this time, Africa became a popular backdrop for Hollywood tales of mystery and romance, and degrading stereotypes of the continent and its inhabitants became more widespread than ever. In the vast majority of these early films, Africa was portrayed as an exotic place filled with unusual wildlife, colorful plant life, and ignorant black savages. Invariably, the white characters were the leaders, and the black characters were the followers.

Even as Hollywood popularized these negative images, some Africans who had been affected by colonization began to have ambivalent feelings about the worth of their own culture when juxtaposed against Western culture. Such feelings prompted one early-twentieth-century African nationalist to write:

We know that even if British rule were to be voluntarily withdrawn from West Africa, we cannot at present rule ourselves. We know further, that every other race which found itself in the predicament in which we are to-day, has had to be under the tutelage of another nation more advanced in the Science of Government than they until such time as they were sufficiently advanced to manage their own affairs, and then the idea of their continued domination by an alien power had to be decided by an overruling Providence. Ancient History is full of instances of this nature, and we have sufficient faith in God to know that we are not going to be an exception to the general rule.[37]

Thus, as twentieth-century African Americans attempted to understand their Americanness and their Africanness, they were assaulted by conflicting views of Africa, a changing balance of power in the world, and related changes on the domestic scene. Barely a generation after the Garvey movement reached its height and large numbers of African Americans identified their African heritage as most important, the civil rights movement of the 1960s began. The hope engendered by the movement convinced many that they truly could be accepted as Americans after all. Yet, the more involved in the movement some became, the more alienated they began to feel from American culture. Once again, to ease their alienation, many African Americans looked to Africa; but as they reached out to embrace the land of their ancestors, many 1960s activists discovered, much to their dismay, that they could not totally identify with Africa either.

The case of Matthew Jones, Jr., a member of the SNCC, clearly illustrates the uncertainty and difficulty that faced him and his contemporaries as they tried to define their identity in a changing America. During the summer of 1964, SNCC unsuccessfully challenged the right of white Mississippians to exclude black voters from the delegate selection process for the Democratic National Convention in Atlantic City, New Jersey. SNCC members were convinced that they were morally, legally, and politically right, but the credentials committee at the Democratic National Convention refused to seat the integrated slate of delegates they sent to the convention. Their unsuccessful challenge left many of the young people in SNCC demoralized, disillusioned, and doubtful that their identity and destiny were, in fact, tied to America.

At this critical point, a delegation of SNCC members was invited to West Africa. The group left the country in September of 1964, and they spent a great deal of their time in the West African nation of Guinea. Jones, who was a member of that delegation, vividly recalled how that trip affected his view of his identity. "I'll tell you what that trip did.... When we first got to Conakry [Guinea] . . . it was exciting for us. We looked at Sekou Toure [Guinea's leader] almost like a father. We decided we wanted to dress up, get our little dashikis, and get our hair cornrowed so we could talk to him."[38] Jones recalled that after the whole SNCC delegation did this to one degree or another,

> he [Sekou Toure] looked at us and he said, uh, he told us that was African culture. That what we had to do was go back to the United States and organize in the black community . . . in other words, he did not give our cultural escapade, or whatever you want to call it, any impetus. He saw us as being Western and going over taking care of business in the United States for the benefit of all.[39]

Jones vividly recalled the reaction of the SNCC delegation to Sekou Toure's comments:

> We felt a little naive because we had done it [embraced African culture in such an overt way]. So that was a little bit, uh, confusing for us. . . . That's when I found out how American I was and that's when I found that I was at that time much closer to Bill Hanson, who was a white fella from Arkansas . . . and myself, I was much closer to him than anybody; any of the Africans.[40]

The longer Jones stayed in West Africa, the more he realized that certain aspects of the culture perplexed him. He recalled, "We were faced with a lot of things . . . that didn't quite fit what I thought were things to do. So I saw then how, number one, how Western I was."[41] Julian Bond, another SNCC staff member who went on the African trip, recalled how amazed he was when he got to Africa and saw black people doing so many things that they were not allowed to do in the United States, such as flying commercial jets. Even though this reality fascinated him, when he boarded a plane that was flown by an African pilot, Bond's years of negative conditioning still made him remark half jokingly and half seriously, "I hope this guy knows what he's doing."[42]

Yes, there was uncertainty about Africa in the 1960s, but there was also excitement. During this era, many African Americans spoke frequently about discovering their roots, learning about their ancestral homeland, glorifying their blackness. One commentator observed, "Finally and equally, if not more importantly, within the past decade of the sixties there has been a significant increase in black pride and self-esteem and concomitant decrease in self-hatred among Afro-Americans. This is especially noticeable in standards of physical beauty, particularly insofar as hair styles, and dress are concerned. One rarely encounters black men with processed hair, and black women increasingly are rejecting hair straighteners."[43] That noisy and enthusiastic expression of pride in African ancestry did not last long. In fact, by the early 1970s, there were clear signs that this celebration of blackness was on the wane. Historian Alphonso Pinkey dated this waning interest from 1972, but he insisted, however, that it was only temporary.[44] (He was writing in 1975.) It turns out that Pinkey's prediction missed the mark: since the publication of his book, chemical hair straighteners have become popular, there is a healthy demand for bleaching creams, and pride in African ancestry has been replaced once again by ambivalence.

It seems that in some ways Americans of African descent have come full circle. The laws have finally changed, granting full citizenship rights, but in many ways, the ambiguity remains. After having come through a Civil War that freed them, and a civil rights movement that abolished legal segregation, African Americans are still wrestling with the same basic issues that plagued their ancestors. It seems that their relationship to this country is still not clear—and it has never been clear.

As we enter a new millennium, because of the commodification of black culture, the issue of black identity has shifted to a global stage. With the advent of music videos, MTV, and the Internet, the worldwide popularity of the negative black stereotypical images that are such an important part of rap music and hip-hop culture have reached unimaginable heights. This latest development has served only to continue to emphasize the gulf between African Americans and the land of their birth, but this time, some African Americans are willing participants in the act of glorifying black stereotypes. At the same time, it is important to note that this celebration of black stereotypes drives a thriving and profitable business. In his insightful work *Race in the Global Era*, Clarence Lusane explains the impact of this business on all of those involved:

> The collaboration between some of the largest transnational corporations in the world and inner-city black youth is not as strange as it may appear. The creation of global market niches in this era is a driving force in the contemporary exploitation of black American cultural forms. The marketing of the "other" as entertainment, an opportunity to experience the dangerously exotic, even if only abstractly, motivates both corporate producer and nonblack consumer. In the middle are "declassed" poor black youth—that is, those who are marginalized perhaps permanently out of the labor force—whose efforts to avoid what are clearly unpleasant destinies generate innovative ways to prosper and survive. Those ways have become new modes of capital accumulation.[45]

Thus, some marginalized African Americans have begun to embrace their "otherness." Instead of denying the stereotypical images that many African Americans have fought against for generations, they celebrate them and allow them to define their identity. But, there is hardly unanimity of opinion among African Americans regarding this latest trend. On the contrary, there are many who see this new trend as dangerous and insulting. They are vehement in their denial that rap music or hip-hop culture has anything to do with the identity of the majority of African Americans in the new millennium.

And so, the search for black identity continues. W.E.B. Du Bois's observation remains every bit as timely now as it was in 1903, when he first articulated it. Many African Americans still feel their twoness: they remain marginal, negative Americans. After 100 years, Du Bois's question remains unanswered: will it ever be possible to be both black and American?

NOTES

1. Bernard Makhosezwe Magubane, *The Ties That Bind: African-American Consciousness of Africa* (Trenton, NJ: Africa World Press, 1987), 3.

2. John Hope Franklin, *From Slavery to Freedom: A History of Negro Americans*, 6th ed. (New York: McGraw-Hill, 1988), 408.

3. *Sweatt v. Painter*, 339 US. 629 (1950), 634, quoted in Donald G. Nieman, *Promises to Keep: African-Americans and the Constitutional Order, 1776 to the Present* (New York: Oxford Univ. Press, 1991), 147.

4. Steven F. Lawson, *Running for Freedom, Civil Rights and Black Politics in America since 1941* (New York: McGraw-Hill, 1991), 19.

5. Steven J. Whitfield, *A Death in the Delta, The Story of Emmett Till* (New York: Free Press, 1988), 22.

6. Ibid., 42.

7. Zohara Simmons, interview with the author, Philadelphia, PA, December 17, 1988.

8. W.E.B. Du Bois, *The Souls of Black Folk* (New York: New American Library, 1969), 45.

9. Winthrop D. Jordan, *White over Black, American Attitudes toward the Negro, 1550–1812* (Baltimore, MD: Johns Hopkins Univ. Press, 1968), 7.

10. Ibid.

11. William Lee Howard, "The Negro as a Distinct Ethnic Factor in Civilization," *Medicine* 9 (January 1903): 423, quoted in John S. Haller, Jr., *Outcasts From Evolution, Scientific Attitudes of Racial Inferiority, 1859–1900* (Urbana: Univ. of Illinois Press, 1971), 55.

12. Wilson Jeremiah Moses, *The Golden Age of Black Nationalism, 1850–1925* (Hamden, CT: Archon Books, 1978), 47.

13. Edward W. Blyden, *Christianity, Islam and the Negro Race* (London: W. B. Whittingham & Co., 1888), quoted in Hollis R. Lynch, *Edward Wilmot Blyden, Pan-Negro Patriot, 1832–1912* (London: Oxford Univ. Press, 1967), 62.

14. *Liberia Bulletin*, no. 16 (February 1900): 93. Quoted in Lynch, *Edward Wilmot Blyden*, 80.

15. Benjamin Brawley, *Early Negro American Writers* (New York: Dover Publications, 1970), 97; also John H. Bracey, Jr., August Meier, and Elliott Rudwick, eds., *Black Nationalism in America* (Indianapolis: Bobbs-Merrill, 1970), 4, 22, 29.

16. Brawley, *Early Negro American Writers*, 97.

17. Prince Sanders, Thomas Jarvis, and Perry Locks to Paul Cuffe, August 3, 1812, Paul Cuffe Papers, Massachusetts Public Library, New Bedford, quoted in Bracey et al., *Black Nationalism*, 22.

18. Brawley, *Early Negro American Writers*, 107.

19. Franklin, *From Slavery to Freedom*, 109.

20. Leon Litwack, *North of Slavery, The Negro in the Free States 1790–1860* (Chicago: Univ. of Chicago Press, 1961), 20.

21. Franklin, *From Slavery to Freedom*, 176.

22. Ibid., 177.

23. Litwack, *North of Slavery*, 253.

24. Jordan, *White Over Black*, 567.

25. Litwack, *North of Slavery*, 21.

26. "Movement among the Colored People of Cincinnati," *African Repository* (Washington, DC) 26 (July 1850), quoted in Bracey et al., *Black Nationalism*, 86.

27. Litwack, *North of Slavery*, 66.

28. Ibid., 60.

29. Henry Highland Gamet, *The Past and the Present Condition, and the Destiny of the Colored Race: A Discourse Delivered at the 5th Anniversary of the Female Benevolent Society of Troy, N.Y., February 14, 1848* (Troy, NY, 1848), 12, quoted in Bracey et al., *Black Nationalism*, 120.

30. Martin R. Delany, *The Condition, Elevation, Emigration, and Destiny of the Colored People of the United States* (New York: Arno Press, 1969), 87.

31. Brawley, *Early Negro American Writers*, 303–304.

32. *African Repository* 53 (April 1877): 75; Ibid. 56 (July 1880): 73–74, quoted in Bracey et al., *Black Nationalism*, 170.

33. Ibid., 170.

34. Marcus Garvey, *The Philosophy and Opinions of Marcus Garvey* (New York: Atheneum, 1969), quoted in Moses, *Golden Age of Black Nationalism*, 263.

35. Garvey, *Philosophy and Opinions*, 59, quoted in Moses, *Golden Age of Black Nationalism*, 235.

36. Benjamin Quarles, *The Negro in the Making of America* (New York: Collier Books, 1969), 196.

37. A Gold Coast leader, May 13, 1916, 5. Quoted in Moses, *Golden Age of Black Nationalism*, 235.

38. Matthew Jones, Jr., interview with the author, Knoxville, TN, April 24, 1989.

39. Ibid.

40. Ibid.

41. Ibid.

42. Julian Bond, interview with the author, Washington, DC, December 16, 1988.

43. Alphonso Pinkney, *Red, Black, and Green: Black Nationalism in the United States* (New York: Cambridge Univ. Press, 1976), 218.

44. Ibid., 223.

45. Clarence Lusane, *Race in the Global Era, African Americans at the Millennium* (Boston: South End Press, 1997), 96–97.

BIBLIOGRAPHICAL ESSAY

Although the literature dealing with African Americans is voluminous, much of it focuses on their subordinate position vis à vis mainstream "white" society and culture and their efforts to integrate themselves into that milieu. Works that focus directly on the evolution of African American society and culture per se are relatively rare and generally recent, although *The Souls of Black Folk* (New York: New American Library, 1969) by W.E.B. Du Bois, originally published in 1903, remains a classic, especially for its perception of African Americans as marginal and negative. A useful introduction to the concept of dual consciousness is Thomas C. Holt, "Afro-Americans," in Stephan Thernstrom et al., eds., *Harvard Encyclopedia of American Ethnic Groups* (Cambridge, MA: Belknap Press of Harvard Univ., 1980), 5–23. An appreciation of the breadth of the literature on the general topic can be gained from four bibliographies: Elizabeth W. Miller, ed., *The Negro in America: A Bibliography* (Cambridge, MA: Harvard Univ. Press, 1970); James M. McPherson et al., *Blacks in America: Bibliographical Essays* (Garden City, New York: Doubleday, 1971); John Szwed and Roger D. Abrahams, eds., *An Annotated Bibliography: Afro-American Folk Culture* (Philadelphia: Institute for the Study of Human Issues, 1978); and Robert L. Clarke, *Afro-American History: Sources for Research* (Washington, DC: Howard Univ. Press, 1981).

The basic facts of African American history can be garnered from four other reference works: John P. Davis, ed., *The American Negro Reference Book* (Englewood Cliffs, NJ: Prentice Hall, 1966); Irving Sloan, *The Blacks in America, 1492–1976: A Chronology and Fact Book* (Dobbs Ferry, NY: Oceana Publications, 1971); W.A. Low and Virgil A. Clift, *Encyclopedia of Black America* (New York: McGraw-Hill, 1981); and Harry A. Ploski and James Williams, eds., *The Negro Almanac: A Reference Work on the African American* (New York: Bellwhether Publishing Co., 1989). The evolution of African American identity and culture is dealt with in varying degrees in a number of single-volume histories. Benjamin Quarles, *The Negro in the Making of America* (New York: Collier Books, 1969), emphasizes the integral role played by African Americans in the development of the United States. So does Peter M. Bergman and Mort N. Bergman, comps., *The Chronological History of the Negro in America* (New York: Harper and Row, 1969). John Hope Franklin, *From Slavery to Freedom: A History of Negro Americans* (New York: Knopf, 1988), traces the history of African Americans from their ancient Old World roots to 1970 and reflects the optimism over progress toward full equality prevalent in the

1960s. August Meier and Elliott Rudwick, *From Plantation to Ghetto: An Interpretive History of American Negroes* (New York: Hill and Wang, 1976), encompasses the path from West Africa to the 1963 march on Washington highlighted by Dr. Martin Luther King, Jr.'s "I have a dream" speech. Much more somberly, Alphonso Pinkney, *Black Americans* (Englewood Cliffs, NJ: Prentice Hall, 1988), views the Afro-American community as an "internal colony."

A number of works concentrate primarily on the views of African Americans held by white Americans. Gunnar Myrdal, *The American Dilemma: The Negro Problem and Modern Democracy* (New York: Pantheon Books, 1975) is the classic statement, by a non-American, of the fundamental disparity between racism and the American Dream. Stanford M. Lyman, *The Black American in Sociological Thought* (New York: Putnam, 1972), places Myrdal's observations in a wider scholarly context. Winthrop D. Jordan, *White over Black: American Attitudes toward the Negro, 1550–1812* (Baltimore, MD: Johns Hopkins Univ. Press, 1968), traces the evolution of American racism from Elizabethan-age contacts with Africa through the end of the slave trade. George M. Frederickson, *The Black Image in the White Mind: The Debate on Afro-American Character and Destiny* (New York: Harper and Row, 1971), examines the continuity and transformation of white attitudes from the colonization movement through the nadir of segregation. John S. Haller, *Outcasts from Evolution: Scientific Attitudes of Racial Inferiority, 1859–1900* (Carbondale: Southern Illinois Univ. Press, 1995) analyzes the deeply flawed efforts of biologists and geneticists to come to grips with their own biases. See also Rayford W. Logan and Irving S. Cohen, *The American Negro: Old World Background and New World Experience* (Boston: Houghton Mifflin, 1967); Lerone Bennett, Jr., *Before the Mayflower: A History of Black America* (Chicago: Johnson Publishing Co., 1969); and Margaret Just Butcher, *The Negro in American Culture* (New York: Knopf, 1972).

Perhaps surprisingly, the subject of African survivals in African American culture has only begun to receive serious scholarly attention within the past few decades. An early exception, in addition to Du Bois, was Melville J. Hersvokits, *The Myth of the Negro Past* (New York: Harper and Brothers, 1941), which traces the survival of thousands of African traits in African American culture. A good general introduction to African culture and character is Basil Davidson, *The African Genius: An Introduction to African Cultural and Social History* (Boston: Little Brown, 1969). More intensive and thought-provoking is John S. Mbiti, *African Religions and Philosophy* (New York: Praeger, 1969). Philip Curtin, *The Atlantic Slave Trade: A Census* (Madison: Univ. of Wisconsin Press, 1969), demonstrates that statistics tell only slightly the terrible human cost of the commerce in human life, while Herbert S. Klein, *The Middle Passage: Comparative Studies in the Atlantic Slave Trade* (Princeton, NJ: Princeton Univ. Press, 1978), examines the argument that the slave trade provided much of the capital for the Industrial Revolution. The theme of continuity versus discontinuity receives considerable stress in the essays contained in Daniel Crowley, ed., *African Folklore in the New World* (Austin: Univ. of Texas Press, 1977). Bernard Makhosezwe Magubane, *The Ties That Bind: African-American Consciousness of Africa* (Trenton, NJ: Africa World Press, 1987), explores "the phenomenon of ambivalence" through a series of essays on back-to-Africa movements, pan-Africanism, the Italian invasion of Ethiopia, post–World War II African independence, and South Africa. In *Positively Black* (Englewood Cliffs, NJ: Prentice-Hall, 1970), Roger D. Abrahams argues that a full appreciation of the meaning and style of African American folklore will convince any reasonable person that African Americans are not "culturally deprived."

The early history of blacks in the United States is told in macroscopic fashion in Donald R. Wright, *African-Americans in the Colonial Era: From African Origins through the American Revolution* (Arlington Heights, IL: Harlan Davidson, 1990), and in microscopic fashion in Peter H. Wood, *Black Majority: Negroes in Colonial South Carolina from 1670 through the Stono Rebellion* (New York: Norton, 1974). The latter is especially useful for its insights into the impact of American slavery on African culture. Several relatively recent works have stressed the positive adaptations to slavery made by African Americans. Chief among these are John W. Blassingame, *The Slave Community* (New York: Oxford Univ. Press, 1972); Eugene Genovese, *Roll, Jordan, Roll: The World the Slaves Made* (New York: Pantheon Books, 1974); Herbert G. Gutman, *The Black Family in Slavery and Freedom, 1750–1925* (New York: Vintage Books, 1976); and Lawrence Levine, *Black Culture and Black Consciousness* (New York: Oxford Univ. Press, 1977). The perspective of those African Americans who avoided or transcended the slave experience is carefully delineated in Leon F. Litwack, *North of Slavery: The Negro in the Free States, 1790–1860* (Chicago: Univ. of Chicago Press, 1961), and Ira Berlin, *Slaves without Masters: The Free Negro in the Antebellum South* (New York: Pantheon Books, 1974).

The trauma of the postemancipation era on those African Americans who remained in the South can be apprehended from a variety of studies. Roger Ransom and Richard Sutch, *One Kind of Freedom* (Cambridge, MA: Cambridge Univ. Press, 1977), investigate the evolution and consequences of the "new slavery" of sharecropping and the crop-lien system. The imposition of legal segregation on southern blacks in the late nineteenth century has been interpreted differently by various scholars. C. Vann Woodward, *The Strange Career of Jim Crow* (New York: Oxford Univ. Press, 1974), argues that legal segregation was not a reaction against Reconstruction or a natural phenomenon but rather the outcome of a conflict between southern white conservatives and radicals. Joel Williamson, *The Origins of Segregation* (Boston: D.C. Heath, 1968), provides the viewpoints of a dozen observers organized around the general topics of genesis, historical and psychological roots, urban patterns of segregation, and the relationship between ethnocentrism and race prejudice. The corresponding disenfranchisement of African American voters in the South has been carefully dissected by J. Morgan Kousser, *The Shaping of Southern Politics: Suffrage Restrictions and the Establishment of the One Party South, 1880–1910* (New Haven, CT: Yale Univ. Press, 1974). The toll taken on southern African Americans by the twin horrors of segregation and disenfranchisement are personalized in Theodore Rosengarten, *All God's Dangers: The Life of Nate Shaw* (New York: Knopf, 1974). The persistent, but generally frustrating, efforts to achieve acculturation and assimilation through formal education are chronicled in Henry A. Bullock, *A History of Negro Education in the South from 1619 to the Present* (Cambridge, MA: Harvard Univ. Press, 1967), and in Vincent P. Franklin and James D. Anderson, eds., *New Perspectives on Black Educational History* (Boston: G. K. Hall, 1978).

The impact of the Great Migration on African American identity and culture has been examined by a number of scholars. Hollis R. Lynch, *Black Urban America since Reconstruction* (Belmont, CA: Wadsworth, 1981), is a pioneer effort to develop a synthesis on the entire experience. Reynolds Farley, *Growth of the Black Population: A Study of Demographic Trends* (Chicago: Markham Publishing Co., 1970), also deals with a variety of social and cultural topics involving urban African Americans. The bittersweet evolution of the country's largest African American community is analyzed in Gilbert Osofsky, *Harlem: The Making of a Ghetto* (New York: Oxford Univ. Press, 1966), while Nathan

Huggins, *Harlem Renaissance* (New York: Oxford Univ. Press, 1973), explores the tremendous explosion of African American creative energy that characterized that black metropolis in the 1920s. Sociologist Kenneth B. Clark lays bare the enervating pathology, psychology, and power structure of the modern black slum in *Dark Ghetto: Dilemmas of Social Power* (New York: Harper and Row, 1965).

Several other studies focus on the evolution of an African American community in some of the country's largest cities. Allan H. Spear, *Black Chicago: The Making of a Negro Ghetto, 1890–1920* (Chicago: Univ. of Chicago Press, 1967), stresses the crucial role played by the Great Migration of 1915–1920 and the building of white resentment culminating in the race riots of the "Red Summer" of 1919. Kenneth L. Kusmer, *A Ghetto Takes Shape: Black Cleveland, 1870–1930* (Urbana: Univ. of Illinois Press, 1976), also assigns major importance to the Great Migration but sees more grounds for optimism by 1930 with the emergence of the "new Negro." Joe William Trotter, Jr., *Black Milwaukee: The Making of an Industrial Proletariat, 1915–1945* (Urbana: Univ. of Ilinois Press, 1985), explores the "proletarianization" of the Cream City's African American population in an age of heavy industrialization. For views of the African American urban experience over time, readers should consult Theodore Kornweibal, Jr., ed., *In Search of the Promised Land: Essays in Black Urban History* (Port Washington, NY: Kennikatt Press, 1981), and Hollis R. Lynch, *The Black Urban Condition: A Documentary History, 1866–1971* (New York: Crowell, 1973). Finally, Charles Kiel explores the significant role played in the city life of African Americans by blues musicians and preachers, in *Urban Blues* (Chicago: Univ. of Chicago Press, 1966).

As with most ethnic groups, politics provided northern African Americans with one of the earliest and most accessible avenues of acculturation and assimilation. One of the first scholars to appreciate and elucidate the importance of that connection was Harold F. Gosnell, *Negro Politicians: The Rise of Negro Politics in Chicago* (Chicago: Univ. of Chicago Press, 1937). James Q. Wilson, *Negro Politics: The Search for Leadership* (Glencoe, IL: Free Press, 1960), also focuses on Chicago and on the organization of Negro political and civic life and the character of Negro public life. The relationship between political adaptation and the struggle for equal rights is deftly explored in Steven F. Lawson, *Running for Freedom: Civil Rights and Black Politics in America since 1941* (New York: McGraw-Hill, 1991). The importance of legal action to that same process is carefully outlined in Donald G. Nieman, *Promises to Keep: African-Americans and the Constitutional Order, 1776 to the Present* (New York: Oxford Univ. Press, 1991). A more microcosmic look at the same phenomenon is found in Richard Kluger, *Simple Justice: The History of* Brown v. Board of Education (New York: Knopf, 1975). The brief springtime of political emergence in the Old South is thoughtfully analyzed by Thomas C. Holt, *Black over White: Negro Political Leadership in South Carolina during Reconstruction* (Urbana: Univ. of Illinois Press, 1977). Its reemergence nearly a century later is the subject of political scientist Everett Caril Ladd's *Negro Political Leadership in the South* (Ithaca, NY: Cornell Univ. Press, 1966).

Efforts to generate a genuine African American nationalism that would blend both sides of their "dual consciousness" antedated the Civil War, as Wilson Jeremiah Moses, *The Golden Age of Black Nationalism, 1850–1925* (Hamden, CT: Archon Books, 1978), painstakingly demonstrates. His analysis focuses on nineteenth-century leadership and programs, as well as on black nationalism in literature. John H. Bracey, Jr., August Meier, and Elliott Rudwick, eds., *Black Nationalism in America* (Indianapolis: Bobbs-Merrill,

1970), concentrate on the institutions that promoted nationalism and on the divergent economic, political, social, and cultural themes that comprised it down to 1968. *Red, Black, and Green: Black Nationalism in the United States* (New York: Cambridge Univ. Press, 1976), by Alphonso Pinckney, locates the roots of the phenomenon in a drive for African American solidarity, pride in cultural heritage, and a desire for political autonomy. The range of opinion on the prevailing outcome of over three centuries of African American adaptation is displayed in Norman F. Whitten, Jr., and John F. Szwed, eds., *Afro-American Anthropology: Contemporary Perspectives* (New York: Free Press, 1970), whose twenty-two essays are organized around cultural patterning, socioeconomic adaptation, and the ghetto ethnography of "black culture." Lorraine A. Williams, ed., *Africa and the Afro-American Experience* (Washington, DC: Howard Univ. Press, 1981) is a series of eight essays on the ongoing connection between the people of the two continents. No study of African American nationalism should ignore John Henrick Clarke and Amy Jaques Garvey, eds., *Marcus Garvey and the Vision of Africa* (New York: Random House, 1974). See also Hollis R. Lynch, *Edward Wilmot Blyden, Pan-Negro Patriot, 1832–1912* (London: Oxford Univ. Press, 1967).

AMERICAN INDIANS

Vine Deloria, Jr.

Among American domestic ethnic groups, the original inhabitants, the Indians, constitute a special case. Their ethnicity is a product of historical process and political ideology rather than racial and cultural homogeneity. Indeed, *Indian* is a generic term akin to *Asian* or *European* in the sense that it refers to a large grouping of diverse peoples who occupy a continental land mass rather than a nationalistic entity with historic, homogenous roots. Western scientists have tried to make American Indians a racial unit by insisting that the western hemisphere was populated by migrants from Asia who traversed the Bering Strait land bridge, a mythical corridor created by the manipulation of water levels during certain of the ice ages. Indian tribes, which each have a particular tradition relating to their origin, migration, or creation, universally reject this origin theory.

The origin/creation emphasis of Indian tribes is important in that tribal ethics, social values, and philosophical perspectives are all grounded in the cosmic beginnings of the people and shape all of their actions. Thus, many tribes see creation as a unified activity that bestows on all life forms a basic personality and knowledge structure. Humans are different in kind than other creatures but not set apart for special purposes. Therefore, religious duties include responsibilities for all nonhuman creatures as well as for individual people and other societies. Lands that a tribe occupies are often given to them in the sacred plan of creation for the present world. Tribes may have been created on these lands or told to migrate to them. When lands and peoples are matched together in a cosmic plan, the attachment to the land by the people becomes something extraordinary and involves a sense of identity and a corresponding feeling of responsibility transcending anything that people outside the tribe can comprehend or experience.

That tribes have been able to maintain their discrete identities as national groups can be attributed to their steadfast adherence to their mission as a distinct people, as revealed to them in creation or upon one of their migrations. In the sense that tribes have a divine function within a specific world period, Indians do not see themselves as an ethnic group within a larger society but as a small yet faithful remnant of a people called to a larger vocation. Prophecies suggest that the tribe is destined to vanish or at least dissipate prior to the ending of each world cycle, and people are content with this knowledge. Presumably, the human race is reconstituted on these occasions and survivors come together to form new tribal groups and receive new commands on how to live in the reconstituted world.

Tribes are, therefore, ultimately guided by internal prophetic instructions rather than external political and economic events, and the success or failure of the tribe in dealing with unexpected problems can be traced to this concern with fulfilling their cosmic responsibilities. But in terms of this discussion, and for a comparison of Indians to other American ethnic groups, the focus must be on the political/historical factors that have created American Indians as a unified ethnic group within the American social fabric.

Europeans' initial penetration of the interior of the continent brought them into contact with powerful Indian confederacies such as the Six Nations, the Creeks or Muskogees, the Miamis, the Powhattans, and the Natchez. These Indian groups had sufficient population to control large areas of the eastern United States and the military prowess to make colonization hazardous, if not impossible, without their goodwill and assistance. For at least half of the five hundred years since the landing of Columbus, Europeans badly needed a military alliance with these groups in order to protect their claims to colonial land areas against other Europeans intent on developing competing colonies. Consequently, in North America, the practice grew up of recognizing the national status of these groups by negotiating informal treaty relationships with them. For a significant period of time, Indian confederacies held the balance of power between the European colonial powers that wished to dominate the continent, and the political status and military potential of Indian tribes was a well-established fact by the beginning of the American Revolution. Indeed, in the 1780s, the Comanches could field a larger fighting force than could the Americans or English.

The Americans assiduously cultivated the neutrality of the Indians during their war for independence, and during the struggle for the adoption of the Constitution, Indians were one of the major issues on the American political agenda. The Founding Fathers, failing to anticipate how quickly they would settle and control the interior of the continent, saw the commerce and treaty-making clauses as adequate for describing and defining their relationships with American Indians in the future. The constitutional question that involved Indians was posed in a state-to-state relationship. The United States, fearful that its own claim to national political independence would be challenged by the established nations of Europe, went to extravagant lengths to demonstrate its political independence by making Indian treaties formal documents of state that were submitted by the president and ratified by the Senate in the same manner that treaties with European nations were accepted as law.

Within this formal setting, the United States then made the claim that it had stepped into the shoes of the European colonial nations insofar as the Doctrine of Discovery gave it the title to lands on the continent. The Doctrine of Discovery was a pillar of emerging international law that briefly stated that a Christian monarch could claim the legal title to lands that his subjects discovered if these lands were unoccupied or if they were occupied by non-Christian peoples. The natives, under this doctrine, had to content themselves with the equitable, as opposed to legal, title to their lands, which meant, in practical terms, that only the monarch who held legal title could validly purchase their property estate. In return, the monarch accepted the responsibility to bring the natives to a full understanding of Christianity and to protect them from the intrusions of other European monarchs.

The United States emphasized protection and could not give Christianity its proper due because of its constitutional prohibition against combining the policies of church and state. This protection matured into a doctrine of American federal law that said that a particular kind of "trust" existed between the national government and the Indian tribes. This trust is nebulous in the sense that its reach and the circumstances under which it must or can be applied have never been clearly articulated by the courts or Congress. Therefore, Indians have a separate and distinct legal and political status within the American system that generally operates as an exclusionary clause. Indians are not presumed to be covered by or included in constitutional and domestic law unless they are specifically mentioned.

Consequently, a separate body of law has grown up dealing with the particularity of tribal and individual Indian rights and the relationship between indigenous peoples. This law does not form a consistent and logical whole and is more akin to a body of equitable maxims than to a regular subdivision of law such as contracts, torts, or criminal law. But it is the body of rules and regulations that distinguish Indians from other ethnic groups. A law dealing specifically with the Irish, Polish, or Jewish people would be unconstitutional on its face. The same law applied to American Indians would be described by the courts as political because of the Indian treaty and trust relationship.

The United States made nearly one thousand treaties with the Indian tribes, but only about half of the treaties negotiated were ever formally ratified. Ratification often depended simply on the manner and speed with which the treaty text was presented for ratification in Washington. Therefore, the record is spotty at best and can be described as so haphazard as to preclude and defy any effort to formulate the principles upon which treaties were actually ratified. Some treaties represent serious and prolonged negotiations over issues critical to tribal survival or American military and property interests; others represent simply a casual meeting between Indian representatives and local field officers of the United States. The result of this confusion is that Indian tribes are presumed to possess a plentitude of aboriginal sovereign political powers unless treaties or subsequent acts of Congress specifically divested them of these rights.

Both the treaties and the trust responsibility have moral and ethical dimensions in that they represent a pledge of national honor. They speak to the spirit of the law rather than its letter. In this century, the combination of treaty rights and trust responsibilities has produced a general acceptance of Indians' legal and moral claims on the federal government and the wholly inconsistent notion that Indian tribes are nevertheless quasi-independent political entities with the power of self-government and inherent sovereign powers in commerce and property usage. Federal law often operates, therefore, on the basis of political and economic expediency, and how it is applied largely depends on how the current presidential administration perceives Indians. American Indians, therefore, are completely at the mercy of forces and personalities beyond their control, and this fact alone distinguishes them from all other American minority groups. No constitutional protections exist for American Indians' ethnic identity. By the same token, federal law recognizes in American Indians certain rights and privileges that it cannot recognize in other minority groups.

This extensive preamble to the discussion of Indian ethnicity is necessary because the history and political status of Indians has created in the modern world a peculiar condition for Indians that relates directly to their own conceptions of ethnic identity and their efforts to preserve it. Since the treaty/trust restrictions have been applied to groups in an indiscriminate manner, it is fair to point out that many Indian communities are Indian in a political sense, but that they are sometimes indistinguishable from other Americans culturally, linguistically, or even religiously. The legal and political nature of Indian ethnicity is thus apparent: some Indian groups would have completely assimilated into the American social fabric a century ago were it not for the special status of dependent nationhood that the law bestows on them.

A further peculiarity results from the application of federal law to Indian communities. If Congress grants formal recognition of a community's Indian identity and allows it to organize under one of the laws recognizing self-government, that community is then vested with all of the aboriginal sovereign powers that other tribes are presumed to possess. Congress cannot arbitrarily choose any American community and "make" them Indians, and the criteria for bestowing this tenuous status on a community is rarely defined with any precision. Here, apparent ethnicity seems to create legal rights and political privileges when properly presented to legislative authority. So culture, at least cultural traits that seem to suggest stereotypical commonality with existing Indian groups, becomes an important asset in itself. In this case, the power of the historical experiences of both Indians and non-Indians prevails.

With Indian's, political and historical context established, American Indians can now be compared with other domestic American ethnic groups. Immediately, abstract principles in two areas appear to be of critical importance in understanding the place of Indians in American society: intermarriage and education. But even these topics are fraught with historical baggage. They appear in history at approximately the same time and have about the same influence today as they did when they first began happening. Because intermarriage seems to be the more influential in terms of its political consequences, that topic is covered first, though with the awareness that education could equally well deserve initial attention and discussion.

Intermarriage can be discussed geographically as well as historically because of the nature of European colonization. Most prominent is the intermarriage between Indians and the Spanish in the American Southwest. A large American ethnic group derives from the Indian-settler marriages in this region. It is important to note that there were few European Spaniards in the Southwest at any point in American history. The class definitions that emerged after Cortez's conquest of Mexico were brought northward by mixed bloods who settled Texas, California, and southern Arizona and New Mexico. Over the generations, the degree of Spanish blood must have become almost infinitesimal, so that most Mexican Americans today are probably genetically full blooded Indians. There is probably a greater degree of Indian blood present in a Chicano barrio than there is in some Indian tribes.

In the Spanish-Mexican communities in the United States today, the strength of Spanish culture and language is evident, testimony of the residual power of Spanish feudal class distinctions. The Indian contribution to Mexican culture primarily occurred on an individual basis as each man or woman left his or her tribe and became a part of the dominant society, adopting whatever behavior patterns were necessary to gain acceptance in Mexican society. Southwestern foods illustrate an Indian heritage, but where are the religious, kinship, and other cultural traits of the Indians that in other parts of the continent proved so resistant to change? Contemporary observers point out how Catholic ceremonies were adapted to local Indian beliefs, but they fail to give credit to the fact that these adaptations are *minor* elements in contemporary Mexican Catholicism. In general, Spanish-Mexican culture swallowed Indian individuals and culture and produced a strong and resilient Mexican ethnic group.

In the areas of former French settlement or domination, such as Louisiana and the upper Great Lakes, we also find a large population of mixed-blood peoples. The French colonial practice was to intermarry with the Indians and to exchange children so that the two groups would more quickly come to understand each other. So fundamental was the French-Indian intermarriage practice that in some tribes today French ancestry is almost the equivalent of Indian ancestry, and only those people who have traceable English ancestry are regarded as whites. Although the Iroquois, who have formally hated the French since Champlain sided with the Hurons against them, are an exception. The Ottawas, Potawatomis, Chippewas, and Sioux all have had extensive intermarriage with Frenchmen or with mixed bloods who themselves had a French ancestor.

The importance of French intermarriage cannot be underestimated when viewed from a historical perspective. The Metis in Canada largely originate from these marriages and form a particular class of people in Canadian society. The fur trade would have been impossible in the West without the French-Indian connection, and most of the knowledge of the western regions that English Americans had in the nineteenth century was derived from the mixed-blood Frenchmen. This group of mixed bloods also played a dominant role in the political affairs of the tribes from the first contact with the United States. French-Indian interpreters were present as brokers of the treaties at almost every treaty north of the Mason-Dixon line, and when treaty making ended, they emerged as the dominant group in the profitable vocations of traders, Bureau of Indian Affairs workers, and ranchers in the Great Plains. By the time the Miami Confederacy encountered the United States, the group's leading political families were primarily of mixed French ancestry. The same can be said to a lesser degree of the Chippewa. Only since World War II has the individual with combined French-Sioux heritage achieved a high position in that tribe.

French intermarriage can be understood as the opposite of Spanish intermarriage. Frenchmen tended to move into the tribe, and only when there was a need for the tribe to deal with English Americans did these mixed bloods emerge as a class. Consequently, the French cultural influence on the Indian tribes was minimal, but its political and economic impact was enormous. Except in French Catholicism, there is little discernible trace of French cultural characteristics in those tribes that intermarried with this nation of Europeans.

English intermarriage is difficult to trace because the people who tended to intermarry did not always regard themselves as Englishmen, although within the larger span of European ethnicity they may be regarded as English. Probably the first large-scale intermarriage activity was between fugitive Scottish and Irish indentured servants and Indians in the South. The Indian frontier was not as threatening to Scotch and Irish men as historians would lead us to believe. As soon as they saw the opportunity available to free men in the New World, indentured servants fled to the Appalachians or the Deep South, usually picking up an Indian wife in the process and settling in remote places where they could not be discovered and brought back to serve out their terms. By the time the major Indian tribes in the South confronted the English settlers in frontier wars, a good many of their political leaders were mixed bloods. In the war of 1814 between the Creeks and Andrew Jackson, for example, the Creeks were led by Red Eagle, otherwise known as William Weatherford, a man who was only one-eighth Creek. Many of the Cherokee, Choctaw, and Chickasaw political leaders were also mixed bloods.

Scottish-Irish intermarriage with the Creeks, Cherokees, and Choctaws produced a separate class of people who could only be said to be protosouthern in the sense that their behavior forecast the manner in which the Southern society developed. By the time of Indian Removal in the 1830s, the leading families of the tribes and the whites in the Southern states were often cousins or could at least trace themselves back to a common ancestor not far removed from their own generation. Intermarriage in the South produced what can only be described as two classes of Indians—so-called respectable and real Indians, the respectable people being only a trace Indian but the trace being sufficient to grant them authenticity and status in white society. Today we find thousands of whites who trace their ancestry back to either Pocahontas or a Cherokee "princess," rather than a real full-blooded Cherokees.

It was the propensity of mixed-blood members of the Southern tribes to play both whites and Indians against each other for their own gain that led to the belief that Indians could probably be civilized. Thus, the five major Indian groups from the South have always been called the Five Civilized Tribes. Very early on, they were insisting on educational benefits in their treaty provisions, and a Choctaw academy was even established for mixed-blood sons and daughters of this elite group of people. With some rare exceptions, mixed bloods have always dominated as leaders in the political affairs of the Five Civilized Tribes, and this is still true today. One man, W. W. Keeler, for example, was chairman of the board of Phillips Petroleum and chief of the Cherokees at the same time, and a good many of the Oklahoma politicians have had some trace of Indian ancestry. Charles Curtis, vice president of the United States under Herbert Hoover and a native of Oklahoma was part Kaw Indian. He was deemed competent to be vice president, and yet his trust land was under the supervision of the Bureau of Indian Affairs. In prereservation days, it was not uncommon to have people of mixed tribal ancestry in every tribe, because Indians had a propensity to adopt captives taken in war to replace family members lost in the conflict. Some famous chiefs were adopted members of the tribes that they led in the closing days of the last century, Washakie of the Shoshones and Spokan Garry of the Coeur d'Alenes being prominent examples of this phenomenon. But marriage between tribes took on important dimensions after the Indians were settled on the reservations and their children were sent to government boarding schools far away from their home reservations. Government boarding schools greatly increased the rate of tribal intermarriage, skewing the numbers far beyond what would normally have occurred. Young Indians meeting at government schools would fall in love and get married, producing several generations of Indians with mixed tribal backgrounds.

Today, when the U.S. census is taken, statisticians have a terrible time establishing the proper categories for tribal population. Probably three-quarters of the Indians in the country have dual ancestry, quite often involving two or more Indian tribes, with some individuals on the West Coast often representing eight or more different tribal groups. This situation is the direct result of government educational programs that have emphasized removing Indian children from their homes to be educated in off-reservation boarding schools. The pattern is predictable. The off-reservation schools were begun in the late 1880s. The first generation of students returned home and achieved some degree of prominence in tribal affairs. Some Indians earned professional degrees in law or medicine as a result of their government education and represented the beginnings of a middle class in some tribes. When their children were of an age to attend school, many of the first generation looked back with some degree of pride on their achievements and insisted that their children attend the same boarding schools. However, the second generation viewed off-reservation education as a means of moving beyond the confines of the tribal community and, with the attitude that they could deal with white society as equals, this generation also broke many of the old clan and kinship restrictions and married people from other tribes who they had met in boarding schools.

The children of the second generation came of age in or after World War II, and these people tended both to marry outside the tribe and to relocate themselves to urban areas in the Bureau of Indian Affairs' relocation vocational program. They were also inclined to marry other Indians who had attended school with them and shared the same attitude toward the larger society. Their children have tended to marry non-Indians with whom they have grown up in urban and suburban areas far from the reservations. If one were to consider the possibilities of permutations and combinations from this typical scenario, it is not difficult to see that an individual could have direct ancestral ties with at least a dozen tribes.

The result of tribal intermarriage is that the sharpness of individual tribal heritages has been lost, and in its place a national sense of pan-Indianism has emerged. Individual Indians have been forced to confront this situation when tribal lines are crossed because of the difference in customs and family responsibilities. For example, a Plains Indian marrying into an eastern or southeastern tribal family would move from the Plains extended family context to the larger clan context of his in-laws. He or she could not completely fulfill the duties that are now expected by the clan and still maintain the original Plains kinship duties also. So a mixing occurs in which the two traditions are still represented, but in the form of personal compromise and choice that changes the shape of individual behavior in all social situations. What may be acceptable social behavior in a naming ceremony in one context, for example, is not proper behavior in the other tribal situation. So the individual, in trying to perform some relevant social role in this dilemma, in effect creates a pan-Indian behavior pattern that subsequently becomes the manner in which people act.

The merging of tribal particularities after World War II produced a general sense of Indian-ness in which similarities shared by tribes gradually merged into a new set of social values that were acceptable in both tribal traditions. Such ceremonies as that which took place in the sweat lodge soon transcended individual tribal practices to become one of the rituals that Indians engaged in regardless of tribal backgrounds. By the 1970s, it was possible to find wholly new kinds of behavior generally accepted as being Indian, when in fact they represented changes that had occurred within the previous generation. Many tribes, for example, had special ceremonies in which friends were made. The acceptance of this friendship required a loyalty and commitment equal to or greater than the duties and support owed a sibling. In a pan-Indian setting, however, making friends became simply an act of identifying fellow Indians within a non-Indian social context; for example, attending an urban Indian center and becoming acquainted with other Indians who lived in the same neighborhood. The hospitality and helpfulness characteristic of Indian tribes was still experienced, but friendship itself had lost its sacred sanction and support.

On the national level, this growing together of many tribal traditions provided the foundation for activist protests by such organizations as the American Indian Movement, which discovered that it could appeal to a wide audience on the basis of Indian racial identity alone by advocating unity on behalf of a larger political cause. Unless a specific goal was established by the activists, such as restoring lands for a particular tribe or insuring fishing rights for tribes in a specific region, issues were generally framed in terms of demanding from the federal government concessions that presumably would improve the lot of all tribes. Pan-Indianism did not, therefore, seek to encourage Indians or tribes to do things for themselves. Rather, it accepted the definition of *Indians* as an American minority group and sought to make the group an identifiable political constituency with recognizable influence, a group to whom successful white politicians owed favors. Thus, today, we often talk about the Indian vote as if it is a monolithic thing that can be courted by the pronouncement of certain emotional slogans representing political sympathy and understanding. We hardly ever speak of tribal voting to achieve specific tribal goals.

Having a multitribal genetic background is not a hindrance to most individual Indians. If a person is enrolled in one tribe, it is usually that of his or her father, and enrollment in a tribe usually means forfeiture of rights in or claims to rights as a member of another tribe. Today, some tribal governments have solved this problem of multitribal background by counting the total degree of Indian blood as if it were coming entirely from the parent who makes the children eligible for tribal membership. This technique clarifies the political status of the individual and also helps to solve another problem. Since federal services are usually restricted to people of one-quarter degree of Indian blood, individuals can be enrolled members of a tribe but not always eligible for some kinds of federal services. Or individuals can have sufficient Indian blood but not be enrolled in any tribe because of tribal requirements. For instance, a tribal enrollment committee might not necessarily regard children of a full-blood mother and a white father as Indians eligible for enrollment. Individuals must pay special attention to their genetic ancestry so that they can continue to receive federal services.

If intermarriage with non-Indians and other tribes has been important in forming the present posture of the American Indian community, education has been nearly as important. Under the Doctrine of Discovery it was the responsibility of the European monarch to teach the Christian religion and bring "civilization" to the natives under his sovereign control. In North America, private citizens voluntarily undertook this task initially, and only in recent times has the federal government assumed the task of "civilizing" the Indians. Most of the early colleges in the New England area started partly as mission schools to help teach the local Indians Christianity. Harvard, Princeton, Dartmouth, and William and Mary are among the more prominent institutions whose initial capital partly was given so that the Indians could be instructed in the Gospel.

Among the lasting benefits of this early concern was the translation of the scriptures, and eventually other works, into some of the tribal languages. This process has continued until the present, when many tribes are still translating materials into their own languages. At first, the effort was directed toward making the Indians familiar with biblical themes so that they could much more easily understand English when it was taught to them. The popular bilingual programs of the War on Poverty during the 1960s also had this goal when encouraging the use of the tribal language. In both instances, however, the effect was to interest the people in using their own language, demonstrating that education should be conceived in terms of the tribal goals and not necessarily in measures pleasing to outsiders.

Education was at first a function of the missionaries, and some tribes insisted that missionary groups be given lands so that they could establish schools for the children of the tribe. Later, as federal services became a greater part of the treaty promises, the federal government embarked on an ambitious educational program for Indians that featured the creation of day schools on the reservations. But these schools generally had a difficult time receiving adequate funding because they did not seem to be producing educated Indians with sufficient speed for Congress. So the program of taking children and placing them in boarding schools was adopted. By World War I, there were nearly sixty of these schools in the United States, but the idea of placing them at great distances from the reservation had changed; the emphasis instead was in providing an education to every child from the reservation.

Vocational education long dominated the federal concepts of the kind of education that Indians should receive, and even until the mid-1960s Congress believed devoutly that Indians could not master academic subjects but greatly preferred to learn skills where they could use their hands. Indians, on the other hand, always sought to learn whatever skills would best enable them to earn a living on or near their reservations, and therefore they liked vocational education, since the area to which they would return had few people with academic credentials. The majority of reservations from which the children came were located in remote areas in the West, where there were few white-collar or professional jobs, and there was no great demand for academic education among Indians until they became aware of the larger society in the 1960s. Since then, Indians have sought academic and professional training in record numbers.

The educational hopes of Indians always represented conflicting goals and a confused image of the substance of white society. Education was seen as a means of getting equality in material goods so that the people could live a better, more prosperous life and as a means of protecting the tribe from the intrusions made by the whites. Indians thus sought technical knowledge without realizing that by changing their cultural values to accept this technology they were reducing the distance between themselves and the whites to such a degree that there would be little Indian substance left to protect. In this manner, the Cherokees reduced their customs to written laws and a constitution, invented an alphabet and written language, made every possible overture to the southern whites and merely earned white resentment to such a degree that it became impossible for the federal government to protect their lands and resources, and they were removed from Georgia to Oklahoma.

Indian societies were tightly organized around the sacred teaching and rituals that, it was believed, had been handed down through the centuries and would ensure the continued existence of the tribe and allow for its participation in cosmic realities. Education made these cosmic realities seem remote and, eventually, superstitious, so that the propensity of most educated Indians was to reject the good things in their tradition and accept the worst aspects of the white culture. The heroic figures of Indian history, seen from the perspective of both whites and Indians, are those Indians who held fast to their traditional ways. Educated Indians were perceived as a people set apart from both whites and other Indians. Whites resented educated Indians and believed they were not "real," while Indians saw education as an experience of alienation that made white people out of tribal members.

A consequence of educated Indians' position midway between Indian and white society is that they have often become brokers of power and interpreters of culture between the two groups. As more Indians have become educated since World War II, this group has grown considerably so that it is fair to say that about half of each tribe consists of educated people who do not quite fit in with the central core of tribal society. One need only glance at the tribal scholarship awards or the Bureau of Indian Affairs lists of scholarship recipients to see that the people getting financial support to continue their education are often not reservation residents but Indians from families who have previously moved off the reservation or away from the community, retaining their tribal enrollment but for all practical purposes living and learning as whites in American society.

One of the most detrimental effects of education on Indians has been the abandonment of the old ways and of the old knowledge about the world. Indian health has greatly deteriorated with the loss of traditional medicines and cures. Some Indians blame the change of diet for their bad health conditions, but there is some evidence that the loss of knowledge about plants and their medicinal uses has contributed even more to the inability of either the Indians themselves or the Public Health Service to improve Indian mortality rates. This condition has become very apparent in some tribes because with the resurgence of interest in traditional ways, people are once again beginning to use traditional medicines and are discovering that they can cure a multitude of illnesses with them. In the tribal context, because of the belief in the basic relatedness of the natural world, the deterioration of health indicates a bad spiritual posture and an abandonment of guiding spiritual principles. Education, many Indians believe, caused the people to lose faith in the things that they knew and followed.

The remedy for this condition is not, as some people would have it, a rejection of Western medicine but the elevation of the medicine man or healer to his proper place in tribal society. Since many Indians fall within the educated class of tribal society, a strange phenomenon has occurred in which people who would otherwise accept Western science are coming to depend on traditional medicines and religion to maintain themselves. If this trend continues, the result will be a group of people who are indistinguishable from other Americans and reasonably well educated but adherents of a modernized version of the old tribal religions.

Education can also be used as a measuring stick to evaluate the spectrum of beliefs and practices within tribal societies. If we were to chart the actual educational achievements of all the members of a tribal group, we might find ourselves with a steep parabolic curve in which we find a few members very well educated and a few members hardly educated at all or refusing any contact with the modern world. The majority of tribal members would have a high school diploma and some vocational training and a few at the bottom would have a government school certificate. But this curve is becoming flattened as reservation community colleges offer advanced programs that enable people to secure degrees while living at home.

The same parabolic curve can equally well represent the degree of assimilation and traditionalism to be found within the tribe. There are always a few people who deny their Indian ancestry and seek to disappear within American society. There is always a small, hard core of traditional people who act as if five hundred years of contact with whites has never happened. The majority of Indians in most tribes, however, characterize their Indian heritage according to the manner in which they see themselves functioning in their home environment. Consequently, there is an ebb and flow within the tribes that governs the degree to which people demonstrate or display Indian traits and characteristics. In this respect, Indians are probably not much different than members of other American ethnic groups in showing pride in their heritage.

The activism of the 1970s made it imperative for many people to emphasize their Indian heritage. Some people with a minimal claim to Indian traditions enthusiastically threw themselves into the activist movement and, unfortunately, a good many non-Indians came to believe they were also Indians. So the number of people who claimed to be Indians increased dramatically. Many reservation people who traditionally had shunned white society and were hesitant to show traditional Indian characteristics took heart at the outpouring of interest in Indians and began sharing their knowledge and beliefs with less traditional people. The result was that the national Indian community took on a more militant posture regarding what it meant to be an Indian, and interest and participation in tribal culture and religion escalated accordingly. Today, a near majority of members of each tribe seem to regard themselves as traditional people or as people who revere tribal traditions.

One symptom of this change has been the increasing emphasis on learning the tribal language. Until the early 1960s, it was presumed that most tribal languages were dying out and, indeed, there was solid evidence that English had made great inroads even in the most conservative tribes. Through the authorization of bilingual programs that sought to teach English, or at least lay the groundwork for teaching English, by emphasizing the native language, many of the tribes have used bilingual education to teach their children the tribal tongue.

But this kind of learning has generally followed the traditional classroom methods of teaching, so that Indian children often had to learn their own language as if it were Latin or Greek. In recent years, some university classes in tribal languages have been offered so that a larger group of people now speak a tribal language.

In the long run, native languages will probably disappear because of the inordinate influence of television on younger children. In the midst of the Navajo reservation in Arizona, at Chin Lee, there are three video tape rental stores, an indication of the widespread degree to which the Navajos already speak and understand English. When English becomes the language of the home, thanks to videotapes, it is very difficult to maintain the native language on a consistent basis. Many tribes now conduct their tribal business meetings in English so they can include the TV generation of Indians. It may not be long before only a few very traditional tribes such as the Iroquois can speak their own language with any degree of assurance and confidence.

The political strategies of American Indians differ quite substantially from those of most other ethnic groups. Until World War II, each tribe more or less handled its own business and dealt with important national legislation according to the way it felt the law would affect the reservation. Even though there were a number of voluntary organizations dedicated to assisting Indians with their problems, Indians had no capability to speak with a united voice on legislation that affected all tribes. At the very end of the war, some of the Bureau of Indian Affairs employees, at the urging of Commissioner John Collier, came together to form the National Congress of American Indians (NCAI). Over the years the NCAI has come to represent the mainstream opinions of tribal councils and informed, interested Indians.

In the early 1970s, a new group, partly competitive with the NCAI, the National Tribal Chairmen's Association (NTCA), was formed. It was originally designed to be the Indian counterpart to the various state and city organizations that work for improved conditions and benefits for state agencies and city councils. The NTCA, however, adopted a stance almost indistinguishable from that of the Bureau of Indian Affairs and usually supported the Bureau in its policies and programs. Since its major funding source was the Bureau it is not surprising that the NTCA followed the government's party line so closely. It did not last, because it had no significant constituency and its usefulness to the government failed miserably.

The 1970s were the years of the Indian activists, having their origins in the fishing-rights struggle in the Pacific Northwest in the 1960s and the occupation of Alcatraz in 1969. Even people who have been involved with Indian activism from its inception have a difficult time writing its chronology or providing an accurate view of the many organizations that emerged during this era. The most persistent groups have been the American Indian Movement (AIM), which was the group that led the occupation of Wounded Knee in 1973, and the Survival of American Indians, which began the fishing rights protests in the mid-1960s.

The Indian activists were indeed activists, and membership in each group at times seemed to boil down to which button an Indian was wearing.

With the conclusion of the Wounded Knee trials in 1976, emphasis began to be placed on seeking an international forum where Indians could align themselves with aboriginal peoples from around the globe. This tendency has grown over the past two decades so that some activist groups are now more interested in the hemispheric problems such as the Indians in Nicaragua than in reservation conditions. The present generation of Indians, as a group, eschews political action, as they seem to fear losing the status they have as professionally educated people. As a result, there is sparse response from Indian country when negative policies are devised for Indians. Unless this attitude changes, Indians will lose many of the gains that were made in the 1960s and 1970s.

The recent political strategies used by Indians can be divided into two broad attitudes that represent two distinct historical periods. From the end of World War II until 1970, the tactic was to pose as America's favorite minority and play off the favorable image of Indians against the stereotypes that whites held of Blacks and Chicanos. Whenever a civil rights protest would stir up a controversy, Indians would point out that they had greater needs but did not feel they should take to the streets and lose their dignity over an issue that could be resolved by a simple demonstration of goodwill on each side. This tactic did produce results, because Indian tribes were made eligible agencies under many of the national poverty program authorizations. Thus, tribes could sponsor programs for areas under their control and benefit from the large managerial overhead fees that such agencies received. By the mid-1970s, tribes were eligible for a bewildering number of programs, so many that they had to start being selective in bringing programs to the reservations. The problem with this strategy was that, because of the peculiar nature of the Indian relationship with the federal government, it did not address the problems that arose.

The activist strategy was to call the government directly to account for its past misdeeds and omissions. Treaty rights rather than eligibility and need became the criteria for protest, and the idea was to play directly on whatever reservoir of cumulative guilt lay hidden in the public psyche. That this tactic was partly successful is evident in the fact that when the Indians occupied the Bureau of Indian Affairs in Washington, doing more damage to federal property than the British did when they sacked Washington during the War of 1812, the public was largely behind them. But collective historic guilt is difficult to transform into contemporary political support, and when the public came to understand that some Indian claims, although just and valid, might upset land titles in the eastern states or curtail hunting and fishing in the western states, support for Indians vanished, leaving behind a few militant anti-Indian groups that sought abrogation of all treaties, unsuccessfully.

Increasing the Indian participation in state and national elections has been a continuing goal ever since World War II, and a good deal of work has gone into increasing the number of Indian votes in critical states and congressional districts.

However, Indians are such a small percentage of any important state or congressional election that it has been difficult to make the Indian vote count. Additionally, Indians seem to be too honest to make maximum use of their voting advantages. Since reservations are located in the most remote areas of each state, it would not be difficult for a number of the large tribes to simply wait out the election night and then return the number of votes needed to determine the outcome of close elections. Although, this vote withholding is not in the best tradition of democracy, it has been practiced by the two major parties in many states of the union and has occasionally proven important in determining the outcome of elections. That Indians do not presently engage in such practices is certainly to their credit.

In recent years, the gaming tribes have contributed heavily to some of the presidential and congressional campaigns. The Indians of California spent a considerable amount of money to ensure that a proposal affecting their gaming privileges received maximum publicity, and they were successful in their efforts. In South Dakota, massive voter registration campaigns ensured that a very high percentage of residents voted. They were so successful that accusations of padding the election rolls were made against them by losing candidates—a sure sign of efficient political participation. Other tribes have suggested holding tribal elections when the national elections are held to increase voting, since people vote much more often in tribal elections.

Indians, at least since the Depression, have tended to vote Democratic, and by the end of the 1960s, most tribes were clearly of Democratic composition. The 2002 elections showed a continued support for the Democrats when the Indians of South Dakota overwhelming supported the Democrat in the Senate race. Prior to the New Deal shift in voting loyalties, it was possible to determine the probable vote of reservation residents by the political allegiance of their agent, who had great influence over how the tribe viewed the political world. This factor may also account for the relative political isolation of reservation people until the 1970s and their refusal to align themselves with other minorities seeking change.

Following World War II, it was almost a standard doctrine among Indians and Bureau of Indian Affairs personnel that Indians and blacks had nothing in common. The elected officers of the NCAI cringed when people suggested that Indians cooperate with blacks on issues of mutual concern. Political folklore dictated that Indians form coalitions with Asians, another silent minority, and until tribal leaders had to deal with black program officers in the poverty-program agencies, there was great suspicion that blacks wanted to integrate Indians into the American social mainstream and abolish the reservations.

The Poor People's March in 1968 had a number of Indian participants and probably broke the informal political color line that had existed during most of this century. With the increasing number of tribal council members in the NCAI in the late 1960s, the organization was forced to deal with isolated tribes in the eastern and New England states who had worked well with the NAACP, so that by the mid-1970s, it was commonplace to have Indian leaders suggesting some kind of alliance with other minorities. When Jesse Jackson began his campaign in 1984 and talked about his "Rainbow Coalition," he was surprisingly well received in Indian country.

Until 1960, Indians did not see themselves in the context of American minorities. The prevailing attitude was that they had a special place near, but certainly not in, American society and the task of tribal leaders was to provide whatever protections could be established to keep the outside at arm's length. Tribal eligibility for social-welfare programs broke this sense of determined isolation once and for all. With a great increase in college scholarships, thousands of young Indians headed for college and saw the world pretty much as non-Indians of the same age saw it. As people became more familiar with the world outside the reservation, there is no question that they began to see themselves as another minority group in American society, but a minority with special rights. The activism of the 1970s only confirmed this viewpoint and made it a regular part of the Indian perspective, even of the reservation people. Tribal leaders began to see that their people were part of the much larger forces of social change occurring in all parts of the world. The favorable publicity that Indians have usually received in their role as the Noble Savage wronged by a larger society was transformed by some Indian leaders into a demand that Indians be included in the various civil rights, ecological, and political coalitions that were forming and fermenting in the larger society.

One gauge of the seriousness and permanence of this movement is the very evident loosening of ties within the extended Indian family. Tribal, family, and clan membership once dominated all other considerations, and it was possible for an informed member of one tribe to know or identify almost every other member of every other tribe. This extensive kind of knowledge seems remote if not impossible, but the basis for it was simple. Through their boarding school experiences, many Indians knew members of other tribes and, correspondingly, their families. Elders kept track of the family relationships and passed the information along to the younger generation so that one needed only to know tribe and last name in order to place an individual and locate his home community. This basic identity has now significantly eroded if not vanished altogether in many tribes.

With family no longer acting as the dominant force in restraining behavior, there is little sense of tribal identity other than enrollment number in many Indian communities. Enrolled members of the same tribe may meet at conferences or pow-wows and discover they have no knowledge of each other's families whatsoever. They may even learn that they have no mutual friends or acquaintances. This condition is unprecedented in Indian country. On the other hand, they may find that they share many friends in other tribes who are in the same or related professions or in the same age group. The connections in Indian Affairs have become networks rather than family relationships, and in this sense, Indians have become an American ethnic group rather than a small collection of distinct tribal nationalities.

The popular practice today is to recite one's clan or kinship allegiance when being introduced. Thus, a young Indian may say they are Muskogee, Wind clan on their father's side, Alligator clan on their mother's side. In the old days, such an introduction would call for immediate response and welcome. Today, it seems more like reciting a social security number to identify one's eligibility in the group. Since this practice is prevalent among urban-dwelling Indians and does not necessarily imply a rigorous adherence to clan practices, it seems premature to identify any particular motive for the practice.

At the same time that the old relationships are breaking down, some form of modern traditionalism is surging in many Indian communities. Modern traditionalism seems a contradiction in terms but it is the best description of how Indians are forging a modern identity as a group. Foremost in modern Indian interest is religion, generated initially by the participation of some well-known medicine men in some of the marches on Washington held during the mid-1970s. Additionally, beginning around 1969 and continuing for most of the 1970s, a group of traditional leaders of many tribes met annually in Canada under the broad rubric of the Ecumenical Council. People from many tribes attended these sessions, listening to a mixture of old teachings and prophecies and demonstrating concern for the loss of language and tradition among the young people.

The Ecumenical Council succeeded in reaching people of all ages, far beyond their most optimistic expectations. An impressive number of young people left their careers in Indian organizational work and returned to their reservations determined to learn the tribal ways and become carriers of the traditions. Since the conditions under which the old ways were practiced no longer exist, the most satisfactory solution for these young people was to derive principles of action and understanding from the traditions and apply them to the modern circumstances in which they found themselves. The movement should therefore be denominated as modern traditionalism because it seeks to transform old ways of behaving into standards of action with definable limits set by the conception of Indian identity itself.

Indians, therefore, find themselves at a unique point in their history. The present generation of tribal leaders can best be described, using Robert Bellah's terminology, as a *managerial elite*. That is to say, they are very competent in the administrative skills of the larger society, being able to complete complex federal application forms with speed and accuracy. They can easily read statutes of great complexity and give a fair rendering of the most complicated procedures required to become eligible for programs. They view the tribe as a sovereign entity but seek to develop it in ways indistinguishable from their white neighbors.

Coming right behind them, and offering a more Indian, alternative way of viewing the world are the new traditionals, who are already having quite an impact on tribal life. A recent example may clarify this development. Since the federal recognition of the right of self-government in 1934, it has become almost a duty of tribal councilmen to reward themselves for their service by establishing a lucrative fee schedule for work on tribal business. Indeed, in some tribes per diem and fees constituted one of the few ways for people on the reservation to earn cash income. Although the rank-and-file tribal members often complained bitterly about this practice, until very recently it was unthinkable that anyone would oppose paying tribal councilmen for their attendance at meetings and other tribal business. But some tribes have now voluntarily reduced the fee schedule for tribal elected officials, leading people to assume that while there is a strong managerial inclination in tribal government, there is also a strong undercurrent of traditional belief still present that argues for the old idea of contributing to the welfare of the community as a matter of personal responsibility.

Some interesting programs have arisen as traditional values have been seen as feasible goals. More than forty tribes now raise buffalo on a financially sustaining basis. The trend is to use buffalo raising in education, economics, and general morale building among the people. The Cheyenne River Sioux tribe has been featured in national magazines for its land-use program, which emphasizes buffalo herding. The Salish and Kootenai tribes of Montana have set aside a large tract of land as a grizzly bear sanctuary. The Oklahoma Cherokees have created a comprehensive course on tribal history and rights for all employees and tribal members who wish to learn about Cherokee traditions. Workshops are held around the country, enabling tribal members who live off-reservation to participate.

Indian gaming has become one of the controversial and widespread activities of the tribes in recent years. Beginning with a bingo hall in Florida authorized under the Reagan administration, gaming quickly developed into full-fledged casino operations. Location has meant everything in the development of Indian gaming. Small tribes located near large urban areas have been very successful in their efforts, while tribes in rural areas have not done nearly as well. Income from Indian gaming is now estimated in the billions annually. There are so many casinos in California that they are basically competing against each other rather than against Las Vegas and Reno.

Some tribes have so much income from gaming that they can give substantial dividend checks to members on a monthly basis. Almost all tribes use some of the gaming funds for social-service programs on the reservations, while others devote the money to land purchase or education. The Pequots of Connecticut have given $10 million to help build the National Museum of the American Indian in Washington, DC. Most of the tribes also contribute significantly to local non-Indian charities, help build roads and parks, and participate in local civic affairs.

Two main attitudes can be discerned in today's Indian world. Indians who used to be called progressive, and who are primarily represented by educated younger people, still believe that with a prodigious effort, tribal economies can be raised to the level of their white neighbors. These people work hard in tribal-development programs, support educational opportunities for the coming generation, and seek participation in state and county activities. By and large, although few Indians would admit it, the foundation of this attitude is the belief that Indians have become an American ethnic group and must accommodate themselves to the American way of doing business.

The problem with this approach to tribal affairs is the inability to understand the immense amount of resources and credit that must be accumulated in order to be successful in the American economic game. Indian tribes simply do not have access to this kind of money, regardless of the glitter and gleam that is present in some of the modern economic opportunities, particularly gaming. At best, American Indians can only become one of the poorer and least favored ethnic groups by following this path. The American economy is geared toward creating massive amounts of capital for reinvestment, and tribes must always be focused on the people in the communities and their desires. Some industries, such as commercial hog farms, were initially embraced and then attacked because they are too far away from the beliefs and desires of tribal members.

The other posture present in the Indian world is the return to traditionalism in some form. Here the spectrum is wide, and it includes representatives of almost every nuance of tradition present. Some people want to return to the old ways in every aspect of life, and in Canada there have been experiments in living in the forests again. When this extreme behavior is found in American Indian communities, it usually manifests itself in a resurgence of traditional medicines, subsistence hunting and farming practices, and revitalization of old religious ceremonies. In general, traditionalism is more influential in religious circles and social organizations than in tribal governments and economic-development practices. It has not yet, to any significant degree, assisted in rebuilding families and communities and seems to be restricted to self-improvement and anti-alcoholism activities. Traditionalism seems to be important to many Indians because it provides a recognizable identity for both individuals and communities without an acknowledgment of the difficult facts of economic and political life. In this sense, it resembles Christian fundamentalism in the larger society. But many Indians see traditionalism as the first step in a reconstitution of the tribal community, and so it offers hope for the preservation of the people without the adoption of distasteful cultural values that connection with the industrial machine inevitably brings.

The ultimate fate of American Indians will probably be the same as that of other rural Americans, with a few variations. In choosing to remain in isolated rural areas, Indians must also learn to forego the frills and gimmicks of modern American urban life and make choices about foods, medicines, entertainment, occupations, and participation in the larger society. The fact that these choices are necessary has not been clearly articulated by or for Indians. Consequently, traditionalism still looks much more attractive than does assimilation as an ethnic group. A stabilizing of rural America would do much to demonstrate to the tribes that a partial accommodation to industrial society can be made without losing a sense of community. Initially, *stabilizing* in the Indian sense can only mean a consolidation and expansion of the reservation land base and proper use of its resources, but neither is far enough along yet to indicate which direction the people will take.

BIBLIOGRAPHICAL ESSAY

Narrowing the voluminous literature on American Indians to those works that deal directly or primarily with their interaction with Euro-American society and culture is a herculean task, especially because both Native Americans and mainstream Americans have been extremely ambivalent and fluctuating about the relative merits of separation and acculturation/assimilation. In more recent years, the leading advocates of the various Native American movements have frequently disagreed over the importance of maintaining the rich historical diversity of tribal and national identities versus the necessity of constructing a generic American Indian identity that might conceivably consolidate and maximize economic and political power. The article "Indians," written by Edward H. Spicer for the *Harvard Encyclopedia of American Ethnic Groups* (Cambridge, MA: Harvard Univ. Press, 1980), 58–114, provides a good introduction to and overview of that dilemma. Also very useful is his *A Short History of the Indians of the United States* (New York: Van Nostrand Reinhold Co., 1969). The diversity and complexity of American Indian identity and culture is best conveyed by a collective reading of a number of relatively recent reference works. *The Dictionary of Indian Tribes of the Americas*, 3 vols., compiled and published by American Indian Publishers (Newport Beach, CA: American Indian Publishers, 1980), provides brief descriptions and histories of all the Indian nations. Francis Paul Prucha, *Atlas of American Indian Affairs* (Lincoln: Univ. of Nebraska Press, 1990), conveys a good sense of their changing geographical distribution and resultant cultural adaptation over time, as does Carl Waldman, *Atlas of the North American Indian* (New York: Facts On File, 1985). Frederick W. Hodge, ed., *Handbook of American Indians North of Mexico*, 2 vols. (New York: Greenwood Press, 1969), gives a brief description of the linguistic stock, confederacy, and settlement patterns of all U.S. and Canadian tribes and subtribes. Barry T. Klein, ed., *Reference Encyclopedia of the American Indian*, 2 vols. (New York: Todd Publications, 1986), provides valuable information on reservations, tribal groups, bands, councils, museums, libraries, schools, college courses, magazines and periodicals, and audiovisual aids, as well as extensive bibliographies. Wilcomb E. Washburn, ed., *Handbook of North American Indians*, 20 vols. (Washington, DC: Smithsonian Institution, 1988), features volumes on geographical regions, Indians in contemporary society, environment, origins, population, history of Indian-white relations, technology and visual arts, and languages. It also includes a two-volume biographical dictionary and an extensive index volume.

Carl Waldman, *Who Was Who in Native American History: Indians and Non-Indians from Early Contact through 1900* (New York: Facts On File, 1990) focuses primarily on prominent individuals, whether Native American or those who interacted with them in important ways. So does Frederick J. Dockstader, *Great North American Indians: Profiles in Life and Leadership* (New York: Van Nostrand Reinholdt, 1977). For a chronology of events and ready references to dates significant in American Indian history, see Henry C. Dennis, ed., *The American Indian, 1492–1976: A Chronology and Fact Book* (Dobbs Ferry, NY: Oceana Publications, 1977). Arnold Marquis, *A Guide to America's Indians: Ceremonials, Reservations and Museums* (Norman: Univ. of Oklahoma Press, 1974), supplies such information for 263 tribes, bands, and groups in the United States.

J. R. Swanton, *The Indian Tribes of North America* (Washington, DC: Smithsonian Institution Press, 1969) is generally considered to be the standard work. Ruth Underhill, *Red Man's America: A History of the Indians in the United States* (Chicago: Univ. of Chicago Press, 1971), focuses on the universality and peculiarity of cultural traits, while Ethel Nurge, ed., *The Modern Sioux: Social Systems and Reservation Culture* (Lincoln: Univ. of Nebraska Press, 1970) uses the tribe as a prism through which to view other tribes. The anthology *North American Indian's Historical Perspective* (New York: Random House, 1971), edited by E. B. Leacock and N. O. Lurie, conveys a strong sense of chronological progression.

The tortured course of changing U.S. policy toward American Indians can be traced in many sources. Calvin Martin, ed., *The American Indian and the Problem of History* (New York: Oxford University Press, 1987) contains twenty expert essays on "the metaphysics of writing Indian-white history" from the Native American perspective. Jane F. Smith and Robert M. Kvasnicka, *Indian-White Relations: A Persistent Paradox* (Washington, DC: Howard Univ. Press, 1976), the product of the National Archives Conference on Research in the History of Indian-White Relations, examines the ongoing ambivalence between assimilationist and separatist policies. The same general focus pervades Larry W. Burt, *Tribalism in Crisis: Federal Indian Policy, 1953–1961* (Albuquerque: Univ. of New Mexico Press, 1982), which demonstrates that the paradox of termination versus tribalism endures. James Axtell, *The European and the Indians: Essays in the Ethnohistory of Colonial North America* (New York: Oxford Univ. Press, 1981) examines the early origins of that phenomenon, while Robert Berkhofer, Jr., *The White Man's Indian* (New York: Knopf, 1978), explores the various stereotypes and misconceptions that have consistently informed Euro-American attitudes toward Native Americans. Roy Harvey Pearce, *The Savages of America: A Study of the Indian and the Idea of Civilization* (Baltimore: Johns Hopkins Press, 1953), traces the evolution of the "superior civilization" rationale for the destruction of Indian culture and identity. Frederick E. Hoxie, *A Final Promise: The Campaign to Assimilate the Indians, 1880–1920* (Lincoln: Univ. of Nebraska Press, 1984) focuses on the era that produced the Dawes Act, the breakup of the reservations, and the use of religion and education as tools for "civilizing" Indians. Francis Paul Prucha's ironically titled *Americanizing the American Indian: Writings by the "Friends of the Indian," 1880–1900* (Cambridge, MA: Harvard Univ. Press, 1973) examines a similar phenomenon, while Basil H. Johnston, *Indian School Days* (Norman: Univ. of Oklahoma Press, 1990), concentrates on the concerted effort to alienate the younger generation from their native culture through enforced education.

Wilcomb E. Washburn, ed., *The American Indian and the United States: A Documentary History*, 4 vols. (New York: Random House, 1973) is a comprehensive collection of the reports of commissioners of Indian affairs, congressional debates, acts, ordinances, proclamations, treaties, and legal decisions that defined Indian–United States relations over two centuries. J. Norman Heard, ed., *Handbook of the American Frontier: Four Centuries of Indian-White Relationships*, 5 vols. (Metuchen, NJ: Scarecrow Press, 1990) provides many insights into both sides of the frequent contact between Native Americans and Euro-Americans. Francis Paul Prucha, *The Indian in American Society: From the Revolutionary War to the Present* (Berkeley: Univ. of California Press, 1985), examines the relationship from the perspectives of paternalism, dependency, Indian rights, and self-determination. Wilcomb E. Washburn, ed., *The Indian and the White Man* (Garden City, NY: Anchor Books, 1964) contains over 100 documents organized around the topics of first contact, personal relations, justification for dispossession, the trade nexus, the missionary impulse, war, governmental relations, and literature and the arts. Vine Deloria, Jr., ed., *American Indian Policy in the Twentieth Century* (Norman: Univ. of Oklahoma Press, 1985) is a collection of essays by eleven scholars on various aspects of federal policymaking and enforcement regarding "the Indian problem." S. Lyman Taylor, *A History of Indian Policy* (Washington, DC: Bureau of Indian Affairs, 1973), presents the U.S. government point of view.

Several other fairly recent works concentrate on the tensions within the American Indian community over acculturation, traditionalism, and progressivism. D'Arcy McNickle, *Native American Tribalism: Indian Survivals and Renewals* (New York: Oxford Univ. Press, 1973), explores the modern origins and paradox of such concepts as Indian nationalism, pan-Indianism and Red Power. Murray L. Wax, *Indian-Americans: Unity and Diversity* (Englewood Cliffs, NJ: Prentice Hall, 1971), contends that the American Indian identity has emerged out of the relationship between the native people of the Americas and their European-descended invaders. Howard M. Bahr, Bruce A. Chadwick, and Robert C. Day, *Native Americans Today: Sociological Perspectives* (New York: Harper and Row, 1972), view American Indians primarily from the standpoint of social class analysis. The growing movement toward self-help and cross-tribal association is documented in Armand S. La Potin, ed., *Native American Voluntary Organizations* (Westport, CT: Greenwood Press, 1987). Providing a variety of answers to the question of "Who is an Indian?" within a historical context, Hazel W. Hertzberg, *The Search for an American Indian Identity: Modern Pan Indian Movements* (Syracuse, NY: Syracuse Univ. Press, 1971), examines several fraternal and religious universalist Indian movements in the twentieth century. See also the chapter on "Pan-Indianism" by Robert K. Thomas in Stuart Levine and Nancy O. Lurie, eds., *The American Indian Today* (Deland, FL: Everett Edwards, 1968).

The persisting conundrum between traditionalism and termination is explored thoroughly in Wilcomb E. Washburn, *Red Man's Land/White Man's Law: A Study of the Past and Present Status of the American Indian*, in which he concludes that "the Indian of the Future" cannot totally return to the past or completely retain the present culture. Robert Burnette, *The Tortured Americans* (Englewood Cliffs, NJ: Prentice Hall, 1971), surveys the tragic history of Euro-American treatment of American Indians and proposes a "Fair Indian Act" to Congress. The peculiar problems of the growing numbers of urban Indians and their greater receptivity to a definition of pan-Indianism have received increasing attention. Jack O. Waddell and O. Michael Watson, eds., *The American Indian in Urban Society* (Boston: Little Brown, 1971) ranks as the pioneer work on the topic. The socioeconomic dimensions of urban settlement are examined in Henry F. Dobyns, Richard W. Stoffle, and Kristine Joes, "Native American Urbanism and Socio-Economic Integration in the Southwestern United States," *Ethnohistory* 22 (Spring 1975): 155–179. The relationship of pan-Indianism to city dwelling forms the perspective of James Hirabayashi, William Willard, and Luis Kemmitzer, "Pan-Indianism in the Urban Setting," in Thomas Weaver and Douglas White, eds., *The Anthropology of Urban Environments* (Washington, DC: Society for Applied Anthropology, 1972).

Over the last two decades, the growing militancy of American Indians has manifested itself in many publications. *Custer Died for Your Sins: An Indian Manifesto*, by Vine Deloria, Jr. (New York: Macmillian, 1969), and *Bury My Heart at Wounded Knee: An Indian History of the American West* by Dee Brown (New York: Holt, Rinehart & Winston,

1971) formed a powerful one-two punch. Close behind came Alvin M. Josephy, Jr., *Red Power: The American Indians' Fight for Freedom* (New York: American Heritage Press, 1971), an analysis of this new militancy. In the years that followed, Deloria also contributed *Of Utmost Good Faith* (San Francisco: Straight Arrow Books, 1971), a study of the disparity between landholding theory and of civil rights; *We Talk: You Listen* (New York: Macmillian, 1970), an impassioned plea for a new civic religion that promotes individualism through tribalism and federalism; and *The Indian Affair* (New York: Friendship Press, 1974), a powerful brief for legal research and support, Indian control of Indian education, and diligent congressional oversight. Attempts by federal law enforcement agencies to suppress the new militancy, specifically the Federal Bureau of Investigation's suppression and the Lakota Indians during the 1970s and 1980s, is the theme of *In the Spirit of Crazy Horse* (New York: Viking Press, 1983) by Peter Mathiessen.

ARAB AMERICANS

Gregory Orfalea

Like many immigrants to America, Arab Americans, or Syrians, as they were universally called well past World War II, experienced difficulties of adjustment due to language, racial discrimination (in the early days, the Syrians were one step lower than the Irish), and different social customs, but they have had it fairly good in America. Although they wished to avoid definition vis-à-vis the growing turmoil and chronic warfare in the lands of their ancestors, not to mention America's inexorable pull into the region because of its relationship with Israel and reliance on oil, Arab Americans are now front and center not only in America's foreign policy but in its domestic life. The stakes are high, if not dire. In the spring of 2003, a member of President Bush's Commission on Civil Rights testified in a public hearing in Detroit that should there be another terrorist attack on the United States by Arabs, the hew and cry for evacuation camps, such as those into which Japanese Americans were thrown in World War II, would be hard to resist. At least one member of the same commission agreed with him.

To have gone in one century from being a community at ease and prosperous in the business environments of America, if generally anonymous and nonpolitical—a kind of "benevolent stranger"[1]—to one of the most politicized ethnicities in U.S. history, subject to radical surveillance, is an incredible thing to behold. One might wonder, post–9/11, if the Arab American is now seen as a malevolent stranger.

There are gradations of the current tension. Certainly, recent Muslim immigrants have had it much harder than Arab American descendants of the original, nineteenth-century Syrian peddlers and factory workers. An overview of the Arab American community's unusual experience as immigrants will be presented—for one thing, they had the longest boat voyage of any ethnic group to America—its life at work, family, religion, politics, and art and literature. In the American way, there were many failures and many successes and patriotism certainly plays a role: just ask Arab American Tony Ismail of Dallas, the largest manufacturer of American flags.

IMMIGRATION

There are many tales of very early Arab adventurers to the New World, including a Moorish translator named De Torre who supposedly accompanied Christopher Columbus. Even earlier and more mysterious are ancient Libyan markings in sandstone in Arizona and New Mexico. There is intriguing evidence of Arab names in cemeteries on the outer banks of North Carolina, where a ship containing Algerian horses replenishing supplies for the American Revolution went aground in 1782. One hotel owner on Okracoke Island, Larry Wahab (pronounced Way-Hab there but Wah-Haab in Arabic), pointed to his grandmother's daguerrotype on the wall. She looked very dark and had a severe Semitic nose. He was convinced of the connection.

But the first documented, and celebrated, Arab immigrants who stayed and died in America were a New Yorker and an Arizonan. The first was a young man named Antonious Bishallany, who, in 1854, showed up on the New York doorstep of a man he had taken around the Holy Land as a dragoman, or tour guide, two years earlier. He was from Lebanon. Ingratiating himself as a butler, he soon became the talk of the town. Two years later, he died young of tuberculosis, one of many diseases of the lungs that would plague Syrians in the cold world. Before medicines for respiratory illnesses were made, Americans coughed a lot in the cold East and North, but no one so much as those used to warm weather, such as the Syrians and the Italians. Bishallany is buried in Greenwood Cemetery in Brooklyn.

The year Bishallany died, 1856, the other noted "first immigrant," a Muslim named Haj Ali, came ashore as a camel driver and soon became known as Hi Jolly. He had been brought over with a herd of camels by Secretary of War Jefferson Davis, who worked for the Union in pre-Civil War days, and was fascinated with the idea of a camel highway from the East through Texas and the Southwest to California, a sort of early Route 66. It didn't work, because the camels didn't take well to America's rocky deserts, but it seems that Hi Jolly adjusted well. He married an American girl and settled in Arizona, where today there is a marker to his name in Quartzite.

The Arabs came to America in essentially three distinct waves. The first wave, from roughly 1878 to 1924, was 90 percent Christian and almost entirely Levantine; that is, from Syria, Lebanon, or Palestine. The second wave, from 1948 to 1967, was probably about half Muslim and half Christian, and it contained a significantly higher number of refugees from Palestine, because of the creation of Israel in 1948, as well as from Arab countries such as Egypt, Iraq, Syria, and Lebanon, which were undergoing independence struggles from colonial powers (England and France) as well as dictatorial takeovers. The third wave, from 1968 to the present, is considered by most scholars to be majority Muslim (at least 60 percent), and is an intensification and diversification of the previous wave: people fleeing civil wars (Yemen, Lebanon, and Morocco), religious repression (Syria and Algeria), and wars of conquest (Israel and Iraq).

What made the first-wave Syrians leave a land of such ancient traditions for one that was brand new? It's the subject of some debate among scholars. Historian Alixa Naff comes down on the side of financial opportunity, downplaying the theories of repression and want that characterized Philip Hitti's early classic on the subject, *The Syrians in America*. Naff thinks Hitti was trying too hard to frame a picture of the Arabs as downtrodden like the Jews and others.

Certainly, the highest rates of immigration in the first wave occurred at the onset of World War I, and there are many memoirists who make no bones about what propelled these people to the New World: starvation. The single most traumatic occurrence in the early Syro-Lebanese experience, reached its depths in 1916 in Lebanon, when a quarter of the population, or 100,000, died of malnutrition.

There were at least five reasons why the Arabs came to the New World in sizeable numbers at the end of the nineteenth century.

First, American Protestant missionaries had preached to Christians in the Levant early in the nineteenth century, but their effect was universally positive. The American spiritual leaders (and medical doctors) were seen as unbiased, and during the Christian-Druze massacres of 1860, both sides took refuge in the home of Reverend and Mrs. Simon Calhoun, to the point of stuffing their jewelry in the Calhoun closets. A Druze businessman in New York later called the early American missionaries in Lebanon, "angels in our land."[2] So American equanimity was a large pull factor to the New World.

Second, the religious mosaic in Lebanon and Syria that shattered in 1860 was never completely repaired. It wasn't only Druze-Christian tension, either. In 1914, Reverend Abraham Rihbany wrote in the *Atlantic Monthly* about a "Hatfield-McCoy" rivalry between Christian sects in El Schweir that propelled his family to a new village (Betater) where they were unknown, having no clan of their own there. " 'Thou shalt not oppress a stranger' is a command which is universally observed in Syria," Rihbany noted.[3] And if it was good to be a stranger in Betater, why not America?

Third, economic gyrations, a land squeeze, and overpopulation propelled the early Syrians outward. Between 1865 and 1871, there was a severe silkworm blight in Lebanon, which negatively affected silk production. Arable land in the rocky Lebanon mountain was always scarce, and eventually there was literally no more land to divide up among families and children. The great international fairs in Chicago (1893) and St. Louis (1904) were a magnetic draw to those seeking a new work life.

Fourth, the hand of the Turkish sultan came down ever harder on the subject Arabs as the nineteenth century waned. In 1880, thousands of books were burned by Sultan Abdul Hamid II, repressing what had been an intellectual ferment. In

1916, fourteen Syrian patriots were hanged in Beirut and seven in Damascus. Many Syrians, especially Christians, had no desire to fight for the Sultan in World War I, nor did they wish to hang around for the final crumbling of Europe.

Fifth, the traumatic event in the collective mind of the original Syrian immigrants remained the starvation that gripped Lebanon during World War I. Peak years of Syrian immigration to America in the first wave were 1913 (9,210) and 1914 (9,023), clearly the onset of the World War I. The population was hit three ways during the war: a blockade of Beirut harbor by the French and British, through confiscation of foodstuffs by Turkish troops, and by Mother Nature in the locust plague in 1916. The man who sold Safeway Foods half its spring potatoes, Amean Haddad, witnessed it as a boy: "All you saw under the plum tree were the pits. It was not only bad; it was a sight you will never forget. You are hungry and here is an animal who came over and ate what you could have lived on. Why did the *jarad*, the locust, come and eat all our food? Our grain, our wheat, barley, corn, vegetables, plums—everything. Why?"[4]

Michael Suleiman spotted in early Syrian immigrant essayists and intellectuals an ambivalence about America: "While it is true that the vast majority were enthralled by the great material wealth and fabulous inventions of American civilization, the more discerning and educated Arab immigrants presented a far more nuanced picture, which praised progress but was not blind to the costs involved."[5] Most, perhaps, were just glad to work and see a crust of bread on the table.

WORK

No one took to peddling in America like the early Syrians. They liked getting out on the open road, where they could play the role of benevolent stranger to the hilt. They were Americanized quickly as they dispersed from the original colonies on Washington Street on the Lower West Side of Manhattan and Atlantic Avenue in Brooklyn.

Peddling helped them learn English. It forced interchange, conversation, and idle banter with customers out across the plains and cities. It encouraged entrepreneurism. Peddling was also prosperous—a $60 million industry for the Syrians by 1910. The average Syrian income ($1,000) that year was three times the American average.

They put the marketplace (*suq*) in one bag (*qashshah*)—notions of all kinds, thread, ribbons, handkerchiefs, laces, underwear, garters, suspenders. Being from the Holy Land, they made sure a Kansas housewife knew that this rosary was from Bethlehem (though it could easily have been Bethlehem, Pennsylvania!), that cross from Jerusalem. The role of the early Syrian peddler in American culture was immortalized in the role of Ali Hakim in the Broadway musical *Oklahoma!* A lesser-known play that nevertheless was a Broadway success, the 1912 *Anna Ascends*, showcased a Washington Street Syrian coffeehouse and the love story of a Syrian waitress named Anna and an Anglo customer. The playwright, Henry Ford Chapman, was inspired by a real Syrian waitress he had observed in a coffeehouse in Boston and a family he had known in Washington, D.C.: "Their family life, their clean way of living impressed me and I decided that the Americanization of such a race was a big factor in making the 'melting pot' one of the greatest nations on earth. I figured here is a people who could read and write probably six thousand years before the northern 'blue eyes.'"[6]

Stubborn, self-propelled, proud, initiating, the Arabs took to the entrepreneurial soil in America and in fact may have carried some overseas themselves. Early on, they got involved in the garment and cloth industries, holdovers from their centuries-old work in silk and lace in Lebanon. By 1924, there were twenty-five Syrian silk factories in Paterson and West Hoboken, New Jersey. The kimono (thirty-five manufacturers) and Madeira lace industries in New York were almost exclusively in the hands of the early Syrians. Half the sweaters made in New York were made by the Syrians. In the Roaring Twenties on Broadway, F. A. Kalil won a national competition to produce sweaters bearing the name of football immortal Red Grange.

Some perspective is needed, however. The chief Syrian competitor in the so-called rag business, their crosstown rivals on the Lower East Side—the Jewish Americans—owned 241 garment factories in 1885, or 97 percent of all such factories. The Syrians cut into this some, but not significantly. In some cases the "if you can't beat 'em, join 'em" mentality held sway.

The love of garment making followed the Arab American migration from New York to California after World War II, in firms named Saba, Jan-Sue, Charm of Hollywood (whose founder, Albert Orfalea, posted the small seed money that his son, my uncle Paul, used to found the giant photocopy store chain Kinko's), and many others. In the 1960s, my own father's company, Mr. Aref of California, originated what was called the granny dress, which was featured in *Time* magazine. Its designer was his Jewish partner, George Wilner. For a time in Los Angeles, it was like the Middle East—Christians, Jews, and Muslims arguing, sqwawking, but ultimately working in harmony to fashion things of beauty that made the body appear better than it was.

Some struck out for parts unknown and started sewing. Two of the oldest and most respected men's clothing manufacturers, Haggar Slacks and Farah, were founded in Texas by two men who were originally first-wave peddlers.

Though most wanted to be their own person, some early Syrians labored in the hard industrial factories such as the woolen mills of New England. Although it was unusual for them to take to the unions, one Syrian led the historic 1906 Bread and Roses strike in the mills of Lawrence, Massachusetts—a harbinger of the labor and consumer activism of Ralph Nader, who had grown up in a Syrian restaurant-running family in Winsted, Connecticut. Nader, who captured 4 percent of the vote in the 2000 presidential election, was polled by Gallup in 1971 as the sixth most popular man *in the world*.

Lured by General Motors and Ford to Flint and Detroit, Michigan, by U.S. Steel to Pittsburgh, by box factories and Willys Auto to Toledo, Ohio, and by looms to Quincy, Massachusetts, Muslim Syrians also were a majority of the workers in Michigan City, Indiana, who fashioned the elegant, velvet-lined train Pullman cars. In 1916, 555 Syrian men were working at Ford car plants.

Some descendants of the original Syrian immigrants, such as Dr. Joseph Jacobs and Dr. Michael DeBakey, applied their native strain of initiative and creativity to science, making in a sense a breakthrough business of their scientific prowess.

Born in the Brooklyn colony, Jacobs worked at first for the giant American pharmaceutical firm Merck and Company, where he played an important role in the development of mass-production processes for making Vitamins B and C, as well as penicillin and DDT. But in the tradition of his Lebanese immigrant father, Yusuf, who had had a monopoly on the manufacture of straight razors in the United States when the German imports were cut off by World War I, son Joe wanted to be his own boss. After World War II, he took off to Pasadena, California, to start what became a mammoth Jacobs Engineering Group, today worth $4.6 billion a year.

Dr. DeBakey, the Lake Charles, Louisiana–native son of Lebanese drug store owners, has been called the most famous doctor in the world. He developed the heart-lung pump and process that led to the first open heart surgery and pioneered surgery for strokes, coronary bypasses, and organ transplants. Even at age eighty he was averaging 500 coronary bypass surgeries a year. He once referred to the "agony and ecstasy" of surgery.[7]

According to the U.S. Small Business Administration, except for one group (Russians, probably early immigrant Russian Jews), Arab Americans have the highest rate of self-employment of any ethnicity in the United States.[8] Recent surveys indicate that the average income of an Arab American is $47,000 versus the $42,000 national average. It might be said that no one took to the bedrock of American economic and social life—owning one's own business—more than those Semitic brothers and sisters, Arabs and Jews. In that sense, no one has been more American. When, after the tragedy of September 11, 2001, more than 700 hate crimes were directed against people of Middle Eastern background, or thought to be so, it was a kind of American self-flagellation.

One last work venue should be noted: the military. About 15,000 Syrians served in World War I, and about double that number served in World War II. Captain James Jabara was the first American jet ace spanning the Second World War and Korea. Najeeb Halaby, who later served as President Kennedy's head of the Federal Aviation Administration, was the first man to fly a jet across the American land mass, a Lindbergh of the continent. This strong patriotic streak in Arab Americans continues to this day: the head of all Allied forces in Iraq is Arab American, General John Abizaid.

FAMILY AND RELIGION

For Arab Americans, family has always been especially valued, to the extent that the quest for self often begins and ends in family. Family life is a vindication of the multiplicity of existence and in it the lessons and responsibilities of life are learned deeply, or not at all.

The paradox of the gregariousness of the Arab American is that it is rooted in ancestral isolation—the isolation of Druze and Christian Lebanese mountaineers, Shiite marsh dwellers in a Sunni state in Iraq, and the more ancient confrontation with empty space that the desert presented to the Arab. The colloidal suspension of minorities in the millet system of Ottoman Turkey made for a fragmented society, but tough families woven as tightly as a prized carpet.

The "cousin" concept is also ever present in the Arab American family. By this continually replenishing well of extended family, cousins fill in when the nuclear family itself is not present, or even when it is. There is a remarkable buoyancy about this cousin network in the Arab American community, a safety net of affection that supercedes anything one could have monetarily.

Saul Bellow, a winner of the Nobel Prize for Literature, wrote about this phenomenon in Jewish American life in his short story "Cousins," but the cousin network is especially pronounced in Arab American life. It often extends to people who are not strictly blood relatives. A cousin network may have become more a part of the American culture, too, softening everyday pressures and romanticisms in a society that gives greater stock to a nuclear family that too often can fall apart. Whether or not it is a gift to American life, it is a bulwark against the darker tides of freedom.

A history of starvation and want can make people cling to each other all the more, especially in a host society of great distances. But another factor was faith. Though there are many Arab American skeptics, and pessimism about things political is rampant, one would be hard-pressed to find too many dyed-in-the-wool atheists. As Helen Thomas, the great United Press International White House reporter once said, "God runs through all our conversation" (*Nishkur Allah*, if God wills; *Allah makoon*, God go with you; *Allah maalak*, God, go slowly; *Ya Allah!*, my God!).

The early Syrians were 90 percent Christian, 10 percent Muslim. The hesitance of early Muslim Arabs to immigrate to America can be summed up in the experience of one woman's father, who in 1885 had gotten as far as buying a boat ticket and boarding. "Shortly before sailing he asked the captain whether America had mosques. Told that it had none, he feared America was *bilad kufr*, a land of unbelief. He immediately got off the boat." This certainly changed over time. By 1988, there were an estimated 200 mosques in the United States. By 2003, 23 percent of Arab Americans were Muslim (Catholics—many joining the Roman Catholic rite out of convenience—comprised 42 percent, Antiochian Orthodox, 23 percent, and Protestants, 12 percent).

By 1890, there was one church for each of the Melkite, Maronite, and Syrian Orthodox communities in Manhattan. By 1988, there were 130 Antiochian Orthodox parishes, 52 Maronite churches, 37 Melkite churches, 9 Iraqi Chaldean (most in Detroit), 8 Syrian or Jacobite Orthodox, and 9 Egyptian Coptic (most in New Jersey and California). Druze, who do not have mosques or imams, numbered 22,500 of an estimated 3 million Arab Americans.

Sociologists Philip and Joseph Kayal have said, "The Syrians do not regard 'place' as the root of their community identification. Rather, they prefer the primordial ties of blood and faith."[9] Certainly the pull of family and religion have buoyed the community in hard times and across many cultures and dominant powers in history, including their life in America. But there is another component that has made for the closeness. In addition to family and faith, there is a simple joie de vivre. Nowhere did this all come together better than in an Arab wedding. As Mary Macron noted of the Cleveland community, "To life! they sang. An Arab wedding was not just a family event. . . . It was, rather, a command performance. Everyone had to sing, everyone had to dance."

James Hughes, a second-generation Arab American, wrote in the short story "An Open House," published in *The New Yorker*, through the character Fig, "People don't lose their lust for life. Anybody who says they've lost it never had it in the first place."[10]

What effect intermarriage has had on close family ties in the community is hard to say. New Census data from 2000 indicates that many Arab Americans are of mixed heritage. This is no surprise; coming from the threshing floor of civilizations, the people of the Levant, in particular, had already intermarried with the Europeans over a millenium. The same would be true of North Africans.

There is no way yet to judge, at least statistically, if the glue of affection in the Arab American family has provided for the community a stronger support than the norm against the worst onslaughts of divorce, drugs, and other troubles in a freedom-based society. Few Arab American families have not by 2003 sustained their share of these tragedies. Meanwhile, the cousin network continues. If "it takes a village" to hold a society together, this is a community with villages inside villages.

POLITICS

Princeton scholar Philip Hitti said in 1924, "Syrians cut no figure in the political life of this nation."[11] For a long time, the community kept its head down, a distrust of great powers and political might still lingering in its collective memory of the Ottoman era and colonialism. They enjoyed participating in democracy but looked upon the maneuverings of the Irish in Tammany Hall, for example, with squinted eyes. By 1972, however, when the first U.S. Senator of Arab descent, James Abourezk of South Dakota, was elected, that reticence began to change. In 2003, there were five U.S. Congressmen with Arab roots—including the man who singlehandedly spearheaded the extraordinary recall of the California governor in 2003, Representative Darryl Issa (R-CA)—and one U.S. Senator. By 2003, participation in American political life was widespread and deep: there were twenty-two Arab American elected state legislators, six mayors, forty-one members of school boards, city councils, or county boards and commissions, and thirty-seven judges or district attorneys. The governor of Maine, John Elias Baldacci (2002–2006), is Arab American, as is the attorney general of Louisiana, Richard Ieyoub (1992–2004).[12]

A natural bridge culture, the Arab American community spawned several important diplomats, including Philip Habib, who worked out the American disengagement from Viet Nam in Paris talks, as well as the withdrawal of the Israelis from Lebanon in 1982; and also Senator George Mitchell of Maine, who negotiated critical cease-fires with the IRA in Northern Ireland, as well as heading up a Commission on the Israel-Palestinian dispute.

To some extent, the Arab American "coming out" in politics was a case of simply growing up through several generations with democracy and accruing in local communities the respect and trust necessary to compete for political power. But there was also an external factor that thrust them out. This was the Arab-Israeli conflict, and in particular, the 1967 "Six Day War," in June in which Israel vanquished the armies of five Arab countries. It was an astonishing victory celebrated with amazement by American politicians, comedians, and political commentators. For Arab Americans, it was a disastrous wake-up call, especially for those from the defeated lands, such as Palestine, Syria, and Egypt. This sense of trauma increased over the Israeli invasion of Lebanon in 1982, aided and abetted directly by the United States, which caused the deaths of at least 19,000 civilians. Something terrible was happening to the people they left behind, in care of the country they loved. Thus, they began to speak out.

The three national political organizations of Arab Americans grew out of these crises: the Association of Arab American University Graduates, or AAUG (1967), the National Association of Arab Americans, or NAAA (1972), and the American-Arab Anti-Discrimination Committee, or ADC (1980). The very phrase and concept Arab American—as opposed to Syrian American—came into being with these groups. A nonmembership think tank, the Arab American Institute (1984) established a network of the community's politicians and political hopefuls inside the Democratic and Republican parties.

Prior to 1967, there had been isolated, ineffectual attempts to raise the community's concerns with the powers-that-be. As early as 1929, poet and novelist Amin Rihani debated the future of Palestine with Meyer Weisgal in New York after massacres of sixty-four non-Zionist Jews in Hebron that year (an Arab American who settled in San Francisco remembered sympathetic Arabs smuggling Jews out of Hebron to spare them).[13] Dr. Philip Hitti, testifying before the U.S. House of Representatives in 1944, suggested that it would be far wiser and more moral to settle Jews fleeing Nazi Germany in spacious places in our own land, such as Arizona or Texas, rather than evict Arabs in the narrow land of Palestine.[14] President Harry Truman, after siding with the Zionists in the establishment of Israel, never met with an Arab American delegation on the matter until 1951, three years after the Jewish state was created and 700,000 Palestinians were expelled or caused to flee. This uncomfortable meeting with leaders of the weak and soon-to-break up Federation of Syrian-Lebanese Clubs was for public relations purposes and lasted only ten minutes.[15]

But 1967 changed that, though it took thirty years to leach more time from a U.S. president (Bill Clinton). Wariness, even out-and-out surveillance, of Arab

American efforts in the political arena was there from the beginning. In 1972, AAUG cofounder Abdeen Jabara, whose father had come from Lebanon in 1920 to work in lumber camps and tanneries in northern Michigan, found himself targeted by President Nixon's Operation Boulder, set up by the FBI to monitor the activities of Arab students and politically active Arab Americans in the wake of the killing of eleven Israeli Olympians. Jabara filed suit with the American Civil Liberties Union; it took a decade to settle.[16]

Around the time of President Carter's Camp David and the Egypt-Israel Treaty, in 1978, the NAAA registered its first lobbyist. The organization's high watermarks were attained in 1979 and 1980 over the issues of the misuse by Israel of American weaponry and its creation of settlements in occupied Palestinian territory. In 1979, Senator Mark Hatfield (R-OR) offered an NAAA-generated amendment to the foreign aid bill to cut aid to Israel by 10 percent over its chronic bombing of southern Lebanon with American jets. The amendment was tabled, 78–7, to the chuckles of lobbyists from the immensely powerful American Israel Public Affairs Committee (AIPAC). In 1980, Senator Adlai Stevenson (D-IL), with leaders in the Chicago Jewish community behind him, offered an amendment to shave $150 million from $3 billion in aid to Israel, equivalent to the cost of West Bank settlements, noting that the Begin government in Israel, sometimes ignored U.S. policy on settlements. Once again, a move the NAAA had pushed came to naught; the Stevenson amendment was tabled, 85–7.

Though some near Begin gloated over the lopsided vote, on June 20, the Israeli daily newspaper *Haaretz* attached significance to Stevenson's attempt:

> What counts is not the Senate rejection of that motion but the very fact that it was introduced by a Senator who has a large Jewish constituency whose record is not anti-Israel, and that the motion was backed by the Senate Majority Leader. All this only goes to show the extent to which the government of Israel's settlements policy turns U.S. statesmen against it. . . . It should come as no surprise if the number of Senators subscribing to Senator Stevenson's stand would increase.[17]

It was not to be. After that, Stevenson's career capsized; he was defeated not only for the Senate but later for the governorship of Illinois. No vote was ever taken again in the U.S. Congress tying objectionable Israeli actions to its U.S. aid. Never a particularly well-subscribed group (founded by a coterie of Washington politicos, its membership never got over 5,000), over time, the NAAA, dogged by internicine squabbles and a diminishing tap from the Arab world, slowly curled up and died. In the 1990s, most of its historic files were lost in a move to smaller quarters, and by 2000, what was left of NAAA was merged with the more energetic and vital ADC.

Founded by former Senator James Abourezk (D-SD) in the wake of Operation ABSCAM, in which the FBI dressed up as oil sheikhs to entrap U.S. congressmen with bogus offers of bribes, ADC attacked the long-festering issue of

Arab stereotyping head on. When a Florida Toyota dealer's billboards read, "Buy a Toyota, drive an Arab crazy!" ADC threatened a lawsuit, and the billboard was withdrawn. When a Massachusetts fuel company sold a charcoal briquet called Sheeks, advertising an immolated Arab, they got blasted. ADC even successfully questioned *Roget's Thesaurus* entries on *street Arab*: "Churl villain, yokel, bumpkin, lout." It took on racist talk show hosts, newspaper cartoonists, and public officials, such as FTC chairman Paul Rand Dixon, who called Ralph Nader "a dirty Arab." With the help of movie critic Jack Shaheen, it took on Hollywood, weighing in on some of the flood of films that demonize Arabs, such as Dustin Hoffman's *Ishtar*,[18] or offensive novels such as Leon Uris's *The Haj*. When NAAA had its leaders fundraising in the Arabian Gulf, ADC slid from stereotyping to the political in lobbying during the Israeli invasion of Lebanon to halt U.S. aid.

It may have been a grim measure of ADC's success that in 1985, its West Coast director, Alex Odeh, a poet and community college teacher, was pipebombed to death at his office. Some of the suspected assassins, members of the Jewish Defense League, escaped across the ocean to Israeli settlements on the West Bank. One, Robert Manning, was finally extradited eight years later and sentenced to life in prison without parole, but for the murder of someone else. Another suspected assassin, Irv Rubin, was said to have committed suicide in jail in 2002. Nineteen years later, the Odeh case is still open.

The 1990s saw a roller-coaster ride through an Israeli-Palestinian peace process that began with great hope (and an Arafat-Rabin handshake at the White House with President Clinton) but fell apart amid abysmal violence. In the decade, the fallout from America's Middle East policies drew ever closer to its shores; Arab Americans felt the heat. During the first Gulf War in 1991, the ADC logged 119 hate crimes against Arab Americans, an unprecedented level of domestic violence against the community. More shocking, in the wake of the 1995 bombing of the Murrah government building in Oklahoma City—though none of the perpetrators was an Arab—the ADC registered 150 hate crimes against Arab Americans. This was one of the most violent cases of mistaken identity in U.S. history. Seven mosques were burned. Soon after McVeigh's horrific deed, *USA Today* ran the headline "Bomb Consistent with Mid-East Terror Tactics." The ADC had its hands full.

Then came the Arab American community's worst nightmare: September 11, 2001. When 19 Arab nationals rammed jets into the World Trade Center and the Pentagon and went down with an airplane in Pennsylvania, Arab Americans felt the same anger and agony of all Americans but added something: a sense of betrayal. Poet and children's author Naomi Shihab Nye caught this acutely in a piece she read for National Public Radio, addressed to "would-be terrorists":

> Because I feel a little closer to you than many Americans could possibly feel, I insist you listen to me. . . . I am humble in my country's pain and furious. . . . Many people, thousands of people, perhaps even millions of people, in the United States are very aware of the long unfairness of our country's policies re-

garding Israel and Palestine. We talk about this all the time. It exhausts us and we keep talking. We write letters to newspapers, to politicians, to each other. . . . This tragedy could never help the Palestinians. . . . Our hearts are broken: as yours may also feel broken in some ways, we can't understand, unless you tell us in words. Killing people won't tell us. We can't read that message.[19]

ADC's president Ziad Assali released an open letter to the American public: "No matter who was responsible for this terrible crime, which no cause or ideology could possibly justify, Arab Americans will be no less moved, no less angry, no less outraged than our fellow Americans."[20] Many, like ADC–Washington, D.C., chapter head Mona Hamoui, felt a kind of shame. Even two years after 9/11, "with the word 'Arab,'" she said, "I feel a twinge in my throat."

The initial outrage in the country began to be replaced by nervous tension, abetted by anthrax letters, rumors of other attacks, and the extraordinary three-week shooting by the D.C. snipers that killed eleven innocent people. But for Arab Americans, the general fear took on another fear, that of standing out as "other." They were not alone. A brown face was not the face to have after September 11. The backlash was the worst in the country's history: 700 violent incidents and hate crimes in the first year alone.[21]

President Bush had spoken out forcefully and responsibly as early as September 17 to head off the backlash, noting in a meeting with Muslim leaders in Washington, D.C., "The face of terror is not the true faith of Islam." Still, as many as eleven people were killed in the United States due to misplaced retribution over September 11. People with brown skin were pulled off planes taxiing on the runway; ADC counted eighty cases of airline discrimination. These ranged from an Arab American member of President Bush's own Secret Service to a Jewish businessman pulled off a flight in Chicago by the pilot.

Fifteen arsons were keyed to 9/11, including the burning of six mosques. A Florida man was arrested and sentenced to twelve years in prison for planning to bomb fifty mosques. Workplace discrimination against Arab Americans increased. Christian right-wing leaders spewed plain bigotry; Billy Graham's reverend son Franklin on network television called Islam "a very evil and wicked religion."[22] The urge to retribution was so deep in some it spilled over into the Arab-Israeli conflict where, as always, the Palestinians took it on the chin. Senator Dick Armey (R-TX) told an incredulous talk show host that he was in favor of expelling the entire population of one million Palestines from the West Bank, an endorsement of war crimes before the fact for which the Texan Senator's office issued a weak retraction.[23]

The paranoia hit its nadir when a Bush-appointed member of the U.S. Civil Rights Commission, Peter Kirsanow, indicated that another Arab terrorist strike on America could easily lead to internment of Arab Americans in camps. Though he didn't support such camps, in the event of another attack Kirsanow said "you can forget about civil rights" and that there would be "a groundswell of opinion" for rounding up Arab Americans as was done to the Japanese in World War II.[24]

Shy of such extremism, but still troubling to the community, was the signing into law on October 26, 2001, of the Patriot Act. Most Arab Americans, like other citizens, accepted tightened airport security. But the Patriot Act's draconian, indefinite detentions, searches, and wiretaps without warrants, and presumptions of guilt by association had more than Arab Americans questioning if 9/11 had changed the core of American freedom and jurisprudence. Of some 315,000 "absconders," that is, people with visa violations, at least 1,200 men of Middle Eastern origin were swept up incommunicado without charges or due process; on one occasion, 132 men were shipped off by plane to Pakistan and told not to come back. Attorney General Ashcroft issued orders that some 8,000 from countries where al-Qaeda was being hunted or active, be "interviewed" (voluntarily, of course!). Some police captains (in Wisconsin and Oregon) refused on constitutional grounds to effect the thinly clad racial profiling. More troubling to Arab Americans were the raids on fourteen Muslim American charities and shutting down of three of them. One Arab American (Yaser Hamdi) was being held as an "enemy combatant" in a Navy brig in Virginia. And most troubling for all Americans was that by May 2003, the Justice Department admitted to Congress it had delayed notifying people of forty-seven searches of their homes and fifteen seizures of their belongings. Under the Patriot Act, it is now possible to enter a private home without a search warrant, insert something called a "magic lantern" into a personal computer, download everything on it, and monitor its activities, without the knowledge of its owner.

These significant abridgements of civil rights had ramifications far beyond Arab Americans. By 2003, the ADC, Irish American groups, the ACLU, and others from the left and right were suing the U.S. Government over the Patriot Act. At the same time, Arab Americans were the recipients of extraordinary kindnesses from their American neighbors and leaders right from the beginning of the crisis. A Green Armband project in Louisville, Kentucky, paired escorts to Arab and Muslim Americans on their way to schools, churches, and mosques. Anya Cordell in Chicago set up the Campaign for Collateral Compassion, endorsed by some victims of September 11, to funnel funds to victims of hate crimes. Actress Patricia Arquette, whose mother is Jewish and whose father is a Muslim, organized 50 actors and other celebrities for a public-service message campaign discouraging racist acts. The AAI and the Ad Council produced a moving replication ad, printed in 10,000 newspapers, of the twin towers as two tall messages of tolerance under the title "United We Stand."

In 1899, the Associated Charities of Boston reported its opinion that "next to the Chinese, who can never in any sense be American [the Syrians] are the most foreign of all foreigners." Whether, after a century of accomplishments in the land of their grateful adoption, Arab Americans were to be seen once again as the indigestible "other" remained to be seen. But there was no denying that the riptide of bigotry had spawned a seawall of goodness.

It was intriguing, to say the least, that for the first time in the community's history, the major U.S. presidential candidates came calling in October 2003, speaking before a leadership convention of the Arab American Institute in Dearborn, Michigan. The press reported that Connecticut Senator Joseph Lieberman was booed at one juncture over the recent erection of the Israeli Wall against the West Bank. What the press did not report were the seven times the crowd applauded the Jewish American candidate, not least for ending with a promise "to work our way to that two-state solution and to peace."

NOTES

1. See Gregory Orfalea, *Before the Flames* (Austin: Univ. of Texas Press, 1988), 60–61.

2. Ibid., 56.

3. Abraham Mitry Rihbany, *A Far Journey* (Boston: Houghton Mifflin, 1914), 74–75.

4. Amean Haddad, quoted in Orfalea, *Before the Flames*, 69.

5. Michael Suleiman, "Impressions of New York City by Early Arab Immigrants," in *A Community of Many Worlds: Arab Americans in New York City* (New York: Museum of the City of New York and Syracuse Univ. Press, 2002), 44–45.

6. Henry Chapman Ford, "Anna Ascends," *Syrian World* 2, no. 1 (July 1927).

7. Stan Reddy, "DeBakey," *Texas Magazine* (*Houston Chronicle*), October 12, 1980, U.S. Small Business Administration.

8. *The Handbook of Small Business*, U.S. Small Business Administration, Washington, DC.

9. Philip and Joseph Kayal, *The Syrian-Lebanese in America: A Study in Religion and Assimilation* (Boston: Twayne, 1975), 122.

10. James Hughes, "An Open House," *The New Yorker*, October 1980.

11. Philip Hitti, *The Syrians in America* (New York: George Doran, 1924).

12. See the Web site of the Arab American Institute, www.aai.org.

13. Alfred Farradj, quoted in Orfalea, *Before the Flames*, 142.

14. Ibid., 144.

15. Ibid., 145, 326.

16. Gregory Orfalea, *The Arab Americans: A Quest for Their History and Culture* (Northampton, MA: Interlink Publishers, forthcoming).

17. Ibid.

18. See Jack Shaheen, *Reel Bad Arabs, How Hollywood Villifies a People* (New York: Olive Branch Press, 2001).

19. Naomi Shihab Nye, "To Any Would-Be Terrorists," in *September 11, 2001: American Writers Respond*, ed. William Heyen (Silver Springs, MD: Etruscan Press, 2002), 287–291.

20. Ziad Assali, MD, "America in Crisis: An Open Letter," *ADC Times* 21, no. 4 (September 2001 Special Edition): 1.

21. See Hussein Ibish, ed., *Report on Hate Crimes and Discrimination against Arab Americans: The Post September 11 Backlash, September 11, 2001–October 11, 2002* (Washington, DC: American-Arab Anti-Discrimination Committee, 2003).

22. *NBC Nightly News*, November 17, 2001.

23. Dick Armey, *National Review*, "Call for Ethnic Cleansing of Palestinians," *ADC Times* 21, no. 7 (March–April 2002): 18.

24. Morak Warikoo, "Arabs in U.S. Could be Held, Official Warns," *Detroit Free Press*, July 20, 2002.

BIBLIOGRAPHICAL ESSAY

Though the community had been in the country for nearly a century, the study of Arab Americans was scant before 1967. Since the 1967 Six Day War, a "lightning" victory by Israel over five Arab nations, one we now know was decidedly Pyhrric, there has been a steady, ever-intensifying interest in Arab Americans, almost as if the Israeli attack brought them to a strange, increasingly urgent light.

I will restrict myself here almost entirely to books in English. The critical texts on the nineteenth-century and early-twentieth-century first wave Syrian migration to America are three: Philip Hitti's *The Syrians in America* (New York: George Doran, 1924); Alixa Naff's *Becoming American* (Carbondale, IL: Southern Illinois Univ. Press, 1985), which delves deeply into the experience of the early Syrian peddlers; and Eric Hooglund's seminal anthology, *Crossing the Waters: Arabic-Speaking Immigrants to the United States before 1940* (Washington, DC: Smithsonian Institute Press, 1987). Hooglund takes issue with Naff's "peddler" thesis (as Naff questions Hitti's victimization push factor for Syrian immigration). My own study, *The Arab Americans: A Quest for their History and Culture* (Northampton, MA: Interlink Publishers, 2004) is a sizeable update of an earlier history, *Before the Flames* (Austin: Univ. of Texas Press, 1988), and is the one text that spans the community's history from early days to the present. It includes a close inspection of the politicized, tension-filled period of 1988–2003.

Several bibliographies are useful, and none as mammoth and extraordinary as Michael Suleiman's forthcoming *Arab Americans: An Annotated Bibliography.* See also Philip Kayal's *An Arab American Bibliographic Guide* (Belmont, MA: Association of Arab-American University Graduates, 1985); George Dimitri Selim of the Near East section at the Library of Congress has compiled *The Arabs in the United States: A Selected List of References* (Washington, DC: Library of Congress, 1983). I have written "On Arab Americans: A Bibliographic Essay" for *American Studies International* (Washington, DC: George Washington University, 1989). Of much practical use is Joe Haiek's *Arab-American Almanac* (Glendale, CA: News Circle Publishing Co., 2003).

Two early sociologists and one missionary give interesting insights into the reasons for Syrian immigration and their first experiences in the New World: Lucius Hopkins Miller, *Our Syrian Population: A Study of the Syrian Community in Greater New York* (1904; repr. San Francisco: R&E Research Associate, 1969); and Louise Houghton, "The Syrians in the United States," an invaluable four-part series in *Survey* 26/27 (1911). The missionary is Henry Jessup, *Fifty-Three Years in Syria* (New York: Fleming H. Revell Co., 1910).

Almost unique in the culture of Arab Americans was *The Syrian World*, a journal published in English between 1926 and 1935. It published poems, essays, fiction, and drama by Syrian American authors and about the community itself. It is a fascinating window on the community's life in the 1920s and 1930s, as people navigated the Great Depression, which ultimately did in *The Syrian World* itself. The journal is on microfilm at the Library of Congress and the University of Minnesota's Immigration History Research Center. In 2002, *Mizna* an outstanding literary quarterly publishing the work of Arab American writers, began publishing in Minneapolis, Minnesota. This is the first publication of its kind since *The Syrian World*.

Virtually none of the classic textbooks on turn-of-the-century immigration touch on the early Syrians. There are derogatory references to eastern-Mediterranean immigrants in the memoir of immigration commissioner Edward Corsi, *The Shadow of Liberty* (New

York: Arno Press, 1969, 1935). A fairer glimpse of the community appears in *One America* (New York: Prentice Hall Inc., 1945), edited by Frances J. Brown and Joseph S. Roucek. A more recent and comprehensive treatment of Arab Americans occurs in *Strangers to These Shores* (Boston: Houghton Mifflin, 1980) by Vince Parillo. Barbara Rico and Sandra Mano, eds., *American Mosaic*, 3rd ed. (Boston: Houghton Mifflin, 2001) presents a piece by Naomi Shihab Nye, "White Coals, Broken Clock, Speaking Arabic."

Anthologies of essays on the community include Michael Suleiman, ed., *Arabs in America* (Philadelphia: Temple Univ. Press, 1999); Baba Abu-Laban and Michael Suleiman, eds., *Arab-Americans: Continuity and Change* (Belmont, MA: Association of Arab-American University Graduates, 1989); Sameer Abraham and Nabeel Abraham, eds., *Arabs in the New World* (Detroit, MI: Wayne State Univ., 1983), which concentrates heavily on Detroit; and George Atiyeh, ed., *Arab and American Cultures* (Washington, DC: American Enterprise Institute, 1977), which contains a lively dialogue that includes author John Updike on the image of the Arab in U.S. society. Two ADC anthologies offer historical portraits of fifteen communities, some of them quite unexpected (i.e., Vicksburg, MS; New Castle, PA; Ross, ND): *Taking Root, Bearing Fruit* (Washington, DC: American-Arab Anti-Discrimination Committee, 1984) and *Taking Root: Arab American Community Studies* (Washington, DC: American-Arab Anti-Discrimination Committee, 1985).

Historically, Arab Americans have not been drawn to self-telling and autobiography, but there are some notable exceptions, including several by successful businesspeople. The first Arab American autobiography and probably the best to date is *A Far Journey* (Boston: Little, Brown, 1914) by the Reverend Abraham Rihbany, parts of which were originally excerpted in *Atlantic Monthly*. For a good look at what a Syrian immigrant went through in World War I serving as a U.S. doughboy, there is Ashad Howie's *The Rainbow Ends* (New York: T. Gaus' Sons, 1942). Dr. Michael Shadid recounts experiences of prejudice on the Great Plains and his life founding the first cooperative hospital in America in *A Doctor for the People* (New York: Vanguard Press, 1939). George Hamid's wild life as a circus tumbler is contained in *Circus* (New York: Sterling Publishing Co., 1953).

More recent years have seen prominent Arab Americans pen their autobiographies, such as UPI White House correspondent Helen Thomas (*Dateline White House*, New York: Macmillan, 1975), Pan Am executive Najeeb Halaby (*Crosswinds*, Garden City, New York: Doubleday, 1978), Nicolas Assali (*A Doctor's Life*, New York: Harcourt, Brace, Jovanovich, 1979), former senator James Abourezk (*Advise and Dissent*, Westport, CT: Greenwood Press, 1989), engineer magnate Joseph Jacobs (*The Anatomy of an Entrepreneur*, San Francisco: ICS Press, 1991), and the celebrated literary critic and Palestinian spokesman Edward Said (*Out of Place*, New York: Knopf, 2000). I should also mention three other striking Palestinian American memoirs: *To Be an Arab in Israel* (London: Frances Pinter, 1975) by Fawzi al-Asmar; *The Disinherited* (New York: Monthly Review Press, 1972), the classic cry of protest by former refugee-camp dweller Fawaz Turki; and the charming *A Taste of Palestine* (Dallas, TX: Taylor Publishing & Co., 1993) by Aziz Shihab, which recounts the newspaperman's early days growing up in Jerusalem, as well as more recent days in Dallas, all through the medium of food recipes. William Peter Blatty wrote two memoirs of his Lebanese peddler mother, *Which Way to Mecca, Jack?* (New York: Random House, 1960) and *I'll Tell Them I Remember You* (New York: Norton, 1973).

The literature by Arab Americans is gathering power. To date, poetry has been the outstanding Arab American genre, though fiction and nonfiction have been catching up. The early Syrian *mahjar* poets, including Kahlil Gibran and Mikhail Naimy, link up with the more contemporary authors in the anthology *Grape Leaves: A Century of Arab American Poetry* (Salt Lake City: Univ. of Utah Press, 1988), edited by Sharif Elmusa and Gregory Orfalea. There is also an anthology of Arab American literature of many genres in *Post Gibran* (Syracuse, NY: Syracuse Univ. Press, 2000), edited by Munir Akash and Khaled Mattawa. A special issue of *Paintbrush* magazine (Kirksville, MO, 1991), "American Jihad for Heritage and Hope" featured Arab American poets.

Among noteworthy collections of poetry are *Jesus the Son of Man* (New York: A. A. Knopf, 1928), by Kahlil Gibran; *Thank a Bored Angel, Selected Poems* (New York: New Direction, 1983) by Samuel Hazo; *The Big Bang* (Richmond, VA: Warwick House, 1999) by Joseph Awad; *Dying with the Wrong Name* (New York: Athne Publication, 1980) by Sam Hamod; *Arabian Nights* (Minneapolis: Coffee House Press, 1986) by Jack Marshall; *Shouting at No One* (Pittsburgh, PA: Univ. of Pittsburgh Press, 1983) by Lawrence Joseph; *The Words under the Words: Selected Poems* (Portland, OR: Eighth Mountain Press, 1995) by Naomi Shihab Nye; *The Capital of Solitude* (Ithaca, NY: Cornell Univ. Press, 1988) by Gregory Orfalea; *Ismailia Eclipse* (New York: Sheep Meadow Press, 1997) by Khaled Mattawa; *The Never Field Poem* (Sausalito, CA: Post-Apollo Press, 1999) by Nathalie Handal; and *Born Palestinian, Born Black* (New York: Harlem River Press, 1996) by Suhair Hammad.

The only novel about the early Syrian immigrant's experience in America is Ameen Rihani's *The Book of Khalid* (New York: Dodd, Mead and Co., 1911). One had to wait a long time to get another by an Arab American, but the dozen novels of Vance Bourjaily, the former director of the fiction workshop at the celebrated University of Iowa Writers Workshop and current head of the MFA program at Louisiana State University, were worth the wait. Bourjaily's indispensable coming-of-age novel about someone half Syrian ("a fractional man") is *Confessions of a Spent Youth* (New York: Arbor House, 1960; repr., 1986). William Peter Blatty produced a shocking book of demonic possession set in Washington, DC, *The Exorcist* (New York: Harper and Row, 1971) that actually begins in Iraq. Samuel Hazo has written an intriguing novel about kidnapping and terrorism that occurred long before 9/11, *The Very Fall of the Sun* (New York: Popular Library, 1979). Of special note are the novels of Mona Simpson, who is Syrian American, especially *The Lost Father* (New York: Vintage Books, 1993), which is about a half-Egyptian woman looking all over America and the Middle East for a father who abandoned her and her mother when she was young. Diana Abu-Jaber managed to weave a love story out of the Iraq disasters of the 1990s, *Crescent* (New York: Norton, 2003), set near UCLA. I should also mention Naomi Nye's delightful children's novel, *Habibi* (New York: Simon and Schuster, 1999), based on her year on the West Bank as a young teen. Finally, to my knowledge, there is only one collection of short stories by an Arab American, Joseph Geha's testament to the Toledo community, *Through and Through* (St. Paul, MN: Graywolf Press, 1990).

That new genre known as creative nonfiction has spawned some interesting examples: Elmaz Abinader's Lebanese family saga that ends up in rural Pennsylvania, *Children of the Roojme* (Madison: Univ. of Wisconsin Press, 1997); Eugene Paul Nasser's *Wind of the Land* (Belmont, MA: Association of Arab-American University Graduates, 1978), a prose-poetry remembrance of growing up in Utica, New York; and the personal essays of Naomi Shihab Nye (*Never in a Hurry*, Columbia: Univ. of South Carolina Press, 1996) cannot be put down. I attempted to weave together my father's life in Cleveland during World War II with his paratrooper battalion days (*Messengers of the Lost Battalion*, New York: Free Press, 1997).

The pickings get slim with drama, though Fred Saidy had much success in the 1940s, 1950s, and 1960s with musicals such as *Finian's Rainbow* (1968). Betty Shamieh has run off-Broadway with her one-woman show, *Chocolate in Heat: Growing Up Arab American* (New York, 2001). The one and only Oscar won by an Arab American for an original screenplay was landed by Callie Khouri for the movie *Thelma & Louise* (1991).

ASIAN INDIAN AMERICANS

Karen I. Leonard

Asian Indian is a category in the U.S. census, so it makes sense to write about immigrants from India. However, a new term, *South Asians*, is gaining popularity, particularly on campuses. This constructed category combines immigrants from a wider geographical region, including people from India, Pakistan, Bangladesh, Sri Lanka, Nepal, Bhutan, the Maldive Islands, and even Afghanistan. By contrasting South Asians to East and Southeast Asians, the category asserts shared cultural characteristics and long-standing traditions of cultural pluralism in the region. While the present essay retreats to the more realistic and well-supported national origin and census category *Asian Indian*, the reader should remember that Britain's colonial empire of India included present-day India and Pakistan and Bangladesh (India and Pakistan gained their independence in 1947, and Bangladesh split off from Pakistan in 1971). Thus, before 1947, the Asian Indian category covered a wider area in terms of immigrant origins than it does now, and the South Asian category pushes back toward that wider area again.

Asian Indian immigrants come from different places, then, before and after 1947, but the more striking differences are between those who came before and after 1965, when the U.S. Immigration and Naturalization Act redressed the historic discrimination against Asians.[1] The contrasts between the "old" and "new (post-1965)" Asian Indian immigrants are many, the old immigrants constituting a relatively homogeneous group. Asian Indians began coming to the United States at the end of the nineteenth century, but their numbers were relatively small in the early twentieth century. The first migrants were almost all men and from only one part of India, the Punjab province along the northwestern frontier where the Punjabi language was spoken by Sikhs, Hindus, and Muslims. From farming backgrounds, most of these men settled in California in the early

1900s and worked in agriculture, striving to become citizens, acquire land and status, and establish families in the United States. Yet the pioneer farmers encountered discriminatory laws that effectively ended immigration in 1917 and affected their rights to gain citizenship, hold agricultural land, and marry whom they chose. The relevant federal policies and laws are the 1917 Barred Zone Act (barring most Asians from legal immigration), the 1924 National Origins Quota Act (setting a quota of 105 immigrants per year from India), and the 1923 U.S. Supreme Court Thind Decision (declaring Indians Caucasians but not "white" and therefore ineligible for U.S. citizenship). State policies and laws included California's Alien Land Laws of 1913, 1920, and 1921 (prohibiting noncitizens from owning and leasing agricultural land, and copied by other states) and various state antimiscegenation laws (prohibiting marriages between people of different races).[2]

These Punjabi men were called Hindus by others in their localities, and this simply meant "people from Hindustan," or India. Because of the legal constraints above, most of them married women of Mexican ancestry: the Punjabi men and Mexican women looked racially similar to the county clerks issuing marriage licenses. The biethnic couples produced a second generation of children with names like Maria Jesusita Singh and Jose Akbar Khan, children mostly Catholic and bilingual in English and Spanish but calling themselves Hindus. These Mexican-Hindu children were extremely proud of their Indian heritage. Later Asian Indian immigrants, unable to imagine the conditions in which the pioneers lived, have found it hard to acknowledge these descendants of the Punjabi pioneers, most of whom were actually Sikhs, as Hindus.[3]

Asian Indian immigration opened up again after 1946, as political changes at the national level in both the United States and India made it possible for the old immigrants to reestablish connections with their homeland and for new immigrants to come. In 1946, successful lobbying by the Indians in the United States secured the passage of the Luce-Celler Bill, which gave Asian Indians the right to become naturalized U.S. citizens and use of the quota of 105 per year set by the 1924 National Origins Quota Act.[4] Then, in 1947, Great Britain's Indian empire gave way to the independent nations of India, Pakistan, Sri Lanka, and Burma. As American citizens, the pioneers could revisit their places of origin and sponsor relatives as immigrants, and their pride in their newly independent nations was an impetus to such reconnections.

An even greater spur to new migration came with the 1965 U.S. Immigration and Naturalization Act. The legislation vastly increased the numbers of immigrants from Asia and set preferences that favored certain types of immigrants. The new Asian Indian immigrants are strikingly diverse: they come from all of India's states and speak many languages (there are at least nineteen vernacular languages, and India's political structure was realigned in 1956 so that state boundaries would reflect linguistic ones). In the United States, the most numerous regional groups are Gujaratis, Punjabis, and Malayalis (from the states of Gujarat, Punjab, and Kerala). The recent immigrants are not rural people but predominantly urban, highly educated professionals. They are migrating in family units, women and children accompanying the men. Many religions are represented, many kinds of Hindus, Muslims, Buddhists, Christians, Sikhs, and Parsis (or Zoroastrians). Also, many "traditional" caste and community categories still have some significance in the lives of the immigrants, particularly in the choice of marriage partners. The diversity of the subcontinent is well represented in the United States.

Asian Indians not only come from all over India but are settled all over the United States and they are doing very well. Like other Asians, they slightly favor California (Asians formed some 10 percent of the state population in 1993), with New York, Texas, and Florida close behind in popularity.[5] Immigrants born in India had the highest median household income, family income, and per capita income of any foreign-born group in the 1990 census. They also had the highest percentage with a bachelor's degree or higher and the highest percentage in managerial and professional fields.[6] Among the skilled South Asian professionals, many are doctors. One estimate puts Indian doctors at more than 20,000, or nearly 4 percent of the nation's medical doctors, and the largest ethnic body of doctors in the United States is the American Association of Physicians from India. In terms of family stability, the immigrants from India lead the foreign born in percent of population married and are at the bottom in per cent of those separated and divorced. The most common household size is four.[7] Asian Indians are not clustered in residential areas but dispersed. Despite this high-status profile, a 1992 compilation of social-science surveys shows that Asian Indians are perceived by Americans as relatively low in social standing,[8] a finding that one must attribute to prejudice.

The high socioeconomic standards outlined above were set by the first wave of post-1965 immigrants, while those arriving since the mid-1980s have brought the averages and medians down somewhat. Many of these later arrivals are coming in under the Family Reunification Act and are not as well qualified or well educated as the earlier ones; there have also been recessions in the U.S. economy. As a result, those arriving since 1985 show a much lower percentage in managerial and professional jobs, a much lower median income, and a much higher unemployment rate. Thus, the percentage of South Asian families in poverty is also high, putting those born in India twelfth on the lists of both families in poverty and individuals in poverty.[9] The U.S. Immigration Act of 1990 might reverse this downward trend, since it has sharply increased the numbers of highly skilled immigrants from India (and Asia generally) at the expense of unskilled workers and nonemployed immigrants (parents and spouses of citizens).

Participation in American political life was a goal for the early Asian Indian immigrants and is becoming one for the newcomers. After the Luce-Celler bill made them eligible for citizenship in 1946, the Punjabi pioneers helped elect Dalip Singh Saund from California's Imperial Valley in 1956, the first Congressman from India.[10] After some hesitation, the post-1965 immigrants also are becoming engaged in U.S. politics. About half of those migrating from India since

1977 have become naturalized U.S. citizens, although they must give up their Indian citizenship to do so. The United States allows dual citizenship but India does not.[11] Initially, immigrants pressured India to change its policy and allow dual citizenship (Pakistan allows it), but India's leaders have encouraged its NRIs (nonresident Indians) to become American citizens and work for themselves and India through the U.S. political system. (India actively encourages the NRIs to invest financially in the homeland, but it has not welcomed some of its overseas citizens' political involvements, in particular the movements for Sikh or Kashmiri independence.) Asian Indians are active in both Democratic and Republican party political funding and campaigning.

All Asian Indian organizations show a progression over time from the individual-level adaptations made by the first migrants to early organizations based on national origin (India, Pakistan, or Sri Lanka) or ecumenical religious categories (incorporating South Asians into various Christian churches or Muslim mosques). As the Asian Indian immigrant population has grown, many linguistic associations, ethnic organizations, and sectarian or guru-centered religious groups have formed.[12] Some of these organizations reproduce divisions important back in India,[13] but at the same time, the organizations are federating at the national level on the basis of Indian ancestry. The leading four national associations are the Association of Indians in America, the National Federation of Indian Associations (NFIA), the Indian American Forum for Political Education, and the National Association of Americans of Indian Descent.[14] These competing national federations reflect not only rivalry among leaders but uncertainty over the best term for the community—*Asian Indian* is the census term, while *Indian American* and *Indo-American* are the other leading contenders.

Political mobilization is based on issues in the United States like crimes against South Asians, individual or institutional discrimination in higher education and business, and problems with municipalities. Thus, merchants may fight to achieve minority business preference status or to name a business area Little India, while those seeking to establish Hindu temples or other religious institutions often must work hard for local permission. In Norwalk, California, a Hindu temple could be built in the 1990s only after being redesigned to look like a Spanish mission!

Coalition building with other groups, such as Asian Americans and/or Muslim Americans, is a promising political strategy. Among Asian Americans, Asian Indians are moving from being the fourth largest group, after the Chinese, Filipinos, and Southeast Asians, to third largest, overtaking the Southeast Asians. The Asian Indian group, expanded to South Asian, includes Indians, Pakistanis, Bangladeshis, Sri Lankans, and Fijians and Guyanese of Indian origin, and while it has been behind most other Asian American groups in participation in educational and political coalitions, that situation is changing fast. Similarly, Islam is the second largest religion in the United States, and South Asian Muslims provide the intellectual and political leadership for Muslim Americans.[15]

Asian Indians are settling into the United States in ways unanticipated only a decade or two ago. The young people are moving into the American mainstream, and elderly parents are leaving India to join their adult children in the United States. This latter trend is a mixed blessing for the parents, who feel isolated from their old friends and former lives and are too often stuck in the suburbs without access to shops or other people. Oftentimes they serve as babysitters, phone answerers, or perhaps even cooks, for their children. However, some of them contribute to changes in American life, helping to make South Asian culture more available. The founder of the Kwality ice cream and restaurant chain famous throughout India migrated to California in the late 1970s and helped set the standard for Indian restaurants there, symbolizing the explosion of Indian fast foods and packaged foods being distributed in South Asian ethnic groceries throughout the country.[16] For purposes of business and popular culture, the South Asian label is often used to attract a broader market or audience. Religious and cultural festivals are observed in the United States, their timing adjusted to those of American holidays; one Indian entrepreneur markets Hallmark cards for Diwali, an Indian festival, in Southern California. "Indian groceries" can be owned by anyone from South Asia and supply full lines of ethnic food, toilet products, and often videos as well. Shops now supply almost everything needed to produce South Asian weddings satisfactorily in America, and this is a booming market niche.[17]

Indian music and dance abounds in the United States, with many signs of integration into the American cultural landscape. Indian dance academies offer classical Bharatanatyam and regional folk dances such as Punjabi *bhangra* and Gujarati *giddha*, along with dances from Hindi films and "hip-hop bhangra."[18] In northern California, Ali Akbar Khan's College of Music enrolls many Euro-American students, while the master musician Ravi Shankar has settled down in Southern California. In Cleveland, Ohio, the annual Thyagaraja Aradhana, or Karnatic music festival, draws more Karnatic artists than any other festival outside India, and probably more than many in India now.

Asian Indian and South Asian religious activity has intensified among post-1965 immigrants. Swami Chinmayananda, one of India's most popular spiritual leaders, died in 1993 in San Diego, California, on one of the extensive overseas lecturing tours he had undertaken; many religious figures from India tour the United States, and fundraising for religious and political activities goes on as well. Interactions among the religions from the Indian subcontinent and among their immigrant and indigenous followers are beginning to be studied, as the bibliographic essay demonstrates.[19] The Sikhs and the Hindus are primarily diasporic communities, their North American converts—the "white" or "gora" Sikhs, the Ramakrishna Mission, the Transcendental Meditation movement, the Hare Krishnas—forming very small parts of the two communities in the United States.[20] These communities continue to be oriented toward India but are also flourishing in the United States.[21]

Many new *Sikh gurdwaras* and Hindu temples are being established in America's urban centers, fueled by relative prosperity and the ease of securing the necessary physical and cultural materials (and artisans to put them together) in this era of global trade and travel. Even though both groups are chiefly reproducing rather than reconfiguring congregations in the diaspora, in fact changes from homeland practices are occurring in homes and religious spaces (one could perhaps argue that bringing together Hindus from different Indian linguistic, caste, and sectarian backgrounds in American settings is analogous to bringing together Zoroastrians from India and Iran in the United States). Unlike Sikhism, Hinduism has not been promoted as a universal or world religion, yet Hinduism has had a major impact on popular culture through numerous yoga and new-age meditation movements, ones often so hybrid that they are no longer recognizably religious or Asian Indian in nature.

Gender issues loom large in Asian Indian religious life in the United States, with some communities strongly upholding patriarchy and gender complementarity (different male and female roles) in family and community, perceiving the dominant American values of gender equality and freedom of sexual expression as serious threats to ordered social life. There is fear of American individualism, interpreted not as a moral ideal but as egoism, as family and societal breakdown. Whether certain practices are required for religious purposes or simply matters of culture is often vigorously debated, and such gendered and generational tensions are shared to some extent by immigrant Hindus, Sikhs, Muslims, and others as they worry about emerging conflicts involving their children and families and whether these should be attributed to cultural and religious values brought from the homeland or to those of the host society.

Despite all the signs of their own adaptation to, and, indeed, of Asian Indian impact on, American life, some immigrants are concerned that their children will lose their culture. This concern, and perhaps a feeling that they themselves cannot ever be more than second-class citizens of the United States, leads some older Indian immigrants to return to India upon retirement. Complexes are being built for senior citizens returning from the United States, and Social Security payments can be sent to India, after ten years of employment. Their return is to some extent a recognition of the importance of context in the shaping of identity, yet the return presents a considerable problem to their children who were born or brought up largely in America.

For first-generation immigrants from India, the "youth problem" looms large. Many conference sessions, public talks, and private conversations are devoted to worrying about the children of Asian Indian descent being raised in the United States. Parental ambitions are high with respect to the economic success of their offspring: children are encouraged to undertake higher education and professional training, particularly in medicine and engineering. Parents also stress the retention and transmission of the culture from home, rather than the adoption of American culture. This places the children in a difficult position, since they are inevitably products of their American cultural context and are comfortable in that context in ways that their parents are not, as one article title, "It Ain't Where You're From, It's Where You're At,"[22] indicates. Both parents and youngsters make this point repeatedly. One Hindu grandmother in Hyderabad, India, when I asked if her grandchildren in Texas are in any way Hyderabadi, replied despairingly, "Hyderabadi? They're not even Indian," and then cried as she told how her granddaughter asked her to wear some other clothing, not a sari, when accompanying her to school.

The second generation's difference, its participation in American culture in all its contemporary diversity and intensity, is borne out in many ways. In campus youth conferences, discussion topics always include interracial marriage, South Asian coalition-building, hip-hop culture, homosexuality, premarital sex, and violence against women, as well as identity formation, discrimination in corporate America, and racism.

Some of the youth-problem concern comes from religious leaders and organizations, both Hindu and Muslim. This concern is ostensibly about the continuity of family, caste, and community religious traditions, but just as clearly, it is about sexuality and marriage, in particular about parental arrangement of marriages and parental control of family life. In a North American edition of *Hinduism Today* (in June 1993), the publisher discussed the threat to Hindu families represented by marriages not arranged by the parents, marriages most often with non-Hindus in the United States. Stating that 80 percent of the young Hindu women in Texas are marrying "outside of Indian tradition," he blamed parents for not arranging marriages soon enough, for permitting their children to pursue personal fulfillment rather than fulfillment of duty. Asian Indian parents often oppose dating on the grounds that it inevitably leads to having sex or to date rape; this view prevailed in a survey of post-1965 Indian immigrants carried out in 1990.[23] While the experience of growing up in America has not been a uniform one, most youngsters of Asian Indian descent go through a cycle of early identification with American culture and then, later, identification with Indian culture. Even after they become more interested in their heritage, these young people do not necessarily see themselves as part of a larger community of Asian Indians. But, one writer asserts, what they do have in common with other Indo-Americans is their parents,

> parents who are overinvolved, overworried, overprotective. Parents who have an opinion on every minor life decision, who make demands, impose guilt, withhold approval. . . . As children of immigrants, the promise we fulfill is our parents' own promise, long-deferred and transmuted now into the stuff of American dreams (and nightmares). So we must become respectable, make money, buy a house, bear children. . . . My parents' love supports me and enfolds me, but sometimes also weighs me down . . . still I carry the burden of their unhappiness.

She writes of becoming interested in her Indian heritage, but

> as this Indian fire flickered and grew—it shed light on my American self, too. . . . I see that I am in love with the complexity of the American culture I grew up

in, and cherish my easy familiarity with it . . . that I love to defend it against detractors, revel in its excesses . . . that after attending many Indian dinner parties . . . I long to be with American friends, because with them I relax and return
to myself.[24]

It is the young women of Asian Indian background, not the young men, who
are of most concern. As a young Indian Muslim woman wrote, "in my culture,
it's O.K. for a man to marry outside our Muslim community, go away to college,
stay out at night, do whatever he pleases. A girl, on the other hand, must learn
to cook, not say what's on her mind, and repress sexual desires. . . . Moslem boys
brought up in America integrate much faster into American society than Muslim girls." And in a "Focus on Youth" feature in *India West*, a young Hindu
woman made a similar point, citing a father who stated that because daughters
can get pregnant they are controlled much more strictly than sons, since it is they
who can damage the family's reputation. This writer asserted that it was time to
face up to the issue of sex in her Indo-American generation, and she quoted a
Hindu woman doctor who said that 40 percent of her Indo-American patients
are sexually active. The writer and the doctor both termed the refusal of parents
to accept this possibility as "extreme denial."[25]

Sexuality is a major theme in powerful new writings by predominantly young
women of Asian Indian descent in America, not only heterosexual feelings and
activities but lesbian ones as well. The strategy of nondisclosure, not telling one's
parents about the significant choices one is making in life, is common. In her
book, Priya Agarwal discusses social issues for second-generation Indo-Americans,
and she opens with a quote from a young man about going with a girl for four
years without telling his parents anything about the relationship. More than half
the young people in Agarwal's survey preferred to date without telling their parents.[26]

It is with respect to that very important life event, marriage, that the gender
and generational differences become magnified. Marriage is sometimes the occasion for crisis in Asian Indian immigrant families. Because of parental opposition to dating and "love marriages," the children of the immigrants are usually
put into an either/or situation. They must trust their parents to arrange their marriages, or they must trust themselves. The stakes are high here, for one knows of
many marriages made by parents for their children that have not worked out, and
the consequences have been tragic. Divorce is now a distinct possibility for Indo-
Americans, and the frequently transglobal marriage and family networks add international legal complications to the emotional costs of divorce for Asian
Indians.

It is time to remember the experiences of the Punjabi pioneers and their
Punjabi-Mexican families, experiences that emphasize the flexibility of ethnic
identity and of culture. For the new immigrants from India, as well, we need to
recognize the historical construction of their identities in both the American and
global arenas. Time and place are very important components here, as changes

in the historical context have powerful consequences for individual, family, and community identity. The turnabouts in U.S. citizenship and immigration policies in the 1940s and 1960s had dramatic consequences for Punjabi-Mexican family life in California,[27] and the changing global economy and society are having dramatic consequences for the much larger and more diverse population of Asian Indian immigrants in the United States now. Just as identities and communities have been constituted and reconstituted over time back in India, new concepts of identity and community are being produced in the United States by Asian Indian immigrants and their descendants in conjunction with other Americans.

NOTES

1. The Immigration and Naturalization Act of 1965 took effect in 1968: see Sucheng Chan, *Asian Americans: An Interpretive History* (Boston: Twayne, 1991), 145–165.

2. For these laws, see Karen Isaksen Leonard, *Making Ethnic Choices: California's Punjabi Mexican Americans* (Philadelphia: Temple University Press, 1992), Bruce La Brack, *The Sikhs of Northern California, 1904–1975: A Socio-Historical Study* (New York: AMS Press, 1988) and Joan M. Jensen, *Passage from India: Asian Indian Immigrants in North America* (New Haven, CT: Yale Univ. Press, 1988).

3. Leonard, *Making Ethnic Choices*.

4. Because of the Supreme Court's Thind decision in 1923, this had been used only by whites born in India until 1946.

5. *India West*, May 6, 1994.

6. See U.S. 1990 census releases reported in *India West*, Oct. 1, 1993, and Feb. 4, 1994. A 1991 five-group survey of Asian American groups showed that Indians held the most IRAs and stocks and were the most highly educated: *India West*, Jan. 25, 1991. Census data released in 1994 showed Indian American families with the second-highest median incomes among major Asian groups, second only to the Japanese: *India West*, Feb. 4, 1994. A study on foreign-born professionals, by Leon Bouvier and David Simcox for the Center for Immigration Studies, released April 15, 1994, showed foreign-born Indians to be the highest paid among foreign-born professionals (with an annual median income of $40,625). Foreign-born Indians numbered 593,423 in the 1990 census, of which 450,406 were born in India: *India West*, April 22, 1994.

7. For the 4 percent figure, *India West*, Feb. 26, 1993; for the information about the American Association of Physicians from India, *India Today*, Aug. 15, 1994, 48l. In 1980, of the 400,000 Indians in the United States, 11 percent of the men and 8 percent of the women were physicians, while 17 percent of the men were engineers, architects, or surveyors and 7 percent of the women were nurses (*India West*, Nov. 27, 1992). There are also the Association of Indian Pharmacists in America, an Indo-American Physicians and Dentists Political Association, and many Indian computer professionals working in the United States. For the marriage and divorce statistics, *India West*, Oct. 1, 1993; for the most common household size (for 29 percent of the Indian population), *India West*, Oct. 8, 1993.

8. This national study used polls done over several years by seven national polling organizations and compared thirty-three ethnic and religious groups (in some tables, fifty-

eight groups); of the thirty-three groups, Indians were highest in educational level, fifth in household income, but twenty-eighth in socioeconomic standing (of the fifty-eight groups, they were thirty-eighth in social standing): *India West*, Jan. 17, 1992.

9. *India Today*, Jan. 31, 1994, 60 c,d,f; *India West*, Oct. 1, 1993.

10. See Dalip Singh Saund's autobiography, *Congressman From India* (New York: Dutton, 1960).

11. For Indians admitted from 1977 to 1991, the naturalization rate was 49.8 percent (*India West*, Dec. 3, 1993).

12. This typology was developed by Raymond Brady Williams, ed., *A Sacred Thread: Modern Transmission of Hindu Traditions in India and Abroad* (Chambersburg, PA: Anima Publications, 1992), 228–257.

13. For example, the Telugu Association of North America is dominated by members of the Kamma caste, while their rivals in the countryside of Andhra Pradesh (the Telugu-speaking state in South India), members of the Reddy caste, have formed the American Telugu Association.

14. There are now also international associations, Global Peoples of Indian Origin being the best known, as well as regional and linguistic ones.

15. See Omar Khalidi, ed., *Indian Muslims in North America* (Watertown, MA: South Asia Press, [c. 1991]), particularly the article by Raymond Brady Williams; also Karen Leonard, "South Asian Leadership of American Muslims," in *Muslims in the West: from Sojourners to Citizens*, ed. Yvonne Yazbeck Haddad, 233–249 (Oxford: Oxford Univ. Press, 2002).

16. The "Kwality" founder, Kapal Dev Kapoor, died in Los Angeles in 1991 (*India West*, Oct. 18, 1991).

17. Astrologers find dates that coincide with Labor Day and the Fourth of July. For information about the wedding economy, see Karen Leonard and Chandra Sekhar Tibrewal, "Asian Indians in Southern California: Occupations and Ethnicity," in *Comparative Immigration and Entrepreneurship: Culture, Capital and Ethnic Networks*, eds. Parminder Bhachu and Ivan Light (New Brunswick, NJ: Transaction, 1993).

18. Rahesh Thakkar argues that Indian classical dance plays a major role in winning a place for Indian culture in the North American scene: "Transfer of Culture through Arts: the South Asian Experience in North America," in *Ethnicity, Identity, and Migration*, eds. Milton Israel and N. K. Wagle (Toronto: Center for South Asian Studies, Univ. of Toronto, 1992).

19. The U.S.-born followers of Sikhism, Hinduism, and Islam often differ strikingly from the Indian immigrants, and, depending on the interpreter, their beliefs and practices can be considered dangerously hybrid or more "authentic (text-based)" than those of the immigrants. For some discussion, see Karen Leonard, "South Asian Religions in the U.S.: New Contexts and Configurations," *Cultural Studies* (forthcoming).

20. Raymond Brady Williams discusses these American cousins briefly in "Asian Indian and Pakistani Religions in the United States," *Annals of the American Academy of Political and Social Science* 558 (July 1998). He includes Jains and Indian Christians in the survey, one of the few scholars to publish on them; also see his *Christian Pluralism in the United States: The Indian Immigrant Experience* (Cambridge: Cambridge Univ. Press, 1996).

Best on the white Sikhs is Verne A. Dusenbery. See, for example, "Punjabi Sikhs and Gora Sikhs: Conflicting Assertions of Sikh Identity in North America," in *Sikh History and Religion in the Twentieth Century*, eds. Joseph T. O'Connell, Milton Israel, and Willard G. Oxtoby, with W. H. McLeod and J. S. Grewal, 334–355 (Toronto: Centre for South Asian Studies, Univ. of Toronto, 1988).

21. Buddhist and Muslim communities of believers in America cannot be considered diasporic; both are extremely diverse in terms of national origin, class, language, and race and ethnicity. In both cases, there are significant American-born components, and, also in both cases, South Asians immigrants have emerged as important participants and leaders of these large and evolving religious communities.

22. Paul Gilroy, "It Ain't Where You're From, It's Where You're At: The Dialectics of Diasporic Identification," *Third Text: Third World Perspectives on Contemporary Art and Culture* 13 (Winter 1991): 3–16.

23. Priya Agarwal, *Passage from India: Post 1965 Indian Immigrants and Their Children* (Palos Verdes, CA: Yuvati Publications, 1991), 48–49. Sakguru Bodhinatha Veylonswami, "Eulogy for the Hindu Family" (June 1993).

24. Gauri Bhat, "Tending the Flame: Thoughts on Being Indian-American," in *COSAW* [Committee on South Asian Women] *Bulletin* 7, no. 3–4 (1992), 1–6.

25. The first quote is from Saba, "Reflections of a Young Feminist," *COSAW Bulletin* 7, no. 3–4 (1992), 8; the second, from Smriti Aggarwal, *India West*, July 30, 1993, 62, quoting a doctor who is clearly speaking of her adolescent patients.

26. For inadequate communication between parents and children, see Agarwal, *Passage From India*, 50–59; for the dating quote and statistics, see ibid., 48–49.

27. For the "old" immigrants, the possibilities opened up by U.S. citizenship and the sponsorship of relatives from India endangered the inheritance rights of some spouses and children in the U.S. and also changed the pool of potential spouses for both first and second generation Hindus. See Leonard, *Making Ethnic Choices*, especially 174–202.

BIBLIOGRAPHICAL ESSAY

For the early pioneers from India, see the political histories by Joan Jensen, *Passage from India* (New Haven, CT: Yale Univ. Press, 1988), and Harish Puri, *Ghadar Movement: Ideology, Organization and Strategy* (Amritsar, India: Guru Nanak Dev Univ. Press, 1983). Bruce LaBrack, *The Sikhs of Northern California, 1904–1975: A Socio-Historical Study* (New York: AMS Press, 1988) and Karen Isaksen Leonard, *Making Ethnic Choices: California's Punjabi Mexican Americans* (Philadelphia: Temple University Press, 1992) focus on the Punjabi farmers in California, many of whom married Hispanic women. Usha R. Jain's 1964 thesis has been published, *The Gujaratis of San Francisco* (New York: AMS Press, 1989). The first and as yet only national elected representative from India wrote his autobiography, Dalip Singh Saund, *Congressman From India* (New York: Dutton, 1960). See also Dhan Gopal Mukherji's reissued 1923 autobiography, *Caste and Outcast* (Stanford: Stanford University Press, 2002), with an introduction by Gordon Chang and afterword by Akhil Gupta and Purnima Mankekar that greatly enhance its value. Sucheng Chan, *Asian Americans: An Interpretive History* (Boston: Twayne, 1991) places the East Indians in the context of Asian American history.

Most work focuses on the post-1965 East Indian immigrants. Leona Bagai, *The East Indians and the Pakistanis in America* (Minneapolis: Lerner Publications, 1968), Parmatma Saran and Edwin Eames, eds., *The New Ethnics: Asian Indians in the United States* (New York: Praeger Special Studies, 1980), and George Kurian and Ram P. Srivastava, eds., *Overseas Indians: A Study in Adaptation* (Delhi: Vikas, 1983), are early studies. New York City has been covered: Maxine Fisher, *The Indians of New York City* (Columbia, MO: South Asia Books, 1980), followed by Madhulika Khandelwal, "Indian Immigrants in Queens, New York City: Patterns of Spatial Concentration and Distribution, 1965–1990," in ed. Peter van der Veer, *Nation and Migration: The Politics of Space in the South Asian Diaspora* (Philadelphia: Univ. of Pennsylvania Press, 1995), and, most recently, Johanna Lessinger, *From the Ganges to the Hudson: Indian Immigrants in New York City* (Boston: Allyn and Bacon, 1995). Karen Isaksen Leonard, *The South Asian Americans* (Westport, CT: Greenwood Press, 1997) covers Indians along with other South Asians. See also Usha Helweg and Arthur Helweg, *An Immigrant Success Story: East Indians in America* (London: Hurst, 1990), for a celebratory overview.

For demographic and socioeconomic profiles, see Surinder M. Bhardwaj and N. Madhusudana Rao, "Asian Indians in the United States: A Geographic Appraisal," in *South Asians Overseas: Migration and Ethnicity*, eds. Colin Clarke, Ceri Peach, and Steven Vertovec, 197–218 (New York: Cambridge Univ. Press, 1990); Manoranjan Dutta, "Asian Indian Americans: Search for an Economic Profile," in *From India to America*, ed. S. Chandrasekhar, 76–85 (La Jolla, CA: Population Review, 1982); Urmilla Minocha, "South Asian Immigrants: Trends and Impacts on the Sending and Receiving Societies," in *Pacific Bridges: The New Immigration from Asia and the Pacific Islands*, eds. James T. Fawcett and Benjamin V. Carino, 347–374 (New York: Center for Migration Studies, 1987). For an update using the 2000 census, see Karen Leonard, "Immigrants from India," in Mary Waters and Reed Ueda, editors, *The New Americans: A Handbook to Immigration Since 1965* (Boston: Harvard Univ. Press, forthcoming).

On religious issues, see Raymond Williams, *Religions of Immigrants from India and Pakistan: New Threads in the American Tapestry* (New York: Cambridge Univ. Press, 1988), and his edited book, *A Sacred Thread: Modern Transmission of Hindu Traditions in India and Abroad* (Chambersburg, PA: Anima, 1992). John Y. Fenton also has two books on the subject: *Transplanting Religious Traditions: Asian Indians in America* (New York: Praeger, 1988) and *South Asian Religions in the Americas: An Annotated Bibliography of Immigrant Religious Traditions* (Westport, CT: Greenwood Press, 1995). Diana Eck edited a CD-ROM, *On Common Ground: World Religions in America* (New York: Columbia Univ. Press, 1997) and wrote *A New Religious America: How a "Christian Country" Has Now Become the World's Most Religiously Diverse Nation* (San Francisco: Harper Collins, 2001). Fred W. Clothey, ed., *Rhythm and Intent* (Madras: Blackie and Sons, 1983) and Carla Petievich, ed., *The Expanding Landscape: South Asians in Diaspora* (Delhi: Manohar, 1999), contain some relevant articles (specifically, those by Narayanan, Venkatachari, and John Fenton in the first book and Kathryn Hansen, Joanne Punzo Waghorne, and Usha Sanyal in the second). For articles on Sikhs, check the collections edited by N. Gerald Barrier and/or Peshaura Singh and Verne A. Dusenbery in the 1980s and 1990s; for example, Verne A. Dusenbery, " 'Nation' or 'World Religion'? Master Narratives of Sikh Identity," and Karen Leonard, "Second Generation Sikhs in America," both in *Sikh Identity: Continuity and Change*, eds. Pashaura Singh and N. Gerald Barrier, 127–144, 275–297 (New Delhi; Manohar, 1999). See also N. Gerald Barrier, "Gurdwaras in the U.S.: Governance, Authority, and Legal Issues," *Understanding Sikhism* 4, no.1 (January–June, 2001): 31–41, D. S. Tatla, *The Sikh Diaspora: The Search for Statehood* (London: UCL, 1999), and Brian K. Axel, *The Nation's Tortured Body: Violence, Representation and the Formation of a Sikh "Diaspora"* (Durham NC: Duke Univ.

Press, 2001). For Muslims, Karen Leonard, "South Asian Leadership of American Muslims," in *Muslims in the West: From Sojourners to Citizens*, ed. Yvonne Haddad, 233–249 (Oxford: Oxford Univ. Press, 2002). For discussions of Hindus, see Prema Kurien, "Becoming American by Becoming Hindu: Indian Americans Take Their Place at the Multicultural Table," in *Gatherings in Diaspora: Religious Communities and the New Immigration*, eds. Stephen Warner and Judith Wittmer, 37–70 (Philadelphia: Temple University Press, 1998); following the lead of the editors, Kurien argues that being more religious is a way of becoming American.

Scholarship on Indian postcolonial and diasporic culture in the U.S. is flourishing, often using the phrase *South Asian* but really covering only Asian Indians. Fiction, poetry, and autobiographies by authors from India have attracted much attention: Pramod Mishra and Urmila Mohapatra, *South Asian Diaspora in North America: An Annotated Bibliography* (Delhi: Kalinga Publications, 2002) are an adequate introduction to these and other topics. Roshni Rustomji Kerns has edited an introductory collection: *Living in America: Poetry and Fiction by South Asian American Writers* (San Francisco: Westview Press, 1995). Interviews and musings can be found in Deepika Bahri and Mary Vasudeva, eds., *Between the Lines: South Asians and Postcoloniality* (Philadelphia: Temple Univ. Press, 1996) and Lavina Dhingra Shankar and Rajini Srikanth, ed., *A Part, Yet Apart: South Asians in Asian America* (Philadelphia: Temple Univ. Press, 1998). R. Radhakrishnan, *Diasporic Meditations: Between Home and Location* (Minneapolis: Univ. of Minnesota, 1996) is a remarkably thoughtful set of essays.

Susan Koshy's "Category Crisis: South Asian Americans and Questions of Race and Ethnicity," *Diaspora* 7 (1998): 285–320, nicely covers these issues. In a long opening essay in their edited book, *Postcolonial Theory and the United States* (Jackson: Univ. of Mississippi Press, 2000), Amritjit Singh and Peter Schmidt explore questions of race, ethnicity, and politics, relating postcolonial theory to American or U.S. Studies, and their themes are picked up by two personal political manifestos urging fellow South Asians to turn away from the model-minority myth and engage in progressive politics with African Americans and other people of color. These manifestos are Vijay Prashad's *The Karma of Brown Folk* (Minneapolis: Univ. of Minnesota Press) and Amitava Kumar's *Passport Photos* (Berkeley: Univ. of California Press), both published in 2000. Prashad invokes selected bits of African American and immigrant Indian history to argue eloquently against conservative religious and racist forces among the post-1965 immigrants. Like Prashad, but with more postcolonial terminology and elegance, Ghosh urges engagement at all levels and in all places with those who control borders; he plays with the form of the passport to make his points.

Perhaps the first close look at the second post-1965 generation was Margaret A. Gibson's *Accommodation without Assimilation: Punjabi Sikh Immigrants in an American High School* (Ithaca: Cornell Univ. Press, 1988). Then came Priya Agarwal's *Passage from India: Post 1965 Indian Immigrants and Their Children* (Palos Verdes, CA: Yuvati Publications, 1991), followed by many other writings by and about members of the second generation, especially the young women. The pioneering collection edited by the Women of South Asian Descent Collective, *Our Feet Walk the Sky: Women of the South Asian Diaspora* (San Francisco: Aunt Lute Books, 1993), has been followed by two edited collections, Shamita Das Dasgupta, *A Patchwork Shawl: Chronicles of South Asian Women in America* (New Brunswick, NJ: Rutgers Univ. Press, 1998), and Sangeeta R. Gupta, *Emerging Voices: South Asian American Women Redefine Self, Family, and Community*

(New Delhi: Sage Publications, 1999). Margaret Abraham has published an insightful book, *Speaking the Unspeakable: Marital Violence among South Asian Immigrants in the United States* (New Brunswick, NJ: Rutgers Univ. Press, 2000), about marital violence, drawing on interviews and on her own experiences with Sakhi, a pioneering organization for South Asian women in New York.

Music, dance, and cultural festivals have been used to demonstrate hybrid identities, sexuality, and crossover or fusion culture. See Gayatri Gopinath, "Nostalgia, Desire, Diaspora: South Asian Sexualities in Motion," *Positions* 5 (1992), Sunaina Maira, "Identity Dub: The Paradoxes of an Indian American Youth Subculture" (New York Mix), *Cultural Anthropology* 14, no. 1 (1999): 29–60, and Sandhya Shukla, "Building Diaspora and Nation: The 1991 'Culturalfestival of India,'" *Cultural Studies* 11 (1997): 296–315, are examples of this growing genre of work.

CHINESE AMERICANS

George Anthony Peffer

INTRODUCTION

Among Chinese Americans, the issue of assimilation has followed a somewhat irregular path, both as a social reality and as a subject of scholarly research. The earliest Chinese immigrants to the United States demonstrated no desire at all to become permanent residents or build stable communities. Also from the beginning, European Americans appear to have decided that newcomers from China represented an undesirable element that the country would be better off without. By the twentieth century, however, a small American-born generation of Chinese Americans clearly viewed themselves as belonging to their adopted rather than their ancestral home.[1] As World War II came to an end, they had redefined Chinatown as a safe and educationally valuable tourist destination, and themselves as studious, intellectually gifted examples of a "model minority."[2] Moreover, members of the dominant culture seemed to have changed their minds about Americans of Chinese ancestry. Although still viewing this ethnic group as "exotic," they no longer expressed concern about what was called yellow peril. Old immigration restrictions were removed, and Chinese Americans increasingly were found in the economy's most lucrative and prestigious professions.

Scholars writing about this image transformation interpreted its meaning in terms of assimilative success, dividing the story of Chinese immigration into three broad periods. Typically, they have pointed to the years from 1852 to 1882 as being dominated by the sojourner, or temporary migrant, looking to get rich and go back home. They have designated 1882–1943 as the exclusion era, when European American racism prevented working-class Chinese from entering the country. Finally, the years since 1943 have signaled an emotional transition toward settlement, when political upheaval in China and growing acceptance in the United States led Chinese Americans to see the United States as their home.[3]

Since the 1980s, however, continuing research has unearthed a much more complex and nuanced history of Chinese Americans. The sojourner remains an important theme, but transnational migration strategies and female shadings of this image have replaced the stories of "bachelor Chinatowns."[4] The negative impact of exclusion laws still occupies a central place, but new scholarship emphasizes the skill of Chinese immigrants in circumventing such restrictions and the particular ways that discriminatory legislation targeted women.[5] While these two new approaches have tended to relocate the emphasis on settlement to a much earlier time frame, explosive and diverse new Chinese immigration since 1943 has altered the present picture as well. The foreign born have become as prominent in the Chinese community of the 2000s as they were at the beginning of the twentieth century. Many of these individuals see themselves as temporary migrants, taking advantage of economic opportunities in the United States while leaving spouses and children at home. These contemporary sojourners may be male or female, depending on the overseas job market, and they often indicate little or no interest in assimilation.[6] For the American born, some of whom can claim a birthright of citizenship that extends back five generations, successful careers and marriage across ethnic boundaries have paralleled an increased emphasis on their Chinese heritage and recovering the histories of their pioneer ancestors. Thus, in recognition of such significant changes, Chinese American history is here divided into six distinct time-periods—at least until what is a particularly active scholarly community argues convincingly that there should be more.

THE SOJOURNER PERIOD: 1850–1868

Chinese explorers may have reached the Pacific coast of what became the United States of America many years before Christopher Columbus arrived in the Western Hemisphere, and individual sailors had jumped ship and established residence in cities along the Atlantic seaboard as early as the eighteenth century.[7] However, the first substantial wave of Chinese immigration to the United States came in response to the discovery of gold at Sutter's Mill, California, in 1848. From a few hundred in 1849 to a few thousand in 1852, Chinese fortune hunters joined their counterparts from other parts of the world and the eastern United States in what constituted the most rapid colonization of new territory in the history of the country's development. Like most in this initial migration, Chinese adventurers came with no intention of staying and, reflecting their short-term agenda, without women or children. Instead, they intended to strike it rich—or at least accumulate a comfortable level of wealth—and then return home. While absent from the clan-village that had blessed their departure, they would send regular remittances to support those left behind.

As the hard work of panning or digging for gold generated little in return for most, Chinese and non-Chinese alike, many gave up and either went back to their families or decided to try their luck in some other venue, such as the British outposts along the Malay Peninsula or the European and American colonial plantations of the Pacific and Caribbean Islands, Central America, and South America.[8] Others joined competitors from different ethnic and national backgrounds in seeking the slower but more stable rewards of helping to develop the new state California's vast potential in agriculture and natural resources. For the Chinese, the long and particularly bloody Taiping Rebellion, which had started in 1850 and would not end until 1864, made repatriation in failure the least attractive of these options. Back home, little awaited them but chronic poverty, the destructive forces of war, and conscription into either the imperial or the rebel army. The best chance for survival, both for themselves and their families, lay in continued labor abroad and the funneling of saved wages through the British colony of Hong Kong. Thus, despite the difficulties of overseas migration, most Chinese men settled into lengthy stays away from home and found California to be as promising a place as any for earning a living if not a fortune.

As an overtly competitive enterprise, gold mining did not lend itself to the building of a multicultural community among the diverse group of people working their claims. In fact, the goldfields proved to be particularly dangerous and violent places where contested extraction rights often led to murder and the first concern of the successful was how to make it to San Francisco to book passage for home with their fortunes and their lives intact. Within this kind of environment, Chinese miners—as perhaps the most "different" of their kind—suffered as frequent victims of both harassment and violence. Moreover, when they decided to stay and build lives—or at least indefinite sojourns—for themselves, California's newly formed governmental branches wasted little time in singling out the Chinese as targets of formal discrimination.

As early as 1852, with the state barely two years old, Governor John Bigler issued a declaration of hostility toward Chinese immigration and called for their future exclusion from California. Bigler's letter, addressed to both houses of the state legislature and released to the press, ushered in an array of local and statewide legislative attacks against these "undesirable aliens."[9] Thus, the anti-Chinese movement in California began almost as early as statehood and was connected more to unadulterated racism than to fears of depressed wages or the drain on the local economy caused by remittances to China.

By 1852, however, a number of California's Chinese residents already had developed a substantial interest, both financial and emotional, in preserving their right of migration to the United States. Merchants had built thriving businesses in multiple areas, from importing necessities for their Chinese clientele, to providing what were considered exotic goods for non-Chinese residents, to serving the needs of the whole community in such enterprises as laundries and restaurants. Agricultural and construction laborers had found steady work in draining marshes, building levees, and raising crops. Miners still managed to eke out a living and a little surplus from the trailings of discarded claims and less promising sites.[10] Collectively, these groups resolved to meet both vigilante and governmental hostility with determined resistance. Led by the merchant elite, they challenged the proponents of discrimination at almost every turn and launched activist campaigns in response to the earliest formal attacks on their freedoms of employment and residence in the state. Governor Bigler had delivered his first anti-Chinese message on April 23, 1852, and leaders of the Chinese community had drafted, translated, and published letters by April 29.[11] Following this effort in media activism, they quickly moved on to defend their human and civil rights in the courts.

Throughout the period from about 1855 to 1868, the California legislature and various municipalities in the state enacted an array of anti-Chinese ordinances, from foreign (i.e., Chinese) miners taxes to special debarkation fees for Chinese passengers arriving in port to prohibitions against Chinese land ownership. The Chinese American community met each of these attacks with a consistent formula for judicial activism that resembled the strategy employed by civil rights leaders in the mid-twentieth century. First, individuals would refuse to meet the demands of a particular discriminatory law, thereby prompting their arrest. Then, an immigrant organization—most often the Chinese Consolidated Benevolent Association (CCBA)—would secure the services of California's most prominent attorneys on behalf of the incarcerated violators. Although they normally lost the subsequent court case at the local level, the legal defense team would pursue appeals through the judicial system and, usually in either the California Supreme Court or federal district court, win their client's release. By utilizing this approach, community activists maximized the effectiveness of their resources by defeating the law itself; that is, by working to have the particular law declared unconstitutional.[12]

THE SETTLER PERIOD: 1868–1875

Chinese Americans already had recorded an impressive string of victories when the federal government inadvertently aided their cause with two important legal changes, both of which were intended to protect the rights of newly liberated African Americans after the Civil War.

The first of these revolutionary developments was the Fourteenth Amendment to the United States Constitution, which was ratified in 1868. The amendment guaranteed "equal protection under the law" to all "persons" residing in the country. Thus, as resident aliens, the Chinese could not be singled out as legislative targets by local and state statutes. The second was the Civil Rights Act of 1870, which guaranteed "all persons within the jurisdiction of the United States" the rights to pursue legal action, to give testimony in court, and to protection of their persons and property, while also prohibiting individual states from exacting taxes or fees that did not apply equally to all immigrants living within their borders.[13] Such sweeping transformations made community activists virtually unbeatable in their resistance against discriminatory legislation and led to multiple and embarrassing defeats for California's anti-Chinese forces.

Even as more Chinese women began migrating to the United States, male immigrants started marrying non-Chinese women as well. With gender balance still far from being a reality, their interracial relationships focused primarily on an ethnic group whose new immigration to the Pacific coast was heavily female: the Irish.[14] Although racial prejudice both within and outside the Irish American community worked against such marriages, newspapers of the late 1860s and early 1870s contain numerous accounts of their existence.[15] In fact, they typically were reported as interesting novelties rather than threats to social stability and often were used as evidence against the industry and character of Irish men. Miscegenation remained an issue to be settled by state law, and California did not criminalize it until 1880.[16] Marriages between Chinese men and Irish women may have generated hostility and perhaps contributed to the leadership of Irish Americans like Dennis Kearney in a growing working-class anti-Chinese movement that joined the rise in female immigration as a symbol of permanent Chinese settlement in the United States.[17]

Despite indications of permanence and their success in the courts, however, Chinese immigrants failed to gain an all-important concession to equality: the right of naturalization. The Nationality Act of 1790 had restricted citizenship for the foreign born to whites, and Congress elected to alter this directive in the Civil Rights Act of 1870 only for individuals "of African nativity and persons of African descent."[18] Since few of their number had been born in the United States, Chinese Americans thus were prevented from building on their judicial victories with political organization. Without the ability to create even a locally influential voting block, they remained vulnerable to tactical innovation by organizations opposed to their continued presence in the country. That new strategy would emerge in the 1870s through the exploitation of two particularly popular negative stereotypes of migrants from China: the coolie and the prostitute.

THE PERIOD OF EXCLUSION'S DOMINANCE: 1875–1937

Having experienced repeated frustration in their efforts to drive out the Chinese through local and state legislation, political organizations in California moved their campaign to the national stage with the aid of their representatives in Congress. In 1875, one of these legislators, Democratic congressman Horace Page, won passage of an immigration law that has come to bear his name. The Page Act prohibited "unfree" Chinese laborers and prostitutes from entering the country and called for the development of an elaborate interrogation and screening process to prevent members of these restricted groups from circumventing the law. The large numbers of male immigrants rendered impossible the implementation of such an approach in the case of suspected "coolies," but women were migrating at a rate that was small enough to permit employment of the "prostitute" label to significant effect.[19]

As an increasing number of male immigrants moved from mining into less lucrative and more long-term occupations, a growing percentage of them began to arrange for their wives and minor children to join them in the United States. In addition to the sojourner mentality of the pioneer generation, a number of factors had worked against female immigration. First, Chinese cultural tradition called for a married woman to remain in her husband's village, caring for her parents-in-law and tending the family shrine. Second, although the hardships created by rebellions and economic collapse in China might have acted to mitigate the requirements of tradition, pursuits like mining, commercial agriculture, and construction favored male immigration, leaving few employment opportunities for women aside from the oppressive prostitution industry. Third, even though the diversification of California's economy had started by the 1860s to create female-friendly industrial enterprises like clothing, shoe, and cigar manufacturing, growing hostility toward Chinese immigrants discouraged the migration of nuclear families.[20]

Notwithstanding such myriad obstacles to gender balance, ratification of the Burlingame Treaty in 1868 had guaranteed freedom of travel between China and the United States. This change in U.S. policy had prompted a substantial increase in the rate of female immigration. Although a significant percentage of these new arrivals had been brought to the country as prostitutes—and a much smaller group had come as the second wives and the concubines of prosperous merchants—most were the first wives of laborers. Establishing working-class families in California, most particularly in San Francisco's Chinatown, these women signaled a fundamental change in the nature of the Chinese American community: more and more of its members intended to stay.[21] Facing the prospects of a reproductively viable entrenchment of "yellow peril" in his state, Congressman Page had seized on the well-known image of the Chinese prostitute to create what functioned as a gender-specific exclusion law. Faced with the challenge of proving female virtue through a series of interrogations directed by U.S. consular officials in Hong Kong, few families could afford the risk of investing in the overseas travel of women who still might be denied entry by port officials in San Francisco. As a result of this new obstacle, female immigration plummeted after 1875. Anti-Chinese forces finally had achieved success by pursuing their goals at the federal level, and an immigrant group denied the right of naturalization could do nothing to punish the legislators who enacted discriminatory laws against people who were ineligible to vote. Activists attempted to battle this new threat to their community's survival, but now that battle was exclusively on a national stage.

Over the next seventeen years, Chinese Americans continued to lose ground in the struggle against a movement of racial bigotry that was determined to exclude them from becoming part of American society. In 1880, the United States government negotiated a new treaty with China's Qing Dynasty that authorized comprehensive immigration restrictions in response to perceived crises like economic recessions, as long they carried a specified and reasonable date of termination. The Angell Treaty thus paved the way for banning the entire Chinese working class and their dependents from entry into the United States, a goal that anti-Chinese forces accomplished with the passage of the first general Chinese Exclusion Act in 1882.[22] Since this new legislation could not be challenged as a treaty violation, because of the Angell Treaty little judicial ground existed for mounting a court fight against its constitutionality. When the Scott Act of 1888 expanded exclusion to include laborers and their dependents who had established residence in the United States prior to 1882, prohibiting those who visited China from returning, the gender-based attack on Chinese community building had reached fruition.[23]

Faced with bleak prospects for the future, the CCBA launched a last-ditch effort to retain its role as primary protector of Chinese immigrants. When the Geary Act of 1892 renewed exclusion for another ten years and required resident Chinese to prove their preexclusion residence and carry government documents verifying their right to remain in the country as laborers, the CCBA instructed its constituents to ignore this requirement and challenge their subsequent arrests in court. Many Chinese Americans honored this directive but were rewarded for their expression of ethnic solidarity with deportation, when the United States Supreme Court upheld the constitutionality of the registration requirement in *Fong Yue Ting v. the United States* on May 15, 1893.[24] Still, the negative impact of this decision proved more symbolic than statistical. Throughout the decade that followed, a pattern that had started in the 1880s merely continued: the Chinese American population declined. With women eliminated almost completely from the trickle of new immigrants, men left the country for less austere environments in other parts of the world.

The judicial defeat of 1893 marked the nadir of the immigrant generation's leadership. American-born Chinese saw political activism as the key to sustained protection from discrimination, and they sought to organize an ethnic voting block through the establishment of organizations like the Chinese American Citizens Alliance (CACA), founded under a different name in 1895.[25] Gradually, this younger group of leaders supplanted the authority of their elders, but the reproductive liabilities of the Chinese American community would make the process of building citizen coalitions a difficult one. Exclusion continued unabated through the first four decades of the twentieth century; in fact, it was made even more oppressive with the Expatriation Act of 1907, which stripped the citizenship of any American-born woman who married a Chinese immigrant.[26] Advocates of women's rights hailed the revision of this law that came in the form of the Cable Act of 1922, because the new statute conferred upon women a legal status independent from that of their husbands—as long as the wives in question had not married men who were ineligible for naturalization (i.e., the Chinese and other Asian immigrants). Thus, anti-Chinese forces ensured that advances in the independence of women before the law did not apply to Chinese American families.[27]

THE PERIOD OF EXCLUSION'S DECLINE: 1937–1943

From 1922 to 1937, organizations like the CACA continued to lobby for the repeal of exclusion and a reversal of its negative impact on a community that was now more than seventy years old. In addition, newspapers in both Chinese and English served all of the urban centers that contained significant Chinese American populations. The American born gradually emerged as a majority and assumed key leadership positions. Focused on gaining their full rights as citizens and organizing politically, this new generation achieved a degree of influence in relation to city governments on both the Pacific and Atlantic coasts.[28] Still, it took the tragedy of war to alter the playing field sufficiently for these groups to realize their full aspirations. When the Empire of Japan occupied China in 1937, sympathy for the suffering of the Chinese people prompted a revision of traditional yellow-peril rhetoric in the United States. Pilots from the United States flew the Flying Tiger missions of the American Volunteer Group in support of the anti-Japanese resistance, and this unofficial alliance established the foundation from which Chinese American political activists launched a reinvigorated campaign against exclusion.

As opposition to exclusion gained intensity, it found ready support from the academic community. Robert Park's Chicago School of Sociology, housed at the University of Chicago, had begun to study America's "Oriental Problem" in the 1920s. Believing in the inevitability of immigrant assimilation, Park sought to explain why Chinese Americans retained their status as different or foreign more than seventy years after they had started entering the country in substantial numbers. Developing the theory of the "marginal man," he argued that members of the Chinese American community had lost themselves temporarily in the margins, the middle ground, between their culture of origin and majority culture in the United States. In order to complete the assimilation process, which was indeed inevitable, this group required the aid of individuals from the American-born generation who could act as cultural bridges, or marginal men, completing the links between their immigrant parents and their adopted country.[29] This task required sophisticated understanding of the social and psychological dynamics that characterized such an in-between existence. So, the Chicago School actively recruited Chinese American doctoral students to conduct research on their own communities. Over the next several decades, scholars such as Paul Siu and Rose Hum Lee produced groundbreaking dissertations, all built on the theory of the marginal man, while at the same time personifying the progress of Chinese assimilation into American society.[30] In fulfilling this dual role, they cast a positive light on the "otherness" of their forebears and reassured the dominant culture of its superiority and security.

American-born business leaders did their part as well to further the cause of immigration reform by reinventing the image of the Chinese American. When San Francisco announced its plans to host a World's Fair in 1939, Chinatown merchants seized the opportunity to transform their public image. Securing the support of city government, these "voting Chinese" constructed a model community for the fair at Treasure Island. This attraction replaced old expectations of prostitutes, gambling halls, and opium dens with restaurants, temples, and import outlets.[31] Building on their venue's popularity among family-oriented tourists, they then converted the model into reality. Chinatown no longer served as the city's vice district; it established itself instead as a preferred destination for travelers seeking cultural enrichment in a safe and welcoming environment. Thus, San Francisco's Chinese American community no longer housed the yellow peril but the model minority.[32] Although still "exotic," scholars from the Chicago School had interpreted its continued differentness as merely a phase of assimilation from the margins. If white Americans could not imagine the eventual disappearance of Chinese cultural distinctions, they at least could accept such foreign elements as part of Chinatown's charm—charm that they wanted to keep rather than destroy through continuing to restrict Chinese immigration.

When Japan attacked Pearl Harbor, on December 7, 1941, bringing the United States into World War II as a formal ally of China, the struggle for repeal of the Chinese Exclusion Acts gained irresistible momentum. Continuing to restrict the immigration of America's "friend" in the battle against Japanese aggression simply made no sense, and the Chinese American press joined community groups at every opportunity to point out such glaring illogic. By 1943, as the heroism of its Chinese military personnel was helping to turn the tide in favor of the United States in both Asia and Europe, Congress replaced exclusion with a quota of 105 immigrant visas per year for citizens of China.[33] Although the numerical impact of this legislation was minimal, the Chinese American community had succeeded in securing its future—an achievement of immense symbolic value.

THE PERIOD OF TRANSITION: 1943–1975

During the war, U.S. soldiers stationed in the Asian theater had established romantic relationships with local women. Following the Allied victory in 1945, many more of these soldiers sought to gain admission for more new wives than could be accommodated by post-1943 quotas. Their efforts persuaded Congress to pass the War Brides Act of 1945, which enabled the spouses of American military personnel to enter the country as nonquota immigrants.[34] Among these war brides were a substantial number of Chinese women, who had married soldiers of Chinese heritage as well as others from various ethnic backgrounds. The result was an annual pool of immigrants that, for the first time in Chinese American history, consisted of more women than men. This development launched an evolutionary movement toward gender parity that U.S. immigration law had prevented for seventy years.[35]

The cold war ushered in a new era for the Chinese American community. When civil war produced both the People's Republic of China (PRC) and the Republic of China (Taiwan) in 1949, refugees from these two war-ravaged countries emerged as new sources of Chinese immigration. While the Korean War (1951–1953) established the PRC as an enemy of the United States, this conflict further strengthened U.S. ties with Taiwan. As a result, the door opened a little wider for this source of prospective immigrants. Then, revision of U.S. immigration law in 1965 replaced the discriminatory national origins quotas of 1943 with a universally applied annual limit of 20,000 standard visas per year from each country in the Eastern Hemisphere and gave high priority to family reunification, for which the opponents of exclusion had been lobbying for more than eighty years. Refugees from cold war devastation were exempted from the standard limits.[36] Together, these developments initiated at least three significant trends in the Chinese American community: rapid population growth, movement toward gender balance, and a substantial foreign-born constituency.

Although the increased immigration of women corrected a long-standing injustice, the influx of people from multiple locations produced significant tensions. Most American-born Chinese had supported the Kuomintang (KMT) of Chiang Kai-shek and continued to advocate U.S. protection of his exiled government in Taiwan. The majority of immigrants from the mainland, however, saw Chiang as weak and corrupt at best, and at worst as a collaborator with Japanese occupation forces. Whether members of the Communist Party or not, they had welcomed Mao Tse-tung's victory in recognition of his leadership of the anti-Japanese resistance.

Many Chinese American leaders viewed the large numbers of new immigrants, hostile toward the KMT, as a threat to their positions. Thus, the McCarthyism of the 1950s endured in American Chinatowns for an extended period. Anti-KMT activists suffered harassment, and sometimes arrest, by the FBI's taskforce against Communist subversion. KMT agents even traveled to the United States and assassinated individuals whom their government considered especially dangerous to the interests of Taiwan. The combined forces of oppression and fear created severe strains within the Chinese American community. In order to protect themselves, some community members "turned in" their neighbors and/or family members to the FBI. These acts of betrayal, in addition to the competing rhetoric of organizations on both sides of China's internal struggles, generated bitter divisions and further eroded the trust afforded to traditional power brokers like the CCBA.[37]

During this period, Chinese American student activists in California joined with their counterparts from other ethnic groups in demanding minority recognition from university administrators. Beginning with San Francisco State University in 1968 and moving quickly to such institutions as the University of California at Berkeley and the University of California at Los Angeles, these students—energized by the civil rights movement and organized protests against the Vietnam War—succeeded in winning for themselves a place in the organizational structures of academic institutions. Ethnic studies and Asian American studies departments and programs merged scholarship and activism in empowering ways. Moreover, universities emerged as focal points for the building of pan-Asian political coalitions, from which the term Asian American derived cultural significance.[38]

THE PERIOD OF MOVEMENT INTO MAINSTREAM SOCIETY: 1975–2004

In 1972, following President Richard Nixon's visit to the People's Republic, restrictions were eased against the flow of people from the Chinese mainland. The Vietnam War, which resulted in the expulsion of more than a million ethnic Chinese from the reunited country following North Vietnam's victory in 1975, produced yet another wave of refugees who moved the foreign born toward the status of an intragroup majority.[39] Throughout the 1970–2000 period, Chinese Americans have provided a significant level of leadership in the advancement of Asian American causes. Many have served in appointed and/or elected office at the local, state, and national levels. Others have developed grassroots organizations that have exerted considerable influence over public policy through both their own initiatives and the cohesion of their voter constituencies. In 1979, the leaders of these organizations joined with academics (several of whom were leaders) to create the Association for Asian American Studies, the first professional organization for specialists in the study of Chinese and other Asian American issues. Since that beginning, AAAS has grown to become an internationally recognized entity that publishes its own academic journal, the *Journal of Asian American Studies*, and engages the greater society at multiple levels.[40]

Despite such impressive achievements, however, the merging of Chinese Americans into a broader pan-ethnic coalition also has produced new sources of tension. In the Association for Asian American Studies, for example, expansion beyond the organization's primarily Chinese American and Japanese American roots has called into question the inclusiveness of its leadership and actions. South and Southeast Asians have challenged both overt and unconscious tokenism in regard to issues ranging from the makeup of the AAAS executive board to the subject matter of articles selected for publication in its journal, the scope of panels offered at its annual conference, and its design of curricula for future study of the field. In 1998, at the association's conference in Honolulu, Hawaii, Filipino Americans protested in response to the announcement that AAAS intended to honor the work of a Japanese American novelist whom they considered guilty of fostering negative stereotypes of Filipino males. When their efforts forced the rescinding of this award by the general membership, individuals serving on the executive board felt compelled to resign en masse in order to protect themselves from possible legal action.[41] Having survived this threat to its existence, AAAS continues to debate and seek resolution regarding a proposal, introduced at the 2002 annual conference in Toronto, to change its name to the Association for Asian/Pacific Islander American Studies. In addition to differences of opinion expressed among the organization's diverse constituencies, its Pacific Islander members are divided over the issue. Some consider the name change to be a vital recognition of their hard-won legitimacy in the academy, while others worry about tokenism, and still others note that inclusion within the term *Asian American* obscures the underrepresentation of Pacific Islanders in higher education and professional occupations.[42] While all of these struggles represent authentic concerns, they demonstrate the difficulties that Chinese Americans are experiencing in negotiating their positions within an increasingly complex pan-Asian environment.

In relation to the greater society, continuing expressions of hostility demonstrate to Chinese Americans that they have not yet escaped the legacy of oppression. Two events, separated by time, place, and class, illustrate this ongoing struggle. The first was a murder, the second an arrest and subsequent trial, but both featured rushes to judgment fostered by racial bigotry. In Detroit, Michigan, on June 19, 1982, a young Chinese American man named Vincent Chin was attacked and killed by two laid-off autoworkers who misidentified him as being Japanese. Seventeen years later, Dr. Wen Ho Lee, a naturalized citizen born in Taiwan, was indicted for passing nuclear secrets to the People's Republic of China, because the U.S. government needed to demonstrate its resolve in the face of a *New York Times* story claiming that Chinese spies had stolen classified information from New Mexico's Los Alamos Laboratory, where Dr. Lee had worked as a scientist until his firing in the wake of this article's release.

A Detroit jury convicted Vincent Chin's killers only of manslaughter, resulting in fines of $3,000 each and sentences of three years' probation. Although they were found guilty of civil rights violations in federal court, subsequent appeals led to their acquittals in 1987.[43] Wen Ho Lee, by contrast, remained in prison for about ten months, most of the time in forced isolation from visitors and other inmates. Eventually, however, all charges but one against Dr. Lee were dropped. He pleaded guilty to a single count of mishandling classified information and was released with time served—and an apology from the presiding judge for his mistreatment by the government to which he had sworn his allegiance.[44]

While each of these injustices has shaken the faith of Chinese Americans in the authenticity of U.S. ideals, they have responded by injecting both their own and the pan-Asian community with renewed commitment to political, judicial, and social activism. The death of Vincent Chin and the release of his assailants sparked the creation of American Citizens for Justice (ACJ), a pan-Asian organization established to underwrite and otherwise support the civil rights case. Although its efforts ultimately ended in failure, ACJ remains active in championing other causes and helping to sponsor commemorations of Vincent Chin's murder as a symbol of the frailty of social justice.[45] As Wen Ho Lee awaited trial, Chinese Americans joined with other supporters in raising money for his legal defense and challenging the racial profiling that had led to his arrest.[46]

CONCLUSION

The cases of Vincent Chin, Wen Ho Lee, and other Chinese Americans who have suffered violence and other violations of their humanity over the past two decades bear an unsettling resemblance to those that marred the lives of Chinese immigrants who came to the United States a century-and-a-half ago. Wrong assumptions and negative stereotypes remain an unfortunate part of their experience. Still, Chinese Americans—as inheritors of a pioneer legacy—have earned a secure place for themselves relative to mainstream society. High levels of educational achievement, employment in the professions, and economic success have come to characterize them as an ethnic group. While the resulting "model minority" label obscures continued struggle and diversity, it nonetheless reflects a generally positive, if not entirely accurate, perception that contrasts sharply with nineteenth-century images. Marriage to individuals of non-Chinese heritage, including European Americans, is common. However, commitment to the preservation of heritage and history has not diminished under the weight of these assimilative characteristics.

Whereas Robert Park's Chicago School influenced a generation of Chinese American scholars to study the Oriental Problem and embrace the inevitability of assimilation, their contemporary counterparts have focused on such issues as agency in the face of discrimination and activism in pursuit both of group-specific and pan-Asian agendas.[47] Many still consider themselves to occupy a middle space between the culture and values of their ancestors and those of the dominant traditions in the United States. Yet today, the image of the marginal man moving inexorably from the former to the latter has given way to the anthropological term *liminality*.[48] This concept redefines life in between cultures as a fluid existence, sometimes uncomfortable but often valuable as a means of navigating the gaps between ethnic and mainstream identities. Whether one chooses to be more or less "Chinese" varies from situation to situation, and such movement is always back-and-forth rather than linear. For Chinese Americans, as for other descendants of immigrants in the United States, the quest for absorption into the melting pot has given way to demands for respect and acceptance as ethnic Americans. This objective constitutes the heart of multiculturalism in the twenty-first century.

NOTES

1. For an excellent discussion of the process through which American-born Chinese developed a distinct Chinese American identity, see Sucheng Chan, "Race, Ethnic Culture, and Gender in the Construction of Identities among Second-Generation Chinese Americans," in *Claiming America: Constructing Chinese American Identities during the Exclusion Era*, eds. K. Scott Wong and Sucheng Chan, 127–164 (Philadelphia: Temple Univ. Press, 1998); see also Judy Yung, *Unbound Feet: A Social History of Chinese Women in San Francisco* (Berkeley: Univ. of California Press, 1995), 106–177.

2. For a useful examination of how the "model minority" label came to be applied to Chinese Americans, see Gloria H. Chun, "Go West . . . to China: Chinese American Identity in the 1930s," in *Claiming America* (see note 1), 165–190.

3. Dividing the nineteenth-century history of Chinese immigration into the free and exclusion periods began with Mary Coolidge's pioneering work, *Chinese Immigration* (New York: Henry Holt, 1909), 499–500. Although many specialists in the post–World War II period rightly would object to the designation of the years after exclusion's repeal as a single period, the basic categories of free immigration (1852–1882), exclusion

(1882–1943), and post-exclusion (1943–present) still influence at least the introductory studies of Chinese American history; see, for example, Uma A. Segal, *A Framework for Immigration: Asians in the United States* (New York: Columbia Univ. Press, 2002), 42–45.

4. For examples of works emphasizing the transnational aspect of Chinese immigration, see Madeline Yuan-yin Hsu, *Dreaming of Gold, Dreaming of Home: Transnationalism and Migration between the United States and South China, 1882–1943* (Stanford, CA: Stanford Univ. Press, 2000) and Adam McKeown, *Chinese Migrant Networks and Cultural Change: Peru, Chicago, Hawaii, 1900–1936* (Chicago: Univ. of Chicago Press, 2001).

5. For representative studies of female agency in relation to the exclusion laws and the impact of such immigration restrictions on Chinese American women, see Erika Lee, *At America's Gates: Chinese Immigration during the Exclusion Era, 1882–1943* (Chapel Hill: Univ. of North Carolina Press, 2003); Sucheng Chan, "The Exclusion of Chinese Women, 1870–1943," in *Entry Denied: Exclusion and the Chinese Community in America, 1882–1943*, ed. Sucheng Chan (Philadelphia: Temple Univ. Press, 1991); and George Anthony Peffer, *If They Don't Bring Their Women Here: Chinese Female Immigration before Exclusion* (Urbana: Univ. of Illinois Press, 1999).

6. Among the better studies of contemporary Chinese American sojourners, which tend to emphasize transnational economic strategies, are Huping Ling, *Surviving on the Gold Mountain: A History of Chinese American Women and their Lives* (Albany: State Univ. of New York Press, 1998); Hsu, *Dreaming of Gold, Dreaming of Home*; and McKeown, *Chinese Migrant Networks and Cultural Change*.

7. Although San Francisco's Chinatown was the first substantial Chinese immigrant community in the United States, John Kuo Wei Tchen notes that New York's Chinese community is actually older because such sailors had taken up residence there in the late eighteenth century; see *New York before Chinatown: Orientalism and the Shaping of American Culture, 1776–1882* (Baltimore: Johns Hopkins Univ. Press, 1999).

8. McKeown, *Chinese Migrant Networks and Cultural Change* offers an informative comparison of immigrant life in some of these various destinations.

9. For an extensive account of Governor Bigler's anti-Chinese efforts, see Charles McClain, *In Search of Equality: The Chinese Struggle against Discrimination in the Nineteenth Century*, 10–22 (Berkeley: Univ. of California Press, 1994).

10. For a representative work on the history of Chinese American miners, see David Valentine, "Chinese Placer Mining in the United States: An Example from American Canyon, Nevada," in *The Chinese in America: A History from Gold Mountain to the New Millenium*, ed. Susie Lan Cassel, 37–53 (Walnut Creek, CA: AltaMira Press, 2002); see also Sucheng Chan, *This Bittersweet Soil: The Chinese in California Agriculture, 1860–1910* (Berkeley: Univ. of California Press, 1986).

11. To learn more about the Chinese elite's public response to Bigler's letter, see K. Scott Wong, "Cultural Defenders and Brokers: Chinese Responses to the Anti-Chinese Movement," in *Claiming America* (see note 1), 15–17.

12. For representative works focusing on the judicial resistance of Chinese Americans, see McClain, *In Search of Equality*; Angelo Ancheta, *Race, Rights, and the Asian American Experience* (New Brunswick, NJ: Rutgers Univ. Press, 1998); and Lucy Salyer, *Laws Harsh as Tigers: Chinese Immigrants and the Shaping of Modern Immigration Law* (Chapel Hill: Univ. of North Carolina Press, 1995).

13. Perhaps the best study of these constitutional changes and their impact on Chinese Americans is McClain, *In Search of Equality*.

14. For an informative introduction to the history of Irish American women, see Hasia R. Diner, *Erin's Daughters in America: Irish Immigrant Women in the Nineteenth Century* (Baltimore, MD: Johns Hopkins Univ. Press, 1983).

15. See, for example, *San Francisco Chronicle*, 1870.

16. The Statutes of California 23 (1880), 121. For a brief discussion of this legislation, see Ancheta, *Race, Rights, and the Asian American Experience*, 30.

17. For both the classic and the revisionist perspective on the role of Kearny and other labor activists in making the anti-Chinese movement a national issue, see Alexander Saxton, *The Indispensable Enemy: Labor and the Anti-Chinese Movement in California* (Berkeley: Univ. of California Press, 1971), and Andrew Gyory, *Closing the Gate: Race, Politics, and the Chinese Exclusion Act* (Chapel Hill: Univ. of North Carolina Press, 1998).

18. Both McClain, *In Search of Equality*, and Ancheta, *Race, Rights, and the Asian American Experience*, offer useful coverage of this legislative history relative to the denial of naturalization rights for Chinese and other Asian Americans.

19. For a comprehensive study of the Page Law and its impact on the Chinese American community, see Peffer, *If They Don't Bring Their Women Here*.

20. For representative discussions of these and other factors inhibiting Chinese female immigration to the United States, see Chan, *Entry Denied* (see note 5); Lee, *At America's Gates*; and Peffer, *If They Don't Bring Their Women Here*.

21. On this point, my own work is perhaps the most extensive. See also Peffer, *If They Don't Bring Their Women Here*.

22. For a discussion of the Angell Treaty and its importance in paving the way for passage of the Chinese Exclusion Act in 1882, see Peffer, *If They Don't Bring Their Women Here*, 41, 134; see also McClain, *In Search of Equality*, 148.

23. For explanations of the Scott Act and its expansion of exclusionary restrictions, see Chan, *Entry Denied* (see note 5), 112–114 and Lee, *At America's Gates*, 45.

24. For an analysis of the Geary Act and the *Fong Yue Ting* case, see McClain, *In Search of Equality*, 201–213.

25. For a history of the Chinese American Citizens Alliance, see Sue Fawn Chung, "Fighting for Their American Rights: A History of the Chinese American Citizens Alliance," in *Claiming America*, 95–126.

26. For a path-breaking study of this legislation, see Ann Marie Nicolosi, "'We Do Not Want Our Girls to Marry Foreigners': Gender, Race, and American Citizenship," *NWSA Journal* 13 (Fall 2001): 1–21.

27. See ibid., 15, 16.

28. For a discussion of the second generation's ability to use the economic importance of Chinatown to influence San Francisco and California politics, see Yong Chen, *Chinese San Francisco, 1850–1943: A Trans-Pacific Community* (Stanford, CA: Stanford Univ. Press, 2000), 60–69.

29. Robert Ezra Park, "Human Migration and the Marginal Man," in *Race and Culture*, vol. 1, ed. Everett Hughes et al. (Glencoe, IL: Glencoe Free Press, 1950). For an insightful examination of Park's Chicago School and its influence, see Henry Yu, *Thinking Orientals: Migration, Contact, and Exoticism in Modern America* (New York: Oxford Univ. Press, 2001).

30. Siu's 1953 dissertation was published more than thirty years later under its original title, *The Chinese Laundryman: A Study of Social Isolation*, ed. John Kuo Wei Tchen

(New York: New York Univ. Press, 1987). Lee's 1947 dissertation, titled "The Growth and Decline of Chinese Communities in the Rocky Mountain Region," never was published.

31. For a superb analysis of the importance of the 1939 World's Fair in transforming the image of San Francisco's Chinatown, see *Claiming America* (see note 1), 180–186.

32. See Ivan Light, "From Vice District to Tourist Attraction: The Moral Career of American Chinatowns," *Pacific Historical Review* 43 (August 1974): 367–394.

33. For a discussion of exclusion's repeal and its relative impact on Chinese immigration to the United States, see Xiaojian Zhao, *Remaking Chinese America: Immigration, Family, and Community, 1940–1965* (New Brunswick, NJ: Rutgers Univ. Press, 2002), 22–25.

34. For a comprehensive look at the War Brides Act and its impact on the Chinese American community, see ibid., 78–93.

35. For a study of this change in the gendered nature of post–World War II Chinese immigration to the United States, see ibid., 78–151.

36. U.S. Statutes at Large 79 (1965). For an analysis of this new legislation's impact on the Chinese American community, see Segal, *A Framework for Immigration*, 75–89.

37. For an examination of these cold war tensions and their effect on Chinese American solidarity, see Zhao, *Remaking Chinese America*, 152–184.

38. For a useful introduction to this history of student activism, see Don T. Nakanishi, Linkages and Boundaries: Twenty-Five Years of Asian American Studies," *Amerasia Journal* 21 (Winter 1995/1996): xvii–xxv.

39. See, for example, Philip Q. Yang, "Sojourners or Settlers: Post-1965 Chinese Immigrants," *Journal of Asian American Studies* 2 (February 1999).

40. For an introduction to the formation and mission of the Association for Asian American Studies, see the association's Web site at www.aaastudies.org.

41. For a more detailed account of the events surrounding the awarding and subsequent rescinding of the association's award for outstanding work of prose to Lois-Ann Yamanaka's *Blu's Hanging* (New York: Farrar, Straus, and Giroux, 1997), see copies of the association's minutes, which may be requested through its Web site, www.aaastudies.org.

42. For useful information relative to this proposal and the debate it has generated among members of the association, see ibid.

43. For a more thorough account of the Vincent Chin case, see www.mindspring.com/%7Elouve/vinchin.html; for additional examples of efforts to address the issue of anti-Asian violence, see Scott Kurashige, "Pan-ethnicity and Community Organizing: Asian Americans United's Campaign against Anti-Asian Violence," *Journal of Asian American Studies* 2 (June 2000).

44. For a comprehensive presentation of the experiences of Dr. Wen Ho Lee, see Wen Ho Lee (with Helen Zia), *My Country versus Me: The First Hand Account of the Los Alamos Scientist Who Was Falsely Accused of Being a Spy* (New York: Hyperion, 2001).

45. For more information on the continuing work of American Citizens for Justice, see the organization's Web site at www.acj.org.

46. See Lee and Zia, *My Country versus Me*.

47. For a useful example of the prominence of the idea of agency in current scholarship, in relation to both Chinese Americans specifically and Asian Americans in general, see Shirley Hune and Gail Nomura, eds., *Asian/Pacific Islander American Women* (Philadelphia: Temple Univ. Press, 2003).

48. For the best application of *liminality* to the history of Chinese Americans pub-

lished to date, see Judy Tzu-Chun Wu, "The 'Ministering Angel of Chinatown': Missionary Uplift, Modern Medicine, and Asian American Women's Strategies of Liminality," *Asian/Pacific Islander American Women* (see note 47), 155–171.

BIBLIOGRAPHICAL ESSAY

The scholarly literature on Chinese Americans is voluminous and growing, especially with the contributions being made by academics of Chinese ancestry. Not surprisingly, the vast majority of studies to date are focused on pre-1965 immigrants and their adaptation to life in the United States. The earliest overview of the topic was *Chinese Immigration* (New York: Holt, 1909) by Mary Roberts Coolidge, who was an outspoken opponent of Chinese exclusion legislation. More dispassionate but equally pro-Chinese is Gunther Barth, *Bitter Strength: A History of the Chinese in the United States, 1850–1870* (Cambridge, MA: Harvard University Press, 1964). Lyman Stanford, *Chinese Americans* (New York: Random House, 1974) concentrates on the background of communal organizations and their transplantation to the New World. After dealing topically with effects of language, family, religion, friendship, adolescence, and prejudice in the United States, Francis L. K. Hsu, *The Challenge of the American Dream: The Chinese in the United States* (Belmont, CA: Wadsworth, 1971), concludes with an intensive discussion of Chinese identity in American society. Equally insightful are Betty Lee Sung, *Mountain Of Gold: The Story of the Chinese in America* (New York: Macmillan, 1972), Jack Chen, *The Chinese of America* (New York: Harper and Row, 1980), and S. W. Kung, *Chinese in American Life: Some Aspects of Their History, Status, Problems, and Contributions* (Seattle: University of Washington Press, 1962). The latter is particularly interesting for its examination of the lives of post-World War II Chinese immigration in Southeast Asia, Canada, and Latin America, as well as the United States.

Especially useful are several studies of Chinese American communities in various locales within the United States. Summarizing his findings concerning the overall conditions in various American Chinatowns, Ivan H. Light, "From Vice District to Tourist Attraction: the Moral Career of America's Chinatowns, 1880–1940," *Pacific Historical Review* 63 (1974): 367–94, argues that this transition was due primarily to efforts of merchants to cultivate the tourist business. Focusing on the country's oldest and most famous Chinese settlement, Victor G. Nee and Brett de Berry, *Longtime Californ': A Documentary Study of an American Chinatown* (New York: Pantheon Books, 1973), divides the history of San Francisco's Chinatown into five stages: the bachelor society, the refugees, the family society, the emergence of a new working class, and the arrival of radicals with a new vision. Looking at the same city from a broader perspective, Yong Chen, *Chinese San Francisco, 1850–1943: A Trans-Pacific Community* (Stanford, CA: Stanford University Press, 2000), stresses the cosmopolitan nature of its population due to ongoing migration and remigration. Expanding his focus to include Stockton and Sacramento, as well as San Francisco, Wilbur W. Y. Choy, *The Chinese in California, Pacific Historian* 11 (1967): 16–22, discusses the efforts of Cantonese immigrants to preserve an ethnic community by maintaining their rural extended kinship system. Sandy Lydon, *Chinese Gold: The Chinese in the Monterey Bay Region* (Capitola, CA: Capitola Book Company, 1985) and George Chu, "Chinatowns in the Delta: The Chinese in the Sacramento—San Joaquin Delta, 1870–1960," *California Historical Society Quarterly*, demonstrate how the failure of cash crops in rural Chinese settlements forced their residents to relocate in larger cities in Northern California. In his "The Chinese Community in Los Angeles," *Social Casework* 51 (1970): 591–98, Pei-Ngor Chen describes the plight of elderly Chinese who are unable to return home after the triumph of the Chinese Communists and thus forced to remain suspended between two cultures, neither of which is within their grasp. Finally, James W. Loewen examines the means by which Chinese immigrants in Mississippi adapted to that state's racial policies by separating themselves from the far more numerous African Americans in *The Mississippi Chinese: Between Black and White* (Cambridge, MA: Harvard University Press, 1971).

Although the first Chinese immigrants were originally engaged in prospecting for gold, scholars are just beginning to realize their eventual occupational diversity and the breadth of their contribution to the economic development of the American West. The most comprehensive study of that phenomenon is Edna Bonacich and Lucie Cheng, eds., *Labor Immigration Under Capitalism: Asian Workers in the United States before World War II* (Berkeley: University of California Press, 1984). Somewhat less broad in scope is Ping Chiu, *Chinese Labor In California, 1850–1880: An Economic Study* (Madison: State Historical Society of Wisconsin, 1963). Sucheng Chan, *This Bittersweet Soil: The Chinese in California Agriculture, 1860–1910* (Berkeley: University of California Press, 1986) documents the role of the Chinese in that highly important economic sector. Of particular interest to labor and women's studies historians alike is Sue Fawn Chung, *Comstock Women: The Making of a Mining Community* (Reno: University of Nevada Press, 1998). Documenting one of the most familiar of Chinese contributions to American expansion is George Kraus, "Chinese Laborers and the Construction of the Central Pacific," *Utah Historical Quarterly* 37 (1969): 41–57.

Even though the first wave of Chinese immigrants were overwhelmingly male, it did not take long before they were joined by substantial numbers of women, a development that signified a growing disposition among erstwhile "sojourners" to remain in the United States on a permanent basis. The most thorough investigation of that condition and of American reaction to it is George Anthony Peffer, *If They Don't Bring Their Women Here: Chinese Female Immigration before Exclusion* (Urbana: University of Illinois Press, 1999). Equally informative is Huping Ling, *Surviving on Gold Mountain: A History of Chinese American Women and Their Lives* (Albany: State University of New York Press, 1998). Benson Tong, *Unsubmissive Women: Chinese Prostitutes in Nineteenth Century San Francisco* (Norman: University of Oklahoma Press, 1994) demonstrates how one segment of Chinese American women earned their livelihood and maintained their self-esteem by engaging in the world's oldest profession. In two complementary works—*Unbound Feet: A Social History of Chinese Women in San Francisco* (Berkeley: University of California Press, 1995) and *Unbound Voices: A Documentary History of Chinese Women in San Francisco*—Judy Yung makes a strong case for the argument that immigration, with all of its difficulties and tribulations, actually liberated many Chinese women. In *Remaking Chinese America: Immigration, Family, and Community, 1940–1965* (New Brunswick, NJ: Rutgers University Press, 2002), Xiaojian Zhao shows how even the small increase in Chinese immigration after 1940 facilitated the construction of families and community. With the aid of Helen Zia, Wen Ho Lee, *My Country versus Me: The First Hand Account of the Los Alamos Scientist Who Was Falsely Accused of Being a Spy* (New York: Hyperion, 2001) graphically illustrates that not even being American-born and highly educated protects women of Chinese ancestry from suspicion and discrimination.

Not surprisingly, a great deal of scholarly attention has been focused on the topic of the exclusion of Chinese immigrants from the 1880s through most of the 1960s. The most comprehensive study is Andrew Gyory, *Closing the Gate: Race, Politics, and the Chinese Exclusion Act* (Chapel Hill: University of North Carolina Press, 1998). Also of significant value are Adam McKeown, "Transnational Chinese Families and American Exclusion, 1875–1943," *Journal of American Ethnic History* 18 (1999): 73–110; Sucheng Chan, *Entry Denied: Exclusion and the Chinese Community in America* (Philadelphia: Temple University Press, 1991); Erika Lee, "The Chinese Exclusion Example: Race, Immigration, and American Gatekeeping, 1882–1924," *Journal of American Ethnic History* 21 (2002): 27–62; and Karen J. Leong, "Foreign Policy, National Identity, and Citizenship: The Roosevelt White House and the Expediency of Repeal," *Journal of American Ethnic History* 22 (2003): 3–30. Also vital to an understanding of Chinese exclusion are *The Unwelcome Immigrant: The American Image of the Chinese, 1785–1882* (Berkeley: University of California Press, 1974); Lucy E. Salyer, *Laws Harsh as Tigers: Chinese Immigrants and the Shaping of Modern Immigration Law* (Chapel Hill: University of North Carolina Press, 1995); Elmer C. Sandmeyer, *The Anti-Chinese Movement in California* (Urbana: University of Illinois Press, 1973); and Alexander Saxton, *The Indispensable Enemy: Labor and the Anti-Chinese Movement in California* (Berkeley: University of California Press, 1971).

In addition to those works already mentioned there are several others of importance to anyone interested in the history of Chinese Americans: Uma A. Segal, *A Framework for Immigration: Asians in the United States* (New York: Columbia University Press, 2002); K. Scott Wong, *Claiming America: Constructing Chinese American Identities during the Exclusion Era* (Philadelphia: Temple University Press, 1998); Henry Yu, *Thinking Orientals: Migration, Contact, and Exoticism in Modern America* (New York: Oxford University Press, 2001); S. W. Kung, *Chinese In American Life: Some Aspects of their History, Status, Problems, and Contributions* (Seattle: University of Washington Press, 1962); Paomin Chang, *Continuity and Change: A Profile of Chinese Americans* (New York: Vantage Press, 1983); Milton Konvitz, *The Alien and the Asian in American Law* (Ithaca, NY: Cornell University Press, 1946); and Betty Lee Sung, *Intermarriage Among the Chinese in New York City* (San Francisco: Chinese Historical Society of America, 1987).

DOMINICAN AMERICANS

Silvio Torres-Saillant

The task of defining any culture is fraught with conceptual dangers, not the least of which is the temptation to construe whole populations as monolithic, uncomplicated blocs, on the mere basis of their sharing a common national or ancestral origin. Every culture harbors subcultural segments within it. But distinct ethnic minority groups who politically and economically occupy marginal spaces in relation to dominant mainstreams in society make the job of outlining a cultural community a bit less daunting than it would otherwise be. Such groups find it necessary to flaunt the trappings of their difference as a key instrument in their struggle for survival. Their perception of living under siege culturally leads to their articulating on their own an identity-focused discourse that the scholar can then draw from in approximating the formulation of a definition. The cultural presence of Dominicans in the United States exhibits simultaneously the traits typical of immigrant, ethnic, and diasporic social formations. Its dual location in a space that is informed by *here-elsewhere* and *us-them* binary oppositions spawns a pervasive tension between the desire to belong in the United States and the yearning to preserve the most cherished of the old country's values and ways. Dominican American culture achieves its distinctness by differing from the cultural expressions associated with the homeland in the Dominican Republic, the forms and practices characteristic of the U.S. mainstream, and the distinguishing traits of the other U.S. ethnic minorities, including the other subsections of the Latino population, while inevitably incorporating and integrating borrowings from all of them.

People who trace their origin to the Dominican Republic have lived in the U.S. population prior to the proclamation of Dominican independence on February 27, 1844, by Juan Pablo Duarte, the ideological architect of the nation, who had studied English in New York.[1] Throughout the nineteenth century, as a result of U.S. involvement in Dominican affairs from as early as the administration of James K. Polk, who took office in March 1845, contact between people from the small Caribbean nation and their powerful neighbor to the north remained constant. After the Civil War, U.S. interest in the Dominican land evolved into a fervent desire to annex the country to the territory of the Union. President Ulysses S. Grant embraced this cause with passion, although the fierce opposition he encountered among influential U.S. legislators and popular nationalist leaders in the Dominican Republic thwarted the plan. Even so, the United States eventually dominated the Dominican economy, controlled fiscal life in the country by means of a protectorate from 1905 to 1940, ruled the nation directly through a military government from 1916 to 1924, disarmed the civilian population, and instilled in Dominicans a predilection for American consumer goods, pastimes, and popular culture.

As a result, the United States also became a natural destination for Dominican migrants, a process that initially involved statesmen, political exiles, entrepreneurs, and intellectuals, on the whole, people with sufficient means to finance their easy transposition to more auspicious surroundings. Among these were the children of poet laureate Salome Ureña and Francisco Henriquez y Carvajal, namely Pedro, Max, and Camila, an intellectual family whose lives Dominican American author Julia Alvarez has captured in her novel *In the Name of Salome*. Most notable among the entrepreneurs was Francis Rebajes, who achieved a degree of distinction unmatched by any other Dominican businessperson until the outstanding success of fashion designer Oscar de la Renta, who would become a household name in the United States toward the end of the twentieth century. Rebajes arrived in New York City's Harlem in 1923, took menial jobs of all sorts, roamed the streets with a gang of penniless intellectuals, and eventually discovered his talent for using the hammer and anvil to make beautiful and marketable tin, copper, and metal images of various kinds and ultimately attracted a large clientele. After opening his first store at 184 West Fourth Street in Greenwich Village in 1934 and single-handedly "centering the craft industry along Fourth Street" by the 1940s, his company opened outlets all over the country. He sold his factory operation and original designs and moved to Spain in 1958.[2]

Among the individuals who came from the Dominican Republic to make their mark on American society before the 1960s, two stand out for their remarkable careers. Maria Montez, known affectionately as the Queen of Technicolor in the heyday of her Hollywood stardom during the 1940s, became a preeminent entertainment personality. Her native city of Barahona, where the airport carries her name, remembers her with utmost pride. Having played major or leading roles in such Hollywood hits as *Arabian Nights* (1942), *Cobra Woman* (1943), *Bowery to Broadway* (1944), *Gypsy Wildcat* (1944), *Tangier* (1944), *Sudan* (1945), *The Exile* (1947), and *Pirates of Monterey* (1947), Montez remains, more than five decades after her death, "the object of an extensive fan cult thirsting for nostalgia and high camp."[3] Another Dominican who achieved celebrity status in the United States, distinguishing himself as an adventurer and playboy, was Porfirio

Rubirosa. This modern-day Dominican Casanova numbered among his successive and famous wives the likes of Doris Duke, from the family of tobacco magnates and philanthropists after whom Duke University in Durham, North Carolina, is named; the show business celebrity Eva Gabor; and the wealthy heiress Barbara Hutton, the granddaughter of Frank W. Woolworth, founder of the famous merchandise store chain. Rubirosa had his life of luxury subsidized by his former father-in-law Rafael Trujillo, who ruled the Dominican Republic as a personal hacienda.

To the aforementioned personalities one should add a vast array of political dissidents and other expatriates who came to the United States during the thirty-year-long rule of the ruthless dictator Rafael Leonidas Trujillo from 1930 to 1961, as well as an equally substantial number of agents of the regime who served the Dominican dictator by promoting his interests in American society. Among the former, the most politically committed organized rallies that repudiated the dictatorship, and they joined the New York chapter of the Dominican Revolutionary Party, which would become a major political institution in their homeland after the fall of Trujillo. Most renowned among the latter was Ambassador Minerva Bernardino, who, after the end of the dictatorship, ironically went on to receive periodic honors for humanitarian service and women's-rights advocacy. Less well-known than she, her brother Felix W. Bernardino, a sanguinary henchman of the tyrant, ran a reign of terror against the anti-Trujillo émigré opposition during his years in New York as Consul General of the Dominican Republic.

The foregoing background no doubt forms part of the overall narrative of the U.S. Dominican experience, but research has yet to establish in precisely what ways this early history enters the cultural memory of the community, because it has evolved in connection with the large immigrant settlements that emerged in the 1960s. One can find a clear link in the voluntary associations, a prominent feature of U.S. Dominican neighborhoods that has received scholarly attention from as early as the mid-1980s.[4] The available data suggest that several of the social clubs and community organizations that gained visibility in Dominican neighborhoods as soon as the group became numerically significant from the 1970s onward actually had their start in associations whose original purpose was to promote or repudiate the Trujillo regime.[5] As time passed, those associations lost touch with their ideological beginnings and became "expressive," "affective," or even "instrumental" venues serving diverse needs for community members.

Turning to the field of literature, the late-nineteenth and early-twentieth-century chapter of U.S. Dominican writing has been explored by scholars.[6] Two of the most salient figures among writers active in 2004, who have contributed decisively to the present visibility and vitality of U.S. Dominican literary expression, belong to families that settled in this country prior to the 1960s. The award-winning poet Rhina Espaillat, whose parents brought her to New York City from La Vega, Dominican Republic, in 1939, at age seven, comes first to mind. Espaillat's commitment to creating forums for the sharing of poetry through various workshops she organizes extends to her working closely with young

Dominican poets who write primarily in Spanish. Similarly, her verse frequently draws from her own immigrant background, even though she neither grew up nor ever lived in a Dominican ethnic enclave. Although she earned her spot in the literary community in isolation from any Dominican settlement, she has nonetheless joined the Tertulia Pedro Mir, a Dominican-led poetry reading series in Lawrence, Massachusetts. Her venturing into poetry precedes the boom of Latino writers that began in the 1980s, when it also became established practice to locate literary artists as voices of their respective ethnic constituencies.

At age sixteen, Espaillat became the youngest person ever to have been inducted as a member into the Poetry Society of America, beginning a string of honors that include the Gustav Davidson Memorial Award, the T. S. Eliot Poetry Prize, the Howard Nemerov Sonnet Award, the 2001 Richard Wilbur Award, and the 2003 Stanzas Prize, as well as her inclusion as one of the eighty writers nationwide invited by the First Lady and the Library of Congress to participate in the National Book Festival held in Washington, DC on October 4, 2003. Espaillat began publishing whole books only after she retired from her teaching job in New York City public schools, though by then she had built an impressive literary dossier with the inclusion of her work in various anthologies, numerous journals, and, occasionally, magazines. The reader will note that her poetry volumes—*Lapsing to Grace*, *Where Horizons Go*, *Rehearsing Absence*, *Mundo y palabra/The World & the Word*, *Rhina P. Espaillat's Greatest Hits*, and *The Shadow I Dress In*—invariably include at least one poem in Spanish. She has also produced an English rendition of *Trovas del mar* (Troves of the Sea), a bilingual volume of poems by the Lawrence-based Dominican poet Cesar Sanchez Beras. Though educated in the United States at a time when the group did not have a community to speak of, Espaillat is today a major contributor to the cultural production of Dominican Americans.

An equally expressive instance of the connection between the cultural experience of Dominicans in the United States "before the diaspora" and the expressive culture of the more recent emergence of the community is to be found in the writing career of Julia Alvarez, the offspring of a family of professionals and diplomats, who was born in New York City on March 27, 1950. The birth of this native New Yorker preceded, by over a decade, the great exodus from the Dominican Republic, a massive and unprecedented emigration beginning in the mid-1960s that would lead to the development of Dominican immigrant settlements in the United States. According to the 1990 U.S. census, 511,297 Dominicans were living permanently in the country, although the actual size of this population is considered to be appreciably larger since the official figures do not account for undocumented residents, whose number is estimated to be high. The number of Dominicans, who outnumbered all other immigrants in New York City and ranked sixth in the entire nation by the 1990s, continued to grow at a fast pace. After endeavoring to correct a problem in the official population census that had led to serious misreporting and, consequently, an undercount of nearly 200,000 people, a report released by the Lewis Mumford Center of State

University of New York at Albany, following the 2000 U.S. census, estimated the total number of Dominicans in the country at 1,121,257. Though over 65 percent of this group resides in the State of New York, and the greater bulk of them in New York City, the members of the community have found their way into every state of the Union. The most numerous non–New York contingents reside in New Jersey, Florida, Massachusetts, Rhode Island, Connecticut, California, Maryland, Texas, and Pennsylvania.

By 1950, when Alvarez was born, only a fraction of today's large U.S. Dominican population was around. Nor does the socioeconomic profile of the community today match the profile of those Dominicans who lived in the United States more than five decades ago. Generally light-skinned and boasting a higher education, they had in common a favorable socioeconomic status even if they occupied opposite ends of the political divide spawned by the dictatorship. Their class positions often fit the description one gets of Alvarez's extended family in such autobiographical essays as "An American Childhood in the Dominican Republic" and "My English," which capture key stages of the writer's early education when she, having been brought to live in her parents' homeland, attended the Carol Morgan School, where American diplomats sent their children. Significantly, though her family's manner of incorporation into U.S. society did not follow the path of most of the more recent generations of immigrants, whose class extraction placed them in a position of social disadvantage from the moment of arrival, her family memories have largely dominated the narrative of the Dominican experience in the United States. Suffice it to mention that when WNET-TV, the prestigious PBS station in New York City, featured the screening of the documentary *The Dominican-American Spirit* in August 1999, in the midst of a membership drive, the station sought to lure new members by offering enticing incentives that included a must-read book about Dominican Americans, *How the Garcia Girls Lost Their Accents*, Alvarez's best-selling 1991 novel. A prolific and talented writer, Alvarez has mined Dominican history, the memory of her family's adjustment to life in the United States, and the old country's folklore in book after book.

Following *Garcia Girls*, Alvarez published *In the Time of the Butterflies*, a moving evocation of the lives of the Mirabal sisters, three women assassinated by the Trujillo dictatorship, *¡Yo!*, a clever return to the Garcia girls' story in which the other characters offer their perspectives on Yolanda, the narrator of the earlier novel, and *In the Name of Salome*, which explores the lives of the Henriquez Ureña family, focusing on parallels between poet laureate Ureña's civic involvement in nineteenth-century Santo Domingo and her daughter Camila's psychologically transformative years in early twentieth-century Poughkeepsie, New York. In her poetry—*Homecoming* and *The Other Side/El Otro Lado*—Alvarez delves into the tensions emanating from her dual Dominican and American cultural background, while her children's books celebrate Dominican history, legend, and the cultural contrast of life in Vermont versus life in the Cibao region of the Dominican Republic: *The Secret Footprints, How Tia Lola Came to Visit/Stay, Before*

We Were Free, and *A Cafecito Story*. Given the literary prominence that Alvarez has accrued, she, more than any other Dominican voice, enjoys the power to give currency to a particular version of the group's collective immigrant experience and to disseminate images that readers will construe as representative of the community's culture.

To some degree, the short fiction of Junot Diaz, the author of the highly acclaimed collection *Drown*; the novels *Geographies of Home* by Loida Maritza Perez; *Soledad* by Angie Cruz; and *Song of the Water Saints* by Nelly Rosario offer competing images of the immigrant experience of Dominicans in the United States. Produced by writers who share the unfavorable class position characteristic of the Dominican immigrant settlements that resulted from the great exodus, these texts tackle the trauma of uprooting as it affects the less empowered, who must contend with the material limitations that their marginal location places on them. The characters who populate these stories face obstacles that emanate from their ending up trapped in settings where they cannot take for granted basic amenities such as quality schools, clean neighborhoods, language-rich environments, adequate health services, amicable support networks, and downright physical safety. Their awareness of having been racialized, their social impediments, and their cultural otherness with respect to a distant and indifferent mainstream are thrust on them by the ordinary drama of their struggle for material and spiritual survival. The concerns that fuel the works of these authors seem to continue in the texts of emerging Dominican American writers who have not yet published their first books. Among these, Annecy Baez, Marielys Divanne-Pichardo, Cleyvis Natera, and Leo Suarez made their literary and social sensibilities known when they joined their better-known colleagues in a reading series held in the spring of 2004 at the Brooklyn Public Library, sponsored by the library's Willendorff Division. Key among their common features is the memory of the Dominican past as a source of strength, even while they indict the less democratic and ecumenical characteristics of the ancestral culture. It is often by reconnecting with Dominican history that their characters enhance their ability to cope with the ethnic, racial, and cultural antipathies they face in the United States.

The writers who have risen to visibility with books issued by mainstream American publishers, with the exception of Diaz, are all women, so the literary construction of Dominican cultural identity that has gained currency thus far draws largely from the location, the perspective, the sensibility, and the experience of women. Their books, thus, evoke traumas associated with the unequal position of women in society, such as the consequences of out-of-wedlock pregnancy, the lurking menace of rape, the suffocating force of social norms bent on limiting women's sovereignty over their own bodies, and the resilience of phallocratic regimes both in the Dominican Republic and in the United States. The gender-inflected quality of Dominican American literature is auspicious, particularly in light of the charge of machismo often imputed to Dominican society, where economic structures, the Catholic Church, and other institutions still cling fiercely to patriarchal norms. Perhaps the fact that women have historically outnumbered men in the successive armies of emigrants from the homeland has thrust women into a socioeconomic reality that makes their leadership inescapable. On the whole, the numerical superiority of women has probably brought to the fore the harshness of gender inequity and the need to forge models of relationships based on partnership rather than domination.

One could argue, then, that U.S. Dominican culture exhibits considerably fewer misogynistic traits than its counterpart in the ancestral homeland. Witness the sympathetic, complex, and psychologically well-developed female characters in the fiction of Diaz, the one male Dominican American writer who has achieved fame. Something similar can be said about Alan Cambeira, the author of the novel *Azucar!: The Story of Sugar*, an evocation of the dehumanized existence of sugarcane workers of both sexes on Esperanza Dulce plantation, a setting that only thinly disguises the inhospitable arena of the notorious Dominican bateyes, (shantytown camps where Haitian sugarcane cutters live) where Haitian migrant and native-born laborers languish in dreadful working and living conditions. With his attention turned almost exclusively to the Dominican Republic and other Caribbean territories, Cambeira locates himself differently than the other Dominican American writers, as his work does not narrate his community's immigrant experience. A native of the city of Samana, he migrated with his family first to Barbados and later to Pennsylvania, where he completed his education, through graduate school. The author of an overview of his country's history and culture, *Quisqueya LaBella: The Dominican Republic in Historical and Cultural Perspective*, he has written widely on social issues in the Dominican Republic. One could conjecture that the author's humble origins and his own self-awareness as an African-descended Dominican motivate his attraction to the horrors of exploited and devalued workers. In that respect—in his choice of subject matter and cultural identification that inclines toward his own working-class perspective—Cambeira coincides with the other writers spawned by the great exodus.

We owe to Josefina Baez, a New York–based performance artist, arguably the most engaging statement on the complexity of Dominican cultural identity. Her collection of poems and performance texts, *Dominicanish*, launches an exploration of Dominicanness that discards nothing, no matter how seemingly alien, from the contours of the group's identity. The logic seems to be that any empirical reality that touches Dominicans must necessarily form part of the arsenal of ingredients that goes into the definition. Thus, experiences she collected during travels in Andhra Pradesh, a region in southeastern India, combine smoothly with the urban immigrant education she receives in her daily contact with such inexorable classrooms as the subway system in New York City. The main character in *Dominicanish* came to the Big Apple as a child, and she owes her knowledge of English more to the classics of jazz that she listened to assiduously than to the questionable efficiency of the public schools she attended. A native of La Romana, Baez; like Cambeira, is ancestrally connected to the bateye experience, and her work reflects a complex sensibility that combines world knowledge with working-class rootedness, a sort of proletarian cosmopolitanism.

As the foregoing discussion illustrates, class position, the chronology of the settlement that one belongs to, and a gender-inflected subject position all necessarily come to the fore in a discussion of the Dominican community's culture. Also connected with the foregoing, one's language use, choice of artistic form, religious practices, involvement with popular culture, racial self-identification, attitude toward the native land, view of sexuality, and sympathy for a heterogeneous model of community identity will inevitably emerge in any sustained reflection on the group's culture. Originally, Dominican settlers traveled to the United States in the company of their household gods and familiar forms of worship. Given their cultural ties through birth or ancestral origins to the island of Santo Domingo, a land conquered and colonized under the banner of Catholic Spain, Dominicans are mostly Catholic, though they simultaneously display African-descended forms of worship. Many Dominican homes in New York, for instance, make provisions for small shrines that pay homage to Catholic saints, especially the Virgin of Altagracia, the patron saint of the Dominican people. However, the accoutrements that normally decorate the small altars (flowers, lighted candles, food, water, rum, and other earthly goods) often recall the trappings of Santeria and other African-descended Caribbean religions, stressing the fundamentally syncretic nature of Dominican religious life.

This configuration of their expression of spirituality accords with the group's socioeconomic profile, which can be summarized through the specific example of those living in New York. The distinguishing socioeconomic characteristics of the Dominican community in New York City indicate that, as of the year 2000, nearly two-thirds of its members were foreign born, close to one-third lived at or below the poverty level, over 10 percent of persons 16 years of age or older were unemployed, 51 percent of persons 25 years of age or older had less than a high school education, and only 9 percent possessed college degrees. The per capita income of Dominican households, the mean age of whose members was 29.2 years of age in 1999, was lower than that of other Hispanics.[7] The occupational distribution for members of the Dominican labor force 16 years of age or older broke down as follows: 30.2 percent operators, fabricators, and laborers; 27.8 percent service workers; 25.7 percent technical, sales, and administrative support; 11.6 percent managerial and professional; and 4.7 percent precision production, craft, and repair.

To a large extent, the texture of the group's daily life, its distinguishing characteristics, its sounds, its smells, its rhythm, in short, the sum of sensory elements that many would deem integral to the community's culture as manifested in predominantly Dominican neighborhoods, correspond fittingly to the preceding economic profile. Dominican-based ethnic enclaves such as one finds in Manhattan's Washington Heights visibly display the community's tropical colors, with numerous bodegas, supermarkets, beauty salons, travel agencies, and restaurants, contributing to what could be regarded as a Dominicanization of the physical surroundings. Observers of the community typically highlight the energy and vitality of the group, especially as the number of neighborhood business establishments has tended to grow apace with the continuous arrival of Dominican residents in formerly depressed areas. However, socioeconomic portraits of the community indicate that Dominican New Yorkers, as a group, are lagging behind blacks and other Hispanics economically. Among the reasons explaining their economic retardation, Dominicans have low levels of English-language proficiency, and they often lack the specialized skills that the job market increasingly requires as the economy of urban centers nationwide has become dependent on service. Exacerbating their precarious economic condition, Dominicans often retain economic commitments to relatives back in the native land (Hernandez 2002).[8]

The linguist Almeida Jacqueline Toribio has usefully explored the extent to which the Dominican community's ethnoracial and cultural identity may be "mediated or ascribed via linguistic attributes."[9] Second-generation U.S. Dominicans apparently assert their loyalty to their heritage by pledging "allegiance" to their "vernacular," even while they evince considerable erosion of "their parents' language practices" as well as "racial attitudes." Naturally, since the collective identity of any given group defies monolithic description, the data also show youths of the same generation strategically deploying a Dominican-inflected Spanish in order to avoid being taken for African Americans. By the same token, light-skinned Dominicans who find it feasible to assimilate into mainstream society may embrace an ethos that resembles an outlook attributable to the conservative segment of the European-descended majority, in that they adopt an ideology that stresses the power of the individual over the influence of social forces. A New York–based middle-class male interviewed by Toribio in New York described the United States as a place "where you can set your goals and accomplish whatever you want," and he decried the tendency of African Americans to remember unpleasant experiences of the slavery period. He felt that the readiness of African Americans to pull out "the race card," which he finds Dominicans and other Latinos aping, stifles their ability to get ahead.[10] Another observer of the community from the perspective of language and identity, drawing on interviews conducted in Providence, Rhode Island, has noted that, through their "on-going contact with African Americans," second-generation individuals transcend the "essentialized ethnic/racial stereotypes of their parents," while exclusion and discrimination by mainstream society may lead them to see themselves in contradistinction to white Americans even as they maintain an ethnolinguistic understanding of their identity that fosters a sense of their difference from black Americans.[11]

Just as language use, linked as it is to issues of ethnic and racial identification, functions as a marker of cultural identity among Dominican Americans, so does their attitude toward their ancestral homeland. Second-generation individuals, the majority of whom reside in an ethnic enclave of their own, remain attached to their native cuisine even as they inevitably develop a taste for "American" food, which for many often becomes synonymous with products from the large fast-food chains. They may call attention to their ethnic difference by waving the flag of the Dominican Republic in parades and at other festivities or public events that feature major Dominican stars, such as baseball games involving the likes of Chicago's Sammy Sosa, Boston's Pedro Martinez, or New York's Alex Rodriguez. The display of Dominican flags on the occasion of the Rolando Paulino All-Stars' participation in the Little League World Series in August 2001 triggered remonstrances among some non-Latino fans who failed to see the success of the Bronx team as a real New York triumph on the grounds that "the kids are Dominican."[12] Second-generation individuals generally consume merengue and *bachata* among their favorite rhythms, reproducing their parents' musical taste while they enjoy the sound of hip-hop and the other popular music forms that the U.S. entertainment industry offers to audiences of every new generation. The dancer Vergi Rodriguez, whose professional credits include work with pop stars such as Whitney Houston, Jennifer Lopez, and Prince, got her first break when Dominican merengue/hip-hop group Sandy & Papo MC commissioned her to choreograph its entire 1995 tour. A graduate of New York High School for the Performing Arts, Rodriguez, a New York native whose flourishing career caused her to relocate to Los Angeles, relishes her growing up in New York City "around different sounds like hip-hop and pop," and she stresses the syncretism of her experience: "And coming from a Dominican background, merengue is very apparent in our culture. It's just a little bit of everything, growing up urban, with a little bit of Latin influence."[13] Their aesthetic education, then, matches the socialization available to every American of comparable class status.

Second-generation individuals who often call themselves just Dominican may not know much of their parents' native land, and when travel becomes a possibility, many think of the Dominican Republic as their first option. Given the relatively young age of their settlement in the United States, rarely will members of the Dominican community lack close kinship ties to people back "home," and quite often the grandparents that young Dominican Americans can look to for affection or permissiveness live across the ocean in an urban Dominican city or rural town. That scenario, probably more typical of families located at the lower ends of the class scale and further complicated at times by the considerable volume of intermarriage with spouses of other ethnicities, makes for a constant balancing of life in the United States and life in the Dominican Republic as a binational space wherein to construct their cultural identity. The interplay of here and elsewhere, then, enters as an inescapable element of Dominican American culture insofar as individuals from that group do not typically regard their loyalty to the United States as requiring a de-linking from their parents' homeland.

Indeed, one might think here of Navy Petty Officer Ruben Rodriguez, one of the 225 victims of American Airlines flight 587, which crashed in Queens, New York, as it took off from JFK Airport on November 12, 2001, bound for Santo Domingo. A veteran of the U.S. military mission in Kosovo who had served for seven months on the USS *Enterprise*, Rodriguez had just returned to New York from participating in the U.S. attack on Afganistan when, before taking on his next military assignment, he decided, as a respite, to go to the ancestral homeland to reconnect with the extended family. This sad example illustrates the condition that has given some scholars cause to think of Dominicans in the United States as a transnational community.[14] But the example also shows a young man deeply grounded in the United States as the country of his citizenship and civic duty, his strong affective ties to the "old country" notwithstanding.

Whether or not Dominican Americans can be regarded as a transnational community, scholars have done little to show to what extent their transnationality differs from that of any other U.S. ethnic minority that owes its development to migratory flows in the aviation era. But, a feature that demands equal attention is the interlaced coexistence of U.S.-born and immigrant individuals in shaping the cultural image of the overall group. A telling detail in this respect is the foreign birth of the Dominican American writers already mentioned, with the exception of Alvarez and Cruz. The same frequency of foreign birth applies to the members of the community who have attained legislative positions, such as New York State assemblyman Adriano Espaillat, New York City Council members Miguel Martinez and Diana Reyna, Montgomery County (Maryland) Council member Thomas Perez, Providence (Rhode Island) Municipal Council member Miguel Luna, and Rhode Island state senator Juan Pichardo, to name only a few of those Dominicans who held public office at the end of 2003.

A notable feature of the political leadership of U.S. Dominicans is their need to remain attentive to the sensibilities of a dual political constituency, one made up of people with their hearts set on the affairs of one of the major parties back in the Dominican Republic, the other made up of people who recognize the American arena as the appropriate place for their political involvement and commitment. As the migratory flow of Dominicans from their homeland to the United States has remained unabated, one cannot escape the scenario in which second- and even third-generation members of the group, who may have little Spanish language proficiency, find themselves sharing room in the cultural arena with individuals who got off the boat or airplane merely ten or even five years ago and have not yet mastered the English language. Yet both partake in the construction of the cultural visage that the community presents to the rest of American society. In the realm of visual arts, for instance, nearly all painters and sculptors who have achieved a measure of visibility belong to a middle-class wave of migrants who left the Dominican Republic beginning in the 1980s.

Two timely documents from Dominican-serving institutions—the 2002 calendar of the Washington, DC–based Dominican American National Roundtable, which used the works of twelve Dominican artists to illustrate its pages, and the catalogue of Crossroads/Encrucijada, an exhibition of "contemporary Dominican American art" held at the City College of New York in mid-March 2004 under the sponsorship of the CUNY Dominican Studies Institute—give a succinct idea of the provenance of the cadre of artists who have gained ascendancy in the community (www.danr.org; www.ccny.cuny.edu/dsi). The list of artists drawn from the aforementioned documents consists of Jose Arache, Hochi Asiatico, Delsa Camacho, Niccolo Cataldi, Luis Cepeda, Jose Guillermo Diaz, Felix Diclo, Scherezade Garcia, Reynaldo Garcia Pantaleon, Francisco Hernandez, Carmen Herrera, Luis Leonor, Luanda Lozano, Dario Oleada, Charo Oquet, Doris Rodriguez, Julia Santos Solomom, and Miguel Tio. Based mainly in New York, Florida, and Rhode Island, these artists, a good many of whom are alumni of the Altos de Chavon School of Design in the Dominican Republic and New York City's Parsons School of Design, came to the United States to pursue their artistic dream. Unlike the majority of individuals who have filled the ranks of the great exodus, they are not typical migrants who left their homeland in order to secure their material survival, but rather individual talents thirsting for a suitable ambience wherein their art could flourish and reach large audiences. This seems to be the predicament of those who pursue a professional interest in the artistic forms associated with "high culture." Witness the case of ballerina Michele Jimenez, a principal dancer of the Washington Ballet who starred at the Kennedy Center's Eisenhower Theater from October 31 to November 4, 2001, in the company's new production of *Carmen*, which artistic director Septime Webre had choreographed especially for her. Discovered in 1997 by Lorraine Spiegler, a teacher who had journeyed to Santo Domingo in search of new talent for the Washington School of Ballet, Jimenez at 17 had already outgrown the opportunities that her school—the Ballet Clasico Nacional de Santo Domingo—could afford her. So, when Spiegler offered her the opportunity to travel to Washington to audition, Jimenez had a clear choice before her: "I really wanted to leave, because I wanted more. And it was getting a little . . . restricting."[15]

Given the mixed profile of the U.S. Dominican population, a characteristic feature of the cultural identity of the group is to be found precisely in the continuous negotiation of traditions, practices, and beliefs inherited from the ancestral homeland and the transformative thoughts, values, and ways emanating from the experience of living as an ethnic minority in the United States. Dominican Americans emerge as a differentiated cultural group, then, in the historical context of the ethnic self-assertion and the affirmation of cultural alterity that minorities in the United States display, the vigorous legacy of the civil rights movement having rendered that self-recognition tantamount to a struggle for full citizenship. Concomitantly, the group's distinct features are similarly shaped by the Dominican Republic's conventional manner of understanding cultural identity and national belonging, which minimizes the significance of internal differences and posits adherence to an official formulation of the contours of Dominicanness as the basis of one's social identity. The creative tension produced by the confrontation of the legacies inherited from the ancestral homeland and the sensibilities forged in the United States largely accounts for the texture of Dominican American culture. The group at times embraces a worldview that breaks with ideologies and ways of thinking owed to the old country and yet at times distances itself from experiences collected within the framework of American society.

Scholars often note that U.S. Dominicans find it hard to accept the prevailing racial code that in this country seems to reduce social identity to a choice between the binary opposition of white or black. They often prefer to adhere to the less rigid code of their ancestral homeland that allows for distinct identity spaces between the extremes of black and white. But they at the same time recognize the need to distance themselves from the Negrophobia and the anti-Haitianism that has conventionally characterized the discourse on nationality and culture in the Dominican Republic. A look at the record of patrons using the research resources of the CUNY Dominican Studies Institute at the City College of New York from 1994 through 2004 reveals that Dominican students care more about the study of the African heritage in Dominican society than about any other subject of scholarly investigation in the human sciences. Similarly, a commemoration of the 155th anniversary of Dominican independence from Haitian rule, held on February 27, 1999, at the Centro Cultural Orlando Martinez in northern Manhattan, sought the cosponsorship of Haitian community and cultural organizations in New York. The program featured a presentation of *gaga*, a musical and spiritual performance born of the experience of Haitian migrant sugarcane workers in Dominican plantations, and concluded with a reading of the poetry of Jacques Viau Renaud, a Haitian-born poet who grew up in the Dominican Republic, where he died fighting for social justice in the revolution of 1965.

Perhaps ultimately the culture of Dominican Americans differs from that of the ancestral homeland as well as the cultures of African Americans and of the other subsections of the Latino population in its continuous wrestling with own internal diversity. The appreciation of the African heritage without skewing the vitality of the Iberian background in the formation of the ancestral culture, the desire to preserve Spanish while refraining from the temptation to privilege that language as a requirement for entering the identity space of the community, and the incorporation of democratic values written into the American creed of equality all emerge as pertinent ingredients in the arsenal of ideas that go into a formulation of the collective identity of the group. The Dominican American propensity to embrace diversity is perhaps best illustrated in the symposium "Up from the Margins: Diversity as Challenge to the Democratic Nation," a multidisciplinary, international undertaking held in New York and Santo Domingo over two consecutive weeks in the latter half of June 2001. Spearheaded by the CUNY Dominican Studies Institute with the support of the Rockefeller Foundation, the symposium brought together Dominican and non-Dominican voices from Santo Domingo, Madrid, San Juan, and various U.S. cities to interrogate the principle of homogeneity that informs official and nationalist discourses on Dominicanness. Over sixty scholars, artists, community advocates, and cultural activists spoke, either at the City College campus in one week or at Hotel Santo Domingo the following week, about the urgent need to recognize ethnic, sexual, social, ideological, and other forms of diversity as a fundamental value for any nation that wishes to call itself democratic today. Collectively, they defended the contention that distinct communities or constituencies have a right to preserve or even assert their difference without having to sacrifice their claim to national belonging and full citizenship.

The papers presented included coverage of Dominicans of Chinese, Haitian, Arab, Anglophone West Indian, and African descent, as well as reports on the Dominican experience of diasporic settlements in Holland, Spain, Puerto Rico, and the United States. The multiple faiths and forms of worship that make up the religious life of Dominicans despite the homogenizing claim that construes the group as fundamentally Catholic, the patriarchal assumptions and misogynistic values that gain the support of the religious and political leadership in Dominican society, the sentiments associated with homophobia and compulsive heterosexuality that inform conventional views of national belonging, and the class biases that seem to exclude the lower strata of the population from renditions of the national community in public discourse came to the fore in an unprecedented conversation about the complex, diverse, multilayered, and heterogeneous constitution of the Dominican people, whether in the ancestral homeland or in the diaspora. Divorced from homogenizing ideas of culture or national belonging, the imagination that conceived the symposium with the purpose of fostering a capacious conceptualization of the visage of the community is arguably a direct product of the living and the learning that U.S. Dominicans have done in their continuous effort to find and assert their place among the multiple, ethnically differentiated segments that make up the American population.

NOTES

1. Rosa Duarte, *Apuntes de Rosa Duarte: Archivo y versos de Juan Pablo Duarte*, 2nd ed., ed. Emilio Rodriguez Demorizi, Carlos Larrazabal Blanco, and Vetilio Alfau Duran (Santo Domingo: Secretaria de Educacion Bellas Artes y Cultos, 1994), 40.

2. Wallace B. Alig, "Man With A Hammer," *Americas* 5, no. 5 (May 1953): 6–8, 43–45; Toni Greenbaum, *Messengers of Modernism: American Studio Jewelry, 1940–1960* (New York: Flammarion, 1996), 70–72.

3. Nicolas Kanellos, Hispanic Almanac (Detroit: Invisible Ink, 1994), 552.

4. Eugenia Georges, *Ethnic Associations and the Integration of New Immigrants: Dominicans in New York City*, Occasional Paper no.41 (New York: Research Program in Inter-American Affairs, 1984); Saskia Sassen-Koob, "Formal and Informal Associations: Dominicans and Colombians in New York," *Caribbean Life in New York City: Sociocultural Dimensions*, ed. Constance R. Sutton and Elsa M. Chaney, 278–296 (New York: Center for Migration Studies, 1987).

5. Silvio Torres-Saillant and Ramona Hernández, *The Dominican Americans* (Westport, CT: Greenwood Press, 1998), 80.

6. See Silvio Torres-Saillant, "Before the Diaspora: Early Dominican Literature in the United States," in *Recovering the U.S. Hispanic Literary Heritage*, ed. María Herrera-Sobek and Virginia Sánchez-Korrol (Houston: Arte Público Press, 2000), 3: 250–267; Silvio Torres-Saillant, "La literatura dominicana en los Estados Unidos y la periferia del margen," *Punto y Coma* 3, no. 1–2 (1991): 139–149 (also published in *Brujula/Compass*

11 [1991]: 16–17); and Daisy Cocco de Filippis and Franklin Gutierrez, eds., *Literatura dominicana en los Estados Unidos: Presencia temprana* (Santo Domingo: Buho, 2001).

7. Marilyn Ramírez, "Selected Socioeconomic Information about Dominicans in the United States," CUNY Dominican Studies Research Briefs (New York, September 2002).

8. See Ramona Hernández, *The Mobility of Labor under Advance Capitalism: Dominican Migration to the United States* (New York: Columbia University Press, 2002).

9. Almeida Jacqueline Toribio, "The Social Significance of Language Loyalty among Black and White Dominicans in New York," *Bilingual Review* (forthcoming).

10. Ibid.

11. Benjamin Bailey, "Dominican-American Ethnic/Racial Identities and United States Social Categories," *International Migration Review* 35 (2001): 703–704.

12. Edward Wong, "Multicultural Bronx Stars Strike Nationalist Chord," *New York Times*, August 23, 2001.

13. Melanie Feliciano, "Dominican Dancer Vergi Choreographer to the Stars," *LatinoLink*, March 16, 2000, www.latinolink.com/musicentertainment/theatreance/0316vrgi.php3.

14. Jorge Duany, *Quisqueya on the Hudson: The Transnational Identity of Dominicans in Washington Heights*, Dominican Research Monographs (New York: CUNY Dominican Studies Institute, 1993); Luis E. Guarnizo, "The Emergence of a Transnational Social Formation and the Mirage of Return Migration among Dominican Transmigrants." *Identities* 4, no. 2 (1997): 281–322; Luis E. Guarnizo "*Los Dominicanyorks*: The Making of a Binational Society," *Annals of the American Academy of Political and Social Sciences* 533 (1994): 70–86; Levitt, Peggy, *The Transnational Villagers* (Berkeley: Univ. of California Press, 2001).

15. Sarah Kaufman, "An Island Treasure: In the Caribbean, Michele Jimenez Became A Dancer. Here, She's Become A Star," *Washington Post*, October 28, 2001, sec. G.

BIBLIOGRAPHICAL ESSAY

Although the scholarly literature on Dominican Americans is still relatively sparse, that scarcity is offset to a significant degree by the amount of autobiographical and semi-autobiographical works written by individuals who are actually living the Domincan-American experience. The best starting point is Sarah Aponte, *Dominican Migration to the United States, 1970–1999: An Annotated Bibliography* (New York: The City Univ. of New York Dominican Studies Institute, 1999), the first of a projected series of Dominican Research Monographs to be published by the Institute. Also extremely useful, if the reader understands Spanish, is Daisy Cocco de Filipis and Franklin Gutierrez, eds., *Literatura Dominicana en los Estados Unidos* (Santa Domingo: Buho, 2001), and Silvio Torres-Saillant, "La Literatura Dominicana en los Estados Unidos y la Periferia del Margen, *Punto y Coma*, 3 (1991):139–141. Torres-Saillant has also published "Before the Diaspora: Early Dominican Literature in the United States" in Volume 3 of *Recovering the United States Hispanic Literary Heritage* (Houston: Arte Publica Press, 2002), 250–267, edited by Maria Herrera-Sobek and Virginia Sanchez-Karrol.

The most comprehensive overview of the Dominican-American experience is Silvio Torres-Saillant and Ramona Hernandez, *The Dominican Americans* (Westport, CT: Greenwood Press, 1998). Also highly informative is Marilyn Ramirez, "Selected Socioeconomic Information About Dominicans in the United States" (New York: City Univ. of New York Dominicans Studies Research Briefs, 2002). Ramona Hernandez supplies an integrative context for understanding the Dominican diaspora in *The Mobility of Labor under Advanced Capitalism: Dominican Migration to the United States* (New York: Columbia Univ. Press, 2001). Given the poverty of most Dominican immigrants, it is important to understand their interactions with the American system of social services, a need that is at least partially filled by two articles written by Ana Paulino: "Dominican Immigrant Elders: Social Service Needs, Utilization Patterns and Challenges," *Journal of Gerontological Social Work*, 30 (1998): 61–74, and "Dominicans in the United States: Implications for Practice and Policies in the Human Services," *Journal of Multicultural Social Work*, 3 (1994): 53–65.

Like all recent immigrants, Dominican Americans are undergoing a complex process of adaptation to mainstream society and culture. Eugenia Georges, *Ethnic Associations and the Integration of New Immigrants: Dominicans in New York City*, Occasional Paper No. 41 (New York: Research Program in Inter-American Affairs, 1984), looks at how the group's network of fraternal and benevolent societies has facilitated the process for many Dominicans. Saskia Sassen-Koob, "Formal and Informal Associations: Dominicans and Colombians in New York," *Caribbean Life in New York City: Societal Dimensions* (New York: Center for Migration Studies, 1987), 278–296, edited by Constance R. Sutton and Elsa M. Chaney examines the operation of these organizations in a comparative framework. Two important studies deal with the critical issues of formal education and language retention: Dulce Maria Gray, *High Literacy and Ethnic Identity: Dominican American Schooling in Transition* (Lanham, MD: Rowman & Littlefield, 2002), and Almeda Jacqueline Toribio, "The Social Significance of Language Loyalty Among Black and White Dominicans in New York," *Bilingual Review* (forthcoming). The manner in which American educational institutions relate to Dominican Americans is the subject of Ramona Hernandez and Silvio Torres-Saillant, "Editor's Preface: Dominican Quiddities in the U.S. Academy," *Punto 7 Review: A Journal of Marginal Discourse*, 3 (1996): 1–10.

The give-and-take of the adaptation process has clearly had a profound impact on identity formation in the Dominican-American community. Benjamin Bailey, "Dominican-American Ethnic/Racial Identities and U.S. Social Categories," *International Migration Review*, 35 (2001): 677–708), examines how the multiracial nature of Dominican identity makes it difficult to fit them into the social categories constructed by mainstream American institutions. Focusing specifically on the challenges faced by Dominicans and other Latinos in American higher education is Dulcie M. Cruz, "Struggling with Labels that Mark my Ethnic Identity," *The Leaning Ivory Tower: Latino Professors in American Universities* (New York: State Univ. of New York Press, 1995), 91–100. Much of the discussion concerning Dominican-American identity stresses the transnational or binational nature of that identity. One of the best treatments of the transnational nature of Dominican-American identity is Jorge Duany, *Quisqueya on the Hudson: The Transnational Identity of Dominicans in Washington Heights* (New York: City Univ. of New York Dominican Studies Institute, 1994). Equally enlightening is Luis E. Guarnizo, "The Emergence of a Transnational Social Formation and the Mirage of Return Migration among Dominican Transmigrants," *Identities*, 4 (1997): 281–322, and "*Los Dominicanyorks*: The Making of a Binational Society," *Annals of the American Academy of Political and Social Sciences*, 533 (1994): 70–86. Also very informative is Peggy Levitt, *The Transnational Villagers* (Berkeley: Univ. of California Press, 2001).

Several other scholars have dealt with the issue of Dominican-American identity by trying to reduce it to the level of individual migrants. Two studies that focus on the career of Francis Rebajes, the artist in metals who enjoyed great celebrity from the 1930s through the 1960s, are: Wallace B. Alig, "Man With A Hammer," *Americas*, 5 (1953): 6–8, 43–45, and Toni Greenbaum, *Messengers of Modernism: American Studio Jewelry, 1940–1960* (New York: Flammarion, 1996). Concentrating on Juan Pablo Duarte, the ideological architect of the Dominican nation is Rosa Duarte, in *Apuntes de Rosa Duarte: Archivo y Versos de Juan Pablo Duarte* (Santo Domingo: Secretaria de Educacion Bellas Artes y Cultos, 1994), edited by Emilio Rodriguez Demorizi, Carlos Larrazabal Blanco, and Vetilio Alfau Duran. Melanie Feliciano profiles the career of another successful Dominican American in "Dominican Dancer Vergi: Choreographer to the Stars," *Latino Link*, 16 March 2000), *www.latinolink.com/music entertainment/theatreance/0316vrgi. php3*, while Sarah Kaufman, "An Island Treasure: In the Caribbean, Michele Becomes a Dancer, Here She Becomes a Star," *Washington Post*, 28 October 2001, examines the rise of another celebrated Dominican American. Examining the reaction of non-Latinos to the participation of the Rolando Paulino All-Star baseball team in the 2001 Little League World Series is Edward Wang, "Multicultural Bronx Stars Strike a Nationalist Chord," *New York Times*, 23 October 2001.

Even though the scholarly work on Dominican Americans is growing, the leading source of information is still the novels and semi-autobiographical books written largely by women. Perhaps the most prolific and famous of these is Julia Alvarez, an American-born Dominican who is best known for her novel, *How the Garcia Girls Lost Their Accent* (Chapel Hill, NC: Algonquin Books, 1991), and her moving evocation of the three Mirabel sisters, who were murdered by the Trujillo regime, *In the Time of Butterflies* (Chapel Hill, NC: Algonquin Books, 1994). She has also written *Yo!* (Chapel Hill, NC: Algonquin Books, 1997), which elaborates on the adventures of the Garcia girls, and *In the Name of Salome* (Chapel Hill, NC: Algonquin Books, 2001), which explores the lives of the Henriquez Urena family during the late nineteenth and early twentieth centuries. She has also written several other books intended primarily for children: *The Secret of Footprints* (New York: Random House, 2000), *How Tia Lola Came to Visit/Stay* (New York: Knopf, 2002), *Before We Were Free* (New York: Knopf, 2002), and *A Cafecito Story* (White River Junction, VT: Chelsea Green Publishing Co., 1987). Her works of poetry include, *Homecoming* (New York: Plume, 1984) and *The Other Side/El Otro Lado* (New York: Dutton, 1995).

Almost as prolific in her own genre is poet Rhina Espaillat. Included in her works are: *Lapsing to Grace* (New York: Bennett and Kitchel, 1992), *Where Horizons Go* (Kirksville, MO: New Odyssey Press, 1998), *Shadows of the Sea* (Santo Domingo: Editora Buho, 2000), *Rehearsing Absence* (Evansville, IN: Univ. of Evansville Press, 2001), *The World and the Word* (Evansville, IN: Univ. of Evansville Press, 2001), and *The Shadow I Dress In* (Cincinnati: David Roberts Books, 2003). Also worth consulting are: Angie Cruz, *Soledad* (New York: Simon and Schuster, 2001), Junat Diaz, *Drown* (New York: Riverside Books, 1996), Loida Maritza Perez, *Geographies of Home* (New York: Viking Press, 1999), and Nelly Rosario, *Song of the Water Saints* (New York: Pantheon Books, 2002). Among male writers, the one whose work presents the most insights into life in the Dominican Republic is Alan Cambeira, *Azucar: The Story of Sugar* (New York: Belcam, 2001), and *Quisqueya La Bella: The Dominican Republic in Historical and Cultural Perspective* (Armonk, New York: M.E. Sharpe, 1997).

FILIPINO AMERICANS

Augusto Espiritu

THE SLEEPING GIANT

Over a hundred years ago, the legend of Bernardo Carpio animated the Filipinos who rose up against Spanish colonialism and ended its 300-year rule of the Philippines. The legend said there was a giant folk hero named Bernardo Carpio, who had been imprisoned in the caves of a mountain in Luzon. One day, he would break loose and emerge from the mountain and free his people, especially in driving out the Spaniards from the country.[1]

Today, there are close to 2 million Filipino Americans in the fifty states, and they are like the sleeping giant, Bernardo Carpio. According to the 2000 census, they are the second largest group among Asian Americans (1.9 million out of 12.5 million), second only to the Chinese.[2] One-fourth of the working population over sixteen years of age is made up of U.S. born Filipinos. Meanwhile, three-quarters of the working population is foreign-born, testifying to the continuing surge in immigration.[3] Unlike many recent migrants, Filipino Americans face few language barriers because of an almost universal knowledge of English.[4]

Meanwhile, they are economically and culturally well positioned to make further inroads into American life. A good proportion of Filipino Americans belong to the professional middle class. They are doctors, nurses, engineers, accountants, lawyers, and teachers. A sizeable number are computer-assembly workers, cannery workers, farm laborers, home caregivers, government employees, and hotel and restaurant workers. Women also slightly outnumbered men in the population, providing the basis for family formation and population growth.[5] Filipino Americans are inveterate organizers, forming several hundred associations that reach out to the population's diverse interests.[6] They are devoted members of the

Catholic and Protestant churches, but they also belong to the Philippine-origin churches, Iglesia ni Kristo and Aglipayan (or Philippine Independent) Church. Some are Muslims, Buddhists, and animists.[7] There are outstanding Filipino American local and state political leaders and heads of national organizations. And not a few are making a direct impact in the entertainment industry.[8]

These positive qualities would suggest community cohesion, but Filipino Americans, like most other ethnic or immigrant groups, face divisions of class, generation, migration, and politics as well as institutional weaknesses that threaten to undermine their cultural identity, racial solidarity, economic development, and political power. The concerns of Filipino airport screeners fired from their jobs, assemblers in the Silicon Valley working under difficult conditions, or home caregivers working long hours and under abysmal conditions hardly touch the lives of the Filipino American middle class, many of whom live in the suburban sprawl of America's largest cities and commute to the urban areas for work.[9] There, they remain unaware of or indifferent to the problems faced by immigrant or inner-city youth—high dropout rates, gang violence, drug addiction, and unemployment.[10] Meanwhile, suburban youth grow up with little awareness of their cultural heritage and speak little of their parents' native languages, especially Tagalog, Visayan, and Ilocano. They either rebel against their parents, whose principal concerns of survival, material wealth, and conspicuous consumption they fail to grasp or, ironically, they become consumed by the very same materialism that preoccupied their parents and led to serious rifts within their families.[11] In school, Filipino immigrant youth are likely to encounter the nativism of American-born Filipinos, who label their immigrant counterparts as F.O.B.s or "fobs" ("fresh off the boat").[12] Or, vice versa, they may have to endure the sense of superiority of immigrant Filipinos who regard their American-born counterparts as linguistically and culturally "ignorant."[13] Politically, Filipinos are divided by personal and regional politics as well as by the legacies of homeland political conflicts, such as the Marcos dictatorship. While many vote, there are still large numbers who remain unregistered, despite high rates of naturalization. There are a small but growing number of undocumented workers, mostly professionals who find various ways to adjust their immigration status, whose basic needs are hardly attended to, except by enterprising immigration lawyers.[14]

Compounding these problems are institutional weaknesses, particularly in the realms of economics, education, and culture, that hamper the growth of an infrastructure for dealing with these social divisions. While there are signs of small-business activity in suburban areas with high Filipino concentrations, the financial base of the community remains relatively weak. Small-business participation remains low, while failure or bankruptcy rates are high. There are painfully few Filipinos who are entrepreneurs.[15] In the realm of education, Filipino Americans remain severely underrepresented in higher education, especially as professors and administrators.[16] And, finally, within cultural institutions, particularly in museums, theaters, libraries, language schools, and so forth, that provide the basis for cultural cohesiveness, there are few Filipinos.[17] All three

weaknesses are interrelated. The absence of Filipino Americans in academia denies businesses the information, insights, and contacts they need from established
business schools, academic programs, and university think tanks. Small-business
failure diminishes the capital that can be invested in educational scholarships,
foundations, or even the construction of centers of value to the Filipino American community. And the paucity of cultural institutions contributes to the lack
of ideological, cultural, and political cohesion of the community, the ignorance
about Filipino American small business that does exist, and the narrowing of cultural horizons among youth.

Altogether, these factors contribute to the chronic invisibility of Filipino Americans in the mainstream of American life.[18] They remain strangers from American life, despite their large-numbers and the fact that Filipinos have been present
on American soil in significant numbers for over one hundred years. Filipino
Americans face the reality of their existence in the United States being unacknowledged or only partially acknowledged, which lends a liminal, alienated
quality to their life in America. That they seem to be assimilating into American
life, at least if one looks at language, is as much a symptom of a larger problem
as it is a seeming indicator of success. It could be a symptom, as sociologist Antonio J. A. Pido has argued, of self-hatred among some Filipino Americans.[19] To
say that the history of Filipino presence in the United States provides the answers
to these problems would be to grant the study of history an explanatory power it
has never had. One can say, however, that both the present conditions of possibility and the limitations faced by Filipino Americans have come about through
a complex evolution that a historical analysis could help to illuminate.

THE "REMONTADO" TRADITION

What today might be regarded as Filipino American history began with the
U.S.–Philippine War, which officially lasted from 1899 to 1903. This single event
laid the basis for the colonial relationship between the two countries and the series of large migrations from the Philippines to the United States throughout the
twentieth century.[20] However, Filipinos sporadically and in small numbers began
arriving in what is now the United States of America from the sixteenth century
to the late nineteenth century, before the Philippines' official incorporation as
American territory. This constitutes a kind of prehistory of Filipino Americans,
one that might be signified by the image of the *remontado*. This is a Spanish
word that referred to the lowland Philippine natives who, in order to escape the
exactions of tribute, forced labor, and conscription, fled to the jungles and the
mountains of the country. There are stories, as in the Maroon ex-slave communities of the Caribbean, of people establishing communities there and continuing to resist the Spanish.[21] The rebel from the island of Bohol, Francisco
Dagohoy, fended off Spanish encroachments into a remontado mountain stronghold for over eighty-five years! While not remontados in the technical sense, the
Igorots, the mountain peoples of Northern Luzon, put up equally stiff resistance

against the Spaniards, utilizing their ability to escape into the forested mountains.[22]

The basis for early Filipino travels to the New World was thus an attempt to escape the exactions of Spanish colonialism and restore some sense of wholeness to a disrupted community life. The galleon trade from Manila to Acapulco was made possible by the creativity of native artists and craftsmen in building ships, the escapees' seafaring skills and labor reserves for manning the ships. The galleon trade emerged in the seventeenth century and would continue until 1813.[23] Some Filipino Americans have claimed that there were native Filipinos in the New World as early as the sixteenth century. Today, for instance, there is a rock in Monterey, California, commemorating the first Filipinos who landed in America during the 1560s, among shipwrecked Spanish soldiers who described them as "Luzon indios," the word *indio* being used to describe the non-Spanish and non-Chinese Malay majority of the Philippine colony.[24]

Perhaps the most interesting, if not controversial, account of Filipinos' prehistory in the Americas is the story of the Manilamen who found their way into Louisiana's bayous and formed coastal communities. How long they have been there and the precise routes they took to get to Louisiana are a matter of dispute. It seems that they were stowaways from the galleons who had first landed in Acapulco. For some reason, they kept on fleeing northward. Historian Marina Espina's account has them moving from Veracruz on the Atlantic Coast until they reached Louisiana, far enough from the Spanish authorities.[25] Espina thinks they arrived there in 1763, although she provides no documentary proof for this dating.[26] In the 1880s, Lafcadio Hearn, the translator and author of Japanese tales, who was visiting the bayous, described a community of "Manilamen" who lived by fishing, drying shrimps, and trading with their multicultural neighbors. Espina sees this community continuing through the twentieth century as a result of intermarriage, the establishment of voluntary associations, fraternities, sodalities that preserved group coherence, and even participation in the Philippine independence movement of the 1920s and 1930s. The group survives today, Espina contends, with mixed-race children going on to the tenth generation.[27]

European Americans, on the other hand, began sailing to the Philippines in the late eighteenth century in the clipper ships that sought out the China trade.[28] The impetus for American trade in the late nineteenth century, however, was abaca, the plant fiber that became known, after processing, as Manila hemp, which was used as cordage for ships and for other industrial purposes.[29] One of the earliest scholars to visit the Philippines was the notorious Dean Worcester, a zoologist who traveled throughout the islands for four years prior to the outbreak of the Spanish-American War. Worcester became Washington's expert on the Philippines during the American invasion, despite his lack of knowledge of the people, and apparently made great profits in gold mining as a colonial administrator.[30] There seems no evidence, however, that Philippine natives, unlike the Chinese, Japanese, and Indians (from British India) ever visited New England or the northeastern United States.

FILIPINO AMERICANS: FORTY YEARS OF HOLLYWOOD?

There is a popular saying that Filipinos spent "[t]hree centuries in a Catholic convent and 50 years in Hollywood."[31] The convent metaphor refers to Spanish colonialism and its hothouse of Catholic conversion and indoctrination. Hollywood stands for the United States and in particular the colonization of the Philippines. There is a great deal of truth to this in the sense that American commodities flooded Philippine markets, outcompeting and destabilizing homegrown industries and creating new consumer desires. American mass culture and popular cultural forms—from ragtime to jazz to bebop, from newspaper culture to radio to television, and from gaslights to automobiles—invaded Philippine shores. Filipinos came under the influence of Americanization rapidly and extensively. Public education and English's de facto status as *the* language of economy, fashion, and modernity facilitated the influx of commodities, and conversely, commodification lent glamour and allure to the study of English and American society. American advertising, as much as America's sentimental imperialism, inflated demand and raised expectations of a utopian land of opportunity among Filipinos.[32] In truth, the "50 years in Hollywood" can only refer to a tremendous propaganda victory for America's colonial mission insofar as it roused the desires of Filipinos and others around the world for America's products as well as for its ideological exports, captured in words and phrases such as "free trade," "democracy," and "civilization." Filipino political leaders were soon advocating for American statehood and American citizenship under the tutelage of its white fathers.[33]

A closer look at America's colonial project and the experience of Filipino migrants to the United States provides a reality check to this filmic, innocuous image of an empire. It is not for rhetorical reasons alone that comparisons have been made between the U.S.–Philippine War and the Vietnam War, and the anti-imperialist movement at the turn of the century with the antiwar movement of the 1960s and 1970s.[34] America's turn-of-the-century excursion into Spain's colonies and its subsequent suppression of an independent nationalist movement in the Philippines was a brilliant, efficient, and overwhelmingly brutal military campaign. Perhaps several hundred thousand Filipinos died as a result of war and the dire conditions created by war, including America's concentration-camp policy, the killing of livestock and other food sources, and disease conditions. American soldiers employed torture, including the infamous "water cure," and conducted the war in a racist manner. In retaliation for the infamous massacre of fifty-four American soldiers at Balangiga, Samar General Otis Smith initiated a "reign of terror" on the island, his explicit orders being, "Kill and burn, kill and burn, the more you kill and the more you burn the more you please me." He ordered his men to convert one of the largest Philippine islands into "a howling wilderness."[35]

At the same time, the stick could not have worked without the carrot. While American soldiers were shooting down an entire community of Muslim men, women, and children in Jolo, American civil administrators were guaranteeing that the elite, landholding class would remain in power.[36] In various stages, they set up local, regional, and national representative institutions in the guise of "Filipinization," while at the same time maintaining their supremacy through political patronage that subverted supposedly democratic institutions.[37] Filipinos, so long denied universal education and economic opportunities under Spanish colonial rule, flocked to the promise of American benevolence, to the American colonial public school system, and to its new seat of higher learning, the public, Protestant-dominated, University of the Philippines in Manila.[38] America constructed a dependent colony, a cash-crop economy habituated to tariff-free entry into American markets and tariff-free American imports. Perhaps most importantly, America shaped the patterns of labor migration to the United States, setting a pattern of seeking escape, exile, and advancement in the colonial motherland—instead of solving the problems at home—that Filipino migrant streams would continue throughout the rest of the century.[39]

The streams of Filipino migration to the United States have always been diverse. Representatives of the two social classes arrived at practically the same time. As a result of the Pensionado Act, the first colonial government–sponsored students arrived in the United States in 1904. They were expected to return to the Philippines at the completion of their studies.[40] The program began at first as a system of undergraduate studies, but after the founding of the University of the Philippines in 1908, it focused on the pursuit of advanced graduate studies. It continued with diminishing numbers until 1941, dispersing Filipino students throughout the United States, but especially in selected, geographically distorted key universities such as the University of Washington, the University of Illinois, and Columbia University. Indeed, a Columbian Association and a Philippine Illini club were both founded in the Philippines to accommodate returning *pensionados*.[41] Perhaps the most famous of the pensionados was Jorge Bocobo, who was among the first batch of pensionados. He arrived in the United States just in time for the St. Louis World's Fair of 1904, which featured the infamous Philippine Pavilion, with its human exhibitions of Igorots and other ethnolinguistic groups that, ironically, included the Christianized Visayans and Tagalogs. All were regarded as tribes in a narrative of civilization that culminated with the coming of the Americans to the Philippines. The exhibit, however, created an uproar among Bocobo's fellow Philippine nationalists at home.[42] After serving as a guide at the fair, Bocobo went on to study at the University of Indiana, completing his bachelor's degree, and attending law school there. Thereafter, he returned to the Philippines to resume his professional and political career, eventually becoming president of the University of the Philippines and a cabinet minister in the Philippine Commonwealth.[43] Bocobo's story is paradigmatic of the earliest pensionados and their essential roles in the making of a modern, English-speaking, professionally trained Philippine elite and middle class. Other famous pensionados included jurist Jose Abad Santos, diplomat Carlos P. Romulo, and author Bienvenido Santos.[44]

Significantly, few women came through this program. Indeed, few Filipino women journeyed to the United States during the 1920s and 1930s, and many of those who did were joining their husbands from whom they had long been separated, or for other personal reasons.[45] Sociologist Ronald Takaki has argued that the number of Filipino women was determined by their fixed destinations, either Hawaii or the mainland, by Filipino culture's Catholic restrictions on women's ability to travel, and by the large proportion of bachelors (over three-quarters) among the migrants.[46] To this, one might add another important cause for women's absence in the pensionado cohort: Philippine patriarchy, which circumscribed Filipinas' educational, economic, and political participation. Despite the increasing knowledge of the women's suffrage movement in America, the rise of a Philippine women's suffrage movement, and advertisements showing the increasing sexual independence of women, women's principal roles as married homemakers and reproducers of children remained strong and unchanged. This exerted tremendous social pressure on Filipino women to resort to part-time work and to give up their professional work, even after a substantial investment in education, in order to marry, raise children, or take care of their aging parents. Long periods of time away from home risked the disruption of these bonds, something difficult for most women to accept in such a male-dominated society.[47]

There were many other Filipino colonial subjects who came to the United States to study or to fulfill individual ambitions but who were never sponsored by the insular government. Many were self-supporting students who eventually became involved in labor activities. Some, as historian Barbara Posadas has shown, played an important part in the Chicago-based union the Brotherhood of Sleeping Car Porters, joining the largely African American organization established by A. Philip Randolph.[48] Meanwhile, the so-called school-boys, a term ascribed to those who lived and worked for an American family, included Philip Vera Cruz, future vice president of the United Farm Workers Union, who for a time attended Gonzaga University in Washington while doing domestic chores for a white couple.[49] Would-be writers such as Carlos Bulosan and Jose Garcia Villa supported themselves in similar ways. In becoming a writer, Bulosan never had formal education in the United States but learned to write from self-study and exposure to the progressive intellectual community. Villa, on the other hand, received his degree from the University of New Mexico and for a time studied in the masters program in English at Columbia, until he quit to pursue his career as poet par excellence.[50]

Meanwhile, in 1905, the first Filipino laborers started arriving in Hawaii Territory after years of unsuccessful recruitment efforts by the Hawaiian Sugar Planters Association (HSPA), particularly in the Ilokos region in Northern Luzon, which was noted for its pioneering and industrious laborers who cleared the forests and built the economies of the Central Luzon area.[51] Ilocanos and others were at first reluctant to leave their homelands, despite the devastation upon human life and agriculture caused by the U.S.–Philippine War and the scarce natural resources of the Ilokos region, whose principal crop was tobacco. However, the unscrupulous recruitment campaign of the HSPA in the Philippines stimulated the desire for migration to other American territory.[52] A large and steady stream of Filipino laborers arrived in Hawaii from the 1910s to the 1940s. With the declining prices of sugar, the demands of commercial agriculture in California and the West Coast, and the restriction on Mexican labor, Filipino laborers in Hawaii started migrating to the continent in the 1920s, and over time formed the backbone of the service industry (as bellhops, domestic workers, chauffeurs, and restaurant workers) in urban areas while becoming one of the mainstays of agricultural labor in the rural areas.[53] Filipinos were particularly concentrated in lettuce, asparagus, and grapes as so-called stoop labor, a stereotype ascribed to them from having worked in a stooped-over position in Hawaii's plantations. Unlike their relatively isolated existence there, Filipino mainland laborers migrated all over the western United States, following the seasonal planting and harvesting of crops. Hence, they became exposed to the human and social landscapes of the West.[54]

Immigration restriction movements, however, which had led to the exclusion of southern and eastern European migrants in 1924, the founding of the Border Patrol against Mexican migrants, and to anti-Oriental laws against the Chinese and the Japanese, found a new enemy in the Filipinos, especially during the Great Depression.[55] Similar nativist arguments used in these campaigns reemerged in the Filipino exclusion movement. White workers, labor leaders, and others regarded Filipinos as a social problem that threatened to take away the jobs of Americans or lowered wages by their status as cheap labor. Moreover, they felt sexually threatened by these Westernized, English-speaking Filipino men who saw themselves as the equal of white men and consorted with white women in "dime a dance" taxi dance halls and in public.[56] There was strong anti-Filipino sentiment from established unions like the American Federation of Labor, which disparaged "ethnic labor," while simultaneously frowning on attempts by Filipinos to form their own unions.[57] They called for the exclusion of Filipinos from American soil. However, since Filipinos were "nationals," inhabitants of a nation under the American flag, such an immigration restriction could not be effected in a direct manner. Labor's solution was to call for Philippine independence, which would change the citizenship status of Filipinos to Philippine citizens and subsequently make them aliens excludable under the law.[58] American labor was joined by agricultural interests threatened by the competition of duty-free products such as sugar, then the Philippines' chief export. Both labor and agricultural interests clamored for Philippine independence, not on the basis of an altruistic desire to see the Philippines as free, but on the basis of these nativist notions.[59]

Ironically enough, the mean-spirited campaign for Filipino exclusion dovetailed with the Philippine independence movement's goal of obtaining a timetable for the end to American colonialism. While in the beginning there were strong Filipino anti-imperialist sentiments, with supporters in the United States, more malleable elite Filipino nationalists like Manuel Quezon and Sergio Osmeña rose to power and called for a parliamentary struggle in the American Congress to convince Americans to grant the Filipinos self-government and independence. Hence, the Philippine colonial government, beginning in 1919 and ending in 1934, sent regular "independence missions" to the United States. While Quezon and the rest of the elites vacillated on independence behind the scenes, the threat of popular conspiracies, revolts, and mass discontent in the Philippines in support of independence kept them on their toes.[60] Moreover, the humiliating experience of anti-Filipino violence on the West Coast, in Exeter and Watsonville, California, in 1929 and 1930, led to nationalist sentiments in the Philippines for separation from the United States, economic protectionism, and Philippine independence.[61] In 1934, the exclusionists and the proindependence advocates alike reached their goal of Philippine independence with the passage of the Tydings-McDuffie Act, which set a timetable of ten years for Philippine independence, set an immigration quota of fifty a year, and modified the status of Filipino nationals to excludable aliens.[62] Virtual exclusion, however, was not enough for the restrictionists. In 1935, while the United States was overseeing the establishment of the Philippine Commonwealth government under President Manuel Quezon, President Franklin Roosevelt issued the Repatriation Act. A disguised deportation law, the act provided Filipinos free passage back to the Philippines, although with the stipulation that they could never come back.[63] In the late 1930s, Filipinos were also excluded from obtaining relief during the Great Depression. Antimiscegenation laws in numerous states prevented them from marrying white and ethnic women and building families and communities, although a few still did manage to circumvent these laws, marry, have families, and raise a second generation of Filipino Americans.[64] The dire conditions faced by Filipinos in the United States who, like the Chinese and Japanese immigrants, could not become U.S. citizens, own land, vote or run for political office, or properly build families led to a citizenship campaign sponsored by Vito Marcantonio, the uncompromisingly radical Italian American congressman from New York who represented the interests of his largely immigrant and minority district. Racist sentiment was strong in Congress, however, and it was not until several years later that a citizenship bill would pass this body.[65]

Forced by circumstances to fend for themselves, Filipinos in the United States responded by organizing. In particular, three institutions became prominent in galvanizing Filipinos during this period: labor unions, fraternal associations, and ethnic churches. During the 1920s and 1930s, both in Hawaii and on the mainland, Filipinos conducted strike actions to protest their working conditions, raise their wages, and create the basis for greater political and economic power. The first strike actions occurred in Hawaii, and there were two notable strikes. The 1920 Filipino and Japanese strike was led in part by Pablo Manlapit, a dynamic unionist, lawyer, and founder of the Filipino Federation of Labor in 1911; this became known as *Vibora Luviminda* in the 1930s.[66] Most likely, Filipino migrant and labor leaders moving from Hawaii to the mainland brought their unionizing experiences to their countrymen in the West. There, Filipino lettuce workers founded the Filipino Labor Union in Salinas, engaged in strike actions in the Imperial Valley under unions influenced by the Communist Party, unionized the cannery workers in Washington and Alaska through the American Federation of Labor (AFL)-chartered Cannery Workers and Farm Laborers Union (CWFLU) and the prototype of the International Ladies Garment Workers Union (ILGWU), and brought themselves together under the Filipino Agricultural and Laborers Association in Stockton, the center of Filipino settlement at the time.[67] There were several fraternal associations, which brought their nationalist, Masonic, and religious traditions from the Philippines, including the Legionarios del Trabajo, with its union origins, the Caballeros de Dimas Alang, named after the pseudonym of national hero Jose Rizal, and the Filipino Federation of America.[68] The last of this group was truly a transnational phenomenon. It was headed by the enigmatic and charismatic folk Christian leader Hilario Moncado, who brought folk Christian elements into the fraternity. Moncado criss-crossed between Los Angeles and Hawaii and even challenged Manuel Quezon for the Philippine presidency in 1934–1935. He also later established "Moncadista" communities in the Philippine island of Mindanao.[69] Finally, churches such as the Filipino Christian Church (FCC), founded by the Protestant leader Silvestre Morales, arose in response to the exclusion of Filipinos from the Catholic Church, particularly in Los Angeles. The FCC provided meals, recreation, and moral instruction to Filipinos who were barred from governmental relief efforts and other religious institutions. Both fraternal organizations and churches preached an abstemious life to their Filipino members or congregations, enjoining them to leave the taxi dance halls, pool halls, gambling joints, and cockfighting arenas, as well as prostitution and alcohol, for a cleaner, moral life.[70]

Despite all of the efforts of Filipinos to better their lives and to expand their cultural and political inclusion into American life, it was not until America's defeat at Pearl Harbor and the surprise Japanese attacks on the Philippines and other Southeast Asian countries that the conditions of their lives in America would change. The heroic stand by Filipino and American soldiers at Bataan and Corregidor, fighting under Douglas MacArthur and the United States flag, won the admiration and respect of Americans. It directly translated into greater social and economic opportunities for Filipinos in the United States, even as the enemy status of Japan led to the violation of civil liberties and internment for Japanese Americans.[71] At first excluded from joining the military, Filipino Americans were allowed to form segregated units—the First and Second Infantry regiments—that played important roles in the American invasion of the Philippines and the attempt to retake the country from Japan. Filipino soldiers in the military were the first Filipino Americans to obtain U.S. citizenship. The opportunity for naturalization was extended to Filipinos in 1946, alongside of the Chinese and the Asian Indians.[72]

Even as Filipinos were clamoring to join the fight against the Japanese in Asia, the Philippine Commonwealth government was fleeing to the United States and setting up its headquarters in Washington, DC, and New York. The exiled government became the center of Filipino life, especially in the eastern United States. Important Anglophone fiction writers, playwrights, and poets such as Villa, Bulosan, Santos, Arturo Rotor, P. C. Morantte, and Severino Montano—who were among their country's prized intellectuals—joined or served their country by working in the Philippine headquarters.[73] Filipino intellectuals found numerous literary opportunities for addressing Americans who were concerned about the fate of their soldiers in the colony. Romulo and Santos racked up thousands of miles traveling through numerous cities in the United States, bringing home the message of the sacrifice of Filipinos in Bataan and the "special relations" between American colonial soldiers and the loyal colonized Filipinos. This was to be an important theme in the postwar and postindependence picture, one perhaps honored in the breach but just as enduring and powerful in its mythic quality.[74]

THE GREASED POLE

In many ways, the postwar situation of Filipinos and Filipino Americans might be seen as one of limited expansion and diversification. The gains Filipinos made during the war might be likened to the game of the greasy pole played by rural youngsters in the Philippines at fiestas, or feasts honoring patron saints. Two poles are greased and two contestants must climb them, and the first one who reaches the top wins. One can imagine the way these contestants slide down every time they appear to climb higher to the top. Citizenship was conferred upon Filipinos as were social and political benefits that other Americans enjoyed. Filipinos in the United States took advantage of the Naturalization Act, the War Brides Act, and the GI Bill to become U.S. citizens, to bring back Filipina brides and establish families, and to educate themselves, which also bettered their chances for obtaining higher-paying jobs than they had held previously.[75] These policies led to the growth of a second generation of Filipino Americans that made its presence felt in the social events and community organizations, as well as the recreational activities frequented by many Filipino bachelors. With the increasing breakdown of housing covenants and the beginning of challenges to discrimination and segregation, Filipino Americans were able to own property, settle in urban or suburban areas beyond ethnic enclaves, and send their children to better schools. Hence, in many ways, Filipino Americans were able to participate in the postwar developments—education, homeownership, domesticity, and material consumption—that Americans everywhere were enjoying.[76] In the Philippines, after the initial shocks occasioned by American neocolonialism and the pro-American policies of the first few administrations, Philippine leaders, especially under the Filipino-first policy of President Carlos P. Garcia, began to develop some domestic industrial capacity, international trade, and infrastructure that allowed the Philippines to be one of Asia's more successful stories. This was built, however, on an export-based strategy, which failed to address rural landlessness and the inequitable economic and political relations in the countryside, upon which the majority of the population still depended for its livelihood. While there were forces impelling Filipinos to leave the Philippines at this time, such as the threat of a domestic insurgency, greater immigration to the United States from the Philippines during this period was hampered by the new, postwar immigration quota of 100 established after the United States granted the Philippines its nominal independence. This was the lowest quota for any nation.[77]

These developments, moreover, need to be examined in the context of the challenges posed by the cold war. Take, for instance, the situation of Filipinos in the U.S. military. Filipinos in the Philippines entered the military in increasing numbers even after World War II. Thousands of young men signed up, especially for the U.S. Navy in Manila and Cavite. The military became their avenue for travel and advancement. During the postwar period, they migrated to the United States in increasing numbers and obtained American citizenship, and many of them sent for family members in the Philippines. This example of the continuation of neocolonialism is a story familiar to most people of color and the poor in the United States.[78] And just as familiar is the story of racism in the military. No matter how long they had been in the military, Filipinos serving with Uncle Sam were relegated to the lowest rungs of the institution, often as stewards and cooks, doing the most menial of occupations, without benefit of advancement. They were ubiquitous and distinguished themselves in their professions, even becoming favored chefs and domestic servants in the White House under various presidential administrations. Nonetheless, they suffered discrimination in the workplace from those who regarded Filipinos as fit only for such work.[79] Indeed, Filipino participation in the military occurred amid increasing strain between the United States and the Philippines over the frankly racist and unjustifiable shootings of Filipinos by American servicemen in or around the U.S. military bases in the Philippines and over the large prostitution industry that emerged for what was referred to as rest and recreation.[80] Filipino servicemen served their terms and reenlisted because of the far greater benefits they could obtain on American ships than living in the Philippines, but it was a long time before Filipinos could be seen in occupations in the military beyond the kitchen. Many of them settled and continue to settle in various military bases all over the United States and Puerto Rico, especially in San Diego, where Filipinos make up the largest group of all the Asian Americans.[81]

Similarly, Filipino Americans, especially among workers, encountered nativism, anti-Communism, and racism in their quest to reach the top, forces that often set them back, or at least seemed to make tenuous whatever social gains they made. There was of course the persistence of discrimination in employment and housing, which tended to circumscribe the opportunities opened up by more access to higher education.[82] There remained, as in Hawaii and the western United States, the continued dominance of large corporations such as the HSPA and California agribusiness, which created despotic conditions for workers, even as their profits soared. And when Filipino Americans issued challenges against the system, they came under the boot of the Bureau of Immigration or J. Edgar Hoover's FBI. In Seattle, for instance, Local 37 of the ILWU faced a life-and-death struggle with the government, as well as against its own members in challenging the domestic and international policies of the U.S. government. Members were interrogated, blacklisted, and even imprisoned for their political beliefs, and for their challenge for better working conditions and higher wages. Likewise, Filipino agricultural workers' fortunes fluctuated with the obstacles placed in the way of their unionization.[83]

Despite these obstacles, however, there were significant gains. Local 37 won a landmark U.S. Supreme Court case in *Mangaoang v. Boyd,* in which the Court ruled that ILWU leader, Ernesto Mangaoang, a militant union leader, could not be deported as an alien because he had arrived in the United States before 1934, when the Philippines was under the U.S. flag. This victory guaranteed Filipino unionists who had arrived in the United States during the same period freedom from deportation and was an important moral victory for the Seattle-based union movement.[84] Likewise, Filipino agricultural workers in California banded together to form the Agricultural Workers Organizing Committee (AWOC), which received organizing help from the AFL-CIO. AWOC waged an untiring war against the grape industry and in 1965 joined forces with the National Farm Workers Alliance of Cesar Chavez and Dolores Huerta to form the United Farm Workers Organizing Committee. Two prominent union activists emerged out of this merger—the fiery Larry Itliong and Philip Vera Cruz—both of whom would be elected vice presidents of the union.[85] Meanwhile, in Hawaii, Filipino American workers, along with other Asian workers, helped to solidify the position of the ILWU in the Democratic Party and to transform not only Hawaii's politics but also the conditions in the plantations for numerous old-time Filipino workers.[86]

Filipino professionals started coming in limited numbers to the United States during this period, but the quotas on Filipino immigration were far too few for them to be able to exert a significant influence in the community's transformation. Many veterans had also decided to return to the Philippines to help in the reconstruction of the country, while others decided to solve the problem of their identity by remaining in the United States for good.[87] At the same time, there were stronger pressures at various times for the Filipino middle class to leave the country, especially during the period of peasant unrest known as the Huk Rebellion, which threatened Manila itself. However, CIA intervention and the counterinsurgency strategies of President Magsaysay reestablished order and confidence in the economy, at the cost of alienating the large peasantry, and restored the predominance of the oligarchy.[88] It was not until 1965, with President Ferdinand Marcos's accession to power, that Filipinos would have an opportunity to leave the country in large numbers. It is indeed ironic that his reform administration and the large-scale emigration of Filipinos would go hand-in-hand, leading not only to a financial drain on the Philippine economy but also to the notorious brain drain.[89]

AMERICAN *BARANGAYS?*

It has been said that thousands of years ago the islands that became known as the Philippines were settled by various people who came on boats known as *balangay*. Each of these transported members of a family to settle in local, riverine communities that subsequently became known as *barangays*. The word has come down among Filipinos as a symbol of the local, a persistent reminder even in the midst of supralocal organizations such as cities, provinces, and even the nation of the persistence of familial ties and the local foundations of politics.[90] Similarly, in the United States, Filipino immigrants after 1965 came to settle throughout the United States and began to form visible but localized communities that joined with the old-timers of another generation. Much has been written about the Immigration Act of 1965, which made large-scale migration from the Philippines, Asia, Latin America, and the rest of the world possible, and about its roots in the civil rights movement. Indeed, the act repealed decades of discriminatory legislation against immigrants of color, vastly increased the numbers of those admitted to the country, and created a seven-category preference system that selected the *kinds* of immigrants who could enter the country.[91] The act has vastly transformed the Filipino American population and has likewise spearheaded the demographic and cultural shift in American society in the last thirty years. It finally made possible the balancing of gender in the population, professional employment, family formation, and community building in the mode of *barangays*, although there were alternative models of community building above or below this transplanted institution.[92]

The 1965 act led to the professionalization of the Filipino American community. Whereas before, the Filipino population had been made up of a large laboring population alongside a small, socially distant elite stemming from the diplomatic corps or the professional class, the post-1965 landscape brought thousands of professionals from the Philippines, especially doctors, nurses, dentists, accountants, engineers, medical support personnel, and skilled workers, who helped to enlarge the middle to upper-middle-class segments of the population.[93] Large numbers settled in Hawaii and the western United States. Just as important, Filipino professionals began settling in the Midwest, especially in Chicago and Wichita, as well as in the New York–New Jersey area. Filipino medical personnel became a visible presence in hospitals and clinics, alongside Koreans, Pakistanis, Indians, and professionals from the Middle East.[94] At the same time, many faced various obstacles. Professional boards—in accounting, optometry, dentristy, and medicine—enacted various restrictions that prevented the full participation of Filipinos. Hence, during the 1970s, Filipinos sued under the provisions of the Civil Rights Act of 1964 to eliminate testing requirements that discriminated against foreign-born and foreign-trained professionals.[95] Various workplace issues, involving race, accent, and language discrimination also affected Filipinos. Two nurses in a Detroit hospital, for instance, were wrongly charged with first-degree murder in the deaths of several patients. The Narciso-Perez case, named after the two nurses, became a cause célèbre in the Filipino American community, and the campaign led to their eventual exoneration.[96] In Hawaii, Manuel Fragante sued his employer, the City of Honolulu, for discrimination based on his accent. In Los Angeles, a determined nurse, Aida Dimaranan, took on a Pomona hospital for harassment on the basis of language and her right to speak Tagalog, where appropriate, in the workplace. Filipino nurses have more recently begun to band into unions to negotiate for better working conditions, particularly in private, Catholic hospitals, where they are often relegated to the graveyard shift.[97] But professionalization was not solely related to the influx of professionals but also to the increase in federal funding that accompanied the so-called War on Poverty, which created a need for social-service providers and change agents in the Filipino community. This has, nonetheless, led to conflicts with other established Asian American groups for leadership positions and the tapping of federal funds.[98]

The Immigration Act also resulted in the influx of larger numbers of women, which transformed the dynamics of the Filipino community. The lifting of immigration restrictions and the preference system that selected for professionals in which Filipino women were concentrated certainly contributed to this trend. The image of the community as old and male changed as if overnight to that of young and female.[99] Women increased not only in population but also in their labor-force participation and in their presence in leadership roles in various movements and institutions. Gone were the days when women could choose only between being to beauty contestants or secretaries. Women in political organizations led the way. Revolutionary groups such as the Union of Democratic Filipinos (KDP) had large numbers of women with vital and influential roles in leadership.[100] Women now could be found leading community-service organizations such as Filipino American Service Group, Incorporated (FASGI) and Search to Involve Pilipino Americans (SIPA) in Los Angeles, Filipino Youth Activities (FYA) in Seattle, and Filipinos for Affirmative Action (FAA) in San Francisco. Others have successfully run for office. Practically invisible as writers before 1965, women writers such as Linda Ty-Casper, Ninotchka Rosca, Jessica Hagedorn, and Cecilia Brainard emerged on the national and international arena, where once only male authors such as Carlos Bulosan, Stevan Javellana, and Jose Garcia Villa had been in the limelight. Businesswomen such as Loida Nicolas-Lewis of Beatrice Corporation, and designer Josie Natori are pioneers among Filipino American entrepreneurs.[101] At any rate, Filipino women entered the field and transformed the Filipino American community with their activity, intellectual and creative talents, and their leadership.

Immigration also led to the creation of islands or pockets of Filipino settlement in urban and suburban areas, although ones never large enough to constitute a stable ethnic enclave, unlike the Chinatowns, Little Tokyos, and Koreatowns that have become such a focus of media attention for everything from their burgeoning small businesses, ethnic cohesion, ethnic isolation, labor exploitation, and urban unrest. In Los Angeles, for instance, Filipino Americans have settled beyond the Temple Street area where the old-timers had been limited to suburban areas like West Covina, Cerritos, Carson, and Long Beach.[102] A similar situation has arisen in the San Francisco area, where the Filipino population has grown to large numbers and has blended in with longtime residents, in Daly City, Oakland, and San Jose, as well as Salinas and Stockton.[103] In many areas, Filipino Americans have established unofficial barangays, neighborhoods with their own Filipino stores, restaurants, supermarkets, dry-goods stores, service centers, and so forth. At times, these have led to efforts at concentration, such as the Filipino Town campaign in Los Angeles, which lasted over a decade and attempted to declare the Temple area an official ethnic enclave.[104]

The influx of the new, however, has not diminished the realities of urban and suburban life, or their unpredictability. Efforts at ethnic town formation paralleled various local initiatives on urban renewal, redevelopment, and gentrification. Business and political leaders' redevelopment of the International Hotel in San Francisco, the Kingdome in Seattle, and Honolulu's Chinatown, as well as projects in other cities, destroyed areas of Filipino settlement without replacing them with low-cost housing for the old-timers. The "dilution" of Filipino community strength in the redistricting of Los Angeles in 1986 adversely impacted attempts at creating a Filipino Town.[105] In the wake of these developments, younger and more politically savvy Filipino Americans have in more recent years begun to assert their interests. The Temple Street area of Los Angeles was declared Historic Filipino Town, a brand new Filipino Community Center (Filcom) has been built in Waipahu, Hawaii, and a coalition of Filipino nonprofits are involved in the SoMa, or South of Market, development in San Francisco. Meanwhile, Filipino small businesses in suburban areas seem to show a resilience that goes against the business failures of past years.[106] These are welcome developments in a Filipino American community that, despite high rates of professional immigration, continues to suffer from various social problems, including economic inequality, underemployment, and discrimination in education and the workplace based on accents or expectations of proper "American" behavior. One random study by the Federal Center for Disease Control in San Diego found that Filipino female students had the highest rates of attempted suicide.[107]

The realities of American urban life thus provided compelling reasons for Filipino Americans to enter into the fray of political organizing, although ironically, it took an international campaign to involve Filipino American participation in these struggles. President Ferdinand Marcos's declaration of martial law in the Philippines affected Filipino Americans in a profound way. The lives and the security of immigrants' families remaining in the Philippines were threatened by martial law, as were Filipino Americans in the United States, because the Philippine state extended its control of local communities through its own intelligence services and active consulates that spied upon, cajoled, and intimidated them.[108] At the same time, the Vietnam War and the antiwar movement's high profile led Filipino American youth to see Marcos's martial law as their own Vietnam, their own anti-imperialist struggle, and a defining moment in their own assertion of identity as Filipino Americans.[109] The anti-Marcos movement in America was thus born, bringing together longtime community-empowerment activists, political exiles and political leaders from the Philippines, and anti-imperialist supporters from the American left into organizations such as the National Coalition for the Restoration of Civil Liberties in the Philippines (NCRCLP) and parallel, ideologically different, formations such as the Movement for a Free Philippines, the KDP, and the Friends of the Filipino People.[110] The fourteen-year struggle against Marcos polarized the community between pro- and anti-Marcos forces, and not until the assassination of Marcos's political rival Benigno Aquino in 1983 and Marcos's eventual overthrow in 1986 in the People Power uprising did this issue cease to be among the predominant concerns of the Filipino American community. The end of the campaign was bittersweet. Numerous political exiles returned to the Philippines, leaving a vacuum in Filipino American organizing. At the same time, Filipino Americans lost a vital focal point when the struggle against the dictatorship ended, and the community needed new goals and new models of organizing a community that had to take a hard look at the issues it faced in America and simultaneously deal with a transnational community that was freed from the obstacles of martial law and traveling across the Pacific in both directions.

THE CLOAK OF INVISIBILITY

Among the reputed powers conferred by amulets, known as *anting-anting* in Philippine cultures, is the power of invisibility. Invisibility allows one to move in and out of the enemy's strongholds without being detected and even to be in several places simultaneously. Hence, it makes one invulnerable and gives one a sense of power and strength.[111] Invisibility, in a sense, is the amulet of Filipino Americans. Despite being a large minority, they have escaped in part the racial and class opprobrium and violence that has been directed at other, more visible minorities such as Koreans, Vietnamese, Haitians, and Arab Americans. Filipino Americans have yet to regard this as a source of power, instead seeing their invisibility as a sign of weakness rather than strength, with few exceptions.[112] Without much fanfare, Filipino Americans have increasingly begun to join the mainstream of American politics and culture. Benjamin Cayetano of Hawaii became the first Filipino American to become governor of the state and, indeed, the first Filipino American to govern any state of the Union. Honolulu's city council has three members, including the most recent, Donovan de la Cruz, who are of Filipino descent.[113] Former anti-Marcos activist women and men have assumed important leadership positions—Melinda Paras as executive director of the National Gay and Lesbian Task Force, Catherine Tactaquin as director of the National Network for Immigrant and Refugee Rights, Luisa Blue as national director of the Asian Pacific American Labor Alliance, Enrique de la Cruz as director of the Asian American Studies program at California State University, Northridge, and Rodel Rodis as Community College Board Member of San Francisco, and many others. There are many Filipino Americans who have been elected to various positions in local, city, and state offices. Filipino Americans have played an active role in restoring veterans' benefits for Filipinos in the Philippines who fought under the United States flag during World War II and in combating anti-Asian violence, including taking action after the death of Joseph Ileto, a Filipino postal worker murdered by a white supremacist. Through an emerging organization, the Filipino Civil Rights Advocates (FilCRA), Filipino Americans are gaining a presence in the civil rights arena.[114] They have also challenged the internal hierarchies of Asian American coalitions and the problematic representations of Filipinos in Asian American texts.[115]

At the same time, new avenues for transnational communication and exchange have been opened up by the democratization of Philippine politics after Marcos and the dismantling of the U.S. military bases Subic Bay and Clark, which led to their economic reconversion.[116] Filipino Americans, for instance, returned in 1998 to campaign for Philippine presidential candidates. There are exchange and study-abroad programs that have opened up between American and Philippine universities.[117] More Filipino Americans are traveling, studying, and even making careers in the Philippines than ever before. Likewise, more Filipinos have continued to visit or to stay in the United States. For some, the Philippines and the United States have become virtual poles for a regular trans-Pacific commute. Even in this arrangement, political activity continues in transnational coalitions to liquidate the Philippine debt, to represent the interests of Filipino women and children, to educate Filipino Americans about conditions in the Philippines, and to combat the impact of national-security measures on Filipino airport screeners in Oakland and struggles for autonomy in Muslim Mindanao. This activity is occurring even as Filipino Americans and Filipino immigrants have been taken as prisoners of war or died in the U.S. war against Iraq and have posthumously been granted American citizenship.[118]

There comes a time when the cloak must come off, when one must cease being an invisible observer and become an active participant that both sees and is seen, that takes responsibility but also can be held accountable, especially if the community is to grow in strength and to exercise a progressive influence in American civic culture. This is a moment of insecurity for many Filipino Americans, as they reach a critical mass in the population and look at their relative powerlessness in American society. The groundwork has been laid by a history of protest and creative adaptation to the challenges they have faced in this country and in the Philippines. It is essential that Filipino Americans see their contemporary challenges in light of the steps that their forebears took over the last century or more, and take hold of the opportunity for self-assertion that this historical moment provides.

NOTES

1. Reynaldo Clemeña Ileto, *Pasyon and Revolution: Popular Movements in the Philippines, 1840–1910* (Quezon City, Philippines: Ateneo de Manila Univ. Press, 1979, 1998), 99–103.

2. *Asia Source: A Resource of the Asia Society,* July 29, 2003. See www.asia source.org/news/at_mp_02.cfm?newsid=53011.

3. Barbara Posadas, *The Filipino Americans* (Westport, CT: Greenwood Press, 1999), 77.

4. Pauline Agbayani-Siewert and Linda Revilla, "Filipino Americans," in *Asian Americans: Contemporary Trends,* ed. Pyong Gap Min, 152 (Thousand Oaks, CA: Sage Publications, 1995). The authors cite a study by Robert M. Jiobu, *Ethnicity and Inequality* (Albany: State Univ. of New York Press, 1988), 101, 103 in which 91 percent of Filipino immigrants reported being able to speak English "well" or "very well." Nine out of ten Filipinos in a study of second-generation youth in San Diego also reported speaking and reading English "very well." See Yen Le Espiritu, *Homebound: Filipino American Lives across Cultures, Communities, and Countries* (Berkeley: Univ. of California Press, 2003), 194. There remains surprisingly little scholarly attention focused on languages among Filipino Americans.

5. In the 1990 census of Filipino occupational characteristics, professional, managerial, technical/sales, and precision, production, and craft categories made up 48 percent of the total number of working Filipinos twenty-five years old and over. Meanwhile, administrative support, service, farm, and operatives and laborers made up 52 percent of the total. See Agbayani-Siewert and Revilla, 151. Also, in the 1990 census, women made up 53.7 percent, or 762,946, of the total Filipino population of 1,419,711. See Harry H. L. Kitano and Roger Daniels, *Asian Americans: Emerging Minorities,* 3rd ed. (Upper Saddle River, NJ: Prentice Hall, 2001), 96.

6. For Filipino American organizations, see Rick Bonus, *Locating Filipino Americans: Ethnicity and the Cultural Politics of Space* (Philadelphia: Temple Univ. Press, 2000), 92–121; and Antonio J. A. Pido, *The Pilipinos in America* (New York: Center for Migration Studies, 1986), 105–107.

7. Posadas, 24, 53–56; Pido, 18, 48; and Steffi San Buenaventura, "The Master and the Federation: A Filipino-American Social Movement in California and Hawaii," *Social Process in Hawaii* 33 (1991): 169–193.

8. See, for instance, the excellent profiles "Notable Filipino Americans" in Posadas, 153–160; the well-reviewed stage productions of Han Ong and Ted Benito, "The Old Times Square, Home for the Hopeless," *New York Times,* June 4, 2001, B5; and "A 'New World' Worth Discovering," *Los Angeles Times,* July 18, 2003. One can also get a sense of prominent Filipino Americans from the glossy but always informative transnational magazine *Filipinas;* see for instance, "Oh, What a Night: The 1999 Filipinas Magazine Achievement Awards," *Filipinas* 8, no. 87 (July 1999): 49–52.

9. According to Samantha Chanse and Gordon Hurd, "Over 75 percent of the 1,250 screeners at the San Francisco, Oakland, and San Jose airports"—who were slated to lose their jobs because they were noncitizens—"are Filipino." See *Colorlines* 5, no. 2 (Summer 2002); David Bacon, "Nightmare Case Now a Legend: Filipino Workers Challenge Silicon Valley's 'Clean Industry,'" *Jinn Magazine* (Pacific News Service), November 4, 1997, www.pacificnews.org/jinn/stories/3.23/971104-toxic.html (accessed August 14, 2003). See also Charlene Tung, "The Social Reproductive Labor of Filipina Transmigrant Workers in Southern California: Caring for Those Who Provide Elderly Care" (PhD diss., Univ. of California, Irvine, 1999).

10. Bangele D. Alsaybar, "'Party Culture,' and Ethnic Identity in Los Angeles," *Second Generation: Ethnic Identity among Asian Americans,* ed. Pyong Gap Min, 129–152 (Walnut Creek, California: AltaMira Press, 2002).

11. See Yen Espiritu, "The Intersection of Race, Ethnicity, and Class: The Multiple Identities of Second-Generation Filipinos," in *Second Generation* (see note 10), 19–52.

12. Jonathan Green, ed., *The Cassell Dictionary of Slang* (London: Cassell Wellington House, 1998), 437, defines *F.O.B.* as a noun that originated in U.S. campuses around the 1970s. It refers to "an Asian not used to American ways," and abbreviation for "fresh off the boat." The word's origin in the 1970s seems to be consistent with the entry of Asians and Asian Americans in larger numbers in college campuses. The dictionary, however, has not caught the derogatory flavor of the word, its strong anti-immigrant connotations, which dovetail with a history of nativism in American life. See, for instance, the classic by John Higham, *Strangers in the Land: Patterns of American Nativism, 1860–1925* (New Brunswick, NJ: Rutgers Univ. Press, 2002).

13. Leny M. Strobel, *Coming Full Circle: The Process of Decolonization among Post-1965 Filipino Americans* (Manila: Giraffe Books, 2001), e.g., 129ff.

14. Madge Bello and Vince Reyes, "Filipino Americans and the Marcos Overthrow: The Transformation of Political Consciousness," *Amerasia Journal* 13, no.1 (1986–1987): 73–83; Don T. Nakanishi, "Asian American Politics: An Agenda for Research," *Amerasia Journal* 12, no. 2 (1985/1986): 1–28; Posadas, 144–145; Concepcion A. Montoya, "Living in the Frontiers: The Undocumented Immigrant Experience of Filipinos," *Filipino Americans: Transformation and Identity*, ed. Maria Root, 112–120 (Thousand Oaks, California: Sage Publications, 1997); and Posadas, 130–133.

15. See Pyong Gap Min, "Filipino and Korean Immigrants in Small Business: A Comparative Analysis," *Amerasia Journal* 13, no.1 (1986–1987): 53–71; and Posadas, 79. Using 1990 census statistics, Posadas found that only 3.2 percent of Filipino Americans were self-employed and that they ranked sixth among Asian Americans in ownership of retail businesses.

16. Filipino Americans, according to Amefil Agbayani, made up but one percent of the "tenured/tenurable faculty" at the University of Hawaii, Manoa, in 1990 and were also underrepresented among staff and clerical workers even as they made up 15 percent of Hawaii's total population for that year. See her article "The Education of Filipinos in Hawaii," *Social Process in Hawaii* 37 (1996): 147, 158.

17. Teresita V. Ramos, "Philippine Languages in Hawaii," *Social Process in Hawaii* 37 (1996): 165.

18. See James F. Allen's discussion of "urban invisibility" in "Recent Immigration from the Philippines and Filipino Communities in the United States," *Geographical Review* 67, no.2 (April 1977): 205–206; and Oscar Campomanes, "Filipinos in the United States and Their Literature of Exile," in *Reading the Literatures of Asian America*, ed. Shirley Lim and Amy Ling, 49–78 (Philadelphia: Temple Univ. Press, 1993).

19. See his essay "The Invisible Minority and the Anti-Pilipino Pilipinos," in *The Philipinos in America* (see note 6) 99–102.

20. Stuart Creighton Miller, "*Benevolent Assimilation*": *The American Conquest of the Philippines, 1899–1903* (New Haven, CT: Yale Univ. Press, 1982); Miriam Sharma, "The Philippines: A Case of Migration to Hawaii, 1906–1946," *Labor Immigration under Capitalism Asian Workers in the United States before World War II*, ed. Lucie Cheng and Edna Bonacich (Berkeley: Univ. of California Press, 1984), 337–358.

21. See Renato Constantino and Letizia R. Constantino, *The Philippines: A Past Revisited* (Quezon City: R. Constantino, 1975), 257, and Reynaldo Ileto's discussion of "bandits" and his challenge to a pueblo-centered Philippine history in "Outlines of a Nonlinear

Emplotment of Philippine History," in *Reflections on Development in Southeast Asia*, ed. Lim Teck Ghee, 144–148 (Singapore: Institute of Southeast Asian Studies, 1988). On the maroon revolts, see, for instance, Peter H. Wood, *Black Majority: Negroes in Colonial South Carolina from 1670 to the Stono Rebellion* (New York: Norton, 1974), 223.

22. Constantino and Constantino, *The Philippines*, 102–105; William Henry Scott, *The Discovery of the Igorots: Spanish Contacts with the Pagans of Northern Luzon* (Quezon City: New Day Publishers, 1974).

23. See Constantino and Constantino, *The Philippines*, 57, 90, 119. Boat-building and seamanship were important to the livelihood and trade of the Philippine population at the time of the Spanish conquest. See William Henry Scott, "Boat-Building and Seamanship in Classic Philippine Society," *Cracks in the Parchment Curtain* (Quezon City: New Day Publishers, 1982), 60–95.

24. Eloisa Gomez Borah, "Filipinos in Unamuno's California Expedition of 1587," *Amerasia Journal* 21, no.3 (1995/1996): 175–183; Letizia R. Constantino, "From Indio to Filipino," in *Issues without Tears: A Layman's Manual of Current Issues*, vol. 4, 24–28 (Quezon City: Karrel, Inc., 1985).

25. Marina Espina, *Filipinos in Louisiana* (New Orleans, LA: A. F. Laborde, 1988), cited in Fred Cordova, *Forgotten Asian Americans: A Pictorial Essay, 1763–circa 1963* (Dubuque, IA: Kendall/Hunt Publishing Company, 1983), 1–7.

26. Cordova, *Forgotten Asian Americans*, 1. Ambeth Ocampo, writing for the *Philippine Daily Inquirer* in September 2000, argues from contrary evidence that the first Filipinos in Louisiana did not land there in 1763 but in 1882, when Jacinto Quintin de la Cruz, originally from Albay, arrived there.

27. Lafcadio Hearn, "Saint Malo: A Lacustrine Village in Louisiana," *Harper's Weekly* 31 (March 1883).

28. Isagani R. Medina, "American Logbooks and Journals in Salem, Massachusetts on the Philippines," *Asian Studies* 11, no.1 (April 1973): 177.

29. See Constantino and Constantino, *The Philippines*, 121–122.

30. Richard Drinnon, *Facing West: The Metaphysics of Indian-Hating and Empire Building* (Minneapolis: Univ. of Minnesota Press, 1980), 280–281; Fidel Reyes, "Birds of Prey," in *Filipino Nationalism: 1872–1970*, ed. Teodoro A. Agoncillo, 251–254 (Quezon City: R. P. Garcia Publishing Company, 1974).

31. Stanley Karnow, *In Our Image: America's Empire in the Philippines* (New York: Random House, 1989), 9.

32. Renato Constantino, "The Miseducation of the Filipino," in *The Philippines Reader: A History of Colonialism, Neocolonialism, Dictatorship, and Resistance*, ed. Daniel B. Schirmer and Stephen Rosskamm Shalom, 45–49 (Boston: South End Press, 1987).

33. Constantino and Constantino, *The Philippines*, 244–245; Vicente L. Rafael, *White Love and Other Events in Filipino History* (Durham: Duke Univ. Press, 2000), 21, 22, 74.

34. Luzviminda Francisco, "The First Vietnam: The Philippine-American War of 1899," *Bulletin of Concerned Asian Scholars* 5, no. 4 (December 1973): 2–16; Gabriel Kolko, "The Philippines: Another Vietnam," *Bulletin of Concerned Asian Scholars* 5, no.1 (July 1973): 47–52; Daniel B. Schirmer, *Republic or Empire: American Resistance to the Philippine War*, (Cambridge, MA: Schenkman Publishing Company, 1972); and Schirmer and Shalom, eds., *The Philippines Reader*.

35. Francisco, 8; David Roediger, "*Gook*: The Short History of an Americanism," *Monthly Review* 43, no.10 (1992): 50–54. Roediger argues that the provenance of the racist term *guk*, so widely used in America's twentieth-century wars in Korea and Vietnam, originated in *googoo*, the slur widely used by American soldiers in the U.S.–Philippine War. See also Richard Drinnon, *Facing West*, 287–291.

36. Mark Twain, "Comments on the Killing of 600 Moros," *In Time of Hesitation: American Anti-Imperialists and the Philippine-American War*, ed. Roger J. Bresnahan, 67–74 (Quezon City: New Day Publishers, 1981).

37. Agoncillo, *History of the Filipino People*, 8th ed. (Quezon City: Gartotech Publishing, 1990), 307–312; Ruby Paredes, *Philippine Colonial Democracy* (New Haven, CT: Yale Univ. Southeast Asia Studies, 1988).

38. John Schumacher, *The Making of a Nation: Essays on Nineteenth-Century Filipino Nationalism* (Ateneo de Manila Univ. Press, 1991), 30–33; Oscar M. Alfonso, ed. *University of the Philippines: The First 75 Years* (Quezon City: Univ. of the Philippines Press, 1985), 4–5.

39. Jonathan Fast, "Imperialism and Bourgeois Dictatorship in the Philippines," *New Left Review* 78 (March-April 1973): 69–98; James P. Allen, "Recent Immigration from the Philippines and Filipino Communities in the United States," *Geographical Review* 67, no. 2 (April 1977): 195–208; James T. Fawcett and Benjamin V. Cariño, eds., *Pacific Bridges: The New Immigration from Asia and the Pacific Islands* (Staten Island, NY: Center for Migration Studies, 1987).

40. Celia Bocobo Olivar, *Aristocracy of the Mind: A Precious Heritage: A Biography of Jorge Bocobo* (Quezon City: New Day Publishers, 1981), 9; Daniel F. Doeppers, *Manila, 1900–1941: Social Change in a Late Colonial Metropolis* (New Haven, CT: Yale Univ. Southeast Asia Studies, 1984), 63. See also W.A. Sutherland, *Not by Might: The Epic of the Philippines* (Las Cruces, NM: Southwest Publishing Company, 1953).

41. Bonifacio Salamanca, *The Filipino Reaction to American Rule, 1901–1913* (Hamden, CT: The Shoe String Press, Inc., 1968), 90–92, 243–244; Cameron Forbes, *The Philippine Islands*, vol. 1 (Boston: Houghton Mifflin Company, 1928), 457–458.

42. Bocobo Olivar *Aristocracy of the Mind*, 12–13; Robert Rydell, *All the World's a Fair: Visions of Empire at American International Expositions, 1876–1916* (Chicago: Univ. of Chicago Press, 1984), 154–183; Paul Kramer, "Making Concessions: Race and Empire Revisited at the Philippine Exposition, St. Louis, 1901–1905," *Radical History Review* 73 (Winter 1999): 74–115; Michael Salman, *The Embarrassment of Slavery: Controversies over Bondage and Nationalism in the American Colonial Philippines* (Berkeley: Univ. of California Press, 2001), 155. See also Christopher A. Vaughan, "Ogling Igorots: The Politics and Commerce of Exhibiting Cultural Otherness, 1898–1913," in *Freakery: Cultural Spectacles of the Extraordinary Body*, ed. Rosemarie Garland Thomson, 219–232 (New York: New York Univ. Press, 1996).

43. Bonifacio S. Salamanca, "Bocobo Fosters a Vibrant Nationalism (1934–1939)," in *University of the Philippines*, 204–206 (see note 38).

44. Ramon C. Aquino, *Chief Justice Jose Abad Santos, 1886–1942: A Biography* (Quezon City: Phoenix Publishing House, 1986), 13ff; General Carlos P. Romulo, *I Walked with Heroes* (New York: Holt, Rinehart and Winston, 1961), 128ff; Bienvenido N. Santos, *Memory's Fictions: A Personal History* (Quezon City: New Day Publishers, 1993), 72ff.

45. Dorothy Cordova, "Voices from the Past: Why They Came," in *Making Waves:*

An Anthology of Writings By and About Asian American Women, ed. Asian Women United of California, 42–49 (Boston: Beacon Press, 1989).

46. Ronald Takaki, *Strangers from a Different Shore: A History of Asian Americans* (Boston: Little, Brown, 1998), 58–59.

47. See Daniel F. Doeppers, *Manila, 1900–1941: Social Change in a Late Colonial Metropolis* (New Haven, CT: Yale University Southeast Asia Studies, 1984), 66, 99, 106; Edna Zapanta Manlapaz, *Angela Manalang Gloria: A Literary Biography* (Quezon City: Ateneo de Manila Univ. Press, 1993), 40ff.

48. Barbara M. Posadas, "The Hierarchy of Color and Psychological Adjustment in an Industrial Environment: Filipinos, The Pullman Company, and the Brotherhood of Sleeping Car Porters," *Labor History* 23 (1982): 349–373.

49. Yuji Ichioka, *Issei: The World of the First-Generation Japanese Immigrants 1885–1924* (New York: The Free Press, 1988), 24; Craig Scharlin and Lilia V. Villanueva, *Philip Vera Cruz: A Personal History of Filipino Immigrants and the Farmworkers Movement* (Los Angeles: UCLA Labor Center, Institute of Industrial Relations, and UCLA Asian American Studies Center, 1994), 60–63.

50. Carlos Bulosan, *America Is in the Heart: A Personal History* (Seattle: Univ. of Washington Press, 1973), parts 3 and 4; and P. C. Morantte, "Two Filipinos in America," *Books Abroad* (1944): 326–327.

51. Miriam Sharma, "Labor Migration and Class Formation among the Filipinos in Hawaii, 1906–1946," *Labor Migration under Capitalism*, 579; John Larkin, "Philippine History Reconsidered: A Socioeconomic Perspective," *American Historical Review* 87, no.3 (June 1982): 614ff.

52. Carey McWilliams, *Brothers under the Skin* (Boston: Little, Brown, 1951), 234–235.

53. Bruno Lasker, *Filipino Immigration* (New York: Arno Press, 1969), 203–269.

54. Benicio T. Catapusan, *The Social Adjustment of Filipinos in the United States* (San Francisco: R and E Research Associates, 1972), 53–55.

55. McWilliams, *Brothers under the Skin*, 241ff.

56. Lasker, *Filipino Immigration*, 92–100.

57. Howard DeWitt, *Violence in the Fields: California Farm Labor Unionization during the Great Depression* (Saratoga, CA: Century Twenty One Publishing, 1980), 3–5.

58. James R. Lawrence, "The A. F. of L. and the Philippine Independence Question," *Labor History* (Winter 1966): 62–69.

59. Emory Bogardus, "Social Problems in the Philippines," *Sociology and Social Research* 21, no.6 (July–August 1937): 565; McWilliams, *Brothers under the Skin*, 243; Shirley Jenkins, "The Independence Lobby," *The Philippines Reader*, 56–57.

60. Bernardita Reyes Churchill, *The Philippine Independence Missions to the United States, 1919–1934* (Manila: National Historical Institute, 1983); Reynaldo Ileto, "Orators and the Crowd: Philippine Independence Politics," *Reappraising an Empire: New Perspectives on Philippine-American History* (Cambridge, MA: Harvard Univ. Press, 1984), 85–116.

61. Emory S. Bogardus, "Anti-Filipino Riots," in *Letters in Exile: An Introductory Reader on the History of Pilipinos in America* 57 (Los Angeles: UCLA Asian American Studies Center, 1976).

62. Jenkins, "The Independence Lobby," 58.

63. Emory S. Bogardus, "Filipino repatriation," *Sociology and Social Research* 21,

no.1 (September–October 1936): 67–71; "*Time* Magazine Reveals Sexual Basis for Filipino Repatriation, 1936," *Major Problems in Asian American History*, ed. Lon Kurashige and Alice Yang Murray, 228–229 (Boston: Houghton Mifflin, 2003).

64. Henry Empeno, et al., "Anti-Miscegenation Laws and the Pilipino," in *Letters in Exile* (see note 61), 65ff; Fred Cordova, 154–165.

65. Bulosan, *America Is in the Heart*, 284–289; Gerald Meyer, *Vito Marcantonio: Radical Politician, 1902–1954* (Albany: State Univ. of New York Press, 1989), 4, 69.

66. Melinda Tria Kerkvliet, "Interpreting Pablo Manlapit," *Social Process in Hawaii* 37 (1996): 4–7; Posadas, *Filipino Americans*, 24.

67. Labor organizations: Howard Dewitt, "The Filipino Labor Union: The Salinas Lettuce Strike of 1934," *Amerasia Journal* 5, no.2 (Fall 1978); Cletus E. Daniel, *Bitter Harvest: A History of California Farmworkers, 1870–1941* (Ithaca: Cornell Univ. Press, 1981), 109, 117; Jack K. Masson and Donald L. Guimary, "Pilipinos and Unionization of the Alaskan Canned Salmon Industry," *Amerasia Journal* 8, no.2 (1981): 10ff; Chris Friday, *Organizing Asian American Labor: The Pacific Coast Canned-Salmon Industry, 1870–1942* (Philadelphia: Temple Univ. Press, 1994), 125–126, 128–132; and Sucheng Chan, *Asian Americans: An Interpretive History* (Philadelphia: Temple Univ. Press, 1990), 89.

68. Chan, 75–77; Melinda Tria Kerkvliet, *Manila Worker's Unions, 1900–1950* (Quezon City: New Day Publishers, 1992), 37, 40.

69. See Steffi San Buenaventura's "The Master and the Federation," *Social Process in Hawaii* 33 (1991): 169–193.

70. Severino Corpus, *An Analysis of the Racial Adjustment Activities and Problems of the Filipino-American Christian Fellowship in Los Angeles* (San Francisco: R and E Research Associates, 1975), 57ff.

71. R.T. Feria, "War and the Status of Filipino Immigrants," *Sociology and Social Research: An International Journal* 31, no.1 (September–October 1946): 51, 52.

72. See Alex Fabros, "The Boogie Woogie Boys," *Filipinas: A Magazine for all Filipinos*, September 1993; and "They Were All Young and Daring: The Bahala Na Batallion, Part I," *Filipinas*, July 1994.

73. P.C. Morantte, *Remembering Carlos Bulosan: His Heart Affair with America* (Quezon City: New Day Publishers, 1984), 134–147; Santos, *Memory's Fictions*, 90–98.

74. Augusto Espiritu, *Five Faces of Exile: The Nation and Filipino American Intellectuals* (forthcoming); Constantino, "The Miseducation of the Filipino."

75. Chan, 122, 139, 140.

76. Caridad Concepcion Vallangca, *The Second Wave: Pinay and Pinoy, 1945–1960* (San Francisco: Strawberry Hill Press, 1987), 12.

77. Jonathan Fast, "Imperialism and Bourgeois Dictatorship in the Philippines," *The New Left Review* 78 (March-April 1973): 87–91; John H. Burma, "Filipino Americans," *Spanish-Speaking Groups in the United States* (Durham, NC: Duke Univ. Press, 1954), 139; McWilliams, *Brothers under the Skin*, 244.

78. Lawrence T. Johnson, "The Migration Waves of Filipinos," *Rice* 1, no.11 (July 1988): 38. See also Jesse Quinsaat, "An Exercise on How to Join the Navy and Still Not See the World," in *Letters in Exile* (see note 61), 96–111.

79. Johnson, "The Migration Waves of Filipinos."

80. Agoncillo, *A History of the Filipino People*, 527–530.

81. Johnson, "The Migration Waves of Filipinos"; Yen Le Espiritu, *Filipino American Lives*, (Philadelphia: Temple Univ. Press, 1995), 22–26.

82. Vallangca, *The Second Wave*, 137.

83. Arleen de Vera, "Without Parallel: The Local 7 Deportation Cases, 1949–1955," *Amerasia Journal* 20, no.2 (1994): 1–25. See also Sam Kushner, *Long Road to Delano* (New York: International Publishers, 1975).

84. De Vera, "Without Parallel," 15–16.

85. For discussions of Itliong, Vera Cruz, and the Agricultural Workers Organizing Committee, AFL-CIO, see Kushner, *Long Road to Delano*, 81–94, 127, 184.

86. Dean Alegado, "Carl Damaso: A Champion of Hawaii's Working People," *Social Process in Hawaii* 37 (1996): 26–35.

87. Feria, "War and the Status of Filipino Immigrants."

88. See Schirmer and Shalom, *The Philippines Reader*, 105–124; Nick Cullather's *Illusions of Influence: The Political Economy of United States-Philippines Relations, 1942–1960* (Stanford: Stanford Univ. Press, 1994); Benedict J. Kerkvliet, *The Huk Rebellion: A Study of Peasant Revolt in the Philippines* (Berkeley: Univ. of California Press, 1977).

89. Allen "Recent Immigration from the Philippines," 198.

90. For the origins of the word, see William Henry Scott, *Barangay: Sixteenth-Century Philippine Culture and Society* (Quezon City: Ateneo de Manila Univ. Press, 1994), 4–6. For local, factional, and family politics, see Carl H. Landé, *Leaders, Factions, and Parties: The Structure of Philippine Politics* (New Haven, CT: Yale University Southeast Asia Studies, 1965); and *An Anarchy of Families: State and Family in the Philippines*, ed. Alfred W. McCoy (Madison: Univ. of Wisconsin, Center for Southeast Asian Studies, 1993).

91. *Major Problems in Asian American History* (see note 63), 359–360.

92. Barbara Posadas, *The Filipino Americans* (Westport, CT: Greenwood Press, 1999), 26–31. The trend toward greater gender balance had begun in the period from 1945 to 1965, although the post-1965 period greatly accelerated it.

93. Posadas, *The Filipino Americans*, 37–40.

94. Posadas, *The Filipino Americans*; Allen, "Recent Immigration from the Philippines"; and Paul Ong and Tania Azores, "The Migration and Incorporation of Filipino Nurses," in *The New Asian Immigration to Los Angeles and Global Restructuring*, ed. Paul Ong, Edna Bonacich, and Lucie Cheng 164–195 (Philadelphia: Temple Univ. Press, 1994).

95. See Vallangca, *The Second Wave*, 232–239; and "Filipina Teacher Fights Discrimination," *Ang Katipunan*, April 1975, 10; "New York Conference Assails Immigrant Discrimination," *Ang Katipunan*, July 1975, 1; "Filipino CPA's Target Discriminatory Practices," *Ang Katipunan*, March 1–15, 1978, 8; "NAFL-FNG Launch Petition Drive," *Ang Katipunan*, June 15–30, 1978, 7.

96. Catherine Ceniza Choy, *Empire of Care: Nursing and Migration in Filipino American History* (Durham: Duke Univ. Press, 2003), 139–165.

97. Ong and Azores, "Migration and Incorporation of Filipino Nurses," 188. For the Fragante case, see Sheila M. Forman, "Filipno Participation in Civil Rights Policies and Practices in Hawai'i," *Social Process in Hawaii* 33 (1991): 5–9. See the biographies of Filipino union organizers for the SEIU in Kent Wong, *Voices for Justice: Asian Pacific American Organizers and the New Labor Movement* (Los Angeles: UCLA Center for Labor Research and Education), 5–18, 45–62.

98. See Yen Le Espiritu, *Asian American Panethnicity: Bridging Institutions and Identities* (Philadelphia: Temple Univ. Press, 1992), 103–109.

99. Agbayani-Siewert and Revilla, "Filipino Americans," 148–150.

100. See, for instance, the example of Melinda Paras in Max Elbaum's *Revolution in the Air: Sixties Radicals Turn to Lenin, Mao and Che* (New York: Verso, 2002), 242–243; and Luisa Blue in Wong, *Voices for Justice*, 5–18. Paras has served as the chair of the National Gay and Lesbian Task Force while Luisa Blue is the current head of the Asian Pacific American Labor Alliance and an officer for the Service Employees International Union (SEIU).

101. Posadas, *The Filipino Americans*, 155–159; Leonard Casper, "Four Filipina Writers: Recultivating Eden," *Amerasia Journal* 24, no.3 (1998): 143–159. See also *Filipina: Hawaii's Filipino Women*, Pepi Nieva, ed. (Hawaii: Filipino Association of Univ. Women, 1994).

102. Rick Bonus, *Locating Filipino Americans: Ethnicity and the Cultural Politics of Space* (Philadelphia: Temple Univ. Press, 2000), 47–56.

103. Benito M. Vergara, "Betrayal, Class Fantasies, and the Filipino Nation in Daly City," in *Cultural Compass: Ethnographic Explorations of Asian America*, ed. Martin Manalansan (Philadelphia: Temple Univ. Press, 2000), 139–158.

104. Augusto Fauni Espiritu, "The Rise and Fall of the Filipino Town Campaign in Los Angeles: A Study in Filipino American Leadership" (master's thesis, UCLA, 1992).

105. Ibid., 14–16.

106. "Garcetti Calls for Official Recognition of 'Historic Filipinotown,'" press release, office of Eric Garcetti, City Council member of Los Angeles, July 22, 2002; "FilCom Center Celebrates its 1st Anniversary!," by FilCom Center Staff, FilCom Waipahu official Web site, www.filcom.org/1st_anniversary.shtml; Rick DelVecchio, "Big Push to Save Little Manila: Filipino Americans try to preserve Stockton's symbols of Immigration History," *San Francisco Examiner*, Wednesday, July 16, 2003, A-15; Bonus, *Locating Filipino Americans*, ibid.

107. Amado Cabezas, et al., found that U.S.-born Filipino American men and foreign-born Filipino men and women earned lower incomes than white men (e.g., in 1980, the first group made only 64 percent of what white males earned) as a result of low returns on their human capital investments, that is, education. The authors theorize that Filipino Americans are clustering into a "secondary labor market." See "New Inquiries into the Socioeconomic Status of Pilipino Americans in California," *Amerasia Journal* 13 (1986–1987): 12–13. See also Jeff Chang, "Lessons of Tolerance: Americanism and the Filipino Affirmative Action Movement in Hawai'i," *Social Process in Hawaii* 37 (1996): 112–146. The San Diego study comes from Angela Lau, "Filipino Girls Think Suicide at Number One Rate," *San Diego Union Tribune*, February 11, 1995, cited in Yen Le Espiritu, *Homebound*, 177, 256.

108. Joseph P. McCallus, "The Myths of the New Filipino: Philippine Government Propaganda during the Early Years of Martial Law," *Philippine Quarterly of Culture and Society* (1989): 90–103.

109. Rene Ciria-Cruz, former anti-Marcos activist, interview with the author, July 7, 2003, San Francisco, California.

110. See Madge Bello and Vince Reyes, "Filipino Americans and the Marcos Overthrow: The Transformation of Political Consciousness," *Amerasia Journal* 13, no.1 (1986–1987): 73–84.

111. Ileto, *Pasyon and Revolution*, 235–236. See also Nenita Pambid, *Anting-Anting: O Kung Bakit Nagtatago sa Loob ng Bato si Bathala* (Quezon City: Univ. of the Philip-

pines Press, 2000). The title of Pambid's book literally translates into "Amulet: Or Why Bathala Dwells inside the Stone." See Alfred W. McCoy, "Baylan: Animist Religion and the Philippine Peasant Ideology," *Philippine Quarterly of Culture and Society* 10 (1982): 141–184.

112. See Pido, *Pilipinos in America*, 100–101, who regards being an "invisible minority" as a conscious strategy among Filipino Americans.

113. Agenda of the Executive Matters Committee, City Council, City and county of Honolulu, Honolulu, Hawaii, July 24, 2003.

114. Helen Zia, *Asian American Dreams: The Emergence of an American People* (New York: Farrar, Strauss & Giroux, 2000), 303–305, 309.

115. Candace Fujikane, "Sweeping Racism under the Rug of 'Censorship': The Controversy over Lois Ann Yamanaka's *Blu's Hanging*," *Amerasia Journal* 26, no.2 (2000): 159–194.

116. Seth Mydans, "Subic Bay, Minus U.S., Becomes Surprise Success," *New York Times*, November 23, 1996, sec. A.

117. Belinda Aquino, "Presidential Derby," *The Fil-Am Courier*, July 16–31, 2003, 3, 6–7; Editorial, "Primer on the Overseas Absentee Voting Act of 2003," ibid.

118. Guil Franco, "RP: World's Top Source of Migrant Workers," *Hawaii Filipino Chronicle*, July 16, 2003, 4–5. Remittances to the Philippines from overseas workers, a large portion of which comes from the United States, now total $6.9 billion. See also Jim Gomez, "U.S. Enters Philippine Combat Zone," *Washington Post*, March 19, 2002; Anastasia Hendrix, "Filipino Citizens Get Chance to Cast Ballot," *San Francisco Chronicle*, Sunday, July 20, 2003; S. Lily Mendoza, *Between the Homeland and the Diaspora* (New York: Routledge, 2002), 130; Rodel Rodis, "The New Filipino American War Heroes," *San Francisco Chronicle*, April 30, 2003.

BIBLIOGRAPHICAL ESSAY

A useful research guide for the study of Filipino Americans is Estela L. Manila, *Filipinos in the United States: A Print and Digital Resource Guide* (San Francisco: Asian American Information, 2000).

For general surveys of Filipino American history and social life, see Royal Morales, *Makibaka 2: The Pilipino American Struggle* (Laoag City, Philippines: Mountainview Publisher, 1998), J.A. Pido, *The Pilipinos in America* (New York: Center for Migration Studies, 1986), and Fred Cordova's pictorial essay, *Filipinos: Forgotten Asian Americans* (Dubuque, IA: Kendoll/Hunt Pub. Co., 1983). See also the references and excellent introductions to Filipino Americans in Sucheng Chan, *Asian Americans: An Interpretive History* (Philadelphia: Temple Univ. Press, 1990) and Ronald Takaki, *Strangers from a Different Shore: A History of Asian Americans* (Boston: Little, Brown, 1998).

For Filipino Americans in the West Coast during the 1920s and 1930s, see the classic survey by Bruno Lasker, *Filipino Immigration* (New York: Arno Press, 1969), first published in 1933; *Letters in Exile: An Introductory Reader on the History of Pilipinos in America* (Los Angeles: UCLA Asian American Studies Center, 1976); Howard DeWitt, *Violence in the Fields: California Farm Labor Unionization during the Great Depression* (Saratoga, CA: Century Twenty One Publishing, 1980), Gail Nomura, "Within the Law: The Establishment of Filipino Leasing Rights in the Yakima Indian Reservation," *Amerasia Journal* 13, no.1 (1986–1987): 99–118; and Dorothy B. Fujita-Rony, *American*

Workers, Colonial Power: Philippine Seattle and the Transpacific West, 1919–1941 (Berkeley: Univ. of California Press, 2003). For Hawaii, see Roman R. Cariaga, *The Filipinos in Hawaii: A Survey of Their Economic and Social Conditions* (San Francisco: R and E Research Associates, 1974) and the excellent reading of this source, Jonathan Okamura, "Writing the Filipino Diaspora: Roman R. Cariaga's *The Filipinos in Hawaii*," *Social Process in Hawaii* 37 (1996): 36–56; Ruben Alcantara, *Filipino Adaptation in Hawaii* (Washington, DC: Univ. Press of America, 1981); Miriam Sharma has also penned two seminal essays, "The Philippines: A Case of Migration to Hawaii, 1906–1946" and "Labor Migration and Class Formation among the Filipinos in Hawaii, 1906–1946," both of them in *Labor Migration under Capitalism*, ed. Lucie Cheng and Edna Bonacich (Berkeley: Univ. of California Press, 1984); Ronald Takaki, *Pau Hana Plantation Life and Labor in Hawaii, 1835–1920* (Honolulu: Univ. of Hawaii Press, 1983); and Edward D. Beechert, *Working in Hawaii: A Labor History* (Honolulu: Univ. of Hawaii Press, 1985). For Alaska, see Chris Friday, *Organizing Asian American Labor: The Pacific Coast Canned-Salmon Industry, 1870–1942* (Philadelphia: Temple Univ. Press, 1994) and Thelma Buchholdt's pictorial essay, *Filipinos in Alaska: 1788–1958* (Anchorage: Aboriginal Press, 1996).

There are excellent autobiographical and biographical works that throw light on Filipino life before 1965. These include Melinda Tria Kerkvliet, "Interpreting Pablo Manlapit," *Social Process in Hawaii* 37 (1996): 1–25; Manuel Buaken, *I Have Lived with the American People* (Caldwell, ID: Caxton Printers, 1948); Carlos Bulosan, *America Is in the Heart: A Personal History* (Seattle: Univ. of Washington Press, 1973); the oral histories in Caridad Concepcion Vallangca, *The Second Wave: Pinay and Pinoy, 1945–1960* (San Francisco: Strawberry Hill Press, 1987); Craig Scharlin and Lilia V. Villanueva, *Philip Vera Cruz: A Personal History of Filipino Immigrants and the Farmworkers Movement* (Los Angeles: UCLA Labor Center, 1994); Steffi San Buenaventura, "The Master and the Federation: A Filipino-American Social Movement in California and Hawaii," *Social Process in Hawaii* 33 (1991): 169–193 [about Hilario Camino Moncado]; Dean Alegado, "Carl Damaso: A Champion of Hawaii's Working People," *Social Process in Hawaii* 37 (1996): 26–35.

Barbara Posadas has written a number of as yet uncollected excellent historical explorations of the lives of Filipino men and women in Chicago. They include "Crossed Boundaries in Interracial Chicago: Pilipino American Families since 1925," *Amerasia Journal* 8, no.2 (1981): 31–52; "The Hierarchy of Color and Psychological Adjustment in an Industrial Environment: Filipinos, The Pullman Company, and the Brotherhood of Sleeping Car Porters," *Labor History* 23 (1982): 349–373; "Will the Real Pinoy Please Stand Up? Filipino Immigration to America: A Review Article," [with Roland Guyotte] *Pilipinas: A Journal of Philippine Studies* 5 (1985): 79–89; "At a Crossroads: Filipino American History and the Old-Timers' Generation," *Amerasia Journal* 13 (1986–1987): 85–97; "Mestiza Girlhood: Interracial Families in Chicago's Filipino American Community Since 1930," in *Making Waves: Writings about Asian American Women*, ed. Judy Yung, ed. 273–290 (Boston: Beacon Press, 1989); "Ethnic Life and Labor in Chicago's Pre-World War II Filipino Community," in *Labor Divided: Race and Ethnicity in United States Labor Struggles, 1835–1960*, ed. Robert Asher and Charles Stephenson, 63–80 (Albany: State Univ. of New York Press, 1990); "Unintentional Immigrants: Chicago's Filipino Foreign Students Become Settlers, 1900–1941," [with Roland L. Guyotte] 9, no.2 (Spring 1990): 26–48; "Aspiration and Reality: Occupational and Educational Choice among Filipino Migrants to Chicago, 1900–1935," [with Guyotte] *Illinois Historical Jour-*

nal 85 (Summer 1992): 89–104; and "Filipinos and Race in Twentieth Century Chicago: The Impact of Polarization between Blacks and Whites," [with Guyotte] *Amerasia Journal* 24:2 (1998): 135–154.

For contemporary developments after the passage of the 1965 Immigration Act, see James P. Allen, "Recent Immigration from the Philippines and Filipino Communities in the United States," *Geographical Review* 67, no.2 (April 1977): 195–208; *Filipino Americans: Transformation and Identity*, ed. Maria Root (Thousand Oaks, CA: Sage Publications, 1997); Barbara Posadas, *The Filipino Americans* (Westport, CT: Greenwood Press, 1999); Rick Bonus, *Locating Filipino Americans: Ethnicity and the Cultural Politics of Space* (Philadelphia: Temple Univ. Press, 2000); Belinda Aquino, "The Politics of Ethnicity among Ilokanos in Hawaii," in *Old Ties and New Solidarities* Charles J-H Macdonald and Guillerno M. Pesigon eds. (Quezon City: Ateneo de Manila Univ. Press, 2000); Yen Le Espiritu, *Homebound: Filipino American Lives across Cultures, Communities, and Countries* (Berkeley: Univ. of California Press, 2003); and Martin Manalansan IV, "Searching for Community: Gay Filipino Men in New York City," *Amerasia Journal* 20, no.1 (1994): 59–73; Theo Gonzalves, "'We Hold a Neatly Folded Hope': Filipino Veterans of World War II on Citizenship and Political Obligation," *Amerasia Journal* 21, no.3 (1995/1996): 155–174.

For Filipino nurses, see Paul Ong and Tania Azores, "The Migration and Incorporation of Filipino Nurses," *The New Asian Immigration to Los Angeles and Global Restructuring*, ed. Paul Ong, Edna Bonacich, and Lucie Cheng (Philadelphia: Temple Univ. Press, 1994); and Catherine Ceniza Choy, *Empire of Care: Nursing and Migration in Filipino American History* (Durham, NC: Duke Univ. Press, 2003). For educational issues, see Jeff Chang, "Lessons of Tolerance: Americanism and the Filipino Affirmative Action Movement in Hawai'i," *Social Process in Hawaii* 37 (1996): 112–146; and Amefil R. Agbayani, "The Education of Filipinos in Hawai'i," *Social Process in Hawaii* 37 (1996): 147–160.

On the anti-Marcos movement that began in the early 1970s, see Madge Bello and Vince Reyes, "Filipino Americans and the Marcos Overthrow: The Transformation of Political Consciousness," *Amerasia Journal* 13, no. 1 (1986–1987): 73–84; Helen Toribio, "We Are Revolution: A Reflective History of the Union of Democratic Filipinos (KDP)," *Amerasia Journal* 24, no. 2 (Summer 1998): 155–178; Barbara Gaerlan, Anti-Martial Law Movement, *Pilipinas* 33 (Fall 1999): 75–98. See also "Welcome to Washington" in Helen Zia's *Asian American Dreams: The Emergence of an American People* (New York: Farrar, Strauss, and Giroux, 2000).

For works on cultural and intellectual developments among Filipino Americans, see Theo Gonzalves, "'The Show Must Go On': Production Notes on the Pilipino Cultural Night," *Critical Mass: A Journal of Asian American Cultural Criticism* 2, no.2 (Spring 1995): 129–144; Barbara Gaerlan, "In the Court of the Sultan: Orientalism, Nationalism, and Modernity in Philippine and Filipino American Dance," *Journal of Asian American Studies* 2, no.3 (October 1999): 251–288; Oscar Campomanes, "Filipinos in the United States and Their Literature of Exile," *Reading the Literatures of Asian America*, ed. Shirley Lim and Amy Ling (Philadelphia: Temple Univ. Press, 1993), 49–78; Leonard Casper, "Four Filipina Writers: Recultivating Eden," *Amerasia Journal* 24, no.3 (1998): 143–159; Rachel Lee, "Journalistic Representations of Asian Americans and Literary Responses, 1910–1920," *Interethnic Companion to Asian American Literature*, ed. King-Kok Cheung (New York: Cambridge Univ. Press, 1997); and Augusto Espiritu, "The 'Pre-History' of an 'Asian-American' Writer: N.V.M. Gonzalez' Allegory of Decolonization," *Amerasia Journal* 24, no.3 (Winter 1998): 126–142.

The literature on Philippine developments is vast and will only be telescoped here. For a survey of Philippine history, see Teodoro Agoncillo, *History of the Filipino People*, 8th ed. (Quezon City: Gartotech Publishing, 1990); Renato Constantino and Letizia R. Constantino, *The Philippines: A Past Revisited* (Quezon City: R. Constantino, 1975); Stanley Karnow, *In Our Image: America's Empire in the Philippines* (New York: Random House, 1989), although Karnow's book should be read against Michael Salman, "In Our Orientalist Imagination," *Radical History Review* (1990). For the colonial encounter with Spain, see William Henry Scott, *Cracks in the Parchment Curtain* (Quezon City: New Day Publishers, 1982); Scott, *Barangay: Sixteenth-Century Philippine Culture and Society* (Quezon City: Ateneo de Manila Univ. Press, 1994); Vicente Rafael, *Contracting Colonialism: Translation and Christian Conversion in Tagalog Society under Early Spanish Rule* (Ithaca, NY: Cornell Univ. Press, 1988). For economic and social developments in various local sites during the Spanish period, see Alfred W. McCoy, ed. *Philippine Social History: Global Trade and Local Transformation* (Quezon City: Ateneo de Manila Univ. Press, 1982). For the rise of Filipino nationalism in the late nineteenth century and the Philippine Revolution, see John Schumacher, *The Propaganda Movement, 1880–1895: The Creation of a Filipino Consciousness, the Making of the Revolution* (1963; repr. Quezon City: Ateneo de Manila Univ. Press, 1997); Schumacher, *The Making of a Nation* (Quezon City: Ateneo de Manila Univ. Press, 1991); and Ambeth Ocampo's *Rizal without the Overcoat* (Quezon City: Ateneo de Manila Univ. Press, 1995). For folk rebellions and the revolution against Spain, see Reynaldo Ileto's seminal works, *Pasyon and Revolution: Popular Movements in the Philippines, 1840–1910* (Quezon City: Ateneo de Manila Univ. Press, 1979); "Outlines of a Nonlinear Emplotment of Philippine History," in *Reflections on Development in Southeast Asia*, ed. Lim Teck Ghee (Singapore: Institute of Southeast Asian Studies, 1988); and *Filipinos and Their Revolution: Event, Discourse, and Historiography* (Quezon City: Ateneo de Manila Univ. Press, 1998). On the U.S.–Philippine War, see Stuart Creighton Miller, *"Benevolent Assimilation": The American Conquest of the Philippines, 1899–1903* (New Haven, CT: Yale Univ. Press, 1982); Luzviminda Francisco, "The First Vietnam: The Philippine-American War of 1899," *Bulletin of Concerned Asian Scholars* 5, no.4 (December 1973): 2–16; Brian McAllister Linn, *The Philippine War, 1899–1902* (Lawrence: Univ. Press of Kansas, 2000); and Angel Velasco Shaw and Luis H. Francia, eds., *Vestiges of War: The Philippine-American War and the Aftermath of an Imperial Dream, 1899–1999* (New York: New York Univ. Press, 2002). For anti-imperialist movements in the United States, see Jim Zwick, "The Anti-Imperialist League and the Origins of Filipino-American Oppositional Solidarity," *Amerasia Journal* 24, no.2 (Summer 1998): 65–86; Robert L. Beisner, *Twelve against Empire: The Anti-Imperialists, 1898–1900* (New York: McGraw-Hill, 1968); Daniel B. Schirmer, *Republic or Empire: American Resistance to the Philippine War* (Cambridge, MA: Schenkman Pub. Co., 1972); and Roger Bresnahan, *In Time of Hesitation: American Anti-Imperialists and the Philippine-American War* (Quezon City: New Day Publishers, 1981).

On the American colonial period, see Daniel B. Schirmer and Stephen Rosskamm Shalom, eds., *The Philippines Reader: A History of Colonialism, Neocolonialism, Dictatorship, and Resistance* (Boston: South End Press, 1987); Renato Constantino, "The Miseducation of the Filipino," in *The Philippines Reader*; Vicente Rafael, ed., *Discrepant Histories: Translocal Essays on Filipino Cultures* (Quezon City: Ateneo de Manila Univ.

Press, 1995); Rafael, *White Love and Other Events in Filipino History* (Durham, NC: Duke Univ. Press, 2000); Ruby Paredes, ed., *Philippine Colonial Democracy* (New Haven, CT: Yale Center for International Studies, 1988); Melinda Tria Kerkvliet, *Manila Workers' Unions, 1900–1950* (Quezon City: New Day Publishers, 1992); Daniel F. Doeppers, *Manila, 1900–1941: Social Change in a Late Colonial Metropolis* (New Haven, CT: Univ. Southeast Asia Studies, 1984); Enrique B. Delacruz and Pearlie Baluyot, eds., *Confrontations, Crossings, and Convergence: Photographs of the Philippines and the United States* (Los Angeles: UCLA Asian American Studies, 1998); *Michael Salman, The Embarrassment of Slavery: Controversies over Bondage and Nationalism in the American Colonial Philippines* (Berkeley: Univ. of California Press, 2001).

On Philippine-Japanese relations and the wartime occupation, see Grant K. Goodman, *Four Aspects of Philippine-Japanese Relations, 1930–1940* (New Haven, CT: Southeast Asia Studies, Yale Univ., 1967); Teodoro Agoncillo, *The Fateful Years: Japan's Adventure in the Philippines, 1941–45* (Quezon City: R.P. Garcia Pub. Co., 1965, 2001); and Ikehata Setsuho and Ricardo Trota Jose, eds., *The Philippines under Japan: Occupation Policy and Reaction* (Quezon City: Ateneo de Manila Univ. Press, 1999).

On the post-war period, see H.W. Brands, *Bound to Empire: The United States and the Philippines* (New York: Oxford Univ. Press, 1992); Nick Cullather, *Illusions of Influence: The Political Economy of United States-Philippines Relations, 1942–1960* (Stanford, CA: Stanford Univ. Press, 1994); Alfred W. McCoy, ed., *An Anarchy of Families: State and Family in the Philippines* (Madison: Univ. of Wisconsin, Center for Southeast and Asian Studies, 1993). On Philippine history and culture and United States policy toward the Philippines during the Marcos dictatorship, see Nick Joaquin, *The Aquinos of Tarlac: An Essay on History as Three Generations* (Metro Manila: Ateneo de Manila Univ. Press, 1983); Fenella Cannell, *Power and Intimacy in the Christian Philippines* (New York: Cambridge Univ. Press, 1999); Raymond Bonner, *Waltzing with a Dictator: The Marcoses and the Making of American Policy* (New York: Vintage Books, 1988); Joel Rocamora, "Lost Opportunities, Deepening Crisis: The Philippines under Cory Aquino," in *Low-Intensity Democracy: Political Power in the New World Order*, ed. Barry Gills, Joel Rocamora, and Richard Wilson (Boulder, CO: Pluto Press, 1993); Mark R. Thompson, *The Anti-Marcos Struggle: Personalistic Rule and Democratic Transition in the Philippines* (New Haven, CT: Yale Univ. Press, 1995); and essays on the Philippines by Walden Bello, in *The Future in the Balance: Essays on Globalization and Resistance*, ed. Anuradha Mittal (Oakland, CA: Food First Books, 2001).

GERMAN AMERICANS

James M. Bergquist

For over 300 years, German ethnicity has been a persistent influence on American culture. For two of those three centuries, the Germans provided the most common example of a separate enclave of non-English-speaking foreigners, and at times the German Americans seemed to other Americans aggressively resistant to adaptation to mainstream American society.

At the beginning of the twenty-first century, however, as the three-century mark of German migration passed and as modern-day migration from Germany dwindled to a comparative trickle, the vast majority of people of German derivation had long since found their way into the mainstream. The more recognizable elements of German separatism in American society had disappeared—the elaborate institutional framework, the ubiquitous German-language newspapers, the colorful business district that catered to German ethnic tastes in so many American cities. Millions of present-day Americans with obviously German surnames would be surprised to be addressed as "German Americans." On the other hand, the story of the Germans' integration into American life also demonstrates forcefully that cultural adaptation works two ways. American culture has accepted many influences from the world of the German immigrants—their beer, their food, their love of good music, their customs of Sunday celebration, and, perhaps most of all, their arguments for acceptance of cultural diversity as a way of American life.[1]

There is no one answer to the question of how the "Germans" adapted to American life because there have been so many different groups who might answer to that name. They came from different regions within Germany, which was still a patchwork of separate states before 1870. They came for a wide variety of reasons and in different waves of migration, each of which was prompted by its own causes. They had had various identities within a very diverse Germany, where differences of class, religion, and occupation had great meaning. Likewise, the America to which they adapted changed over time: American culture in 1730 was quite different from what it was in 1850 or 1900.[2]

Americans, over centuries, perceived a solid, presumably stable, and long-enduring institutional framework called German America, which, they often concluded, sheltered an ethnic group that remained immersed in its traditional cultural concerns and resistant to adaptation to American society. Since Americans knew of German neighborhoods that had persisted for many decades, German newspapers nearly a century old, and German societies that had continued the same festivals every year within memory, it was easy to understand these phenomena as symbols of the group's determined adherence to the culture of the fatherland and its resistance to assimilation. These appearances, however, were illusory.

In any serious attempt to analyze the process of adaptation of German ethnic culture to American life, it is important to separate the German institutions from the successive waves of immigrants and their descendants who passed through them and made use of them, quite often as stepping-stones into the mainstream of American life. The institutions themselves survived for a long time because the supply of newcomers, who needed them most, was frequently reconstituted by fresh waves of migration. While the many German Americans of the country were still heavily populated by newly arrived immigrants at the end of the nineteenth century, the second- and third-generation descendants of those who had used these institutions earlier in the century had to a large extent passed on into the broader institutional networks of the society at large.

Only a few of the German organizations functioned to serve descendants of Germans as genealogical or historical societies or as institutions seeking to preserve a culture for later generations. By far, the greater number served more pragmatic ends of particular importance to the newly immigrated and their children. And many such institutions reflected the dual purpose common to all immigrant organizations: they preserved and re-created some aspects of the culture of the fatherland, yet at the same time they also assisted the immigrant in making the necessary adjustments to American life.[3] The German newspapers, for example, brought a daily or weekly visit from someone speaking the native language, but they also told the newcomer of the way American society worked, the strange political practices that had to be dealt with, and the economic opportunities that were available. Most German organizations embodied in various proportions these dual functions of cultural preservation and social adaptation. The political clubs, of course, were directly aimed at mastering the intricacies of American politics; the singing societies, at the other end of the spectrum, clearly offered a comforting refuge where old-country tradition held sway.

In the last decade of the nineteenth century, the flow of immigrants from Germany decreased sharply, never to return to the level of the peak years of the 1850s and the 1880s. The effect upon the German institutional structure was fairly immediate, and the leadership in various sections of German America began to

complain of the lack of support, especially from the second and third generations. Those institutions, which managed to survive until World War I did so with
increasing effort, and often with fervent appeals to German cultural pride and
ethnic solidarity. Disillusioning as the experience was for the caretakers of German ethnic institutions, it also showed that persons of German ethnic descent
were not, on the whole, slower than other immigrants to adapt to American life.[4]

The story of the cultural assimilation of German Americans, then, is actually
many, separate stories pertaining to various groups that entered the country
through the course of American history. Understanding those stories involves
consideration of the changes in the flow of migration, and also of the rise and
decline of various institutional structures, some of which served several waves of
migration. German ethnicity as it was experienced at any one time really was
connected to two traditions: the German American one derived from previous
generations in America, and the German one, continuously renewed by the most
recent immigrants. Thus, this ethnicity continued to develop and change and
showed considerable diversity within it at any given time.

Colonial times gave America its first examples of German America, a term
scarcely used before 1850. Beginning with the settlements in eastern Pennsylvania in the 1680s, German communities began to appear in the interior of Pennsylvania and southwestward along the backcountry of Maryland, Virginia, and
the Carolinas. These communities had characteristics of insularity and cultural
durability that would not always prevail in later German settlements. Most were
in rural areas receiving the first influx of white Europeans. The Germans could
occupy such places exclusively and have a free hand in determining the cultural
framework. The churches dominated the communities, and there was little need
for voluntary organizations—such as those that later German immigrants established—which were designed to shelter German culture within a society dominated by other groups.[5] Those Pennsylvania German communities dominated by
the pietistic sects could enforce cultural separatism as a part of religious doctrine.
But these examples, which developed into cultural islands and in some cases endured to become tourist attractions in the twentieth century, were not typical
even of the Pennsylvania Germans as a whole. The more numerous Lutheran
and Reformed groups might cling to their particular dialect—itself so modified
by American influences as to be nearly incomprehensible to native German
speakers—but they were rapidly Americanized in other ways. They were drawn
into American politics, into the economic system within which they functioned,
and into the frontier process, as many descendants of the Pennsylvania Germans
migrated westward and mixed with other populations in the newer communities
being formed in these new settlements. In Pennsylvania German regions outside
the original Pennsylvania heartland, the use of the German language was fading
fast by the 1820s.[6]

By the mid-nineteenth century, Pennsylvania Germans, although still clearly
possessing a distinct regional American culture, did not identify with the newer
German immigrants and their desire to re-create German ways in America. The

Pennsylvania Germans considered themselves Americans, and their ethnicity after over a century was more an outgrowth of their American experience than of their ancestral German origin.[7] Even in the colonial period, Germans found their way into heterogeneous urban areas such as Philadelphia, Baltimore, and Lancaster. Urban Germans often found their place within the economy as skilled craftsmen, tradesmen, and storekeepers, and these services within the urban context facilitated their integration into American society even more rapidly than might happen in rural areas.[8]

German immigration fell off in the years before the American Revolution and remained at a low ebb until the end of the Napoleonic Wars in Europe.[9] Thus, a period of nearly half a century separated the colonial German migration from the first major wave of Germans to enter the new republic. The German newcomers of the 1820s and 1830s were vastly more diverse than the colonial migrants had been. The economic opportunities they pursued, whether urban or agricultural, were largely in regions other than those where the colonial Germans had settled. Only a small number of nineteenth-century Germans settled in the Pennsylvania German region. Thus, the new German migration established its communities and institutions in newer areas of the United States. Those who sought homes on the developing agricultural frontier found themselves in communities much less isolated and homogeneous than did the German farmers of colonial days. Their farms depended on a widening network of transportation and communication that connected them with a national economy. The American environment and marketplace provided strong pressures for Germans to adapt to the agricultural practices of America. Although some old customs might prevail in their practices, the Germans adapted to American ways in the major aspects of farming, abandoning European farm-village models of settlement and adopting the crops that the marketplace demanded. After two or three generations on the land, the German-descended farmers exhibited few differences in their practices from their neighbors of other backgrounds.[10]

The nineteenth-century immigrants found their way to American cities more frequently than had their colonial predecessors. By 1850, 27 percent of the German born were found in urban places, a proportion larger than Germans were in the total American population.[11] Their urban character reflected the effects of the commercial and industrial revolutions taking place in Germany: the migrants included both artisans replaced by factory production and workers who had had experience in the factories of Europe. American cities, especially the newer ones just taking root in the West, offered opportunities at different levels of the socioeconomic ladder that Germans were able to fill, and many could use their place in the American social structure as stepping-stones to greater social mobility. A greater number of German workers could be categorized as artisans or skilled craftsmen than was true of the Irish, the other largest immigrant group of the time. In 1850, 63.6 percent of the German workers in Philadelphia were skilled workers; in Milwaukee, 51 percent were classified as skilled; in New York, 60.7 percent. By 1860, Germans held over 58 percent of the skilled craftsmen's jobs in Milwaukee.[12] The Germans in many cities came to dominate certain trades and crafts that served the entire population and so were not limited merely to the German community. Other Americans came to depend on the Germans as tailors, shoemakers, pharmacists, furniture makers, tobacconists, bakers, and, of course, brewers. While ethnic solidarity sometimes reinforced certain German sectors of the economy, these strengths also worked to integrate them into the larger American economy and speeded their adaptation to the American business system.[13]

The nineteenth-century migration created societies in some midwestern cities that seemed to outsiders heavily dominated by German culture—first Cincinnati, then St. Louis, later Milwaukee. But although cities like these boasted some well-known and highly visible German districts as centers of German ethnicity, the dynamic growth of such cities usually promoted both geographic and social mobility for individual Germans. No one core German district could contain all of the newcomers, and inevitably there was some process of moving outward into other areas of the city, as well as movement to other cities and rural areas.[14] Stability of the German population was not a feature of any of the great urban centers of German America, and changes of status and location tended to speed the process of integration into American life.[15]

The growing, highly mobile, diverse, and sometimes turbulent German-born population of the mid-nineteenth century laid the basis of institutional German America as it would emerge at its zenith just before the end of the century. This was an essentially new organizational structure; only in a few coastal cities did institutions of the 1700s overlap with those of the post-1815 era. These organizations for the most part served the needs of a German ethnicity seeking to preserve some aspects of its culture while surrounded by other, dominant cultures. It was an elaborate and complex organizational structure, in part because it had to cope with the complexities of American life, and in part because it had to serve many specific and often conflicting subgroups within German America.

Americans perceived a monolithic German America turned in upon itself, but the reality was a very fragmented German America. The churches were still the central social institutions for many Germans, yet they were divided among Catholic and many Protestant sects and included as well a small but influential Jewish element. Obviously, no one faith could serve to unite Germans, and religious conflict often hindered efforts to rally them to ethnic solidarity. There were also increasing numbers of immigrants with no church affiliation, especially when liberal and radical refugees fled after the failure of the revolutions of 1830 and 1848. The mutual suspicions between religious and free-thinking Germans helped to multiply the separate institutions.

In the larger cities and in the smaller communities as well, growth in the numbers of German immigrants fostered the development of societies and institutions that served specific subgroups of German America. Between 1830 and 1850, there were at least fifty-six different mutual-aid societies among the German population of Philadelphia, and the number continued to grow thereafter.[16] The constituency of each of these might be defined by religious affiliation, regional origin, occupational group, or ideological inclination. The same kind of subdivision might be found among the proliferating singing societies so dear to the Germans. In the relatively small German community of San Francisco, thirty of these were founded between 1851 and 1890.[17] The Turner societies, founded originally for purposes of maintaining the physical culture through gymnastics and for intellectual development by refugees from the failed revolution of 1848, began as institutions of the liberal nationalist Germans, but other elements fostered competing social and athletic organizations.[18] Lodges, literary societies, dramatic groups, shooting societies, labor unions, militia companies, bands—the list was endless, but most of these groups catered to a specific subgroup of German Americans rather than to the whole. The burgeoning German press, which expanded from seventy newspapers in 1848 to 144 in 1860 and 546 by 1880, reflected the increasing diversity of German Americans in matters of politics, ideology, culture, and religion.[19]

Did these complex institutional structures hold Germans apart from American society by providing them with a separate cultural world? Or did they merely provide the Germans with a variety of instruments with which to deal with American life and thereby speed their integration into it? One can cite forces working in both directions, and obviously there were many motivations among the people who participated in these organizations. On the one hand, the elaborate institutional framework could be used to formulate some broad sense of common German identity to replace the narrower loyalties that many Germans had brought with them. Many German leaders arriving after the 1848 revolutions did strive to develop this broader sense of German ethnicity. Such a purpose was vital to the German-language press, which had to forsake separate regional dialects for one common German language.[20] In the face of hostile anti-German pressures, there was an effort to define German ethnicity as a culture worth preserving and capable of making its own contribution to American life. Considerable debate went on among German leaders, beginning in the 1840s, about the value of maintaining a separate culture, but the argument generally moved toward what in the twentieth century would be called a theory of pluralism: American society did not have to insist on some necessary homogeneity of culture, but could accept a diversity of cultural groups, all of which could contribute to American life.[21]

On the other hand, these ideals of cultural retention set forth by German American leaders were not always those pursued by many of the rank and file. They might be more interested in narrower goals that held in place the fragmented structures of German America. The chronic disunity of German America, based on religion, provincial origin, class, and ideology, did not of itself hasten integration into American life, but it did weaken efforts to rally behind one cultural standard upon which to base ethnic solidarity, and the separate goals of the myriad German institutions often had more to do with adaptation to American life than with cultural preservation. Mutual-aid societies and building-and-loan associations helped to provide security and upward mobility within the American economic framework. Labor organizations grappled in various ways with the American industrial structure. Literary and discussion groups dealt with American social and political problems as frequently as with German philosophical ones. The German-language newspapers, dependent like all American newspapers on political-party support for operating expenses, pursued no other goal as consistently as that of indoctrinating immigrants in the ways of American politics and integrating them into the political system. The fact that institutions like these dealt with German immigrants in a familiar language and by means separate from those that served other Americans was secondary to the basic function of adaptation that most of them served.

During the period of remarkable German population growth just before the Civil War, no force drew the new immigrants into American life more strongly than the turbulent politics of the period. In the late 1820s and early 1830s, a pattern of German political loyalty had been set when the new Jacksonian party enlisted them as an element in the country's first mass-political organization. That loyalty was usually easily maintained, since the party opposed to Jackson and his successors, the Whig party, often seemed nativistic and hostile to the immigrants. Jacksonian Democratic politicians, especially in the urban Northeast, habitually paid their respects to the German voters, but the predictability of the overwhelmingly Democratic German vote sometimes made these appeals a perfunctory ritual. All of this changed, however, in the early 1850s. During the general breakup of the old party system in those years, the German vote became more divided, and in many western states the Germans appeared to be a critical element hanging in the political balance. The new Free-Soil Republican party appealed to their interests, but the Germans were often torn in their party loyalties over issues such as slavery, nativism, and temperance. Nevertheless, these vital issues of the time and the constant appeals of competing politicians involved the Germans inexorably in the workings of politics at one of the most critical periods of American political development. The new element of German leaders that had entered the country after the revolutions of 1848 played a role in these political changes as well. Once they had abandoned hope of a revival of the European revolutions, they applied their liberal principles to the problems of American politics. A majority of the "Forty-Eighters" aligned themselves with the anti-slavery cause and the new Republican party. The historical accidents of the time took German leaders and many of their followers beyond German American interests to involvement in crucial matters affecting all of American society.

The 1850s were, however, also a period when Germans were called on to defend their own way of life against social and political attack. The largest wave of immigration so far in American history produced a strong nativist reaction, which culminated in the formation of a party with an openly nativist platform, the American, or Know-Nothing, party. Germans regarded other reform movements of the time, especially the temperance crusade and the agitation for strict enforcement of Sunday laws, as part and parcel of the nativist assault. Taken together, these appeared to be attacks on their traditional way of life and attempts to subordinate the ethnic culture to a more narrowly defined American culture imposed by Anglo-Saxon Protestant standards. The German response had to rest on something more than their traditional liking for beer, music, and Sunday conviviality. They cast their defense in terms of the freedom promised by American ideals to all individuals; the sumptuary laws advocated by temperance reformers, German leaders said, were reflections of outmoded social systems that did not recognize individual rights. In arguing for such rights, which were essentially the rights of individuals to pursue their own cultural traditions, the German spokesmen were contributing to the new theory of a pluralistic society in which all played a role in the society but were able to retain their own cultural ways and in which republicanism was not rooted in one culture but in many. The natural conclusion of this, of course, was that new peoples could be integrated into American life even while preserving some of their own traditions and some of their separate social structures.

The Civil War was a period of considerable change in German ethnic life, as well as in American life generally. The flow of immigration into the country was greatly reduced, and the great numbers who had arrived in the 1850s were forced to deal with the upheavals caused by the country's greatest crisis. For many young men, service in the army, whether Union or Confederate, was an experience that drew them forcibly from ethnic concerns and immersed them in a common American cause. While there were German regiments, the great majority of the 200,000 German immigrants in the Union army served in the regular military units, side by side with other American soldiers.[22] Many German-born soldiers returned to American environments far different from the ethnic communities they had left. And for those who stayed home, the war's call to a common purpose, entreaties to patriotic duty for the American nation, and demands on both the agricultural and industrial economies to produce for the needs of the country served as strong integrating factors. The contribution of the Germans also tended to discredit the nativists' attacks on them that had been heard frequently in the prewar years. Germans could point to their service in the Civil War as proof that they deserved a place in American society.

The post–Civil War period thus found many of the prewar immigrants in new places in American life that they had not imagined or anticipated being in. This increasing geographical and social mobility of the German population was augmented by the arrival of a new influx of migrants. From 1877 to 1887 a major wave of German migration to the United States occurred; the peak year, 1881, with a quarter of a million arrivals from Germany, was the greatest year of German migration in all of American history. As always, the influx of newcomers would serve to extend German America and to inject new life into its social and cultural institutions. It was still possible for the new German immigrants to start new and relatively isolated communities of their own. Many of these were on the Great Plains, where the railroads were opening up new lands, encouraging immigrants to come and colonize new towns. Some such communities (including many settled by Russian Germans) were centered on immigrants of a particular religious group, with the church serving as the center of community life. The elements were present in such communities to create isolated German "language islands," where the inhabitants could persist in their traditional ways for a long time.[23] But even in such relatively ideal conditions there were influences working the other way. The railroads that made these communities possible also were the necessary link to the national economy, offering markets for agricultural products and a supply line for the necessities of life. Groups with little background in politics were inevitably drawn into it, whether to exercise control over their local governments, to protect their way of life from cultural attack, or to combat the hardships that economic forces might place on them. And there was always the question of the second and third generation, which as in all of the rural communities of the time might be impelled to leave in order to pursue their livelihoods in other, more cosmopolitan regions, whether rural or urban.

Migrants to new rural areas, however, were a decreasing proportion of the last great wave of German immigration. These were years of vast industrial development in America and a majority of German newcomers found themselves in the cities, where industrial employment was more frequently their lot. The character of German migrants was changing somewhat; an increasing number came from the eastern parts of Germany, and fewer of them were from the skilled-worker class. Even Germans who possessed skills frequently found less employment for them, especially when factory mass production had made these skills obsolete.[24] The result of all this was that the great urban concentrations of Germans had a growing working-class element, particularly among the recently immigrated, whose lives would of necessity be dictated by concerns of industrial occupation, the workplace, and class status. Though many might still treasure the old, ethnic traditions, these could only be cultivated in a limited, part-time way.

In the last two decades of the nineteenth century, the phenomenon of German America could be seen at its peak in the great urban centers of German concentration. Particularly impressive was the number and scope of its organizations and institutions. The numbers of these—mutual-aid societies, social groups, musical organizations, political clubs, labor organizations—multiplied rapidly and generally reached a peak in the early 1890s. But this organizational complexity did not always reflect a structure that was oriented either toward German solidarity or toward slowing their integration into American life. For one thing, the great diversity of organizations heightened the possibility of splintering of the German groups, because individuals had more opportunities to seek out their own particular type of German. "Wherever there are four Germans, there will be five opinions," was the complaint common to many German ethnic leaders.[25]

It is also true that many of these institutions served more to educate the immigrants in American ways than they did to maintain a separate German culture. Institutions with the overt aim of preserving German culture, such as language schools and theater societies, were not usually the ones with the widest support from the rank-and-file German Americans.[26] While organizations devoted to recreation, economic security, religious devotion, occupational advancement, and civic affairs might well have their roots in a separate German ethnic community, many such organizations that survived into the first half of the twentieth century eventually evolved beyond that community and became part of a more general, integrated society, just as individual German Americans and their descendants moved into the broader community.

Some of the growth of institutional German America was related to the dispersal of its population, especially within the urban centers. The previously existing German centers in the older cities could not contain the growing population of German Americans. New German neighborhoods inevitably began to develop in outlying sections of the city, and upwardly mobile Germans found their way into newer sections of the city that were not always as ethnically homogeneous as the neighborhoods they had left. Even a city like Detroit, which more than some other cities retained a pattern of neighborhoods that each had a distinct ethnic character, the German districts in the early decades of the 1900s were losing their tightly knit character as second- and third-generation Germans moved on into other, less-concentrated neighborhoods.[27]

There is no one model pattern of the dissolving and integration of the German ethnic communities in the American urban context. They differ because of many factors: the age of the city, the character of its commerce and industry, the nature of the geography, the quality and ease of use of public transportation, and the varieties of other ethnic groups that might be present in the same environment, to name a few. But it is clear that the dynamics of the rapidly changing American city and the very fluid and mobile nature of the German Americans within them were working in the long run against the maintenance of the homogeneous German neighborhood.[28] By the early part of the twentieth century, the normal, everyday experience for the first- or second-generation German immigrant in the city was not in the very close-knit German district but in a more cosmopolitan urban environment. While some could still live, work, and achieve success within a German environment, perhaps never even having to speak English,[29] by far the greater number had to spend most of their lives outside the German cultural enclave.

The peak of German institutional life in the 1890s also reflected the demography created by the particular history of the German immigration. In the 1890s, most of the immigrants of the two great waves of the 1850s and the 1880s were still alive. This gave the German organizations, businesses, and newspapers an unusually high number of clients. But death would begin to remove the pre–Civil War immigrants at a more rapid rate by the beginning of the twentieth century, and many organizations began to experience a decline in membership. The German newspapers in the United States numbered nearly 800 about 1893; by 1900, the number was down to 613 and, by 1910, to 554. In Milwaukee, daily German-language newspapers circulated 92,000 copies in the mid-1880s; by 1910 they circulated about 45,000.[30] Figures like these were reinforced by the frequent complaints of German leaders that the second generation was indifferent to the old cultural traditions. It was clearly the first generation that was the great force that held German America together; when fewer newcomers came after 1885 and the older generation began to pass from the scene, the separate ethnic community began to yield rather rapidly to the wider society.

Some of the same demographic changes were reflected in the nature of the leadership of the Germans as a group. The dynamic element of the Forty-Eighters was, after 1890, quickly passing from the scene. A new element of leadership came out of the post–Civil War generation of immigrants. They were less frequently idealists with specific ideological goals like those of some of the pre–Civil War generation. Rather, they were more frequently influenced by a German nationalism stemming from the creation of a unified German state under Prussian rule in 1871. The events of German unification did have their effects on German Americans, and the emergence of a great modern, unified nation served as a point of pride for Germans who had themselves never lived in a united Germany. Even many of the old Forty-Eighters abandoned their traditional hostility to the Prussian monarchy and joined in the celebration of a united German state.[31] Unification also made it possible to assert a common German culture and to appeal to Germans of different origins to associate themselves with that common German culture. This concept of a common cultural heritage and a common great nation of origin became a useful instrument for ethnic leaders as they forged an aggressive defense for institutional German America when it passed its peak and began a steady decline.

In the last two decades of the nineteenth century, there thus developed the anomaly of the emergence of a strong defensive mentality in organized German America, at a time when its institutional structure seemed to be at its strongest. The reasons for this anomaly came both from outside and from within German America. From American society in the 1880s and 1890s there emerged one of the country's periodic upsurges of antiforeign sentiment; although it was directed more toward the newer waves of eastern and southern European immigrants, it had its implications for all groups who were not deemed fully assimilated.[32] The rising demand for adherence to Anglo-American cultural standards also seemed to be an assault on German cultural pride. This was reflected in efforts to forbid the use of German (or any language other than English) in school instruction and in the renewed drives of temperance and prohibition reformers. German leaders who sounded the cry to rally around the standards of German pride and to unite in support of institutional German America were, however, also aware that the German American social structure needed defense against deterioration from within. Only a minority of second-generation German Americans retained the language or continued their association with German organizations. With the rapidly declining numbers of first-generation German Americans, the leadership increasingly directed a campaign toward the younger generations, in an effort to keep them within the cultural community. While some doubtless did maintain their ties to German America, there were not enough of them in the long run to maintain the vast institutional structure at the level at which it had existed in the early 1890s.

The efforts to revive and maintain the German language and ethnic culture, and to keep them as rallying points to secure the loyalties of German Americans, involved a leadership that to a great extent was closely tied to that institutional structure. Editors of German-language newspaper, leaders of German singing societies, businessmen who catered to the ethnic community, and a variety of types who might loosely be called professional German Americans mounted vigorous appeals to defend German ethnicity. While their defenses seemed addressed to those outside the ethnic community, in an effort to persuade other Americans of the cultural benefits that German American brought to American society, their principal concern was more often with those German Americans, especially of the second generation, who seemed to be on the margins of ethnic life and drifting farther away from it. The many German Americans who had moved from the core ethnic neighborhoods and remained in touch with only one or two German societies or institutions were the ones who perhaps aroused most concern. It was now not uncommon to find social societies, sporting clubs, and churches that no longer used the German language in their functions and in whose membership increasingly did not speak or understand German. Some Turner societies, for example, started an emotional debate in the early 1890s over whether the commands for their gymnastic exercises might be given in English. Many German Protestant congregations about the same time entered stages of critical debate over what role, if any, the German language should play in their services.[33]

Language preservation was, however, one of the rallying points that German leaders found useful in awakening the sensitivities of the group and making its influence felt in politics. In the late 1880s and early 1890s, various public debates arose over whether to require that compulsory education be conducted only in English. Such proposals threatened public and parochial schools in both rural and urban areas of the Midwest, where instruction in all subjects was carried on mainly in German. In 1890, efforts in Illinois and Wisconsin to forbid non-English instruction brought a major reaction against the Republicans who advocated the idea; the resulting upheaval in political alignments had repercussions far beyond those states and even played a role in the Democrats regaining control of Congress in the 1890 elections.[34] While such attacks could be used to rally Germans to fend off hostility against them, it was another matter to persuade Germans to get their children into voluntary German-language classes, and increasingly the younger generation's acquaintance with the language weakened.[35]

By the turn of the century the German defenses were focused more on the threat of the temperance movement, whose efforts in favor of liquor-prohibition laws had been increasing in the preceding two decades. Ever since the temperance crusades of the 1850s, the Germans had been sensitive on the point of liquor restriction. The drinking of beer had always been an important part of their traditional culture, which had very often used the tavern and the beer garden as central institutions of the ethnic community. The German traditions of sociability—gathering to eat and drink, with noisy singing and dancing, and exuberant public celebration on Sundays—were just the kinds of things that clashed with old-fashioned Yankee Protestant cultural values. This liking for spirited public celebration was in the long run probably a means by which German Americans brought a change in the American culture in general. At the turn of the century, however, German *Gemütlichkeit* (congeniality) and its free-flowing use of beer became one of the objects of native-born temperance reformers. The German response was encouraged by the brewing industry, which had developed in the previous half-century as an almost exclusively German enterprise and which had close ties with the German ethnic community. Beer played a vital role in the meetings and festivals of countless German organizations, and both the brewers and the German organizations stood to be drastically affected by liquor regulation or prohibition laws.[36]

The principal effort to achieve some unified organization nationally for German America came to fruition in 1901 and was strongly influenced in subsequent years by controversies over prohibition. The National German-American Alliance eventually claimed to include over 2 million members, but most of these were scarcely aware that they were members. The actual structure was that of a federation of many German societies, and the Alliance claimed that all members of these constituent groups were its members. But the policies of the Alliance were made by the leaders of German organizational life, and much of the financing of its activities came from the brewing industry.[37] While many in German America might endorse the struggle of the Alliance against prohibitionists, the Alliance did rather little otherwise to strengthen or enhance the cultural world of German America. While beer was one of the few points of unity among nearly all German Americans, concentration on that issue only served to conceal the great diversity and conflict that still divided the German ethnic group in many other ways.[38]

The slow but accelerating dwindling of institutional German America, and with it the increasing movement of many German Americans into the larger social structures of American society, was well under way long before the guns of August 1914 sounded the opening of the World War I and thereby created further strain on the ethnic bonds of Germans in America. The natural course for many Americans of German descent in the early years of the war, when the United States was not a participant, was simply to hope for and advocate the country's continuing neutrality. There seemed little possibility that the United States as a country would aid Germany, and the practical ways in which individuals might lend support to Germany were very limited. For some German American leaders and newspaper editors, however, especially those active in the National German-American Alliance, the support of German culture in America became identified with support of Germany's position in the European conflict. It did not seem unreasonable to them to defend the "German side" when America was officially neutral and others within American society praised the

French and English war efforts while denouncing Imperial Germany as barbaric and militaristic. The statements of German American newspaper editors and speakers who sought to defend German positions in such controversies would of course come back to haunt them in 1917 when America was drawn into the war against Germany. Nor did it help that German government agents had sought to provide propaganda and to otherwise assist the National Alliance in its efforts to defend German views.[39]

The inevitable reaction of American public opinion against German America in 1917 and 1918 provides one of the prime examples in American history of an assault on a single ethnic group during a period in which emotions were heated by war. The details of that assault do not need retelling here. They included, among other things, censorship and the closing down of newspapers, prohibitions and restrictions on the use of the German language, violent intimidation of individuals, the hounding of institutions and businesses with "German" in their names, and the denigration of any cultural practice that suggested German origin. By the end of the war, the National German-American Alliance had been dissolved under pressure from Congress, and the number of German-language newspapers and social institutions had been drastically reduced.

Clearly, the events of the war struck a blow at the institutional structures of the German Americans. However, one should not overstate the war's influence in forcing many Germans out of their ethnic communities and into the mainstream of American life. The ties of many German-stock people to their ethnic traditions were already tenuous; the heated emotions and the public controversy over symbols of loyalty may have simply served to cut the last few ties. Many nominal German Americans may have simply stopped referring to themselves as such, dropped a membership or two in German organizations, cancelled their subscriptions to a German newspaper, and felt relieved when the German Bank changed its name to something more innocuous. To quietly become "less German" in this fashion was of course following the line of least resistance, but for many marginal German Americans, it was probably not a matter of great pain or loss. Much of the effect of World War I on the vast and differentiated body of German America was simply to accelerate a process of merging into American life that was already well advanced.[40] No doubt, others abandoned their German traditions and practices with difficulty, and some sought to recover them after the end of the war. The census of 1920 records a decrease of over 25 percent in the number of German born in the United States. Such a decline hardly seems to be corroborated by migration and mortality statistics; in actuality, the numbers seem to be evidence that many German born were denying the place of their nativity to the census takers in 1920. There was a mild revival of German institutions and German newspaper circulation in the 1920s, which would seem to reflect that World War I suppressed some German ethnicity abnormally.[41] Before long, however, the decline of German America was continuing in the same inexorable fashion that had shown itself in the years before 1914. The 1930s showed an even sharper decline in German American life. The pressures came from several sources: the economic impact of the Great Depression on many weak and faltering institutions, the absence of any significant new immigration, and the rapid decline in the numbers of first-generation immigrants as those of the late-nineteenth century wave of immigration died off. It is very hard to put a date on the end of German America, but it is safe to say that by the time of America's entry into World War II, institutional German America was hardly a factor in the lives of the great majority of Americans who were of German background.

Despite their reputation among many other Americans for clannishness and isolation, the German Americans throughout their history were among those groups who had a relatively easy process of adaptation to American society and its ways. Some of the reasons for this lie in the particular nature of the group itself, and some in the particular history of its migration—a pattern of migration that was spread out and renewed over a period extending well beyond two centuries.

The vast majority of German Americans who came to America came with firm intentions of staying and beginning a new life. Relatively few of them came as sojourners. That means that most Germans came fully expecting to have to alter their lives and hoping to find a permanent place within a new social and economic system, whether by owning a farm, practicing a trade, or finding some other occupation within the context of American society. Some Germans as late as the 1830s may have held some hope for establishing an enclave of a "new Germany" somewhere in America, but by the time of the flood of migration of the 1840s and 1850s, that dream had dwindled and was never really revived. Pragmatically, most German immigrants recognized that they and their children would have to be a part of American society and accepted the changes that were implied by that.

The social composition of the German Americans during most of the periods of heavy migration meshed well with the makeup of American society in general and with its needs, especially during eras of American economic growth and territorial expansion. The Germans were not just a peasant people or a proletarian people, all concentrated at one particular social stratum or one particular point of entry into the American socioeconomic system. Rather, they included farmers able to buy land, farmhands waiting to obtain farms, industrial workers with previous experience in Europe, common laborers new to industry, skilled artisans, small businessmen, and a significant element of professionals, intellectuals, and persons of wealth. All of these different elements could make use of a variety of opportunities at various levels, when new agricultural regions were opened, when new towns were begun in the West, or when new industries arose. Because the ethnic community of German America itself, with its considerable complexity, very often included economic opportunities at many occupational and economic levels, it was possible for some to make a start within German America and then to move laterally into a comparable place in the American social structure.

German America, like American society in general, had its divisions of class and status, but it was often comparable to the American social structure in the predominance of middle-class values within it. The concerns of German Americans with stability, the family, the work ethic, self-discipline, and a striving for success and security for themselves and their children were compatible with the values that prevailed among many in mainstream America. In the long run, these cultural similarities far outweighed the cultural conflicts with some Americans over matters of drinking, language, and Sunday behavior. German Americans' problems of adaptation were considerably moderated by this similarity in values.[42]

At almost any particular point in its long history, German America might consist of people at many different stages of adaptation—those of the first generation, recently arrived and still considerably dependent on German American institutions; those who had been in the country for two or three decades; those of the second generation, most of them with no direct memories of Germany; and those of subsequent generations with various stages of ethnic awareness. At any one time, there was usually a wide continuum of people at various points in the transition from ethnic separation to full integration into American life. An individual could very often make a comfortable transition at his own pace from membership in a pervasive ethnic environment through more tenuous ties to specific organizations to perhaps a few lingering gestures toward German America. Kindred spirits could be found at any point along the way. It was seldom necessary to undergo the sudden shock of an irrevocable plunge from a warm, enveloping ethnic environment to the cold outside world of American society. German Americans usually had the luxury of being able to go home again to their previous culture; if nostalgia, guilt, or a longing for former stability overtook them, they could take a step backward and revisit the ethnicity they had once known. The impressive world of German America was so complex that it made possible an almost endless variety of structures and experiences for those within it. Except for those in small and isolated rural communities, the individual could make his own choice about participation in German societies and institutions, and seldom could any one institution demand the adherence of all who claimed to be German Americans. Thus individuals could create their own version of German America to suit themselves, and no one membership or institutional tie could be made the absolute standard of one's loyalty to the ethnic community. Those who wanted to use the structures of German America to retain the ethnic traditions and insulate themselves from the strange world of American life could do so. For those, on the other hand, who wished to use the institutions as instruments of transition in the process of adjustment to American life, the ethnic community seldom enforced strong demands that the process of adaptation be slowed.

The world of German America in its most prosperous and thriving times was a world of considerable movement and change for those within it. While some might cling to a church or neighborhood or singing society as a secure link to an older culture, most realized that their children and others would loosen those ties. New generations would pass through, while the old institutional structures might or might not remain. The frequent conflicts within the German community raged on over matters of religion, politics, class, and ideology; seldom, however, were there conflicts over loyalty to the German community, for the natural passage through it was taken for granted by many. The story of the latter half of the twentieth century was that of the final crumbling of most of the old institutions as the new migration that had made them possible dwindled to a trickle and the descendants of earlier migrations moved on into American life.

NOTES

1. James M. Bergquist, "Germans and the City," in *Germans in America: Retrospect and Prospect*, ed. Randall M. Miller (Philadelphia: Temple Univ. Press, 1984), 53–54.

2. Kathleen N. Conzen, "Patterns of German American History," in *Germans in America* (see note 1), 15–18.

3. James M. Bergquist, "German Communities in American Cities: An Interpretation of the Nineteenth-Century Experience," *Journal of American Ethnic History* 4 (1984): 16–17; Milton Gordon, *Assimilation in American Life* (New York: Oxford Univ. Press, 1964), 105–114.

4. The principal argument for a German America that was slow to adapt to the mainstream is John A. Hawgood, *The Tragedy of German-America: The Germans in the United States of America during the Nineteenth Century—and After* (New York: G.P. Putnam's Sons, 1940).

5. Aaron Fogleman, *Hopeful Journeys: German Immigration, Settlement, and Political Culture in Colonial America, 1717–1775* (Philadelphia: Univ. of Pennsylvania Press, 1996), 69–99; Marianne S. Wokeck, *Trade in Strangers: The Beginnings of Mass Migration to North America* (University Park: Pennsylvania State Univ. Press, 1999), 37–58; A.G. Roeber, *Palatines, Liberty and Property: German Lutherans in Colonial America* (Baltimore: Johns Hopkins Univ. Press, 1993), 135–174.

6. Heinz Kloss, "German-American Language Maintenance Efforts," in *Language Loyalty in the United States*, ed. Joshua R. Fishman et al. (The Hague: Mouton, 1966), 215–222.

7. For a stimulating discussion of Pennsylvania German ethnicity, see Don Yoder, "The Pennsylvania Germans: Three Centuries of Identity Crisis," in *America and the Germans: An Assessment of a Three-Hundred Year History*, ed. Frank Trommler and Joseph McVeigh (Philadelphia: Univ. of Pennsylvania Press, 1985), 1:41–65. For a general discussion of their development as a group, see William Parsons, *The Pennsylvania Dutch: A Persistent Minority* (New York: Macmillan, 1950).

8. Stephanie G. Wolf, *Urban Village: Population, Community and Family Structure in Germantown, Pennsylvania, 1683–1800* (Princeton: Princeton Univ. Press, 1976), 127–153; Wolf, "Hyphenated America: the Creation of an Eighteenth-Century German-American Culture," in *America and the Germans* (see note 7), 1:66–84.

9. For detailed discussion of the immigration of the period, see Hans-Jürgen Grabbe, *Vor der grossen Flut: Die Europäische Migration in die Vereinigten Staaten von Amerika, 1783–1820* (Stuttgart: Steiger, 2001).

10. For a thorough study of one example of German agricultural adaptation, see Terry B. Jordan, *German Seed in Texas Soil: Immigrant Farmers in Nineteenth-Century Texas* (Austin: Univ. of Texas Press, 1966), especially 192–203. See also A.J. Petersen, "The

German-Russian Settlement Pattern in Ellis County, Kansas," *Rocky Mountain Social Science Journal* 5 (1968): 52–67; and Walter D. Kamphoefner, *The Westfalians: From Germany to Missouri* (Princeton, NJ: Princeton Univ. Press, 1987), 122–134.

11. John G. Gazley, *American Opinion of German Unification, 1848–1871* (New York: Columbia Univ. Press, 1926), 428; Conzen, "Patterns of German-American History," 22–23.

12. Leslie Ann Kawaguchi, "The Making of Philadelphia's German-America: Ethnic Groups and Community Development, 1830–1883" (PhD diss., Univ. of California at Los Angeles, 1983), 155–156; Kathleen N. Conzen, *Immigrant Milwaukee, 1830–1860: Accommodation and Community in a Frontier City* (Cambridge, MA: Harvard Univ. Press, 1976), 65–74; Stanley Nadel, *Little Germany: Ethnicity, Religion and Class in New York City, 1845–80* (Urbana: Univ. of Illinois Press, 1990), 171.

13. George H. Kellner, "The German Element on the Urban Frontier: St. Louis, 1830–1860" (PhD diss., Univ. of Missouri, 1973), 275–290; Nadel, *Little Germany*, 62–87; David Gerber, *The Making of an American Pluralism: Buffalo, New York, 1825–1860* (Urbana: Univ. of Illinois Press, 1989), 176–181; Laurence A. Glasco, "Ethnicity and Social Structure: Irish, Germans and Native-born of Buffalo, New York, 1850–1860" (PhD diss., Univ. of Rochester, 1973), 84–96; Nora Faires, "Ethnicity in Evolution: The German Community in Pittsburgh and Allegheny City, Pennsylvania, 1845–1885" (PhD diss., Univ. of Pittsburgh, 1981), 219–220. For general discussion, see Nora Faires, "Occupational Patterns of German-Americans in Nineteenth Century Cities," in *German Workers in Industrial Chicago, 1850–1910: A Comparative Perspective*, ed. Hartmut Keil and John B. Jentz, 37–51 (De Kalb: Northern Illinois Univ. Press, 1983).

14. Audrey V. Olson, *St. Louis Germans, 1850–1920* (New York: Arno Press, 1980), 248–249; Joseph M. White, "Religion and Community: Cincinnati Germans, 1814–1870" (PhD diss., Univ. of Notre Dame, 1980), 17–31; Conzen, *Immigrant Milwaukee*, 131–136; Kellner, "German Element on the Urban Frontier," 118–145. White points out (p. 29) that even in heavily German Cincinnati the Germans were not more than half the population in any single ward in the city in 1840.

15. Jay Dolan, studying a sample of German Catholics in New York City, found that 58 percent of those present in 1850 had left the city by 1869. Dolan, *The Immigrant Church: New York's Irish and German Catholics, 1815–1865* (Baltimore: Johns Hopkins Univ. Press, 1975).

16. Kawaguchi, "The Making of Philadelphia's German-America," 257.

17. Irving Bobow, "The Singing Societies of European Immigrant Groups in San Francisco: 1851–1953," *Journal of the History of the Behavioral Sciences* 5 (1969): 16–18. See also Mary Jane Corry, "The Role of German Singing Societies in Nineteenth-Century America," in *Germans in America: Aspects of German-American Relations in the Nineteenth Century*, ed. E. Allen McCormick, 155–168 (New York: Columbia Univ. Press, 1983).

18. Augustus J. Prahl, "History of the German Gymnastic Movement of Baltimore," Society for the History of Germans in Maryland, *Twenty-Sixth Report* (Baltimore: Society for the History of Germans in Maryland, 1945), 16–29; Guido Dobbert, "Disintegration of an Immigrant Community: The Cincinnati Germans, 1870–1920," (PhD thesis, Univ. Of Chicago, 1965), 16–29.

19. James M. Bergquist, "The German-American Press," in *The Ethnic Press in the United States: A Historical Analysis and Handbook*, ed. Sally M. Miller, 136, 142 (Westport, CT: Greenwood Press, 1987). The figures are for newspapers only and exclude magazines and other special-interest publications.

20. Kawaguchi, "The Making of Philadelphia's German-America," 248–296, 404–406.

21. The evolution of a broader concept of German ethnicity in America is described in detail in a ground-breaking essay by Kathleen N. Conzen, "German-Americans and the Invention of Ethnicity," in *America and the Germans* (see note 7), 1:131–147.

22. William L. Barton, *Melting Pot Soldiers: The Union's Ethnic Regiments* (Ames: Iowa State Univ. Press, 1988), 110.

23. LaVern J. Rippley, "German Assimilation: The Effect of the 1871 Victory on Americana-Germanica," in *Germany and America: Essays on Problems of International Relations and Immigration*, ed. Hans L. Trefousse, 121–128 (New York: Columbia Univ. Press, 1980).

24. Hartmut Keil, "Chicago's German Working Class in 1900," in *German Workers in Industrial Chicago*, ed. Keil and Jentz, 21–29; Mack Walker, *Germany and the Emigration, 1816–1885* (Cambridge, MA: Harvard Univ. Press, 1964), 181–194; Nadel, *Little Germany*, 66–74.

25. Guido Dobbert, "German-Americans between Old and New Fatherland, 1870–1914," *American Quarterly* 19 (1967): 665–666, quoting *Deutsche Pionier* 11 (June 1879): 140.

26. Olson, *St. Louis Germans*, 133–168.

27. Olivier Zunz, *The Changing Face of Inequality: Urbanization, Industrial Development, and Immigrants in Detroit, 1880–1920* (Chicago: Univ. of Chicago Press, 1982), 348–349.

28. For some review of the complex literature on ethnic dispersion, see Kathleen N. Conzen, "Immigrants, Immigrant Neighborhoods and Ethnic Identity: Historical Issues," *Journal of American History* 66 (1979), 603–615; Zunz, *The Changing Face of Inequality*, 40–60; and Alan N. Burstein, "Immigrants and Residential Mobility: The Irish and Germans in Philadelphia, 1850–1880," in *Philadelphia: Work, Space, Family and Group Experience in the Nineteenth Century*, ed. Theodore Hershberg, 174–203 (New York: Oxford Univ. Press, 1981). For other discussions of German population movement, see Dobbert, "Disintegration of an Immigrant Community," 37–42; Nadel, *Little Germany*, 29–46, 161–162; Gerd Korman, *Industrialization, Immigrants and Americanizers: The View from Milwaukee, 1866–1921* (Madison: State Historical Society of Wisconsin, 1967), 41–43.

29. Zunz's study of Detroit, *Changing Face of Inequality*, 186, found that 15 percent of the German-born there in 1900 did not speak English. Two thirds of these were women, who presumably could remain more consistently within the limits of the German neighborhood.

30. James M. Bergquist, "The German-American Press," 143; Carl F. Wittke, *The German Language Press in America* (Lexington: Univ. Press of Kentucky, 1957), 206–209. The decline of the German newspapers in the 1890s was also hastened by a major economic depression.

31. Dieter Cunz, *The Maryland Germans: A History* (Princeton, NJ: Princeton Univ. Press, 1948), 374–377; Dobbert, "Disintegration of an Immigrant Community," 148–156; Carl Wittke, *Against the Current: The Life of Karl Heinzen* (Chicago: Univ. of Chicago Press, 1945), 276–281.

32. John Higham, *Strangers in the Land: Patterns of American Nativism, 1860–1925* (New York: Atheneum, 1963), 35–105.

33. Bergquist, "German Communities in American Cities," 22–23.

34. Robert J. Ulrich, "The Bennett Law of 1889: Education and Politics in Wisconsin" (PhD diss., Univ. of Wisconsin, 1965); Richard Jensen, *The Winning of the Midwest: Social and Political Conflict, 1888–1890* (Chicago: Univ. of Chicago Press, 1971), 122–153; Paul J. Kleppner, *The Cross of Culture: A Social Analysis of Midwestern Politics, 1850–1900* (New York: Free Press, 1970), 158–178.

35. Kloss, "German-American Language Maintenance Efforts," 233–237; Ernest J. Becker, "History of the English-German Schools of Baltimore," Society for the History of the Germans in Maryland, *Twenty-fifth Report* (Baltimore, 1942), 13–17; Olson, "St. Louis Germans," 91–132.

36. William L. Downard, *The Cincinnati Brewing Industry: A Social and Economic History* (Athens: Ohio Univ. Press, 1973), 64–78.

37. LaVern J. Rippley, "Ameliorated Americanization: The Effect of World War I on German-Americans in the 1920s," in *America and the Germans* (see note 7), 2:220–221.

38. Clifton J. Child, *German-Americans in Politics, 1914–1917* (Madison: Univ. of Wisconsin Press, 1939); David W. Detjen, *The Germans in Missouri, 1900–1918: Prohibition, Neutrality, and Assimilation* (Columbia: Univ. of Missouri Press, 1985), 31–71.

39. Frederick C. Luebke, *Bonds of Loyalty: German Americans and World War I* (DeKalb: Northern Illinois Univ. Press, 1974).

40. Conzen, "Immigrants, Immigrant Neighborhoods and Ethnic Identity," 614.

41. Rippley, "Ameliorated Americanization," 223–229.

42. Frederick C. Luebke, "Images of German Immigrants in the United States and Brazil, 1890–1918: Some Comparisons," in *America and the Germans* (see note 7), 1:209–212.

BIBLIOGRAPHICAL ESSAY

Kathleen Neils Conzen's essay on Germans in Stephan Thernstrom et al., eds., *Harvard Encyclopedia of American Ethnic Groups* (Cambridge, MA: Harvard Univ. Press, 1980), 405–425, is a convenient starting point for an understanding of the German American experience. Comprehensive bibliographical coverage can be found in Henry A. Pochman, comp., *Bibliography of German Culture in the United States to 1940* (Madison: Univ. of Wisconsin Press, 1953), and Pochman's *German Culture in America: Philosophical and Literary Influence, 1600–1900* (Madison: Univ. of Wisconsin Press, 1957). These are supplemented by Arthur R. Schultz, *German-American Relations and German Culture in America: A Subject Bibliography, 1941–1980,* 2 vols. (Millwood, NY: Kraus International Publication, 1984). Two other useful bibliographies are Michael Keresztesi and Gary Cocozzoli, eds., *German-American History and Life: A Guide to Information Sources* (Detroit, MI: Gale Research Co., 1980); and Don Heinrich Tolzman, *German-Americans* (Metuchen, NJ: Scarecrow Press, 1975), which contains a discussion of major German-American archives. The pattern of German dispersion in the United States can be seen in Heinz Kloss, *Atlas of 19th and Early 20th Century German-American Settlement* (Marburg: Elwert, 1974).

General treatments of German American history include La Vern J. Rippley, *The German-Americans* (Boston: Twayne Publishers, 1976); Robert Henry Billigmeier, *Americans from Germany: A Study in Cultural Diversity* (Belmont, CA: Wadsworth Publishing Co., 1974); Richard O'Connor, *German-Americans: An Informal History* (Boston:

Little, Brown, 1968); and Theodore Huebener, *The Germans in America* (New York: Chilton Co., 1962). John A. Hawgood, *The Tragedy of German America* (New York: G. P. Putnam's Sons, 1940), stresses the events of mid-nineteenth century nativism and of World War I. For details, one can still consult the classic survey, Albert B. Faust's *The German Element in the United States*, 2 vols. (New York: Arno Press, 1927). Several compilations of essays cover the sweep of German American history: Frank Trommler and Joseph McVeigh, eds., *America and the Germans: An Assessment of a Three-Hundred Year History*, 2 vols. (Philadelphia: Univ. of Pennsylvania Press, 1985); Frank Trommler and Elliott Shore, eds., *The German-American Encounter: Conflict and Cooperation between Two Cultures, 1800–2000* (New York: Berghahn Books, 2001); Randall M. Miller, ed., *Germans in America: Retrospect and Prospect* (Philadelphia: The Society, 1984); and Frederick C. Luebke, *Germans in the New World: Essays in the History of Immigration* (Urbana: Univ. of Illinois Press, 1990).

The original German migrations to America entered mostly through Pennsylvania and moved down the back country through Maryland, Virginia, and the Carolinas. These colonial-era experiences are covered in Marianne Wokeck, *Trade in Strangers: The Beginnings of Mass Migration to North America* (University Park: Pennsylvania State Univ. Press, 1999); Aaron S. Fogleman, *Hopeful Journeys: German Immigration, Settlement and Political Culture in Colonial America, 1717–1775* (Philadelphia: Univ. of Pennsylvania Press, 1996); George Fenwick Jones, *The Georgia Dutch: From the Rhine and the Danube to the Savannah, 1733–1783* (Athens: Univ. of Georgia Press, 1992); Ralph Wood, ed., *The Pennsylvania Germans* (Princeton, NJ: Princeton Univ. Press, 1941); and William T. Parsons, *The Pennsylvania Dutch: A Persistent Minority* (Boston: Twayne, 1976), which follows the account into more recent times, as do Dieter Cunz, *The Maryland Germans: A History* (Princeton, NJ: Princeton Univ. Press, 1948), and Klaus Wust, *The Virginia Germans* (Charlottesville: Univ. of Virginia Press, 1969). Hartmut Lehmann et al., eds., *In Search of Peace and Prosperity: New German Settlements in Eighteenth-Century Europe and America* (University Park: Pennsylvania State Univ. Press, 2000) also discusses emigration from Germany. The early German community in Philadelphia is dealt with in Stephanie G. Wolf, *Urban Village: Population, Community and Family Structure in Germantown, Pennsylvania, 1683–1800* (Princeton, NJ: Princeton Univ. Press, 1976). Stephen M. Nolt, *Foreigners in their Own Land: Pennsylvania Germans in the New Republic* (University Park: Pennsylvania State Univ. Press, 2002) carries the story forward into the nineteenth century.

Mack Walker, *Germany and the Emigration, 1816–1885* (Boston: Harvard Univ. Press, 1964), deals with the pressures behind the flow of immigrants out of Germany. See also the discussion in Wolfgang Köllmann and Peter Marschalck, "German Emigration to the United States," *Perspectives in American History* 7 (1973), 499–554. Geographical patterns of German settlement are traced in Eberhard Reichman et al., *Emigration and Settlement Patterns of German Communities in North America* (Indianapolis, IN: Bobbs, Merrill, 1995). An excellent resource for the personal experiences of German immigrants is Walter D. Kamphoefner et al., eds., *News from the Land of Freedom: German Immigrants Write Home* (Ithaca, NY: Cornell Univ. Press, 1991). A useful collection of essays on nineteenth-century migration is Dirk Hoerder and Jörg Nagler, eds., *People in Transit: German Migrations in Comparative Perspective, 1820–1930* (Washington, DC: German Historical Institute, 1995). The nineteenth-century German experience in the United States can be seen through a variety of local studies. For generalizations about the urban experience see James M. Bergquist, "German Communities in American Cities: An Interpretation of the Nineteenth-Century Experience," *Journal of American Ethnic History* 4 (1981): 9–30; and Kathleeen N. Conzen, "Immigrants, Immigrant Neighborhoods and Ethnic Identity: Historical Issues," *Journal of American History* 66 (1979): 603–615. Studies of specific urban environments include: Kathleen Conzen, *Immigrant Milwaukee, 1830–1860: Accommodation and Community in a Frontier City* (Cambridge, MA: Harvard Univ. Press, 1976); John F. Nau, *The German People of New Orleans, 1850–1900* (Leiden, Netherlands: E. J. Brill, 1958); Robert Ernst, *Immigrant Life in New York City, 1825–1863* (New York: Octagon Books, 1949); David A. Gerber, *The Making of an American Pluralism: Buffalo, New York, 1825–1860* (Urbana: Univ. of Illinois Press, 1989); and Stanley Nadel, *Little Germany: Ethnicity, Religion and Class in New York City, 1845–80* (Urbana: Univ. of Illinois Press, 1990). Works carrying the story forward into the twentieth century include Guido Dobbert, *The Disintegration of an Immigrant Community: The Cincinnati Germans, 1870–1920* (New York: Arno Press, 1980); Audrey L. Olson, *The St. Louis Germans, 1850–1920* (New York: Arno Press, 1980); Robert T. McCaffrey, *Islands of Deutschtum: German-Americans in Manchester, New Hampshire, and Lawrence, Massachusetts, 1870–1942* (New York: P. Lang, 1996); Peter Connolly-Smith, *Translating America: An Ethnic Press and Popular Culture, 1890–1920* (Washington, DC: Smithsonian Books, 2004), about New York's Germans; and Russell A. Kazal, *Becoming Old Stock: The Paradox of German-American Identity* (Princeton, NJ: Princeton Univ. Press, 2004), about Philadelphia.

There are fewer regional and rural studies of German settlements. A model study of "chain migration" is Walter D. Kamphoefner, *The Westfalians: From Germany to Missouri* (Princeton, NJ: Princeton Univ. Press, 1987). Terry G. Jordan, *German Seed in Texas Soil: Immigrant Farmers in Nineteenth-Century Texas* (Austin: Univ. of Texas Press, 1966) deals with the changes in agricultural practice that took place in the process of migration. Other studies include Russell L. Gerlach, *Immigrants in the Ozarks: A Study in Ethnic Geography* (Columbia: Univ. of Missouri Press, 1976); Rudolph L. Biesele, *History of the German Settlements in Texas, 1831–1861* (Austin: Univ. of Texas Press, 1930); and Carol Coburn, *Life at Four Corners: Religion, Gender, and Education in a German-Lutheran Community, 1868–1945* (Lawrence: Univ. Press of Kansas, 1992).

Many works on nineteenth-century developments dwell on the German American involvement in political life. Much attention has been given to the "forty-eighters," who made their impact on the German communities in the 1850s and after. The classic monograph is Carl F. Wittke, *Refugees of Revolution: The German Forty-Eighters in America* (Philadelphia: Univ. of Pennsylvania Press, 1952). One useful collective work, Adolf E. Zucker, ed., *The Forty-Eighters: Political Refugees of the German Revolution of 1848* (New York: Columbia Univ. Press, 1950), includes a listing of the more prominent refugees. Another collection of essays is Charlotte F. Brancaforte, ed., *The German Forty-Eighters in the United States* (New York: P. Lang, 1989). On the 1850s, see Bruce Levine, *The Spirit of 1848: German Immigrants, Labor Conflict, and the Coming of the Civil War* (Urbana: Univ. of Illinois Press, 1992). The election of 1860 is the subject of Frederick Luebke, ed., *Ethnic Voters and the Election of Lincoln* (Lincoln: Univ. of Nebraska Press, 1971). The German military experience in the Civil War is dealt with in William L. Burton, *Melting Pot Soldiers: The Union's Ethnic Regiments* (Ames: Iowa State Univ. Press, 1988). For late-nineteenth-century political matters, see Frederick C. Luebke, *Immigrants and Politics: The Germans of Nebraska, 1880–1900* (Lincoln: Univ. of Nebraska Press,

1969). Much of the German political activity can be traced through biographies. The most famous German in American political life is thoroughly dealt with in Hans Trefousse, *Carl Schurz: A Biography* (Knoxville: Univ. of Tennessee Press, 1982). See also Chester V. Easum, *The Americanization of Carl Schurz* (Chicago: Univ. of Chicago Press, 1929); Claude M. Fuess, *Carl Schurz, Reformer (1829–1906)* (Philadelphia: Carl Schurz Memorial Foundation, 1932); and *The Reminiscences of Carl Schurz*, 3 vols. (New York: The McClure Co., 1907–1908). Other important biographical material is in Thomas J. McCormack, ed., *Memoirs of Gustave Koerner, 1809–1906*, 2 vols. (Cedar Rapids, IA: The Torch Press, 1909); Frank Freidel, *Francis Lieber, Nineteenth-Century Liberal* (Baton Rouge: Louisiana State Univ. Press, 1947); Stephen D. Engle, *Yankee Dutchman: The Life of Franz Sigel* (Fayetteville: Univ. of Arkansas Press, 1993); Carl F. Wittke, *Against the Current; The Life of Karl Heinzen (1809–80)* (Chicago: Univ. of Chicago Press, 1945), and Carl F. Wittke, *The Utopian Communist: A Biography of William Weitling, Nineteenth-Century Reformer* (Baton Rouge: Louisiana State Univ. Press, 1950).

The German Americans developed a great variety of ethnic institutions that served both to assist them in the transition to American life and to preserve the culture of their homeland. The German churches, which reflected the religious divisions among the Germans, were among the most important. German Catholics are dealt with in Emmet H. Rothan, *The German Catholic Immigrant in the United States, 1830–1860* (Washington, DC: Catholic Univ. of America Press, 1946); Jay P. Dolan, *The Immigrant Church: New York's Irish and German Catholics, 1815–1865* (Baltimore: Johns Hopkins Univ. Press, 1975); Colman J. Barry, *The Catholic Church and German Americans* (Milwaukee, WI: Bruce, 1953); Philip Gleason, *The Conservative Reformers: German American Catholics and the Social Order* (Notre Dame: Univ. of Notre Dame Press, 1968); and Stephen J. Shaw, *The Catholic Parish as a Way-Station of Ethnicity and Americanization: Chicago's Germans and Italians, 1903–1939* (New York: Carlson Publishing, 1991). On German Lutherans, see A. G. Roeber, *Palatines, Liberty and Property: German Lutherans in Colonial British America* (Baltimore: Johns Hopkins Univ. Press, 1993); and Walter O. Forster, *Zion on the Mississippi: The Settlement of the Saxon Lutherans in Missouri, 1839–1841* (St. Louis, MO: Concordia Publishing House, 1953). Other German Protestants are dealt with in Carl F. Schneider, *The German Church on the American Frontier* (St. Louis, MO: Concordia Publishing House, 1939); Paul F. Douglas, *The Story of German Methodism* (New York: The Methodist Book Concern, 1939); Carl F. Wittke, *William Nast, Patriarch of German Methodism* (Detroit, MI: Wayne State Univ. Press, 1959).

On the prolific German American press, see Carl F. Wittke, *The German-Language Press in America* (Lexington: Univ. Press of Kentucky, 1957); James M. Bergquist, "The German-American Press," in Sally M. Miller, ed., *The Ethnic Press in the United States: A Historical Analysis and Handbook* (Westport, CT: Greenwood Press, 1987), 131–159; Henry Geitz, ed., *The German-American Press* (Madison: State Historical Society of Wisconsin, 1992), a collection of essays. A bibliography cataloging the immense diversity of German newspapers in America is Karl J. R. Arndt and May E. Olson, *The German-Language Press of the Americas, 1732–1968; History and Bibliography*, 3rd ed., 2 vols. (Munich: Verlag Dokumentation, 1973). On German American book publishing, see Robert E. Cazden, *The Social History of the German Book Trade in America to the Civil War* (Columbia: Univ. of South Carolina Press, 1984). A book of essays about the German language in America is Glenn Gilbert, ed., *The German Language in America: A Symposium*

(Austin: Univ. of Texas Press, 1971). An excellent book on German America's material culture is Charles Van Ravenswaay, *The Arts and Architecture of German Settlements in Missouri: A Survey of a Vanishing Culture* (Columbia: Univ. of Missouri Press, 1977). E. Allen McCormick, ed., *Germans in America: Aspects of German-American Relations in the Nineteenth Century* (New York: Columbia Univ. Press, 1983), contains essays on several aspects of the culture of German Americans.

The period before and during World War I has been seen as a crucial turning point in the history of German America. The best interpretation of the period is Frederick C. Luebke, *Bonds of Loyalty: German-Americans and World War I* (DeKalb: Northern Illinois Univ. Press, 1974). An older work is Clifton J. Child, *German-Americans in Politics, 1914–1917* (Madison: Univ. of Wisconsin Press, 1939). The cultural conflicts of the same period are dealt with in David W. Detjen, *The Germans in Missouri, 1900–1918: Prohibition, Neutrality and Assimilation* (Columbia: Univ. of Missouri Press, 1985). See also Carl F. Wittke, *German-Americans and the World War (with special emphasis on Ohio's German-Language Press)* (Columbus: The Ohio State Univ. Press, 1936). Germans felt fewer accusations of disloyalty before World War II, but German involvement in those events is discussed in Sander A. Diamond, *The Nazi Movement in the United States, 1924–1941* (Ithaca, NY: Cornell Univ. Press, 1974), and in Susan Canedy, *America's Nazis, a Democratic Dilemma: A History of the German American Bund* (Menlo Park, CA: Markgraf Publications Group, 1990).

HAITIAN AMERICANS

Marc Prou

One important phenomenon of the last four decades in the United States has been the tremendous growth of immigrant and other refugee populations. A significant percentage of this immigrant/refugee population came from many Third World countries as a result of international political and economic crises. Haiti is one such country that has been affected greatly by these world affairs. This essay focuses on the process of migration and adaptation of the Haitian American population and the dynamic incorporation of Haitian ethnic culture into American society. It looks at the patterns of migration, particularly the kinds of strategies and institutional apparatuses, that Haitian Americans have used to adapt and forge community in the United States. In addition, the essay analyzes how the various informal Haitian Americans institutions establish intracommunity networks and institutions that characterize their lives and dreams in the diaspora. Among the questions this essay raises are: Do Haitian Americans follow the same trends of other immigrant groups in the United States? What tactics do they use to respond to acculturation or assimilation? How do they overcome the stigmas of their identification as the "boat people," or "HIV carriers"? How do U.S. immigration policies affect Haitian Americans? And lastly, how do they respond to or cope with these challenges in the course of adaptation and community formation?

Although these questions are complex, it is important to analyze them, especially in the case of recent demographic profiles of Haitian Americans, which tend to focus on the adaptation process. The notion of assimilation, which many earlier, primarily European, immigrant groups had used in the past, is not relevant or applicable to understanding recent Haitian immigrants. Many of these immigrants and refugees enjoy and maintain both their native culture and their newly adopted American culture.

To place the Haitian immigrants in perspective, an examination of their history in the United States seems warranted. Anthropologist Susan Buchanan reported that the U.S. Immigration and Naturalization Service (INS) has no record of any Haitian immigrants to the United States prior to 1910. The first major flight of Haitians in the twentieth century was a direct result of U.S. interference in the politics and economy of the country, and in particular, of the U.S. occupation.[1]

From 1915 to 1934, significant numbers of Haitian peasants were deprived of their lands in estate-consolidation projects that passed for agrarian reforms, but that actually involved the dispossession of small farmers in favor of large, foreign-owned companies and large, single-crop farms. According to economist Paul Moral, "these deprived farmers fled to U.S.-owned plantations in Cuba and the Dominican Republic."[2] They were joined by others who sought to escape rising rural violence resulting from U.S. Marine occupation forces and native guerilla movements. Some fled forced labor gangs, and many were lured away by labor recruiters promising higher wages. Political Scientist Ira Reid's account reported that during this period of occupation "the United States received its first group of Haitian immigrants." Specifically, there were about fifty Haitian university students sponsored by the U.S.-led occupation government. These first Haitian immigrants were representative of the vast majority of those who came to the United States prior to the mid-1970s. They were upper class, urban, relatively prosperous, professional, and well educated.[3]

Reid described Haitian immigrants to the United States in the 1920s and 1930s in the following terms:

> These émigrés are from urban rather than rural areas of Haiti and are more literate than other non-English speaking immigrants. . . . Haitian workers in New York are usually engaged in industry, trade, or the professions. Few, if any, are found in domestic service. Many of these "up-scale" Haitian immigrants were involved in the great Harlem Renaissance. Particular examples include Marie Duchâtelier, Napoléon Frances, and Eliézar Cadet to name a few.[4]

Subsequent Haitian immigration to the United States during the Depression and World War II was negligible. For the most part, the elite or aspiring elite of Haiti during this period had no reason to abandon their privileged positions. The few politically active refugees who did have good reasons to flee their homeland chose destinations other than the United States, which at that time, "had an unsavory reputation for racism."[5] If anything, the Depression years saw a reversal of large-scale Haitian immigration, as most of the 300,000 workers who had fled to Cuba from 1915 to 1930 returned to Haiti. Accordingly, Cuba's 1953 census recorded only 28,000 Haitians.

Because Haiti shared in the post–World War II economic boom that the United States experienced, immigration during this period was low. In 1952, the new Immigration and Naturalization Act gave favored-immigrant status to certain national groups, including the Haitians. Susan Buchanan found that from 1953 to 1956, the Immigration and Naturalization Service recorded "1,812 Haitian immigrants, of whom 1,009 were women and 803 were men."[6] This numerical gap between male and female Haitian immigrants may have been a consequence of the growing demand in the United States for women in the garment industry as dressmakers and in the service industry as housekeepers and maids. Because the Haitian elite and emerging middle class stayed home to enjoy the new prosperity, the new group of immigrants tended to be poorer and less educated than their predecessors.

In 1965, the McCarran-Walter Act was amended to abolish quotas for immigrants from the Eastern Hemisphere. The cold war definition of an acceptable refugee remained in effect. It is worth noting at this point that a major inconsistency existed between the definition of a refugee as specified in immigration law and the definition to which the United States subscribed in international agreement. For instance, the United Nations' "Convention Relating to the Status of Refugees" of 1951, in which ninety-three nations, including the United States, were parties, defines *refugees* in the following terms:

> Any person who, owing to a well-founded fear of being persecuted for reasons of race, religion, nationality, membership of particular social group or political opinion, is outside the country of his nationality and is unable or, owing to such fear, is unwilling to avail himself of the protection of that country, or who, not having a nationality and being outside the country of his former habitual residence, is unable or, owing to such fear, is unwilling to return to it.[7]

In 1967, the United Nations brought the 1951 convention up to date. It included a "Declaration of Territorial Asylum," establishing a "bill of rights," specifying such protections as the right not to be subjected to *refoulement*, or forcible repatriation. In fact, by signing the 1975 Helsinki Accord, the United States accepted "the principles of humanitarianism, some of which have definite application to refugees. Among these were: 1) Respect for human rights and freedom; 2) Fulfillment in good faith of obligations under international law, and; 3) Cooperation in international humanitarian endeavors, some of which relate directly to immigration and refugees."[8]

Demographer Nina Barnett Glick provides a statistical breakdown of annual Haitian immigration to the United States in the 1960s (Table 1). It is evident from the data in Table 1 that Haitian immigration to the United States rose steadily throughout the decade, with spectacular increases during the late 1960s. These figures represented only documented entries into the United States. Many undocumented immigrants obtained temporary visas and simply remained in the country after their visas expired. Thus, these figures understate the total immigration during the 1960s.[9]

Emigration from Haiti in the 1960s, when university-educated professionals and skilled workers fled the island at the rate of 288 per year, was essentially an

Table 1
Haitian Immigration to the United States from 1960 to 1969

Year	Immigrants	Non-Immigrants*	Students
1960	931	4,107	—
1961	1,025	1,025	95
1962	1,322	4,699	87
1963	1,851	6,341	124
1964	2,082	8,050	182
1965	3,609	9,271	201
1966	3,801	10,990	234
1967	3,567	17,259	371
1968	6,806	19,209	601
1969	6,542	—	—
Total	31,536	80,951	1,895
Average	3,154	8,994	237

Source: Glick, N. B. (1975). *The Formation of a Haitian Ethnic Group*. PhD diss., Columbia Univ., p. 68.

upper-class and middle-class brain drain. Taking place during the period from 1957, following François Duvalier's (Papa Doc) rise to power, until 1967, this massive exodus can be attributed to Duvalier's failure to live up to his electoral campaign promises. Faced with this massive flight, Duvalier created a kleptocratic regime that relied heavily on the use of terror to intimidate the population.

Economist Robert Rotberg explained the impact of this brain drain when he noted that by the mid-1960s, about eighty percent of Haitian doctors, lawyers, engineers, teachers, and other professionals had fled to Canada, the United States, or Africa. By 1968, there were approximately 75,000 Haitians in the United States. According to Jervis Anderson in his 1975 article in the *New Yorker*, the majority of these Haitians were mostly undocumented aliens; they represented the "intelligentsia of their country" who were forced to live a meager and precarious existence without the benefits of work permits, welfare, educational assistance, and legal protection.[10]

The influx of Haitian immigrants to the United States continued in the 1970s. Initially, many of these immigrants went to the Bahamas. About 50,000 Haitians initially sought sanctuary there in the early 1970s. However, with independence and worsening economic conditions, the Bahamas inaugurated Operation Cleanup in 1978 to expel 400 Haitians each month. In June 1978, the first month of this operation, 600 Haitians arrived on the coast of Florida.[11]

These were not the first Haitian "boat people" to arrive in the United States. Documents verify that the invasion of the Haitian "boat people" actually began on December 12, 1972, with the arrival, in Florida, of the first boat loaded with more than forty Haitian refugees. However, until 1978, the number was a mere "trickle." Then, in 1978 alone, about 1,810 Haitian refugees arrived in Florida. The next year, the total was 2,522. In September 1981, the *New York Times* estimated that more than 44,000 Haitians had arrived illegally in the United States over the previous nine years. Seven months later, the same source estimated that there were at least 60,000 illegal Haitian immigrants in the United States.

In 1981 and into early 1982, Haitian immigration to this country averaged nearly 2,300 people a month. If this rate had remained constant, more than 27,000 Haitians would have immigrated illegally to the United States in 1982. It was estimated in the early 1980s that officially there were only about 100,000 Haitians in the country. However, unofficial estimates that included illegal immigrants placed the number between 300,000 and 500,000. U.S. officials accepted Haitian immigration as long as it was negligible or showed only modest rates of increase, but when, in the late 1970s and the early 1980s, a trickle of immigrants became a deluge, the situation changed drastically.[12]

At the time of this dramatic increase in Haitian immigration, the U.S. had a web of antiquated immigration legislation and contradictory refugee policies. At the same time that Haitian immigration was taking place, the United States was in the process of responding to a substantial number of Cuban immigrants. The INS's immigration policies toward, and different treatment of the Cuban and Haitian refugees made clear that a double standard was in effect, which further exacerbated an already complicated situation. About 125,000 Cubans arrived between April and September 1980. Instead of seizing the opportunity to formulate some sort of consistent refugee policy, the U.S. government response to these refugee groups was inconsistent, accepting some but refusing many. Further, the economic recession in the United States in the late 1970s and early 1980s compounded the immigration issue. Many Americans were concerned about being displaced by foreigners who, they feared, would work more cheaply than the current workforce. Low-income U.S. workers were competing with refugees not only for jobs but also for that rare find in the United States: cheap housing.[13]

With all of these economic, social, political, and legal factors marshaled against them, it is not surprising that from the very beginning, Haitian refugees encountered substantial difficulties and challenges on their journey. "The Nixon, Ford, and Carter administrations," according to one summation, "have treated the Haitians with hostility instead of hospitality. Prejudged to be economic and not political refugees, they were given cursory interviews upon their arrival, with no attorney permitted. They were imprisoned, often on a $1,000 bond, and those released were denied work authorization. Thirteen years ago in October, 1980, the Immigration and Naturalization Service had a backlog of over 10,000 asylum cases."[14]

Haitian immigration grew most dramatically during the Carter administration, and so did the controversy surrounding it. The government continued to classify

Haitians as illegal aliens and subject them to arrest, summary deportation hearings, expulsion, and denial of work permits and government assistance. Differential treatment of Haitian immigrants was no longer based on cold war refugee definitions. On March 17, 1980, the U.S. government, mainly in response to the plight of Indo-Chinese refugees, brought its definition of a refugee into line with the protocol of the United Nations. The term *refugee* then embraced all persons who were forced to flee their country because of persecution based on religion, race, nationality, political affiliation, or membership in a particular social group. The Refugee Act of 1980 eliminated the old restrictions that favored eastern European anti-Communists and Middle Eastern refugees.

What, then, was the justification for welcoming Cubans and denying asylum to Haitians after the removal of restrictions from the government's working definition of a *refugee*? This was a crucial question that the Carter administration faced in 1980. Confronted by mounting pressures from the Governing Board of the National Council of Churches, the Congressional Black Caucus, the National Urban League, and public reactions to newspaper and television coverage of the issue, on June 20, 1980, the Carter administration reversed its position on the status of Haitian immigrants. This change of policy was not a complete turnabout but a grudging concession to public pressure. Thus caught between the Cubans, whom it did not wish to refuse, and the Haitians, whom it did not wish to admit, the government devised a new category of parole "entrant status" as a way of granting temporary refuge to the Haitians without having to determine whether they were political or economic refugees and without altering its treatment of the Cubans. By this maneuver, the Haitians were granted employment authorization, as well as government financial assistance. This measure applied only to Haitians who had arrived on or before June 19, 1980, and was to remain in effect for only six months. A government spokesmen proclaimed that by this policy the United States maintained the "strong humanitarian tradition of this nation" and that it was "totally unacceptable to return people to countries where we know they would be persecuted." Yet, U.S. authorities continued to maintain that a distinction existed between Cuban "political" refugees and Haitian "economic" ones. To many critics, it seemed as if the U.S. government was cynically manipulating the United Nations definition of *refugee* in order to exclude Haitians.[15]

Surprisingly, one month after the Carter administration included Haitians in its "open arms" policy, U.S. federal district judge James King, after hearing a class-action suit brought by 4,000 Haitians, found that the INS had violated the Haitians' rights to due process under the Constitution. "Haitians who came to the United States seeking freedom and justice," Judge King stated, "did not find it." He also suggested that there had been racial bias against "part of the first substantial flight of black refugees from a repressive regime to this country." Finally, the judge chastised U.S. government officials for their failure to comprehend that the "dramatic poverty" from which the Haitian refugees had fled was largely "a result of Duvalier's effort to maintain power." In other words, Judge King found the dichotomy between economic and political refugees to be a specious one. According to him, "The manner in which the INS treated the more than 4,000 Haitian plaintiffs violated the Constitution, the immigration statutes, international agreements, INS regulations and INS operating procedures. It must stop."[16]

All protections of the Carter amnesty program were scheduled to expire on October 10, 1980, and later, by extension, on July 15, 1981. However, the Reagan administration, primarily in response to the public opinion and pressure from the State of Florida, resolved to take a hard-line approach to the Haitian immigration problem before the law's expiration date.

On June 6, 1981, the *New York Times* noted that, "Haitian Deportation Starts; U.S. Orders Open Hearings." The U.S. government began mass deportation hearings for 6,000 Haitians who had arrived after October 1980 and thus were exempt from President Carter's "amnesty program." These hearings were held behind closed doors, and private attorneys were barred from the proceedings. The INS began to process up to 35 cases a day. On June 7, 1981, the resumption of deportations from the Miami Krome Avenue Detention Center was announced. That same day, Attorney General William French Smith ordered an end to mass exclusion hearings and opened the proceedings to the public. On June 9, 1981, the INS temporarily suspended deportation hearings, pending a complete review of procedures. In the meantime, large numbers of Haitians were transferred to detention centers, mainly in New York and Puerto Rico.[17]

The Reagan administration had merely duplicated the actions of previous administrations in resorting to detention and deportation. On September 30, 1981, a new method of dealing with the Haitians was announced. President Ronald Reagan issued an executive order permitting agreements between the United States and foreign governments to prevent undocumented immigration by interception at sea. According to the United States Committee for Refugees, there were "between 35,000 and 45,000 Haitians who came to the United States by boat between 1971 and 1981." Now, the Coast Guard was ordered to intercept and turn back vessels that were suspected of carrying illegal aliens. By maneuvering to deal with the refugees beyond the borders of the United States, the Reagan administration sought to avoid having to account to the judicial branch for its failure to grant due process to the immigrants. By turning the Haitians back before they reached the United States, the government technically avoided accusations of refoulement. But in terms of the international law of the high seas, the United States' interdiction policy was highly questionable. At least one refugee advocacy group declared with some justification that the interception of vessels on the high seas was a violation of international law. While the interdiction policy was effective in stemming the flow of undocumented aliens, it also revealed the U.S. government's intense hostility toward Haitian immigrants. Of the 22,651 Haitians intercepted by the Coast Guard from September 1981 to October 1990, fewer than one dozen were allowed to apply for asylum in the United States. The data presented by the INS reveals how U.S. treatment of Haitian refugees contrasted sharply with its treatment of refugees from other nations ruled by authoritarian regimes. From 1983 to 1990, for instance, the United States approved only 2 percent of all Haitian asylum claims. During the same period, the United States granted asylum to 17 percent of those seeking refuge from Cuba, 34 percent of those from Vietnam, 61 percent of those from Iran, and 65 percent of those from China.[18]

The legal wrangling between the judicial and executive branches over proper treatment of Haitian immigrants continued through May 1982. At that time, the government finally agreed to "parole" Haitian detainees in the United States until individual deportation hearings could be arranged. On July 24, 1982, the first Haitian detainees were released. The process was inexcusably slow and as of September 1982, some Haitians were still in custody. In Westchester County, New York, among other places, deportation hearings were still in progress as late as February 1983.[19]

For all intents and purposes, the Haitian immigration crisis had passed by December 1981, when a *New York Times* headline proclaimed that the "Sea Patrol Has Slowed Haitian Entries." Whether the decrease in the number of Haitian entries was directly attributable to the United States interdiction policy is debatable. As one source pointed out, the U.S. government spent $2 million on interdiction to catch only thirty-seven Haitians. What seemed evident was that there was a combination of repressive anti-immigration measures and public international pressures on the Haitian government to end the flow of Haitian refugees. The biased measures of both the Haitian and the U.S. governments may have decreased the flow of Haitian immigrants, but it did not stop it, and with the political and economic situations in Haiti deteriorating under the imposed Organization of American States (OAS)–United Nations (UN) embargo, the pressure to leave the island increased.[20]

Once on U.S. soil, the Haitian refugees, like all other immigrants, had to cope with and adapt to U.S. society. The bulk of these refugees came from rural and coastal communities in Haiti. Josh Dewind's article "Alien Justice: The Exclusion of Haitian Refugees," provides a blunt description of the new breed of undocumented entrants. He also points out that many of them had never been allowed to work before entering the United States and were now forced to survive on annual incomes of less than $100. They suffered from illiteracy, malnutrition, sickness, and premature mortality.[21]

Immediately following the Army coup d'état on September 30, 1991, against the government of Jean Bertrand Aristide, thousands of people left Haiti. It was estimated that tens of thousands crossed the border into the neighboring Dominican Republic. Several thousands fled by boat, with some 1,500 landing in Cuba and many more apparently intending to seek asylum in the United States. By the end of 1991, more than 8,000 of these Haitian asylum seekers were intercepted by U.S. Coast Guard ships before reaching U.S. territorial waters.

In early November 1991, the U.S. government asked countries in Latin America and the Caribbean to accept Haitian asylum seekers; Honduras, Venezuela, Belize, and Trinidad and Tobago each agreed to grant temporary refuge to some of them. The others, who had been halted on the high seas by U.S. Coast Guard vessels, were interviewed by U.S. authorities to assess whether they had a valid claim for asylum in the United States. On November 18, 1991, the State Department issued a statement announcing that only those who might qualify for asylum would be allowed to proceed to the United States to lodge an asylum claim and that about fifty such individuals had been identified so far. On the next day, November 19, 1991, the U.S. authorities returned over 500 asylum seekers against their will to Haiti. The others, apart from those who had been granted temporary refuge by other countries in the region, would be sent back to Haiti eventually. The statement added that the U.S. government did not believe that the asylum seekers sent back to Haiti would face persecution there.

Ironically, on that same day, November 19, 1991, a federal court in Miami issued an order temporarily prohibiting the U.S. authorities from returning any more asylum seekers to Haiti pending further examination of the issue. The U.S. government appealed the decision, but a series of court rulings continued to prevent the U.S. government from forcibly returning any Haitian asylum seekers who had been intercepted at sea. The government's appeal was heard on January 22, 1992. By mid-January 1992, only 1,600 Haitians intercepted by the U.S. authorities had been "screened in" and were allowed to proceed to the United States to lodge an asylum claim.

The screening procedure lacked certain essential safeguards that international standards required be allowed to asylum seekers. These included the right of every asylum seeker to appropriate legal advice and, if their application for asylum was rejected, the right to have a thorough review of their case before being expelled from the country where they sought asylum. Militating against these safeguards was the 1981 bilateral agreement between the governments of Haiti and the United States, which had permitted the U.S. authorities to intercept Haitians who were trying to reach the United States outside of U.S. territorial waters and return them to Haiti. Thus, getting caught by the INS reduced the chance for immigrants to file an application for permanent-resident status or even a tourist visa. It is reported that "of the more than 22,651 Haitians intercepted and interviewed at sea from September 1981 to September 1991, only about 30 were allowed to enter the U.S. and apply for asylum in the U.S."[22] President Aristide, on April 4, 1994, notified Washington that he intended to end the thirteen-year-old bilateral agreement that allowed the U.S. to intercept Haitians at sea and repatriate them. The letter of notification, which President Aristide sent to the White House, served a six-month notice of the end of the agreement.[23]

In 1992, faced with another large influx of Haitian refugees, President George H.W. Bush described the situation as "dangerous and unmanageable," and on May 24, 1992, introduced a policy that effectively prevented further Haitian immigration. Pursuant to Bush's executive order, the U.S. Coast Guard had been intercepting Haitian refugees and turning them back to Haiti without allowing hearings for asylum claims. Even without the agreement, the Coast Guard maintained that it could legally stop the rafts and dinghies because they are not registered vessels.[24] Although Bush administration was likely to return some legitimate political refugees in the process, it contended that its main concern was to discourage Haitians from risking their lives on the high seas. President Bush's executive order to tighten refugee policy was only the latest episode in Washington's discriminatory treatment of Haitian refugees. Even before the president's policy decision was announced in May 1992, the administration showed that it was willing to backtrack on its earlier commitment to support a trade embargo in order to discourage the flow of Haitian boat people heading to Florida. Although the president partially relaxed the embargo in February 1992—for example, by allowing some U.S.-owned assembly plants to resume business in Haiti—that action was not sufficient to slow the flow of Haitian immigrants and/or refugees.

In 2004, the Bush administration's policy vis-à-vis the Haitian immigration dilemma, crafted by Attorney General John Ashcroft, has remained identical to the policy of the Clinton administration, when the situation was no better than it had been. For instance, immediately after his victory, Clinton broke a campaign promise to Haitian Americans. In a joint television appearance, President Clinton and the then-exiled President Aristide urged the Haitian boat people not to risk their lives on the high seas because they would be returned to Haiti. At the very least, the Clinton administration could have issued an executive order directing the INS and its agencies to end their insensitive treatment of Haitian refugees under the current interdiction program, and allowing all fleeing Haitians to make claims for asylum. That initiative was indeed urgent, especially given the perennial state of human-rights abuses and violations in Haiti. The inhumane policy of returning politically repressed Haitians to their brutal oppressors should have been replaced with a more open immigration policy consistent with traditional democratic American values. Because of the severity of the conditions in Haiti, due in large part to misguided U.S. foreign policy, immigration restrictions should have been relaxed to allow consideration of economic, as well as political, claims to asylum. In a move responding to mounting public pressures, particularly from the Black Caucus and TransAfrica, President Bill Clinton finally ordered the Coast Guard on May 10, 1994, not to return Haitian refugees without processing their claims. Finally, Haitian American voters felt the reward of their ballots.

The aforementioned analysis helps to shed some light on the Haitian immigrants' challenges and tribulations. It would be of little value to debate the U.S. government actions vis-à-vis the Haitian immigration question, since these actions have already been condemned by the judicial and legislative branches, as well as by the media and public opinion. Overall, the Haitian American migration continues to challenge U.S. immigration policies toward people from the Caribbean, particularly in the case of Cuban and Haitian "boat people." Both groups arrived at the same time on the shores of Florida. One (Cuban) was granted asylum, the other (Haitian) was sent to detention camps.

This kind of treatment is terrifying to Haitian American immigrants in their new society. Despite enduring all kinds of racial discrimination and overcoming difficulties of immigration formalism, Haitian Americans have been able to adapt to their new society. Now they have to face the realities of an alien society that offers them some opportunities to enhance their sociocultural capital. Thus, they have to learn new norms and values in order to adapt and survive in their newly adopted country. For Haitian Americans, their journey is just beginning, and by emphasizing their cultural identity and social values, they are making the transition.

While those who are critical of an influx of Haitian American immigrants contend that their arrival could upset local economies and produce an increase in crime, many community leaders in South Florida, for instance, view Haitian American immigrants as law-abiding and hardworking individuals. In fact, the Haitian American immigrants have built growing and productive communities; Miami's "Little Haiti" is considered one of the safest neighborhoods in the city. One Miami police officer reported that, "newly arrived Haitians are most likely [to be] victims of crimes than perpetrators."[25] Furthermore, the view that Haitian immigrants would drag down the economy and have little to contribute to the community are being allayed by the fact that Haitians rarely receive welfare benefits and exhibit strong belief in education, as demonstrated by their high rate of registration for classes and high school attendance. In fact, Haitian American immigrants are raising their own standard of living as well as that of the members of the communities in which they live and work.

Assimilation is "the process . . . in which persons and groups acquire the memories, sentiments, and attitudes of other persons or groups and by sharing their experiences and history, are incorporated with them in a common cultural life."[26] It is assumed under the assimilation theory that migrants must absorb all the characteristics of their host culture while forgetting or rejecting their old ways of life. Thus, "classical assimilation perspective . . . posits that immigrants must divest themselves of their previous cultural patterns, including their ethnic identifica tions and languages[,] and adopt those of the host society to become assimilated as full members of their country."[27]

The assimilation model has been used to describe how new immigrants have more than one choice of success in comparison with earlier, twentieth-century immigrants' melting pot ideology. Instead of opting for assimilation or the melting pot ideology, new immigrants tend rather to integrate through a transnational or a diasporic community. Thus, the common ideological belief expressed was that the more "assimilated" the people became, the more economically successful they were. Indeed, this was true when considering the European immigrants of the early twentieth century, who were characterized as "poor immigrants becoming working-class ethnics and then over time successful ethnic Americans." They quickly became part of the "melting pot" and Anglo conformity, which "was associated with upward socioeconomic mobility in American society."[28]

However, after the 1965 Immigration Act it became clear that the old assimilation process does not work for contemporary immigrants. Thus, ideas like "melting pot" and "Anglo conformity" can no longer be used to explain the adaptation process of recent immigrants. This new phenomenon may be related to the existence of international networks of these scattered geographical communities. But today, an immigrant's adaptation is considered to be a segmented assimilation, because the immigrant group may well develop an ethnic economy. Or, it may involve socioeconomic disadvantages, particularly for groups in which members' skin color is different from that of the dominant majority.

For Haitian Americans and other nonwhite immigrants, discrimination poses another problem with the assimilation model. For instance, Caribbean immigrants view assimilation in America as "becoming African Americans and, therefore, enduring stigma and diminishing opportunities."[29] Many Haitian Americans would, at times, rather identify themselves as Jamaicans or Trinidadians instead of African Americans because of the complex nature of discrimination in American society against blacks, in contrast to European immigrants who made their transitions to Anglo America to become white Americans. In fact, "[i]f white immigrants tend to gain status by becoming American—by assimilating into a higher status group—black immigrants may actually lose status if they lose their cultural distinctiveness." Therefore, Caribbean American and Haitian American immigrants in particular have made a conscious decision to "use their ethnicity and their cultural distinctiveness . . . to increase their chances of making it in the new environment." Otherwise, they would lose their status when they assimilate or become black in America.[30]

Haitian Americans are the second largest black immigrant group in the United States after the Jamaican Americans. Upon arrival in their new society, Haitian Americans began to experience the paradox of American realities, which are characterized by race relations and institutional racism. Race matters, since it shapes the life chances of every U.S. inhabitant. Thus, the racial dilemma adds a new dimension to the everyday problems Haitian American immigrants must face. The skin complexion that accompanies their ethnicity suddenly becomes a burden, one that cannot be overcome.

Haitian American immigrants know that they ought to adjust to the American way of life. However, the following question remains: would adaptation mean Americanization to become black Americans? If so, Haitian Americans show no tendency toward assimilation by becoming black Americans because "they don't want to be Black twice."[31] Many Haitian Americans feel stigmatized by national stereotypes and labels of HIV, high illiteracy, "boat people," or *voodoo*. At the same time, they feel that becoming black Americans would place them in a double jeopardy, thus amplifying their problems. Instead, they tend to rely on and promote Haitian ethnic pride. Their ethnicity, which can be expressed through language, food, religion, music, crafts, and visual arts, is the only chance they have for surviving in the United States. In fact, many Haitian Americans have realized that by maintaining their ethnic identity, they increase their chances to achieve success by setting themselves apart from other minority groups, which have a history of disempowerment in the society. Thus, Haitian

Americans adjust to necessary elements of the American system while keeping their native ethos, which represents their diasporic citizenships and transnational identities.

Social anthropologist Michel Laguerre cited Randolph Bourne, the author of the essay "Transnational—America," published in 1916, to build the foundation of transnationalism in *Diasporic Citizenship*. He asserted that Bourne's prediction was right when he wrote that assimilation in the context of immigrants is "the failure of the melting pot and the need to assert a higher ideal than the melting pot." In addition, "America is coming to be, not a nationality but transnationality, a weaving back and forth, with the other hands, of many threads of all sizes and colors."[32]

Transnationalism can be defined as transcending or reaching beyond national borders; it involves migrants moving back and forth between their host country and their homeland. These migrants also are classified as people who live across borders. They may reside primarily in the United States while remaining involved in many activities back home through friendship, business, religion, family, or even politics. The reality is that these practices transcend societies and nation-states in a way that transforms not only the individual but both societies in different venues.

Haitian Americans represent the best-case scenario of transnationalism at work. They belong to a contemporary migration movement in which people going back and forth regularly between the two countries. In fact, the transnational ties maintained by Haitian Americans help sustain Haiti's economy. The explanation is simple: Haitian Americans send large amounts of money and goods as remittances to their country. This remittance assistance goes directly to families or "headquarters-households" all over the country and has been the most effective system of economic aid in Haiti.

Haitian Americans continue to take on major responsibilities in the political and economic affairs of Haiti while they participate in the development process from the mainland. After being overthrown on September 30, 1991, President Aristide maintained his government from abroad, and the network of Haitian American activists dispersed throughout the world continued to influence politics "at home." Haitian Americans represent a paradoxical case when it comes to cross-border politics, however. On the one hand, Haiti has instituted formal representation of Haitian Americans living abroad by creating a deterritorialized administrative district known as the Tenth Department to represent migrants. A cabinet minister for Haitians living abroad served in the Haitian government since the early 1990s. However, Haiti does not permit dual citizenship. A Haitian-born person who acquires another nationality must formally renounce it before Haitian nationality is restored. This issue appears to have created tensions in the first Aristide administration, as many of his supporters were abroad during the military regime following the coup d'état but have subsequently returned to participate in politics. Other Haitian Americans, whose emigration predates Aristide's first election, have also returned to Haiti with an interest in participating in politics. Many Haitian Americans who returned may still have economic or other interests in the United States and would be hesitant to give up their U.S. citizenship and the political rights they have acquired. Thus dual citizenship remains one of the most prominent demands of Haitian Americans, along with the right to vote in Haitian elections. From the initial years of Aristide's presidency in 1991 until his last days in power, Haitian lawmakers debated a dual-citizenship bill, but it was never voted into law.

The transnational process does not manifest itself only in the forms of identity and remittances. It also occurs in others maintaining different kinds of businesses that serve both the homeland (Haiti), and the home country (the United States). These various kinds of activities provide a broad market for the sale of Haitian products in the United States, and vice versa. Above all, transnationality helps create all kinds of necessary global exchanges between both the United States and Haiti. It is in that context that the "diasporic subject is located vis-à-vis two states: the host state where he is considered to be a hyphenated citizen, and the homeland where he is identified as an insider/outsider, not a foreigner, but someone whose allegiance is shared with another nation-state."[33]

Alongside transnationalism, a diaspora is viewed as individuals or communities living in a country other than their own. Though *diaspora* implies the notion of dispersion, large numbers of migrants have contacts with the home country. Those who have contacts with the homeland differ in degree between passive and active. An active diaspora, maintains its relationships with the homeland in real and not simply in symbolic terms. Active diasporics keep good contacts with the family members in the homeland by using calling cards, taped messages, letters, and even e-mails.

Scholars are beginning to question traditional explanations of a diaspora as a community of dispersed individuals who originate in the same place called a homeland. The term *diaspora* is understood as a category that describes a set of complex practices and relations that form a globally mobile category of affiliation, creating possibilities for new political action. In their various guises, conflicts between different diaspora groups and nation-states provide new perspectives from which to inquire about issues of ethnicity, gender, sovereignty, and citizenship.

Haitian diasporic citizens tend to commit to both of the countries to which they are. For instance, a diasporic individual may fulfill his citizenship duty in the newly adopted country but go to Haiti to participate in political, culture, or social activities. For many Haitian diasporic citizens, the kinds of activities in which they engage in the home country are needed, given the impact of the brain drain caused by massive immigration during the past three decades. Maintaining such relationships is helpful for finding strength and resistance while facing the American odds. It also reflects their willingness and sense of responsibility to look after their immediate families back home.

The Haitian Americans' challenges with racism, ethnicity, and nationality differ from those of other immigrants, such as Asian Americans and European-Americans. They experience continued difficulties as a result of being immigrants of African descent, and there is not yet a cohesive Haitian American community because Haitian immigrants to the United States are geographically scattered. At the same time, they are occasionally rejoined with their loved ones in their homeland. Above all, they have established networks throughout the United States that set the stage for the formation of a Haitian American community.

The formation of Haitian American communities in the United States follows the patterns of their migration process. Haitian immigrants at first had no intention of building communities because they saw the United States "as having very little to offer [them] besides a temporary haven." Indeed, those who migrated immediately after Duvalier assumed power in Haiti belonged to the upper class that included professionals and intellectuals. They thought that Duvalier would not last long in office before a general or the military could overthrow him. Years later, many of these political exiles in the United States who thought they would be returning to Haiti in a matter of months found themselves with their suitcases still unpacked.[34]

There was a preoccupation with playwright and poet Aimé Césaire's idea of "return to the native land," and this attitude remains unchanged even today. In an article published in the *New York Times* on September 14, 1997, a group of second-generation Haitian Americans stated that "[leaders of the old generation] place [too much] stress on affairs back home in Haiti." The first generation of Haitian immigrants did not care much about their conditions in the United States. In other words, they were living like "*yon pye anndan yon pye deyò*," as they say in Haitian-Creole, meaning "one foot inside, one foot outside." This phenomenon might help explain how they were physically dislocated in the United States and they dreamed of life back in the homeland. Thus, they did not want to assimilate into U.S. culture. Even those who came later on to join the underground undocumented immigrant community still focused on life back in Haiti.

Consequently, because early Haitian immigrants did not see the United States as a permanent home, they did not try to become citizens. For them, naturalization meant a loss of identity, so the best way to maintain their identity was to not get involved in any activity that would make them Americans. Indeed, "community leaders who dared to urge Haitians to become citizens were loudly assailed as turncoats."[35] People of this movement still shared the dream of "returning home." Although many of them made it back and forth, there are those who have cut off the migratory process and remained in the United States. But they have grouped themselves, forming private social clubs and relying heavily on their ethnicity to form niches for those who share similar political views, cultures, immigrant status, and economic status.

Despite numerous obstacles, Haitians Americans have developed many small but vibrant communities across the United States. The vibrancy of the scattered communities can be observed during the week of May 18, which is Haitian Flag Day. Yearly, some city governments across the United States sponsor cultural and public activities to honor the Haitian American presence. Mayors in major urban areas such as New York, Boston, and Miami have declared that week Haitian

American Week. These scattered Haitian American communities reflect different aspects of the Haitian American diaspora; they play significant roles in helping immigrants retain their ethnicity but make the necessary adaptations to the host culture. New York City has the oldest and by far the largest Haitian American enclave in the United States. The Haitian American community in New York differs from other Haitian communities across the Northeast because it is composed of immigrants from all social and economic backgrounds.

Florida has the second largest group of Haitian Americans in the United States. In the early 1980s, a Haitian American community known as "Little Haiti" emerged in Miami, located just north of the downtown area; it has become the geographical hub of Haitian American presence in continental United States. Unlike New York and other northeast states, Florida attracts, for the most part, Haitian Americans who had limited or no education before coming to the United States. Many immigrants were from rural communities and had never been in any urban center. For these people, American urban life was an especially new and frightening experience. Yet, the Haitian American community in south Florida has been growing rapidly, and it reflects many facets of the life of Haitian immigrants in the United States. Massachusetts, Rhode Island, Connecticut, Illinois, New Jersey, and Washington, DC, also have large concentrations of Haitian Americans.

Within the Haitian American communities across the United States, different kinds of institutions help preserve some cultural values and norms of the homeland; they also help in the process of adaptation to American cultural norms and life. Some of these institutions are the churches, media, and businesses, which together play a significant role in the formation of Haitian American communities.

Haitians Americans have developed many formal and informal networks to assist in their diasporic and transnational communities. These networks have been established to instill a sense of pride and dignity in the community and to facilitate understanding of U.S. mainstream culture. The Haitian American media provides an illustrative example. It provides information and helps demystify the mainstream media, which has spread many negative stereotypes of Haiti and Haitians in general. These stereotypes come both from newspapers and television, which have perpetuated a series of particularly potent myths about Haiti and Haitians. Sociologist Sidney W. Mintz cogently reminds us that, "few countries in modern times have received as bad a press at the hands of foreign observers as Haiti." For instance, in the 1980s, the Centers for Disease Control (CDC) accused Haitians of being one of the primary groups at risk of HIV/AIDS (one of the "Four Hs," along with hemophiliac, homosexual, and heroin user). Though later, the CDC withdrew Haitians from the list, this kind of accusation was a result of prejudice and racial profiling against Haitians.[36]

In response to the bad press from the mainstream U.S. media, and to provide an alternative voice, the Haitian American diasporic media has emerged as a very visible force in these communities. These media assumed the role of informing, entertaining, and demystifying myths regarding Haiti and Haitians in the diaspora, as well as promoting and reaffirming cultural pride. They are in fact transnational media, according to Michel Laguerre, because they "interconnect various diasporic sites to each other and the homeland." Their programming covers a variety of events and news in the diaspora as a whole, while paying attention to what is happening in Haiti. Moreover, the Haitian American media uses three languages—Haitian Creole, French, and English—to attract readers and listeners of different backgrounds and generations.[37]

For the most part, the Haitian American diasporic communities present interesting media venues that capture their diverse audiences. There now are several well-known newspapers, magazines, and academic journals that maintain transnational ties. Among the most popular news weeklies are the *Haiti-Observateur, Haiti-Progress*, and *Haiti en March*. In addition, there are other important diasporic newspapers that are more locally oriented, for example, the *Haitian Times* and the *Haitian Boston Reporter*. In general, these newspapers explore the experiences of the Haitian people. They also report important events in the American mainstream as well as world events and politics.

Radio is also important. There are well over a hundred Haitian American radio programs in many cities and communities where Haitian Americans reside. Prominent radio programming is available in the New York City boroughs of Brooklyn, Queens, and Manhattan as well as in suburban Long Island communities. In addition, such programs can be heard in suburban New Jersey, in the Boston area, in Connecticut and Rhode Island, in Chicago, in the nation's capital, and in Florida. They report on the news in Haiti and are a way for community leaders to gain access to the Haitian American community. Many of these radio programs give information on American life and society that helps in the integration and adaptation process of Haitian Americans. Haitian American radio broadcasting is considered one of the most effective ways of communicating with the Haitian American community because it is readily accessible. Also, radio is a good medium for talk shows.

In addition to newspapers and radio programs, local-access television is another effective means of communication. Haitian American television programs report news from Haiti and about the African and Caribbean diasporas. Through television networks, many Haitian music videos and documentaries are aired. In New York for example, 96 percent of such television programming is done through nonprofits or public access. This is also true for other Haitian American communities in Boston and Miami. Powerful Web sites also inform, promote, and even foster business activities in the Haitian American community. Internet access, which carries information between remote villages and urban centers, is used extensively among Haitian Americans because it provides quick and easy access to relatives and friends across the waters.

Thus, the Haitian American media are emerging as a means of providing information necessary for adaptation as well as for the maintenance of transnationality. Their primary focus is to serve and to bring messages of cultural understanding to the community providing easy access to information that helps to remove some of the cultural barriers that people may face as outsiders. Yet, media outlets in the Haitian American community are small and tend to face financial crises as they struggle to continue programming. Many Haitian pastors, priests, and religious organizations have subcontracted air time to broadcast their weekly sermons, thus using the media to evangelize and communicate with the Haitian American community. As with other institutions, the church serves the community by helping to sustain immigrants' spiritual identity and providing ways and means for coping with adaptation.

Religion can be defined as a particular system, like an institution of beliefs, practices, and values concerning the existence, nature, and worship of God. But besides its spiritual role, religion can provide social and economic services that will improve the quality of socioeconomic life. Most Haitian Americans practice Catholicism, which often syncretizes with *voodoo* practices. There are also a growing number who share some Protestant faith.

At first, Haitian Americans attended English-speaking churches because there was no Haitian church. But, after a few years, churches in New York, Boston, and Miami started serving the Haitian community by conducting masses in Haitian Creole. Later, Haitian churches of different denominations served the communities. In addition to these services, *voodoo* ceremonies are held periodically in these cities. Many of these ceremonies are performed within the family compound during the celebration of the feast of some Catholic saint. The Catholic Church plays a significant role because it has been the state church in Haiti for a long time and because most Haitians, urban and rural, are baptized Catholics.

Alongside the Catholic Church, Protestant churches such as Baptist, Pentecostal, Jehovah's Witness and Seventh-Day Adventist assist the Haitian American community with its spiritual needs. Some Haitian Americans make a strategic choice to convert to Protestantism, because they see it both as a social move toward the center and as an advantage when facing societal adversity. In fact, many of these Protestant churches call upon migrants "to renounce their ancestral gods and 'worship of Satan.' In return, the church promises the certainty of a place in heaven and protection against evil in this life."[38]

In general, Haitian American churches reach out in many ways to the local community they serve to offer a spiritual message, social networking, and financial assistance. Spiritually, it is like therapy where individuals come to sing, pray, dance, and put their faith into action. This is indeed the spiritual side, with heaven as the reward. But, the societal form of *demele* helps to alleviate different conditions that individuals face. In this sense, it helps in the networking of individual members of the congregation who are in search of employment and housing. These types of activities demonstrate how the church can be used as an institution to help Haitian Americans retain their values and at the same time adapt to mainstream American culture.

Schiller, Basch, and Blanc-Szancton remind us that "Haitians prefer to transfer capital back to Haiti rather than open business in the United States, because in Haiti one does not have to worry about extensive regulations and taxes."[39] This observation is no longer sufficient (if it ever was) to explain the Haitian diasporic community's socioeconomic actions toward those in Haiti. If the above quote was partly true in explaining the dynamics of the Haitian American community's socioeconomic links with Haiti, it is less true now than ever before. While at one time illegal and undocumented immigrants might have invested in Haiti because it was less risky in Haiti than in the United States, after years of reflecting on their experience, they have realized the necessity of creating businesses and entrepreneurial activities in the United States.

These entrepreneurial activities take place in various cities in New York, Florida, Massachusetts, New Jersey, Illinois, Connecticut, Rhode Island, and other places, particularly where an ethnic enclave supports and helps to boost the economic well-being of this ethnic community. Haitian Americans are striving to turn Little Haiti in Miami into an economic enclave similar to the Cuban-Americans' Little Havana in Miami. Among the small businesses being started are restaurants, money-transfer shops, dry-cleaning establishments, barbershops, laundries, grocery stores, jewelry shops, bakeries, real-estate offices, beauty salons, travel agencies, furniture stores, photography studios, bookstores, record shops, and businesses that promote cultural entertainments (e.g., concerts and dances).

These Haitian American businesses provide services to members of their community and attract other minority groups such as Caribbean Americans, African Americans, and some Francophone African immigrants from Senegal, Zaire, and the Ivory Coast. Whether these businesses are transnational or not depends on the nature of the business; for instance, shipping *rad pèpè* ("used clothes" in Haitian Creole) would sell more in Haiti than in the United States, where there are many sidewalk merchants and peddlers already in the market. For that reason, certain businesses are not transnational, but others, like money transfer and travel agencies, "conduct transnational businesses with the home country or serve the Haitian community."[40]

In reality, the Haitian American business community, as with any other institution within any other ethnic community, helps provide ways to adapt and acculturate. It "provide[s] employment mainly for members of the proprietor's families and for undocumented immigrants," offers services that members of the community would not easily find anywhere else, and carries some products to attract people from the mainstream culture. The business institution is growing, yet lack of good marketing skills and managerial know-how are why some business entrepreneurs fail. Despite all odds, there are many successful, well-operated Haitian American businesses that work for the well-being of the community.[41]

Several studies have been conducted on Haitian American immigrants and adaptation of second-generation Haitian Americans in America. The majority tend to focus on Haitian American immigrants' transnational links, adaptation process, language, family kinship, and schooling. But the idea of new orientations is also very important because it demonstrates how the group has shifted away from temporary migration toward a transnational *habitus*. As French sociologist Pierre Bourdieu argues, "Habitus, the inhabited space—and above all the house is the principal locus" for those socially constituted motivating principles that generate cultural practices. Earlier Haitian immigrants of the 1960s through the early 1980s, constructed transnational practices of a "return to my native land," the notion of going back to *lakay* (the homeland). However, since the mid-1990s, the focus for second-generation Haitian Americans has been to develop and improve the Haitian American ethnic community, which in turn will have an impact on the politics of both the (United States and Haiti). Bourdieu investigates what he calls the premises—both physical and figurative—on which people inhabit and carry out everyday life. Bourdieu's work helps explain how Haitian American transnational *habitus* and *class habitus* constitute sustainable attitudes and spirits that are a consequence of one's position within socioeconomic space.[42] The new orientations in Haitian migration and adaptation processes, as Laguerre asserts, seem mainly "shaped by structural constraints imposed on the ethnic community and by the adaptive strategies developed by the community to improve its lot."[43]

Local community improvement through hometown associations has been one of the results for this new way of adaptation. Another factor is the mind-set of the new generation of Haitian Americans who see themselves as American first in the pursuit of their dreams and Haitian second in claiming a national identity. This new generation includes both Americans born of Haitian parents and those who migrated from Haiti at an early age and have been schooled primarily in the United States. Other reasons for this new adaptation process relate to Haiti's political and socioeconomic conditions, which are characterized by insecurity, gross inflation, corruption, weak institutions, and global inequities. After years of resisting, the younger generation of Haitian Americans have chosen to reside in the United States, unlike some of their elders who decided to go back to live in their homeland after the fall of the Duvalier regime in 1987, a few younger Haitian Americans opt to go back and forth, maintaining transnational links.

Today, the majority of second-generation Haitian Americans, born in the United States, understand the necessity of being actively involved in American political, social, and cultural life. They represent "a growing number of Haitian Americans [who] have been engaged in American politics. They are found mainly among the educated middle class and especially among Haitian immigrants who arrived in [New York] before 1956," according to Laguerre. This group is involved in the politics of the host country. They identify themselves as a Haitian ethnic group, partly as the effect of discrimination experiences against blacks. Though Haitians and other blacks share lots in common, Haitians are seen as another ethnic group.[44]

Second-generation Haitian Americans have begun active involvement in American public life in order to improve the services provided to the Haitian immigrant community. They seek to build bridges between Haitian Americans and other ethnic minority communities. They witnessed the harsh treatment that their parents endured, and for that reason many of them were encouraged to learn English and attend colleges and universities, which can be interpreted as a form of integration and acculturation—looking outside of the Haitian American enclave for ways of reaching for the American dream within the larger community. The new generation of Haitian Americans is taking more interest in local elections, tackling issues such as affordable housing, economic development, health care, and public social policy.

Haitian Americans are running for elected public office to serve their newly adopted country. They want to be part of the American political process and to take a different path than their elders took during the past thirty years. It is often acknowledged that some Haitian Americans did not want to participate in American politics because they assumed they would return to Haiti at any time. Therefore, politics in their host country did not matter much to them. However, the new generation is critical of them for taking this stance of noninvolvement. When looking at the past, "the younger generation feels that Haitians should be more concerned with conditions in this country, while the older generation of leaders places its stresses on affairs back home in Haiti."[45]

Though more Haitian Americans show interests in American politics, this is not consistent across all regions of the United States. For instance, Haitians are active politically in New York, Florida, and Massachusetts, but those who live in the Midwest or the West Coast do not yet prioritize politics high on their American agenda. Many of them still consider being U.S. citizens a betrayal of Haiti. "They [feel] disloyal to Haiti and would be embarrassed to tell their friends [about their American status]." Though the number of Haitian Americans in these areas is the smallest among different communities in the country, they are now experiencing what people in New York, Florida, and Boston had faced already. They believe this is the beginning of their adaptation process, since people from these areas are still concerned about politics in the country of origin.[46]

For more than three decades, Haitian residents have avoided taking an active part in the cultural life and political process of the United States. That is no longer the case. Scattered throughout the United States, are many vibrant and active Haitian American communities. What is clear is that Haitian Americans are not homogenous in their orientation and/or adaptation to living in the United States. For many communities, the focus is no longer Haiti only. Many events clearly demonstrate how they have overcome the syndrome of returning to *lakay* by becoming more involved in U.S. public and political life. Although many Haitian Americans maintain a transnational *habitus* form of identity, they see themselves as participants in the American game. They no longer perceive the United States as a safe heaven; rather, it is a place for them to achieve their aspirations, to live the American Dream. They are now investing in the United States by purchasing real estate and owning businesses, while at the same time helping to build homes and support loved ones in Haiti. This, indeed, is a sign of progress toward their full integration and adaptation in a global context. Today, the new generation of Haitian Americans is encouraging people of the older generations to become American citizens and to vote on Election Day, because this new generation is aware that ballots can make a big difference in improving the place of the Haitian American community in the larger American society.

NOTES

1. For a stimulating discussion, see Susan Buchanan, "Scattered Seeds: The Meaning of Migration for Haitians in New York City," (PhD diss., New York Univ., 1980).

2. For a thorough study of the Haitian peasantry and flight to U.S-owned plantations in Cuba and the Dominican Republic, see Paul Moral, *Le Paysan Haitien, Etude sur la Vie Rural d'Haiti* (Port-au-Prince: Editions Fardin, 1978), 60.

3. Ira Reid, *The Negro Immigrant: His Background, Characteristics and Social Adjustment, 1899–1937* (New York: Columbia Univ. Press, 1939), 62.

4. Ibid., 81, 96.

5. Susan Buchanan, "Scattered Seeds," 65.

6. Ibid., 66–67.

7. Cited in L. Anderson, *Immigration* (New York: Franklin Watts, 1981), 38.

8. See William Korey, *Human Rights and the Helsinki Accord HS 264* (New York: Foreign Policy Association, 1983), 16–18.

9. See Nina Glick, "The Formation of a Haitian Ethnic Group" (PhD diss., Columbia Univ., New York, 1975), 58, which provides a compilation of annual breakdown numbers of Haitian immigration to the United States in the 1960s. Note in Table 1 that the non-immigrants' category represents the bulk of all other entries. These people entered the United States as businessmen, tourists, merchants, ship crewmen, contracted maids, and the list goes on. They overstayed their temporary visa status.

10. See Robert Rotberg, *Haiti: The Politics of Squalor* (Boston: Houghton Mifflin, 1971), 243–249. See also Jervis Anderson's article, "The Haitians of New York," *New Yorker*, March 31, 1975, 50–55. Also refer to Paddy Poux, "Haitians' Assimilation in the Life and the Future of the City of New York" (master's thesis, Fordham Univ., 1973); T. W. Weil, "Trouble Beset Haitian Refugees," *New York Times*, September 1, 1970, 35, col.1; and Rotberg, "Why the Boat People," *Newsweek*, June 2, 1980, 53.

11. For a stimulating discussion, see James Bentley, *American Immigration Today: Pressures, Problems, Policies* (New York: Julian Messner, 1981), 98. Also refer to Dawn Marshall, "The Haitian Problem: Illegal Migration to the Bahamas" (master's thesis, Institute of Social and Economic Research, Univ. of the West Indies, 1979).

12. For an in-depth analysis, see Josh Dewind, *Aiding Migration: The Impact of International Development Assistance on Haiti* (Boulder, CO: Westview Press, 1990), 123. Also, see Paul Lehman, "The Haitian Struggle for Human Rights" *Christian Century*, October 8, 1980, 941–943. Also see F. Lewis, "Ellis Island South," *New York Times*, February 11, 1982, 35, col. 5. Also refer to Anderson, *Immigration*, 51. A very useful documentation can be found in the MacNeil/Lehrer NewsHour program titled "Haitians: Why they Leave," (New York: WNET/13, October 13, 1981), transcript.

13. Lehman, "Haitian Struggle for Human Rights," 941–943.

14. Cited in Anderson, *Immigration*, 52.

15. Ibid.

16. See Amnesty International, "Reasonable Fear: Human Rights and the United States Refugee Policy," March 1990. Also, Amnesty International, "Haiti, the Human Tragedy: Human Rights Violations since the Coup d'Etat," January 1992. See also

Haitian Refugee Center et al. v. Benjamin Civiletti et al., 503 F.Supp. 442 (S.D. Florida 1980): final order granting relief.

17. See "Haitian Deportation Starts; U.S. Orders Open Hearings," *New York Times*, June 6, 1981; "Haitian Refugees in Miami Are Warned of Immigration Arrest Threat," *New York Times*, June 7, 1981; and an article in the *New York Times*, September 30, 1981, 1, col. 2 reporting that "President Ronald Reagan issued an order authorizing the Coast Guard to intercept and turn around ships on the high seas that are suspected of carrying illegal immigrants."

18. See M. Taft-Morales, *Haiti: Prospects for Democracy and U.S. Policy Concerns*, Congressional Research Service Issue Brief, (January 29, 1992), 13.

19. For a detail account of the nature and process of the hearing policy effects on Haitian Immigrants/refugees, see the case of a Haitian woman in (Amnesty International, March 1990, page 13).

20. See the *Washington Post*, February 8, 1992, A1.

21. See Josh Dewind, "Alien Justice: The Exclusion of Haitian Refugees," *Journal of Social Issues* 46, no.1 (Spring 1990): 124.

22. See Taft-Morales, *Haiti*, 2–3.

23. See Steven Greenhouse's article "Aristide to End Accord That Allows U.S. to Seize Refugee Boats," *New York Times*, April 8, 1994, A6.

24. See Anne Devroy's article, "U.S. to Halt Haitians on High Seas: Bush Orders Refugees Forcibly Returned," *Washington Post*, May 25, 1992, A1.

25. Ernest H. Preeg, *Haiti and the C.B.I.: A Time of Change and Opportunity* (Coral Gables, FL: North-South Center, University of Miami, 1985), 5–18.

26. For a discussion on the assimilation process of immigrants, see Robert E. Park and Ernest Burgess, *Introduction to the Science of Sociology: The Unexplored Connection* (Boulder, CO: Westview Press, 1924).

27. Min Zhou and Carl Bankston, "Social Capital and the Adaptation of the Second Generation: The Case of Vietnamese Youth in New Orleans," *International Migration Review* 28, no. 4 (1994): 822.

28. Mary Waters, *Black Identities: West Indian Immigrant Dreams and American Dreams* (Cambridge, MA: Harvard Univ. Press, 1999), 4, 193.

29. Maria Patricia Fernandez-Kelly and Richard Schauffler, "Divided Fates: Immigrant Children in a Restricted U.S Economy," *International Migration Review* 28, no. 4 (Winter 1994): 662–689.

30. Phillip Kasinitz, *Caribbean New York: Black Immigrants and the Politics of Race* (Ithaca, NY: Cornell Univ. Press, 1992), 36. See also Flore Zéphir, *Haitian Immigration in Black America: A Sociological and Sociolinguistic Portrait* (Westport, CT: Bergin & Garvey, 1996), 45.

31. Zéphir, *Haitian Immigration in Black America*, 69.

32. Michel Laguerre, *Diasporic Citizenship: Haitian-Americans in Transnational America* (New York: St. Martin's Press, 1998), 6.

33. Ibid., 10, 26.

34. See Nina Glick-Schiller, Linda Basch, and Cristina Blanc-Szancton, eds., *Towards a Transnational Perspective on Migration: Race, Ethnicity, and Nationalism Reconsidered* (New York: Academy of Sciences, 1991), 158.

35. Pierre-Pierre Gary, "For Haitians, Leadership Split Is a Generation Gap," *New York Times*, September 24, 1997, sec. B.

36. See Sidney Mintz, *Caribbean Transformations* (Baltimore: John Hopkins Univ. Press, 1974), 267. Also, for additional information on the issue of Haiti's bad press, see Paul Farmer, *The Uses of Haiti* (Monrode, Maine: Common Courage Press, 1994), 45. For an in-depth analysis, refer to Robert Lawless' book, *Haiti's Bad Press* (Boston: Schenkman Books, 1992).

37. Laguerre, *Diasporic Citizenship*, 131.

38. Rose-Marie Chierici, *Demele, 'Making it': Migration and Adaptation among Haitian Boat People in the United States* (New York: AMS Press, 1991), 263–264.

39. Ibid; Basch, Glick-Schiller and Blanc-Szancton, *Towards a Transnational Perspective on Migration* (September 24, 1997). 1991: 1.

40. Alex Stepick, *Pride against Prejudice: Haitian in the United States* (Needham Heights, MA: Allyn & Bacon, 1998), 50–52.

41. Michel Laguerre, *American Odyssey: Haitians in New York City* (Ithaca, NY: Cornell Univ. Press, 1984), 93.

42. See Pierre Bourdieu, *The Logic of Practice*, trans. Richard Nice (Stanford, CA: Stanford Univ. Press, 1977: 89, 1984: 169–225, 1990: 271–283). See also Bourdieu *Outline of a Theory of Practice* (Cambridge: Cambridge Univ. Press, 1977); Bourdieu "Distinction: A Social Critique of the Judgment of Taste" (Cambridge, MA: Harvard Univ. Press, 1984).

43. Laguerre, *American Odyssey*, 151.

44. Ibid., 150. Also, see Flore Zéphir, *Haitian Immigration in Black America.*

45. Gary "For Haitians, Leadership Split Is a Generation Gap," New York *Times.*

46. See Marjorie Valbrun, "Haitian-American Politics in Chicago." *APF Reporter* 20, no. 2 (2002): 60–63.

BIBLIOGRAPHICAL ESSAY

The indisputable massive presence of Haitian Americans in the last three decades has changed the way scholarship on black immigrants from the Caribbean and the African Diasporas has taken shape. Haitian Americans' presence has serious implications for U.S. society, its institutions, and public policies. The existing body of literature dealing with ethnic Haitian Americans, although not as voluminous as that of other recent ethnic groups in the United States, reflects a vast array of perspectives. Much of the literature centers on the history of immigration and the adaptation process of Haitian immigrants and Haitian Americans in many urban areas of the United States.

From reviewing the literature, three general impressions emerge. First, the literature describes the trials and tribulations of Haitian immigrants and refugees and provides historical and political perspectives to understand the legal wrangling and the activism of Haitian Americans who challenge U.S. immigration policies and processes. Second, the literature addresses issues of integration and acculturation and the efforts of Haitian Americans to adapt and survive in the new milieu through ethnic identity and community formation, viewed from sociological and sociolinguistic perspectives. Third, the literature focuses on second-generation Haitian Americans, their journey through the American landscape, incorporation in the cultural, political, and social life of the United States through schooling and work, and perceptions on diasporic issues and transnational dynamics. Penned by both Haitian American and non–Haitian American scholars, these distinct strata in the literature bear witness to the scope, challenges, and complexity of the historiography of Haitian Americans in North America.

The presence of Haitian Americans in early-nineteenth-century Maryland has been documented in the writings of Moreau de Saint-Mery's, *American Journey* (New York: Doubleday, 1947); and Rodolphe L. Desdunes's, *Our People and Our History* (Baton Rouge: Louisiana State Univ. Press, 1973). Walter C. Hartridge's article, "The Refugees from the Island of Saint Domingo in Maryland," *Maryland Historical Magazine* 38 (1943):103–22. The active presence of Haitian American during the Harlem Renaissance can be found in Ira Reid's, *The Negro Immigrant: His Background, Characteristics and Social Adjustment 1899–1937* (New York: Columbia Univ. Press, 1939). Equally important is David P. Geggus's, *Haitian Revolutionary Studies: Blacks in the Diaspora* (Bloomington: Indiana Univ. Press, 2002), 179–203. By bringing together an unparalleled variety of facts drawn from archival research in six countries, Geggus sheds light on this phenomenal upheaval and its aftermath. As such, these works are important in reconstructing the Haitian American journey, as well as in highlighting an understanding of Haitian affinity to America.

A handful of scholars have contributed topical essays on the origins, status, and development of the Haitian American experience in the United States. Some of these essays are the work of Claude Souffrant, "Les Haitiens aux Etats-Unis" in *Population* 29 (1974):133–146. Michel Laguerre's essay, "Haitians," in *The Harvard Encyclopedia of American Ethic Groups*, ed. Stephan Thernstrom et al. (Cambridge, MA: Harvard Univ. Press, 1980); also, James Allman's article "Haitian Migration: Thirty Years Assessed," *Migration Today* 10, no.1 (1982): 7–12. For a more comprehensive exploration, see Michel Laguerre's article "Haitian Immigrants in the United States: A Historical Overview," in *White Collar Migrants in the Americas and the Caribbean*, ed. Arnaud F. Marks and Hebe M. C. Vessuri, (Leiden: Royal Institute of Linguistics and Anthropology, 1983), 119–169. Also, J. C. Miller, *The Plight of Haitian Refugees* (New York: Praeger, 1984); Alex Stepick, *Haitian Refugees in the United States*, (London: Minority Rights Group, 1982) provide a critical sociohistorical perspective in the context of diverse conflicting immigration policies. Also, Alex Stepick's essay "The Roots of Haitian Migration," in *Haiti Today and Tomorrow*, ed. Albert Valdman et al. (Maryland: Univ. Press of America, 1984), 337–350. In a pioneering effort, each of these writers provides a historical account of the presence of Haitian Americans, as well as their dreams and aspirations as expressed in the types of institutional networks they have constructed.

In fact, Michel Laguerre's *American Odyssey: Haitians in New York City* (Ithaca, NY: Cornell Univ. Press, 1984), is a classic introduction to the Haitian American experience in the United States. It assesses the development and adaptation of the Haitian American enclaves in Brooklyn, Manhattan, and Queens. Also useful are Michele Klopner's "A Composite Profile of Haitian Immigrants in the United States Based on Community Needs Assessment" (PhD diss., Rutgers Univ., 1985); and Brian Marvis' *The Haitian Americans: The Immigrant Experience* (New York: Chelsea House, 2003).

A handful of dissertations, articles, and book chapters examine Haitian American ethnic identity and community formation with an understanding of the conflicted notions of race and ethnicity in the United States. This is explored within the context of the idea of the melting pot and cultural pluralism theories in immigrant studies. Among them are Jessie Marie Colin's dissertation, "My Body in Miami, My Soul in Haiti: Understanding the Adolescent Who Is Haitian" (PhD diss., Adelphi Univ., 2000); Susan H. Buchanan's article, "Language and Identity: Haitians in New York City" (*International Migration Review* 13, no. 2 (1979): 298–313), which explores the correlation between language and identity by examining Haitian American attitudes toward the use of Haitian Creole,

French, and English in the New York City areas. Also, Nina Glick's doctoral dissertation, "The Formation of a Haitian Ethnic Group" (PhD diss., Columbia Univ., 1975), provides an analysis of the Haitian immigrant ethnic group formation by identifying particular characteristics in the establishment of dual mediating institutions, agencies, and organizations within sending states. In the same vein, a groundbreaking and thought-provoking analysis of Haitian American identity formation can be found in Flore Zéphir's book *Haitian Immigration in Black America: A Sociological and Sociolinguistic Portrait* (Westport, CT: Bergin & Garvey, 1996). Zéphir suggests including recent immigrants in the larger discussion on race and ethnicity in the United States and, also, ceasing the practice of grouping together different minority groups on the basis of common racial heritage. The significance of this text is its examination of the very core and the essence of Haitian American ethnicity and culture. It also documents and demonstrates how the historical meaning of racial identity is grounded in national pride and how this world-view shapes the psychological disposition of many Haitian Americans and determines their behavior and action. Lastly, Alex Stepick et al., *This Land Is Our Land: Immigrants and Power in Miami* (Berkeley: Univ. of California Press, 2003), examines the interactions between Haitian American immigrants and established Americans in order to address fundamental questions of American identity and multiculturalism. It looks at Miami's development over the last four decades, to convey the salient message that immigration in America is not simply an "us versus them" phenomenon.

Several works document demographic and socioeconomic studies on Haitian Americans with local particularities. Among them are Pierre-Michel Fontaine's "Haitian Immigrants in Boston: A Commentary," in *Caribbean Immigration to the United States*, ed. Royce S. Bryce-Laporte et al. (Washington, DC: Research Institute on Immigration and Ethnic Studies, Smithsonian Institution, 1976), 111–129; Charles Radin, "From Haiti to Boston: A Portrait of the Nation's Third Largest Community of Haitian Immigrants," *Boston Globe Magazine*, December 15, 1995, 18–30, which provides a chronological history of Boston Haitian Americans, reasons for migration, and the different skills Haitian Americans brought to Massachusetts; and Susan H. Buchanan's, "Scattered Seeds: The Meaning of the Migration for Haitians in New York City" (PhD diss., New York Univ., 1980), which analyzes existing statistical data to answer questions centered on ethnicity, language, value systems, social mores, and common history. For an analysis of the incorporation of Haitian Americans into U.S. social structure, their level of consciousness, and patterns of identification that impede their assimilation or enhance their integration see Nina Glick-Schiller et al., "All in the Same Boat?: Unity and Diversity in Haitian Organizing in New York," in *Caribbean Life in New York City: Socio-Cultural Dimensions*, ed. Constance Sutton and Elsa Cheney (Staten Island, NY: Center for Migration Studies, 1987), 182–201; and Joel Dreyfus's article "The Invisible Immigrants," *New York Times Magazine*, May 23, 1993.

Anthony V. Cantanese's book, *Haitian Migrations and Diaspora* (Boulder, CO: Westview, 1994), utilizes census data and INS statistics to explain the Haitian American migratory process and the ensuing diasporization dynamics. Chantale F. Verna, "Beyond the Immigration Centers: A History of Haitian Community in Three Michigan Cities (1966–1998)" (PhD diss., Michigan State Univ., 2000), presents an excellent analysis of the origin and development of the Haitian American community in Michigan. Using a typology, she demonstrates how the three different groups of migrants who arrived in three successive waves settled in three Michigan cities. Teklemarian Woldemikael's,

Becoming Black American: Haitians and American Institutions in Evanston, Illinois (New York: AMS Press, 1989), provides a detailed look at this specific community of Haitian Americans and discusses the effects of African American culture on Haitian American identity and cultural values. Thomas D. Boswell's article "The New Haitian Diaspora, Florida's Most Recent Residents," *Caribbean Review* 11, no. 1 (1979): 18–21. Brian Walsh's article, "Haitians in Miami," *Migration Today* 7, no. 4 (1979): 42–44. Michel Laguerre's article, "Haitians in the Southern States" in *Encyclopedia of Southern Culture*, ed. William Ferris and Charles Wilson, (Chapel Hill: Univ. of North Carolina Press, 1988). Alex Stepick and Alejandro Portes's article "Flight into Despair: A Profile of Recent Haitian Refugees in South Florida," *International Migration Review* 20, no. 2 (1986): 329–350. For an analysis of civic engagement, and lack thereof among Haitian Americans in Miami-Dade County, see Alex Stepick, et al. *Civic Engagement of Haitian Immigrants and Haitian Americans in Miami-Dade County*, (Miami, FL: Immigration and Ethnicity Institute, Florida International Univ., 2001).

As happens with every immigrant group in post-1965 immigration, Haitian Americans, in their search for survival, adaptation, and community formation in the United States, have also established a series of formal and informal mediating networks and transnational ties with the homeland. A handful of dissertations, essays, and books have contributed critical insights on many aspects of Haitian American transnationalism. From that perspective, Carolle Charles's outstanding dissertation, "A Transnational Dialectic of Race, Class and Ethnicity: Patterns of Identities and Forms of Consciousness among Haitian Migrants in New York City" (PhD, diss. State Univ. of New York at Binghamton, 1990), persuasively argues that, "the multiple racial identities which Haitian migrants to New York city display in their organizations and their public discourse is not an expression of ambiguity and/or denial of a racial consciousness. Rather, it is an expression of the different meanings of blackness that informs the consciousness and identity of Haitian immigrants" (102). Also, Rose-Marie Chierici's, *Demele, 'Making it': Migration and Adaptation among Haitian Boat People in the United States* (New York: AMS Press, 1991) focuses on the adaptation process of refugees and Haitian Americans by analyzing the establishment of various mediating institutions. Karen Richman's dissertation, "They will Remember Me in the House: The Pwen of Haitian Transnational Migration" (PhD diss., Univ. of Virginia, 1992), focuses on the Miami Haitian American transmigrant community. Pierre-Louis François's "Transnational Organizations and Citizen Participation: A Study of Haitian Immigrants in New York City" (PhD diss., City Univ. of New York, 2001), examines the experience of the sizeable Haitian American population of New York and their involvement in homeland associations and community-based organizing. Also, Tatiana Kaw-Siu Wah's "Expatriate Reconnection: An Alternative Approach to Expatriate Recovery and Engagement for Homeland Development: The Case of Haiti." (PhD diss., Rutgers Univ., 2001), argues for the importance of Haitian Americans actively engaging in the homeland and helping reverse the brain drain by pursuing venues in which to reconnect with Haiti. Also, Nina Glick-Schiller and Fouron, "EveryWhere We Go We Are in Danger": Ti Manno and the Emergence of a Haitian Transnational Identity," *American Ethnologist* (1989) 13 4:329–347, examines the central role Haitian Americans played in the opening up of transnational ties. For a methodical analysis of Haitian Americans' racial categories of identity through an exploration of the interaction between immigrants' forms of values in the context of race, ethnicity, and nationalism see Carolle Charles's article "Transnationalism in the Construct of Haitian's Migrants Racial Categories in New York City," in *Towards a Transnational Perspective on Migration: Race, Ethnicity, and Nationalism Reconsidered* ed. Nina Glick-Schiller, Linda Basch, and Christina Blanc-Szancton (New York: New York Academy of Sciences, 1991). Also, George Fouron's essay "The Black Dilemma in the U.S.: The Haitian Experience," *Journal of Caribbean Studies* 3, no. 3 (1982): 242–265.

The most comprehensive analysis of Haitian American transnationalism is Nina Glick-Schiller and Georges Fouron's, *Georges Woke up Laughing: Long-Distance Nationalism and the Search for Home* (Durham, NC: Duke Univ. Press, 1994), in which Glick-Schiller and Fouron present a portrait of the Haitian experience of migration to the United States that explains the phenomenon of long-distance nationalism. Nancy Foner's essay "What's New About Transnationalism? New Immigrants Today at the Turn of the Century," in *Diaspora* 6, no. 3 (Winter 1997): 355–375, attributes the slow integration of immigrants to the pressures of transnational ties and diasporic citizenship.

She explores how many Haitian Americans continue to be intimately and integrally connected to their relatives back in Haiti, sometimes even after they become legal citizens. The authors expose the realities and quandaries that underlie the efforts of long-distance nationalists to redefine citizenship, race, nationality, and political loyalty; also highlighted are the forces that shape Haitian Americans' experiences of government and citizenship to create a transborder citizenry.

As Haitian Americans claim their space in the social landscape of the United States, they become more visible in the political arena, actively engaging in politics both at home and abroad. However, not much writing exists on this topic. It seems almost impractical and even impossible to clearly disassociate, or even to separate, the literature that focuses on Haitian Americans as diasporic or as transnational from the literature focusing on political participation in the United States. In fact, Haitian Americans' political activism comes primarily out of an ethnic political identity formed within the American social and racial space. Karen Richman's provocative essay "A *Lavalas* at Home/A *Lavalas* for Home: Inflections of Transnationalism in the Discourse of President Jean Bertrand Aristide," in *Towards a Transnational Perspective on Migration*, ed. Glick-Schiller et al., 189–200, analyzes the double meaning implicit in the political discourse of leaders who encourage political participation and activism both at home and abroad. Another insight comes from Michel Laguerre's essay "The Role of the Diaspora in Politics," in Robert Rotberg, *Haiti Renewed: Political and Economic Prospects*, ed. Robert Rotberg, 170–183 (Washington, DC: Brookings Institution Press, 1997), which "analyzes the transnational political field that links the diaspora to the homeland, the transnational circuit of social mobility, and informal transnational practices as they influence the local Haitian political reality" (170). Nina Glick Schiller's article "The Implications of Haitian Transnationalism for U.S–Haiti Relations: Contradictions of the De-territorialized Nation-State," *Journal of Haitian Studies* 1, no. 1 (Spring 1995): 111–123, explores the way in which Haitian transnationalism is effecting U.S.-Haitian relations and looks at how Haitian Americans have responded to this deterritorialized context by maintaining and developing familial, political, religious, social, and economic interconnections with Haiti. Michel S. Laguerre's essay "State, Diaspora and Transnational Politics," *Millennium: Journal of International Studies* 28, no.3 (1999): 663–651, analyzes five models of state-diaspora relations—namely, reincorporation, ethnic, economic, political opposition, and transnational—in the context of the history of Haitian American experience in the United States. Also, Opitz Gotz-Dietreich, "Transnational

Organizing and the Haitian Crisis, 1991–1994," *Journal of Haitian Studies* 8, no. 2 (Spring 2002): 114–126, argues that "transnational organizing as a bilateral relations between Haiti and the U.S. represents a social field of bi-directional and reciprocal patterns of stimuli and responses, which was affected by both international actors and transnational formations" (115). Worthy of mention also are two articles that provide factual information and data on the Haitian-Americans' emerging American identity, civic involvement, and political activism in Miami and Chicago: Marjorie Valbrun, "Haitian-Americans: Their Search for Political Identity in South Florida," *The APF Reporter* 20, no. 1 (2001): 60–66; and Valbrun, "Haitian-American Politics in Chicago," *The APF Reporter* 20, no. 2 (2002): 60–63.

Generally speaking, research on the impact of education and schooling on Haitian American students has received little attention, except for sparse coverage in journal articles and in book chapters dealing with black immigrants, West Indian, or Caribbean, other language minority groups, Latinos, and Asians. However, Flore Zéphir's, *Haitian Immigrants in Black America: A Sociological and Sociolinguistic Portrait* (Westport: CT, Bergin & Garvey, 1996) is a significant sociological work that examines the educational issues of Haitian American students. In addition, an entire chapter on the urban schooling experiences of Haitian Americans in the United States can be found in Michel Laguerre's seminal text *Diasporic Citizenship: Haitian Americans in Transnational America* (New York: St. Martin's Press, 1998). Mary C. Waters' *Black Identity: West Indian Dreams and American Realities* (Cambridge, MA: Harvard Univ. Press, 1999) argues that "black immigrants from the Caribbean come to the United States with a particular identity/culture/worldview that reflects their unique history and experiences" (6). In the chapter "Neighborhoods and Schools," Waters addresses the tension between first-generation Haitian American students and other ethnic groups in New York's urban schools. Emphasis is also given to the "division in the ways in which the second generation balanced their race and ethnic identity" (286). Flore Zéphir's, *Trends in Ethnic Identification among Second Generation Haitian Immigrants* (Westport, CT: Bergin & Garvey 2001), assesses the identity formation among second-generation Haitian American students and their sense of integration in American society. Except for the few studies mentioned above, there is a dearth of research in the field of education with an emphasis on Haitian American students.

A few scholars have documented efforts to develop strong community ties between Haitian Americans and African Americans that benefit both groups in their struggle for equality, justice, and the fight against prejudice. Alex Stepick's thought-provoking *Pride against Prejudice: Haitians in the United States* (Needham Heights, MA: Allyn & Bacon, 1998) describes the struggle of Haitian Americans, the devastating impact of cultural conflict with other ethnic minority groups in the United States; the strained relations with African Americans; and the prejudice against Haitian Americans. Also on this topic, see Henriette Gomis, "The Impact of the Congressional Black Caucus on United States Foreign Policy: Haiti and the Haitian Refugees, 1991–1994" (PhD diss., Univ. of Miami, 2000). For a preeminent historical account of the U.S. occupation of independent Haiti, see Mary Renda's *Taking Haiti: Military Occupation and the Culture of U.S. Imperialism* (Chapel Hill: Univ. of North Carolina Press, 2001). It also addresses the emergence of a Haitian American transnational community that was formed in New York as a result of links established through the emigration of African Americans to Haiti in the previous century. Perhaps the most comprehensive is Leon Pamphile's *Haitians and African*

Americans: A Heritage of Tragedy and Hope (Miami: Univ. of Florida Press, 2002), which analyzes the relations between Haitians and African Americans from the colonial period to the present; it explains how historical ties between these two communities of the African diaspora have influenced their respective histories, cultures, and community lives. Further, it examines U.S. perceptions of Haiti in the first half of the nineteenth century, during the debate over slavery and emancipation, and Haiti's role as a model in the struggle for liberation and then an asylum for many escaping oppression in the United States.

A thematic review of the literature reveals some remarkable interdisciplinary work while helping to capture the scope of the existing literature on Haitian Americans. For an introduction to understanding Haitian Americans' ethnic health beliefs and practices, Michel Laguerre's article "Haitian-Americans," in *Ethnicity and Medical Care*, ed. Alan Harwood, 172–210 (Cambridge, MA: Harvard Univ. Press, 1981) is a must. In the area of religious manifestations, faith-based communities and health beliefs and practices, Karen McCarthy Brown's classic, *Mama Lola: A Voodoo Priestess in Brooklyn* (1991; repr. Berkeley: Univ. of California Press, 2002) provides a detailed and sympathetic account of the world of Haitian Voodoo among Haitian Americans in Brooklyn, New York. In addition to exploring the importance of women's religious practices, attendant with themes of family and of social change, it demystifies Hollywood's stereotypes on Haitian vodoo. Also see Elizabeth A. McAlister's *Rara: Vodou, Power, and Performance in Haiti and Its Diaspora* (Berkeley: Univ. of California Press, 2002), which focuses on Afro-Caribbean religion, music, and Haitian culture. Academically researched and engagingly written, the chapter "Rara in New York City: Transnational Popular Culture," exposes the reader to Afro-Caribbean religious manifestations, namely Haitian vodoo through rara, a form of Haitian popular music. Other significant noted works are: Nina Glick Schiller, "What's Wrong with This Picture? The Hegemonic Construction of Culture in AIDS Research in the United States," in *Medical Anthropology Quarterly* 6 (1992) 3: 237–254; and Paul Farmer's, *Aids and Accusations: Haiti and the Geography of Blame* (Berkeley: Univ. of California Press, 1993) describes some of the complicated historical and ethnographic connections between illness and racism and the longstanding ignorance and racist misunderstandings about Haitian vodoo. Farmer points out how stereotypes and racial profiling of Haitian citizenship as a risk factor (one of the Four *H*s along with hemophiliacs, homosexuals, and heroin user), contributed to public policies penalizing Haitian immigrants. Also see Robert Lawless, "Haitian Migrants and Haitian Americans from Invisibility into the Spotlight," *Journal of Ethnic Studies* 14, no. 2 (1990): 29–70, explores the meaning of ethnic and racial invisibility for Haitian Americans.

Finally, there is a body of research on Haitian American business with a focus on ethnic entrepreneurship, capital formation, and the diaspora economy. This new line of inquiry can be found in Michel S. Laguerre, "Rotating Credit Associations and the Diasporic Economy" *Journal of Developmental Entrepreneurship* 3, no. 1 (1998); and Marilyn Halter, "Staying Close to Haitian Culture: Ethnic Enterprise in the Immigrant Community," in *New Migrants in the Marketplace: Boston's Ethnic Entrepreneurs*, ed. M. Halter (Amherst, MA: Univ. of Massachusetts Press, 1995). The problems that older Haitian Americans are confronting in their adaptation to American society are reported in Michel S. Laguerre, "Diasporic Aging," in *Age through Ethnic Lenses*, ed. Laura Katz Olson (Lanham, MD: Rowman & Littlefield, 2001): 103–112.

IRISH AMERICANS

Lawrence J. McCaffrey

Hunger, poverty, political and religious oppression, and searches for adventure and opportunity have dispatched the Irish throughout the world, generally to English-speaking countries, usually North America, particularly the United States. According to the 1990 census, almost 39 million Americans claimed Irish, and about 5 million Scots-Irish, heredity. During the eighteenth and early nineteenth centuries, hundreds of thousands of Irish Protestants, mostly Ulster Presbyterians, crossed the Atlantic, escaping excessive rents, land shortages, paying of tithes to the established Church of Ireland, and religious persecution. And they expected a better life in the New World. They tended to leave Ireland as families, sometimes as total communities, and they settled in various places. New England Calvinists were not hospitable to their rowdy Irish brethren; Pennsylvania, Virginia, and the Carolinas were more welcoming. Ulster Presbyterian émigrés pioneered America's western frontier, serving as farming buffers between Indians and Tidewater whites on the Atlantic coast.[1] In 1790, of the 447,000 Irish in the United States, 295,000, or approximately two-thirds, came from Ulster Presbyterian stock. They have been industrious, not only as tillers of the soil but as industrialists and merchants such as the Carnegies and Mellons. At least eleven American presidents had Ulster Scots-Irish roots: Andrew Jackson, James K. Polk, James Buchanan, Andrew Johnson, Ulysses S. Grant, Chester Alan Arthur, Grover Cleveland, Benjamin Harrison, William McKinley, Theodore Roosevelt, and Woodrow Wilson.[2]

In the eighteenth and early nineteenth centuries, few Catholics journeyed to America. Many who did were either convicts who were being transported or indentured servants with little knowledge of or commitment to their religion. Before and after indentures or sentences, they resided in places where Catholicism lacked a presence. As a result, the vast majority became Protestant, usually Evangelical.[3] Most Irish Catholics who left Ireland at this time went to England and Scotland as seasonal farm laborers or more permanently as unskilled workers amid Britain's industrial and transportation revolutions.

After 1820, the religious profile of Irish emigration changed radically. Over the next hundred years, 75 percent of the 5 million who left Ireland for the United States were Catholic. Following the Napoleonic Wars, Irish agriculture changed from predominantly tillage to predominantly pasture, resulting in land scarcity at a time of a massive population increase and diminishing feelings of security and hope for the future.[4] In addition to an underdeveloped agrarian economy and industrial-employment alternatives being limited to Northeast Ulster, the three-quarters Catholic majority's resistance to paying tithes to an established Protestant Church that served only 13 percent of the population, and fears of rural secret-society violence—agricultural laborers against tenant farmers, and tenant farmers against landlords—also contributed to desires to leave a troubled land. During the 1820s, 1830s, and early 1840s, most Catholics emigrants were tenant farmers with financial resources to pay passages and to sustain themselves through their early days in the United States.

In 1845, a potato virus originating in the United States reached Europe. Since millions in rural Ireland were almost totally dependent on that root crop for nourishment, they suffered more than peasants in other countries. The disease also devastated harvests in 1846, 1848, and 1849, and the aftershock persisted until 1851. At least 1.5 million perished during the Great Hunger from starvation and associated diseases such as cholera, fever, and scurvy. A million desperate refugees found their way to the United States. Early Famine emigrants tended to be relatively well off; in its later years, most were impoverished souls in flight from hunger and death. A large number, usually those involved in landlord-sponsored exoduses, arrived literally naked in the New World. Many, already sick when they boarded the over-crowded, filthy "coffin" ships, died at sea and found watery graves. Others perished on arrival, and perhaps as many as 30,000 Famine fatalities rest on Grosse Isle near Quebec.[5]

The Famine institutionalized Irish immigration as a safety valve for a country unable to feed or employ many of its people. Only one son could inherit the farm, one daughter could have a marriage dowry, some lads could join the Royal Irish Constabulary or the British army or navy, and a few lassies could work as servants in Protestant Big Houses, so mothers and fathers in rural Ireland raised most of their children for export. In the vast majority of cases, leaving home for America was a one-way trip. The "American Wake," a departure ceremony lasting into the 1950s, represented its finality.

Before and during the Famine, Irish Catholic emigrants tended to leave as families. But following the Great Hunger they usually departed as singles, unlike most other European groups emigrating to the United States at that time. Since women in Ireland had fewer economic or marriage prospects than their brothers, by the end of the nineteenth century they, more than men, sought American futures.[6] Despite fears of Irish bishops, priests, and prominent laymen on both sides of the Atlantic that the temptation of urban America endangered immigrant faith and morals, the vast majority of these immigrants settled in cities or towns.[7]

While it is true that poverty restricted many new Irish immigrants to port cities, few who could afford to purchase land at a dollar-and-a-quarter an acre took advantage of the opportunity. Small tenant farmers or agricultural laborers from Ireland's primitive agrarian economy lacked necessary skills to cultivate and harvest successfully America's spacious and fertile fields. Contrasts between rural areas of Ireland, where closely built cottages encouraged socializing, and rural regions of the United States, where distant neighbors and harsh winters bred isolation, also discouraged rural settlement. City life was morally and physically parlous but consoling in that it offered the company of one's own kind. Religion also factored in the urban choice. Like Judaism, Catholicism is liturgically and theologically more communal and less individualistic than Protestantism. Other Catholic peasant groups, for example, Poles, Italians, and Croatians, also have preferred urban to rural America. And Catholics from Germany, more than Protestants, seem to have preferred New World cities.[8]

Few early Irish immigrants had either educational backgrounds or physical skills to be more successful in urban than rural America. To survive, men engaged in hard, often dangerous, physical labor on docks, in horse barns, on riverboats. They dug foundations, mixed cement, and carried bricks on building sites; mined coal, iron, gold, silver, and copper; dug canals; and laid railroad tracks. Their occupations plus such diseases as alcoholism and tuberculosis abbreviated life spans. In Ireland, the call to adventure, the desire to escape the dull routines of puritan Catholic rural life, the prospect of a few shillings, the appeal of flashy uniforms, and the promise of a pension led many a lad to join the British army. American military and naval life held a similar attraction.

Irish women worked in shoe and textile factories or, more often, became domestics, dusting, sweeping, serving meals, and caring for children in the homes of affluent Anglo-Protestant Americans. While sometimes demeaning and sexually hazardous, domestic service was usually cleaner and healthier than factory employment and provided a taste of the good life. Because of this experience, former Irish maids and housekeepers propelled their husbands and children in the direction of middle-class respectability. No matter where they worked, Irish women were more likely than men to save money that raised the standard of living of their families back in Ireland and paid passage fares for siblings who then followed them to the United States.[9]

As pioneers of urban-ethnic ghettos in the United States, Irish Catholics were a massive social problem. Their traumatic passage from rural Ireland to American cities affected their conduct as well as mental and physical health. Alcohol addictions, that had disrupted families and triggered violent behavior in Ireland became a bigger problem in America. Drink and poverty nourished crime; violence, often domestic; delinquency; and a variety of neuroses. Along the East

Coast, and, later, other parts of the country, the Irish filled jails, hospitals, mental institutions, and orphanages. Quite often, fathers deserted wives and children, adding to family destitution and children and adolescent misbehavior. To Anglo-Americans, and even French Catholics in New Orleans, Irish Catholics were a social plague devastating their cities, multiplying the expenses of public institutions and the costs of maintaining law and order.

For Americans of British lineage, social disorder was a lesser Irish evil than was their religion. The anti-Catholicism of those of English, Scottish, Welsh, Ulster Presbyterian, and Anglo-Irish heritage became an essential ingredient of American nativism. Since at the beginnings of the Republic the shy, deferential American Catholic Church, with its one bishop, thirty priests, and 30,000 members (of whom 10 percent were black slaves), was virtually invisible, early "no-popery" contested a mythical rather than a real enemy.[10]

But after 1820, when Irish Catholics became the largest immigrant group, the enemy had a public face. For Protestant Americans or those committed to the rationalism of the Enlightenment, slaves of Roman authoritarianism and superstition could never become trusted fellow citizens, and their existence constituted a perceived danger to the country's values and institutions. Some of the most vehement anti-Catholics came from Ulster Presbyterian stock. To distinguish themselves from the despicable papists, they took on a Scots-Irish identity, guaranteeing that until very late in twentieth-century America, *Irish* and *Catholic* would be integrated identities. Anti-Irish prejudices took on racial as well as religious dimensions, with cartoon depictions of the Irish as an inferior, ape-like species, brutal as well as ignorant.[11]

Although authoritarian, aristocratic, and reactionary governments in European Catholic countries, including the papal states, seemed to confirm American nativism's fear of Catholicism as subversive of American liberties, Ireland was different. While Catholicism in Ireland was deeply devotional, short on aesthetic and intellectual content, strongly puritanical in regard to sex, and extremely loyal to Rome in matters of religion, thanks to the influence of Daniel O'Connell, the founding father of modern Irish nationalism, it was not antithetical to American political values. Instead, it accepted the democratic, freedom-of-conscience, separation-of-church-and-state principles of its ally, Irish nationalism. When Gustave de Beaumont and Alexis de Tocqueville visited early nineteenth-century Ireland, they were amazed to hear priests express commitments to popular sovereignty and preferences for the political ideas of British radicals and Whigs to those of Continental Catholic political theorists.[12] Since they had been schooled in O'Connell's version of Irish nationalism, Irish Catholic immigrants found it easy to adjust to American political culture. Later, they led ethnic co-religionists into similar accommodations.

Although it was an obstacle to acceptance and success, Catholicism compensated the Irish by offering them solace in a hostile atmosphere. Attending Mass and religious devotions and receiving the sacraments were bridges of familiarity between rural Ireland and urban America. Anti-Catholic agitations strengthened bonds between Catholicism and Irish cultural identity. In social as well as religious spheres, city parishes came to resemble old-country peasant communities. Irish American parents contributed many of their best and brightest daughters and sons to the Catholic Church as priests, nuns, and brothers. As in Ireland, entire families acquired respect and status if sons wore Roman collars and daughters nun's habits. By the close of the nineteenth century, two-thirds of the American Catholic hierarchy was Irish and so were a vast majority of nuns, priests, and brothers. And the Irish were as generous with their money as they were with their children. Working-class dollars built churches, rectories, convents, and schools. More than any other group, the Irish built the infrastructure and superstructure of the American urban Catholic Church.[13]

Deep into the twentieth century, from birth to burial Irish Americans lived their lives within a Catholic context. They worked with those of other faiths but worshipped and socialized with their own kind. From primary school through college and university, Catholic education emphasized loyalty to country but insisted on a religious distinctiveness that distrusted what it described as America's mainstream "secularism, materialism, and pragmatism." In a rote-memory, apologetic approach to learning, Catholic education succeeded in teaching fundamentals but discouraged intellectual exploration or creativity. And an Irish puritanical obsession with sex rather than Christian charity pervaded instructions on Catholic morality.[14]

A shortage of Christian charity has at times been evident in the Irish reaction to other races, religions, and nationalities. They vehemently opposed abolitionism and turned against O'Connell when he censured them for supporting such a vile institution as slavery.[15] Irish soldiers fought to preserve the Union, not to liberate blacks. Irish Catholics were prominent in mobs protesting the Draft Act of 1863. In New York, they murdered eleven blacks and an Indian mistaken for one, and burned down a black orphanage.[16] Later in the nineteenth century, the San Francisco Irish opposed Chinese immigration. In many parts of the country, especially in the East, they have had a long record of anti-Semitism. Whiteness theorists, such as Noel Ignatiev, have attributed Irish antiblack sentiment as an aspiration for whiteness in racist America.[17] Eric Arneson effectively rebuts this thesis by pointing out that neither the Irish nor the institutions of the United States ever disputed Irish whiteness. Although many other Americans viewed them as inferior it was because of their Catholic culture and religion and their early social misconduct, not their skin color.[18] There are much more historically correct and plausible explanations for Irish racial prejudice than the quest for whiteness: ignorance, competition for lower-level jobs, adoption of general American attitudes, and something common among many defensive minorities, the compulsion to inflict their miseries on others, especially those on lower rungs of the economic and social ladder.

Experiences with poverty, alienation, and Anglo-Protestant and Scots-Irish hostility physically and psychologically ghettoized the Irish in the United States and spurred them to liberate the mother country from British occupation. Irish American nationalism not only expressed anger over Ireland's painful past but also bitterness over the immigrant experience. American Irish blamed Britain for the hunger, poverty, political, and religious oppression that forced them or antecedents to depart from what became a mythical Emerald Isle and to journey to another land, where they would again confront hostility and discrimination. In many ways, Irish American nationalists hated Britain more than they loved Ireland. From the 1840s until recent events in Northern Ireland, that passionate detestation and the dollars that it engendered nourished both physical force and constitutional efforts to free Ireland.[19]

Obstructed by anti-Catholicism from business, commerce, and, to a lesser extent, the professions as avenues to affluence and success, Irish American talent sought power and influence through politics and religion. As previously mentioned, Irish Catholicism and nationalism approved of democratic government and the separation of church and state, indoctrinating immigrants in what were fundamental American political values before they left home. And throughout the nineteenth century, many of the Irish coming to America had participated in a variety of mass agitations to gain Catholic civil rights, eliminate the tithe, repeal the union with Britain, guarantee security of tenure on their farms at fair rents, and home rule. Politics was a familiar game, and they played it with gusto and skill.

Self-interest rather than ideology attached the vast majority of Irish Catholic immigrants to the Democratic Party. Whigs, American Party Know-Nothings, and Republicans appealed to anti-Catholics. Democratic politicians met immigrants at the pier, speeded their naturalization, and found them jobs. In gratitude, the Irish voted for their benefactors but weren't content to be mere foot soldiers in the Democratic army. Quickly, they took control over neighborhood political organizations, and by the close of the nineteenth century were in charge of most of cities north of the Mason-Dixon line and had considerable influence in New Orleans in the South, giving them considerable weight in the national Democratic Party.

In and out of the halls of academia, Irish political power has been a subject for debate. Nativists and reformers have found it deplorable that Irish Catholics transformed much of urban America into fiefs of graft and corruption. More recently, some historians have credited Irish political machines with bringing people of other disadvantaged ethnicities into the American political process and providing the poor with food baskets, coal for their stoves, medical and funeral expenses, bail money, and jobs. Others have complained that Irish political power blocked significant social improvement.[20] For example, Steven P. Erie, an expert on Irish American politics, argues that Irish politicians, except in cities such as Chicago and Pittsburgh, where ethnic diversity and equality demanded coalitions with other groups, have tended to parcel out most of the benefits of power to their own people and tried to satisfy others with mere token gestures of concern. He also insists that employment related to politics froze the Irish in low-paying, blue-collar and white-collar bureaucratic jobs, closing off more interesting and lucrative possibilities.[21]

On balance, the Irish impact on American politics appears to have been more positive than negative. Most late-nineteenth- and early-twentieth-century reformers were far more interested in good, efficient, and moral, rather than generous, government. While they campaigned against liquor, gambling, prostitution, and the corruption and wastefulness of ethnic politics, Irish politicians took care of constituents' daily needs. The attention to constituents' needs and problems provided by such machine politicians as New York's George Washington Plunkett and Chicago's Johnny Powers indicate that they cared for the non-Irish as well as their own kind.[22] Erie certainly exaggerates the economic and professional opportunities for the Irish in anti-Catholic America. For many, politics brought jobs as well as power. Perhaps the most important benefit that the Irish brought to American politics was their redirection of the character and purpose of the Democratic Party. In an appeal for voter loyalty, and perhaps out of Catholic corporatist views of social justice, they led their party away from individualistic and toward communal liberalism. From 1912 to 1916, Governor Edward F. Dunne of Illinois steered bills though the state legislature that improved the rights and working conditions of laborers and the health of the state's citizens. He also proved that an Irish American Catholic politician could be as concerned with efficient government as progressive, Anglo-Protestant reformers.[23] In the 1920s, New York's governor, Al Smith, a Tammany Hall product, with the guidance of Jewish and Anglo-Protestant advisers, pioneered important legislation, much of which improved the work environment.[24] At the same time, Monsignor John Ryan, codirector of the Social Action Department of the National Catholic Welfare Conference, authored a social justice agenda that anticipated the New Deal.[25]

In the second half of the nineteenth century, Irish America's economic and social standing obviously improved, partly because of better educated, more affluent immigrants who were products of a changing Ireland that featured a rising standard of living, a "Devotional Revolution" in Catholicism, and a tremendous increase in literacy.[26] By the beginning of the twentieth century, only about 5 percent of the Irish arriving in the United States could not read or write, making them more literate than the American average. Most of the men still had to accept lower-level employment on building sites, in mines, and in factories, and women, in textile mills, in the homes of Anglo-Protestants, or as restaurant waitresses. But even some qualified immigrants, like an expanding number of second- and third-generation Irish Americans, were able to join the skilled labor force as plumbers, painters, plasterers, electricians, railroad engineers, firemen, signal supervisors, and clerks. Irish Americans were visible as motormen and conductors on streetcars and subways, bureaucrats in city governments, and postal workers. Serving in police and fire departments became Irish family vocations. Although this wave of immigrants had more going for them even prior to their arrival in the United States than earlier immigrants, other factors were probably more important to Irish American progress: the morality and discipline imposed by Catholic institutions, politically associated jobs, and immigrants from eastern and southern Europe, who replaced the Irish in the lower levels of employment, escalating their climb to better jobs.

By the beginning of the twentieth century, Irish Americans usually were in the skilled working class, with a significant penetration of the middle class as teachers, nurses, lawyers, doctors, dentists, and owners of small businesses. Nuns were teachers, school principals, college presidents, and hospital nurses and directors. In leading the professional advance of American women, they inspired female students to follow their examples. In many cities, especially Boston, Chicago, New York, and San Francisco, Irish American women have been prominent in the ranks of public school teachers and on hospital staffs.[27]

Although Irish Americans improved their economic situation, they still felt insecure about their status. Consequently, they added another dimension to their nationalism. For many, hate for the hereditary Sassenach enemy remained vivid, but for others, those achieving economic mobility, Ireland's independence was a key to American social acceptability and respectability. They believed that their mother country's bondage related to their exclusion from the full benefits of American citizenship. In liberating Ireland, they expected to free themselves from the afflictions of prejudice.[28]

Irish Americans contributed political skills to the labor movement, agitating for decent wages, a shorter day of toil, and a healthy workplace. In 1879, Terence V. Powderly became the first Grand Master of the Knights of Labor, the original effort to nationally organize the workforce. Founded in 1886, the American Federation of Labor (AFL) quickly surpassed the Knights in membership. By 1910, Irish Americans held 45 percent of its presidencies.[29] Irish and Jewish labor leaders, like Irish politicians, concentrated on the grievances and needs of white ethnics to the neglect of African and Hispanic Americans.[30] Irish American women as well as men were active in the labor movement. Among them, Kate Kennedy (San Francisco), and Margaret Haley and Catherine Goggins (Chicago) organized public school teachers. Leonora Barry had a leadership role in the Knights of Labor, as did Elizabeth Flynn Rogers. Leonora O'Reilly and Agnes Nestor organized garment and glove workers.[31]

Irish American progress displayed regional variations. They did better in the cities of the Midwest and West, where economies were more varied and dynamic, anti-Catholicism was less intense, and social structures more flexible than in the East, especially New England.[32] But even the East, glimmers of positive change were apparent. In Edward McSorley's 1946 novel, *Our Own Kind*, which is set in the second decade of the twentieth century, a County Leitrim immigrant named Ned McDermott recalls earlier days in Providence, Rhode Island, where signs like No Irish Need Apply were common. But he observes an increasing number of Irish businessmen and professionals and pride replacing defeat in his community: "Yes God bless them, today the spires of their churches reached higher into the skies than anything in the city, proud and enduring with their altars of Carrara and Connemara marble, their stained glass and their loud defiant bells. There was hardly a parish now without its own school."[33]

McSorley's novel represents the middle of an Irish American literary tradition that began in the 1890s with Finley Peter Dunne's Mr. Dooley essays in the *Chicago Evening Post*, although there were Irish American writers before Dunne. In the 1870s, John Boyle O'Reilly gathered a literary coterie around him at the *Boston Pilot*, but its work reflected the genteel idealism of the New England literary establishment and Young Ireland's romanticism and never really penetrated the harsh existence of urban Irish America. In contrast, Dunne presented the first realistic literary portrait of an American ethnic group.[34] In discussions with Hennessey and McKenna, two of his customers, Martin Dooley, immigrant saloon-keeper from County Roscommon, revealed the lives of Chicago's Bridgeport and Canaryville neighborhoods: mill workers, firemen, policemen, priests, housewives, widows, and politicians. James T. Farrell, another Chicago realist, described the generation of Irish Americans that followed, still insecure, but often middle class and living in finer neighborhoods, though constantly moving to avoid integration with an expanding African American population. In time, Irish American writers such as Eugene O'Neill, William Kennedy, Alice McDermott, Maureen Howard, Elizabeth Cullinan, J. F. Powers, Peter Quinn, Frank Gilroy, Jimmy Breslin, and Pete Hamill, inspired by the Literary Revival in Ireland and interpreting the journey of their own people from working-class ghettos to middle-class suburbs, would produce some of the best work in American literature and theater.

In efforts to make it in the United States, the Irish established many precedents, including sports as a safety valve in explosive social situations and as a path to fame and fortune. From the early days of boxing until the June 1941 night in New York when heavyweight champion Joe Louis knocked out his light-heavyweight challenger, Billy Conn, the Irish were a dominant force in the ring, so much so that many other ethnics fought under Hibernian monikers. In the late nineteenth and early twentieth centuries, Irish stars shone on baseball diamonds. Mike "King" Kelly, Ed Delahanty, Charles Comiskey, John McGraw, and Connie Mack are among many in Cooperstown's Hall of Fame. At first, the American public associated college football with Ivy League schools, but in the 1920s it developed a less elitist aura, and Catholic colleges and universities with largely Irish student bodies—especially Notre Dame, when its nickname, the "Fighting Irish," was more appropriate than it is now—played a much better and tougher brand of the game than did Yale, Harvard, or Princeton.

As well as being athletes, Irish Americans performed as entertainers: actors, singers, dancers, and comedians. Historian William B. Williams argues that Irish songs, particularly those in the musical sketches of Harrigan and Hart, did much to lift their ethnic image.[35] Multitalented George M. Cohan became the king of Broadway.

Despite positive changes in their incomes and class standing, Irish Americans remained defensive, sometimes to the point of paranoia, well into the twentieth century. Because of their control of urban politics, the Catholic Church, and a large portion of the labor movement, they continued to be a leading target of nativism, sharing the burden with their coreligionists and African and Jewish Americans. The popularity of the Ku Klux Klan, mostly in the South and Midwest, and the anti-Catholic rhetoric directed against Al Smith in his 1928 bid for the presidency convinced them that they were a long way from acceptable. A considerable amount of Catholic newspaper sympathy for Fascist dictatorships in Catholic countries in Europe and South America, and substantial, if not a majority, of Irish support for pro-Mussolini, anti-Semitic Father Charles Coughlin in the 1930s indicated their insecurities and seemed to substantiate suspicions that they were not trustworthy Americans. During World War II, disciples of Father Coughlin and members of the hate-mongering Christian Front assaulted Jews in Boston.

However, during the 1930s and 1940s, sectarian and ethnic barriers lowered when all sections of the American populace shared economic insecurity during the Great Depression and patriotism during World War II. Franklin D. Roosevelt's administration rewarded the Irish for their long-standing loyalty to the Democratic Party with a fair proportion of government positions.[36] Irish American congressmen and senators supported, administered, and added new ideas to the New Deal's quest for social justice, and Irish American labor leaders were prominent in efforts of the AFL and the Congress of Industrial Organizations (CIO) to improve the wages, working conditions, and lifetime security of the working class. As the United States battled Germany, Italy, and Japan, Irish and other Catholic ethnics proved their love of country in Europe and the Pacific.

Popular entertainments, especially the cinema, also elevated the Irish image and self-confidence. During the Depression and World War II, audiences packing movie houses saw an on-screen Catholicism, mostly portrayed by Irish characters, that was a constructive rather than a dangerous, alien force in American life. Popular and respected actors such as Spencer Tracy, Pat O'Brien, and Bing Crosby played Irish American priests more as manly, problem-solving social workers than sacramental ministers. In 1944, Crosby, the country's leading vocalist and box-office draw, played Father Chuck O'Malley in *Going My Way*; a year later he reprised the role in *Bells of St. Mary's*. The former won seven Academy Awards. Both films drew massive viewers and were the leading money-makers for their respective years.[37]

Movies not only portrayed Irish Catholics and their religion in a favorable light, they also emphasized their loyalty to the United States. *Yankee Doodle Dandy* (1941), the fictionalized biography of George M. Cohan, the talented singer, dancer, actor, playwright, and composer of songs that Americans sang in two world wars, was a testament to Irish patriotism. In the scene where FDR awards Cohan (James Cagney) with the Congressional Medal of Honor, the president remarks: "That's one thing I've always admired about you Irish Americans. You carry your love of country like a flag, right out in the open. It's a great quality."[38] Directors liked to cast Irish American priests as heroic chaplains in war films. Pat O'Brien was Father Francis Duffy in *The Fighting 69th* (1940), and

Preston Foster played Father Ignatius Donnelly in *Guadalcanal Diary* (1943); both characters were based on the lives of real clerics. *The Fighting Sullivans* (1944), which told the story of five Waterloo, Iowa, brothers killed when the Japanese sunk their cruiser, the *Juneau,* in the South Pacific, was another film featuring Irish American devotion to the United States. In it, the working-class Sullivans are conscientious Catholics as well as patriots.

World War II and its consequences did much to erode Irish America's defensive, isolationist subculture. Its soldiers, sailors, and marines associated with and shared danger with comrades of different nationalities, religions, and, to a lesser extent, races. Training and combat experiences broadened perspective and increased tolerance. A large percentage of Irish American veterans took advantage of the 1944 Serviceman's Readjustment Act (GI Bill of Rights) to attend college. After earning undergraduate degrees, a good number went on to graduate and professional schools. Eventually, they became a significant portion of America's intellectual, academic, and professional classes, completing Irish America's transition from unskilled workers to members of the middle class and speeding its residential transition from urban to suburban.

Not all Irish Americans were on the move. Some continued to live in densely ethnic city neighborhoods, in such places as Queens, South Boston, Cambridge, and the southwest side of Chicago. Their parishes, once spiritual, social, and psychological comfort zones, often became defensive garrisons against black intrusion.[39] However, the majority of Irish Americans increasingly scattered into suburbs or prosperous, sometimes newly developed sections of cities. The 2000 census indicated that most Chicago Irish were living in affluent sections of the southwest and northwest sides or along Lake Michigan to the north. Suburban, fringe of the city, and gentrified neighborhood Irish have enjoyed the fruits of higher incomes, but a good number had parents who retreated from racial tensions and social unrest in older urban areas.[40]

Unlike old city parishes, those in the suburbs tend to be multiethnic and play a diminished role in the lives of their congregations. Irish Americans have Jewish, Protestant, and other Catholic-nationality friends and neighbors. For many, the country club or golf club is more important than the parish hall. Parents increasingly take advantage of public schools, which tend to be better funded than parochial schools and don't hesitate to send children off to state and other non-Catholic universities. In 1952, and more so in 1956, a considerable number of Irish Americans, cast ballots for the Republican presidential candidate Dwight Eisenhower rather than his Democratic opponent, Adlai Stevenson, thereby voting according to class and economic interests rather than heritage, historical experience, and memory. But almost all returned to the Democratic fold in 1960 to vote for one of their own, John F. Kennedy. But since then, there has been a significant suburban switch to the Republican fold.[41] Many who make the change argue that Democratic support for abortion offends their Catholic values, but their positions for the death penalty and unrestricted gun ownership are, in fact, in contradiction to the Catholic right-to-life position.

Many Irish American political leaders blanched at Kennedy's candidacy, fearing that the presidential campaign would trigger an outburst of anti-Catholicism, and it, combined with possible defeat, would resurrect insecurities that followed Al Smith's loss in 1928. And some feared that if Kennedy won and an economic depression followed, Catholics, particularly the Irish, would take the blame. But Mayor Richard J. Daley of Chicago, the prototype of the Irish political boss, decided that Kennedy was the right man and 1960 was the appropriate time for Catholic Irish America to finally capture the highest office in the land.[42] Despite the anti-Catholicism apparent in the presidential race and Kennedy's close victory, his subsequent national and international popularity transformed Irish America, smashing status anxieties and defensiveness and convincing most of the community that they were indeed first-class Americans.

But for some, doubts remained. A good portion of those who had endorsed Senator Joseph McCarthy's anti-civil-liberties campaign against the "Red menace," including New York's Francis Cardinal Spellman, attempting to emphasize their patriotism as well as their Catholicism, remained obsessed with communism into the 1970s. They were a force behind America's involvement in Vietnam. Before and after Kennedy's presidency, Irish and other Catholics in declining urban neighborhoods balked at racial integration, but the new spirit of confidence that came with the Kennedys' days in the White House liberalized Irish American attitudes. Priests and nuns, along with Catholic college students, marched for civil rights in Selma, Alabama, and against the Vietnam War. Many young Catholics with higher-education backgrounds joined the Peace Corp to bring a better life to people in underdeveloped countries. Senator Eugene McCarthy of Minnesota had the political courage to challenge Joseph McCarthy at the height of his influence and Lyndon Johnson in the 1968 presidential primaries. His strong showing in New Hampshire and the probability of his win in Wisconsin factored in the president's decision not to seek another term. Eugene McCarthy's success gave New York senator Robert F. Kennedy the spunk to enter the race as well. Sirhan Sirhan's assassination of Kennedy after Kennedy defeated McCarthy in the California primary resulted in Hubert Humphrey's nomination and subsequent defeat by Richard Nixon.

While protests against integrated schooling and housing in Boston and Chicago indicated that racism still permeated some Irish Catholic minds, according to sociologist Andrew Greeley and researchers at Chicago's National Opinion Research Center, contemporary Irish Americans, next to Jewish Americans, are the best educated and most liberal ethnics on racial and a score of other issues.[43] Certainly, inner-city Catholic schools, staffed by many Irish American religious and lay teachers, have provided urban, predominantly not Catholic, African Americans with alternatives to struggling public schools.[44]

Much of the confidence and idealism that American Catholics felt with the election of Kennedy benefited their church as well as political and social causes. Large numbers of young men and women (usually Irish) flooded into convents and seminaries. People crowded churches to attend Mass and stood in long lines to hear confession and receive communion. And they were magnanimous in contributing to Sunday collections and supporting Catholic institutions. In Rome, at Vatican II, American bishops, mostly Irish, made few contributions to discussions of liturgy and theology but had a strong voice in the Council's decisions to accept the principles of separation of church and state and the primacy of the private conscience. They also helped persuade their church to abandon vestiges of anti-Semitism and to seek dialogues with Protestants, Jews, and members of the Eastern Orthodox Churches.

Most Irish Americans and other Catholics expected that Vatican II would be a prelude to significant reforms beyond liturgy and regulations concerning fasting and abstinence. They hoped that in the wake of the contraception pill the church would reconsider its position on birth control. Since most American Catholics wanted to provide a comfortable standard of living for their families and send their children on to higher education, limiting dependents became a financial necessity. The church-approved rhythm system was so ineffective that it earned the sobriquet Roman Roulette. Not only failing as contraception prevention, it denied husbands and wives affection needed to preserve matrimonial harmony and love. When John XXIII appointed a commission to investigate the issue of contraception, a majority of Catholics in the Western world looked forward to the church accepting that sex in marriage should be more than just a means of producing children. In 1968, Paul VI dashed these hopes when his encyclical *Humanae Vitae* rejected the commission's majority support of the contraceptive pill, confirming traditional church disapproval of any means of birth control except the rhythm system.

Outraged, a majority of American and European Catholics defied the pope's ruling and used the pill and other contraceptive methods. Contesting Rome's authority on birth control spread to other issues: the questioning of the need for a celibate, all male priesthood and of the exclusion of divorced and remarried Catholics from the sacraments. At present, most Irish and other American Catholics are not pro-choice in matters of abortion, but many are prepared to accept flexible situational decisions on the subject—in the case of rape, incest, and the mother's health, for example—and many are unwilling to employ legal restraints against those whose private consciences differ with theirs.[45]

Once loyal, devout, and generous Catholics, the Irish are now the most rebellious. No longer do they offer their best and brightest to the church or jam parish churches for Mass and devotions, stand in long lines for confession, contribute as much to Sunday and other collections, or send as many of their children to Catholic schools or colleges. Consequently, there is a massive shortage of priests, nuns, and brothers; many dioceses are closing churches and schools; and Catholic institutions are short on funds to support their missions. Recent exposures of a significant number of priests, often Irish, who sexually abused boys, young men, and women, and of bishops, also frequently Irish, who covered up their crimes by moving ephebophiles, pedophiles, and exploiters of women from parish to parish, and conjectures that the priesthood has become an increasingly homosexual vocation, have further alienated respect for church authorities. Many believe that Catholicism has lost moral credibility.[46]

Following the lead of Pope John Paul II, traditionalists brand rejecters of church authority as cafeteria Catholics, corrupted by American materialism and secularism, picking and choosing what to believe and practice. Escaping from a psychological ghetto may be a better explanation for American Catholic behavior. Once they lost their defensive paranoia and realized that they had become first-class American citizens, the Irish and other Catholics recognized and resolved their contradictory loyalties to the most authoritarian religious and the most politically liberal systems in the Western world in favor of the latter. They expect their church to be as respectful of reason and the individual conscience as their nation is.

To replace Catholicism as its essence, the Irish American identity search has turned to history and culture: literature, theatre, music, and dance. College and university Irish studies programs flourish. The American public has warmed to things Irish; folk music, dancing, theater, and Irish literature continue to attract critical acclaim and devotees. But much Celtic enthusiasm is often more romantic than real, exalting a pastoral Ireland that no longer exists, if it ever truly did. Today's land of the economic "Celtic Tiger" resembles contemporary America more than it does the land of Irish Literary Revival poetry. So much of sentimental Irishness is a reluctance to accept how uncomfortable it is for middle-class Irish Americans to acknowledge and understand the true stories of their painful Old and New World experiences at their worst: poverty, hunger, and oppression on one side of the Atlantic; crime- and disease-infested urban slums on the other. And then, in the face of anti-Catholic bigotry, the long climb up from the bottom rungs of American society to the comforts of American suburbia. Present-day Irish Americans watch *Riverdance*; listen to the Chieftans; read the poems of Seamus Heaney, Paul Muldoon, John Montague, and Edna O'Brien; and attend the plays of Brian Friel, Hugh Leonard, and Tom Murphy, but most of these are modern adaptations rather than traditionals or authentic Irish survivals. Their immigrant parents or grandparents read Charles Kickham's popular and nostalgic *Knocknagow or the Homes of Tipperary*, not Joyce or Yeats, but they lived an Irish life on a day-by-day basis. Their progeny no longer possess the old religious and political attitudes or the communal spirit that defined Irish America.

Ethnic identity is fading in the United States, faster for the Irish than most others of European stock. Despite an increase in the national population, much of it representing immigrants from Asia, Latin America, and the Caribbean, census evidence (based upon self-identification) indicates a drop from 1990 to 2000 of 30 million Americans claiming ethnicity. In New England, 228, 7,000 fewer people acknowledged being Irish than ten years earlier, 35,000 in Massachusetts, 12,000 in Boston. Deaths, decline in western European immigration, and mixed parentage account for some of the seepage, but probably most of those who claim to be just American feel no connection with long-ago immigrant ancestors.[47] After abandoning or diminishing traditional ties to Catholicism and the history and values it symbolizes, it is difficult for the Irish and other ethnics connected to that faith to maintain their identities in a majority non-Catholic, culturally pluralistic America. Actually, the Irish American experience is more of a case study in assimilation and acculturation than in ethnic preservation. After shedding much of their religious and political loyalties—voting by class rather than heritage, except for things green and an abundance of liquor on St. Patrick's Day—Irish America is virtually indistinguishable from Anglo-America.

NOTES

1. Trevor Parkhill, "Emigration: 17th and 18th Centuries," in *The Encyclopedia of the Irish in America*, ed. Michael Glazier, 253 (Notre Dame, IN: Univ. of Notre Dame Press, 1999); David Doyle, "Scots Irish or Scotch Irish," *Encyclopedia of the Irish in America*, 842–851 contains considerable information on Scots-Irish emigration, religion, culture, and settlement.

2. Leroy V. Eid, "Scotch Irish and American Politics," *Encyclopedia of the Irish in America* (see note 1), 839–842; Patrick Fitzgerald, *Encyclopedia of Ireland* (Dublin and New Haven, CT: Gill and Macmillan and Yale Univ. Press, 2003), 952; and Kevin Kenny, *The American Irish: A History* (New York: Longman, 2000), 41.

3. For information on early Irish Catholic emigration to North America see Audrey Lockhart, *Some Aspects of Emigration from Ireland to the North American Colonies between 1660 and 1775* (New York: Arno Press, 1976).

4. Kerby Miller, *Emigrants and Exiles: Ireland and the Irish Exodus to North America* (New York: Oxford Univ. Press, 1985) is the best and most detailed study of Irish emigration. Kenneth Connell, *The Population of Ireland, 1750–1845* (London: Oxford Univ. Press, 1950) explains the Irish population boom and its relationship to the potato as a food source.

5. The Famine has produced a bevy of books, especially during the mid-1990s. Among the best are James S. Donnelly, Jr., *The Great Irish Potato Famine* (London: Sutton, 2001); Christine Kinealey, *This Great Calamity: The Irish Famine* (Dublin: Gill and Macmillan, 1994); Cormac O'Grada, *The Great Irish Famine* (Atlantic Highlands, NJ: Prentice Hall, 1988); and Robert James Scally, *The End of Hidden Ireland, Rebellion, Famine and Emigration* (New York: Oxford Univ. Press, 1995). In *The Great Hunger: Ireland 1845–1849* (New York: New York Univ. Press, 1962), Cecil Woodham-Smith estimated that 6,000 famine victims lie in the soil of Grosse Isle. A more recent study, Padraic O'Laighin, "The Holocaust Revisited," in *The Untold Story: The History of the Irish in Canada*, ed. Robert O'Driscoll and Lorna Reynolds (Toronto: Celtic Arts, 1988), claims that the British government falsified the number of graves to disguise the extent of the Famine disaster. He believes that at least 30,000 Famine victims are buried a Grosse Isle.

6. Hasia Diner, *Erin's Daughter in America: Irish Immigrant Women in the Nineteenth Century* (Baltimore: Johns Hopkins Univ. Press, 1983), 30–42; and Janet Nolan, *Ourselves Alone: Women's Emigration from Ireland, 1885–1920* (Lexington: The Univ. Press of Kentucky, 1989), 47–51, discuss the numbers of men and women leaving Ireland and their motives for emigrating.

7. In several publications, including *Being Had: Historians, Evidence, and the Irish in North America* (Toronto: Queen's Univ. Press and Toronto Univ. Press, 1985); *Small*

Differences: Irish Catholics and Irish Protestants, 1815–1922 (Kingston and Montreal: Queen's University Press, 1988); and "Data: What Is Known about the Irish in North America," in *The Untold Story* (see note 5), Donald Harman Akenson accuses historians, mainly Kerby Miller, William Shannon, and me, of exaggerating Irish American urbanization. He points to the 1870 census, which has only 44.5 percent of the Irish resident in cities of over 25,000 people. In reviewing *Small Differences* in *Labour/Le Travail*, David Miller pointed out that the 1870 census pointed to the urbanization of Irish America. That year, only 15 percent of Americans lived in cities over 25,000 and only 30.8 percent of non-Irish immigrants, compared to the Irish 44.5 percent, lived in such urban places. Miller also emphasizes the increasing urbanization of the Irish. From 1891 to 1900, the number of Irish in cities of over 25,000 people escalated to 74.3 percent, and another 19.2 percent settled in towns with less than 25,000 people, leaving only 6 percent in rural areas. In *The Irish in Philadelphia: Ten Generations of Urban Experience* (Philadelphia, PA: Temple Univ. Press, 1973), 62, Dennis Clark described 85.4 percent of Irish immigrants as being from rural backgrounds. Patrick Blessing, "The Irish," in the *Harvard Encyclopedia of American Ethnic Groups*, ed. Stephan Thernstrom et al., 530 (Cambridge, MA: Harvard Univ. Press, 1980), estimates that in 1920, Irish America was 90 percent urban. For a discussion of the efforts of Buffalo's Bishop John Timon to settle the Irish in rural areas and small towns, see Leonard R. Riforgiato, "Bishop John Timon, Archbishop John Hughes, and Irish Colonization: A Clash of Episcopal Views on the Future of the Irish and Catholic Church in America," in *Immigration to New York*, ed. William Pencak, Selma Berrol, and Randall M. Miller, 7–26 (Cranberry, NJ: Associated Univ. Press, 1991). Archbishop John Ireland's efforts to settle the Irish in rural Minnesota is the subject of James Shannon, *Catholic Colonization on the Frontier* (New York: Arno Press, 1976).

8. See the bibliographical essay for studies of Irish communities in various parts of the United States.

9. Nolan, *Ourselves Alone*, 87–88; Diner, *Erin's Daughter in America*, 125, 137.

10. For information on the pre– and post–Irish American Catholic Church, see Charles R. Morris, *American Catholic: The Saints and Sinners Who Built America's Most Powerful Church* (New York: Random House, 1997); Jay P. Dolan, *The American Catholic Experience: A History from Colonial Times to the Present* (Garden City, NY: Doubleday, 1985); and *In Search of an American Catholicism: A History of Religion and Culture in Tension* (New York: Oxford Univ. Press, 2002); and James Hennessey, S. J., *American Catholics: A History of the American Catholic Community in the United States* (New York: Oxford Univ. Press, 1981).

11. In *Paddy and the Republic: Ethnicity and Nationality in Antibellum America* (Middletown, CT: Wesleyan Univ. Press, 1986), Dale T. Knobel argues that anti-Irishness was based more on ethnicity than religion. If so, why didn't nativism also target Anglo-Irish Protestants or Scots-Irish Presbyterians? According to Kevin Kenny, *American Irish*, 80–82, 115–116, 158–159, the Scots-Irish were in the vanguard of anti-Irish-Catholic nativism.

12. Fergus O'Ferrall, *Catholic Emancipation: Daniel O'Connell and the Birth of Irish Democracy, 1820–1830* (Dublin: Gill and Macmillan, 1985), 277–278, discuss the reactions of Beaumont and de Tocqueville to the democratic opinions of Irish priests and bishops. For de Tocqueville's observations on Irish Catholicism and its political and social attitudes, see Emmet Larkin, ed. and trans., *Alex de Tocqueville's Tour in Ireland, July–August, 1925* (Washington, DC: The Catholic Univ. Press of America, 1990), 39–47, 61–67, 78–80.

13. According to Morris, *American Catholic*, 52: "The ethnic background of American bishops consecrated between 1850 and 1910 clearly show the rise in Irish influence. From the 1850s through the 1880s, the Irish, including native priests of Irish descent, accounted for half the consecrations, rising to 60 percent in the 1890s, and to 75 percent by the early 1900s, where it remained until the 1960s."

14. John Tracy Ellis, *American Catholics and the Intellectual Life* (Chicago: University of Chicago Press, 1956); and Thomas O'Dea, *The American Catholic Dilemma* (New York: The New American Library, 1958) discuss the paucity in American Catholic intellectual life before 1960. Sean O'Faolain, *The Irish: A Character Study* (New York: Devin-Adair, 1956), 116–119, 146, blames exiled French theologians teaching Jansenism at the seminary in Maynooth for much of Irish Puritanism. While this position has had many echoes, in fact, Irish Catholicism teaches nothing about sex that doesn't originate in Rome. Although, the Irish have perhaps taken it more seriously, according to Eugene Hynes, "The Great Hunger and Irish Catholicism," *Societas* 8 (Spring 1978): 137–156, because the Famine persuaded people to follow Catholic guidelines on sex as a method of limiting population. In *The Irish: Emigration, Marriage, and Fertility* (Berkeley: Univ. of California Press, 1973), 13–15, 145–151, Robert E. Kennedy, Jr., examines relationships between religion and celibacy in modern Ireland and concludes that economic motives persuaded the Irish that Catholic sexual morality justified and strengthened their decision to postpone marriage until they were financially secure.

15. For information on O'Connell's condemnation of slavery and Irish American support for such a vile institution, see Lawrence J. McCaffrey, *Daniel O'Connell and the Repeal Year* (Lexington: Univ. of Kentucky Press, 1966), 73–75.

16. Iver Bernstein, *The New York City Draft Riots: Their Significance for American Society and Politics in the Age of the Civil War* (New York: Oxford Univ. Press, 1990).

17. Noel Ignatiev, *How the Irish Became White* (New York: Routledge, 1995).

18. Eric Arneson, "Whiteness and the Historians' Imagination," *Historically Speaking* (February 2002):19–22; and Arneson, "Whiteness and the Historian's Imagination," *Labor and Working Class History* 60 (Fall 2001): 3–92.

19. For information on Irish American nationalism, see Thomas N. Brown, *Irish American Nationalism, 1870–1890* (Philadelphia and New York: Lippincott, 1966); Terry Golway, *Irish Rebel: John Devoy and America's Fight for Ireland's Freedom* (New York: St. Martin's Press, 1998); Lawrence J. McCaffrey, ed., *Irish Nationalism and the American Contribution* (New York: Arno Press, 1976); and Michael F. Funchion, *Chicago's Irish Nationalists, 1881–1890* (New York: Arno Press, 1976).

20. John Paul Bocock, "The Irish Conquest of Our Cities, *Forum* 17 (April 1894): 195, is a reformist, nativist hostile opinion on Irish political power. Daniel Patrick Moynihans's essay "The Irish," in his and Nathan Glazier's *Beyond the Melting Pot* (Cambridge, MA: MIT Press, 1963), 229, credits the Irish with great skill in acquiring political power but criticizes them for lacking the vision to employ it in constructive ways. For favorable estimates of the Irish as politicians expanding opportunities for other ethnics as well their own people, see J. Joseph Huthmacher, "Urban Liberalism and the Age of Reform," *Mississippi Valley Historical Review* 49 (1962): 231–241; John D. Buenker, *Urban Liberalism and Progressive Reform* (New York: Norton, 1978); and Robert Dahl, *Who Governs? Democracy and Power in an American City* (New Haven, CT: Yale Univ. Press, 1961); and Elmer E. Cornwell, "Bosses, Machines, and Ethnic Groups," *Annals* 353 (May 1964): 27–39.

21. Stephen P. Erie, *Irish Americans and the Dilemmas of Urban Machine Politics,*

1840–1845 (Berkeley: Univ. of California Press, 1988). Like Erie, Dennis P. Ryan, in his *Beyond the Ballot Box: A Social History of the Boston Irish, 1845–1917* (Amherst: Univ. of Massachusetts Press, 1989), 106, believes that too much of a focus on politics steered the Irish away from other occupational and financial possibilities.

22. Both Plunkett and Powers were there to provide food, clothing, shelter, funeral expenses, jobs, and wedding gifts for needy constituents, Irish and non-Irish alike. Jane Addams of Hull House, an enemy of Powers in Chicago's nineteenth ward, had to admit that he won elections because he did far more for the poor than political reformers did. *Plunkett of Tammany Hall: A Series of Very Plain Talks on Very Practical Matters*, recorded by William L. Riordan, introduction by Peter Quinn (New York: Signet Classic, 1995); Jane Addams, "Why the Ward Boss Rules," *Outlook* 58 (1898), 879–882; and Allan F. Davis, "Jane Addams and the Ward Boss," *Journal of the Illinois State Historical Society* 53 (1960): 247–265.

23. John D. Buenker, "Edward F. Dunne, The Urban New Stock Democrat as Progressive," *Mid-America: An Historical* Review 50, no.1 (January 1968): 3–21; and "Edward F. Dunne: The Limits of Municipal Reform," in *The Mayors: The Chicago Political Tradition*, ed. Melvin G. Holli and Paul Green, 33–49 (Carbondale: Southern Illinois University Press, 1986).

24. Robert Slayton, *Empire Statesman: The Rise and Redemption of Al Smith* (New York: Free Press, 2001); and Christopher M. Finan, *Alfred E. Smith, The Happy Warrior* (New York: Hill and Wang, 2002).

25. Francis L. Broderick, *Right Reverend New Dealer, John A. Ryan* (New York: Macmillan, 1963).

26. Emmet Larkin, "The Devotional Revolution in Ireland, 1850–1875," in his *The Historical Dimensions of Irish Catholicism* (Washington, DC: The Catholic Univ. of America Press, 1997), 57–89.

27. Diner, *Erin's Daughter in America* 71, 73, 96–99; and Janet Nolan, "Education and Women's Mobility in Ireland and Irish America 1880–1920: A Preliminary Look," *New Hibernian Review* 2, no.3 (Autumn 1998): 78–88.

28. Brown, *Irish-American Nationalism*, 23–24.

29. David Montgomery, "The Irish and the American Labor Movement," in *America and Ireland, 1776–1976: The American Identity and the Irish Connection*, ed. David Noel Doyle and Owen Dudley Edwards (Westport, CT: Greenwood Press, 1980), 206.

30. Herbert Hill, "Race and Ethnicity in Organized Labor: The Historical Sources for Resistance to Affirmative Action," in *Ethnicity and the Work Force*, ed. Winston A. Van Horn and Thomas V. Tonneson (Madison: Univ. of Wisconsin System American Ethnic Studies Coordinating Committee/Urban Corridor Consortium, 1985), 19–64.

31. Diner, *Erin's Daughter in America* 39, 83, 100–102, 77; Nolan, *Ourselves Alone*, 85.

32. Jo Ellen McNergney Vinyard, *The Irish on the Urban Frontier: Detroit, 1850–1880* (New York: Arno Press, 1976); and Timothy Meagher, ed., *From Paddy to Studs: Irish-American Communities at the Turn of the century Era, 1880–1920* (Westport, CT: Greenwood Press, 1986) provide strong evidence that the Irish on the urban frontier, Buffalo and points west, prospered more than those on the East Coast.

33. Edward McSorley, *Our Own Kind* (New York: Harper and Brothers, 1946), 17.

34. Charles Fanning, *Finley Peter Dunne and Mr. Dooley: The Chicago Years* (Lexington: Univ. of Kentucky Press, 1978); and Fanning, *Mr. Dooley and the Chicago Irish:*

The Autobiography of a Nineteenth Century Ethnic Group (Washington, DC: The Catholic Univ. of America Press, 1987).

35. William H. A. Williams, '*Twas Only an Irishman's Dream: The Image of Ireland and the Irish in American Popular Song Lyrics* (Urbana and Chicago: Univ. of Illinois Press, 1996); and Williams, "From Lost Land to Emerald Isle: Ireland and the Irish in American Sheet Music, 1800–1920," *Eire-Ireland* 26 (Spring 1991): 43.

36. George Q. Flynn, *American Catholics and the Roosevelt Presidency* (Lexington: Univ. of Kentucky Press, 1968), discusses relationships between Irish America and the Roosevelt administration.

37. For information on Irish American priest roles in the movies, see Joseph M. Curran, *Hibernian Green on the Silver Screen* (Westport, CT: Greenwood Press, 1989), 52–58; Morris, *American Catholic*, 196–200, 208–209; and Lawrence J. McCaffrey, "Going My Way and Irish-American Catholicism: Myth and Reality," *New Hibernian Review* 4, no.1 (Autumn 2000): 119–127.

38. Curran, *Hibernian Green*, 87.

39. The transition of the parish from community to defensive garrison is a thesis in John McGreevey's *Parish Boundaries: The Catholic Encounter with Race in the Twentieth-Century Urban North* (Chicago: Univ. of Chicago Press, 1996).

40. Mark Skertic and Curtis Lawrence, "Ethnics Disappearing in Chicago Melting Pot," *Chicago Sun Times*, August 21, 2002, Metro section.

41. The Chicago area is a good example. In Cook County, Irish Catholics still have a major role in Democratic politics. As the *Chicago Tribune* noted in an editorial on November 13, 2002, it is almost a requirement to be a Democratic Irish American woman to be elected a Cook County judge. But in the collar counties, the Irish are prominent in the Republican Party. Among quite a few Republican candidates, in the 2002 November election, Jim Ryan ran for governor and James Durkin for the U.S. Senate.

42. Eugene Kennedy, *Himself! The Life and Times of Mayor Richard J. Daley* (New York: Viking Press, 1978), 156–158, 160, 169, 171–175, 178–187.

43. Andrew Greeley, *Irish America: The Rise to Money and Power* (New York: Harper & Row, 1981), 167–168. Greeley takes his information from the National Opinion Research Center. Considering the Irish American political shift to the right, perhaps in 2002 they are not quite as liberal as they were in 1981.

44. An excellent discussion of how Catholic nuns, mostly Irish American, adapted to urban color change in the 1950s and contributed to racial and social justice are Suellen Hoy's "No Color Line at Loretta Academy: Catholic Sisters and African Americans on Chicago's East Side, *Journal of Women's History* 14, no.1 (Spring 2002), 8–33; and Hoy "Ministering Hope to Chicago," *Chicago History* 37, no.2 (Fall 2000): 4–23.

45. According to a 1993 General Social Survey, 42 percent of Catholics compared to 38 percent of Protestants agreed that a woman should have the option of abortion to terminate a pregnancy, no matter what the reason. The national approval average was 43 percent. Forty-eight percent of Catholics with higher degree credentials agreed, compared to the Protestant 53 percent.

46. A May 6, 2002, *Newsweek* poll discusses Catholic discontents with Church authority on a number of issues. A May 15, 2002, CBS poll reported that 79 percent of Catholics thought the hierarchy was doing a poor job in responding to the sex-abuse scandals. A September 27–29, 1995, *Time*/CNN survey printed in the October 9, 1995, issue of *Time* indicated that 70 percent of Catholics favored a married clergy, 60 percent ap-

proved of ordaining women, 69 percent thought that divorced people should be able to remarry in a Catholic ceremony, only 20 percent disapproved of premarital sex, 79 percent viewed contraception as a private conscience decision, 59 percent practiced birth control, and 80 percent believed they could disagree with the pope and remain good Catholics.

47. Cindy Rodriguez and Bill Dedman, *Boston Globe*, May 31, 2002.

BIBLIOGRAPHICAL ESSAY

Michael Glazer, ed., *The Encyclopedia of the Irish in America* (Notre Dame, IN: Univ. of Notre Dame Press, 1999), which contain valuable essays by distinguished scholars on a variety of subjects, is essential for anyone interested in Irish America. There are a number of general interpretations of the Irish American experience, including John B. Duff, *The Irish in America* (Belmont, CA: Wadsworth, 1971); Dennis Clark, *Hibernia America: The Irish and Regional Cultures* (New York: Greenwood Press, 1986); Michael Coffey and Terry Golway, eds., *The Irish in America* (New York: Hyperion, 1997); Maureen Dezell, *Irish America, Coming into Clover: The Evolution of a People and Culture* (Garden City, NY: Doubleday, 2000); Marjorie Fallows, *Irish Americans: Identity and Assimilation* (Englewood Cliffs, NJ: Prentice Hall, 1977); Andrew M. Greeley, *The Irish Americans: The Rise to Money and Power* (New York: Harper and Row, 1981); William D. Griffin, *A Portrait of the Irish in America* (New York: Scribner, 1981); Griffin, *The Book of Irish-Americans* (New York: Times Books, 1990); Kevin Kenny, *The American Irish: A History* (New York: Longman, 2000); Lawrence J. McCaffrey, *The Irish Catholic Diaspora in America* (Washington, DC: Catholic Univ. of America Press, 1997); McCaffrey, *Textures of Irish America* (Syracuse, NY: Syracuse Univ. Press, 1998); Joseph P. O'Grady, *How the Irish Became American* (New York: Twayne Publishers, 1973); William V. Shannon, *The American Irish* (New York: Macmillan, 1974); and Carl Wittke, *The Irish in America* (New York: Russell and Russell, 1970). Wittke's book, the pioneer scholarly study of Irish America, is rich in detail and still holds up well. Shannon provides solid and perceptive essays on many Irish American subjects and personalities. Greeley views Irish America from historical and sociological perspectives, insisting that it is a liberal, progressive community that retains a unique ethnic identity. Fallows also blends historical and sociological evidence into a readable, lively book. O'Grady's and Duff's interpretations are brief but useful. Clark shows how urban physical and psychological ghettos delayed Irish American economic and social progress and assimilation but once removed from them, success and regional cultures, particularly in the West, dimmed Irish identity. Kenny's up-to-date study of Irish America includes interesting information on the Scots-Irish. Dezell asks important questions, sometimes without conclusive answers, and challenges clichés about Irish America. The essays in Coffey and Golway are uneven, but the latter writes lucid prose and Ellen Skerrett's piece on Catholicism, Maureen Murphy's look at Irish servant girls, and Thomas Flanagan's view of John Ford's movies are well worth reading. McCaffrey's *The Irish Catholic Diaspora in America* attempts to explain the influence of the Irish historical experience on Irish America. His *Textures of Irish America* focuses on the three most important dimensions of Irish American identity: Catholicism, politics, and nationalism. In both books he agrees with Greeley's thesis that Irish America has been a success story and with Clark's position that Irish America's residential, social, and economic mobility and its success has diminished the essences of its identity. In two essays, "The Irish," in the *Harvard Encyclopedia of American Ethnic Groups*, ed. Stephan Thernstrom (Cambridge, MA: Harvard Univ. Press, 1980) and "The Irish in America," *The Encyclopedia of the Irish in America*, Michael Glazer ed. (Notre Dame, IN: Univ. of Notre Dame Press, 1999). Patrick Blessing offers succinct, highly intelligent, and statistical information on Irish America. He has also put together the valuable *The Irish in America: A Guide to the Literature and Manuscript Collections* (Washington, DC: Catholic Univ. of America Press, 1992). Seamus P. Metress, *The Irish-American Experience: A Guide to the Literature* (Washington, DC: Catholic Univ. Press of America, 1981) is another bibliographical guide. Two volumes containing perceptive examinations of aspects of the Irish American experience are *America and Ireland, 1776–1976*, ed. David Noel Doyle and Owen Dudley Edwards (Westport, CT: Greenwood Press, 1980) and *The Irish in America*, ed., P. J. Drudy (New York: Cambridge Univ. Press, 1985). Drudy's is more consistent in quality.

In *Going to America* (New York: Cambridge Univ. Press, 1985), Terry Coleman describes the physical and psychological challenges and miseries that nineteenth-century emigrants, mostly Irish, experienced on their journey from Liverpool to the United States. Philip Taylor's *The Distant Magnet* (New York: Harper and Row, 1971) covers the entire scope of European emigration, dealing with the voyage to the United States and problems that newcomers faced on their arrival. David Fitzpatrick's *Irish Emigration, 1801–1921* (Dundalk, Ireland: Economic and Social History Society of Ireland, 1984) looks at the variety of reasons that young people decided to leave Ireland for opportunities in other parts of the world. In his influential, prize-winning *Emigrants and Exiles: Ireland and the Exodus to North America* (New York: Oxford Univ. Press, 1986), Kerby Miller, employing an extensive use of emigrant letters, details the reasons that sent Ulster Presbyterians and Irish Catholics out of Ireland and what awaited them in their new homes. He came to the conclusion that religious and Gaelic cultural influences rendered premodern Irish Catholics psychologically incapable of contentedly adjusting to Protestant, urban, industrial America. In rebuttal, Donald H. Akenson's *The Irish Diaspora: A Primer* (Toronto: P.D. Meany Co., 1994) insists that Catholic and Gaelic cultural values did not impede Irish progress in the United States and many other parts of the English-speaking world. McCaffrey's *The Irish Catholic Diaspora in America* and *Textures of Irish America* also reject the position that the Irish in the United States were exiles looking backward rather than forward. Miller's and Paul Wagner's *Out of Ireland* (Washington, DC: Elliott and Clark Publishing, 1995), a very good Public Broadcasting Corp. documentary, qualifies the alienated exile thesis, pointing out that the Irish were less likely than other European immigrants to return home, and some who did return to visit found that reality clashed with memories and were happy to return to the United States. Prior to Miller, Arnold Shrier made good use of emigrant letters in *Ireland and the American Emigration* (New York: Russell and Russell, 1970) to clarify the immigrant experience in various parts of the United States. Audrey Lockhart's *Some Aspects of Emigration from Ireland to North America between 1660 and 1775* (New York: Arno Press, 1976) brings attention to the Catholic minority who emigrated in the eighteenth century. They usually came to North America as indentured servants or transported convicts and located where their church had little or no presence. Therefore, they and their descendents became Protestant. W. F. Adams entertained an Anglo-Protestant bias against Irish Catholics, but his *Ireland and Irish Immigration to the New World from 1815 to the Famine* (New York: Arno Press, 1967) is a good look at pre-Famine immigration. Like

Adams, George W. Potter in *To the Golden Door* (Westport, CT: Greenwood Press, 1974) concentrates on pre-Famine Irish immigration. The book is loaded with interesting and useful information, but the author exaggerates Irish progress in the New World. Unfortunately, Potter died before he completed *To the Golden Door*, leaving readers in the dark concerning sources for much of his information and conclusions.

Irish immigration was unusual in that it consisted of large number of singles and women who entered the United States. Robert F. Kennedy, Jr., *The Irish: Emigration, Marriage, and Fertility* (Berkeley, CA: Univ. of California Press, 1973) intelligently analyzes why young people emigrated. His evidence indicates that both Catholics and Protestants used emigration, late marriages, and permanent celibacy as economic and social safety valves to lift and then raise their standard of living. Because they had fewer marriage or employment prospects than men, women increasingly decided to seek their future in the United States. This position is supported in Janet Nolan's *Ourselves Alone: Women's Emigration from Ireland, 1855–1920* (Lexington: Univ. Press of Kentucky, 1989); and Grace Neville's "'He Never Then After That Forgot Him': Irishwomen and Emigration to the United States in Irish Folklore," *Mid-America* 74 (October 1992): 217–290. Linda Dowling Almeida's *Irish Immigrants in New York City, 1945–1995* (Bloomington: Indiana Univ. Press, 2001) is an exceptionally well-written study of post–World War II Irish immigrants to New York City. In distinguishing between three generations of newcomers to the city, she emphasizes that each left a different Ireland and settled in a changing America.

Lacking skills and temperaments to be successful farmers in rural America, the vast majority of Irish immigrants settled in cities and towns involved in industry and commerce. Oscar Handlin's *Boston's Immigrant's: A Study in Acculturation* (Cambridge, MA: Harvard Univ. Press, 1941; repr. New York, 1968; Cambridge, MA: Belknap Press), remains a valuable study of the pioneer Irish American urban ghetto. Boston has attracted the attention of other scholars. As his title suggests, Dennis P. Ryan's *Beyond the Ballot Box: A Social History of the Boston Irish, 1845–1917* (Rutherford, NJ: Fairleigh Dickinson Univ. Press, 1983) politics is only one dimension of the Boston Irish experience. Thomas H. O'Connor's *The Boston Irish: A Political History* (Boston: Northeastern Univ. Press, 1995) is an articulate and informative examination of the Irish political impact on Boston and their position in the city. Shaun O'Connell's *Imagining Boston: A Literary Landscape* (Boston: Beacon Press, 1990), a beautifully written and perceptive history of Boston's literary tradition, contains "Irish-America's Red Brick City: Edwin O'Connor's Boston," 108–140. In *Poverty and Progress* (Cambridge, MA: Harvard Univ. Press, 1964), Stephan Thernstrom concludes that the Irish in Newberryport, Massachusetts, from 1850 to 1880, were slow in achieving economic and social mobility because they chose to invest in property rather than education. In a later volume, *The Other Bostonians: Poverty and Progress in the American Metropolis, 1860–1970* (Cambridge, MA: Harvard Univ. Press, 1970), Thernstrom found that the Boston Irish, like those in Newberryport, had difficulty climbing the ladder to success. But Thernstrom's findings do not establish that the failures of the New England Irish typified all of Irish America. As Dennis Clark's *Hibernia America*; Timothy J. Meagher, ed., *From Paddy to Studs* (Westport, CT: Greenwood Press, 1986); and Lawrence J. McCaffrey's *The Irish Catholic Diaspora in America* and *Textures of Irish America*, as well as other studies in this bibliographical essay, indicate that Irish success depended on regional and gender variations. Those in the West and Midwest did better than those in the East, and women tended to reach middle-class status a bit faster than men.

There are a number of local studies that put Irish America in a more complete perspective than Handlin's and Thernstrom's evaluations of the Boston-area Irish. The New York Irish have received attention in Linda Dowling Almeida's *Irish Immigrants in New York City, 1945–1995* (Bloomington: Indiana Univ. Press, 2001); Ann M. Shea and Marion R. Casey, *The Irish Experience in New York City: A Select Bibliography* (Syracuse, NY: Syracuse Univ. Press, 1995); and Ronald H. Bayor and Timothy J. Meagher, eds., *The New York Irish* (Baltimore: Johns Hopkins Univ. Press, 1996). Essays in the Bayor and Meagher volume cover various aspects and periods of New York Irish historical and cultural experiences. Many have great value, especially Charles Fanning's "The Heart's Speech No Longer Stilted: New York Irish Writing Since the 1960s," 508–549. The Irish in other places are subjects in R. A. Burchell, *The San Francisco Irish 1848–1880* (Berkeley: Univ. of California Press, 1980); Dennis Clark, *The Irish in Philadelphia* (Philadelphia, PA: Temple Univ. Press, 1973); David N. Emmons, *The Butte Irish: Class and Ethnicity in an American Mining Town, 1875–1925* (Urbana: Univ. of Illinois Press, 1989); Lawrence J. McCaffrey, Ellen Skerrett, Michael Funchion, and Charles Fanning, *The Irish in Chicago* (Urbana: Univ. of Illinois Press, 1987); Grace McDonald, *History of the Irish in Wisconsin in the Nineteenth Century* (New York: Arno Press, 1976); Timothy Meagher, *Inventing Irish America: Generation, Class, and Ethnic Identity in a New England City, 1880–1928* (Notre Dame, IN: Univ. of Notre Dame Press, 2000); Brian C. Mitchell, *The Paddy Camps: The Irish of Lowell, 1821–61* (Urbana: Univ. of Illinois Press, 1988); Earl F. Niehaus, *The Irish in New Orleans 1800–1860,* (New York: Arno Press, 1976); Douglas V. Shaw, *The Making of an Immigrant City: Ethnic and Cultural Conflict in New Jersey, 1850–1877* (New York: Arno Press, 1976); and Jo Ellen McNergney Vinyard, *The Irish on the Urban Frontier: Detroit, 1850–1880* (New York: Arno Press, 1976). Vinyard provides convincing evidence that the Irish on the urban frontier, from Buffalo west, achieved more social and economic mobility as well as acceptability and respectability than those in the East. The American Conference for Irish Studies gave Emmons' Portrait of the Butte, Montana, Irish its best-book award in 1990. The Irish in that city owned as well as worked the copper mines. David T. Gleeson's *The Irish in the South, 1815–1877* (Chapel Hill: Univ. of North Carolina Press, 2001) is a significant contribution to Irish American regional historiography, demonstrating the similarities as well as the regional diversity that colors Irish America. Below the Mason-Dixon line, the Irish blended Irish and southern identities. A number of scholars describe Irish achievements in the trans-Mississippi West in Timothy J. Sarbaugh and James P. Walsh, eds., *The Irish in the West* (Manhattan, KS: Sunflower Univ. Press, 1993).

Hasia Diner's *Erin's Daughter in America: Irish-Immigrant Women in the Nineteenth Century* (Baltimore: Johns Hopkins Univ. Press, 1983) discusses women as immigrants; employees; labor activists; wives, widows, and mothers; nuns; teachers; nurses; and the force propelling their community toward middle-class respectability. Janet Nolan's *Ourselves Alone* explains why women emigrated. Diner pays considerable attention to nuns as guides and examples for the young women they taught in Catholic schools. This subject inspires Eileen Brewers, *Beyond Utility: The Role of Nuns in the Education of American Catholic Girls* (Chicago: Microform, 1987). In "Charity, Poverty, and Child Welfare, *Harvard Divinity Bulletin* 25, no. 4 (1996): 12–17, Maureen Fitzgerald claims that social work by nineteenth-century New York nuns preserved many families and established patterns for the coming of the welfare state. Sue Ellen Hoy's "Walking Nuns: Chicago's Irish Sisters of Mercy," in *At the Crossroads: Old St. Patrick's and the Chicago*

Irish, ed. Ellen Skerrett, 39–51 (Chicago: Wild Onion Books, 1997), convincingly argues that the Sisters of Mercy engaged in comprehensive social work earlier and on a larger scale than Jane Addams and her Hull House colleagues.

In addition to poverty, a shortage of skills, frequent illiteracy, and the trauma of moving from rural to urban settings, Irish progress in the United States was also impeded by anti-Catholic nativism. Leading examination of American anti-Catholic prejudices are Ray Allen Billington, *The Protestant Crusade, 1800–1860* (1938; repr. Chicago: Quadrangle Books, 1964); John Higham, *Strangers in the Land: Patterns of American Nativism, 1860–1925* (1955; repr. Chicago, Univ. of Chicago Press, 1965); Donald L. Kinzer, *An Episode in Anti-Catholicism: The American Protective Association* (Seattle: Univ. of Washington Press, 1964); and Kenneth Jackson, *The Ku Klux Klan in the City* (New York: Oxford Univ. Press, 1967); Dale T. Knobel's, *Paddy and the Republic: Ethnicity and Nationality in Antebellum America* (Middletown, CT: Wesleyan Univ. Press, 1986) claims that nativists targeted the Irish for their ethnicity rather than their religion. If that is true, why didn't they also discriminate against non-Catholic Irish? Brutal looking, simian-featured Irish cartoon figures, common in English publications, also appeared in American newspapers and periodicals. John J. and Selma Appel present examples and discuss them in "The Distorted Image," an Anti-Defamation League of New York slide collection.

Irish Americans were victimizers as well as victims of prejudice. The 1863 New York Draft riot was an early example of Irish antiblack sentiment. It is well described in Adrian Cook, *The Armies of the Street: The New York Draft Riots of 1863* (Lexington: Univ. Press of Kentucky, 1974); and Iver Bernstein, *The New York City Draft Riots: Their Significance for American Society and Politics in the Age of the Civil War* (New York: Oxford Univ. Press, 1990). Peter Quinn's novel *The Banished Children of Eve* (New York: Viking, 1990) is a beautifully written portrait of the New York Irish in the 1860s and their relationships with Anglo-Americans and African Americans. Irish New Yorkers also rioted in 1870 and 1871, changing targets from blacks to the city's Orange parades. Like Bernstein, in *The Orange Riots: Irish Political Violence in New York City, 1870 and 1871* (Ithaca, NY: Cornell Univ. Press, 1993), Michael A. Gordon explains Irish Catholic urban mob violence as lower-working-class hostility to nativist elites that frustrated their advance in American society. Ronald H. Bayor's *Neighbors in Conflict: The Irish, Germans, Jews, and Italians of New York, 1921–1941* (Baltimore: Johns Hopkins Univ. Press, 1978) describes how the Great Depression incited a great deal of anti-Semitism among the New York Irish in the 1930s and 1940s. Although racism and anti-Semitism declined as Irish America became suburban middle class, racism remained a potent force a number of urban centers. The most detailed, informative, and well written book on the subject is Anthony J. Lukas's *Common Ground: A Turbulent Decade in the Lives of Three Families* (New York: Vintage Books, 1985), a careful and objective view of the 1970s bussing crisis in Boston that has considerable sympathy for all involved. Racial tensions in Chicago provide the background for Arnold R. Hirsh's *Making the Second Ghetto: Race and Housing in Chicago, 1940–1960* (New York: Cambridge Univ. Press, 1983); and Eileen McMahon's *What Parish Are You From? A Chicago Irish Community and Race Relations* (Lexington, KY: Univ. Press of Chicago, 1995), a well-told, relevant story of the transition of St. Sabina's parish from Irish to black. John T. McGreevy's *Parish Boundaries: The Catholic Encounter with Race in the Twentieth Century Urban North* (Chicago: Univ. of Chicago Press, 1996) pays tribute to Catholic parishes that gave a sense of security to the Irish and other ethnics in their early encounters with American hostility, but it laments that they evolved into white fortresses resisting neighborhood and school integration.

For Irish Americans, Catholicism was spiritual and psychological comfort and the essence of their ethnic identity, the bond of community. Irish Americans were instrumental in shaping the character, values, and structure of the American Catholic Church. The three leading surveys of the church are Jay P. Dolan, *The American Catholic Experience* (Garden City, NY: Doubleday, 1985); James Hennessey, S.J., *American Catholics: A History of the American Catholic Community in the United States* (New York: Oxford Univ. Press, 1981) and Charles R. Morris, *American Catholic: The Saints and Sinners Who Built America's Most Powerful Church* (New York: Times Books, 1997). Stylistically and content-wise, the last mentioned is the best of the three. John Cogley, *Catholic America* (New York: Dial Press, 1973); John Tracy Ellis, *American Catholicism* (Chicago: Univ. of Chicago Press, 1956); and Andrew M. Greeley, *The Catholic Experience* (Garden City, NY: Doubleday, 1967) are satisfactory but briefer interpretations. Specific references to the Irish presence in American Catholicism can be found in Thomas N. Brown and Thomas McAvoy, *The United States of America*, vol. 6 of *A History of Irish Catholicism*, ed. Patrick Corish (Dublin: Gill and Macmillan, 1970); Jay P. Dolan, *The Immigrant Church, New York's Irish and German Catholics, 1815–1865* (Baltimore: Johns Hopkins Univ. Press, 1975); Ellen Skerrett, Edward R. Kantowicz, and Steven M. Avella, *Catholicism, Chicago Style* (Chicago: Loyola Univ. Press, 1993); and Ellen Skerret, ed., *At the Crossroads: Old Saint Patrick's and the Chicago Irish*.

A number of biographies feature Irish American prelates. Marvin O'Connell's *John Ireland and the American Catholic Church* (St. Paul: Minnesota Historical Society Press, 1988) reviews the life of the most liberal, Americanist voice in the church. His conservative, ultramontaine New York opponent is the subject of Robert Emmet Curran's *Michael Augustine Corrigan and the Shaping of Conservative Catholicism in America, 1878–1902* (New York: Arno Press, 1978). For many decades, William Henry Cardinal O'Connell of Boston cast a conservative shadow over his archdiocese. James M. O'Toole reveals his incompetent, cantankerous, and scandalous ecclesiastical career in *Militant and Triumphant: William Henry O'Connell and the Catholic Church in Boston, 1859–1944* (Notre Dame, IN: Univ. of Notre Dame Press, 1992). Other valuable studies of Irish American leaders of the Church are Peter Guilday, *The Life and Times of John England: First Bishop of Charleston, 1786–1842* (New York: The America Press, 1927); John Tracy Ellis, *The Life of James Cardinal Gibbons, Archbishop of Baltimore, 1834–1921*, 2 vols. (Milwaukee, WI: Bruce Pub. Co., 1952); Richard Shaw, *Dagger John: The Unquiet Life and Times of Archbishop John Hughes of New York* (New York: Paulist Press, 1977); and James P. Gaffey, *Citizen of No Mean City: Archbishop Patrick Reardon of San Francisco, 1841–1914* (Wilmington, NC: Consortium Books, 1976). He wasn't a bishop, but no Catholic cleric had a bigger impact on Catholic social thought or American life in general than St. Paul native Monsignor John A. Ryan, the subject of Francis L. Broderick's *Right Reverend New Dealer, John A. Ryan* (New York: Macmillan, 1963). Catholicism's impact on social thought and action during the 1930s is also the subject of David J. O'Brien's *American Catholics and Social Reform: The New Deal Years* (New York: Oxford Univ. Press, 1968).

Irish-influenced American Catholicism functioned as a powerful subculture in the United States. It is the focus of Phil Gleason's *Catholicism in America* (New York: Harper and Row, 1970) and *Keeping the Faith: American Catholicism Past and Present* (Notre

Dame, IN: Univ. of Notre Dame Press, 1977); James Terence Fisher, *The Catholic Counter Culture in America, 1933–62* (Chapel Hill: Univ. of North Carolina Press, 1987); Paula M. Kane, *Separatism and Subculture: Boston Catholicism, 1900–1920* (Chapel Hill: Univ. of North Carolina Press, 1994); and Gary Wills' fascinating *Bare Ruined Choirs* (Garden City, NY: Doubleday, 1972). In *Religion, Culture and Values: A Cross-Cultural Analysis of Motivational Factors in Native Irish and American Irish Catholicism* (New York: Arno Press, 1976) Bruce Francis Biever quantitative research finds that while there are similarities between the way Irish Americans and the Irish practice their religion, the former is much more likely to reject clerical authoritarianism and demand democratic and pluralistic controls of their church.

Stephen P. Erie's *Rainbow's End: Irish-Americans and the Dilemmas of Urban Machine Politics, 1840–1885* (Berkeley: Univ. of California Press, 1988) is the most comprehensive examination of American politics. Although it corrects some of the exaggerations of the benefits of Irish American political machines to the Irish and others, it also underestimates both. John B. Buenker's *Urban Liberalism and Progressive Reform* (New York: Scribners, 1973) and Robert Dahl, *Who Governs? Democracy and Power in an American City* (New Haven, CT: Yale Univ. Press, 1961) take the position that Irish politicians did escalate the economic and social mobility of their own people and improved the lives of other ethnics and assimilated them into the American political mainstream. New York's Tammany Hall, the first, powerful Irish political machine, has attracted a considerable amount of attention, including Alfred Connable and Edward Silberfarb, *Tigers of Tammany* (New York: Holt, Rinehart and Winston, 1967); and Oliver E. Allen, *The Tiger: The Rise and Fall of Tammany Hall* (New York: Holt, Rinehart and Winston, 1993). A recent paperback edition of *Plunkett of Tammany Hall: A Series of Very Plain Talks on Very Practical Matters*, recorded by William L. Riordan (New York: Bedford Books, 1995) has an interesting and informative introductory essay by Peter Quinn surveying the history of Tammany, the tactics of its leaders, and their close relationships with constituents. He effectively rebuts Daniel Patrick Moynihan's thesis in "The Irish" section of his and Nathan Glazer's *Beyond the Melting Pot: Jews, Italians, and Irish of New York City* (Cambridge, MA: Harvard Univ. Press, 1963), 229, that insists that while the Irish were skilled at acquiring political power they were ineffective in its use. In *Charles Francis Murphy, 1858–1892: Respectability and Responsibility in Tammany Politics* (Northampton, MA: Smith College, 1968), Nancy Joan Weiss explains how Murphy's leadership moved Tammany beyond the search for and preservation of power toward social reform. Al Smith, the many-term governor of New York and the first Catholic candidate for president of the United States, was the most important product of Tammany. He is the subject of two recent biographies: Robert A. Slayton, *Empire Statesman: The Rise and Redemption of Al Smith* (New York: Free Press, 2001); and Christopher M. Finan, *Alfred E. Smith, The Happy Warrior* (New York: Hill and Wang, 2002).

Boston never produced the same kind of well-organized Irish political machines as New York and later Chicago but has had colorful, flamboyant characters, most notably James Michael Curley, thoroughly depicted in Jack Beatty's *The Rascal King: The Life and Times of James Michael Curley, 1874–1958* (Reading, MA: DaCapo Press, 1992). Thomas H. O'Connor treats the whole range of Irish politics in *The Boston Irish: A Political History* (Boston: Northeastern Univ. Press, 1995). On the national level, the most powerful Boston Irish politician in Congress was Speaker of the House Thomas P. O'Neill. With William Novak, he wrote his autobiography, *Man of the House: The Life and Memoirs of Speaker Tip O'Neill* (New York: Random House, 1987). Unlike his political foe, President Ronald Reagan, O'Neill reminds readers that he never forgot where he came from. Without a doubt, another Bostonian, John Fitzgerald Kennedy, is the most important Irish American politician, not for what he accomplished but for what he symbolized. His election and presidency convinced Catholics that at last they were first-class Americans. Herbert S. Parmet's *Jack: The Struggles of John F. Kennedy* (New York: Dial Press, 1980) and *JFK, The Presidency of John F. Kennedy* (New York: Dial Press, 1983) is an exceptionally good two-volume biography of the first Catholic presidency. Thomas C. Reeves's *A Question of Character: A Life of John F. Kennedy* (New York: Free Press, 1991) describes flaws that prevented JFK from living up to his promise but concludes that his presidency improved with time. Garry Wills in *The Kennedy Imprisonment* (Boston: Little, Brown, 1982), decides that Kennedy males were far more influenced by upper-class Anglo-Protestant values than Catholic ones.

Chicago perfected the Irish political machine. Unlike Boston or New York, Chicago's Irish politics thrived under the New Deal, using federal money to increase its power and efficiency. The beginning of the machine's power and efficiency began with Mayor Edward J. Kelly, it reached its peak during the twenty-year-plus rule of Mayor Richard J. Daley. In *Big City Boss in Depression and War: Mayor Edward J. Kelly of Chicago* (DeKalb: Northern Illinois Univ. Press, 1984) Roger Biles describes how Kelly winked at graft and corruption but effectively managed and beautified the city and through his commitment to civil rights brought African Americans into the Democratic fold. Mike Royko's *Boss* (New York: Dutton, 1970) is the best-known biography of Daley; William F. Gleason's *Daley of Chicago: The Man, the Mayor, and the Limits of Conventional Politics* (New York: Simon and Schuster, 1970), the most underrated; and Roger Biles's *Richard J. Daley: Politics, Race, and the Governing of Chicago* (DeKalb: Northern Illinois Univ. Press, 1995) the most scholarly. Biles appreciates Daley's managerial skills but like other critics chastises his neglect of African Americans. There are a number of good studies of the character of the Chicago Irish machine, especially Milton Rakove's *Don't Make No Waves—Don't Back No Losers* (Bloomington: Indiana Univ. Press, 1975) and *We Don't Want Nobody That Nobody Sent* (Bloomington: Indiana Univ. Press, 1979); and Edward M. Levine, *The Irish and Irish Politicians* (Notre Dame, IN: Univ. of Notre Dame Press, 1965).

Irish America produced villains as well as heroes, namely Father Charles Coughlin, anti-Semitic, pro-Mussolini radio rabble-rouser, and Senator Joseph McCarthy, whose more phony than real search for communists in government seriously jeopardized American civil liberties. Coughlin is featured in Alan Brinkley's *Voices of Protest: Huey Long, Father Coughlin, and the Great Depression* (New York: Knopf, 1982); Charles J. Tull's *Father Coughlin and the New Deal* (Syracuse, NY: Syracuse Univ. Press, 1965); and Donald Warren's *Radio Priest: Charles Coughlin, the Father of Hate Radio* (New York, 1995). Thomas C. Reeve's *The Life and Times of Joe McCarthy* (New York: Stein and Day, 1982) is a solid and detailed biography of the late Wisconsin senator. Donald F. Cosby's *God, Church, and Flag: Senator Joseph R. McCarthy and the Catholic Church, 1950–57* (Chapel Hill: Univ. of North Carolina Press, 1978) covers McCarthy's relationship with fellow Catholics.

Irish American nationalism expressed bitterness against Britain's oppression of Ireland that factored in emigration. It also reflected frustrations with American nativism that blocked Irish progress in the United States. Irish American passion and money endowed both constitutional and physical force nationalism in Ireland, guaranteeing its energetic survival. *Irish Nationalism and the American Contribution*, ed. Lawrence J. McCaffrey (New York: Arno Press, 1976) contains four valuable essays: Thomas N. Brown, "Nationalism and the Irish Peasant," and "The Origin and Character of Irish-American Nationalism" (Brown's essays were originally published in *The Review of Politics*, October 1953 and July 1956); Alan J. Ward, "America and the Irish Problem, 1899–1921 (reprinted from *Irish Historical Studies*, March 1968); and Lawrence J. McCaffrey, "Irish Nationalism and Irish Catholicism: A Study in Cultural Identity" (reprinted from *Church History*, December 1973). Fenianism represented the switch of Irish American nationalism from constitutional to revolutionary tactics. R. V. Comerford's *The Fenians in Context: Irish Politics and Society 1848–82* (Atlantic Highlands, NJ: Humanities Press, 1985) is the most complete study of the Irish Republican Brotherhood and its American Counterpart and funding arsenal. The American dimension of early revolutionary Irish republicans is the topic of William D'Arcy's *The Fenian Movement in the United States, 1858–1886* (New York: Russell and Russell, 1971). Brian Jenkins describes one of the few occasions before the recent Northern Ireland troubles when Irish American nationalism played an effective role in Anglo-Irish relations in *Fenians and Anglo-American Relations during Reconstruction* (Ithaca, NY: Cornell Univ. Press, 1969). Patrick Ford, an Irish American journalist, and the Clan na Gael were key authors of the New Departure in Irish nationalism, a strategy combining agrarian agitation with more radical elements in the Irish Parliamentary Party as a prelude to revolution. This is one of the topics in Thomas N. Brown's *Irish-American Nationalism* (Philadelphia: Lippincott, 1976). Others are Irish American nationalism pursuing respectability by freeing the mother country as much if not more than with vengeance and the impact of the Parnell divorce scandal on Irish America. For a time, Chicago was the Clan na Gael base. This is the subject of Michael Funchion's *Chicago's Irish Nationalists, 1881–1890* (New York: Arno Press, 1976). John Devoy, an IRB refugee from Ireland, was the dominant Clan na Gael personality. Terry Golway describes his long nationalist career in *Irish Rebel John Devoy and America's Fight for Ireland's Freedom* (New York: St. Martin's Press, 1999). C. C. Tansill's *America and the Fight for Irish Freedom, 1886–1922* (New York: Devin-Adair, 1957) details Irish America's financial contributions to Ireland's liberation efforts. Although Irish America has had a powerful voice in American politics, until relatively recently it has had little impact on American relations with Britain. However, its efforts are the subject of Joseph Patrick O'Grady, *Irish-Americans and Anglo-American Relations, 1880–1888* (New York: Arno Press, 1976); Joseph Edward Cuddy, *Irish-America and National Isolationism, 1914–1920* (New York: Arno Press, 1976); Alan J. Ward, *Ireland and Anglo-American Relations, 1899–1921* (London: Weidenfeld and Nicholson, 1969); John Patrick Buckley, *The New York Irish: Their View of American Foreign Policy, 1914–1921* (New York: Arno Press, 1976); and Francis M. Carroll, *American Opinion and the Irish Question, 1910–1923* (New York: St. Martin's Press, 1978). In *Dublin's American Policy: Irish-American Diplomatic Relations, 1945–1952* (Washington, DC: Catholic Univ. Press of America, 1998), Troy Davis explains how the Irish government failed to persuade the United States to support its antipartitionist campaign. In exchange, Dublin hinted at joining NATO, but Washington refused to alienate its British ally, telling the Irish we got along without you in World War II and can do so again. Finally, during the Northern Ireland troubles that began in 1968 Irish America brought the United States into the mix of Anglo-Irish relations. Its role is featured in Jack Holland, *The American Connection:*

U.S. Guns, Money, and Influence in Northern Ireland (New York: Roberts Rinehart Publishers, 1987); Dennis Clark, *Irish Blood: Northern Ireland and the American Conscience* (Port Washington, NY: Kennikat, 1977); Sean Cronin, *Washington's Irish Policy, 1916–1986: Independence, Partition, and Neutrality* (Dublin: 1986); and Andrew M. Wilson, *Irish America and the Ulster Conflict, 1968–1993* (Washington, DC: Catholic Univ. of America Press, 1995). Wilson's nicely written study is the most comprehensive examination of Irish America's impact on the Northern Ireland situation.

Irish nationalism had a quicker impact on American labor radicalism than on foreign policy. Secret agrarian societies in Ireland, more interested in achieving a moral economy than Irish independence, influenced the character of the Molly Maguires in Pennsylvania coal fields, the subject of Kevin Kenny's *Making Sense of the Molly Maguires* (New York: Oxford Univ. Press, 1998), the best examination of a complicated subject. Boycotting began as a strategy in the Irish land war of the 1880s and became an American labor tactic to achieve just wages, a civilized workday, and decent working conditions. This is discussed in Michael Gordon's "Irish Immigrant Culture and the Labor Boycott in New York City, 1880–1886," in *Immigrants in Industrial America, 1850–1920*, ed. Richard L. Ehrlich 11–22 (Charlottesville, NC: Balch Institute, 1977). According to Joshua B. Freeman, "Catholics, Communists, and Republicans: Irish Workers and the Organization of the Transport Workers Union," in *Working Class America: Essays on Labor, Community, and American Society*, ed. Michael A. Frish and Daniel Walkowitz (Urbana: Univ. of Illinois Press, 1983) immigrant veterans of the Anglo-Irish and civil wars in Ireland cooperated with Communists in the founding of the New York Transport Workers Union. In *The Catholic Church and the Knights of Labor* (New York: Arno Press, 1976), Henry J. Brown covers the dispute between progressive Irish prelates, Archbishop John Ireland and James Cardinal Gibbons and their conservative foe, Archbishop Michael Corrigan, over the Irish influenced Knights of Labor effort to organize working-class America on a national basis. Eliot Gorn's *Mother Jones: The Most Dangerous Woman in America* (New York: Hill and Wang, 2001) is an excellent biography of Cork Born Marry Harris Jones, "The Miner's Angel."

Unfortunately, the many contributions of the Irish to American athletics, especially boxing and baseball, haven't received enough attention, but Jerrold Casway's *The Times and Tragedy of Ed Delahanty in the Emerald Age of Baseball* (Notre Dame, IN: Univ. of Notre Dame Press, 2003) helps fill the gap. The Irish presence in American entertainment has also been formidable. In *'Twas Only an Irishman's Dream: The Image of Ireland and the Irish in American Popular Song Lyrics, 1800–1920s* (Urbana and Chicago: Univ. of Illinois Press, 1996), William H. A. Williams makes the case that Irish American songs, particularly those of Harrigan and Hart, did much to improve their standing with other Americans. Gary Giddens's *Bing Crosby: A Pocketful of Dreams: The Early Years* (Boston: Little, Brown, 2001) the first volume in a two-volume biography, is a thorough examination of the early career of pre-Sinatra America's most popular vocalist-jazz singer and crooner. It emphasizes Irish family and cultural influences on Bing. In addition to being a great singer, Crosby was one of many highly regarded Irish American movie stars. They and their work is the theme of Joseph M. Curran's *Hibernian Green on the Silver Screen* (Westport, CT: Greenwood Press, 1989). Curran discusses all facets of the Irish role in the making and acting of movies and pays special attention to the directing genius of John Ford, as does Joseph McBride, *Searching for John Ford* (New York: St. Martin's Press, 2001), and Thomas Flanagan in two reviews of McBrides's work,

"Western Star," *New York Review of Books*, Nov. 29, 2001; and "John Ford's West," *New York Review of Books*, Dec. 20, 2001.

From Finley Peter Dunne's Mr. Dooley essays in the 1890s to the recent triumphs of William Kennedy and Alice McDermott, Irish America has made valuable contributions to the nation's literature. A variety of Irish American literary portraits appear in Lawrence J. McCaffrey's "Fictional Images of Irish America" in Tom Dunne, ed., *The Writer as Witness* (Cork, Ireland: Cork Univ. Press, 1987). Daniel J. Casey and Robert E. Rhodes have edited two anthologies concerning Irish American literature: *Irish-American Fiction: Essays in Criticism* (New York: AMS, 1979) and *Modern Irish-American Fiction: A Reader* (Syracuse, NY: Syracuse Univ. Press, 1989). In Eugene O'Neill, Irish America contributed one of the country's leading playwrights. Stephen A. Black's *Eugene O'Neill: Beyond Mourning and Tragedy* (New Haven, CT: Yale Univ. Press, 1999) investigates the many family and personal experiences that colored O'Neill's Work. In *Eugene O'Neill, Irish and American: A Study in Cultural Context* (New York: Arno Press, 1976), Henry Cornelius Cronin makes the case that although he rejected the church, O'Neill saw life from an Irish-Catholic original-sin and guilt perspective. Charles Fanning, the leading scholar of Irish American literature, has contributed a number of valuable studies on the subject, beginning with *Finley Peter Dunne and Mr. Dooley: The Chicago Years* (Lexington: Univ. Press of Kentucky, 1978). He edited two important anthologies: *Mr. Dooley and the Chicago Irish: The Autobiography of a Nineteenth-Century Ethnic Group* (Washington, DC: Catholic Univ. of America, 1987), and *Exiles of Erin: Nineteenth Century Irish-American Fiction* (Notre Dame, IN: Univ. of Notre Dame Press, 1987). In a Spring 2001 review in *The Irish Literary Supplement*, 18–20, I described his *The Irish Voice in America: 250 Years of Irish-American Fiction* (Lexington: Univ. Press of Kentucky, 2000) as "the most important book yet published in Irish-American Studies."

ITALIAN AMERICANS

Dominic Candeloro

Though sometimes referred to as the Children of Columbus, Italian Americans as a people played only a minor role in American history prior to the 1880s.[1] Columbus did trigger intellectual, economic, and social revolutions with his discovery of the Western Hemisphere for Europe. Though his heroism endures as a symbol for Italian Americans, the gap between Columbus' time and when Italians became present in significant numbers in the United States spanned almost four hundred years. On the other hand, there were reports of Venetian glassblowers among the early settlers in Virginia, Italian-named missionaries such as Father Eusebio Kino and Father Samuel Mazzuchelli operating in what is now Arizona and in the Wisconsin-Michigan area, respectively, and Enrico Tonti leading the LaSalle explorations.

The Founding Fathers and educated Americans of that time held Italian art and culture in high esteem. Thomas Jefferson and Benjamin Franklin were familiar with the Italian language and with Roman history. Jefferson was a sponsor of Filippo Mazzei in the early 1770s and encouraged him to bring Italian vintners to Virginia. Though not successful in that venture, Mazzei became actively involved in the colonists' struggle with England. Writing in the Virginia newspapers under the name Furioso, he was one of the first to urge Americans to declare independence and form a unified constitution to govern all thirteen colonies. Some of his phraseology later found its way into Jefferson's Declaration of Independence.[2] Italian-named William Paca, an early governor of Maryland, was one of the signers of the Declaration of Independence.

Though the presence of Italian individuals in the United States was sparse before 1850, the historian Giovanni Schiavo has documented the accomplishments of scores of Italian clerics and musicians active in that period.[3] Lorenzo da Ponte, librettist for Mozart, taught Italian language and literature at Columbia University. In 1825, he produced his *Don Giovanni* in New York. Music teachers, architects, and the artists who embellished the capitols built throughout the United States were imported from Italy in that period, and Italian was one of the most frequently studied foreign languages in America. A few of these figures achieved the kinds of things that sometimes merit brief mention in survey textbooks.[4] The design of buildings in Washington, D.C., was heavily influenced by Italian style and Italian artisans. Costantino Brumidi painted the splendid frescoes in the U.S. Capitol between 1855 and 1880.

There was a modest migration of Italians to California during and after the Gold Rush. Many in this group became prosperous farmers, vintners, and business leaders, including Domenico Ghirardelli, (the chocolate maker), the Gallo and Mondavi families (wine producers), and Amadeo Giannini (the founder of the Bank of America). Most historians consider the experience of Italians in California to be exceptional because immigration there was early and agricultural. This combination made possible relatively fast entry into the middle and upper classes of California society. The California Italian experience is also characterized by the relative intensity with which the government sought to repress and relocate Italians as "enemy aliens" in the early stages of World War II.[5]

The 1850 census reported a total of 5,000 Italians in America, mostly in and around New York City. During that period, the Italian revolutionary Giuseppe Garibaldi resided briefly on Staten Island with Antonio Meucci, an inventor of the telephone. St. Anthony's, the first Italian church in America, was founded in New York in 1866. When the Civil War began, Garibaldi approached President Lincoln and volunteered to become the Commander in Chief of Union armies but was turned down.

In the 1880s, Italian migration to the United States began in earnest and continued until immigration restriction in the 1920s. As refugees from an overpopulated rural nation, Italian emigrants joined millions in Western Europe and North America in experiencing the rough transition to modernization. Estimates of the number of Italian immigrants are made murky by individuals' repeated crossings, the undocumented entry of untold thousands, and inconsistencies in the spelling of names. The Ellis Island Web site provides fascinating primary source documentation of each immigrant who passed through. About 4.5 million Italians made the trip to the United States in that forty-year period. With some notable exceptions, they came for economic reasons, looking for *pane e lavoro* (bread and work), and often depended on *padroni* (labor agents) to find them any kind of work.[6]

America needed the immigrants as much as the immigrants needed America. Between 1900 and 1910, 2 million Italians emigrated. The numbers peaked at 285,000 in 1907, 284,000 in 1914, and 222,000 in 1921.[7] After 1900, Italian immigrants began in earnest to bring their families to join them, and Italian neighborhoods in large cities became more stable. In this "chain migration," *paesani* (townspeople) from a particular town in Italy, transferred, over varying time periods, to specific neighborhoods and suburbs in the United States. In this manner, they created a near-replica of their home town, adhering more or less to the

social customs, dialect, and family patterns of the old country, even while beginning their journey toward Americanization.

Italians brought with them an agrarian, Catholic, and family-based culture.
Hard work and self-sufficiency were facts of life. Of all the social institutions in
Italian society, the family was the only one that could be relied on consistently,
even though the early immigrants had to leave their families in order to save
them.

Italian immigrants were ambivalent toward the church. On the one hand, they
were all baptized Catholics, they believed in the saints, and were devoted to the
Blessed Virgin Mary; on the other hand, the church was a large landholder,
deeply involved in Italian politics in coalition with the upper classes, and opposed to unification. In contrast to Irish and Polish immigrants whose national
identity was championed by the church, Italian nationalists saw the church as
their enemy. As a result the immigrants brought with them a certain anticlericalism, a casual attitude toward strict rules, and a devotion to folk practices.

Although southern Italy and Sicily sent the most immigrants, all parts of Italy
contributed to the migration. The early migrants were mostly illiterate, unskilled
male workers, birds of passage, many of whom returned to Italy several times before they decided to stay in America permanently and to bring their wives and families with them. A good number returned to live in their native villages. The impact
of these *rimpatrioti* (returnees) on Italian social mobility and culture is a fascinating aspect of the unexpected consequences of emigration. These men often served
as unofficial agents, expediting the chain migration process and helping to revital-
ize it in the post–World War II period. Sometimes the *rimpatrioti* successfully advanced their family fortunes by investing savings accumulated in the United States
in small businesses or farms. Occasionally, aspects of Italian modernization can be
traced back to emigrants who returned from industrialized America.[8]

Restrictive immigration laws, Benito Mussolini's policies, the Depression of
the 1930s, and World War II reduced Italian migration to a trickle from the 1920s
to the late 1940s. A second wave of migration to the United States followed World
War II, as residents of war-torn sections of Italy used every possible connection
to find opportunities to migrate to the United States and other countries, such
as Canada, Argentina, and Australia. Waiting lists for migration to the United
States were lengthy. Through all the periods of the Italian exodus there developed chains and networks of migration from Italian clans, towns, and regions to
specific states, towns, and urban neighborhoods in the United States. For
instance, many from the Abruzzi region ended up in the Philadelphia area, and
a good percentage of the New Orleans Italians are of Sicilian origin. There are
dozens of U.S. towns and neighborhoods whose population of descendants from
an Italian town far exceeds the current population of that town of origin. With
the exception of New Orleans; Tampa, Florida; and parts of West Virginia, Italian immigrants tended to avoid the South. Because they were sojourners without capital and because most of the good agricultural land was spoken for, most
of these agrarian migrants ended up in the industrialized northeastern and north-

central cities. A significant segment also settled in the West as a result of work on the railroads and in the mines of that region.[9] Perhaps the most established Italian Americans today are the descendants of the Piedmontese vintners who migrated to California shortly after the Gold Rush. The Italian experience in America was influenced by the mix of ethnic groups, class relationships, and economic structure of the geographic areas where they settled. Thus, Joseph Bernardin (later Cardinal Bernardin) had a different experience growing up in rural North Carolina, where there were few Italians, than did former New York State governor Mario Cuomo, who grew up in New York City. And Italians in Chicago have played a lesser role in politics than those in New York or Rhode Island, where Italian ethnics make up a larger portion of the population.

Like other immigrant and minority groups, Italians suffered discrimination. They were poor, illiterate, considered a problem, and stereotyped as criminals, radicals, and buffoons. The largest single lynching in American history took place in New Orleans in 1891 and had as its victims eleven Italians.[10] More subtle discrimination persists into the twenty-first century, in the form of negative stereotypes in the mass media, and is the only significant deprivation of sorts of this well-heeled group that has moved from urban slums to middle-class status in barely three generations.[11] An analysis of the nature and completeness of that transformation—of five million immigrants into sixteen million ethnics—is the subject of this chapter.

Italians brought with them a lively rural-*paesani* culture that, though imbued with class distinctions, lent itself to cooperative survival strategies in their New World. And the failing agricultural economy from which they were fleeing gave them the habit of hard work. The class consciousness of Italians who participated in strikes in Paterson, New Jersey; Lowell, Massachusetts; and Tampa, Florida is additional evidence of their inner-directedness. The establishment by Bishop Giovanni Battista Scalabrini of the Missionary Fathers of St. Charles Borromeo in the 1880s was the first concentrated effort by the Catholic Church to minister to the needs of Italian migrants. Over the century that followed, the Scalabrinians have built and staffed hundreds of churches, schools, and hospitals in the United States, Canada, Latin America, and Australia. Among the disciples of Scalabrini was Mother Cabrini, who led the Chicago Italian American community in building their own local institutions, like hospitals and schools. This mix of forces developed a substantial cultural base that belies the too-sympathetic notion espoused by the historian Oscar Handlin that the immigrants were hapless victims of the brutal process of migration.[12] Moreover, it is that very strength of the Italian cultural base that goes far toward explaining the retention of ethnic identity by Italians and other groups.

SELF-HELP ORGANIZATIONS

Like other ethnic groups, Italian immigrants developed a range of self-help organizations. Their mutual-benefit societies were based on their towns of origin and provided the early immigrants with minimal sick and death benefits before Medicare and before Social Security. These Societé di Mutuo Soccorso (Mutual Benefit Societies) often hired a physician on retainer and provided modest benefits to survivors in case of a death.

Their neighborhoods, their extended family, *paesani* networks, leisure clubs, church groups, and unions also helped them cope with the challenges of urban life in the new country. Various national groups, such as the Order of Sons of Italy of America (OSIA), tried to combine or federate the thousands of small lodges (those with an average membership of 250) but experienced only moderate success. Heavy involvement by the OSIA in Mussolini's Fascist propaganda campaign in the 1920s and 1930s had obvious disastrous consequences for the organization after the outbreak of World War II, and any hope of organizational unity through OSIA was dashed.

The Italian American press can also be considered a self-help organization. From the time of the founding of the first Italian newspaper in America by Francesco Secchi De Casali in 1849 (*L'Eco d'Italia*), the immigrant press was there, providing the news of the day in the immigrants' own language, promoting local political bosses, providing advice for learning English and coping in the New World, preaching fascism, preaching socialism, pushing Protestantism, and acquiescing in Americanization. Dozens of Italian American Socialist, anarchist, religious, Fascist, anti-Fascist, unionist, and literary magazines have been published in the period since then. *Il Progresso Italo-Americano*, (New York, 1880–1989) and the *L'Italia* (Chicago, 1888–1940s) in particular, because of their longevity, provide continuous coverage of Italian American history. Since *Il Progresso*'s daily circulation was above 100,000, Generoso Pope, its editor during the 1930s and 1940s, was perhaps the most influential Italian American leader of his time. These newspapers depended on an Italian-speaking public, and the radical newspapers also depended on a sizeable Socialist following. By the 1930s, the monocultural Americanization policy had begun to have its effect. The second generation preferred their newspapers in English. This same phenomenon hit radio broadcasting about twenty years later.

Current Italian American journalism reflects continued changes in the marketplace. The *Italian Tribune* of Newark, New Jersey, is an English-language weekly founded in 1931, and *America Oggi* is an Italian-language daily that serves the New York–New Jersey area. On the West Coast, the weekly bilingual *L'Italo-Americano*, founded in 1908 by Gabriello Spini, continues to serve the Los Angeles community. *Fra Noi* (Among Us) is a monthly founded in 1961 by Father Armando Pierini to promote his senior citizens' home, Villa Scalabrini, in suburban Chicago. Slick magazines launched in the 1980s, like *Attenzione*, *I-AM*, and *Identity*, could never quite decide whether their target constituency was upscale Italophiles or second- and third-generation old-neighborhood types. Though they served a purpose in enhancing the awareness of Italian ethnicity, those slick magazines are gone now. The current selection of Italian American magazines includes the monthly *Primo* published out of Pittsburgh, the Order of Sons of Italy's *Italian America*, and the National Italian American Foundation's *Ambassador*.

Much has been written about Italian radicals.[13] This is both because their story is exciting and because they were by far the most literate element in Italian American society, and the most literate are always overrepresented in history. Those few Italians who left Italy for reasons other than economic ones tended to be Socialists and "anarchists," (perhaps better described by the term *"radical democrat"*). Leaders of these movements, such as Carlo Tresca and Arturo Giovannitti, had a respectable following in a series of clothing-workers strikes in Paterson, New Jersey, and Lowell, Massachusetts, around 1910. The Italian section of the American Socialist party was one of the strongest prior to the Russian Revolution (1917) and the Nicola Sacco and Bartolomeo Vanzetti executions (1927).

The controversial trial of Sacco and Vanzetti for a murder-robbery in Braintree, Massachusetts, in 1920 haunted the headlines for over seven years. Their execution in 1927 was a dark day in Italian American history, because it proved to Italian Americans that the system was so prejudiced against Italians that even their most righteous causes could not get a fair hearing in this country. The execution of the pair crippled Italian-American radicalism and many of the Italian-language publications that espoused that philosophy.

The flamboyance and style of Italian American bootleggers during Prohibition helped shape the image of gangsters of that period and has since become the baseline stereotype of Italian Americans. The thousands of books and media productions on the subject of Italian gangsters include some of the best and some of the worst artistic expression in American culture. But whatever the quality of the art, in the eyes of the Italian American leadership, the result was the same: the intensification in the public's mind of a negative image of Italian Americans.

In addition to mutual-benefit societies and newspapers, Italian American organizations cover a wide range of activities. Italian American self-help organizations abounded in the post–World War II era to the point of excess. The Center for Migration Studies in the 1980s published the *National Directory of Italian American Organizations* and a New York City directory listing almost a thousand organizations of every imaginable size and scope.[14]

Each new group presented itself as the one that would bring the elusive unity to the community. One of the roots of Italian American disunity can be traced to *campanilismo*, an intense loyalty to one's Italian town of origin. This feeling often undermined national allegiance. Italians who were never really unified in Italy should not have expected unity within their immigrant colonies. From a group that had to stretch itself to develop loyalties beyond family, it would be too much to expect a well-developed sense of national patriotism. Moreover, from 1922 to 1941, the two most articulate elements among Italian Americans, the Fascists and the anti-Fascists (mostly Socialists), were at each others' throats.[15] Flashes of unity appeared during and after World War II in the relief efforts toward the war-torn old country and in later relief efforts following major Italian earthquakes. Since 1960, however, Italy has been prosperous. There is no need for Italian American groups to jump to its defense or to lobby the U.S. government on behalf of its survival, as Jewish Americans do for Israel and as Polish Americans did for many years to pry their homeland away from Soviet domination.

In the past two decades, however, thanks to the creation of the National Italian American Foundation (NIAF), based in Washington, DC, the brainchild of Father Geno Baroni (former undersecretary of the U.S. Department of Housing and Urban Development), bankrolled by Jeno Paolucci (of Jeno's Pizza Rolls), and promoted by Italian American political figures such as John Volpe (former governor of Massachusetts), and Chicago congressman Frank Annunzio, there has been an established national representative for Italian Americans. As always, Washington politicians are delighted to have only one entity to deal with in satisfying the desires of an ethnic group, especially one that is perceived as an emerging and complex one. By remaining bipartisan, by creating alliances with existing Italian American organizations, and by developing a broad program of scholarships and cultural endeavors and links to Italy, the NIAF has gone further toward achieving a genuine, unified voice of Italian Americans than any previous organization. During each U.S. presidential election campaign, the appearance of Democratic and Republican presidential and vice presidential candidates at the NIAF banquet demonstrates the prestige of the organization. Moreover, NIAF's apparent ability to play a role in the nomination and appointment of high-ranking political figures such as congresswoman and one-time Democratic vice presidential nominee Geraldine Ferraro, Clinton chief-of-staff Leon Panetta, Supreme Court justice Antonin Scalia, and secretary of defense Frank Carlucci adds to the self-fulfilling process of image building.

Founded in 1908, the Order of the Sons of Italy in America continues to be a major voice for the ethnic group. The organization recovered in the postwar period and today claims 600,000 members in 700 chapters across the nation. Some observers believe that the OSIA's large membership and wide geographic penetration make it a sleeping giant. The traditional orientation of OSIA has been toward the ceremonial, although their lodges also provide social programming and group life insurance. In recent years, its Committee on Social Justice and its publications have generated a sophisticated defense against defamation and an interest in promoting Italian-language education and the popularization of Italian American culture. The success of these national institutions will reinforce the retention of ethnic identity among Italian Americans far into the future and will act to counterbalance such antiretention trends as ethnic intermarriage.

The Italian government's attempts to organize the Italian American community have been confused and ineffective. In the 1980s, complicating the organizational scene among Italian Americans was the establishment Co. Em. It. (Commitato d'Emigranti Italiana), an elective group devised to advise the consul general in each of a half-dozen major U.S. cities. Created by a vote of the Italian parliament, Co. Em. It. was clearly an effort to keep recent Italian immigrants to the United States in the Italian sphere, both legally and culturally.

Co. Em. It. focused on those who continue to hold Italian citizenship. Though often ignored by older Italian American groups, the post–World War II immigrants consider themselves to be the natural leaders of Italian Americans because of their close ties with contemporary Italian culture. The 1980s efforts were marked by a counterproductive, heated political scramble. The recent establishment of the Italian Ministry of Italians Abroad under the leadership of Mirko Tremaglia, combined with the passage of laws allowing Italian citizens abroad to vote in some Italian elections, indicates both a cultural and political interest in Italian Americans. Italian consulate officers and local Italian-language and culture support groups like *Italidea* in Chicago and *WisItalia* in Wisconsin have had success in lobbying state government to expand the teaching of Italian in public schools.

RELIGION

The relationship of Italian Americans to their religion is a complicated one. Italians are implicitly Roman Catholics. Rome is the seat of the church. Evidence of the role of Catholicism in Italian culture and Western culture has been pervasive in the architecture, literature, and folkways of the Italian people for almost 2,000 years. The church has also been a political entity, with the popes of Rome scrambling and competing with local strongmen and foreign potentates for political domination of central Italy.

This kind of activity kept Italy from being unified as a modern nation until the latter part of the nineteenth century. The papacy was the last holdout, the final stumbling block to unification. When its temporal power was stripped away in 1870, the church withdrew not gracefully but with a curse of excommunication on all the leaders in the unification movement. Thus, to be an Italian patriot was to be anticlerical. It was not until 1929 that the papacy recognized the legitimacy of the Italian government in return for the government's guarantee of papal sovereignty over the Vatican City and the establishment of Catholicism as the official state religion.

Just as important was the role that the church played in the social and economic structure of the woebegone towns from which the emigrants fled. The church was a landlord allied with the establishment, and had no motivation to encourage reform. Moreover, until the Scalabrini movement, few priests joined the waves of migrants to the New World. When Italians reached American cities in the 1890s and after, they found a Roman Catholic Church dominated by the Irish, who sent them to the church basement to pray. This proverbial insult was probably due more to their differences in style of worship than to their language differences. Italians didn't care about church rules so much; they didn't take to the catechism and puritanical bent of Irish Catholicism; and they were not in the habit of tossing their hard-earned cash into the collection basket. Anticlericalism was strong among the Socialists and others. Since large numbers were virtually unchurched, a variety of Protestant denominations targeted Italian immigrants for their brand of salvation. Yet, for the most part the considerable effort by American Protestants to convert Italians failed.

Probably the most important reason for this failure is that the Italians brought their folk religion with them. The cult of the virgin, devotion to patron saints of each village, and even the superstitious practices associated with the *mal occhio* (evil eye curses) constituted a virtually indestructible imported core culture.

Religious street festivals have been the most outstanding characteristic of old Italian religiosity in America. Italians parading the graven images of saints and madonnas laden with money pinned to their garments as a way of supporting the church was shocking to Protestant Americans and not a little disturbing to the Irish hierarchy and even some Italian priests. The San Rocco feast in the movie *Godfather II* was a masterly portrayal of the tradition. One would have thought that such maudlin folk practices would have been an early casualty to the Americanization process.

Twenty years ago the number of such feasts had dwindled to a mere handful, but in recent times there has been a resurgence in the number and intensity of these celebrations. For instance, in Chicago in the 1920s you could attend a different festival each Sunday at the Sicilian St. Philip Benizi Church. In the twenty-first century in the Chicago area you can still attend a *festa* each Sunday, but you have to travel to different parts of the metropolitan area to do so. Although they are promoted as religious events, these clan-oriented activities also have strong charitable and commercial aspects that keep them viable. In the Chicago area, and especially Milwaukee for the past few decades, the commercialized Festa Italiana has featured big-name Italian American entertainers, food, art, merchandise, rides, and Sunday mass on the lakefront. The organizers have attracted hundreds of thousands of people and have used the proceeds to encourage and support Italian American culture and charitable activities—thus intensifying and perpetuating the identification of all participants and beneficiaries with things Italian. Ethnicity is nothing if not symbolic, and the festivals themselves, laden with both ancient and modern symbolism, proclaim a convincing challenge to all who would dismiss the importance of Italian ethnicity in the United States.

The anticlerical, superstitious, unchurched aspects of Italian American religiosity were tempered by the presence in Chicago, New York, and New England of the Scalabrini order. Officially known as the fathers of St. Charles Borromeo, the order was founded in 1887 by Bishop Giovanni Scalabrini of Piacenza, who was moved by the church's insensitivity to the needs of the immigrant masses. Scalabrini is credited with inspiring Mother Cabrini to shift her attention from Chinese missionary duties to work with Italian immigrants in the Americas.

In the first quarter of the twentieth century, Scalabrini priests led the Italian immigrants in the establishment of approximately one hundred schools and churches. The process of organizing to build churches and schools contributed mightily to the development of a sense of community within the Italian sections of larger cities. In Chicago, the term *Italian community* would have been inconceivable without the leadership of the Scalabrini fathers, especially Armando Pierini, who established a seminary, a senior citizens' home, and a newspaper (*Fra Noi*), which today form the centers of the Chicago Italian community. Gary Mormino, in *Immigrants on the Hill*, credits St. Ambrose Church and its priests with maintaining the community identity of St. Louis Italians.[16] In short, the Scalabrini fathers did for the Italians what other religious orders have done for other ethnic groups: they preserved and strengthened Italian national culture and language through religion. Though the forces of suburbanization have scattered Italian Catholics, and though the Scalabrini dedication to the immigrants in America has now extended to Mexican Americans, the Scalabrini fathers and their five hundred members around the world continue to play an important role in the maintenance and advancement of Italian ethnicity.

EDUCATION AND SOCIAL MOBILITY

Formal education was not an important part of the experience of the early Italian immigrants. Well over 50 percent of the immigrants from Italy at the turn of the century were illiterate in their own language. And their own language was not likely to be standard Italian, but one of its hundreds of dialects. Illiteracy and the isolation created by Italy's mountainous geography encouraged the development of local dialects significantly different from standard Italian. Even today in Italy, with its mass media and effective universal education, differing language patterns are a means of social distinction. The illiteracy of Italian immigrants and their sojourner mentality retarded their mastery of American English and blocked easy access to education as a stepping-stone to social mobility. The need of parents to supplement their own incomes with those of their children was often crucial.

The immigrants valued hard work and family solidarity, and many of them had no intention of remaining long in the United States. They distrusted the conscious and unconscious messages sent back through their children by the middle-class, Anglo-oriented school system. The kids got the message, too. Seventy-five years ago Italian American kids dropped out of and caused trouble in the schools at rates that today plague other minority teens.[17] This disconnection with the school system was compounded by conflicts between the immigrant generation and their children. The second generation was Americanized enough to understand the cult of success at any price. This and the opportunities presented by bootlegging help to explain why some Italian American youth turned to gangsterism.[18]

Italian American achievers are divided on the attitudes of their parents toward education. Leonard Covello, a New York City educator, and Helen Barolini, a New York writer, both report that their parents discouraged them from "wasting time reading books."[19] On the other hand, many successful Italian Americans report that their parents respected education and scrimped and saved and vowed that their kids would not have to do the heavy manual work that they themselves were condemned to do. While the attitudes are debatable, the results are not. Italian immigrants were not very successful at passing their language on to their children and grandchildren. In addition, few Italian Americans attended college before the late 1940s, when the GI Bill began to take effect. Many Italian American veterans chose to use GI benefits to get vocational training. College attendance by Italian American youth was far below average well into the 1970s.[20] And while the ethnic group made inroads into the professions of law, medicine, and dentistry in the post–World War II era, the majority of Italian Americans who reached middle-class status in the 1960s did so by means other than higher education.

Hard work at steady, unskilled jobs in an America that needed unskilled labor, long hours in small family business, and underconsumption of material goods were the elements crucial to Italian American success in the first two generations. Upwardly mobile Italians turned to small businesses such as groceries, barbershops, shoe-repair shops, fruit vending, and restaurants because they required little capital, and could be established near home and staffed by family members. Capitalizing on the role of foodways in Italian culture, Italian Americans are overrepresented in food-related businesses. In common with other immigrant groups, early on Italians focused on achieving home ownership. Paychecks of all family members were turned over to the mother, as portrayed in Mario Puzo's book *Fortunate Pilgrim*, and the welfare of individual family members was subordinated to that of the family. Gardening skills and construction skills applied to two flats or duplexes over time yielded modest accumulations of capital. Mutual assistance within the extended family meant never having to buy in-season produce, to pay for a haircut, hire a plumber, or call a cab. Reciprocity in doing favors and in giving money gifts at birthdays, christenings, confirmations, weddings, and funerals gave extended family members access to cash at critical moments in the life cycle.

The other side of the coin is that family solidarity might be stifling. Young people, especially girls, were either subtley or directly discouraged from going away to school. Parents and relatives often pressured the upwardly mobile to refuse promotions that might take them out of town and out of their lives. Perhaps second-generation Italian Americans, as the children of migrants who had split from their families in order to survive, were especially sensitive to the psychic costs of migration. Many were survivors of the Depression who valued security above all else. In any case, until the 1970s Italian Americans did not use higher education as their major tool of social mobility into the middle class, and, consequently, the group was underrepresented in the ranks of corporate leadership, for example.

Times have changed. The statistics show Italian Americans attending college at a rate roughly proportional to their presence in the general population.[21] While there might be some variation in their majors and the relative prestige of the schools they are attending, modern Italian Americans are worshipping at the shrine of higher education. Upward ripples in the number of students enrolled in Italian-language classes reflect a sensitivity on the part of Italian American students and their parents to the importance of the maintenance of their ethnicity.[22] It also reflects the fact that instruction in the Italian language is no longer available in the homes and neighborhoods of Italian Americans. The language, the culture of Italy, and even the immigrant heritage are available only in the classroom and from cultural institutions. The migrating generation of the first wave is gone. The semighettoized Italian neighborhoods and their institutions, such as athletic clubs, settlement houses, candy stores, and churches, which shaped the lives of second-generation Italians, have disappeared or been gentrified. It is ironic that many of the keys to the content of Italian American ethnicity are no longer in the hands of the ethnics themselves but in the possession of educational and formal cultural institutions.

Like other ethnic groups, Italians have formed an historical association, the American Italian Historical Association (AIHA), to promote the study and dissemination of information about the Italian American experience. In 1967, Leonard Covello, the first Italian high school principal in New York City, and a hardy group of academics organized the group in New York. The founding president was Rudolph J. Vecoli, who went on to become one of the most important scholars in the field of ethnic/migration history, as director of the Immigration History Research Center at the University of Minnesota. The AIHA transposed *Italian* and *American* in its name to emphasize the continuity of *Italianitá*. The name suggests that the immigrants and their descendants constituted an American brand of Italians rather than a hyphenated American group on the verge of melting into nondescript Americans. AIHA membership has grown to four hundred college professors, students, and community researchers in various fields of the humanities and social sciences. The organization holds annual conferences, publishes its proceedings, maintains a Web site (http://www.aiha.fau.edu) and a listserv (H-ItAm) and has been directly or indirectly involved in almost all of the scholarship on the subject of Italian Americans in the past thirty-five years. But to say that it is a household name to the sixteen million Italian Americans in the United States would be a gross exaggeration. The Calandra Institute at Queens College, the Italian Studies program at State University of New York at Stony Brook, and several other university centers in the United States also focus on Italian American studies.

ITALIAN AMERICAN LITERATURE

Another indication of a lack of development among Italian Americans of an intellectual curiosity about themselves is the plight of Italian American literature. Aside from Pietro di Donato, Jerre Mangione, and Helen Barolini, few Italian Americans have become self-sufficient by writing on authentic Italian American themes other than the Mafia. Mario Puzo himself was nearly destitute before writing *The Godfather*, having previously written critically acclaimed but commercial failures like *Fortunate Pilgrim*. Fred Gardaphe's essay "In Search of Italian American Writers," in the spring 1997 issue of *Italian America* summarizes the work of more recent Italian American writers. Yet, even the exquisite poet laureate of Italian Americans, Joseph Tusiani, is almost unknown among his compatriots.

Beginning with the publication of *From the Margin: Writings in Italian Americana*, edited by Anthony Tamburri, Paolo Giordano, and Gardaphe, an appreciation for the standard Italian American writer and second-, third-, and fourth-generation writers began to flourish. Another breakthrough publication was *Dream Book: An Anthology of Writings by Italian American Women*, edited by Helen Barolini, brought to light dozens of women writers. Other developments included establishment of the Italian American Writers Association and the awakening of Italian American feminism. This same growing circle of literati supported the emergence of outlets like Bordighera Press, Guernica Publishers (Canada), and *VIA: Voices in Italian Americana and Italian Americana*, which have provided a vast increase in the quantity and diversity of publications by and about Italian Americans. Lawrence DiStasi and the Western Regional Chapter of the American Italian Historical Association's documentation of the federal government's violation of the rights of Italian Americans in World War II has also stirred up the kind of interest that might create demand for books on Italian American subjects.

In 2003, the publication by Morrow of *The Italian American Reader*, edited by Bill Tonelli, offered hope that the market was changing. Finding an audience for these writers and bringing their writings to the mass media are continuing challenges. Especially when compared to Jewish Americans and African Americans, Italian Americans, even the college educated, cannot claim a body of literature that has led them to a learned and sophisticated appreciation of their ethnic history or the humanistic heritage of their nation of origin. Whether this will change among the current generation of Italian American students is yet to be seen.

Some of the most creative and successful literary products of Italian Americans have emerged from film and television. Unfortunately for the Italian American image, the bulk of these productions, like *The Godfather*, *Goodfellas*, and *The Sopranos*, have reinforced the stereotype of the Italian American connection to organized crime. The Mafia mystique has become so pervasive in the mass media that many Italian American activists find themselves spending the vast majority of their energy and resources in fighting *against* the stereotype rather than devoting themselves to the positive task of preservation of authentic Italian American culture. One immediate response to *The Sopranos* in New Jersey, however, was the funding in 2003 of a modest state-supported Italian American studies program in the public schools.

LABOR UNIONS

Italian Americans have had considerable success in the labor movement. Though unions no longer represent radical class-consciousness as they did ninety years ago, union membership and leadership have added to the welfare and security of a good part of the American population, including Italian Americans. Italian Americans have played prominent roles in a number of major unions. The International Laborers' Union (LIUNA) has a membership of 500,000 and was dominated by the Fosco family of Chicago (formerly of Molise, Italy) for several decades. Peter Fosco served as president from the 1960s to the 1980s and was succeeded by his son Angelo until Angelo was removed by federal authorities in the 1990s. Though the national and local leadership of the LIUNA often handled business affairs in a scandalous manner, damage to individual members was limited. On a basic level, LIUNA got the job done, improving wages and working conditions and providing pensions.

In the field of music, James "Caesar" Petrillo (1892–1984) emerged in the 1920s on the Chicago scene. In 1940, Petrillo was elected president of the American Federation of Musicians (AFM), a position he served in until 1958. Petrillo was tough. He protested to Chicago politicians and even to Mussolini when events that they sponsored failed to use union musicians. His campaign against "canned music" and the strike actions he took against NBC and the Boston Symphony, for example, drew a lot of criticism from the public. For a period in 1942, he banned union musicians from making recordings until the record industry would agree to his demand to create a Music Performance Trust Fund (derived from record sales) to pay musicians to give free concerts. Twice Petrillo's image graced the cover of *Time* magazine. He has earned a place in the history of Italian Americans because of his feisty defense of his interest group—the musicians—a sizeable number of whom were Italian Americans.

It appears that ethnic, even regional, Italian considerations were important in the recruitment of membership and the growth of leadership in the unions. Italians have shared leadership with the Jews in the Amalgamated Clothing Workers Union and in the Garment Workers Union (ILGWU). One of the most effective and yet one of the most notorious unions in the nation is the Teamsters' Union. Italians have played a prominent role on both the local and national level. Jimmy Hoffa became the president of the International Brotherhood of the Teamsters in 1957.

Both New York and Chicago boast Italian American Labor Councils, which are composed of the ethnic group's leaders from a wide range of unions. While they are not always the most prominent among ethnic organizations, unions are among the best financed and organized of the Italian Americans support organizations. Thus, the backing of Italian American union leaders for a fund-raiser is often the key to success. This association has a darker side, however, because many of the union leaders have image problems that are even more severe for Italian Americans.[23]

POLITICS

Francis B. Spignola, a Civil War officer from Brooklyn, became the first Italian American congressman (1886–1892), and Andrew Houston Longino, a native of Virginia, was the first Italian American governor (Mississippi 1889–1904). The immigrants after 1880 participated in politics as pawns of the big-city bosses who got to the immigrants before social workers did. By giving out food baskets to the needy, attending wakes, helping youth out of scrapes with the police, and finding jobs for the immigrants, the bosses won their confidence, helped them apply for citizenship, and saw that they voted the right way. A key Italian American political hero is Fiorello LaGuardia, who represented Italians and others as a New York City congressman for a decade before becoming mayor of New York in the 1930s. His ethnic-coalition brand of politics was a model for all who followed. John O. Pastore of Rhode Island was the first Italian American elected to the U.S. Senate, in 1950, based on his popularity in what is now the most ethnic Italian state in the Union. Michael Di Salle served as governor of Ohio in the post–World War II period.

Italian Americans appear to be well represented in politics today. The most heavily Italian American states are New Jersey (1.5 million, or 18.5 percent of the total population), Connecticut (653,000, or 19.8 percent) and Rhode Island (202,735, or about 20 percent). The Italian American population of New York is about 2.7 million, or 14.8 percent; Pennsylvania, 1.5 million, or 13 percent; Nevada, 142,658, or 7.3 percent; California, 1.4 million, or 4.3 percent; and Massachusetts, 890,000, or 14.5 percent. Other states with significant Italian American populations are Illinois, 706,000, or 5.8 percent; Florida 1 million, or 6.5 percent; Ohio, 713,015, or 6.7 percent; and Louisiana, 360,333, or 5.2 percent. (National Italian American Foundation, "Italian Population in all 50 States.")

This ethnic concentration during the past century has resulted in the election of Italian American political leaders, including LaGuardia, Pastore, Mario Cuomo, Geraldine Ferraro, U.S. senator from New York Alphonse D'Amato, Connecticut governor Ella Grasso, and former New York City mayor Rudolph Giuliani. A partial list of political achievers continues with Justice Antonin Scalia, the first Italian American on the U.S. Supreme Court, Frank Carlucci, Leon Panetta, poet Dana Gioia, head of the National Endowment for the Arts, and Anthony Principi, secretary of Veterans Affairs.

Contemporary Italian Americans rarely vote as a bloc. Their politics seem to be based on social class and income rather than on ethnicity. There appear to be few overriding ethnic-based issues as there might be for African American or Jewish American voters. Moreover, in many places on the East Coast, it is not uncommon to see Italian American candidates from diverse parties and philosophical camps running against each other for political office at different levels.

Italian American voting strength in New York, New Jersey, Pennsylvania, and some New England states is significant. Politically speaking, it appears that Italian Americans have arrived. Yet when compared to other ethnic groups, Italian Americans lack unifying issues. They have not been the persistent victims of racist oppression, as have been African Americans, and they lack the forces of unity that motivate Jewish American and Polish American activism in the political arena. Earlier in the century, Italian Americans had some working-class solidarity, and Italians were part of the Roosevelt Coalition that made the Democratic Party dominant from the 1930s through the 1960s. They voted for fellow Catholic John F. Kennedy. Increasingly prosperous, middle-class, and small-business-oriented Italian American voters most recently backed Ronald Reagan in the 1984 presidential election, snubbing their own Geraldine Ferraro, who was on the Democratic ticket as Walter Mondale's vice presidential running mate. Catholic leaders balked at supporting Ferraro because of her pro-choice stand on abortion. And, perhaps because she was a woman running in a hopeless race, grassroots and midlevel activity on her behalf by Italian Americans was surprisingly absent.

Ferraro's experience in dealing with allegations that her husband and a long-dead relative had some connection to organized crime demonstrates another unique aspect of Italian American political participation. Although organized crime is a multiethnic industry, and only a minuscule percentage of the sixteen million Italian Americans could possibly be part of the organized crime network, the specter of Al Capone and his ilk casts a shadow over the public perception of Italian Americans, especially politicians. This image is reinforced by the exciting media images of gangsters that, ironically, are often created by Italian American writers, actors, and filmmakers. And the image is further intensified by the very real infiltration of organized crime into the political establishment in order to gain protection against strict law enforcement.

The result is the popular perception that politicians, especially Italian American politicians, are "connected." Even a seasoned and well-meaning journalist like Sam Donaldson lent credence to thoughtless Mafia stereotyping when he stated on the *Oprah Winfrey Show* that, of course, investigative journalists would look for Mafia connections in the past of any Italian American candidate for high office. Perhaps the most vicious aspect of this phenomenon is that Italian Americans distrust each other. Politically ambitious Italian Americans are often satisfied to settle for appointed judgeships rather than subject themselves to the ordeal of Mafia innuendoes. The NIAF has been successful in encouraging higher ambitions among Italian Americans by promoting Italian Americans without regard to political philosophy to see "some of their" in high government positions. Even the NIAF has been frustrated, however, in trying to develop among Italian Americans a habit of contributing substantial amounts to the political campaigns of their coethnics. For the foreseeable future, the group will not come anywhere near the political funding patterns of Jewish Americans and Greek Americans.

Aside from power considerations, the chief reason for Italian Americans to enter the political arena appears to be the desire for respect. Italians are not poor, not unemployed, not grossly discriminated against, or significantly disadvantaged in any other way except for the negative or trivialized image that the larger society has of them and that they sometimes have of themselves. The major task of Italian American organizations is to get the general society to take an objective look at them, free of the easy stereotypes.

Many people inside and outside of the Italian community are convinced that if only they had an Italian American president like Mario Cuomo or Lee Iaccoca, unfair stereotypes would disappear as they did with the election of our first Catholic president. This is the miraculous solution that would make unnecessary the slow process of building positive self-images based on solid cultural knowledge.

SUBURBANIZATION

Modernization has definitely assaulted Italian American ethnicity. Suburbanization destroyed the ethnic neighborhoods. They no longer exist as self-perpetuating enclaves but, where they have partially survived, as ethnic theme parks. Ethnic retention can no longer be geographically based. Ethnic newspapers, metropolitan-based ethnic professional organizations, radio and TV broadcasts, and the teaching of the Italian language in schools and universities are the only basis on which ethnicity can rely if it is to survive. Though still the best carrier of ethnicity, the Italian American extended family is not immune from the effects of divorce, birth control, exogamy, and fragmentation.

Some aspects of modernization might strengthen Italian American ethnicity. The growing fascination of yuppie America with food and travel leave them with a positive attitude toward Italian food customs, language, and lifestyle. And Italian Americans stand tall in the reflected light of the mother country. Easy international travel and satellite television will keep post–World War II Italian immigrants bound more closely to Italian culture than were previous generations of immigrants. The spectacular success of the direct broadcast via satellite of Italian soccer matches to Italian American sports clubs is hard evidence of the potential of satellite communication for keeping Italy's immigrants in all parts of the world in touch with their culture. And since it is clearly in the commercial, political, and cultural interest of Italy (population 57 million) to maintain cultural links with its perhaps 50 million immigrants and their descendents in the United States, Canada, Argentina, Australia, and elsewhere, modernization can be expected to facilitate the maintenance, and perhaps even growth, of Italian culture among Italian Americans.

What will be lost through modernization are the Italian American ethnic neighborhood folkways that played such an important role in shaping previous generations of Italian Americans. In short, modernization can help us conquer the geographic space between America and Italy, but it has the opposite effect on our ability to conquer time and link up with the ethnic neighborhoods of fifty years ago. Popularized ethnic history and the blockbuster authentic Italian American novel or motion picture are the only ways of recapturing the "old neighborhood" for the modern Italian American consciousness.

Italian American ethnicity has come a long way from the time when upwardly mobile immigrants routinely changed their names to avoid identification with the wretched refuse. Italian American identity has survived the ignominy. Third- and fourth-generation Italians seem fairly comfortable with—if not terribly knowledgeable about—their ethnic identity. They are thoroughly American and only part-time consumers of their Italian American ethnicity. A small minority are Italian American activists who can gain entry to the larger social arena through their leadership in ethnic organizations or who have support in their professions from fellow Italian Americans. The latest emigrants, through organizations sponsored by regional governments, satellite-television links, and airplane travel back to Italy, may achieve a kind of émigré status.

An idyllic vision of Italian ethnicity in the United States is projected for a third- or fourth-generation, college-educated group. This group would learn the Italian language in high school and college. They would gain an appreciation for their roots in the migration process and of the ethnic neighborhoods through Italian American cultural institutions, which would give them a creative and tolerant understanding of all ethnic groups. Their education would be punctuated by early and frequent trips to Italy. They would approach biculturalism, and their contacts with Italians all over the world would give them a global perspective.

The range of Italian American modalities is wide, but there are few indeed among them who would deny their identity. American policy on ethnicity seems to have settled into a halfhearted acceptance of the harmless aspects of multiculturalism. For most Italian Americans, that is all the approval they need. Italian American ethnicity is formed by the sociopsychic needs of individuals and groups to create a comfortably scaled arena for their lives and the current positive image of Italy in American public opinion.

NOTES

1. Erik Amphiteatrof, *The Children of Columbus: An Informal History of the Italians in the New World*, 3–38 (Boston: Little, Brown, 1973).

2. Margherite Marchione, *Selected Writings and Correspondence of Philip Mazzei* (Millwood, NY: Kraus International Publication, *passim*, 1982).

3. Giovanni Schiavo, *Four Centuries of Italian American History* (New York: Vigo Press, 1952).

4. Alexander DeConde, *Half Bitter, Half Sweet: An Excursion into Italian American History*, 1–76 (New York: Scribner, 1971).

5. Lawrence Di Stasi, ed. *Una Storia Segreta: The Secret History of Italian American Evacuation and Internment during World War II* (Berkeley: Univ. of California Press, 2001).

6. George Pozzetta, ed., *Pane e Lavoro: The Italian American Working Class* (Toronto: Multicultural History Society of Ontario, 1980).

7. Luciano Iorizzo and Salvatore Mondello, *The Italian Americans* (Boston: G. K. Hall, 1980), 17–163.

8. Betty Boyd Caroli, *Italian Repatriation from the United States* (New York: Center for Migration Studies, 1974), 23–50, 91–100.

9. Andrew Rolle, *The Immigrant Upraised* (Norman: Univ. of Oklahoma Press, 1968), 89–292.

10. Richard Gambino, *Vendetta: A True Story of the Worst Lynching in America* (Garden City, NY: Doubleday, 1977).

11. Stephen Hall, "Italian Americans: Coming into Their Own," *New York Times Magazine*, May 15, 1983.

12. Oscar Handlin, *The Uprooted: The Epic Story of the Great Migrations That Made the American People*, 203–299 (Boston: Little, Brown, 1951).

13. Rudolph Vecoli, "Pane e Giustizia," *La Parola del Popolo* (September–October 1976).

14. Silvano Tomasi, *Italian Culture in the United States: A National Directory of Research Centers, Repositories, and Organizations of Italian Culture in the United States* (New York: Center for Migration Studies, 1979); and Andrew Brizzolara, *A Directory of Italian and Italian American Organizations and Community Services in the Metropolitan Area of Greater New York* (New York: Center for Migration Studies, 1980).

15. Gaetano Salvemini, *Italian Fascist Activities in the United States* (New York: Center for Migration Studies, 1977), Philip Cannistraro, "Generoso Pope and the Rise of Italian American Politics, 1925–1936," *The Italian Americans: New Perspectives in Italian Immigration and Ethnicity*, ed. Lydio Tomasi (New York: Center for Migration Studies, 1985), 264–288.

16. Gary Mormino, *Immigrants on the Hill: Italian Americans in St. Louis, 1881–1920* (Chicago: Univ. of Chicago Press, 1986), 56–194.

17. Leonard Covello, *The Social Background of the Italia American School Child* (Leiden: E. J. Brill, 1967).

18. Humbert Nelli, *The Business of Crime* (New York: Oxford Univ. Press, passim, 1976).

19. Leonard Covello, *The Heart Is the Teacher* (New York: McGraw-Hill, 1958), 92–275.

20. Richard Gambino, *Blood of My Blood: The Dilemma of Italian Americans* (Garden City, New York: Doubleday, 1974), 223–342.

21. Nampeo McKenney, Michael Levin, and Alfred Telia, "A Sociodemographic Profile of Italian Americans," in *Italian Americans: New Perspectives* (see note 15), 3–31.

22. Edoardo Lebano, "Report to the Conference Lingua e Cultura Italian negli Stati," Rome, March 30–April 1, 1987.

23. Schiavo, *Four Centuries*.

BIBLIOGRAPHICAL ESSAY

The best brief introduction to Italian Americans is Humbert S. Nelli, "Italians," in *Harvard Encyclopedia of American Ethnic Groups*, ed., Stephan Thernstrom et al. (Cambridge, MA: Harvard Univ. Press, 1980), 545–560. The most impressive collection of exhaustive and authoritative factual information about Italian Americans is Salvatore LaGumina, Frank Cavaioli, Salvatore Primeggia, and Joseph Varacalli, editors, *The Italian American Experience: An Encyclopedia* (New York: Garland, 2000). Also covering a broad scope is the work of Giovanni Schiavo, especially Schiavo's, *Four Centuries of Italian American History* (New York: Vigo Press, 1952). During the past few decades, there has been a significant outpouring of reference works on Italian Americans, beginning with Wayne Moquin and Charles Van Doren, eds., *A Documentary History of the Italian Americans* (New York: Praeger, 1974), which includes documents originating from a range of people from Columbus to Vince Lombardi, organized around the topics of the age of discovery, the period of mass migration, making a living, organized crime, discrimination, and the emergence of the Italian American. The record made and the institutional structure developed by generations of Italian Americans was captured by Silvano Tomasi, *Italian Culture in the United States: A National Directory of Research Centers, Repositories, and Organizations of Italian Culture in the United States* (New York: Center for Migration Studies, 1979). The ongoing interest of those remaining in the old country in understanding the immigrant experience has led to the publication of Fondazione Giovanni Agnelli, *The Italian-Americans: Who They Are, Where They Live, How Many They Are* (Turin: Fondazione Giovanni Agnelli, 1980). Andrew Brizzolara, *A Directory of Italian and Italian American Organizations and Community Services in the Metropolitan Area of New York* (New York: Center for Migration Studies, 1980) graphically illustrates the significant impact of Italian American culture on the country's largest city.

The impressive outpouring of literature can best be apprehended in a number of bibliographies. C. M. Diodati et al., *Writings on Italian-Americans: A Bicentennial Bibliography* (New York: Italian-American Center for Urban Affairs, 1975) reflects the ethnic revival of the 1970s. Francesco Cordasco, ed., *Italians in the United States: A Bibliography of Reports, Texts, Critical Studies, and Related Materials* (New York: Oriole Editions, 1972) is an unannotated compilation designed to present a sufficient representation of Italian American literature to afford both orientation and resources for further study. His *The Italian-American Experience: An Annotated and Classified Bibliographical Guide, With Selected Publications of the Casa Italiana Educational Bureau* (New York: Burt Franklin, 1974) contains a list of bibliographies and archives, as well as a bibliography of works dealing with Italian immigration to America, general and regional studies, and analyses of social, political, and economic structure and institutions. His *Italian Mass Immigration: The Exodus of a Latin People: A Bibliographical Guide to "Bolletino dell Emigrazione," 1902–1927* (Towata, NJ: Rowman and Littlefield, 1980) focuses directly on studies dealing with the peak migration years.

Single-volume overviews of Italian immigration and ethnicity date from the publication of Robert F. Foerster, *The Italian Emigration of Our Times* (New York: Harvard Univ. Press, 1919, repr. Arno Press, 1968), primarily a detailed examination of the causes of emigration that is highly critical of the Italian government. Michael Musmanno, *The Story of the Italians in America* (New York: Doubleday, 1965), stresses the socioeconomic successes of Italian America in a highly uncritical manner. Two books by Andrew F. Rolle, *The Immigrant Upraised: Italian Adventurers and Colonists in an Expanding America* (Norman: Univ. of Oklahoma Press, 1968) and *The American Italians: Their History and Culture* (Belmont, CA: Wadsworth, 1972), both focus on immigration to the western states before the onset of the twentieth century. Silvano Tomasi and Madeline H. Engel, eds., *The Italian Experience in the United States* (Staten Island, NY: Center for Migration Studies, 1970) is a collection of essays by ten scholars dealing with settlement patterns, institutions, political activity, religion, and return migration. Joseph Lopreato, *Italian Americans* (New York: Random House, 1970), investigates settlement patterns, the impact of continuing immigration on social institutions and intergroup relations, and the process of adaptation and achievement. Luciano J. Iorizzo and Salvatore Mondello, *The Italian Americans* (New York: Twayne, 1971), survey the varieties of Italian American experience on farms, small towns, and large cities, focusing on politics, occupations, crime, religion, and reaction to Mussolini. Alexander De Conde's *Half Bitter, Half Sweet: An Excursion into Italian-American History* (New York: Scribners, 1971) explores the paradoxical relationship between the Italian and the American peoples, institutions, and cultures, in both the Old World and the New. Jerre Mangione and Ben Morreale's, *La Storia* (New York: HarperCollins, 1992) presents the saga with a broad sweeping literary flair. Erik Amphiteatrof, *The Children of Columbus: An Informal History of the Italians in the New World* (Boston: Little, Brown, 1973), stresses the rich diversity of Italian Americans, as well as their sense of "being looked down upon." In a highly personalized blend of scholarship and experience, Patrick J. Gallo attempts to correct many myths and stereotypes in *Old Bread, New Wine: A Portrait of the Italian-Americans* (Chicago: Nelson Hall, 1981). Gallo has also thoughtfully explored the causes of Italian American discontent in *Ethnic Alienation: The Italian Americans* (Rutherford, NJ: Fairleigh-Dickinson Univ. Press, 1974) and edited the proceedings of the eighth annual conference of the American-Italian Historical Association under the title *The Urban Experience of Italian Americans* (Staten Island, NY: American Station Historical Association, 1976).

An appreciation of the importance of locale to the formation of Italian American identity and culture can be gained from a collateral reading of some of the many works on specific communities. Robert F. Harney and Jean Vincenza Scarpaci, eds., *Little Italies in North America* (Toronto: Multicultural History Society of Ontario, 1981) includes essays on New York, Toronto, Montreal, Philadelphia, Baltimore, Tampa, St. Louis, and Oswego, New York. The Federal Writers Project of the Works Progress Administration produced a detailed study of the country's largest Little Italy in *The Italians of New York: A Survey* (New York: Arno Press, 1969). Almost a half century later, armed with insights from the new social history, Donna R. Gabaccia, *From Italy to Elizabeth Street: Housing and Social Change among Italian Immigrants, 1880–1930* (Albany, NY: State Univ. of New York Press, 1984), explored the changes in family, housing, customs and living conditions of Sicilians immigrating to the same metropolises. Farther north in the Empire State, John W. Briggs, *An Italian Passage: Immigrants to Three American Cities, 1890–1930* (New Haven, CT: Yale Univ. Press, 1978) compares and contrasts the communities formed in Utica and Rochester, as well as their counterpart in Kansas City, Missouri. In *Mount Allegro: A Memoir of Italian American Life* (New York: Columbia Univ. Press, 1981), Jerre Mangione describes the phenomenon of growing up Sicilian in Rochester, New York, where the immigrant generation either gradually displaced Italian solutions with American ones or retained the former while allowing their children to make a free choice. Their counterparts in Buffalo, according to Virginia Yans-McLaughlin, *Family and Community: Italian Americans in Buffalo, 1880–1930* (Ithaca, NY: Cornell Univ. Press, 1977), resisted outside pressures toward independence and individualism and maintained strict sex-role definitions and adult-centered family structures. The Lombards and Sicilians who immigrated to St. Louis built an enduring community by combining extensive ethnic clustering, physical and social isolation, and deep roots with limited geographical and social mobility, according to Gary Mormino, *Immigrants on the Hill: Italian Americans in St. Louis, 1881–1920* (Urbana: Univ. of Illinois Press, 1986). Joseph J. Barton, *Peasants and Strangers: Italians, Rumanians, and Slovaks in an American City* (Cambridge, MA: Harvard Univ. Press, 1975), contends that Italians and Slovaks perpetuated particular cultural values that kept them in the working class for two generations while the Rumanians experienced much greater upward social mobility. Carlo Bianco, *The Two Rosetos* (Bloomington: Indiana Univ. Press, 1974), chronicles the migration of an entire village in southern Italy to southeastern Pennsylvania and analyzes their efforts to keep much of their culture, folklore, and dialect intact. Finally, Humbert S. Nelli, *Italians in Chicago, 1880–1930: A Study in Ethnic Mobility* (New York: Oxford Univ. Press, 1970), explores settlement patterns, economic and political life, community institutions, crime, and assimilation, and a dissertation and a series of articles by Rudolph Vecoli focused on cultural retention and Italian radicalism in Chicago.

Other scholars have focused their attention primarily on the Italian American social structure and on the mores that underlie it. Edward C. Banfield, *The Moral Basis of a Backward Society* (Glencoe, IL: Free Press, 1958), generalizes from his own experiences in a small southern Italian village that an "amoral familialism" prevents the development of "public-regarding" civic consciousness among Italian Americans. That same familial bond, according to Francis A. J. Ianni, *A Family Business: Kinship and Social Control in Organized Crime* (New York: Russell Sage Foundation, 1972), accounts for the marked similarity in crime families that leads outsiders to see a nationwide network of organized crime. By the same token, Humbert S. Nelli, *The Business of Crime: Italians and Syndicate Crime in the United States* (New York: Oxford Univ. Press, 1976), insists that the syndicate is really a loose, multiethnic federation. Similarly, according to William F. Whyte, *Street Corner Society: Social Structure of an Italian Slum* (Chicago: Univ. of Chicago Press, 1955), the kinship bonds formed in street gangs in the "Cornerville" section of "Eastern City" carry over into careers in the rackets and in politics. Francesco M. Cordasco and Eugene Bucchioni, *The Italians: Social Backgrounds of an American Group* (Clifton, NJ: Augustus M. Kelley, 1974), examine chain migration patterns, responses to American life, employment, health, social needs, and the educational experience of Italian children in American schools. Herbert J. Gans, *The Urban Villagers: Group and Class in the Life of Italian Americans* (Glencoe, IL: Free Press, 1962), examines Boston's West End, its internal social structure, and its relationship with the larger metropolis. Lawrence Frank Pisani, *The Italians in America: A Social Study and History* (New York: Exposition Press, 1957), stresses the role played by Italian Americans in labor, religion, arts, science, and the urban scene.

The place of community institutions in the adaptive process of Italian Americans has also received increasing attention. Silvano Tomasi, *Piety and Power: The Role of Italian Parishes in the New York Metropolitan Area, 1880–1930* (Staten Island, NY: Center for Migration Studies, 1975), contends that the Italian national parish was the primary building block of the ethnic community and the main conservator of culture. Tomasi and Edward C. Stibili, *Italian Americans and Religion: An Annotated Bibliography* (New York: Center for Migration Studies, 1978), provide an organized guide to numerous parish histories and to over 800 books and articles on religion. In two related works, *The Heart Is the Teacher* (New York: McGraw-Hill, 1958) and *The Social Background of the Italo-American School Child* (Leiden, Netherlands: E. J. Brill, 1967), Leonard Covello provides the historical background and the technical analysis to understand the conflict between Old World culture and public education faced by young Italians. Edwin Fenton, *Immigrants and Unions, a Case Study: Italians and American Labor, 1870–1920* (New York: Arno Press, 1975), argues that while union membership accelerated acculturation and assimilation, Italian workers also forced unions to alter their programs and tactics in significant ways. In *Pane e Lovoro: The Italian American Working Class* (Toronto: Multicultural History Society of Ontario, 1980), George E. Pozzetta, ed., and others explore their role in well-known strikes and nine disasters, the conflict between the padrone system and labor unions, and their reactions to Fascism and to the Vietnam

War. Although the title is somewhat restrictive, John H. Mariano, *The Italian Contribution to American Democracy* (New York: Arno Press, 1975) deals with a range of socioeconomic and demographic issues and draws conclusions regarding acculturation and assimilation, based largely on responses from questionnaires.

Throughout all the processes of acculturation and community building, Italian Americans never lost their connections to the homeland. Many Italians continued to function as "birds of passage" as Betty Boyd Caroli, *Italian Repatriation from the United States, 1900–1914* (New York: Center for Migration Studies, 1974), clearly demonstrates. Although some of this migration was forced by one government or the other, most of it was voluntary on both sides of the ocean. John P. Diggins, *Mussolini and Fascism: The View from America* (Princeton, NJ: Princeton Univ. Press, 1972) examines the degree to which the values, symbols, and images of Fascism appealed to American Italians of various backgrounds. Gaetano Salvemini, *Italian Fascist Activities in the United States* (New York: Center for Migration Studies 1977) demonstrates that Mussolini was more attractive to economically successful Italian Americans than he was to working-class people.

As with every ethnic group, debates still rage over the pace, degree, and contours of the adaptation process. Almost a half century ago, Irvin L. Child, *Italian or American? The Second Generation in Conflict* (New York: Russell and Russell, 1943), posed the dilemma of the acculturation in psychological terms. In *An Ethnic at Large: A Memoir of America in the Thirties and Forties* (New York: Putnam 1978), Jerre Mangione resolves that dilemma by becoming an "ethnic-at-large," with one foot in his Sicilian heritage, the other in the American mainstream, a "cultural gymnastic stance" that enables him to gain strength from his past and hope from his present. In her biography *Rosa: The Life of an Italian Immigrant* (Minneapolis: Immigration History Society, 1970), Marie Hall Ets concludes that what Rosa had learned in America was not to be afraid. Confronting the dilemma in 1975, Richard Gambino, *Blood of My Blood: The Dilemma of Italian-Americans* (Garden City, NY: Doubleday, 1975), argues that to be Italian in the United States means to develop hyphenated values concerning work, sex, sex roles, family, religion, education, and politics. Silvano M. Tomasi, ed., *Perspectives in Italian Immigration and Ethnicity* (Staten Island, NY: Center for Migration Studies, 1977), is a collection of papers by sixteen American and Canadian scholars on new Italian American identity, the state of research on Italian Americans, and new directions in that research. Richard Alba's important *Italian Americans: Into the Twilight of Ethnicity* (Englewood Cliffs, NJ: Prentice Hall, 1985) stresses that the intensity of ethnic identity is challenged by demographic trends toward intermarriage. Italian Americans and other ethnics must consciously work to preserve their heritages.

The proceedings of the annual conferences of the American Italian Historical Association (New York, 1970–present) contain some 500 articles on all aspects of Italian American life. Many additional resources are available through the association's Web site www.aiha.fau.edu and its listserv, H-ItAm. Part of H-Net, this listserv of 300 members also has a searchable archive at www2.h-net.msu.edu/~itam containing over 30,000 items. *The Italian American Review: A Social Science Journal of the Italian American Experience*, published by the John Calandra Institute, Queens College, and *Italian Americana: A Cultural and Historical Review*, from the University of Rhode Island (since 1982), and *VIA: Voices in Italian Americana*, a literary and cultural review (since 1989) are the current scholarly journals devoted to Italian American studies.

JEWISH AMERICANS

Edward S. Shapiro

Over two hundred years ago in *Letters From An American Farmer*, Hector St. John de Crevecoeur, the French observer of American mores, asked, "What then is the American, this new man?" His answer stressed both the biological and intellectual uniqueness of the transplanted European. The American was an amalgamation of the ethnic strains of Europe, or at least of those of Western Europe. "I could point out to you a family whose grandfather was an Englishman, whose wife was Dutch, whose son married a French woman, and whose present four sons have now four wives of different nations." The true American had also discarded European modes of thought. He is an American who, leaving behind him all the ancient prejudices and manners, "acts upon new principles, entertains new ideas, and forms new opinions."

Crevecoeur waxed poetic as he contemplated the future of this new, American man and his land. "Here individuals of all nations are melted into a new race of men, whose labors and posterity will one day cause great changes in the world." American writers of the nineteenth century followed Crevecoeur's cue and stressed the theme of the newness of America and the American. Thus, Ralph Waldo Emerson, in his famous 1837 "American Scholar" address delivered before Harvard's Phi Beta Kappa Society, declared that American dependence on the learning of other lands had ended. "The millions that around us are rushing into life cannot always be fed on the sere remains of foreign harvests. Events, actions arise, that must be sung, that will sing themselves." He concluded with a well-known sentence in American literature: "We must have listened too long to the courtly muses of Europe. What is the remedy? . . . We will walk on our own feet; we will work with our own hands; we will speak our own minds."

It is no coincidence that America's Jews, perhaps more than any other group, have followed the advice of Crevecoeur and Emerson to leave behind the prejudices and manners of Europe and to sing of American events. This has been true not only in the defining of American nationality but also in the defining of American Jewish identity. Crevecoeur's "new mode of life" was especially new for the Jew. The definitions of Jewish identity developed elsewhere, "the sere remains of foreign harvests," were hardly relevant for America. In Europe, Africa, and Asia, status and citizenship were based on religion, anti-Semitism was pervasive, Jews were denied citizenship until the nineteenth century, and the *kehillah*, the self-contained Jewish community, played a vital role and had an official, or at least semiofficial, position. In America, there was little public (as distinct from private) anti-Semitism, citizenship was a matter of right and not sufferance, there were few significant barriers to a Jew's social and economic advancement, and the Jewish community had no standing in law, nor did it perform any official tasks. The Jewish attitude toward America was best expressed by Irving Baline (later Americanized as Irving Berlin), a resident of New York City's Lower East Side Jewish ghetto, who wrote "God Bless America."

Pulled in seemingly opposite directions by the force of American hope and the power of Jewish memory, America's Jews were forced to define what it meant to be a Jew in America, to articulate the relationship between American and Jewish identities, and to develop lifestyles both fully American and fully Jewish. No other ethnic group has been as concerned with defining their relationship to America. It is no coincidence that Jews wrote three of the most popular expressions of American identity: Emma Lazarus's poem "The New Colossus," Israel Zangwill's play *The Melting Pot*, and Horace Kallen's essay "Democracy versus the Melting Pot." A disproportionate number of America's most prominent sociologists of ethnicity have been Jews: Arnold Rose, Milton Gordon, and Nathan Glazer, to name just a few. The Harvard historian Oscar Handlin wrote an important monograph on the history of America's Irish, and Jewish historians such as Gilbert Osofsky, Allan Spear, Lawrence Levine, and Herbert Gutman provided much of the intellectual framework for understanding black history and culture. No American novel has probed more perceptively the costs of immigrant acculturation than *The Rise of David Levinsky*, written by Abraham Cahan, the longtime editor of the *Jewish Daily Forward*, which is the most widely read foreign-language paper in American history.

Jews have had a more difficult problem in defining their status as Americans than any other major ethnic group. Not only did Jews have to adapt to a culture radically different from what they had known in Europe and the Arab lands, they were also entering a society in which they were both a religious and an ethnic minority. Other ethnic groups were at least Christian and thus had a religious bond with fellow Americans. Furthermore, Jews in Europe, Africa, and Asia were the most isolated, communally organized, and encapsulated of groups and had to make the radical adaptation to the individualistic and liberal ethos of America.

From the beginning, America's Jews sought to demonstrate that they were at home in America, and that, at least for them, the travail of the wandering, homeless Jew had ended. In 1841, at the dedication of the Beth Elohim synagogue in Charleston, South Carolina, Rabbi Gustav Poznanski rebuked Jews who longed for a return to Zion. "This synagogue is our temple, this city our Jerusalem, this happy land our Palestine." The compatibility of Jewish and American identity was not something that could be taken for granted; it had to be asserted and defended. This became the life's work of Rabbi Isaac Mayer Wise, the greatest Jewish figure in nineteenth-century America and the founder of Reform Judaism in America.

Wise preferred to use the phrase "*American Judaism*" rather than "*Reform Judaism*" to describe the changes in Jewish theology and ritual he sought in order to reconcile Judaism with the temper of America. His 1857 prayer book was titled *Minhag America* (American Custom), his organization of synagogues was called the Union of American Hebrew Congregations, and his organization of rabbis was named the Central Conference of American Rabbis. The word *Hebrew* was frequently used by German Jews in describing themselves and in naming their institutions, partially to distinguish themselves from the eastern European immigrant "Jews," whom they saw as backward and less Americanized. This Americanization of Judaism reached its logical conclusion in a seminal document drawn up by a group of Reform rabbis in Pittsburgh in 1885.

The Pittsburgh Platform not only emphasized the compatibility of Judaism with modern science and biblical criticism, it also stressed the harmony between Judaism and America. It rejected those elements of Judaism that distinguished Jews from other Americans and cast doubt on their Americanness. "We consider ourselves," the rabbis solemnly said, "no longer a nation, but a religious community, and therefore expect neither a return to Palestine, nor a sacrificial worship under the sons of Aaron, nor the restoration of any of the laws concerning the Jewish state." Rabbi Kaufmann Kohler called the Pittsburgh Platform the Reform movement's declaration of independence, because it freed America's Jews from the nationalism and cultural and social separatism of what was referred to as Mosaico-Talmudical Judaism.

Most Reform spokesmen were intense opponents of Zionism. They strongly opposed Zionism's emphasis on Jewish nationalism, its belief that anti-Semitism was a permanent aspect of European and American life, and its call for the gathering of Jews into Palestine. Reform, in contrast, stressed the religious element of Jewish identity, claimed that the dispersion of the Jews was part of God's plan to spread the ethical teachings of Judaism, believed that American anti-Semitism was insignificant and transitory, and feared that Zionism would result in the raising of legitimate doubts about the patriotism of Jews. "As an American," Jacob Schiff wrote in 1907, "I cannot for a moment concede that one can be at the same time a true American and an 'honest' adherent of the Zionist movement. . . . The Jew should not for a moment feel that he is in exile and that his abode here is only a temporary or passing one."

For some German Jews, even the tepid Judaism of the Reform movement was too much. Felix Adler, the son of Rabbi Samuel Adler of New York, carried the rationalism and universalism of the left wing of Reform Judaism to their logical conclusion when he founded the Society for Ethical Culture in 1876. Wishing to free the Jew from any lingering effects of the ghetto, and skeptical of traditional religion, Adler favored a humanistic religion that would transcend all racial and religious particularism. To this day, a disproportionate percentage of the members of Ethical Culture and the Unitarian Universalist Church are Jews seeking to escape from the remnants of an unwanted religious-ethnic heritage.

Despite the ideological challenge of Adler, the vast majority of nineteenth-century German Jews maintained that a denationalized Judaism was perfectly compatible with American identity. Rabbi David Philipson asserted, "From the hills of Palestine the prophet's voice floated down the vestibule of time, enjoining the soulful command, 'Here O Israel, the Eternal is our God.' From the broad plains of the United States, the answer is sent back, 'God is one.'" Reformers believed a universalistic Judaism shorn of any distinctive ethnic characteristics could make great strides in the United States, and Wise even rashly predicted that it could eventually become the majority American religion and lead to the salvation of the world.

From the Reform perspective, the mission of the Jew was no longer to preserve a distinctive religious culture and to observe Jewish law. Rather, it was to convert the Gentiles and to usher in the Messianic age. Reformers modified the Jewish liturgy to resemble upper-class Protestantism. Sermons became a central part of the religious service, decorum was stressed, and ethical behavior was emphasized. These services were often conducted in buildings called temples, implying that the Reform temple was here in America now and not in Zion at some future date.

Other Jews besides rabbis were also intent on showing that there was no incompatibility between being an American and being a Jew. In 1892, the American Jewish Historical Society, the nation's oldest ethnic historical society, was established to refute the claims that Jews were not patriotic, were interested solely in making money, could not be integrated into American life, and lacked ties to the colonial period of American history. One of its earliest publications had the revealing title *Christopher Columbus and the Participation of the Jews in the Spanish and Portuguese Discoveries*. The society's first president was Oscar Straus, who fancied himself an amateur historian. In 1885, Straus had published *The Origins of the Republican Form of Government in the United States*, which argued that the Founding Fathers had been influenced by the political ideas of the Jewish commonwealth.

Jewish writers during the late nineteenth and early twentieth centuries both challenged and supplemented the attempt of the society to demonstrate that there was no inherent conflict between American and Jewish identity. The sociologist Milton Gordon in his *Assimilation in American Life* (1964) argued that the most important paradigms of American immigrant acculturation have been Anglo-conformity, the melting pot, and cultural pluralism. Jews provided the most popular expressions of each model. Anglo-conformity, the belief that America was permanently shaped by the English character of the colonial period and that immigrants should make themselves over into good Yankees is one of the motifs of Emma Lazarus's 1883 sonnet "The New Colossus." This poem was engraved on a memorial plaque and placed on the pedestal of the Statue of Liberty in 1903.

Lazarus was born in 1849 into an old, respected, and almost completely assimilated Sephardic New York family. One of her earliest references to Jews was in her poem "In the Jewish Synagogue at Newport," which appeared in her 1871 collection, *Admetus and Other Poems*. The volume was dedicated to "My Friend, Ralph Waldo Emerson." The poem somberly contemplated the fate of Newport Jewry and, by implication, all of American Jewry.

> No signs of life are here: the very prayers
> Inscribed around are in a language dead.

Lazarus's nearly comatose Jewish identity was revived in the early 1880s when she read George Eliot's novel *Daniel Deronda*, learned of the Russian pogroms of 1881–1882, and witnessed the beginning of a massive immigration of eastern European Jews into New York City. She involved herself in immigrant relief work and defended the Jewish immigrants against their detractors. To quote the historian John Higham, she became "the first modern American laureate of their history and culture." In 1882, Lazarus wrote a series of essays in *Century Magazine* attacking anti-Semitism and describing Jews as the agents of progress. In that same year, she published a volume of poems titled *Songs of a Semite*, which contained the pro-Zionist "The Banner of the Jew":

> O deem not dead that martial fire,
> Say not the mystic flame is spent!
> With Moses' law and David's lyre,
> Your ancient strength remains unbent
> Let but an Ezra rise anew,
> To life the *Banner of the Jew*!

In *An Epistle to the Hebrews*, which appeared in 1883, Lazarus argued for a Jewish national and cultural revival in Palestine and the United States. She thus undoubtedly had the immigrant Jews primarily in mind in "The New Colossus."

For Lazarus, the Statue of Liberty was a symbol of hope and welcome for Jews and other immigrants:

> Mother of Exiles. From her beacon-hand
> Glows world-wide welcome; her mild eyes command
> The air-bridged harbor that twin, edges frame.

And yet the words spoken by the statue seemingly conflict with the vision of an America whose "golden door" welcomes the immigrants:

Give me your tired, your poor,
Your huddled masses yearning to breathe free.
The wretched refuse of your teeming shore.

Historians have puzzled over Lazarus's seemingly condescending description of the immigrants as "wretched refuse." One interpretation has argued that Lazarus did not use the phrase in a pejorative sense, since in the 1880s *wretched* was often used as a synonym for *distressed*, and *refuse* often described objects considered to be valueless as well as worthless. There was no doubt, however, as to the attitude of Lazarus's sister toward the immigrant Jews. She forbade the inclusion of "anything Jewish" when Emma's collected works appeared posthumously in 1889. Whatever the original intention of "The New Colossus," the poem was compatible with the ideology of Anglo-conformity that contended that Jews and other immigrants were acceptable only to the extent that they adopted the dominant social and intellectual patterns of American life. Otherwise, they remained "wretched refuse."

Israel Zangwill's 1908 play *The Melting Pot* was the most important literary answer to the doctrine of Anglo-conformity. Zangwill was born in 1864 in the London Jewish ghetto of Whitechapel, the son of poor and Orthodox Russian immigrants. He was the most prominent Jewish writer of his generation in the English-speaking world. In 1856, eight years before his birth, Parliament had granted complete civil rights to Jews. In a series of "ghetto" novels, essays, and plays, Zangwill explored the challenge this presented to Jewish identity.

Zangwill described himself as a man of "violent contraries." Deeply attached to Jewish history and the spiritual values of Judaism, he also believed Judaism was not a viable faith for modern man. The Jew, he wrote, was "like a mother who clasps her dead child to her breast and will not let it go." Although he translated portions of the Jewish liturgy into English, he also published *The Next Religion*, an attack on Judaism. Zangwill wrote nostalgically of the ghetto while proclaiming to be a militant assimilationist. He was one of the founders of British Zionism and was a friend and supporter of Zionist Theodor Herzl, yet he advised Western Jews to forego any thought of settling in Palestine and to follow the path of assimilation that he himself had taken.

Zangwill yearned to be accepted as an English writer, not as a Jewish writer. Shortly before his marriage to Edith Ayrton, an English Christian, he defended intermarriage as the solution to anti-Semitism. "With Israelitish stiffneckedness we have spurned intermarriage, the only natural process by which two alien races can be welded into one. To speak most dispassionately, we have in the long run got only what we deserved." His wife shared his universalism, and the couple rejected all sectarian identification such as Judaism and Christianity, preferring to support such general causes as peace and feminism. Their first son was neither baptized nor circumcised, and belonged, as did his parents, to an abstract humanity. The biological assimilation that Zangwill experienced in his own life was the theme of *The Melting Pot*.

Zangwill the Englishmen was entranced by the vision of an American nationality that combined the best that all of the world's ethnic groups had to offer. The purpose of the *The Melting Pot*, he said, was to show how "the most violent antitheses of the past may be fused into a higher unity." Contrary to popular belief, Zangwill's melting pot did not refer to a process whereby immigrants were to be transformed into good Anglo-Saxons but rather to a process whereby native Americans and immigrants alike were to be thrown together into the pot to create something entirely new. "America is God's crucible, the great melting pot where all the races of Europe are melting and reforming. . . . A fig for your feuds and vendettas, Germans and Frenchmen, Irishmen and Englishmen, Jews and Russians—into the Crucible with you all. God is making the American."

For Zangwill, intermarriage was the fuel that kept the melting pot bubbling. His play recounted the romance between two immigrants—David, a Russian Jew, and Vera, a Russian Christian whose father was responsible for the pogrom that had claimed the lives of David's parents. The play's dramatic focus is whether the love of David and Vera will survive amid the bitter memories of Europe and the opposition of their relatives. David's last name is Quixano, an unusual name for an eastern European Jew. Some scholars have speculated that Zangwill was alluding to Cervantes' hero's hopeless belief in the power of love to conquer all. At one point, David rejects Vera: "Christian love! For this I gave up my people—darkened the home that sheltered me. . . . Let me go home, let me go home." But, as could be predicted, love triumphs. In its melodramatic finale, David proclaims to Vera his vision of an American national identity being shaped in the crucible of New York City:

> Yes, East and West, and North and South, and palm and the pine, the pole and the equator, the crescent and the cross-how the great Alchemist melts and fuses them with his purging flame! Here shall they all unite to build the Republic of Man and the Kingdom of God. Ah, Vera, what is the glory of Rome and Jerusalem, where all nations and races come to worship and look back, compared with the glory of America, where all races and nations come to labor and look forward!

The Melting Pot made a deep impression on American audiences and was a great commercial success. President Theodore Roosevelt said, "I do not know when I have seen a play that stirred me as much." Social worker Jane Addams observed that Zangwill's obituaries in 1926 emphasized his authorship of *The Melting Pot*. The New York *Herald Tribune* declared, "Seldom has an author so molded thought by the instrumentality of a single phrase." And the magazine *Independent* praised Zangwill for allowing Americans "to see ourselves as others see us, to learn how the fair Goddess of Liberty looks to those who have fled to her protection from Russian pogroms."

Zangwill was not alone in favoring Jewish assimilation through intermarriage. Although Hollywood was dominated by Jewish producers, directors, and owners during the era of the silent screen, that did not prevent (and perhaps it caused) the production of dozens of films endorsing intermarriage. Most of these featured marriages between Jews and Irish. Love can conquer all, even religious differences, was the message of *Romance of the Jewess* (1908), *Becky Gets a Husband* (1912), *The Jew's Christmas* (1913), *For the Love of Mike and Rosie* (1916), *The Cohens and the Kellys* (1926), *Private Izzy Murphy* (1926), *Kosher Kitty Kelly* (1926), *Clancy's Kosher Wedding* (1927), and *Abie's Irish Rose* (1927).

The most famous treatment of intermarriage was *The Jazz Singer* (1927). The jazz singer, played by Al Jolson, changes his name from Jackie Rabinowitz to Jack Robin, rejects the religion and culture of his ancestors, sings in the Winter Garden and not in the synagogue, and marries the Gentile Mary Dale. "You're of the old world," he tells his father. "Tradition is alright, but this is another day." In these films, the young Jews symbolize Americanization and the melting pot, while their parents personify the irrelevant traditions of Europe.

Not all Americans, however, were so enthusiastic regarding the concept of the melting pot. Spokesmen for Anglo-Saxon Protestant America had no objection to immigrants throwing themselves into the melting pot to purge themselves of their foreign impurities, but they had no intention themselves of jumping into the pot. Nor did they believe that American identity was still in the process of being formed. Rather, they maintained, the creation of American nationality had ended with the close of the eighteenth century.

The nativist *Forum's* review of *The Melting Pot* suggested that its definition of American nationality could only have come from "an author who is himself foreign in 'nationality' and alien in race." And in *The Melting Pot Mistake*, which appeared in the year of Zangwill's death, Henry Pratt Fairchild, a fervent advocate of immigration restriction and a future president of the American Eugenics Society, warned that "a preponHering influence of foreigners . . . take away from a people its most precious possession—its soul."

Zangwill's message of "E Pluribus Unum" was particularly directed at America's Jews. He thought the future held out only two options to them. They could either renationalize themselves and migrate to Palestine, or they could renounce Jewish identity and throw themselves into the American melting pot. Zangwill did not believe that a strong Jewish identity could be reconciled with a strong American identity, and he was convinced that Jewish assimilation was inevitable, although it could be slowed down by continued immigration from Europe and by anti-Semitism. For America's Jews, Zangwill's message was a prescription for cultural and religious extinction. As the *American Hebrew* noted, "Not for this have the million refugees from Russia sought America."

Mary Antin, a Jewish immigrant writer, agreed with Zangwill that American and Jewish identities were incompatible. Four years after the appearance of *The Melting Pot*, Antin published *The Promised Land*, one of the most famous of American Jewish autobiographies. Born in Plotzk in White Russia, Antin had immigrated to Boston with her family when she was a child. Her memoir recounts how the promised land of America replaced the promised land of Zion. The autobiography's chapter recounting her passage across the Atlantic was appropriately titled "The Exodus." For Antin, life in America was a rebirth, and she was entranced by what she learned about America in her American *yeshiva*, the Boston Public Library. Her book ended with a panegyric to her new nation. "America is the youngest of the nations, and inherits all that went before in history. And I am the youngest of all America's children, and into my hands is given all her priceless heritage, to the last white star—espied through the telescope, to the last great thought of the philosopher."

For Antin, as well as for David Quixano, the demands of American life required the putting aside of Old World traditions and hatreds. She married Madeus V. Grabau, a Columbia University professor of paleontology and the son of a Lutheran minister. One can only wonder whether she questioned her idealized view of America or her faith in assimilation when her husband left her in 1920 and settled in China.

In contrast to Antin, most American Jews sought to be both American and Jewish. They welcomed Horace Kallen's 1915 essay "Democracy versus the Melting Pot," which argued that this was not mere wishful thinking. Born in Silesia, Kallen settled in Boston with his family at age 5. Although his father was an Orthodox rabbi, Kallen gave up any belief in God when he was a youth. Breaking with Judaism was part of Kallen's repudiation of his Jewish identity, a repudiation that left him permanently estranged from his father. Initially, he believed Jewish identity was an encumbrance to full integration into American life and to becoming a Yankee.

Harvard, and particularly Barrett Wendell, a professor of American literature, showed Kallen the great influence that the Hebraic spirit had had on American literature and culture. While Harvard acquainted him with America's ideals, teaching at the University of Wisconsin prior to World War I acquainted him with America's reality. He was impressed by the extent to which German, Scandinavian, and Irish immigrants had maintained their ethnic identities, and he mistakenly concluded that America was developing as a federation of nationalities similar to Switzerland. Rejecting his earlier efforts at assimilation, Kallen now claimed that being a good American and a good Jew were not antagonistic as Zangwill had proclaimed, but complementary.

But how did Kallen define Jewishness? An atheist, his loyalties were not to Judaism but to Hebrew culture, and he referred to himself as a Hebraist rather than a Judaist. Defining Hebraism as "the total biography of the Jewish soul," Kallen became a secular Jewish nationalist, a fervent Zionist, and America's most important advocate of "cultural pluralism." In contrast to Reform Judaism's emphasis on the religion of Judaism, Kallen looked to the ethnic and nationalistic elements of Jewish identity. His was a message of ethnic and not religious survival.

In "Democracy versus the Melting Pot," which was a direct answer to Zangwill, Kallen replaced the metaphor of a melting pot with that of an orchestra. Just as the beauty of an orchestra stems from the different sounds of dozens of instruments harmonizing with one another, so the richness of American culture derived from the contributions of dozens of separate ethnic groups to the American mosaic. The American spirit, he argued, consisted of "this union of the different," and was sustained by the equality among ethnic groups and by "the free trade between these different equals in every good thing the community's life and culture produce."

While comforting to some Jewish spokesmen, it is questionable whether Kallen's belief in a national mosaic of ethnic and religious groups was either accurate or desirable. There is much truth to Nicholas Roosevelt's (cousin of both Theodore and Franklin Roosevelt) complaint that Kallen's scenario would have Balkanized America and that ethnic identity was an unimportant factor in the lives of many Americans. Kallen argued that ethnic identity was the most intimate, important, and permanent element of a person's life, "the efficacious natural milieu or habitat of his temperament . . . the center at which he stands, the point of his most intimate social relations, therefore of his intensest emotional life." A person could change many things, he argued, but he could never change the ethnic character of his grandfather. This might be true, but perhaps a more important consideration was whether he could predict the ethnic and religious identity of his grandchildren.

As the historian Arthur Mann has noted, Kallen did not anticipate the widespread intermarriage suggested and encouraged by Zangwill. "Democracy versus the Melting Pot" appeared during the heyday of American immigration from eastern and southern Europe. In 1915, ethnic loyalties remained strong, immigrant groups congregated together in ethnic neighborhoods, and exogamy was relatively rare. Jewish intermarriage in particular was quite low. Zangwill's own life should have alerted him to the malleability of American ethnic patterns.

He had married the daughter of a Methodist minister and hymn writer, his own daughter married a lapsed Quaker, and his grandchild was raised as a Jew. Today, the intermarried couples depicted in the movie *Abie's Irish Rose* and the 1970s television show *Bridget Loves Bernie* are a common phenomenon. If Irving Berlin could write "White Christmas" and "Easter Parade," if Leonard Bernstein could compose his "Mass," and if Stephen Schwartz could write the popular musical *Godspell* (based on the Gospel according to St. Matthew), then it is possible to forget, if not to change, one's grandparents. And, of course, it is always possible to change one's own name and identity. Bernie Schwartz became Tony Curtis, Jules Garfinkel became John Garfield, Theodosia Goodman became Theda Bara (an anagram of "Arab death"); and Max Aronson became Bronco Billy, America's first cowboy movie star.

All definitions of Jewish identity in the twentieth century inevitably have had to confront Zionism and, after 1948, the Jewish state of Israel. Both Zangwill and Kallen were Zionists. For Zangwill, Zionism was the negation of the eastern European diaspora, a movement with little or no relevance for Jews living in the West who had no intention of exchanging the good life of America, Canada, and Great Britain for the problems of Palestine. For Kallen, Zionism was an expression of that nationalistic cultural pluralism basic to American identity. American

Zionists accepted neither of these formulations, preferring to develop a Zionism that was appropriate both for Americans who had no plan to emigrate to the Holy land and for a nation in which permanent national divisions were frowned upon.

The major figure in "Americanizing" Zionism was Louis D. Brandeis, the progressive reformer, advisor to Woodrow Wilson, and first Jew to sit on the U.S. Supreme Court. The great mystery surrounding Brandeis is why he ever became a Zionist in the first place. There was little in his life prior to 1914, when he became a leader of the American Zionist movement at age 58 to suggest such a possibility. A descendant of German Jews who had settled in Louisville, Kentucky, in the mid-nineteenth century, Brandeis had not previously exhibited any particular interest in things Jewish. He was not a member of a synagogue or a Jewish fraternal group, he did not observe Jewish religious rituals, and he opposed the retention of ethnic differences. In 1910, for example, he stated, "Habits of living or of thought which tend to keep alive differences of origin or classify men according to their religious beliefs are inconsistent with the American ideal of brotherhood and are disloyal." And yet, two years later, he joined the Federation of American Zionists and became an advocate of cultural pluralism. Various interpretations, ranging from the influence of Kallen to Brandeis's political ambitions, have been offered to explain such seemingly bizarre behavior. There is, however, no confusion as to his impact on American Zionism. He helped transform American Zionism from a plaything of unassimilated Jewish nationalists into a movement that could attract acculturated American Jews.

Under the Brandeis's influence, American Zionism was shorn of both its nationalistic thrust and its underlying assumption that the essence of Zionism is *aliyah*, a Hebrew term signifying immigration to the land of Zion. Brandeisian Zionism resulted in philanthropy to provide a refuge for persecuted Jews of other lands. American Jews had already migrated to the promised land of America, and they had no intention of migrating once more. Brandeisian Zionism, one humorous definition put it, was a movement in which one person gave money to a second person so that a third person could reach Palestine. As a result, American Zionism has been most popular when the needs of non-American Jews have been greatest, such as during World War I and World War II, from 1946 to 1948, and the period after 1967 when Israel was directly threatened by her Arab neighbors. For most contemporary American Jews, Zionism rather than Judaism has become the most important manifestation of their Jewishness, the single most important element shaping their identity as Jews. And yet only a tiny number of American Jews have resettled in the Holy Land—the thing which, more than anything else, defined one as a Zionist, according to classic European Zionist ideology.

European Zionists lamented this transformation of American Zionism into a charity emphasizing refugee relief, arguing that Brandeisianism had divested the movement of its nationalistic raison d'etre. They were convinced that anti-Semitism was so strong and economic conditions so perilous for Jews that *aliyah* was the only realistic Jewish option. For eastern European Zionists such as Chaim

Weizmann and David Ben-Gurion, any movement that rejected Jewish nationalism and the "negation of the diaspora" was hardly Zionistic. Their European Zionist ideology, however, did not resonate in America, where there was no "Jewish question" nor any serious attempt to deny American Jews the rights and responsibilities of full citizenship.

For Brandeis, the legitimacy of American Zionism stemmed precisely from what European Zionists objected to—its denial of Jewish nationalism and its definition of Zionism as a political and social movement whose values and goals were similar to those of America. He was careful to describe Jews as a people and not a nation, in part because he did not want Zionists to appear un-American and guilty of dual loyalty. American Jews who wished to succor Jews in Europe and elsewhere but did not wish to have their Americanism questioned welcomed Brandeis's revision of Zionism.

Brandeis argued that the basic impulses of Zionism resembled those of the American Progressive Movement of the early twentieth century. Just as Zionism sought freedom, social justice, and democracy for the oppressed Jews of Europe, so Progressivism sought freedom, social justice, and democracy for abused Americans. He was particularly impressed by the voluntary kibbutz movement and helped found a kibbutz that was later named for him, Kibbutz Ein Ha Shofet, Hebrew for "spring of the judge." An American Zionist, Brandeis argued, was not only a better Jew but also a better American, because Zionism exhibited precisely those impulses that Americans characterized as uniquely American. Zionism was thus a fulfillment and not a derogation of Americanism. "To be good Americans," he told a Jewish audience, "we must be better Jews, and to be better Jews, we must become. Zionists." An American Zionist was thus by definition an ardent American patriot.

Brandeis's own life demonstrated this symbiosis between Zionism and Americanism. This leader of American Zionism was also the first Jew to give the Fourth of July oration in Boston's Faneuil Hall. Brandeis and his supporters refused to turn their backs on America or Americanization. The relative unimportance of American anti-Semitism has been compared to that of Europe, and the improving social and economic status of America's Jews and the American democratic political and social traditions warranted neither a blanket condemnation of the nation nor a wholesale exodus to Palestine.

Supporters of classic Zionism strongly opposed the Brandeisian synthesis of American identity and Zionism. Chaim Weizmann, the future first president of the state of Israel, accused the Brandeisians of being ignorant of "all those questions in Zionism which have contributed so much towards the real life of the movement, like the Hebrew revival, like the desire of the Zionists to 'judaize' the Jewish communities of the world . . . in short, for all those imponderabilia which form a national movement of which Palestine is merely a territorial aspect of a national political upheaval," Louis Lipsky, an American supporter of Weizmann, described Brandeisianism as "a form of opiate for the Jewish masses, which would keep them in the bondage of a culture that could never lead to political rebirth."

From his perspective, Lipsky was correct, but he failed to realize that the political rebirth he sought for American Jews was already taking place in America. The character of Jewish immigration clearly showed the extent to which American Jews identified with their new homeland. Of all the major immigrant groups, Jews had a larger percentage of children and, next to the Irish, a larger percentage of women. When Jews came to the United States, they came with their families, and they came to stay. Their rate of repatriation was far lower than other immigrant groups. With nothing to return to in Europe, Jews had decisively broken their ties with the old country. And once in America, Jews rapidly learned English, flocked to the public schools, and became citizens with alacrity. Only a minuscule minority ever contemplated exchanging the benefits of life in America for a problematic existence in the Middle East. Their support for a Jewish homeland would be restricted to philanthropy, political lobbying, and tourism.

Undoubtedly, the most important manifestation of Brandeisian Zionism was Hadassah, the women's auxiliary of the American Zionist Organization. Established by Henrietta Szold of Baltimore in 1912, Hadassah's mission was medical work in Palestine. Hadassah's eschewing of Jewish nationalism and *aliyah*, its ignoring of the political abstractions and ideology so dear to the hearts of European Zionists, and its emphasis on practical and concrete activities to alleviate suffering reflected the fundamental, nonnationalistic, charitable thrust of American Zionism. The Hadassash ideal, Szold correctly stated, "can be embraced by all, no matter what their attitude may be to other Jewish questions." Hadassah would become the largest and arguably the most powerful Jewish organization in the world. By 1980, it had 400,000 members, approximately ten times the membership of the National Organization of Women.

The middle-of-the-road Zionism that identified with Brandeis and Szold was strongly opposed by a variety of ideological purists. Elements within the Reform movement, particularly at the Hebrew Union College in Cincinnati, believed all forms of Zionism were tainted, to a greater or lesser extent, by Jewish tribalism. For them, the Pittsburgh Platform remained the last word regarding Zionism, and they continued to oppose it even when, in 1937 in Columbus, Ohio, a new set of principles were adopted by the Central Conference of American Rabbis, the national association of Reform rabbis.

The Columbus Platform sharply revised the traditional American Reform position on Jewish identity and Zionism. No longer was Jewish identity viewed as solely a religious matter, and no longer as Zionism rejected out of hand. "We recognize in the group-loyalty of Jews who have become estranged from our religious tradition," the rabbis declared, "a bond that still united them with us." Furthermore, they affirmed, "In the rehabilitation of Palestine, the land hallowed by memories and hopes, we behold the promise of renewed life for many of our brethren. We affirm the obligation of all Jewry to aid in its upbuilding as a Jewish homeland by endeavoring to make it not only a refuge for the oppressed but also a center of Jewish culture and spiritual life."

The Columbus Platform was, of course, a response to the European catastrophe that by 1937 was threatening to engulf European Jewry. The ideological consistency that had marked the Pittsburgh Platform retreated before the tragic reality of the Holocaust. The Reform rabbinate realized that there were more important things than ideological consistency. American Jews had a responsibility for European Jews not because they were members of the same religion but because of "group-loyalty." Some Reform spokesmen, however, remained anti-Zionist platonists.

They refused to allow facts, however disagreeable, to modify that classic Reform ideology that had emptied Jewish identity of any particular ethnic or nationalistic characteristics and had defined Judaism solely as a voluntaristic religion. In 1943, a dissenting group of Reform rabbis organized the American Council for Judaism after the Central Conference of American Rabbis in 1942 had gone on record in support of the formation of a Jewish Army composed of Palestinian Jews. The initial statement of the Council supported the concept of Palestine as a refuge for Jews, but it adamantly opposed the creation of a Jewish state or a Jewish army. Such a state, the Council contended, would detract from the universal teachings of Judaism, would lead to accusations of dual loyalty among Jews, and would confuse "our fellow men about our place and function in society and also divert our own attention from our historical role to live as a religious community wherever we may dwell." As the manichean-like title of Rabbi Elmer Berger's book *Judaism or Jewish Nationalism* (1957) indicated, the American Council for Judaism believed the alternatives facing America's Jews were unambiguous.

The debate regarding a Jewish state became moot with the creation of Israel in 1948. American Jewry in general, and American Zionism in particular, then faced a vigorous challenge from Israeli officials and intellectuals who partially blamed American Zionism for the failure of American Jewry to migrate en masse to Israel. For them, American Zionism was a mere fund-raising operation and unable to instill into American Jewry either a love of Zion or a commitment to make *aliyah*. Israeli diplomat Abba Eban expressed the contempt of the Israelis for American Zionism in his quip that American Zionism demonstrated the truth of that fundamental religious belief that there can be life after death.

The confrontation between the Israelis and Americans came to a head in 1950 and 1951 over the Israelis' claim that all Jews were obligated to migrate to Israel. American Jewish leaders promptly demanded that Israel officially acknowledge that American Jews had no political obligations toward Israel. Because of their concern for the future of Israeli-diaspora relationships, David Ben-Gurion, Israel's prime minister, backed down in August 1950. He publicly acknowledged that Jews in America were not living in exile and that "the state of Israel represents and speaks only on behalf of its own citizens and in no way presumes to represent or speak in the name of Jews who are citizens of any other country. We, the people of Israel, have no desire and no intention to interfere in any way with the internal affairs of Jewish communities abroad." Jacob Blaustein, then president of the American Jewish Committee, welcomed Ben-Gurion's statement but warned that it was insufficient unless accompanied by unmistakable evidence that Israel's leaders realize relations between Israel and American Jews "must be based on mutual respect for one another's feelings and needs, and on the preservation of the integrity of the two communities and their institutions."

The attempt to define a proper American Jewish stance toward Israel that would allow for a close identification between American Jews and the Jewish state but not derogate from their Americanism masked a growing ideological, psychological, and emotional commitment to Israel. The secularization of American Jewry, the numerical decline in the number of American Jews professing orthodoxy, and the atrophying of Jewish socialism, Yiddish culture, and other forms of Jewish identity prevalent among first-generation Jews left a vacuum in Jewish identity that was filled by Zionism, American-style. That Zionism was the major expression of American Jewish identity became clear only after Israel's incredible victory in the 1967 Six-Day War. It was during the dark days of May and early June 1967 that American Jews realized the extent of their emotional identification with Israel and the degree to which support for Israel had become the lowest common denominator of American Jewish life.

This identification has been strengthened by another element within recent American Jewish culture—a growing interest in the Holocaust and a passion to learn its lessons. American Jews attend numerous Holocaust remembrance events, write and read a continuing flow of novels and histories of the European catastrophe, avidly view television shows and movies such as *The Holocaust, The Sorrow and the Pity, The Pawnbroker, Diary of Anne Frank, The Wall, Playing for Time,* and *Shoah,* endow university chairs and lecture series on the Holocaust, establish Holocaust museums and erect Holocaust statues, pressure state departments of education to establish Holocaust studies programs in high schools, and engage in numerable other Holocaust-related activities. The most popular course in many Judaic departments in American universities is one relating to the history of the Holocaust. The Hebrew word *zachor* (remember) has become the code word for this obsession with the Holocaust.

By the 1970s, the American Jewish community was defining its agenda and judging its accomplishments partially by the extent to which these conformed to the Holocaust's teachings. The most important American explicator of the meaning of the Holocaust has been the writer Elie Wiesel, the 1986 winner of the Nobel Peace Prize and himself a survivor of Auschwitz. His book *The Jews of Silence* (1966), which condemned the failure of world Jewry to work for the freedom of Russian Jews, evoked bitter memories of the 1930s and 1940s, when American Jews supposedly stood passively aside and allowed the slaughter of European Jews to occur unimpeded. Wiesel argued that the greatest sin of Jews in the post-Holocaust era was the sin of silence, the failure to hear the cries of help of fellow Jews.

Another eloquent voice in defining the meaning of the Holocaust has been Emil Fackenheim, a refugee from Hitler's Europe and a theologian at the University of Toronto. Fackenheim proclaimed in his *The Jewish Return into History:*

Reflections in the Age of Auschwitz and a New Jerusalem (1978) the need for a 614th commandment to go with the 613 other commandments that devout Jews observe: "The authentic Jew of today is forbidden to hand Hitler yet another, posthumous victory." The book was dedicated to Yonatan Netanyahu, the hero of the 1976 Israeli Entebbe rescue of one hundred hostages held by Palestinians, and it concluded with a segment from the official Israeli prayer for the state: "Our Father in Heaven, the Rock of Israel and her Redeemer, bless thou the state of Israel, the beginning of the dawn of our redemption. Shield her with the wings of Thy Love, and spread over her the tabernacle of Thy peace." This determination not to allow Adolf Hitler another victory explains the outrage of American Jews in 1985 when President Ronald Reagan visited the Bitburg cemetery.

Some American Jews have suggested that this consuming interest in the Holocaust has been counterproductive. Rabbi Daniel Silver of Cleveland, Ohio, for example, complained in 1986 that "the Holocaust cannot, and does not, provide the kind of vitalizing and informing myth around which American Jews could marshal their energies and construct a vital culture." Martyrs command respect, he argued, but the Jewish community's sense of sacred purpose must consist of something "more substantial than tears." Silver especially questioned the decision to build a Holocaust museum in Washington, DC. "Such a museum," he fears, "will speak of death, not of life, of victimization, not civilization—a less than appropriate statement of the spirit of a people who, throughout their long history, have obeyed God's command: 'Choose life.'" He concluded that "the fires of Hell are mesmerizing" but Jews would be mistaken to organize their future solely by this light.

While there is merit in Silver's concern, it fails to take into consideration the fact that the meaning of the Holocaust for America's Jews is intimately related to the greatest life-giving event in modern Jewish history, the establishment of the state of Israel. For American Jewry, Israel is a contra-Holocaust, rescuing recent Jewish history from its bleakness and providing meaning and purpose to Jewish existence. To emphasize the relationship between the Holocaust and the Jewish state, missions sponsored by the United Jewish Appeal will often first visit Auschwitz before going to Israel. Many of the most popular post–World War II novels by American Jewish writers examined implicitly or explicitly the connection between Israel and the Holocaust. Among the most notable were Herman Wouk's *War and Remembrance* and Leon Uris's *Exodus*. The American-Jewish response to *Exodus* was particularly intense, and one observer dubbed it the Jewish *Uncle Tom's Cabin*.

The relationship between Israel and the Holocaust only became clear for most American Jews in 1967, when Israel and world Jewry were faced with possibility of another holocaust from a united Arab world. For Jews, the Gentile world in 1967 exhibited the same apathy toward Jewish suffering that had marked its behavior during the 1930s and 1940s when, American Jews were convinced, the destruction of European Jewry could be explained in large part by the indifference of bystanders—officials in the Franklin D. Roosevelt administration fearful of the unfavorable political impact of welcoming a large number of Jewish immigrants to America, American Jewish organizations interested only in their own petty agendas, and British politicians concerned with preserving British interests in the Middle East. A series of historical and quasi-historical books with such titles *While Six Million Died: A Chronicle of American Apathy* (Arthur D. Morse, 1967), *The Abandonment of the Jews: America and the Holocaust, 1941–1945* (David Wyman, 1984), and *Were We Our Brothers' Keepers?: The Public Response of Jews to the Holocaust, 1938–1944* (Haskell Lookstein, 1985) catered to this almost morbid obsession with allocating blame for the Holocaust among the Nazis' opponents.

The frantic response of American Jewry to the crisis of 1967—the unprecedented fund-raising for Israel, the ears continually glued to radios in search of the latest news, the exultation at the amazing victory of Israeli arms—is understandable only against the backdrop of World War II. It was as if American Jews had spontaneously resolved to prevent another Holocaust, to wash away the strain of guilt carried by American Jewry because of the apathy they and their parents had demonstrated a quarter of a century earlier, and to demonstrate to the non-Jewish world that the period of Jews going like sheep to the slaughter, as the popular description put it, had ended. Since the 1960s, there has been an upsurge of militancy within American Jewry, ranging from acts of violence to a vigorous and blatant political lobbying unknown prior to 1967, on behalf of distinctly Jewish causes. Throughout, the major concern of Jewish spokesmen has been that seemingly ancient and parochial question, "But is it good for the Jews?"

This militancy has encompassed all strains of American Jewish life. Members of the Jewish Defense League and other organizations have bombed pro-Palestinian and Soviet offices in the United States. Other Jews have participated in giant demonstrations on behalf of Soviet Jewry and Israel. Jewish organizations and political action committees put unprecedented pressure on Congress and the White House to encourage the Soviet Union to allow its Jews to emigrate, to guarantee the military and economic security of Israel, and to speak up for Jewish interests in Ethiopia and elsewhere. This new Jewish militancy even modified individual behavior.

In the 1930s, the operative principle in Jewish life was *shah* (low profile). Jews were advised to be as inconspicuous as possible for fear of provoking anti-Semitism. Beginning in the 1960s, however, it became common to see Jewish men wearing skullcaps outside the home, Jewish women wearing stars of David, members of both sexes wearing buttons proclaiming "Kiss me, I'm Jewish," and Jewish comedians such as Lenny Bruce and Woody Allen telling Jewish jokes to largely Gentile audiences.

Jews also came out of the cinematic coast. In the 1960 film *Exodus*, the Israeli Ari Ben Canaan (Paul Newman) tells the Gentile Kitty Fremont (Eva Marie Saint) that she is wrong in believing that people are the same no matter where: "Don't believe it. People have a right to be different." And in the 1979 movie *Norma Rae*, the character Reuben Warshovsky, a northern union organizer, tells Norma Rae that they are different: "History makes us different." Indians speak

Yiddish in *Cat Ballou* and *Blazing Saddles,* a black cabbie speaks Yiddish in *Bye Bye Braverman*, and a Japanese career woman speaks Yiddish in *Walk, Don't Run*. Barbara Streisand virtually built her Hollywood career playing Jewish characters. In *Funny Girl, The Way We Were, Yentl,* and other films, she refused to dilute the Jewishness of the characters she portrayed, and she refused to get a nose job to modify her less than classic profile. In one song in *Funny Girl* she asks, "Is a nose with a deviation a crime against the nation?"

While these movies were being released, there was a dramatic upsurge of interest in Judaica on the American campus, and no major university was without its Jewish studies program offering courses in Jewish history, theology and philosophy, and Hebrew language. In the fall of 1985, the *New Yorker* magazine even published a lengthy three-part essay titled "Holy Days," which described in favorable terms a Hassidic sect in Brooklyn.

The overriding concern of this new Jewish militancy has been Jewish survival. While the dread of anti-Semitism has receded, it has been replaced by a fear of cultural assimilation and intermarriage. American Jewish leaders have come to realize that the marriage altar rather than the pogrom is the most immediate threat to American Jewish identity. This fear even affected television programming in the early 1970s with the appearance of the sitcom *Bridget Loves Bernie*, which featured the tribulations of an intermarried couple (and interestingly enough, the show's hero and heroine—the Jewish David Birney and the Gentile Meredith Baxter—were a couple off the show as well as on it). Despite their long-standing commitment to freedom of speech, Jewish organizations succeeded in having the program taken off the air.

During the 1970s and 1980s, Jewish task forces examined the condition of the Jewish family and Jewish education, particularly the extent to which they were barriers to intermarriage and transmitters of Jewish identity. The studies of the task forces were generally somber in their conclusions, although Jewish sociologists such as Steven M. Cohen and Calvin Goldscheider claimed that the evidence was more ambiguous than generally assumed and that optimism was as warranted as pessimism regarding the future of the American Jewish community. Pessimism, however, fit the new mood of American Jewry, with its urgent concern for demographic and cultural survival. This mood resulted in some startling changes on the American Jewish scene, particularly within the Reform movement, which had always been the segment of American Jewry most willing to make the greatest modifications in Jewish law and practice to conform to the temper of American life.

The Reform movement, which had not welcomed Zionism and had remained unsympathetic to a Jewish state until World War II, now has a branch of its seminary in Jerusalem that all rabbinical students must attend prior to ordination. An even more startling development, because of its tradition of strong support of public schools and distrust of parochial education, has been the establishment under Reform auspices of several Jewish day schools. But Reform's most controversial change has been its modification of the very definition of what it is to be a Jew.

For millennia, to have been considered a Jew required that one either have had a Jewish mother or have been converted according to traditional Jewish law. In 1983, the Reform movement officially stated that it would consider a child of a Jewish father and a non-Jewish mother to be Jewish if the child was being raised Jewishly. The decision on behalf of patrilineal descent was due to a perceived skyrocketing intermarriage rate among American Jews. The Reform movement hoped the revised definition of a Jew and a more open attitude toward religious conversion would provide a sufficiently large enough pool of people to insure a vibrant American Jewish community in general and strong Reform congregations in particular.

For representatives of the Conservative and particularly Orthodox wings of American Jewry, the Reform movement's approval of patrilineal descent was a direct challenge to the integrity of the Jewish legal process and to fundamental Jewish tradition. Traditionalists were adamant that Jewish law could not be made to conform to the Reform movement's latest sociological concerns, particularly when it encouraged a fraudulent Jewish identity. "We can't go half-way," Rabbi Nosson Scherman declared. "I believe Torah is God-given, and I can't compromise on that." Traditionalists pointed out that if the Reform movement did not overturn its decision, no longer could prospective marriage partners assume that their prospective spouses were Jewish. Some marriages between supposed Jews would turn out to be intermarriages, and this would present observant Jews and their children with a whole host of Jewish legal problems, including questions of illegitimacy.

One prospect was that some Jews might not accept others as authentic Jews unless they provided family pedigrees. Orthodox rabbis predicted dire consequences would flow from the patrilineal decision unless the Reform movement recanted. In December 1985, Rabbi Haskell Lookstein claimed the divisions within the American Jewish community were so deep that they threatened "to isolate Jew from Jew and to rend the fabric of Jewish peoplehood so that we will no longer be one people." Rabbi Irving Greenberg predicted that by 1990 "there will be between three-quarters of a million and a million people whose Jewishness is contested or whose marriageability is denied by a larger group of other Jews." You have, he lamented, "a situation ripe for schism."

This pervasive concern with Jewish survival and Jewish identity arises out of the revolutionary situation in which American Jews found themselves. While America was not the Promised Land, it was the land of promise. America's Jews have been perhaps the major beneficiaries of America's liberal and capitalist social, political, and economic order. America's Jews today comprise the wealthiest and most influential diaspora community in history. Denied none of the benefits America has to offer, the nation's Jews have flocked to the universities, businesses, and professions in search of their share of the American Dream. Overall, they have not been disappointed. But the price Jews have had to pay for their rapid economic and social ascent has been an increasingly attenuated Jewish identity. "The threat of Jewish oblivion in America," Herman Wouk warned in the 1950s, "is the threat of pleasantly vanishing down a broad highway at the wheel of a high-powered station wagon, with the golf clubs piled in the back."

Most American Jews have eliminated those aspects of Jewish existence, such as distinctive dress and diet, that are barriers to economic and social mobility. Attendance at college, and approximately 85 percent of Jewish high school graduates enter college, places Jews at an impressionable age in an intellectual and social environment in which parochial ethnic and religious identities and values are viewed as anachronistic. The secularism of American life and the religious skepticism characteristic of the campus have undermined the Jewish identities largely derived from Judaism. The slogan of the United Jewish Appeal is "We Are One." But the oneness that holds Jews together is no longer Judaism or anti-Semitism but Israel. "For those without a sense of the Jewish past," the historian Luch Dawidowicz said, "Israel serves as the positively charged nucleus of Jewish identity." Israel provides the link that binds Jews together, no matter how remote they might be from any involvement in Jewish social or religious life. The Jewish thing most Jews have in common is not attendance at the synagogue (even on Yom Kippur) or providing a Jewish education for their children or supporting liberal political causes but contributing at least a nominal sum to United Jewish Appeal. In this respect, the UJA's slogan is apt.

The popularity of the UJA stems from the manner in which it distributes the over half a billion dollars it raises every year from America's six million Jews. While some of the money finances local institutions and some aids impoverished Jews in Europe, Asia, and Africa, over 50 percent of the UJA's allocations support social, welfare, educational, and economic development projects in Israel. And the importance of Israel and the UJA to the individual contributor defines his or her status within the Jewish community.

With fund-raising the major priority, the emphasis in contemporary Jewish life is on philanthropy rather than Jewish learning or piety. The local Jewish federation, rather than the synagogue or the *yeshiva*, has become the major focal point of Jewish life and the major dispenser of prestige. The fund-raising activity of the federation is supplemented by that of a host of other organizations working independently to raise money for Israeli institutions. Finally, there is the Israel Bond Organization, which every year sells about half a billion dollars in Israeli bonds to American Jews and their friends. Many observers have severely criticized this "checkbook" Judaism, but they have been unable to suggest any alternative to even this attenuated Jewish identity that would appeal to acculturated and sophisticated Jews. The sociologist Charles S. Liebman predicted in his *The Ambivalent American Jew: Politics, Religion, and Family in American Jewish Life* (1973) that if Judaism in America was to perpetuate itself, "it must, at least to some extent, reject the value of integration, which I see as sapping its very essence." It is highly unlikely that this will take place.

In 1900, Jacob David Wilowsky, the prominent rabbi of Slutsk, Russia, told a New York audience that Jews who had migrated to America were sinners, since they had placed the spiritual welfare of themselves and their children in mortal peril. In coming to America, Jews had left behind "their Torah, their Talmud, their yeshivoth—in a word, their Yiddishkeit, their entire Jewish way of life." Three years later, Wilowsky settled in Chicago and became chief rabbi of a group of Orthodox congregations. If Wilowsky, one of the rabbinical giants of his age, could not resist the call of America, it was asking too much of less pious Jews to forego migrating to the "golden land." For every Jew who migrated to Palestine during the late nineteenth and early twentieth centuries, perhaps fifty risked their souls and came to the United States.

It has been the hospitality of a free and open society to Jewish aspirations that has provided the major challenge to American Jews—to be simultaneously both Jewish and American, to withstand the allure of cultural assimilation while affirming the right to be an integral part of America. Certainly, Jews still bear the imprint of the Jewish cultural legacy—in addition to liberal and at times Messianic politics, an educational elitism, and an occupational profile heavily tilted toward business and the professions. What is problematic is the ability of Jews to pass on to future generations a religious and cultural tradition that for many is no longer operative in their daily lives. Although valuable in themselves, cherishing Israel and contributing to Jewish charities are, in the long run, not weighty enough to support a strong Jewish identity. The problem that confronts today's Jews is the same one that confronted the first Jewish migrants to America: to establish the delicate balance that can satisfy the demands of both Jewishness and American-ness. Should the center cease to hold, it will not be because Jewishness has assumed a new importance.

BIBLIOGRAPHICAL ESSAY

The history of America's Jews is surveyed in Oscar Handlin, *Adventure in Freedom: Three Hundred Years of Jewish Life in America* (New York: McGraw-Hill, 1954); Henry L. Feingold, *Zion in America: The Jewish Experience from Colonial Times to the Present* (New York: Twayne, 1974); Arthur A. Goren, *The American Jews* (Cambridge, MA: Belknap Press of Harvard Univ. Press, 1982); Abraham J. Karp, *Haven and Home: A History of the Jews in America* (New York: Schocken Books, 1985); Arthur Hertzberg, *The Jews in America: Four Centuries of an Uneasy Encounter: A History* (New York: Simon and Schuster, 1989); Howard M. Sachar, *A History of the Jews in America* (New York: Knopf 1992); and Gerald Sorin, *Tradition Transformed: The Jewish Experience in America* (Baltimore: Johns Hopkins Univ. Press, 1997). The most comprehensive history is Henry L. Feingold, ed., *The Jewish People in America*, 5 vols. (Baltimore: Johns Hopkins Univ. Press, 1992).

The story of the German Jews in America is told in Naomi W. Cohen, *Encounter with Emancipation: The German Jews in the United States* (Philadelphia: Jewish Publication Society, 1984) and Alan Silverstein, *Alternatives to Assimilation: The Response of Reform Judaism to American Culture, 1840–1930* (Hanover, NH: Univ. Press of New England, 1994). The East European immigration is examined in Moses Rischin, *The Promised City: New York's Jews, 1870–1914* (Cambridge, MA: Harvard Univ. Press, 1962); Irving Howe, *World of Our Fathers: The Journey of the East European Jews to America and the*

Life They Found and Made (New York: Simon and Schuster, 1976); Thomas Kessner, *The Golden Door: Italian and Jewish Immigrant Mobility in New York City, 1880–1915* (New York: Oxford Univ. Press, 1977); and Neil M. Cowan and Ruth Schwartz Cowan, *Our Parents' Lives: The Americanization of Eastern European Jews* (New York: Basic Books, 1989). The often difficult relationship between German Jews and the eastern European immigrants is one of the themes of Arthur A. Goren, *New York Jews and the Quest for Community: The Kehillah Experiment, 1908–1922* (New York: Columbia Univ. Press, 1970). The second- and third-generation descendants of the eastern European immigrants are discussed in Deborah Dash Moore, *At Home in America: Second Generation New York Jews* (New York: Columbia Univ. Press, 1981); Jenna W. Joselit, *New York's Jewish Jews: The Orthodox Community in the Interwar Years* (Bloomington: Indiana Univ. Press, 1990); and Eli Lederhendler, *New York Jews and the Decline of Urban Ethnicity, 1950–1970* (Syracuse, NY: Syracuse Univ. Press, 2001).

Perceptive interpretations of post–World War II American Jewish life include Marshall Sklare, *America's Jews* (New York: Random House, 1971); Charles S. Liebman, *The Ambivalent American Jew: Politics, Religion, and Family in American Jewish Life* (Philadelphia: Jewish Publication Society of America, 1973); Daniel Elazar, *Community and Polity: The Organizational Dynamics of American Jewry* (Philadelphia: Jewish Publication Society of America, 1976); Marshall Sklare and Joseph Greenblum, *Jewish Identity on the Suburban Frontier* (Chicago: Univ. Chicago Press, 1979); Steven M. Cohen, *American Modernity and Jewish Identity* (New York: Tavistock Publication, 1983); Stuart E. Rosenberg, *The New Jewish Identity in America* (New York: Hippocrene Books, 1985); Charles E. Silberman, *A Certain People: American Jews and Their Lives Today* (New York: Summit Books, 1985); Calvin Goldscheider, *Jewish Continuity and Change: Emerging Patterns in America* (Bloomington: Indiana Univ. Press, 1986); Jonathan S. Woocher, *Sacred Survival: The Civil Religion of American Jews* (Bloomington: Indiana Univ. Press, 1986); Leonard Fein, *Where Are We? The Inner Life of America's Jews* (New York: Harper & Row, 1988); Jerold S. Auerbach, *Rabbis and Lawyers: The Journey from Torah to Constitution* (Bloomington: Indiana Univ. Press, 1990); Sylvia B. Fishman, *A Breath of Life: Feminism in the American Jewish Community* (New York: Free Press, 1993); Jenna W. Joselit, *Wonders of America: Reinventing Jewish Culture, 1880–1950* (New York: Hill and Wang, 1994); Seymour Martin Lipset and Earl Raab, *Jews and the New American Scene* (Cambridge, MA: Harvard Univ. Press, 1995); Samuel C. Heilman, *Portrait of American Jews: The Last Half of the 20th Century* (Seattle: Univ. of Washington Press, 1995); Robert M. Seltzer and Norman J. Cohen, eds., *The Americanization of the Jews* (New York: New York Univ. Press, 1995); J. J. Goldberg, *Jewish Power: Inside the American Jewish Establishment* (Reading, MA: Addison-Wesley, 1996); David Biale, Michael Galchinsky, and Susannah Heschel, eds., *Insider/Outsider: American Jews and Multiculturalism* (Berkeley: Univ. of California Press, 1998); Peter Novick, *The Holocaust in American Life* (Boston: Houghton Mifflin, 1999); Samuel G. Freedman, *Jew vs. Jew: The Struggle for the Soul of American Jewry* (New York: Simon and Schuster, 2000); and L. Sandy Maisel and Ira N. Forman, *Jews in American Politics* (Lankam, MD: Rowman & Littlefield Publishers, 2001).

The history of American Zionism is covered in Melvin I. Urofsky's two-volume work, *American Zionism from Herzl to the Holocaust* (Garden City, NY: Anchor Press, 1975) and *We Are One! American Jewry and Israel* (Garden City, NY: Anchor Press, 1978). Hillel Halkin's *Letters to an American Jewish Friend: A Zionist's Polemic* (Philadelphia: Jewish Publication Society of America, 1977) argues that a Jewish life is possible only in Israel. American Judaism is explored in Charles S. Liebman, "Orthodoxy in American Jewish Life," *American Jewish Year Book* (1965), 21–97; Marshall Sklare, *Conservative Judaism: An American Religious Movement* (New York: Schocken Books, 1972); Nathan Glazer, *American Judaism* (Chicago: Univ. of Chicago Press, 1972); Marc Lee Raphael, *Profiles in American Judaism: The Reform, Conservative, Orthodox, and Reconstructionist Traditions in Historical Perspective* (San Francisco: Harper & Row, 1985); Jack Wertheimer, ed., *The American Synagogue: A Sanctuary Transformed* (New York: Cambridge Univ. Press, 1987); Michael A. Meyer, *Response to Modernity: A History of the Reform Movement in Judaism* (New York: Oxford Univ. Press, 1988); Lynn Davidman, *Tradition in a Rootless World: Women Turn to Orthodox Judaism* (Berkeley: Univ. of California Press, 1991); and Jack Wertheimer, *A People Divided: Judaism in Contemporary America* (New York: Basic Books, 1993).

The nature of American identity in general and American Jewish identity in particular are discussed in Milton Gordon, *Assimilation in American Life: The Role of Race, Religion, and National Origins* (New York: Oxford Univ. Press, 1964); Howard Brotz, *The Black Jews of Harlem: Negro Nationalism and the Dilemma of Negro Leadership* (New York: Free Press of Glencoe, 1970); John Higham, *Send These to Me: Jews and Other Immigrants in America* (New York: Atheneum, 1975); Arthur Mann, *The One and the Many: Reflections on the American Identity* (Chicago: Univ. of Chicago Press, 1979); Joseph A. D. Sutton, *Magic Carpet: Aleppo-in-Flatbush: The Story of Unique Ethnic Community* (New York: Thayer-Jacoby, 1979); Egon Mayer, *From Suburb to Shtetl: The Jews of Boro Park* (Philadelphia: Temple Univ. Press, 1979); Werner Sollors, *Beyond Ethnicity: Consent and Descent in American Culture* (New York: Oxford Univ. Press, 1986); Charles L. Liebman and Steven M. Cohen, *Two Worlds of Judaism: The Israeli and American Experiences* (New Haven: Yale Univ. Press, 1990); Arthur M. Schlesinger, Jr., *The Disuniting of America: Reflections on Multicultural Society* (Knoxville, TN: Whittle Direct Books, 1991); and Philip Gleason, *Speaking of Diversity: Language and Ethnicity in Twentieth-Century America* (Baltimore: Johns Hopkins Univ. Press, 1992).

American Jewish novels have perceptively examined the often-conflicting demands of being Jewish and American. The most important of these include Abraham Cahan, *Yekl: A Tale of the New York Ghetto* (New York: Appleton, 1896); and *The Rise of David Levinsky* (New York: Harper & Brothers, 1917); Anzia Yezierzka, *Hungry Hearts* (Boston: Houghton Mifflin, 1920); and Henry Roth, *Call It Sleep* (New York: R. O. Ballow, 1934). An overall view is Allen Guttmann, *The Jewish Writer in America: Assimilation and the Crisis of Identity* (New York: Oxford Univ. Press, 1971). For the Jewish identity of Emma Lazarus, see Bette Roth Young, *Emma Lazarus in Her World: Life and Letters* (Philadelphia: Jewish Publication Society, 1995); and "Emma Lazarus and Her Jewish Problem," *American Jewish History* (1996), 291–313. Recent essays on Horace Kallen include Erika Sunada, "Revisiting Horace M. Kallen's Cultural Pluralism: A Comparative Analysis," *Journal of American and Canadian Studies* (2000), 51–76, and June Sochen, "Jewish American Identity: The Views of Horace Kallen and Will Herberg," *Michael* (2000), 18196. For Zangwill, see Isaac M. Fein, "Israel Zangwill and American Jewry: A Documentary Study," *American Jewish Historical Quarterly* (1970), 12–36, and Neil L. Shumsky, "Zangwill's 'The Melting Pot': Ethnic Tensions on Stage," *American Quarterly* (1975), 29–41.

KOREAN AMERICANS

Kyeyoung Park

In New York City in the late 1980s, a progressive group in the Korean American community organized a Korean cultural program in the Asian village at the famous Queens Festival.[1] This mammoth festival attracts as many as 300,000 visitors on a weekend. After the festival was over, controversy arose over the Korean cultural exhibit. Did it fairly represent Korean culture? Some people were indignant about the exhibit. They chided the organizers and said that the strong political messages—evident in posters, paintings, woodblock printings, and wall hangings—had little to do with the elegance of Korean culture. For them, the artwork depicting Korean workers demanding higher wages and democracy was a disgrace for Koreans in the United States. They questioned why exhibit organizers ignored the other aspects of Korean culture. They also declared that performance of farmers' dances and other folk dances misrepresented Koreans.

The lingering questions of this controversy have to do with the presentation and representation of Korean homeland culture in the context of a festival in the United States. In other words, what is really "Korean" in the Korean transnational community, and why does this matter provoke such heated arguments among Korean Americans?

As Koreans leave Korea and settle in other nations, the name *Korea* becomes enigmatic, much different than in the homeland. In Korea, when people marry, they tend to verify their identity through references to region, birthplace, family background, educational level, and other factors.[2] In contrast, in the United States, the reference point for Koreans becomes ethnicity. It is not uncommon to hear conversations between immigrants about whether their daughter is marrying another Korean or not.

In addition to the problems of retaining the particularities of Korean culture and ethnicity, there is a problem of measurement. A Korean immigrant is often asked, How Korean are you? People raise this question as if one could measure the degree of Koreanization or Americanization.[3] But more important are the implications of this question: what do people mean when they identify a person as not being Korean enough or being too Korean?

This article examines the construction of culture in diaspora communities; in particular, what happens to Korean culture and identity among Korean immigrants living in the United States, and how Koreanness is re-created and reinterpreted in the Korean American community.[4] It analyzes Korean immigrant discourse on culture and argues that the making of Korean American culture is a creative and critical process drawing from Korean, American, and other cultures. Specifically, it argues that Korean American culture is rooted in Korea, but that its parameters are set by the political economy of the United States (i.e., by the impact the U.S. economy has on the restructuring of the immigrant community).

The data comes from ethnographic fieldwork done in the late 1980s on the Korean immigrant community in New York City, where some 200,000 ethnic Koreans reside.[5] In Queens, New York City, the county population in 1987 was 49 percent white, 21 percent black, 16 percent Hispanic, and 14 percent Asian. In New York City, which has the second-largest Korean community in America, over two-thirds of the Koreans work in small businesses as either employers or employees. As a Korean-born woman and an anthropologist, I will also add my own perspective as a new-immigrant researcher to this discussion.[6]

TRANSNATIONAL DIASPORA AND THE QUESTION OF AGENCY

An increasing number of new approaches to studying immigrants and their communities are shifting their focus from international migration to an examination of transnational diaspora. In their book on Chinese diaspora, Nonini and Ong viewed diaspora: as a pattern of communities, persons, and groups, separated by space but sharing a common condition; a community that is continually reconstituted by the travel of Chinese persons across and throughout the regions of dispersion; and a community characterized by multiple and varied connections via family ties, kinship, commerce, sentiments, and values related to the "homeland," shared memberships in transnational organizations, and so forth.[7]

In addition, as presented in new journals such as *Diaspora*, *Public Culture*, and *Identities*, writers and researchers no longer interpret the contemporary global movement and flow of people, information, and commodities within the outmoded framework of unidirectional assimilation.[8] Instead, they write about migration that is transnational rather than international, that is circular rather than just one-way, and that follows multifarious trajectories and diverse networks.

This approach also reflects a new understanding of nation-states as borderlands of shifting and contested boundaries and presents migrant networks and communities in this context. These developments occur within the context of late capitalism, or what David Harvey called the condition of postmodernity. A constellation of technical, financial, and institutional innovations that have occurred since the early 1970s has led to a shift in capitalism from mass industrial production to globalized regimes of "flexible accumulation."[9] According to Harvey, "Flexible accumulation rests on flexibility with respect to labor processes, labor markets, products, and patterns of consumption. It is characterized by the emergence of entirely new sectors of production, new ways of providing financial services, new markets, and, above all, greatly intensified rates of commercial, technological, and organizational innovation."[10]

Fundamentally, these changes are associated with the enhanced and increased mobility of people, commodities, ideas, and capital on a global scale, and one of the major consequences is the migration of people. For example, Asian countries are producing more highly trained members than they can absorb, while the United States produces fewer than it needs. These imbalances are a product of the contradictions of capitalism, the resulting class struggles, and efforts to restructure the global economy.[11] Since the late 1970s, large numbers of, mainly middle-class professional Koreans have come to the United States. Their departure from Korea and their entrance into the United States reflect the late-capitalist relationship between the United States and Korea.

Korean immigrant culture has been shaped by the diaspora experience. It is transnational and deterritorialized. Following Nina Glick-Schiller and George Fournon's (1989) model in their study of Haitians, the Korean diaspora experience can be analyzed in terms of multiple and overlapping identities. For Korean immigrants, these separate identities allow them to both accommodate and resist the realities of race, class, and gender both in Korea and the United States.[12] Korean American culture, thus, is very fluid, and similar to what some scholars have described as creole cultures. According to Ulf Hannerz, creole cultures "are intrinsically of mixed origin, the confluence of two or more widely separate historical currents which interact in what is basically a center/periphery relationships."[13] Perhaps the best American example of a creole culture is found in New Orleans, where Europeans, Americans, Indians, and Africans have intermingled. Can Korean Americans be one of the many new creoles in New York?

Hannerz's creolization concept helps in an analysis of the creation of Korean immigrant culture. However, the concept lacks important historical and political dimensions such as time, place, and context. Also, although the government plays a major role in resocializing or acculturating ethnic immigrants, people are not passive but rather dynamically engaged in the process of developing their own particular identity and culture, and the definition does not adequately acknowledge this.

In her much-celebrated study of Asian American diasporas, Anthropologist Lisa Lowe argues that interpreting Asian American culture exclusively in terms of conflict between generations and filial relationships oversimplifies that culture, obscuring the particularities and differences created by class, gender, and nationality among Asians. Instead, basing on her study of Asian American customs and practices, she suggests, "The making of Asian American culture may be a much 'messier' process than unmediated vertical transmission from one generation to another, including practices that are partly inherited and partly modified, as well as partly invented."[14]

Similarly, Andrew Apter explains cultural construction as a dynamic process, as evidenced by his study of religious practices such as Haitian voodoo, Brazilian Candomble and Cuban Santeria. In his deconstruction of Linguist Melville Herskovits's much-celebrated essentialized syncretic paradigm on the repossession of Africa's heritage in the New World, Apter states, "The relation between implicit social knowledge and political economy . . . defines the horizon of Africanity in the New World: not as core values or cultural templates but as dynamic and critical practices."[15]

Nonetheless, Eric Gable, Richard Handler, and Anna Lawson insightfully note that ongoing construction of culture can be politically damaging to underrepresented (or misrepresented) peoples who are in the process of claiming their collective rights. More significantly, lost in the deconstructive orgy is the more crucial point that majority or mainstream traditions are equally invented.[16]

This article examines the construction of culture in diasporic communities, emphasizing the creative and critical practices relating to the idea of agency. How do transnational people maintain their identities, and what strategies do they adopt? In the creation of a hybrid culture, what efforts are made to retain original characteristics and customs?

Part of the transnational experience is "the prices people pay and are forced to pay by all of this, the blood on the floor and immense suffering and anguish and ambiguity."[17] Amid this context of "anguish and ambiguity" lies Korean American culture in multiethnic America.

KOREAN AMERICAN CULTURE

A researcher who studied cultural differences and communication styles between Korean merchants and employees and black patrons in south Los Angeles listed the following values and characteristics of Korean immigrants, based on her observations. "Respect of hierarchy; racial pride; reverence for lineage-loyalty, honor and duty; introspection and self-control; age orientation; emphasis on collective responsibility; formalism in behavior and logic of the heart; circular (indirect) ways of thinking; avoidance of confrontation; and high regard for education.[18]

In addition, she stated that Asian tradition assumes that all humans are created unequal.[19] Although some of these characteristics may be true, the concept of culture is broader than a list of values and traits.

Other scholars have approached the concept of culture through acculturation studies. In Los Angeles, Won Mao Hurh and Kwang Chung Kim studied patterns of Korean immigrants' acculturation by measuring the following variables: English proficiency, exposure to American printed mass media, and Anglicization of Korean names (first names). "In sharp contrast to the findings on acculturation, most of the dimensions of ethnic attachment are not related to the length of residence in the United States. . . . [R]egardless of the length of residence, a high proportion of our respondents subscribe to Korean newspapers, prefer to associate with Koreans, and prefer to attend the Korean ethnic church."[20]

One problem with these acculturation studies is that "they often involved a rather weak sense of the political economy of culture, of the overwhelming power of the Western expansion and of the material bases of change."[21] In addition, in the studies already discussed, we do not know what each Korean thought of the survey. Here, the measure of Korean culture is limited to the variables of language, names, and media. One of the most important keys to understanding Korean immigrants is the notion of *anjong* (establishment, stability, or security) related to small business ventures.[22] As used by immigrants, anjong refers to a definition of success that is different from becoming rich or attaining status as a member of high society. Anjong was developed by Korean immigrants to make sense of the American ideology of opportunity. Included in the concept are the immigrant community's analysis of causes and consequences of social relations and prescriptions to take advantage of opportunities. Korean immigrants see establishment of their own small business as a shortcut to the American Dream. In striving for this ideal, they remind themselves of the proverb "One will be rewarded as hard as one works."

In their pursuit of anjong, they alter traditional gender and kinship relations, as seen in the rise of a women-centered and sister-initiated kinship structure in Korean American small business. Also as a result of their focus on anjong, Korean immigrants have developed a new understanding of class, ethnicity, and race, as well as new religious ideas and practices. Anjong, therefore, plays a central role in the lives and foundational thinking of first-generation Korean Americans.

This description reveals certain aspects of Korean culture that have been reconfigured in the formation of a Korean American community. However, unless these concepts are related to how members of that community perceive their culture, how cultural reproduction occurs, and what aspects of the culture remain intact will not be clear. Is Korean immigrant culture, broadly speaking, Korean, or is it American culture? For the most part, immigrants tend to identify American culture with lifestyles of the white American middle class. However, they are also familiar with other ethnic cultures in America. For instance, given the importance of small-business activities, many Korean immigrant men in New York are familiar with Latino and other cultures, through bars and restaurants. Nonetheless, for Korean immigrants, there seems to be a gap between their perception of America and their multiethnic experience. As a result, in their testimonies, they do not yet seem to recognize American multiethnic culture.

Professors Kim and Hurh suggest that an adhesive mode of adaptation—meaning that the immigrant group remains tightly knit—allows Korean Americans to incorporate elements of American culture and social relations into their indigenous culture, *without replacing or modifying any significant part of that culture*.[23] However, even if one imagines that culture is a static unit or entity that is absorbed whole, it is not easy to add elements of American culture, while keeping Korean culture intact.

At the same time, one should avoid oversimplifying Korean or American culture. The process of acculturation/assimilation doesn't necessarily mean a linear evolutionary process from the immigrant culture to host culture. Moreover, Korean and U.S. culture have been interlocked since the Korean War; Koreans are exposed to the hegemonic U.S. culture long before they immigrate. Another related problem is defining what immigrants mean by "America." "American" culture is composed of so many cultural elements that there is no one, true American culture.

According to the interviewees, the making of Korean American culture is a gradual process, but more importantly, it is a moral and political process. Koreans often comment on the gradual process of Americanization when they refer to their eating habits.[24] For instance, an immigrant who enjoys a sour grapefruit is said to be more Americanized than an immigrant who prefers the Korean taste of a sweet mandarin orange. Similarly, an immigrant who drinks coffee black is more Americanized than an immigrant who drinks coffee with milk and sugar. In these cases, the process of Americanization is thought to be accompanied by rejection and denial as well as lack of familiarity. On the other hand, an immigrant who is said to be "smelling butter" is thought to be Americanized with the added connotation of having forgotten his Korean culture.

Thus, the making of Korean American culture in the United States turns out to be a complex, selective, contradictory, and ambiguous process, encompassing a broad spectrum of change. There is great deal of heterogeneity in the way each Korean American performs, practices, or interprets Korean and American culture. Often it is said that men do not change greatly from the way they behaved in Korea, whereas women change a lot in America. Also, it is often said that Americanization in the Korean immigrant family occurs most quickly in children. So, the younger generation and women tend to Americanize much faster than the older generation and men, which may create tension in the family. Perhaps educational level—particularly U.S. education—occupational category, and length of residence in the United States make a further difference. However, the way Koreans are Americanized is not limited to these factors.

There are three important angles from which to study the cultural production and reproduction of Korean American culture. The first angle is generation change: from immigrant parents to children, from an immigrant community to ethnic Americans. The second angle, which is the major focus of this article, is the way immigrants in their daily lives tear apart Korean culture and reconstruct it. In other words, they constantly use Korean culture as their cultural reference for digesting American culture. The third angle is identifying contradiction, confusion, and struggle. As immigrants understand implications of American culture, they develop a fear for their culture's future. As a consequence, they constantly draw from both American and Korean culture as a way of producing the third alternative, Korean immigrant culture. The only way to overcome this contradiction is to create this new alternative: redefining Korean as well as American culture.

With these approaches in mind and based on the interviewees' responses during fieldwork that was conducted, there are four main types of value judgments made by immigrants about Korean American culture. These value judgments occur over a wide spectrum of daily life, in matters of aesthetics; problems of virtue/morals/ethics/righteousness; concepts of time and space; language and speech patterns; behaviors and mannerisms; work relations; social and human relations; gender relations and sexuality; experiences with government agencies such as schools, police, and courts; patterns of consumption, leisure, and customs; and so forth. As they redefine their culture, or it is redefined, Korean immigrants employ their moral framework as a strategy for making sense of aspects of both cultures.[25] For Korean immigrants, what does not fit into existing rules or stereotypes is described as wrong, bad, dirty, or dangerous. For some Korean immigrant men, the phrase "Americanized Korean women" implies loose sexual morality.

Korean immigrants often refer to "drinking different water," when they change their residence. Accordingly, they view their new life in the United States as "drinking American water" (*mikukmulul masida*). However, they also distinguish between good or foul water. If one develops the reputation of "drinking foul water," it implies that one is not properly Americanized. Immigrants focus on the negative aspects of U.S. culture when they speak of those who are "thinly Americanized," compared with "truly deeply Americanized." Similarly, when they call someone a "true Korean," compared with someone who is "thinly Koreanized," they refer to the negative aspects of Korean culture.

Furthermore, many Korean immigrants talk about the "grafting" (*chobmok*) of Korean American culture. A Korean immigrant woman, an art therapist, wrote:

> In my hometown, there were many fruit trees, particularly persimmon trees, "kam namu." Early morning on summer days, I used to gather all the fallen persimmon flowers and wear it as a necklace. Later I used to eat one after another. A persimmon tree is not originally a persimmon tree. First, one should find a young koyom namu (a kind of persimmon tree, but considered inferior in quality to a true persimmon tree). Three years later, often in early spring, one cuts the stem of the young tree and grafts it to the real persimmon tree. I found the whole process to be poetic and mysterious, and it used to appear often in my drawings. Our immigrant life is exactly this process of grafting, chobmok.[26]

Korean immigrants see a persimmon tree and koyom tree as equivalent to Korean and American cultures, respectively, which through grafting can ultimately produce delicious persimmons. The underlying message is that one has to be careful to select good trees in order to complete the grafting process. In the grafting process, some immigrants add negative aspects of American culture to negative aspects of Korean culture. Others adopt negative aspects of American culture but keep positive aspects of Korean culture. Still others adopt positive aspects of Amer-

Figure 1
Four Types of Responses to the Formation of Korean American Culture

Maturity	Types
High	4 (ideal cosmopolitan)
Medium High	3 (confused or contradictory)
Medium Low	2 (confused or contradictory)
Low	1 (marginalized)

ican culture but lose positive attributes of Korean culture, and some adopt positive aspects of American culture and also keep positive aspects of Korean culture. Here, this moralistic and aesthetic way of understanding change can also include dimensions of either affirming or negating or adding to or forgetting each culture. As seen in Figure 1, the last type, type 4, can be called the cosmopolitan outlook, while the first category, type 1, refers to the estrangers, marginal people. *Cosmopolitanism* means a willingness to put the future of every culture at risk through the critical, sympathetic scrutiny of other cultures and the willingness to contemplate the creation of new affiliations.[27] These typologies describe the efforts of Korean immigrants to create a third culture that is neither Korean nor American. This emphasis is similar to the analysis of Ling-chi Wang, who looked at the two dominant concepts in the study of the Chinese diaspora: in the Western world, that of assimilation, or Anglo-conformity, and in China, the notion of loyalty.[28] Similarly, some Korean immigrants hope to liberate themselves from pressures of either conforming to U.S. society or remaining faithful to Korea. Others might come to the realization that being American does not disqualify one from being Korean. In selecting and reinterpreting certain aspects of Korean and/or American culture, immigrants do not define their lives according to clear lines of demarcation. Instead, these aspects combine to form an integrated whole.

By measuring the frequency of positive and negative attributes of Korean and American culture and continuing to consider cultural change in terms of grafting, we come up with a four-way classification (see Figure 2). These categories stem from Korean immigrants' efforts to make sense of their host American culture through references to their prior Korean experience. Like the Hegelian system of dialectics, they identify a thesis (Korean culture); an antithesis (American culture); and the synthesis (Korean American culture). However, this process does not occur smoothly. Immigrants are often torn apart by conflicting cultural repertoires. In addition, they often find these cultures contradictory.

It is important to note that most immigrants remain at the intermediate levels, halfway, *yolch'igi*: Americanized positive and Koreanized negative; or Americanized negative and Koreanized positive.[29] Although there are different levels of maturity, the developmental process is a continuum, evolving over time. More importantly, it is fluid, moving in different directions at different times.[30] It might

Figure 2
Four-Way Classification of the Formation of Korean American
Culture and "Grafting"

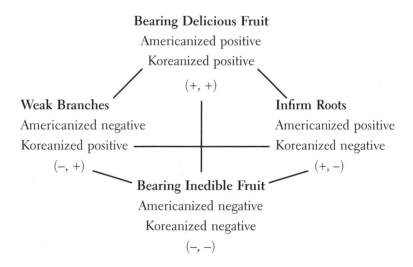

be expected that all immigrants move toward Americanization, but that is contingent on political and economic factors relating to the status of Koreans in American society.

For Koreans, becoming American has a special meaning that goes beyond holding U.S. citizenship. Many speak about their dream of material success in the idiom of Americanization. They see this as a process of joining the best parts of Korean culture with the best parts of American culture. The person who is "truly deeply Americanized" belongs to the highest stage of development. These idealized individuals have moved beyond the individualistic and selfish attitudes that many see in thinly Americanized immigrants. Immigrants' criticisms of fellow Koreans' behavior, and their contradictory views about positive and negative aspects of American behavior lead to an interesting social commentary about life in America.

BEARING INEDIBLE FRUIT

At worst, an immigrant loses, denies, or forgets the good aspects of Korean culture and adopts the bad aspects of American culture. For example, there are Koreans who are not able to speak either English or Korean fluently. Mrs. Kwon, who runs a Korean dress shop, sees this trend, particularly in young people. "Young ladies smoke and young guys have long hair and assume loose attitudes, adopting the American way. I wish that these were not identified as traits in Koreans by other ethnic groups. I want Koreans to keep their own culture."[31] It remains a major concern of many Koreans to retain their cultural tradition, including language and proper behavior between generations. Some immigrants fear that if they adopt some aspects of American culture, they will lose Korean culture in the process.

WEAK BRANCHES, "YAKHAN KAJI"

At the intermediate level of Americanization, Mr. Chun, a fish-market owner, explains how some Koreans tend to adopt only bad, egotistical, individualistic, and materialistic aspects of American culture.

> Some Koreans tend to be Americanized too soon. They pretend to be American as soon as they arrive in America adopting an arrogant attitude. Without considering any obligations to other Koreans, once they make some money, they try to isolate themselves by living in the suburbs. They do not think of the well-being of the second- or third-generation Koreans. That's why, despite my ten-year residence in America, I am reluctant to be Americanized.

Here, Mr. Chun suggests that even Americanized Koreans should be concerned about the future of the Korean American community. Similarly, Mr. Kim recognizes other Koreans' thin Americanization as he struggles to select only good aspects of the American culture for himself:

> As Koreans live longer in America, they also become individualistic. If someone is robbed, now Korean onlookers, like Americans, neither call the police nor help the person. While I was shopping yesterday, I thought about the serious competition among Koreans. This is sad; there were too many green groceries all on the same block. In my analysis, Koreans seem to become inhumane. As they live in a difficult situation, they learn to satisfy only their own accumulated wants.[32]

It should be noted that individualism, materialism, and competition have been deemed American traits. But the more that immigrants pursue their dream of owning small businesses, the more likely it is that they become materialistic, competitive, and individualistic—traits that conflict with their ideal of true Americanization.

Meanwhile, other immigrants strive to retain some positive elements from Korean culture. In the following statement, Mr. Pai, a Yellow Cab driver, critiques American society: "What is negative about American society is the dependence on government. Whereas Americans seem to be content with their lives, Koreans always try to have a better life, focusing on savings. In that sense, I want to keep working hard. I plan to run a grocery in two or three years."[33]

His statement reflects Koreans' unfamiliarity with the welfare state. South Korea has no such concept. Similarly, Ms. Hong, a twenty-three-year-old, college student wrote:

> I am proud of my three siblings. I am not saying that I have no conflict at all with them. Since I left Korea for Brazil at the age of eight, my younger sisters

remember little about Korea. In addition, they made many friends with Americans, mikuk saramdul,[34] so they became more Americanized. Therefore, I often try to talk to them after seeing movies together. "We are forever Koreans. Tradition or customs might change but never disappear. To remember and respect our hard work and the suffering of our parents, we need to be careful. Don't ever forget Korean etiquette and manners. Do you understand?" Then, my 16 and 19 year old sisters say, "Older sister, we are aware. Don't worry."[35]

To Ms. Choi, who works at a coffee shop, Americanization is just a term, not a reality. She points to racial and ethnic discrimination against Korean Americans and to the American concepts of no privacy and private property as major stumbling blocks to Koreans' Americanization.

No matter how long one has been in America, there seems to be a barrier in terms of race and culture. It is difficult for a Korean to go beyond this barrier. For instance, if one ignores our customs—if one kisses a lover in public, or if one eats in public without sharing food with others—one usually gets criticism. When Americans eat in public—and they often offer you some of their food—I am sure that they have a clear notion of "my food" and "your food," which we do not have.[36]

To her, Koreans neither can nor should be fully Americanized. They retain their Korean cultural baggage. Even if they try, they will not be accepted easily by Americans. She adds, "If Americans treat them (Koreans) as a new sort of American, it is only when it is in their interest, and no more. Many second-generation Korean Americans have problems when they enter college. They are not regarded as American, but they are not accepted by Koreans either.

INFIRM ROOTS, *HUNDULINUN PPURI*

The interviewees constantly compare different social systems and cultures, assessing pros and cons. In this typology, they are able to find some positive elements from the American culture while discarding some bad elements in Korean culture. Mr. Kwon, who arrived in America ten years ago, says, "The quality of education itself, I think, is better here. In Korea, emphasis is given to cramming; in America, although students don't listen to their teachers, there is more emphasis on creativity and using a different method of teaching."

Others agree that American culture has positive values, often associated with rational and liberal values, while Korean culture needs some reform. Aiming at becoming "truly deeply Americanized," Mr. Park states that he will lead a more American life in the future while discarding bad aspects of Korean culture:

I want to adopt the way of life Americans live, but more so internally than externally.[37] I came here with an understanding of Korean culture, having been educated in Korea. This would be a chance for me to correct the bad aspects of Korean culture, such as excessive formalism and Korean time [failure to be punctual]. For instance, in the past, if my nephew here ate food alone, I felt unsettled, because in Korea food should be shared, never eaten alone. But now I understand it well. Also, I now object if someone is not punctual.[38]

As far as the American family is concerned, many immigrants are struck by the differences in gender and generation relationships. To Mr. Nam, American family life is epitomized by its high divorce rate yet, he feels that, depending on their level of income, many American husbands and wives seem to enjoy life together a great deal. He also sees less discrimination between the sexes. "American women seem to make many important decisions—at least 60 percent of family decisions."[39]

BEARING DELICIOUS FRUIT

To many Korean immigrants "true Americanization" is multifaceted. They mean a state where one holds on to the positive aspects of Korean culture and, at the same time, incorporates the best aspects of American culture. As a goal, true Americanization comes after the realization of the dream of establishment of a small business. However, the quest for this dream brings out both negative aspects of Korean and American culture, especially individualism, materialism, and other traits. Only if one adopts American values selectively and critically can one be said to be truly Americanized.

It should also be emphasized that this creative process will not be complete until Korean immigrants are able to be critical of both Korean and American cultures. It is not easy to add American culture to Korean culture. Only when they review Korean culture critically and decide which aspects to keep and which to radically remove is there room for American culture and, subsequently, a new, Korean immigrant culture. Here, the Buddhist concept of emptiness can be helpful.[40] In other words, in order to gain something, one first has to empty oneself.

Therefore, the interviewees consider the political dimension crucial in their making of Korean American culture. For them, Americanization means becoming familiar with the American social structure, particularly the legal system—in other words, becoming integrated into the American system.[41] James, a Certified Public Accountant, observes, "(Initially) Koreans seem to be obsessed with the idea that they should not pay taxes in America. They thought of America as a free country, and, if at all possible, they want to avoid paying taxes. However, as children grow up and get educated, they realize their mistake, and are ready to pay taxes fully."[42] Mr. Hwang, a bakery owner, holds what is perhaps the most widespread view among established Korean immigrants. What Americanization means to him is a blend of the best values of each culture, striving for the ideal of "true Americanization":

In addition to understanding the laws here, we have to try to learn the language and the culture. For instance, if we do not do so, our children will not listen to what their parents say, and will become too individualistic. But we must not forget our own cultural tradition. We should not do any shameful things, and not forget Asian pride and virtues. However, as long as we live in America, we must also try to adapt ourselves to this new environment.[43]

A second-generation Korean American wrote about his own process of acculturation:

> My renewed love for Korean culture has simplified my life because I can focus my efforts on carving out a new bicultural identity. My new awareness of Korean American issues causes many internal conflicts. I have become overtly sensitive to the second-class treatment all minorities seem to tolerate. . . . I assert myself against misconceptions others have about Asian American males, and I begrudgingly let others know I am Asian and American. . . . I am always homesick. Despite my American citizenship, my disappearing Korean accent, and all my late-night humor derived from David Letterman, I did not feel like I was American. I wanted to go home, but I felt like I had no homeland. Korea was no longer home. I knew I was a foreigner the moment I was charged more for taxi fare. I realized I had to make America my home.[44]

Some definitely feel that Korean immigrants should be more interested in political life beyond their individual economic concerns. Mr. Pyo, a medical technician, worries about the lack of unity in the Korean community, especially compared to Chinatown, or to the Jewish and Italian communities. But he notes some progress in Haninhoe, "The Korean Association of Greater New York. We knew at first only for its name. After going through a period of transition, now it is getting in better shape, working on juvenile delinquency, senior citizen problems, and for contact with other ethnic groups."[45]

THE SUTURING OF CULTURES

However, the process of grafting does not tell much about immigrants' conceptions of morality and historicity. Here, perhaps, we need to shift our metaphor by referring to two different kinds of surgery: imbricating and suturing.[46] Imbricating implies having the edges overlapping in a regular arrangement like the scales of a fish, or sewing pieces of cloth, emphasizing plausible appearance only, regardless of function. In contrast, suturing (or articulating) is the process of joining by means of a seam of stitches. Theoreticians who argue for the suture model agree that it provides the agency whereby the subject emerges within discourse, and, at least ideally, takes up a position congruent with the existing cultural order.[47] The process of grafting seems to be more similar to imbricating than to suturing. Although Korean immigrants see culture making in terms of grafting, this scheme lacks a sense of historicity. However, their construction of culture also involves struggle, confusion, and contradiction in a creative, heterogeneous, and dynamic process.

CONCLUSION

Korean immigrants' world is an interconnected social space in which every day they figuratively travel back and forth between Korea and the United States. Korean/U.S. borderless social space emerged as a result of transnational capitalism, especially modern transportation and communication technologies rather than geographical contiguity, in this era of Pacific Rim affluence.

Within this setting, Korean immigrants see establishment of their own small businesses as a shortcut to realizing the American dream. In pursuit of anjong in their economic lives immigrants mobilize kin networks, participate in voluntary associations, and organize home life. Korean culture is retained and reconfigured selectively, in relation to historical, political, and economic conditions in the United States.

Thus, the making of Korean immigrant culture is historically situated, politically charged, and creative. Immigrants visualize this process in terms of tree grafting. As anthropologist Michael Taussig notes, many of our cultural explanations are based on body and biology.[48] For immigrants, Korean culture is selectively, and contradictorily, remembered and forgotten, transformed and reconfigured. Therefore, Korean immigrant cultural formation involves contradiction, hybridity, and heterogeneity—all aimed at creating a creole culture. As their main strategy, Korean immigrants rely on cultural and ideological criticism of both Korean and American cultures. Their strategy results in four different outcomes: bearing inedible fruit; grafting good Korean tree on to a bad American tree; grafting a bad Korean tree on to a good American tree; and bearing tasty fruit.

Why do we talk about Korean or American culture at all? Why is culture important? As Renato Rosaldo[49] notes, North American notions of the melting pot make immigration a rite of cultural stripping.[50] Moreover, for racial minorities, including Korean immigrants, culture represents their economic and political power in the United States, and hence culture becomes a weapon in helping them struggle to attain self-esteem and empowerment.

Unlike in Korea, in the multicultural society of America, Korean norms are consistently questioned and challenged. Korean immigrants have to change and adapt, and a new Korean American culture emerges in the process. Korean American culture is also greatly influenced by other cultures and will also eventually influence other cultures in America. Who knows? Perhaps one day Korean-American culture may integrate elements from Latino and African-American culture, and vice versa. By that time, we may envision Korean American culture as only having its origins in the Korean peninsula. Its development and elaboration will be in America.

NOTES

1. The progressive group was YKASEC (Young Korean American Service and Education Center).

2. Regionalism plays a strong role in Korean culture—in marriage, employment, and housing. For instance, in deciding on marriage partners, people from the southeastern part of Korea tend to avoid those from the southwestern part.

3. Similarly, Korean immigrants develop cultural constructions of generation identity. For instance, one-third of the Koreans in America are said to be 1.5 generation (those who came to the United States as children or teenagers). In addition, Koreans further distinguish 1.3, 1.7, and 2.5 generation Korean Americans. These distinctions have much to do with characteristics of Korean immigration history, each individual's immigrant experience, and their political participation in U.S. society.

4. In this article, I use the terms "Korean immigrants" and "Korean Americans" interchangeably. Although *Korean American* generally refers to people born in the United States, I expand its usage to Korean immigrants. My usage reflects the way Korean immigrants use the term, which might be due to the small number of Koreans born in the United States (less than 13 percent).

5. I collected narratives through the cultural model method on the topic "being and becoming American." Naomi Quinn and Dorothy Holland, "Culture and Cognition" in Dorothy Holland and Naomi Quinn eds, Cultural Models in Language and Thought," Cambridge: Cambridge Univ. Press, 3–42.

6. On the one hand, I felt tension due to the ways that Koreans are Americanized in the United States. For instance, I remember feeling awkward when my friend insisted that I dress more formally—i.e., that I wear suits—as if that were the proper dress of Americanized Koreans in the States. However, in order to conduct research on the Korean immigrant community, I tried to fit into their definition of ideal behavior.

7. Donald Nonini and Ong Aihwa, "Introduction: Chinese Transnationalism as an Alternative Modernity," in *Edges of Empire: Culture and Identity in Modern Chinese Transnationalism* (Lanham, MD: Rowman & Littlefield, forthcoming), 1–54.

8. See Khachig Tololyan, "The Nation-State and Its Others: In Lieu of a Preface," *Diaspora* 1 (1991): 3–7.

9. David Harvey, *The Condition of Postmodernity: An Enquiry into the Origins of Cultural Change* (Oxford, England, and Cambridge, MA: Basil Blackwell, 1989).

10. Ibid., 147.

11. Paul Ong, Edna Bonocich, and Lucie Cheng, "The Political Economy of Capitalist Restructuring and the New Asian Immigration" *The New Asian Immigration in Los Angeles and Global Restructuring*, ed. Paul Ong, Edna Bonacich, and Lucie Cheng, 270 (Philadelphia: Temple Univ. Press, 1994): 1–31.

12. In this sense, Korean immigrants will have to deal with gender discrimination, national chauvinism, and ethnocentrism in Korea as well as racism and sexism in the United States.

13. Ulf Hannerz, *Cultural Complexity: Studies in the Social Organization of Meaning* (New York: Columbia Univ. Press, 1992), 264.

14. Lisa Lowe, "Heterogeneity, Hybridity, Multiplicity: Marking Asian American Differences," *Diaspora* 1 (1991): 27.

15. Andrew Apter. "Herskovits's Heritage: Rethinking Syncretism in the African Diaspora," *Diaspora* 1 (1991): 251.

16. Eric Gable, Richard Handler, and Anna Lawson, "On the Uses of Relativism: Fact, Conjecture, and Black and White Histories at Colonial Williamsburg," *American Ethnologist* 19 (1992): 802.

17. Lauria-Perricelli Antonio, "Towards a Transnational Perspective on Migration: Closing Remarks" in *Towards a Transnational Perspective on Migration: Race, Class, Ethnicity, and Nationalism Reconsidered*, ed. Nina Glick-Schiller, ed. Linda Basch, Christina Blanc-Szanton, 251–258 (New York: The New York Academy of Sciences, 1992).

18. Stewart, Ella, "Ethnic Cultural Diversity: An Interpretive Study of Cultural Differences and Communication Styles Between Korean Merchants/Employees and Black Patrons in South Los Angeles," (master's thesis, California State Univ., Los Angeles, 1989), 17–19.

19. I do not deny that there is inequality in Asian societies; however, I find this statement problematic, because it stereotypes and oversimplifies Asian cultures.

20. Won Moo Hurh and Kwang Chung Kim, *Korean Immigrants in America: A Structural Analysis of Ethnic Confinement and Adhesive Adaptation* (London: Associated Univ. Press, 1984).

21. Hannerz, *Cultural Complexity*, 262.

22. For further discussion on this ideology of *anjong*, see Kyeyoung Park, *The Korean American Dream* (Ithaca, NY: Cornell University Press, 1997).

23. Hurh and Kim, *Korean Immigrants in America*.

24. Besides eating habits, there are many other ways to measure Americanization; for example, mannerisms and expressions. If an immigrant shrugs his shoulder and says, "I can't help it," or, "God bless you" when someone coughs, he is described as being Americanized.

25. Mary Douglas, *Purity and Danger: An Analysis of the Concepts of Pollution and Taboo* (London: ARK Paperbacks, 1966).

26. Kyeyoung Park, "The Cultivation of Korean Immigrants on American Soil: The Discourse on Cultural Construction" *Yosong Ch'ongu*, Korean American Women for Action 3 (Spring 1986).

27. David A. Hollinger, *Postethnic America: Beyond Multiculturalism* (New York: Basic Books, 1995), 83.

28. Wang, Ling-chi, "The Structure of Dual Domination: Toward a Paradigm for the Study of the Chinese Diaspora in the U.S.," *Amerasia Journal* 21 (1995): 149–170.

29. Generally, immigrants strive to reach the ideal state of "Americanized positive" and "Koreanized positive." If they cannot, they try to avoid the worst situation—that of losing good aspects of Korean culture and adopting only the bad aspects of American culture.

30. Although it is not clear how an immigrant moves in one direction, to what degree he or she has become established in the United States certainly makes a big difference. However, anjong is not the only factor affecting change.

31. Interview with Mrs. Kwon.

32. Interview with Mr. Kim.

33. Interview with Mr. Pai.

34. Many Korean immigrants refer to Americans as white Americans. When they talk about African Americans, they invoke the racial category of black.

35. Park, "Cultivation of Korean Immigrants," *Yosong Ch'ongu II*, (Spring 1986).

36. Interview with Ms. Choi.

37. Here, external adoption refers to superficial or cosmetic change, whereas inner change is more fundamental change, for instance, moral innovation.

38. Interview with Mr. Park.

39. Interview with Mr. Nam

40. I owe this insight to Dr. Cho Manchul, Korean psychiatrist.

41. In this sense, acculturation is regarded as assimilation—that is, integration into the American legal system in terms of knowledge of and participation in the tax and welfare systems as well familiarity with police, court, and government.

42. Interview with James, a Certified Public Accountant.

43. Interview with Mr. Hwang, a baker.

44. Bobby Kim, *Korean Journal* (September 1993): 20.

45. Interview with Mr. Pyo.

46. I owe this insight to Mr. Lee Manwoo, Korean sociologist.

47. Kaja Silverman, *The Subject of Semiotics* (New York: Oxford Univ. Press, 1983), 236.

48. Michael Taussig, *The Nervous System* (New York: Routledge, 1992).

49. Renato Rosaldo, *Culture and Truth: The Remaking of Social Analysis* (Boston: Beacon Press, 1989).

50. The immigrants, or at any rate their children or grandchildren, supposedly become absorbed into the dominant culture that erases their tradition—autobiography, history, heritage, language, and other parts of their so-called cultural baggage (Rosaldo, *Culture and Truth*, 210).

BIBLIOGRAPHICAL ESSAY

During the past two decades there has been an unprecedented outpouring of literature on Korean Americans, much of it written by scholars of that ethnicity. The most thorough overview of the Korean American experience is Won Moon Hurh, *The Korean Americans* (Westport, CT: Greenwood Press, 1998). It can be supplemented with several other studies, most of which bear the same prosaic title: Brian Lehrer, *The Korean Americans* (New York: Chelsea House Publishers, 1996); Lauren Lee, *Korean Americans* (New York: Marshall Cavendish, 1995); Ann Hagen Griffiths, *The Korean Americans* (New York: Facts on File, 1992); Nichol Bryan, *Korean Americans* (Edina, MN: Abdo Publications, 2004); Alexandra Bandon, *Korean Americans* (New York: New Discovery, 1994); Tamara Orr, *The Korean Americans* (Philadelphia: Mason Crest, 2003), and Bong-Yuon Choy, *Koreans in America* (Chicago: Nelson Hall, 1979). Two very recent studies provide important new insights: Sheila Smith Noonan, *Korean Immigration* (Philadelphia: Mason Crest Publishers, 2004) and Ilpyong Kim, ed., *Korean-Americans: Past, Present, and Future* (Elizabeth, NJ: Hollym International Corp., 2004).

Several other studies have attempted to provide insights into the processes of acculturation and assimilation that have and are affecting Korean immigrants and their progeny. One of the most detailed analyses is Won Moo Hurh and Kwang Chung Kim, *Korean Immigrants in America: A Structural Analysis of Ethnic Confinement and Adhesive Adaptation* (London: Associated Universities Press, 1984). See also Won Moo Hurh, "Toward a Korean-American Ethnicity: Some Theoretical Models," *Ethnic and Racial Studies* 3 (1980): 444–464; *Assimilation of the Korean Minority in the United States* (Elkins Park, PA: Philip Jaison Foundation, 1977); and *Comparative Study of Korean Immigrants in the United States: A Typological Approach* (San Francisco: R and E Research Associates, 1977). A more recent effort is Nazli Kibria, *Becoming Asian American: Second Generation Chinese and Korean American Identities* (Baltimore: Johns Hopkins Univ. Press, 2002). Particularly useful in understanding the adaptive process is Moon H. Jo,

Korean Immigrants and the Challenge of Adjustment (Westport, CT: Greenwood Press, 1999). Using the Korean-descended population of Hawaii as his study group, Peter Hyun, *In the New World: The Making of a Korean American* (Honolulu: Univ. of Hawaii Press, 1995), finds some significant differences in the speed and degree of assimilation from those scholars who have concentrated on the Koreans who have settled on the United States mainland.

Since Hawaii was the area of first settlement for the earliest immigrants from Korea, Myongsup Shin and Daniel B. Lee, eds., *Korean Immigrants in Hawaii: A Symposium on Their Background History, Acculturation, and Public Policy Issues* (Honolulu: Univ. of Hawaii Press, 1978) is indispensable reading. So too is Brenda L. Kwon, *Beyond Ke'eaumoku: Koreans, Nationalism, and Local Culture in Hawaii* (New York: Garland Publishing, 1999). See also several studies by Wayne Patterson, especially *The Ilse: First-Generation Korean Immigrants in Hawaii, 1903–1973* (Honolulu: Univ. of Hawaii Press, 2000) and *The Korean Frontier in America: Immigration to Hawaii, 1886–1910* (Honolulu: Univ. of Hawaii Press, 2000). Those seeking a variety of analyses on the adaptation process should consult Hyung-Chan Kim, ed., *Korean Diaspora: Historical and Sociological Studies of Korean Immigration and Assimilation in North America* (Santa Barbara, CA: ABC-Clio Press, 1977). Another vital perspective is provided by Chang-soo Lee, "The United States Immigration Policy and the Settlement of Koreans in America," *Korea Observer* 6 (1975): 412–451. The economic dimensions of recent Korean immigration to the United States is examined thoroughly in Paul Ong, Edna Bonacich, and Lucie Cheng, eds., *The New Asian Immigration in Los Angeles and Global Restructuring* (Philadelphia: Temple University Press, 1994). Although Hawaii and California have been the principal destination of Korean immigrants, there are sizeable settlements in other large cities, especially New York and Chicago. See, for example, Kyu Park, *Korean Americans in Chicago* (Chicago: Arcadia Press, 2003) and Kyeyoung Park, *The Korean American Dream: Immigrants and Small Business in New York City* (Ithaca, NY: Cornell University Press, 1997).

One of the biggest developments in Korean American communities has been the change in the status of women. See Eui-Young Yu and Earl H. Phillips, eds., *Korean Women in Transition: At Home and Abroad* (Los Angeles: California State Univ., 1987). For a highly positive interpretation of that development in the early years of immigration, see "Korean Women of America: From Subordination to Partnership, 1903–1930," *Amerasia Journal* 11 (1984): 1–28. See also Alice Y. Chai, "Korean Women in Hawaii, 1903–1945," Nobuya Tsuchida, ed., *Asian and Pacific American Experiences: Women's Perspectives* (Minneapolis: Asian/Pacific American Learning Resource Center, 1982); Haeyun Juliana Kim, "Voices from the Shadows: The Lives of Korean War Brides," *Amerasia Journal* 17 (1991): 15–30; and Mary Paik Lee, *Quiet Odyssey: A Pioneer Korean Woman in America* (Seattle: Univ. of Washington, 1990).

One of the most important results of immigration to the United States has been the outpouring of a distinctive Korean American literature. See, for example, Kyhan Lee, "Younghill Kang and the Genesis of Korean-American Literature," *Korea Journal* 31 (1991): 63–78; Elaine H. Kim and Eui-Young Yu, *East to America: Korean American Life Stories,* (New York: New Press, 1996); and Elaine H. Kim, *Echoes upon Echoes: New Korean American Writings* (New York: Asian American Writers' Workshop, 2002). Another result has been tensions in the area of religion. See especially Ho-Youn Kwon, Kwang Chung Kim, and R. Stephen Warner, *Korean Americans and their Religions: Pilgrims and*

Missionaries from a Different Shore (University Park: Pennsylvania State Univ. Press, 2001) and Sharon A. Suh, *Being Buddhist in a Christian World: Gender and Community in a Korean American Temple* (New Haven: Yale Univ. Press, 2000).

One of the most unfortunate outcomes of immigration to the United States has been the developing antipathy between Korean shopkeepers and African Americans in the inner cities of large metropolitan areas. That phenomenon has been analyzed from a number of perspectives in Molefi Kete Asante and Eungjun Min, eds., *Socio-cultural Conflict Between African American and Korean American* (Lanham, MD: Univ. Press of America, 2000). Focusing on the second largest Korean American community in the nation, Claire Jean Kim, *Bitter Fruit: The Politics of Black–Korean Conflict in New York City* (New Haven: Yale Univ. Press, 2000), examines an important aspect of that continuing antipathy. A more positive outlook for the future is Patrick J. Joyce, *No Fire Next Time: Black-Korean Conflicts and the Future of America's Cities* (Ithaca, NY: Cornell Univ. Press, 2003).

MEXICAN AMERICANS

Matt S. Meier

For a century, Mexicanos have been taking back the borderlands acquired forcibly by the Yanquis in 1848. Not with force or warfare, but slowly and surely with the enduring and long-suffering patience of farm workers, gardeners, sweatshop workers, housemaids, waiters, barbers, and shopkeepers.

Professor Lawrence Kinnaird
Department of History
University of California at Berkeley
Conversation with the Author, 1954

Today, half a century later, Professor Kinnaird most certainly would have added "and with the leadership of congressmen, businessmen, lawyers, diplomats, writers, poets, artists, and others who have become a highly visible part of American culture. And by mere numbers." According to the 2000 census today there are over 20 million people of Mexican cultural background living in the United States. The overwhelming majority are immigrants who arrived during the 1900s, and their children. Some, on the other hand, have been here, in situ as it were, before the Southwest became part of the United States. They form the only ethnic group that came into the United States as a conquered people, a circumstance that continues to affect Mexican Americans today. They are to be found in all fifty states. The great majority is located in the Southwest, but today there are also sizeable numbers in Illinois, Kansas, Florida, Washington, and Michigan. Referred to as Mexican Americans or Chicanos, they are part of a broader ethnic classification that is sometimes applied to them and are variously labeled *la raza* (the race), U.S. Latinos, and Hispanic Americans, that is, people whose culture is in part derived from the Iberian Peninsula. Racially, their makeup varies widely. Although their ethnicity is not determined by racial makeup, certainly the racial aspect is a conspicuous element in their ethnic identification.

The 1848 Treaty of Guadalupe Hidalgo created Mexican Americans as an identifiable group within the U.S. population, but their formative history, of course, goes back far beyond that date. The story of their experience falls readily into five broad and chronologically unequal periods: 1540–1848, three centuries of Spanish and Mexican rule; 1848–1910, Treaty of Guadalupe Hidalgo to the Mexican Revolution; 1910–1940, two decades of heavy U.S. immigration, as well as the great repatriation of the 1930s; 1940–1965, World War II and the postwar period; 1965 to the present, the Chicano Movement and continuing heavy immigration to the United States. The early Mexican experience, taking place at the junction of Mexico's northern frontier and the U.S. western frontier, began in antagonism, escalated to conflict, and ended in conquest, subjugation, and subordination.

COLONIAL

This essay begins in 1540, with the search for mineral wealth in Nueva España's (Mexico's) far northern reaches by the Spanish explorer Francisco Vasquez de Coronado. However, colonization did not follow in the steps of the first explorers, mainly because they discovered no precious metals, as they had hoped, or other incentives for settlement. Only toward the end of the 1500s, after learning of England's reported presumed activity on the northern frontier, did Spain begin to encourage colonization in order to safeguard its claims to the land. Francis Drake's voyage up the west coast of South America and across the Pacific Ocean in the late 1570s led Spain to believe he had found the long sought-after Northwest Passage, or Straits of Anian, as the Spaniards called the hoped-for sea route through North America to Asia. As a result of Drake's voyage and renewed rumors of mineral wealth, further reconnoitering was undertaken, and in 1598 Juan de Oñate led an expedition that ultimately resulted in the permanent occupation of what became known as Nuevo Mexico. However, no rich mineral deposits were found and the fancied English threat faded, leaving physical control and missionary activity among the Pueblo Indians as the principal motives for continuing settlement of an area so isolated and so far from central Mexico. Santa Fe was founded in 1610. Nearly three quarters of a century later, in 1680, an uprising among the Pueblos forced the settlers out of Nuevo Mexico south to El Paso del Norte (Ciudad Juarez today) on the Rio Grande. A decade and a half later Spain had regained control of the area. In the succeeding century, population growth was steady but limited to the Rio Grande valley because of aggressive raiding by Apache and Comanche Indians. In 1821, at the end of the colonial period, Nuevo Mexico had by far the largest northern frontier area population, with about 40,000 settlers, nearly all of whom were engaged in animal husbandry and irrigated farming.

In adjacent Arizona, a very limited colonization developed. Settlement was in large measure a result of Jesuit priest Eusibio Kino's missionary activities at the end of the 1600s. However, the discovery of some silver deposits in the next century attracted a few settlers. In 1776, a presidio was established at Tucson to protect the sparse settlements from foraging Apaches. The rugged area north of Tucson remained largely unexplored, the habitat of nomadic Indians. By the end of the colonial period, Arizona had only about 2,000 settlers, who were nearly all located in small villages along the Santa Cruz River, close to the present border, and maintained close economic and social ties to adjacent Sonora.

Mexican settlement in California and Texas developed a bit later and followed a slightly different pattern. In these two areas, it was the genuine threat of foreign intrusion that initiated settlement. Sieur de La Salle's 1682 expedition down the Mississippi River and his fort on Matagordo Bay two years later heralded French attempts to settle in the East Texas area. In response to French trading and colonizing activities, Spain began to establish missions on the Neches River beginning in 1690. Under nearly constant assault from Comanches, the missions had very limited success, and settlers were few. The founding of a mission and presidio at San Antonio de Bexar in 1718 gave the faltering colony a more secure base. However, Franco-Spanish rivalry in eastern Texas continued until Spain acquired Louisiana from France by treaty in 1763. At the end of the colonial period, the Tejano population was less than 3,000.

Alta California settlement was initiated in the second half of the 1700s because of activity in the area by Russia and England. Their interest in the area led to the so-called Sacred Expedition from Baja California, headed by Gaspar de Portola and Junipero Serra. In 1769, Serra founded the first Alta California mission at San Diego, and the twenty-one missions he and his successors subsequently established came to dominate the province both culturally and economically. Partly because of its extreme isolation from the Mexican heartland and the difficulty of communication by both land and sea, the area attracted only a limited numbers of settlers, most of whom established themselves in coastal ranchos and pueblos. By the end of the colonial period, California boasted a population of some 3,000.

The settlement of Mexico's far northern frontier spanned more than two centuries of the colonial era, a period of cultural adjustment and change and of racial and ethnic intermixture both in central Mexico and on the frontier. Except for a handful of leaders, the colonists were virtually all of mixed blood. The four areas of frontier settlement developed in isolation from both the Mexican heartland and each other. Because of Spain's mercantile policy, there was only limited trade with foreign nations, adding to the northern frontier's isolation. In each region, the settlers brought with them distinct cultural baggage that was adapted to frontier environments which spanned from the Gulf of Mexico to the Pacific Ocean. At first, subsistence agriculture was necessarily the predominant activity. However, diverse geographic and economic conditions determined how the individual areas developed and molded the settlers' lives. Nuevo Mexico and Arizona developed primarily around missionary activity and the search for minerals.

In Texas, cattle raising became preeminent, while in California, mission agriculture created and perfected by the Franciscan friars had, by the end of the colonial period, become as important as stock raising. All four areas of Mexico's northern frontier offered settlers a relaxed social system and economic opportunity.

INDEPENDENCE

In 1821, Mexico established its independence from Spain, a change that aroused little passion on its northern frontier because of limited connection to the Mexican heartland. Government oversight, which was quite loose and limited under Spain, soon deteriorated even further as political leaders in the capital of the new country quarreled about the kind of government to create: monarchy or republic, and when they decided on a republic, federalist or centrist. By 1823, Emperor Agustin I (de Iturbide) had been ousted, and chaos developed as liberal federalists and centrist conservatives struggled for control of the new republican government. By the mid-1830s, after more than a decade of political wrangling and sixteen presidencies, centrists took control of the national government.

Meanwhile, Mexico's frontier settlements received little or no attention and were left largely to making their own decisions in solving their problems, a situation to which they had become accustomed and that now they came to prefer. The new government's scrapping of Spain's mercantile policies brought U.S. traders following in the wake of earlier fur trappers and mitigating the area's extreme isolation. The Santa Fe Trail, which started in Missouri, gave U.S. merchants relatively easy access to Nuevo Mexico, and the Pacific Ocean provided a longer and indirect but usable route to California. In reality, by 1821, Alta California was virtually independent of Mexico City. In both areas, U.S. traders and trappers became residents; some individuals, like Kit Carson, intermarried, applied for and received Mexican citizenship, obtained land grants, and adapted to Mexican culture. In Texas, on the other hand, small cotton planters brought along their slaves and settled in colonies made possible by government *empresario* land lords grants. By 1830, Texas counted about 4,000 Mexicanos and 15,000 largely unassimilated Anglos who owned 2,000 slaves.

In Texas, considerable cultural and political differences between Anglos and Mexicans created a basis for potential conflict. The Americans correctly viewed Mexico's outlawing of slavery in 1829 by executive decree as aimed at them, and they protested strongly. As a result, the decree was suspended for Texas, but the next year the government issued a law prohibiting the importation of slaves and further Anglo immigration. In 1834, Mexican president Antonio Lopez de Santa Anna's abolition of Mexico's Liberal Constitution of 1824 and his "conversion" to centralism led to unrest and uprisings in all border regions, north and south. The revolt in Texas was the most successful. At first, its leaders, Mexican and Anglo, demanded only a return to the local political authority provided for by the 1824 constitution. Santa Anna's efforts to suppress this opposition to his centralism included his siege and victory at the Alamo, where Tejano and Anglo defenders died. Overconfident as a result of his Alamo victory, Santa Anna was taken prisoner in the subsequent battle of San Jacinto and was forced to sign the Treaty of Velasco, which ended hostilities and accepted Texas independence. The government in Mexico rejected this treaty that had been made under duress and for the next few years continued ineffectual military efforts to regain control of Texas. In this situation, many Tejanos found a position of neutrality no longer tenable, suffering discrimination from both Anglo civilians and Mexican soldiers. Meanwhile, Anglo leaders of the de facto Texas republic pushed for annexation to the United States. Beginning in the mid-1830s the United States began to show great interest in acquiring Alto California as part of its Manifest Destiny. As the United States and Mexico drifted inexorably toward war, in 1841 Texas leaders sent a military-merchant expedition to Santa Fe in an effort to tap the trade on the Santa Fe trail and to persuade the Nuevomexicanos to join them in independence. The expedition was a complete fiasco. In March 1845, Texas's admission to the Union by the U.S. Congress brought mounting tensions between Mexico and the United States to a first climax.

The focus of conflict then shifted to the issue of the boundaries of Texas, which claimed the Rio Grande all the way from southern Colorado to the Gulf of Mexico. When President James K. Polk's efforts in 1845 to buy Nuevo Mexico and California failed, he sent troops under General Zachary Taylor into the Nueces Triangle, an area near the mouth of the Rio Grande that was claimed by both Mexico and Texas. As the result of a clash between Mexican and U.S. forces in the disputed territory, on May 11, 1846, the United States declared that a state of war with Mexico existed. While General Taylor won a series of victories in northeastern Mexico, Colonel Stephen Kearny, invading via the Santa Fe trail with 1,500 troops, took over Nuevo Mexico with little resistance at first. However, latent hostility soon surfaced, and an aborted revolt in late December was followed by the Taos rebellion of January 19, 1847, which was put down bloodily by U.S. troops. In Alta California, American forces, aided by "Bear Flagger" (Republic of Texas) support, similarly encountered limited initial opposition. However, unnecessarily harsh controls in southern California and insensitivity to cultural differences soon led to an uprising there, which was suppressed by American forces after four months of fighting. In both California and New Mexico, some opposed the U.S. takeover and some welcomed it; many, probably a majority, remained indifferent and uninvolved.

Elsewhere also, the war went badly for Mexico. The country was still seriously divided by partisan bickering. Early in 1847, General Winfield Scott landed 10,000 men at Veracruz and by mid-September had captured Mexico City, despite gallant last-ditch resistence by the "Ninos Heroes," six young cadets from the National Military Academy. The ensuing Treaty of Guadalupe Hidalgo, signed in February and ratified in May 1848 by the two governments, achieved the territorial objectives of Polk's policy of expansion of the United States' Manifest Destiny. In exchange for $15 million, the United States acquired title to Texas with the Rio Grande boundary she claimed, plus approximately one-third of Mexico's national territory, comprising the present states of California, New Mexico, Arizona, Nevada, Utah, and parts of adjacent states. A key document in Mexican American history, the treaty gave the 80,000 inhabitants of the area a year to decide whether they wished to keep their Mexican citizenship or become U.S. nationals with all the rights of eventual citizenship. They were guaranteed freedom of worship as well as rights to their fixed and moveable property. The first guarantee was broadly observed; the second was not. By the end of the century, the political rights of most Mexican Americans had largely been lost, and a legacy of conflict and rancor had been created.

MEXICAN AMERICANS

After the signing of the Treaty of Guadalupe Hidalgo, the new American nationals had the difficult task of adjusting to the Anglo economic and political system. In Texas, where Anglos had become an overwhelming majority except for San Antonio, Laredo, and Brownsville, Mexican Americans quickly lost the political power they needed to protect their rights. When Texas was admitted to the Union in 1845, Jose Antonio Navarro was the sole la raza delegate representing the interests of Tejanos in the state's constitutional convention. At only about 5 percent of the state's population by 1850, Tejanos were highly susceptible at the polls to the problem of language barriers, economic dependence, and Anglo intimidation. In some areas, especially upstate, many were denied the vote on racial grounds, a practice legalized in many counties in the 1890s by the institution of so-called white primaries. In 1902, Texas instituted a poll tax that discouraged the poor from voting, and by the beginning of the twentieth century, a large majority of Tejanos had become effectively disenfranchised. They reacted to political and economic abuse with resistance and confrontation, sometimes violent, as in the raids led by Juan Cortina at the end of the 1850s and the Salt War near El Paso in 1877. Their difficulties were intensified by the law enforcement of the Texas Rangers, who continued on into the twentieth century their regular practice of brutal treatment of suspected Mexicano miscreants. Generally, Mexican Americans in Texas found it extremely difficult, if not impossible, to obtain even minimal justice.

After the Guadalupe Hidalgo Treaty, Mexican Americans continued to create organizations for their mutual welfare, participated in politics where possible, and struggled to retain their lands. As Anglos poured into the former Mexican territory, land ownership became the dominant theme throughout the borderlands. Most of the nearly 80,000 Mexicans who became American by the Treaty of Guadalupe Hidalgo owned land; some held vast tracts granted for grazing by the governments of Spain and Mexico. They were forced to fight interminable law suits that required the hiring of Anglo lawyers whose fees contributed to their impoverishment. Still, by the late 1800s, they had lost most of it. The great cattle boom of the 1870s and 1880s and the spread of cotton culture exerted further pressures on Texas lands. The Cortina raids of the 1850s were in part a response to loss of land to Anglos.

In California, land ownership problems were more complex. There, in addition to missing and disputable records, problems were complicated by the large number of squatters who had come initially to get rich in the goldfields and had turned to farming. Their pressure on the government was an important factor leading to the 1851 creation of a federal Board of Land Commissioners whose basic tenet on land ownership was essentially "Guilty until proven innocent." Nevertheless, 614 claims out of 813 filed with the board ultimately were confirmed. However, the heavy expenses of lawyers, personal expenses in pursuit of their claims, loans at ruinous interest rates, high land taxes, and mortgage foreclosures still led to loss of lands and of Californio influence by the end of the century. In New Mexico, the story was similar; because many land grants were very old, only 20 percent of the Hispano grantees were able to prove title. Their loss of lands was a factor in the violence of the Gorras Blancas (White Cops or dispossessed land owners) in the 1880s and the politics of the People's Party in the 1890s. Both efforts to protect land rights were ultimately futile.

The entire history of the confirmation of Spanish and Mexican land grants is one of misunderstanding, greed, chicanery, and outright despoliation that violated the declared intent of the Treaty of Guadalupe Hidalgo. It created a hardship on both Mexican Americans and on Anglo newcomers, increased the hostility between them, and encouraged social banditry, particularly in California and Texas. By 1900, Mexican Americans had become a small minority, a majority of whom were reduced to second-class citizenship, in some measure because they had lost their lands to Anglo newcomers.

In California, the gold rush had brought in about 333,000 Anglos by 1850, reducing Spanish speakers to some 15 percent of the state's population. Twenty years later, they accounted for about 4 percent. Although eight of the forty-eight delegates to the state's constitutional convention in 1849 were elite Californios who worked to safeguard la raza's interests, reduced population and loss of lands led in turn to loss of political clout. In the northern mining regions, robbing, beating, and lynching Mexicanos was routine; in 1850 the legislature passed the Foreign Miners' Tax law, which was applied to citizen Californios as well as foreigners; and five years later, the legislature passed the Anti-Vagrancy Act, commonly known as the Greaser Law, and also failed to provide funds for the translation of laws into Spanish, a provision of the 1894 constitution. Two years later, delegate Miguel Dominguez was barred from testifying in a San Francisco court because he was a dark-skinned mestizo.

In southern California, Spanish speakers were able to retain a degree of local control, largely the result of the influx of Latino gold seekers and continuing immigration from Mexico. However, even in the south, the Anglo settlers that the transcontinental railroads had brought in the last quarter of the nineteenth century soon dominated politics and overwhelmed all but limited traces of Mexicano culture. In Arizona, considerable trade with the adjacent Mexican state of Sonora and a common enemy, the Apaches, created conditions for greater interethnic cooperation until the 1880s. Except for isolated pockets, elsewhere in the Southwest Mexicano culture was sustained only minimally by Spanish-language newspapers, parochial groups like the Penitentes in New Mexico, the spreading mutualista (mutual aid or benevolent) societies, various associations such as livestock groups and labor unions, and increasing immigration from Mexico toward the end of the century.

PRE-1965 IMMIGRATION

At the end of the nineteenth century, just as Anglo in-migration seemed about to completely overwhelm Mexicano culture in the Borderlands, early stages of what was to become a massive tide of Mexican immigration developed. In the 1880s, some migrant Mexicans became cotton pickers, replacing sharecroppers and tenants on farms in north-central Texas, while others found work in the new lettuce fields of the Winter Garden area. In the first decades of the twentieth century, the volume of this immigration rapidly took off as a result of deteriorating economic conditions in Mexico and its subsequent violent 1910 Revolution, and because of labor needs of the United States during World War I and after 1924 quota legislation limited European immigration. Between 1917 and mid-1920, some 150,000 raza workers came into the country, partly as the result of extensive recruitment in Mexico. Later in the 1920s, another million, more or less, crossed the border. By 1930, after some thousands had returned to Mexico as a result of the incipient U.S. Depression, the Mexico-born population still exceeded 600,000, according to the Census Bureau.

Immigration to the United States and the associated struggle to be accepted into the U.S. mainstream have been constant, related themes in the Mexican American experience. Mexican Americans have been doubly affected by immigration: first as immigrants themselves and, second, as the sector of American society most affected by further immigration. Except for the 1930s, every decade of the twentieth century has seen a sizeable immigration from Mexico. For a variety of reasons, but principally economic and political, thousands moved across the border into an environment that was culturally and topographically familiar to them. Their Mexican ancestors had founded Santa Fe in 1610, initiating four centuries of trekking northward from central Mexico. Only a small percentage of today's Mexican American population is descended from these early settlers. Most are descendants of twentieth-century immigrants who, like their predecessors, came primarily in response to economic opportunity in the Borderlands and its absence in Mexico for the middle and lower classes. As historian Oscar Martinez has written, "The twenty million Mexicans and Mexican Americans living in the United States today are predominantly a product of post-1900 growth. One large portion traces its presence here to migratory flows from Mexico between 1910 and 1930, an even larger immigrant contingent entered between 1940 and 1965, and the largest cohort by far arrived during the years 1965 to 2000."

The incorporation of the Southwest into the national economy by the early twentieth century created a need for a large supply of labor. The flood tide that began at the dawn of the twentieth century was made up almost entirely of poor, landless farmhands and unskilled workers with little or no formal education, plus a few artisans and clerks. Up to 1900, the immigrants were employed mostly in harvest agriculture, ranching, mining, and railroad construction and maintenance. Because of their low social and economic position, they were viewed with mixed feelings by second- and third-generation Mexican Americans, many of whom reacted by stressing the Spanish roots of their cultural heritage. In the first decades of the 1900s, following ancient migratory patterns, Mexican agricultural workers crossed into Texas in increasing numbers. The migrants thought of themselves as sojourners, having the full intention of returning every year to their beloved *patria chica* (little nation) after the harvest was over. Ultimately, many remained, presenting Mexican American communities of new infusions with peasant culture.

Of the three principal areas of the Southwest—Texas, California, and New Mexico—only New Mexico was not completely overwhelmed by the heavy immigrant influx between 1900 and 1930. As a result, in New Mexico the traditional Hispano culture of the Apodaca, Martinez, Montoya, and other elite families, as well as of isolated rural folk, remained largely unaltered. As the immigrant wave lapped at New Mexico at the beginning of the twentieth century, Nuevomexicano elites began stressing their Spanish heritage by identifying themselves as Hispanos or Hispanic Americans in order to set themselves apart from the newcomers of low social and economic status. Elsewhere, in the subregions of Texas and California, basic Mexican American culture patterns and parameters were determined by religion, class, and the patria chica region of origin in Mexico of the more than one million immigrants who entered the country between 1910 and 1930, and their descendants. Further heavy immigration up to the present has largely resulted from Mexico's continuing inability to provide its citizens with a minimally acceptable standard of living. While the majority of these "new" immigrants are undocumented and come from the working class, increasing numbers of professionals are to be found among them. There are also many more women and families than in earlier Mexican immigration waves. These new, urban-based immigrants have given the community an abiding feeling of optimism and have modified the basic culture of Mexican Americans in many other ways as well. So has the incorporation of the region fully into the national economy.

The rapid growth in Mexican immigration during the 1900–1920 period is illustrated, for example, by the soaring of Los Angeles's Mexican-descent population from 5,600 in 1910 to 97,000 in 1930. The increase in all immigration after World War I led to widespread alarm and growing demand for greater restriction. It led to the immigration acts of 1921 and 1924, which established a quota system for European countries and completely excluded Japanese and Chinese workers. Corporate agriculture and other industries relying on cheap labor were able to fight off the inclusion of Western Hemisphere countries (i.e., Mexico) in the quota schema. However, in 1924, the Border Patrol was created with a $1,000,000 budget and a staff of 75 to control a 2,000 mile border, and by the end of the decade, undocumented entry was made a misdemeanor but without legal penalty. Because of the intense demand for their labor, Mexicans continued to pour into the country during the 1920s. After the repatriation of the 1930s, a large majority of Mexican Americans were native born whose first language was English.

WORKERS

As the Southwest became increasingly a part of the national economy after 1900, Mexicans began replacing Europeans and Asians as cheap labor. Mexican immigrants found employment in light manufacturing and the service sector as well as in mining and seasonal labor on large irrigated farms, Sociologist Carey McWilliams's "factories in the fields." As late as the 1920s, a majority of Mexicanos still lived outside the mainstream in a rural or semirural environment. Although the Southwest remained the favorite initial settlement area, by the 1920s barrios began to develop elsewhere, especially in towns of the Midwest where both sugar-beet expansion and industry provided jobs, usually at higher wages than were available in the Borderlands. In the Northwest, the immigrants also discovered increasing opportunities in fields other than agriculture.

By the mid-1920s, Mexicanos had little difficulty finding employment in the industrial centers of the Midwest. Here they shared factory jobs with earlier European immigrants. Hundreds worked in the steel and automobile industries, oil refineries, packing houses, textile mills, and factories in Chicago, Detroit, Kansas City, Saint Louis, Des Moines, Omaha, and other smaller midwestern industrial towns. In their new roles, many were able to advance from unskilled labor to better-paying semiskilled and skilled jobs. By 1930, there were persons of Mexican descent in all of the then forty-eight states and Alaska. Ten years later, midwestern urban workers comprised nearly 10 percent of the total Mexicano population.

URBANIZATION

Urbanization of the Mexican American was in part a by-product of the economic changes that began at the end of the nineteenth century. By 1930, approximately half of Mexican American families lived in towns and cities. During the Great Depression, many poverty-stricken rural Mexican Americans in the Southwest were attracted to urban centers by various New Deal work programs. Although the Southwest was less affected by the Depression than were other areas of the United States, many Nuevomexicanos lost their land through their inability to pay taxes or conservation assessments and found it necessary to move to the city to survive. Inevitably, World War II created a massive movement to the city, and after World War II the benefits of urban life reinforced the trend. The urban *barrio* or *colonia* remained the center of raza life even for the less than 10 percent of Mexicanos who remained in farm work at the beginning of the 1990s. It was also a place where immigrants could find familiar customs and language. With populations constantly renewed by the immigrant influx, some barrios seemed almost like Mexican villages. The urban movement had an impact on the Mexican American family, which now approached the Anglo model. Partly as a result of increased urbanization, considerable strides have been made in employment, especially in the blue-collar sector.

The recession of 1953–1954 after World War II nearly doubled the U.S. unemployment rate and caused many Americans in the Southwest to view their new Mexicano neighbors as a threat to their economic well-being. One of the results was the massive roundup and deportation of undocumented Mexicans in 1954 by a special mobile force organized in the Attorney General's office for what became known as Operation Wetback. Human rights and civil liberties of Mexican Americans were often ignored by the militarized special force, and the more than 1 million deportees were intimidated by harsh and often contemptuous treatment. While Mexican Americans benefited overall in the job market, the impact on some families was devastating. At the end of Operation Wetback, the Immigration and Nationalization Service (INS) assured the nation that the problem of undocumented entry had been solved. That was a premature conclusion. Following a decade of diminution, undocumented immigration began to soar again after the end of the bracero (temporary labor) arrangements in 1964.

POST-1965 IMMIGRATION

Daunted by the expenses, delays, and increasing bureaucratic red tape of legal entry, encouraged by a virtually open border, and abetted by institutionalized migratory patterns and traditions, as well as the absence of legal penalties, Mexicans by the tens of thousands crossed the frontier without documents. As the demand for their labor continued and especially following the demise of the bracero programs in 1964, more entered without documentation despite greater efforts to keep them out. Mexican migration has become profoundly embedded in the economic structure of some areas of the United States as well as Mexico. From Matamores to Tijuana, smuggling of undocumenteds, sometimes referred to as *moiadas* or *alambristas*, became a thriving business for "coyotes" (those who smuggle people across the border for pay). Rounded up in the barrios and colonias that provided temporary refuge but also isolated them, nearly six million undocumented Mexican nationals were repatriated during the 1970s.

Heavy migration from Mexico in the past half century has continuously created new, largely unassimilated generations. Virtual exclusion from the Americanizing influence of the educational system by segregation practiced in the

Southwest until well after World War II has had an inhibiting affect on acculturation and citizenship. Naturalization rates also remained low because of segregation, racism, isolation from the mainstream, various tactics such as the poll tax and at-large elections, the ease of continued regular contact with Mexico, and the widespread idea of eventually returning to Mexico. However, in the late years of the twentieth century, increased participation in American political life, greater upward mobility, and the work of organizations like the League of United Latin American Citizens led to a rapid increase in citizenship.

Between 1980 and 2000, approximately 3 million Mexican migrants established themselves in the United States. Increasingly, they came from urban Mexican environments and included women and families. Many, particularly the undocumenteds who planned to return, continued to identify with Mexico and to think of themselves as *mexicanos de afuera* (Mexicans outside of Mexico). Because of this attitude, a certain amount of friction and conflict developed between them and the 12 million members of the Mexican American community over issues of Americanization and further undocumented immigration. A poll in the early 1990s indicated that Mexican Americans were more strongly opposed to undocumented immigration than the general population was.

During the 1990s, the INS was arresting and deporting over 1 million undocumenteds each year. Despite soaring border apprehensions, in 1996 the INS estimated that there were 2.7 million Mexicans without documents in the United States. The failure of immigration legislation and the INS to reduce undocumented entry, plus a nationwide move into an era of greater conservatism during the 1990s, resulted in a dramatic increase in popular concern about Mexican immigration, especially of undocumenteds. In Texas, this opposition was seen in the case of *Hopwood v. State of Texas*, 1992–1996. In California, it led to passage of Propositions 187, 209, and 227, coming on top of Proposition 67, which declared English to be the state's official language. Aware of limitations inherent in ethnic and linguistic isolation, most Mexican Americans accept that fluency in English is basic to functioning successfully in the United States. At the same time, most wish to preserve certain aspects of their Mexican culture.

LABOR

In the latter 1800s, Mexicanos formed a large part of the labor force in the Southwest and were active in the union movement. Limited labor organization began to develop from the mutualist groups that arose in that period throughout the towns and villages of the Southwest. At the end of the nineteenth century, expansion of large-scale industry in the Southwest stimulated further labor organizing, a trend especially notable in mining. Although not generally accepted in established unions, Mexicanos were actively recruited by the Western Federation of Miners. The first decade of the twentieth century saw considerable labor unrest as a result of union organizations, especially in California and Arizona. In 1903–1904, strikes by both the Clifton-Morenci Copper mine workers in Arizona and of Colorado coal miners against wage discrimination were unsuccessful. A decade later, the Los Angeles street-railway strike over wages failed; in 1910 and again in 1919 the railway workers were unsuccessful.

In California agriculture, the 1903 Oxnard strike of beet workers won Mexicano (and Japanese) workers the right to deal directly with growers rather than through labor contractors. Ten years later, publicity about the brutal conditions of workers at the Durst Ranch in northern California resulted in the creation of a state commission on immigration and housing. The subsequent waiver of immigration requirements during World War I led to intense recruitment of Mexican workers, and by the time of the peace treaty they dominated California's farm labor force. In 1928, a number of local Los Angeles unions formed the Confederation of Mexican Labor Unions, which clearly articulated their views but languished soon thereafter when the Depression hit.

At the end of the 1920s, U.S. prosperity turned into the Great Depression, which was to persist until World War II. The limited strike activities of the 1920s, sometimes supported by Mexican consuls, gave way in the 1930s, despite depression conditions, to numerous strikes involving Chicanos. California alone experienced over 150 farm strikes between 1930 and 1938; at the peak in 1933, there were over 30 strikes in California agriculture. Of these, the 1933 Joaquin Valley cotton strike was the most notable. Led by the leftist Cannery and Agricultural Workers Industrial Union, 18,000 pickers, three-fourths of whom were Mexicanos, demanded increased wages and laid down their sacks. The strike was ended by a state fact-finding commission; however, it also led to the organization of an active anti-union growers group, the Associated Farmers of California. Relying on police power and other more direct forms of intimidation, growers largely succeeded in limiting efforts toward improvements in working conditions and pay. During the 1930s, Mexican Americans gained union organizing experience rather than labor victories. Anglo workers replaced Mexicanos in many jobs that they had previously felt were suitable only to Third World peoples. The hard times caused a dramatic increase in racism and discrimination; in addition, Mexicanos suffered the same misery as the rest of the population as jobs disappeared. Fortunately, various New Deal agencies helped alleviate the worst problems of the Depression for many Chicanos.

For Mexican Americans, the most dramatic event of the 1930s was the repatriation of thousands of Mexicans and some Americans of Mexican descent. Even after some 200,000 Mexican nationals returned voluntarily, local governments, faced with mounting relief costs, began pressuring the rest, who had been encouraged to come in the 1920s, to repatriate. Perhaps as many as half a million persons of Mexican provenance crossed the border into Mexico between 1929 and 1939. In the process of repatriation, intimidation was common and civil rights were abused. Repatriation left a legacy of disillusionment, ill feeling, and resentment among Mexican Americans but also helped push their leaders a hesitant step closer to demanding their rights as the war in Europe created a renewed demand for Mexican workers.

WORLD WAR

World War II resulted in both urban industrialization and agricultural expansion. It created a far greater demand for southwestern agricultural products, manufactured goods, and soldiers than World War I had. Although World War I had found many recent immigrant citizens hesitant about serving, Mexicanos had volunteered in the war at a higher rate than any other ethnic group. Armed service became an early factor in the Americanization of Mexicanos. Unlike their World War I predecessors, few World War II Chicanos were seriously ambivalent about who they were and what they were, despite great diversity within Mexican American communities arising from geography, class, gender, and race. Nearly all of the World War II generation recognized that they were American citizens; most felt a degree of affection for Mexico but no sense of allegiance.

World War II affected Mexican Americans in a myriad of ways. About 333,000 served in the various branches of the armed forces. They fought in North Africa, Italy, and the attack on Fortress Europa, but probably the majority served in the Pacific theater. They made up more than 25 percent of the prisoners of war who underwent the murderous Bataan death march in the spring of 1942. By the end of the war, seventeen of them had won Congressional Medals of Honor. Although the military reflected societal biases, generally they found less discrimination, greater recognition, and easier advancement within its ranks.

On the home front, Chicano-Anglo relations were strained in Los Angeles by the Sleepy Lagoon case, in which the court convicted (though the convictions were later overturned) seventeen Chicano youths of assault and murder, and by the subsequent so-called Zoot Suit riots. Many second-generation teenagers adopted as a badge or uniform of unity the sartorial style known as the zoot suit. Their gangs often took the place formerly filled by family and the community, both now profoundly beset by urbanization, alcoholism, and broken homes. Although rejected by Anglos and most adult Mexican Americans, zoot suiters, or *pachucos*, as they were also known, were viewed by most Anglos as representing the community. Early in May 1943, street brawls that broke out in Los Angeles between military personnel and zoot-suited youths, often over girls, escalated into vicious, indiscriminate attacks by Anglo sailors and soldiers on Mexican American youths. Only after several weeks of rioting, sensationalized by the Los Angeles press, and pressure from the Mexican Embassy did the authorities take steps to halt the assaults by canceling military passes. The Zoot Suit affair left a deep scar on Mexican American–Anglo relations, despite conservative barrio disapproval of Zoot suiters.

The war brought on undreamed-of urban industrialization and agricultural expansion in the Southwest. Early on, it became apparent that U.S. agriculture was going to be in dire need of workers in order to meet wartime requirements of the country and its allies. The bracero program, a 1942 executive agreement between Mexico and the United States to provide the needed labor, imported about

250,000 Mexican males to work in agriculture and on the railroads during the war years. Braceros benefited from the program, and so did corporate agriculture and the railroads. After the war, the importation of braceros continued on a less formal basis. Throughout the program's twenty-two-year history, the Mexican American community attitude toward the use of braceros was divided. By the late 1950s, increased mechanization in the fields had reduced the demand for workers, and in 1964 the bracero program, under vigorous liberal attack, was ended.

World War II had a deep impact on Mexican Americans. It provided second-generation Mexican Americans with opportunities for improving their economic and social well-being. Many learned skills that would serve them well in postwar civilian life. After the war, the GI Bill enabled them to obtain college educations or job training as well as business and home loans. It served to create a budding generation of professionals, especially in education, and greatly enlarged the middle class, whose leaders now joined the struggle to achieve civil rights for all. Some leaders realized that only by entering the political arena could they hope to preserve the limited gains made. For many, serving in the armed forces was a practical way to enter the American mainstream. For Chicanas, the war had special importance.

CHICANAS

Chicanas have been centrally involved in all aspects of the Mexican American experience from its inception. Although most found their societal role largely limited to the home and family, some, like Lucia Gonzalez Parsons, Jovita Idar, Maria L. Hernandez, Emma Tenayuca, and Luisa Moreno, achieved positions of importance outside family and home. Mexico-born Josefina Fierro de Bright was one of the founders of the Los Angeles–based Congreso del Pueblo de Habla Española in 1938. Moreno, the Guatemala-born Mexicana labor organizer and civil rights leader, was also a leader in the Congreso until its demise during World War II. Fierro de Bright was one of the principal organizers of the Sleepy Lagoon Defense Committee.

Previous to World War II, Chicanas worked in a variety of jobs, supplementing the family income and taking over the roles of male family members who were unable to work. Most worked in agriculture, but some were employed at subsistence wages in canneries, packinghouses, restaurants, laundries, clothing factories, retail sales, and offices. Some older women contributed significantly to the support of their families by operating boarding houses for single men who came to work in the United States.

During World War II, Chicanas took jobs in war industries as their fathers, husbands, and sons went into service; they also assumed active roles in other home-front activities, such as participating in war-bond drives and collecting scrap metals and other industrial materials needed for the war effort. For the first time, some found themselves the de facto heads of the family. For many, the experience was liberating and even exhilarating. When the civil rights struggle developed in the postwar years, Chicanas participated actively as feminists, often viewing themselves as victimized by the *movimiento*'s (civil rights movement) male leadership as well as by Anglos, and asserting their right to full equality within the movement.

By the mid-1990s, Latinas exceeded the number of raza males in college and university graduating classes and in the professions. Of special note also is their increased participation in politics and office holding. Bright young women like Lucille Roybal-Allyard and Linda Chavez at the national level, Gloria Molina in Los Angeles, Debbie Ortega in Denver, and Maria Berriozabal and Virginia Musquiz in Crystal City, Texas have followed in the footsteps of earlier role models like Polly Baca and Mari Luci Jaramillo. Their achievement of national prominence has added a valuable dimension to the long Mexican American struggle for complete equality. They have unabashedly asserted the right to voice their opinions and have developed a variety of support organizations, academic and community based. However, despite their best efforts, they have been unable to create a national umbrella association.

RIGHTS STRUGGLE

The fight for equality and acceptance began in the mid-1830s in Texas and continues today. In support of their struggle, Mexican Americans developed many local, regional, and national organizations. Early groups were of a mutualist cast, centered on service, benefits, and community programs; in matters concerning discrimination and racism, they tended to be limited to ad hoc solutions. World War I, the 1930s repatriation, World War II, and the civil rights movement of the 1960s were all important in creating more aggressive and effective organizations for social and political advancement. In 1921, the early efforts of middle-class Tejano World War I veterans led in the creation of the Sons of America, which metamorphosed by the end of the decade into the highly successful League of United Latin American Citizens.

Refusing to accept the status of second-class citizens, World War II veterans had a very different set of expectations from those of their parents. They initiated a spirited struggle against discrimination in education, employment, and housing that became a central part of a complex political, cultural, and social movement known as the Chicano movimiento. They created organizations like the American GI Forum, Mexican American Political Association, and Community Service Organization as well as other regional and national groups, most of which became politically active on a nonpartisan basis. By the 1950s, these Mexican American organizations were increasingly using the courts in the fight to end racial segregation, particularly in the schools. After the 1960s, bias and discrimination declined somewhat; but de facto segregation, both residential and in education, has proven extremely difficult to eradicate and has not disappeared, despite the successes of the movimiento.

MOVIMIENTO

The movimiento was a multifaceted political and social development in the Chicano struggle. With its demands for human dignity and rights, it erupted in the mid-1960s, but its roots may be found as far back as the immediate post–Treaty of Guadalupe Hidalgo years. Phoenix-like, it arose in large part out of turbulent circumstances of the 1960s: out of the Black power, civil rights, and feminist movements and was part of a widespread climate of distrust, disillusion, civil ferment, and demonstrations. These conditions climaxed in a strong opposition to the Vietnam War, in which Chicano casualty rates were disproportionately high, nearly double that of the general population.

The movement's leaders positioned it in the mainstream of American life, bringing the problems of Mexican Americans sharply to the attention of the majority society with radical rhetoric and confrontational tactics. In its widest scope, it included Reies Lopez Tijerina's semirural Alianza Federal de Pueblos Libres in New Mexico, "Corky" Gonzales's urban Crusade for Justice in Colorado, Jose Angel Gutierrez's ethnic Raza Unida Party in Texas, and Cesar Chavez's farm workers' union in California. All four leaders addressed themselves to the goal of creating community; to that end, each used an organization he personally created and directed. Most successful was Chavez, who became the most widely known and universally admired Mexican American leader. Initially concerned with farm workers, he came to espouse the basic rights of all individuals and helped politicize many in the Mexican American community. Unfortunately, his social conservatism and quite modest education prevented his becoming the sole, unchallenged leader. In all four groups, angry young militants caught the public's attention and made headlines.

Central to the early stages of the movement were Chicano complaints leading to the Los Angeles high school "blowouts" in 1968 and the Chicano Moratorium march two years later. High school and college students were in the front ranks of movimiento protesters and agitators, particularly in California and Texas. Los Angeles high school students boycotted classes, and their example was quickly followed by similar eruptions elsewhere in the Southwest. Student leaders demanded that educational institutions recognize the value of Mexican American culture and history and that they provide high school and college courses more relevant to Chicano students.

Ultimately, they demanded full acceptance as Americans. None of their demands was especially new; all were part of the nineteenth-century search for solutions to the problems that Mexicanos faced in American society. After initially rejecting student demands outright, ultimately the educational system responded. As a result, Chicano classes, programs, and studies departments were established in many high schools, colleges, and universities. Nevertheless, the Chicano high school dropout rate remains at an intolerable 40 percent. Nearly all raza members recognize that education is the most likely path to both personal achievement and upward social mobility. However, at both high school and college levels poverty and economic hardship form notable stumbling blocks. Various studies show clearly that most Mexican American parents place a high value on education; however, many do not understand how to use the system to help their children maximally. Education is central to the incorporation of la raza into the U.S. mainstream. Reaction within the Mexican American community to the movement revealed considerable diversity. Older community members and recent immigrants tended to view the youthful movimiento activists with some apprehension. Others who were generally in sympathy with the goals of the militants sometimes decried the means used. Some older and more affluent Mexicanos, Nuevomexicanos particularly, and middle-class workers neither agreed with all the goals nor endorsed the tactics of movimiento leaders. Their often Marxist rhetoric and regular use of confrontation greatly upset many in the community; and some, like representative Henry B. Gonzalez of Texas, actively opposed and publicly condemned them. However, many members of the community were influenced by the movement to take a more active role in civic affairs. Heavy-handed police actions during the 1970 Chicano Moratorium march in Los Angeles and the killing of Ruben Salazar won support for the movement and energized the Mexican American community to adopt a firm anti-Vietnam War stance. There were other, long-term results.

The movement furnished the climate in which Chicano organizations were born and flourished: the Mexican American Legal Defense and Education Fund, 1968; Nosotros, 1969; the Southwest Voter Registration Education Project, 1974; and the Congressional Hispanic Caucus, 1975. It fostered the creation of numerous other community-service organizations. Finally, it created a sense of profound pride in all aspects of Mexican culture and was largely responsible for a Mexican American cultural revitalization that has developed in the past quarter century.

In large measure, enabled and influenced by the movement, the descendants of immigrants from Mexico have made notable contributions to American culture in the fine arts, music, theater, and literature. Many Chicanos have achieved national recognition as writers, poets, dramatists, actors, singers, musicians, and painters. In the cinema, they have found increasing recognition as actors and directors; Edward James Olmos, George Lopez, and others have joined the company of distinguished old-timers Ricardo Montalban and the late Anthony Quinn. Luis Valdez has carved his unique niche in the theater. Striking murals, perhaps the most popular of Chicano arts, decorate hundreds of walls in dozens of U.S. cities, and the canvases of Carlos Almaraz, Alfredo Arreguin, and Carmen Lomas Garza may be found in many museums, galleries, and private collections. Their poetry, short stories, novels, and dramas, often poignantly personal and introspective, both interpret and explicate the Mexican American experience and at the same time often offer the reader a universal message. Some writers, such as Sandra Cisneros and Richard Rodriguez, have achieved a broad national recognition; in the Chicano community, the literary works of Tomas Rivera, Francisco Jimenez, Rolando Hinojosa-Smith, and Rudolfo Anaya are widely known and loved.

TODAY

As one result of the movement, the professions and politics have opened up more widely to Mexican Americans. Greater pride in Mexicano culture developed, as did greater acceptance of that culture by the majority society. Today, Chicanos are encountered routinely in the educational, professional, business, and political sectors. During the past quarter century, they have found increased opportunities in all areas of American life, but especially in the political arena. This development has largely been the result of the Chicano movimiento, the overall civil rights movement, and particularly of voter registration drives, get-out-the-vote drives, and other civic activities by organizations like the Southwest Voter Registration Education Project, American GI Forum, and Mexican American Legal Defense and Education Fund. In California, since the early 1990s there has been a nearly 50 percent increase in the number of Mexican Americans registered to vote.

Chicanos have made impressive gains in meaningful political participation at local, state, and national levels. At the end of the 1970s, Henry Cisneros and Federico Pena became the popular mayors of San Antonio and Denver, respectively. In 1974, Mexico-born Raul Castro was elected governor of Arizona while Jerry Apodaca became governor in New Mexico, and in the 1980s, Toney Anaya followed Apodaca as the state's governor. In January 2003, Bill Richardson took over as the latest Mexican American governor of New Mexico. California Mexican Americans have occupied high positions in state government, including that of lieutenant governor. In the 1990s, President Bill Clinton appointed three Mexican Americans to cabinet posts: Henry Cisneros, Federico Pena, and Bill Richardson. In the past decades, more than a dozen Mexican Americans have served the country as ambassadors to foreign nations, and a growing number of Chicanos have become important federal department principals. In 2001, Latinos held 5,138 elected government positions, including nineteen seats in the House of Representatives.

In overall economic status, Mexican Americans have also achieved some improvement. However, higher income levels for some are still beclouded by continuing widespread poverty in the barrio. The expectation that the gains made in the 1960s and 1970s would continue into the 1980s led to that decade being prematurely labeled the Decade of the Hispanic. Despite some gains made in the 1980s and 1990s, more Mexican Americans were living below the poverty line at the beginning of the new millennium than at the beginning of the widely touted Decade of the Hispanic. One out of four Mexican American families, a majority of them headed by women or persons over 65, falls below the poverty level.

While some overall betterment has taken place, particularly in the second half of the twentieth century, Mexican Americans as a group continue to face a variety of problems. The more overt forms of racism and discrimination have diminished; the subtler forms of ethnic rejection remain. The dropout rate in our high schools has declined only minimally, and a xenophobic nativism seems to be on the increase. Passed handily in 1994, California Proposition 187 disallowed ordinary educational and health services to the children of undocumenteds. Two years later, Californians voted in favor of Proposition 209, which effectively aimed to dismantle affirmative action programs, and in 1998 they also passed Proposition 227, which prohibited teaching in the public schools in any language other than English, and which its supporters hoped would end bilingual education programs.

Meanwhile, vigilantes like the "light up the border" group in California and counterparts in Arizona have shown renewed vigor. Economic improvement since World War II has visibly slowed down in the 1980s and 1990s. Discrimination and racism are still with us, and continuing determined efforts need to be made to wipe out stereotyping and racial stigma. Government policies must assure that all citizens receive equal treatment and must open wider the door of opportunity at all levels. Although Mexican Americans continue to make economic and cultural contributions to U.S. society, a large majority continues to face economic, educational, political, and social barriers. For many, full equality of opportunity still seems a distant goal.

In spite of continuing shortcomings of life in the United States for many persons of Mexican descent, they clearly retain high expectations and hope of betterment. The vast majority of over 20 million Mexicanos counted in the 2000 census are voluntary immigrants of the past century and their descendants. Faced with deep-seated poverty and extremely limited economic opportunity in their native land, Mexicans have crossed and continue to cross the border to El Norte, with or without documentation. Although in recent years the worlds of established Mexican Americans and of the recent immigrants have increasingly diverged, the ongoing migration continues to reshape in many positive ways the Mexican American community, the Southwest, and increasingly, the entire country. The Mexican American community continues to be a dynamic part of the daily political, social, cultural, and economic life in the United States.

BIBLIOGRAPHICAL ESSAY

Any bibliographical essay on the Mexican American experience must begin with Carey McWilliams's sympathetic and still useful pioneering work, *North from Mexico: The Spanish-Speaking People of the United States* (New York: Greenwood Press), published in 1948, coming into its own in the 1960s, and updated in 1990. Companion to it for an excellent brief but more comprehensive survey of Mexicans in the United States through the 1970s is Carlos Cortes's "Mexicans" in the *Harvard Encyclopedia of American Ethnic Groups*, ed. by Stephen Thernstrom, (Cambridge, MA: Harvard Univ. Press, 1980), a tightly organized and useful introduction to all aspects of the Mexican American experience. An even-handed recent survey of the Mexican American experience may be found in *Mexicanos: A History of Mexicans in the United States* (Bloomington: Indiana Univ. Press, 1999) by Manuel G. Gonzales.

In the second half of the 1960s, the overall civil rights movement and a rapidly developing academic interest in the Chicano experience created a need for instructional materials and resulted in the compiling of a number of books of readings. University of Notre Dame sociologist Julian Samora led this development in 1966 with *La Raza: Forgotten Americans*, a collection of articles from various academic fields. It was followed at the end of the decade by historian Manuel Servin's *The Mexican Americans: An Awakening Minority* (Beverley Hills, CA: Glencoe Press, 1974) by John Burma's *Mexican Americans in the United States: A Reader* (Cambridge, MA: Canfield Press, 1970) and by Joan Moore's socioeconomic survey, *Mexican Americans* (Englewood Cliffs, NJ: Prentice Hall, 1970). In 1971, Wayne Moquin, in collaboration with Charles Van Doren, edited *A Documentary History of the Mexican Americans* (New York: Praeger, 1971), and in the next year, Luis Valdez and Stan Steiner came out with *Aztlan: An Anthology of Mexican American Literature* (New York: Knopf, 1972). The year 1973 saw the publication of three timely collections: *Viva la Raza: Readings on Mexican Americans*, edited by Julian Nava (New York: Van Nostrand); *Introduction to Chicano Studies: A Reader* (New York: Macmillan), by Livie Duran and H. R. Bernard; and *Chicano: The Evolution of a People* (Minneapolis: Winston), by Renato Rosaldo, Robert A. Calvert, and Gustav L. Seligmann.

Meanwhile, in the late 1960s, Leo Grebler, Joan Moore, and Ralph Guzman headed a team of scholars who developed, with the support of a Ford Foundation grant, *The Mexican American People: The Nation's Second Largest Minority* (New York: The Free Press). Published in 1970, it was a comprehensive sourcebook stressing the Chicano urban experience. Half a decade later Carlos Cortes served as general editor for Arno Press's two extensive reprint series: *The Mexican-American*, 1974 and *The Chicano Heritage*, 1976. The reprints in both series were, and still are, of great value for understanding the earlier Mexicano experience in the United States.

Meanwhile, there had also appeared the first general histories of the Mexican Americans since McWilliams's 1948 work. *The Chicanos: A History of Mexican Americans* (New York: Hill and Wang, 1972), a narrative account by historians Matt S. Meier and Feliciano Rivera, stressed the themes of immigration and labor, conflict, and adjustment, as McWilliams had. In that same year, historian Rodolfo Acuña broke new interpretive ground in *Occupied America: The Chicano Struggle toward Liberation* (San Francisco: Canfield Press) by postulating an internal colonialism, a concept that he dropped in later editions while continuing to stress Mexicano victimization. These two broad surveys were followed in the next year by Ellwyn Stoddard's *Mexican Americans* (New York: Random House), which analyzed the Chicano experience in the twentieth century, centering on immigration, occupations, and problems of self-identification. In 1979 Mario Barrera's heavily economic *Race and Class in the Southwest: A Theory of Racial Inequality* (Notre Dame, IN: Univ. of Notre Dame Press, 1979) stressed societal conditions and victimization. That same year, Arnulfo D. Trejo edited *The Chicanos: As We See Ourselves* (Tucson: Univ. of Arizona Press, 1979), in which a dozen Mexican Americans, most of them scholars who identified with the Chicano Movement, presented their varying views on select topics in the Chicano experience.

These broad general works were accompanied in the 1970s and 1980s by a profusion of topical studies, nearly all authored by youthful post–World War II Chicano scholars whose historical approach was strongly influenced by the movimiento of the 1960s and early 1970s. Many of these studies were regional and urban. Already in 1967, Julian Samora and Richard Lamanno had published *Mexican Americans in a Mid-West Metropolis: East Chicago* (Los Angeles: McNally and Loftin), and in the following decade

Louise Ano Nuevo Kerr completed her excellent University of Illinois doctoral study, "The Chicano Experience in Chicago, 1920–1970." In 1981, added impetus to urban studies was given by *Desert Immigrants: The Mexicans of El Paso, 1880–1920* (New Haven: Yale Univ. Press, 1981), Mario T. Garcia's revised 1975 doctoral thesis.

California Chicanos turned toward urban history after the 1966 vanguard *Decline of the Californios: A Social History of the Spanish Speaking Californians* (Berkeley: Univ. of California Press) by Leonard Pitt. Alberto Camarillo's *Chicanos in a Changing Society: From Mexican Pueblos to American Barrios in Santa Barbara and Southern California, 1848–1930* (Cambridge, MA: Harvard Univ. Press) and Richard Griswold del Castillo's *The Los Angeles Barrio, 1850–1890: A Social History* (Berkeley: Univ. of California Press), both published in 1979, furthered interest in the Chicano urban experience. Four years later, Ricardo Ramo published *East Los Angeles: History of a Barrio* (Austin: Univ. of Texas Press, 1983), which stressed the impact of the heavy immigration of the 1920s on that *colonia*. George J. Sanchez's *Becoming Mexican American: Ethnicity, Culture and Identity in Chicano Los Angeles, 1900–1945* (New York: Oxford Univ. Press), published in 1993, explored ethnic changes in this important period of Southern California history. *Mexican Los Angeles: A Narrative and Pictorial History* (Los Angeles: Floricanto Press, 1992), by Antonio Ríos-Bustamante is a useful work with excellent photographs.

In 1974, to help explain the Mexican American experience in Texas, Arno Press in New York republished Pauline Kibbe's trailblazing 1946 study, *Latin Americans in Texas*, and in the same year, John Schockley's study of urban Chicano militancy in Crystal City, *Revolt in a Texas Town*, was published. In 1975, Oscar J. Martinez came out with *Border Boom Town: Ciudad Juarez Since 1848*, the first of half a dozen excellent studies he has made of Mexican Americans in the border region. Seven years later, Arnoldo de Leon issued *The Tejano Community, 1836–1900* (Albuquerque: Univ. of New Mexico Press, 1982), the first of various monographs he has written centering on Tejano-Anglo interaction over the years. The year 1987 saw the publication of David Montejano's outstanding survey, *Anglos and Mexicans in the Making of Texas, 1836–1986* (Austin: Univ. of Texas Press), and of Guadalupe San Miguel's equally authoritative *"Let All of Them Take Heed": Mexican Americans and the Campaign for Educational Equality in Texas, 1910–1981* (Austin: Univ. of Texas Press, 1987), both regional and topical, as its title indicates.

In New Mexico, the pioneering work of George I. Sanchez, *Forgotten People: A Study of New Mexicans* (Albuquerque: Univ. of New Mexico Press, 1940), provided the basis for Nancie Gonzalez's updated and amplified 1969 survey, *The Spanish Americans of New Mexico: A Heritage of Pride* (Albuquerque: Univ. of New Mexico Press). Three years later, Robert J. Rosenbaum completed his excellent study of ethnic conflict, "Mexicano versus Americano: A Study of Hispanic-American Resistance to Anglo-American Control in New Mexico Territory, 1870–1900," which he reworked and published in 1981 under the title *Mexicano Resistance in the Southwest: The Sacred Right of Self-Preservation* (Austin: Univ. of Texas Press). Meanwhile, Roxanne Dunbar Ortiz came out with her 1980 study of land conflict in *Roots of Resistance: Land Tenure in New Mexico, 1680–1980* (Los Angeles: Univ. of California Press), and twenty years later Erlinda Gonzales-Berry and David R. Maciel authored *The Contested Homeland: A Chicano History of New Mexico* (Albuquerque: Univ. of New Mexico Press, 2000).

As these excellent regional studies were being written, previously neglected fields of research were also being examined by a post–World War II generation of Mexican American scholars. Beginning in the 1970s, the Chicana historical experience became an important new field. In 1976, Martha P. Cotera published *Diosa y Hembra: The History and Heritage of Chicanas in the U.S.* (Austin, TX: Informats System Development). Her introductory work was followed three years later by *La Chicana: The Mexican-American Woman* (Chicago: Univ. of Chicago Press, 1979), by Alfredo Mirande and Evangelina Enriquez, and then in 1980 by two collections, *Mexican Women in the United States: Struggles, Past and Present* (Los Angeles: Univ. of California Press), edited by Magdalena Mora and Adelaida R. Del Castillo, and *Twice a Minority: Mexican American Women* (St. Louis: Mosby), edited by Margarita B. Melville. In 1986, *Chicana Voices: Intersections of Class, Race, and Gender* (Austin: Univ. of Texas Press), a compilation of outstanding essays from the twelfth annual conference of the National Association for Chicano Studies, was published. Seven years later, Norma Alarcon and others edited a collection of readings, *Chicana Critical Issues* (Berkeley: Third Woman Press, 1993), which explored historical intellectual activity among Mexican American women. Their contributions to American life were even more extensively detailed in 1998 by Vicki Ruiz in her *From Out of the Shadows: Mexican Women in Twentieth Century America* (New York: Oxford Univ. Press).

The Chicano Movement of the 1960s and 1970s itself quickly became a subject of research and interpretative writing. Gilberto Lopez y Rivas described the origins of the movement in his 1973 book *The Chicanos: Life and Struggles of the Mexican Minority in the United States* (New York: Monthly Review Press). Twelve years later, Alfredo Mirande published *The Chicano Experience: An Alternative Perspective* (Notre Dame, IN: Univ. of Notre Dame Press, 1985) which stressed the movement's social and economic background. Four years after that, Mario T. Garcia discussed various aspects of the movimiento in his book *Mexican Americans: Leadership, Ideology and Identity* (New Haven: Yale Univ. Press, 1989), and Carlos Munoz, Jr., came out with *Youth, Identity, Power: The Chicano Movement* (New York: Verso, 1989), which concerned itself largely with the problems of internal factionalism and ethnic identity issues. In 1991, Marguerite V. Marin published *Social Protest in an Urban Barrio: A Study of the Chicano Movement, 1966–1974* (Lanham, MD: Univ. Press of America), and five years later, Juan A. Garcia stressed politics in his article "The Chicano Movement: Its Legacy for Politics and Policy," published in *Chicanas/Chicanos at the Crossroads: Social, Economic, and Political Change* (Tucson: Univ. of Arizona Press, 1996), edited by David R. Maciel and Isidro D. Ortiz. More recently, Maciel and Ortiz, with Maria Herrera-Sobek, edited *Chicano Renaissance: Contemporary Cultural Trends* (Tucson: Univ. of Arizona Press, 2000), which deals broadly with cultural changes resulting from the movement.

The topic of immigration and border history has attracted great interest and considerable research ever since Manuel Gamio's 1930 pioneering work, *Mexican Immigration to the United States*, reprinted by Arno Press, New York in 1970. *By the Sweat of Their Brow: Mexican Immigrant Labor in the United States 1900–1940* (Westport, CT: Greenwood Press), Mark Reisler's outstanding study of immigration by Mexican workers early in the twentieth century came out in 1976. Two years later, Wayne Cornelius published his *Mexican Migration to the United States: Causes, Consequences, and the U.S. Response* (San Diego: Univ. of California Press, 1978); he has remained a distinguished contributor to Mexican immigration studies ever since. Mexican historian Jorge A. Bustamante has also been prolific in researching and writing on the topics of borders and immigration. Abraham Hoffman's 1974 *Unwanted Mexican Americans in the Great Depression: Repatriation Pressures, 1929–1939* (Tucson: Univ. of Arizona Press), may be supplemented with *Decade of Betrayal: Mexican Repatriation in the 1930s* (Albuquerque: Univ. of New Mexico Press), by Francisco Balderrama and Raymond Rodriguez. In 1990 Frank Bean, Barry Edmondston, and Jeffry S. Passel edited a study of the important 1986 Immigration Reform and Control Act in *Undocumented Immigration to the United States: IRCA and the Experience of the 1980s* (Lanham, MD: Univ. Press of America). More recently, Leo R. Chavez has expanded our knowledge of border politics in his *Covering Immigration: Popular Images and the Politics of the Nation* (Berkeley: Univ. of California Press, 2001). Earlier works by researchers Arthur Corwin, Alejando Portes, and Stan Ross still retain great value for the student of border and immigration topics.

In addition to more recent publications in various fields of history there are, of course, many valuable older works. In 1971, Armando Rendon published a passionate activist's interpretation of the Chicano experience in his *Chicano Manifesto: The History and Aspirations of the Second Largest Minority in America* (New York: Macmillan). Writers F. Chris Garcia, John Shockley, Rodolfo O. de la Garza, Ralph Guzman, Ignacio Garcia, Carlos Muñoz, and others have made important contributions to our understanding of the changing Mexican American political role in local, state, and national affairs. In the field of labor history, specialists such as Ernesto Galarza, Juan Gomez-Quinones, Charles Wollenberg, Vicki L. Ruiz, and David Macias provide insights into various aspects of the Chicano work experience. Gomez-Quinones's *Mexican American Labor, 1790–1990* (Albuquerque: Univ. of New Mexico Press, 1994), is particularly useful for an overview; *Las Obreras: Chicana Politics of Work and Family* (Los Angeles: Univ. of California Press, 2000), edited by Vicki Ruiz, illuminates the role of Mexicanas in the U.S. labor market. During the 1990s, Patricia Zavella and Camille Guerin-Gonzales also published extensively on the role of Chicanas as workers.

A number of general bibliographies are available for more extensive information on the works of scholars. *Mexican American Bibliographies* (New York: Arno Press, 1974), edited by Carlos Cortes, reprinted five significant earlier bibliographies. Frank Pino's *Mexican Americans: A Research Bibliography* (East Lansing: Michigan State Univ., 1974), is a two-volume computer-generated guide to Chicano materials in various disciplines. In his insightful 1975 work, *Biblioarafica Chicano: A Guide to Information Sources* (Detroit: Gale Research Co.), Arnulfo Trejo carefully annotated about 500 entries. In *The Mexican American: A Critical Guide to Research Aids* (Greenwich, CT: JAI Press, 1980), Barbara and J. Cordell Robinson provide excellent annotated guidance to various sources. *Bibliography of Mexican American History* (Westport, CT: Greenwood Press, 1984), by Matt S. Meier, remains a useful comprehensive work of about 40,000 entries, only partially and briefly annotated. There are also various valuable bibliographies for specific topics.

POLISH AMERICANS

Edward R. Kantowicz

Polonia, the community of Polish Americans, embraces both old and new immigrants. The great majority of the 9 million people in the United States with Polish surnames or a Polish heritage are descendants of peasants who emigrated from eastern Europe about a century ago.[1] Fleeing the land, they settled in industrial cities of North America, forming tightly knit working-class communities clustered around Roman Catholic parishes staffed by Polish-speaking priests. These peasant, working-class, Catholics worked hard and long in unionized industries, increasing their incomes and pouring their savings into home ownership. Typically, however, they assigned a lower value to education and professional occupational status than did some other European immigrant groups. Still, judging them by their own goals, Polish Americans from the century-old emigration have been very successful. If they came to America seeking primarily bread, a home, and a better standard of living for their families, the conclusion is inescapable that they got what they wanted.

In the last two decades of the twentieth century, these well-established Polish Americans were joined by a new wave of immigrants from Poland. The failure of the Solidarity uprising against the Communist Party in 1981 sent a wave of political refugees to America, and the end of Communist domination in 1989 unleashed a flood of economic migrants seeking a better life. Between 1980 and 1993, 174,664 Polish immigrants were admitted legally into the United States, including at least 33,000 granted asylum as political refugees. Many more came as visitors on temporary visas. At any given point in time, about 250,000 Poles were living supposedly temporarily in the United States. Some of these would return to Poland after the expiration of their visas, but an unknown, probably large, number remained resident illegally.[2]

The new immigrants from Poland came from a higher socioeconomic class than the peasant immigrants of a century ago. Most recent migrants had at least some higher education, and many had been employed in professional or intellectual occupations in Poland. The overwhelming majority had been city dwellers. In America, they often experienced downward social mobility at first, accepting more menial jobs than they would have in Poland. Many women found work as cleaning ladies, and men tended to work in the building and home improvement trades, as roofers or handymen. Though most were fiercely opposed to the Communist Party and had rallied around the leadership of Pope John Paul II (born Karol Wojtyla) and the Solidarity movement, religion was generally less central to the lives of the recent immigrants than it had been to their peasant predecessors.

Today, the old and new migrants in Polonia eye each other warily. They cannot even agree as to which group holds higher class status. Recent migrants compare their own educational backgrounds favorably with those of "the sausage-selling grandchildren of the early peasants," whereas Polish Americans comfortably ensconced in suburbia look down on the ghetto-dwelling newcomers "wearing funky nail polish," and "living like animals in a barn."[3] Most descendants of the century-old emigration do not speak Polish, or else they speak a fractured, ungrammatical mix of Polish and English. The two groups even suffer from different ethnic stereotypes. The peasant immigrants and their working-class descendants have long endured the stereotype of the "dumb Polack" with a strong back and a weak mind. The new migrants from Poland picked up a different stereotype, both in Europe and America. They are considered sneaky, manipulative, and overly clever to the point of dishonesty. An official of the Polish Welfare Association who aided recent immigrants in America concluded that "growing up in Poland under Communism you get to be very manipulative. . . . And if it means in Poland you bribe an official for a better house, you do."[4] Truly, as sociologist Mary Erdmans has said, the two groups resident in Polonia today represent "opposite Poles."

The first of these groups of opposite Poles, those who immigrated to America about a hundred years ago, were largely of peasant origin, became overwhelmingly working-class in America, and adhered to a militant brand of Roman Catholic religion. Peasant, working-class, and Catholic: these three social realities and the system of values they imply summarize most of Polish American history until recent decades.

PEASANT ORIGINS

The Poland that immigrants left a hundred years ago was a divided country in several senses. First of all, the country was divided politically; in fact, Poland did not exist as a political entity throughout the nineteenth century. In 1795, Poland's three powerful neighbors, Prussia, Russia, and Austria, had carved up what was left from two earlier partitions, and the name *Poland* disappeared from the map of Europe for over a century, until after World War I.[5] Perhaps more important, however, than this political partition was the deep social division in Polish society, the great chasm separating the gentry from the peasant classes.

In the days of its independence and in the early years of the partitions, Poland was a nobility nation. The Polish *szlachta,* or gentry, were the most numerous noble class in Europe, forming 8 percent of the country's population. Politically, culturally, and economically, the Polish gentry *were* the Polish nation—only they held political rights, only they felt deep nationalist longings. In addition, they held a virtual monopoly on Poland's principal economic activity, the grain trade.

Beneath the gentry were the mass of Polish peasants, still serfs bound to the soil they tilled but with no property rights to their land.[6] They owed their gentry landlord burdensome labor services and were subject to him in matters of civil and criminal justice. Though economically bound together, peasant and gentry could not be more divided socially. Some *szlachta* even believed they were descendants of the ancient Sarmatians, a different race than the peasants, and insisted that their personal servants come from impoverished gentry families, so that their bodies would not be touched by peasants. Poland contained two other social classes: the clergy (often drawn from among peasants but more closely allied with the gentry) and the townsmen and shopkeepers (usually Jews or Germans). Peasants respected the clergy and patronized the local Jewish innkeeper when necessary, but they kept their distance from both. As a character in Ladislas Reymont's great novel, *The Peasants,* philosophized: "Things have to be so. The husbandman lives on the land he tills, the tradesman on what he sells, the Squire on his estate, the priest on his parish, and the official, on everybody. It must be so."[7]

Peasants in nineteenth-century Poland were thus not Poles in any meaningful sense. Though they spoke Polish, they had little national feeling. As the leading historian of nineteenth-century Poland has phrased it: "Centuries of feudal oppression had resulted in isolating the peasants from the rest of society. Those who were not peasants were either oppressors (landlords, overseers) or aliens (the government official, the local Jew, the travelling townsman)." Peasants deeply resented the economic advantages of the lords and the aliens ("Plough with a goose-quill, sow paper with sand; ye will get much more pelf [wealth] than by tilling the land"); and most did not support the gentry in their various rebellions against the partitioning powers. Indeed, in 1846 in the Austrian province of Galicia, Polish peasants around the city of Tarnow reacted to a gentry uprising against the partitioning powers by attacking the gentry. Rampaging peasants looted 400 manor farms and killed over 1,200 people. They felt their class grievances far more strongly than any national grudges against the Austrians ("The gentry rebel and drive our folk to ruin; but who has to pay, when payday comes? Why we peasants!"). Thus, they confirmed their isolation from the rest of Polish society in "a lake of blood."[8]

Occasionally today, well-meaning individuals will try to flatter a Polish American by reciting a list of notables from Polish history: Copernicus, who first theorized that the earth revolves around the sun; King John Sobieski, who saved Vienna from a Turkish invasion; Prince Adam Czartoryski, a European diplomat;

Ignace Paderewski, an internationally renowned pianist. In a burst of political correctness, the city of Chicago and its surrounding county of Cook have recently declared the birthday of Casimir Pulaski a local holiday for schoolchildren and government workers. Such flattery is ahistorical and misses the point. To compliment a Polish American descended from peasants on his noble Polish ancestors is like complimenting an African American on his illustrious ancestors George Washington and Thomas Jefferson. Polish peasants were as different from the *szlachta* as American slaves were from plantation owners.

Large social and economic forces eventually transformed the three partitions of Poland and set the peasant masses in motion. In an attempt to modernize their economy, the Polish gentry gradually emancipated the peasantry in the nineteenth century and consolidated their landholdings into more efficient farms. Emancipation followed different timetables in the various sectors of divided Poland. In Prussian Poland and in the large body of central Poland that Russia administered (the so-called Congress Kingdom of Poland), serfdom was technically abolished in 1807. This theoretical freedom, however, was not followed immediately by a grant of land title to the peasants, so it remained largely symbolic. Indeed, the first effect of the peasant's "freedom" was that the landlord could now evict him from the land he had previously farmed as a serf. Eventually, Prussia granted land title to many of the more ambitious peasants, in a gradual process completed by about 1850; Russia did not confirm peasant title until 1864. In Galicia, freedom and landowning both came together as a result of the revolution of 1848.

The gradual Prussian emancipation resulted in a highly polarized peasant economy. About 5 percent of the peasants managed to buy enough land to become efficient, productive capitalist farmers, much like the gentry; but over two-thirds of the masses lost their land or else clung to small, inefficient landholdings. In Austria, the process produced a different result. Few became landless, but most peasant landholdings were so small that starvation constantly faced the masses. In Russian Poland, the economic situation fell somewhere between the other two cases. Most peasants became medium-sized landowners; but even here the number of landless swelled by over 600,000 between 1870 and 1891.

Despite these different circumstances in each of the partitions of Poland, we can generalize to some extent about the fate of the emancipated peasants. Some peasants became moderately prosperous farmers as a result of emancipation, but the majority became landless or impoverished or both. The landed peasants stayed where they were, bought more land if possible, acquired some education, and assimilated to the Polish national consciousness preached by the city intelligentsia and some of the more enlightened gentry. The landless, on the other hand, were reduced to marginal subsistence, driven to migratory labor or industrial work in the cities, or else pushed out of Polish territory altogether as emigrants.

The waves of immigration began in the 1870s in the Prussian partition of Poland, where the forces of economic modernization struck earliest. The emigration fever spread to Russian and Austrian Poland after 1890. The process of peasant impoverishment and displacement was greatly accelerated by the general collapse of grain prices in the 1880s, when vast quantities of imported American wheat undercut Poland's traditional markets for grain. By the time of World War I, 1.2 million Poles had left the Prussian provinces east of the Oder-Neisse line; more than 600,000 Poles left Galicia; and 1.3 million abandoned the Russian sector of Poland. Not all of these migrants went to the United States. Some explored other new lands, such as Brazil or Australia, and many settled in industrial cities of western Germany. Yet in the last boom years of unrestricted American immigration, between 1900 and 1914, over 100,000 Poles a year arrived in the United States. According to one careful estimate, between 1,148,649 and 1,780,151 Polish immigrants entered America permanently between 1899 and 1932.[9]

The immigrants from Poland after 1870 came overwhelmingly from the peasant class. The United States Immigration Commission reported in 1911 that over 80 percent of the Polish immigrants had been farmers or farm laborers in the old country. There had been politically motivated Polish immigrants before 1870—each unsuccessful Polish rebellion had sent a small number of gentry patriots into exile in western Europe or America—but their numbers were small and they had little to do with the peasant masses that came after 1870. The peasant migration was economic in its motivation; in the phrase current at the time, Polish peasants went to America *za chlebem*, after bread. Many emigrating peasants probably intended only a temporary stay in America, long enough to earn money to buy land back in Poland. More than are generally recognized did return to Poland (perhaps 30–40 percent), but through a combination of circumstances, the majority stayed in the United States.[10]

The peasant nature of Polish immigration had important consequences. A peasant solidarity, which was neither nationalistic nor socialistic but simply familial and communal, gave the immigrants from Poland a sense of collective fellow-feeling. Their first loyalty was neither to Poland nor to the United States but simply to themselves and their families. Peasant origins made them clannish, conservative, fearful of change, intensely land-hungry, and economically acquisitive. Most of all, however, peasant origins largely determined where the Poles would settle in America and what kind of work they would do here. Polish immigrants came looking for bread, but all they had to offer was their peasant strength. This ensured that most of them would work long and hard as unskilled laborers in America.

WORKING-CLASS LIFE AND VALUES

Ironically, the fact that most Polish immigrants were peasants made it nearly inevitable that they would not settle on farms in the United States. As landless peasants in Europe, they had no money to buy land in America; furthermore, they found American farming uncongenial, too individualistic, and too lonely.

European peasants lived in villages; and though they owned and worked individual farms, they performed many tasks communally and could always count on a family and village support system in times of need. American prairie farming, with the nearest neighbor miles away, held no allure for them. Besides, many of the Polish peasants wanted to return to Poland and buy land there, so they chose the quickest way to earn money in America, and that was in industrial cities. Most Polish immigrants, therefore, settled in cities of the Northeast or the Midwest, in the industrial heartland of the nation.

Polish immigrants did not settle in just any city. They gravitated to the newer, fast-growing cities of heavy industry, where the demand for unskilled labor was the greatest. As peasants, they had few skills that were useful in an industrial society, but they were strong and they knew how to work hard. Thus, they offered their labor in steel mills, stockyards, mines, tanneries, or other heavy industries where machine technology had reduced most tasks to a simple routine requiring just brute strength. It is not surprising, then, that Chicago—"the city of the broad shoulders; the hogbutcher to the world," as the poet Carl Sandburg phrased it—attracted the largest number of Polish immigrants. By 1930, there were over 400,000 Polish Americans in Chicago; today there are 900,000 people of Polish ancestry in the state of Illinois, and most of these in the Chicago metropolitan area.[11] Other large industrial cities, such as Detroit, Cleveland, Pittsburgh, and Buffalo, also attracted large numbers of Poles, as did many small mill and mining towns scattered across the landscape of Pennsylvania.

The cities Poles did not settle in are instructive. Like most immigrants, they avoided Southern or semi-Southern cities, such as Richmond, Baltimore, or St. Louis, where the African American population would have provided stiff competition for the lowest-paying, unskilled jobs. They also avoided cities such as Philadelphia, where industries were old and well-established and put a premium on skilled workers. Though several hundred thousand remained in the New York area after passing through Ellis Island, most settled along the docks of Brooklyn or near the factories of New Jersey rather than in the commercial heart of Manhattan.[12]

The peasant solidarity of the Poles eased their transition into the working class and made them good union members. In the early days of trade unionism, union leaders badly misread the Poles' clannishness and considered them unorganizable. The union's mistake was understandable. Polish peasants had come primarily as temporary laborers, intending to stay only long enough to earn a nest egg and buy land back home. They willingly worked the longest hours, for any wage, and tried to save every penny. Under normal circumstances, then, their limited aspirations in the New World and their peasant submissiveness and dedication to hard work put them at cross-purposes with the militant aims of union organizers. Yet peasants remained submissive only up to a point. If they felt their fundamental rights were being violated, they would resist fiercely, and communal solidarity proved a tremendous asset in a strike situation.[13]

This counterpoint between general peasant submissiveness and occasional bursts of fierce communal struggle carried over directly from Europe. After emancipation of the peasants, some vestigial feudal rights and obligations remained as bones of contention. Among the most important were the peasants' forest rights. Though the landlord owned the forests, villages of peasants retained the right to gather firewood in specific sections of the forest, and the lord was obliged to consult with them before selling or felling any trees. Reymont's novel, *The Peasants*, climaxes with a tremendous peasant *jaquerie* (revolt) when the local squire cuts down a portion of his forest to sell to outsiders. The entire village of Lipka, men, women, and children included, marches to the forest to prevent the sale.

> There were hand-to-hand fights, there were mass attacks; men were seized by the throat or by the hair of the head, and they tore at each other like wild beasts. The manor servants . . . [were led] by the forester, a man of gigantic size, who dearly loved a fight, and had, besides, many a bone to pick with the Lipka folk. He darted onward fighting alone against multitudes, cracking their skulls with the butt of his gun, and making them fly on every side: a scourge to them all, and a terror. . . . But he was assailed by a host of women, who flung themselves on him with shrieks, clawed his face, pulled out his hair by handfuls, and piling themselves one upon the other, bore him to the earth along with them: like a lot of curs attacking a shepherd's dog, plunging their fangs in his flesh, and dragging him this way and that way.[14]

Similarly, in America the violent strikes of the Polish workers involved the whole community. In 1921, at the 43rd and Ashland Avenue gate to the Chicago Stockyards, pitched battles broke out between Polish strikers and the packers' strikebreakers. When mounted police charged the strikers, like so many Cossacks in the old country, the Polish women threw red pepper and paprika in the eyes of both police and horses.[15]

In 1915 and 1916, Bayonne, New Jersey, refinery workers mounted two bitter strikes and forced their middle-class community members, mainly local storekeepers, to support them. When violence broke out, the seemingly uncontrolled crowd exercised great selectivity in choosing targets. They sacked three Jewish businesses and an Irish saloon but did not touch any Polish-owned stores.[16]

The peasant background of immigrant laborers proved to be a two-edged sword. Their initial peasant docility lured employers into hiring them in preference to more skilled American workers, but their fierce communal solidarity made them formidable foes when aroused. Once union organizers broke through the language and cultural barriers, as well as their own craft union limitations, and began to organize the unskilled in industrial unions, they found the Polish immigrant communities fiercely loyal to the workers' cause. Poles and other eastern Europeans with similar peasant backgrounds have formed the backbone of many CIO industrial unions since the 1930s.

As industrial workers, Polish Americans developed what might be called a working-class mentality. That is, they tended to value good wages and job security more than occupational status or education for their children. In 1890, a young Polish immigrant wrote to his father back in Poland, warning him not to waste any money educating his younger brother: "If he wants to earn a living here with a pen that is not for America. America does not like writers but hard-working people." This attitude persisted in the first two generations of Polish Americans. In Pittsburgh, two-thirds of the Poles remained in the same low-skill, working-class occupations between 1930 and 1960; in Detroit in 1970, 75 percent of the employed males in a typical Polish neighborhood were blue-collar workers, and the average number of years of schooling was 10.1; in Chicago in 1970, census data showed Polish families with a higher-than-average median income but a low percentage of professionals and managers.[17]

As former peasants, they still had an intense desire to own land, which led them to a high degree of home ownership. In Polish working-class wards of Milwaukee, Wisconsin, around the beginning of the twentieth century, the immigrant laborers harbored such a strong desire to own their own houses that they bought small frame houses in an undeveloped area. Despite their low wages they met the payments on these cottages by taking in boarders and by consistently voting down tax assessments for street paving and sewer connections. In other words, these Polish workers made a trade-off: they deferred middle-class amenities in order to own a home.[18]

Success for Polish Americans with this working-class mentality meant a good-paying, unionized job, with no fancy title but with lots of overtime, and a neat, well-kept house and garden. First-generation Polish Americans were more likely to send their sons to work in the mills at an early age in order to help pay the mortgage than to forego home ownership and send them to college. The second generation held more ambiguous attitudes toward work and education. Indeed, many raised their children to have lives significantly different from their own. Yet, as one close student of this phenomenon has described it, "Even though mothers and fathers would like their children to become members of the professional middle-class, or middle-level executives, the prevailing patterns of child-rearing are based on what parents, especially, fathers, have learned about the qualities that insure success in the blue-collar world: obedience, self-control, respect for authority, and determination." Such traits do not translate into advantages in the professional world.[19]

CATHOLIC SOLIDARITY

The religion of the Polish immigrants reinforced their peasant communalism and their working-class solidarity. Polish peasants were fervent Catholics, though they mixed their religion with numerous vestiges of magic and superstition. Language and religion, far more than any concept of secular nationalism, gave the peasant his identity and distinguished him from foreigners. "Praised be Jesus Christ" was the standard peasant greeting in Poland; "for ever and ever" the ritual reply.

The Roman Catholic Church in the nineteenth century propounded an aggressively defensive brand of dogma that vigorously condemned the modern trends of unbridled individualism and materialism and political and intellectual liberalism. This "circle the wagons" style of religion aptly suited the situation of the Polish peasant. Like the Catholic Church, the Polish peasant felt beleaguered on all sides. In the peasant world of capricious nature, rapacious landlords, and invading armies, the Catholic Church was a rock of solidity and certainty. The Church was eternal and universal, but at the same time it was tangible and concrete, with its rich liturgy, music, and incense. In the midst of political partition and agrarian reform, religion remained a fixed point defining who the Polish peasant was. The Catholic priest stood as a pillar in the center of the Polish peasant community.[20]

Upon immigration to America, the Polish peasant needed such a pillar all the more. If it were merely a question of religious services, the Polish immigrant could easily have attended one of the Irish or German Catholic parishes in the United States. Indeed, the Mass was offered in a language equally incomprehensible to all: Latin. But the immigrants' parish church was more than a place for religious services; it was a community center, perhaps even an attempt to reestablish the old peasant community itself.

Polish Americans made the church the central institution of their communities in American cities. These communities formed cities within cities, and the string of Polish churches formed a sort of denomination within a denomination. Father Vincent Barzynski, C.R., who served as pastor of the oldest Polish parish in Chicago, St. Stanislaus Kostka, from 1872 to 1899, provides a good example. Father Barzynski and his flock built a massive, cathedral-like church that still stands today; they also built a convent, rectory, school, and parish credit union. In the year of Chicago's World's Fair, 1893, St. Stanislaus billed itself as the largest Catholic parish in America, with over 20,000 parishioners organized into seventy-four different parish societies. Nearby, in the same neighborhood, church-related groups also built a Polish-Catholic hospital, high school, orphanage, and publishing company.[21]

Polish peasants had been respectful and deferential to the clergy in the old country, often kneeling to hug their legs and kiss their feet; and the clergy held considerable influence over them. On many occasions, when peasant riots threatened, the priest would walk through the village with the Holy Viaticum, the Body of the Lord, and quiet their turbulence. Yet, the priest could not oppose the peasants' most fundamental economic interests. In the *jaquerie* already described from Reymont's novel, the local priest had tried to stop the peasants but was swept aside.

So too in America. Chicago's Father Barzynski, and many other strong-willed pastors, often faced opposition from their parishioners. The Polish laymen had usually taken the initiative in founding a parish in America, forming a confraternity or religious society that bought land and began building a church. These lay trustees of the parish often resisted turning over legal title to the bishop and the pastor. In 1873, for instance, when overcrowding at Chicago's St. Stanislaus Kostka necessitated the building of another church, a lay society founded the Holy Trinity church three blocks away and tried to retain title and find a pastor more to their liking than Father Barzynski. The bishop and the Resurrectionist religious order (which Father Barzynski belonged to) wanted the new church to remain a mission of St. Stanislaus. This dispute dragged on for nearly twenty years, several people were excommunicated, and Holy Trinity was padlocked for long periods of time. Finally, a papal representative had to settle the quarrel personally in 1893. Sometimes, these parish disputes between Polish laity and clergy ended in permanent schism. Father Francis Hodur of Scranton, Pennsylvania, eventually gathered together many of these dissident congregations into a new church denomination, the Polish National Church.[22]

Polish Americans took church politics seriously and played for high stakes. "Salvation was not an individual affair but the consequence of a way of life that could only be lived in a community organizing existence on earth. . . . Parish organizations could function as artificial families for immigrants separated from the extended family which had offered help and support in the old village."[23]

St. Stanislaus in Chicago, and most large Polish communities in America, attained a high degree of what sociologists call "institutional completeness." This means that the Polish ethnic group built such a wide range of institutions (most of them church-related) that it could perform most of the services its members required—religious, educational, recreational, and cultural—without recourse to the host society. Within their ethnic enclaves, Polish Americans could not only ignore most non-Catholic Americans, they could even remain separate from non-Polish Catholics.[24]

The peasant, working-class, and Catholic background of Polish Americans, and the resulting separatism of the community, all affected their attitudes toward politics. Poles in America voted overwhelmingly Democratic from the beginning, because they viewed the Democrats as the outsider's party, more sympathetic to working men and more tolerant of the Catholic religion. Republicans, on the other hand, were perceived as puritanical and plutocratic. In Chicago, for example, the identifiably Polish voting precincts gave a majority to the Democratic candidate in all but two of the thirteen presidential elections from 1888 to 1936. The two exceptions reinforce the point. In 1904, Republican Theodore Roosevelt seemed more sympathetic to workers than the conservative Democrat Alton B. Parker, and in 1912 Democrat Woodrow Wilson alienated many immigrant voters with an ethnic slur from his published historical writings.

More significant, perhaps, than the voting record is the political strategy pursued by Polish Democratic leaders, a strategy of clannish solidarity politics. Just as it was initially difficult to unionize the Polish peasant immigrants, it was hard for political leaders to incorporate them into political coalitions. Instead, the Polish politicians organized around parochial concerns, constantly tried to perfect the unity and solidarity of the bloc, and neglected the politics of building bridges to other groups. Polish leaders were misled by their large numbers in some industrial cities into thinking that political power would fall to them like a ripe fruit if only they would stick together. Sometimes this worked. In the small Polish enclave of Hamtramck, an industrial suburb of Detroit, Poles have dominated politics since the 1930s. So too in the city of Buffalo. But in larger and more diverse cities, such as Chicago, they have enjoyed little success. Since Polish voters never formed a majority in Chicago, their solidarity strategy was doomed to failure. Polish Americans never elected a mayor of Chicago, and they remained weak in the councils of the Democratic central committee until the late 1970s.[25]

Polish immigrants, then, built communities that were worlds unto themselves. But they were never completely successful in transplanting the Old World peasant village. Their New World communities were neither completely Polish nor completely American but, instead, Polish American. The people inhabiting these Polish American worlds, collectively called Polonja Amerykanska, or simply Polonia, were peasant in origin, unskilled industrial workers by occupation, and fiercely Roman Catholic in their values and loyalties.

POLONIA AND POLAND

The inhabitants of Polonia gradually grew distant from Poland. Many, perhaps most, had originally intended to remigrate once they had earned enough money to buy some land in the mother country, but either success or lack of success in America could trap them in their new lives. Before World War I, when Poland was still partitioned politically, many American Poles had said that if only their homeland were free and independent they would return in an instant. At the end of the war, the Polish National Alliance, the most nationalistic of the various Polish American fraternal organizations, challenged them to make good their boast: "Every one of us must presently decide whether he wishes to return to Poland and thus remain a Pole, or whether he wishes to live out his life in the land of Washington. . . . There is no middle ground."[26]

Not very many took up the challenge. In the four years after World War I, about 100,000 of the 2.5 million Polish Americans returned to Poland.[27] Many of these, not finding the Poland of their dreams, were swiftly disillusioned and came back to America. Both the leaders and the ordinary inhabitants of Polonia subtly changed the way they talked about themselves in the interwar years. Increasingly, the term "Polish Americans" replaced "We Poles." When a new war broke out and Poland was brutally invaded by the Nazis in 1939, Polish Americans were shocked and dismayed, but there was little they could do to aid their homeland. When the United States joined the conflict after Pearl Harbor, Polish immigrants and their descendants fought as Americans.

The end of World War II and the rise of Communism in Poland raised new concerns for Polish Americans. The major fraternal organizations of Polonia formed a new umbrella organization, the Polish American Congress (PAC), on May 5, 1944, to coordinate lobbying activities on behalf of postwar Poland. The PAC immediately adopted a vociferously anti-Communist stance, from which it did not deviate for over two decades. When the Big Three Allies, the United States, Great Britain, and the Soviet Union, met at the Yalta Conference in February 1945, they acknowledged the existence of a Soviet sphere of influence in the Eastern European territories liberated from Nazism. This meant that Stalin's Russia would hold decisive influence over any government formed in Poland after the war. The leaders of the Polish American Congress felt betrayed by the American government and mounted a sharp campaign of vilification against President Franklin D. Roosevelt.

Polish Americans who became citizens had given their votes to the Democratic Party from the very beginning, long before Franklin Roosevelt's New Deal. This political allegiance was rooted in a perception that the Democrats were the party of average working men and women and that they had broad-minded toleration for the Poles' Catholic religion and ethnic customs. The Yalta Conference and the American government's supposed "abandonment" of Poland to the Communists after World War II gave Polish American voters another agonizing issue. Many voted Republican in 1948, and some never forgave Franklin Roosevelt and the Democrats. Generally speaking, however, the mass of Polish Americans remained Democratic in their orientation, but foreign policy issues could occasionally shake their allegiance.[28]

World War II had devastated Poland, killing millions and setting many more adrift as refugees. The country's very borders were uprooted as the Soviet Union took a huge slice of eastern Poland and the Allies compensated Poland with territory in the west, at the expense of Germany. The United States accommodated a number of war refugees, including more than 120,000 Poles, through the Displaced Persons Act of 1948. After these DPs were admitted, however, immigration from Poland virtually ceased. The Communist domination of Eastern Europe pushed Polish Americans decisively away from their homeland and its concerns. When I was doing research for my doctoral dissertation in the 1960s, I found that the library of the Polish National Alliance did not hold a single book published in Poland after World War II. Poles in America had become Polish Americans during the interwar years, and now they thought of themselves simply as Americans of Polish heritage.

The peasant, working-class, and Catholic culture of Polonia remained vital in many industrial cities after World War II, but it gradually eroded as factories closed and second- and third-generation Americans of Polish descent joined the exodus to the suburbs. An era came to an end in the largest Polish American city, Chicago, when the Union Stock Yards closed forever on August 1, 1971. By this time, however, Polish Americans had found niches in the middle class. Indeed, priest-sociologist Andrew Greeley discovered that Polish Catholics, though earning less than Irish or German Catholics, made more money than all Protestant ethnic groups, except those of British ancestry. Other studies based on 1980 and 1990 census figures similarly found that Polish American workers tended to earn more than the national average income and registered outstandingly low levels of officially measured poverty.[29] Furthermore, few Polish Americans retained any contact with Poland and of the 8 million individuals who identified themselves as Polish American in the 1980 census, only 5 percent had been born in Poland.[30]

Events in Europe, however, soon rocked Polonia and sent a new influx of immigrants to America. On October 16, 1978, the College of Cardinals elected Karol Jozef Wojtyla, archbishop of Krakow, as pope of the Roman Catholic Church. Wojtyla, who took the name John Paul II, was the first non-Italian pontiff in over 400 years. When he toured major cities of the United States, including the Polish American stronghold of Chicago, in October 1979, Polish Americans swelled with immense pride. Earlier that year, in June of 1979, Pope John Paul II made an even more important journey, to his native country, which proved to be a dress rehearsal for the overthrow of Communism in Eastern Europe and the Soviet Union. Wojtyla's Polish pilgrimage marked the 900th anniversary of the martyrdom of St. Stanislaus, Poland's patron and a powerful symbol of the Church's resistance against tyrants. The Polish Communist authorities stalled the pope and tried to envelop his visit in red tape, but ultimately Wojtyla spent nine triumphant days in his homeland. Church volunteers planned the pilgrimage and kept remarkable order, despite crowds of over a million people on several occasions. This peaceful organization of the journey demonstrated to Poles that they could function as a civil society outside of state control, and provided a refreshing experience of community solidarity. The Pope's boldly repeated message, "Be not afraid," further heartened the long-repressed masses. The Polish journey of Pope John Paul II stimulated memories of how important the Catholic Church had been throughout Polish history and provided a model of communal solidarity and nonviolent action.[31]

Emboldened by the pope's words and actions, a nonviolent strike wave hit Poland in the summer of 1980 when the government attempted to raise the price of meat nearly 100 percent. Then, on August 14, 1980, the management of the Gdansk shipyard on the Baltic seacoast fired a popular worker, Anna Walentynowicz, for political action, and her coworkers marched out of work en masse. Another recently dismissed worker, Lech Walesa, rallied the shipyard workers, who soon expanded their list of demands beyond economic and personnel issues to more fundamental matters, such as the recognition of independent trade unions and the right to strike. Walesa and the other striking workers named their spontaneous coalition of trade unions, Solidarnosc, or Solidarity. In order to emphasize the feeling of communal responsibility that Poles had first demonstrated during the pope's visit in 1979, Solidarity adopted an official logo that displayed the letters of the group's name leaning against each other. No letter, or person, could stand alone, but needed support from a neighbor. Solidarity proved to be more than a trade-union federation: it was a movement for freedom of speech, religion, and assembly in Communist Poland.[32]

After a turbulent year and a half of relative freedom, the Communist government of Poland cracked down in December 1981, arresting Walesa and the other Solidarity leaders and declaring martial law. Communist rule resumed in its full severity. Yet within a few years, Walesa and his coworkers were quietly released and Pope John Paul II made two further visits to Poland during the 1980s. When Mikhail Gorbachev loosened up the system of repression in the Soviet Union in the late 1980s and signaled that he would no longer dominate the Eastern European satellite states by force, Poland's Solidarity activists came out of hiding and won the Soviet bloc's first free elections in June 1989. By the end of that year, a Solidarity-led government had replaced the Communists in Poland, the Berlin Wall had fallen, and the Soviet Union was on its way to extinction. Pope John Paul II first opened the doors of Communism during his Polish pilgrimage of 1979, and a year later Solidarity came crashing through. The Communist authorities soon banged the doors shut, but when Gorbachev cracked them ajar once again, they flew open for good.

These epoch events had repercussions in American Polonia. After decades of virtually no contact with Communist Poland, Americans of Polish descent followed the riveting events in their homeland with increasing fascination. The economic hard times that had given rise to Solidarity, and the political repression that followed its suppression, sent new waves of migrants from Poland to America. The Refugee Act of 1980 facilitated this movement of political exiles. The new law admitted refugees outside the standard immigration quota system if they were unwilling to return to their country of origin because of a well-grounded fear of persecution based on race, religion, nationality, or political opinion. In actual practice, during the heightened cold war years of the Reagan presidency, any immigrant fleeing a Communist state, such as Poland, was admitted with few questions asked. Immigrants from other dictatorships, such as the military regimes of Central and South America, experienced much more difficulty in gaining admittance. During the 1980s, 33,889 Poles were granted official refugee status. Many more arrived as quota immigrants or as "temporary" visitors.[33]

In absolute terms, these new immigrants from Poland were still greatly outnumbered by the descendants of the peasant immigrants from a hundred years earlier. For example, in 1990 the census takers estimated that 962,827 people in the state of Illinois considered themselves Polish by descent, yet only 80,594 of these (8 percent) were foreign born. In the city of Chicago, however, fully 20 percent (52,669) of the 261,899 who identified themselves as Polish were foreign born. Only the Mexicans were more numerous among Chicago's foreign born.[34]

These Solidarity immigrants revitalized older Polish neighborhoods in major cities such as Chicago. Sociologist Mary Patrice Erdmans has studied intensively one such neighborhood, the so-called *Jackowo*, or St. Hyacinth's neighborhood on Chicago's northwest side.[35] At the time the Berlin Wall fell and Communism disappeared from Eastern Europe, St. Hyacinth's parish in Chicago consisted of almost 4,000 families, more than half of whom had arrived in the previous ten years. Three of the six priests serving the parish had been born in Poland, and five of the nine weekend masses were said in Polish. Erdmans surveyed 183 businesses on the commercial strip of Milwaukee Avenue, near St. Hyacinth's, and found that 40 percent of the business owners were Polish immigrants and 22 percent were Polish Americans. Erdmans concluded: "*Jackowo* is more of an 'immigrant' community than an 'ethnic' community, and this is reflected in the type of businesses found in the community: overseas shipping and money transit services, passport and visa offices, and employment agencies for immigrants without 'green cards.' "[36] Except for the language spoken, the Jackowo neighborhood is remarkably similar to the Hispanic neighborhoods that surround it.

At the beginning of the twenty-first century, therefore, Polonia consists of a large mass of well-assimilated, middle-class Americans of Polish descent, leavened with a small but significant number of recent migrants who have fled Europe during or after its massive transformation from Communism to freedom. Polonia embraces both old and new immigrants.

NOTES

1. According to the 2000 U.S. census, an estimated 9,053,660 Americans claim Polish ancestry. See www.census.gov, Quick Table – 02, Profile of Selected Social Characteristics, 2000.

2. Mary Patrice Erdmans, *Opposite Poles: Immigrants and Ethnics in Polish Chicago, 1976–1990* (University Park: Pennsylvania State Univ. Press), 64–65.

3. Ibid., 113.

4. Ibid., 91.

5. The best overall history of Poland is a translation of a Polish work, Aleksander Gieysztor et al., *History of Poland* (Warsaw: Polish Scientific Publishers, 1968). The volume on the nineteenth century is written by Stefan Kieniewicz. Some of my remarks about the history of Poland are drawn from two series of lectures Kieniewicz delivered at the University of Chicago from January to June 1968.

6. For the condition of Poland's peasantry at the time of partition, see Stefan Kieniewicz, *The Emancipation of the Polish Peasantry* (Chicago: Univ. of Chicago Press, 1969), 3–43.

7. Ladislas Reymont, *The Peasants*, 4 vols. (New York: Alfred A. Knopf, 1925), 4: 201. Reymont's novel was originally published in Polish as *Chlopi* between 1902 and 1909. Unless otherwise identified, all peasant sayings or aphorisms in this chapter are quoted from this novel.

8. The entire discussion of Polish peasant origins is drawn from Kieniewicz, *Emancipation of the Polish Peasantry.*

9. Helena Znaniecki Lopata, "Polish Immigration to the United States of America: Problems of Estimation and Parameters," *Polish Review* 21, no. 4 (1976): 105.

10. *Reports of the Immigration Commission*, 61st Congress, 2nd Session, 1911, 4: 338–39, 373–75.

11. Ernest W. Burgess and Charles Newcomb (eds.), *Census Data of the City of Chicago, 1930* (Chicago: Univ. of Chicago Press, 1933), 626–634; www.census.gov, Quick Table – 02, Profile of Selected Social Characteristics, 2000. For background on Poles in Chicago, see Edward R. Kantowicz, *Polish American Politics in Chicago, 1888–1940* (Chicago: Univ. of Chicago Press, 1975), 12–27, and Kantowicz, "Polish Chicago: Survival through Solidarity," in *Ethnic Chicago: A Multicultural Portrait*, 4th ed. (Grand Rapids, MI: Wm. Eerdmans Publishing, 1995), 173–198.

12. Caroline Golab, *Immigrant Destinations* (Philadelphia: Temple Univ. Press, 1977), 1–27, ably describes these Polish settlement patterns.

13. Victor Greene, *The Slavic Community on Strike* (Notre Dame: Univ. of Notre Dame Press, 1968), was the first to study Polish labor attitudes in detail. John J. Bukowczyk, "Polish Rural Culture and Immigrant Working Class Formation, 1880–1914," *Polish American Studies* 41 (Autumn 1984): 23–44, has described sensitively the complexities of these attitudes.

14. Reymont, *The Peasants* 2 (Winter): 280.

15. Dominic A. Pacyga, *Polish Immigrants and Industrial Chicago: Workers on the South Side, 1880–1922* (Columbus: Ohio State Univ. Press, 1991), 250–251.

16. John J. Bukowczyk, "The Transformation of Working-Class Ethnicity: Corporate Control, Americanization, and the Polish Immigrant Middle Class in Bayonne, New Jersey 1915–1925," *Labor History* 25 (Winter 1984): 70.

17. Paul Wrobel, *Our Way: Family, Parish, and Neighborhood in a Polish-American Community* (Notre Dame: Univ. of Notre Dame Press, 1979), is a sensitive study of a typical Polish American working-class neighborhood in Detroit by an anthropologist participant-observer. Dominic Pacyga, *Polish Immigrants and Industrial Chicago*, focuses on two primarily working-class areas, the Back of the Yards and South Chicago. John Bodnar, Roger Simon, and Michael P. Weber, *Lives of Their Own: Blacks, Italians, and Poles in Pittsburgh, 1900–1960* (Urbana: Univ. of Illinois Press, 1982), studies three working-class groups over time. All information in this paragraph is from these three works.

18. Roger D. Simon, "Housing and Services in an Immigrant Neighborhood: Milwaukee's Ward 14," *Journal of Urban History* 2 (August 1976): 435–438; and Simon, *The City-Building Process: Housing and Services in New Milwaukee Neighborhoods, 1880–1910* (Philadelphia: American Philosophical Society, 1978).

19. Wrobel, *Our Way*, 77–84.

20. William I. Thomas and Florian Znaniecki, *The Polish Peasant in Europe and America*, 5 vols. (Chicago: Univ. of Chicago Press, 1918), 4:103–120.

21. Kantowicz, *Polish American Politics*, 30–33; Joseph Parot, *Polish Catholics in Chicago, 1850–1920* (DeKalb: Northern Illinois Univ. Press, 1981), 59–94; Victor Greene, *For God and Country* (Madison: State Historical Society of Wisconsin, 1975).

22. Greene, *For God and Country*, 74–82; Parot, *Polish Catholics in Chicago*, 40–64; Kantowicz, "Polish Chicago," 182–185.

23. Mary Cygan, "Ethnic Parish as Compromise: The Spheres of Clerical and Lay Authority in a Polish American Parish, 1911–1930," Cushwa Center for the Study of American Catholicism, University of Notre Dame, Working Paper Series 13, no: 1 (Spring 1983): 11–12, 23–24.

24. Raymond Breton, "Institutional Completeness of Ethnic Communities and the Personal Relations of Immigrants," *American Journal of Sociology* 70 (1964) 193–205; Kantowicz, "Polish Chicago," 177–182.

25. This entire discussion is developed more fully in Kantowicz, *Polish American Politics*.

26. *Dziennik Zwiazkowy*, March 24, 1919, 4.

27. Joseph A. Wytrwal, *America's Polish Heritage* (Detroit: Endurance Press, 1961), 236–237.

28. James S. Pula, *Polish Americans: An Ethnic Community* (New York: Twayne Publishers, 1995), 106–109.

29. Andrew M. Greeley, *Ethnicity in the United States: A Preliminary Reconnaissance* (New York: John Wiley, 1974), 42–43; Pula, *Polish Americans*, 139–140.

30. Mary Erdmans, *Opposite Poles*, 56.

31. There are many biographies of John Paul II. Two journalistic studies, Tad Szulc, *Pope John Paul II: The Biography* (New York: Scribner, 1995), and Carl Bernstein and Marco Politi, *His Holiness: John Paul II and the Hidden History of Our Time* (New York: Doubleday, 1996), emphasize the world-historical importance of this pontiff's reign. George Weigel, *Witness to Hope: The Biography of Pope John Paul II* (New York: Harper-Collins, 1999), probes more deeply into the pope's philosophical and theological ideas.

32. Timothy Garton Ash, *The Polish Revolution: Solidarity* (New York: Scribner, 1983), presents a lively narrative of the movement. For a concise summary, see Edward R. Kantowicz, *Coming Apart, Coming Together* (Grand Rapids, MI: Wm. Eerdmans, 2000), chap. 20.

33. Mary Erdmans, *Opposite Poles*, 63–65.

34. U.S. Bureau of the Census, 1990 Census of Population, Social and Economic Characteristics, Illinois, Tables 19 and 168 and Place of Birth of Foreign-Born Persons, Tables 31 and 166.

35. In Polish, the addition of the suffix *owo* to a parish name turns it into a regional or neighborhood name. Thus, the neighborhood surrounding *Swieto Jacek* (St. Hyacinth) is called *Jackowo*, or the St. Hyacinth's district. Lest anyone miss the point, the city of Chicago has recently posted honorary street signs that identify the area as Polish village.

36. Mary Erdmans, *Opposite Poles*, 78–79.

BIBLIOGRAPHICAL ESSAY

Background History of Poland

Aleksander Gieysztor et al., *History of Poland* (Warsaw: Polish Scientific Publishers, 1968), is a multivolume history, with each volume written by a separate author. For a more concise, up-to-date history, see M. B. Biskupski, *The History of Poland* (Westport, CT: Greenwood Press, 2000). The peasant background may be studied in the five-volume sociological classic by William I. Thomas and Florian Znaniecki, *The Polish Peasant in Europe and America* (Chicago: Univ. of Chicago Press, 1918; reprinted in various editions), and in Stefan Kieniewicz, *The Emancipation of the Polish Peasantry* (Chicago: Univ. of Chicago Press, 1969). A two-volume historical dictionary is useful for looking up individuals and events from Poland's long history: George J. Lerski, *Historical Dictionary of Poland, 966–1945* (Westport, CT: Greenwood Press, 1996), and Piotr Wrobel, *Historical Dictionary of Poland, 1945–1996* (Westport, CT: Greenwood Press, 1998).

Overviews of Polish Americans

The best interpretive history of Polish Americans is by John J. Bukowczyk, *And My Children Did Not Know Me: A History of the Polish Americans* (Bloomington: Univ. of Indiana Press, 1987), and the best sociological study is Paul Wrobel, *Our Way: Family, Parish, and Neighborhood in a Polish-American Community* (Notre Dame, IN: Univ. of Notre Dame Press, 1979). Two brief overviews (the first by a historian, the second by a sociologist) are also useful: James S. Pula, *Polish Americans: An Ethnic Community* (New York: Twayne Publishers, 1995), and Helena Znaniecka Lopata, *Polish Americans: Status Competition in an Ethnic Community* (1976; repr. New Brunswick: Transaction Press,

2nd rev. ed., with a new chapter by Mary Patrice Erdmans, 1994). See also, Victor Greene, "The Poles," in *Harvard Encyclopedia of American Ethnic Groups*, ed. Stephan Thernstrom et al. (Cambridge, MA: Harvard Univ. Press, 1980), 787–803.

Specialized Monographs on Polonia

Victor R. Greene was a pioneer in the exploration of Polish American history. His publications include *The Slavic Community on Strike* (Notre Dame, IN: Univ. of Notre Dame Press, 1968); *For God and Country: The Rise of Polish and Lithuanian Ethnic Consciousness in America* (Madison: The State Historical Society of Wisconsin, 1975); and *American Immigrant Leaders, 1800–1910: Marginality and Identity* (Baltimore: The Johns Hopkins Univ. Press, 1987). Chicago, the largest Polish American settlement, has been studied by Joseph J. Parot, *Polish Catholics in Chicago: 1850–1920* (DeKalb: Northern Illinois Univ. Press, 1981); Dominic A. Pacyga, *Polish Immigrants and Industrial Chicago: Workers on the South Side, 1880–1922* (Columbus: Ohio State Univ. Press, 1991); Edward R. Kantowicz, *Polish American Politics in Chicago, 1888–1940* (Chicago: Univ. of Chicago Press, 1975); and Mary Patrice Erdmans, *Opposite Poles: Immigrants and Ethnics in Polish Chicago, 1976–1990* (University Park: Pennsylvania State Univ. Press, 1998). Polish Americans in other cities have been studied in Caroline Golab, *Immigrant Destinations* (Philadelphia: Temple Univ. Press, 1977); John Bodnar, Roger Simon, and Michael P. Weber, *Lives of Their Own: Blacks, Italians, and Poles in Pittsburgh, 1900–1960* (Urbana: Univ. of Illinois Press, 1982); Laurence D. Orton, *Polish Detroit and the Kolasinksi Affair* (Detroit: Wayne State Univ. Press, 1981); and Anthony J. Kuzniewski, *Faith and Fatherland: The Polish Church War in Wisconsin, 1896–1918* (Notre Dame, IN: Univ. of Notre Dame Press, 1980). Donald E. Pienkos has published two wide-ranging studies: *PNA: A Centennial History of the Polish National Alliance* (Boulder, CO: East European Monographs, 1984), and *For Your Freedom through Ours: Polish-American Efforts on Poland's Behalf, 1863–1991* (Boulder, CO: East European Monographs, 1991).

SCANDINAVIAN AMERICANS

John Robert Christianson

Scandinavian acculturation in America was not a one-way street of assimilation into a dominant Anglo-American community. Rather, it was a process of fragmentation into a variety of ethnic communities, each with its own particular identity and institutions. These localized communities varied considerably, and they all changed as time passed. A broader ethnic identity finally emerged out of the very processes of acculturation and assimilation, so that, as the Scandinavian American communities became more "American," they came to consider themselves more "Scandinavian."

Look at any ethnic group within this nation of great cultural diversity and you will find a nation in miniature, composed of numerous subgroups that differ from one another by social class, regional origins, religion, time of arrival in America, or other factors. Scandinavians in America, like other American ethnic groups, shared this diversity from the very beginning.

COLONIAL SETTLEMENT

Their Viking ancestors had established colonies on Greenland around 985, and on Newfoundland before the year 1000.[1] Both islands are part of North America geologically and geographically. Scandinavian Greenland became an outpost of medieval Christian Europe for nearly 500 years. This was longer than any other Scandinavian settlement in the New World until the present, but not long enough to establish links with later European colonies in America. Unable to survive in the deteriorating late-medieval climate, the Scandinavian settlers on Greenland vanished around the middle of the fifteenth century.[2]

Less than 200 years later, in 1638, Finnish and Swedish colonists established New Sweden on the Delaware River. These colonists brought two distinct ways of life to America. The Swedes were mainly peasant farmers, soldiers, and former estate administrators who built permanent communities along the Delaware estuary in what later became Pennsylvania, southern New Jersey, and Delaware. The Finnish colonists, on the other hand, were skilled backwoodsmen with a mobile wilderness culture admirably preadapted to American frontier conditions.[3] Together, these two groups established the first effective settlement in the Middle Atlantic region and set the pattern for its later development.

Lutheran authorities in New Sweden demanded peaceful coexistence with the native people, encouraging Fenno-Swedish frontiersmen to interact with the Lenape (Delaware). The years 1640–1680 saw the emergence of a syncretic Fenno-Indian frontier culture, based on Indian maize (instead of Finnish rye), squash, pumpkins, maple syrup, and domestic turkeys, together with Finnish log cabins, split-rail fences, iron axes, long rifles, split-wood basketry, double-woven textiles, free-range swine and cattle, homemade vodka, hunting hounds, long hunting expeditions, and a fondness for bear meat. North European herbal and gathering lore was adapted to the flora of the Mid-Atlantic region and combined with Indian herbal medicine.

During the years 1680–1720, the essentials of this backwoods culture were adopted by a host of settlers newly arrived in the region: English and Welsh Quakers, Dutch, Germans, Swiss, Moravians, and Scotch-Irish. Those who moved to the frontier took to wearing Finnish fur caps and buckskins, picked up Finnish woodsmen's lore, learned how to build log structures using broad axe and adze, and adopted the Finnish practice of swidden agriculture, including frequent movement to new clearings. As for the scattered frontier Finns, they soon shifted to speaking English. In this way, a syncretic frontier culture emerged, English in its language, largely Scandinavian in its material culture, and adopted by settlers of diverse racial and ethnic backgrounds. By the nineteenth century, this dynamic American frontier culture rapidly outpaced the expansion of other colonial cultures to become the cutting edge of the Anglo-American Manifest Destiny, and the Scandinavian log cabin became a powerful symbol of American frontier values, adopted widely by Indian, African, and European peoples throughout the continent.

Scandinavian colonists came to America with dissimilar backgrounds, and they were fragmented even more by the process of acculturation. Along the Delaware, they still spoke Swedish in the late eighteenth century and still imported their Lutheran clergymen from Sweden, while the Finns of the frontier had long since switched to English.[4] Along the Hudson River, they learned to speak Dutch.[5] In Pennsylvania and North Carolina, Scandinavian Moravians assimilated into the predominantly German language and customs of the Moravian colonies.[6] In virtually every seaport of North America were scattered Scandinavian seamen and middle-class colonists. The latter were numerous enough in Philadelphia to form a Scandinavian Society in 1768, and they were also among the early pillars of the Lutheran congregation in New York.[7] Generally, however, Scandinavians assimilated without much trace into the local colonial society. As a colonial minority group, they had little choice.

By 1776, Scandinavian American colonists were speaking Dutch, German, English, and in a few communities, Swedish. Under these circumstances, little could remain of a shared Scandinavian ethnicity. For Scandinavian Americans, colonization had already become a process of cultural fragmentation.

SCANDINAVIAN IMMIGRATION TO 1865

The one common characteristic of all Scandinavian Americans is their origin in Scandinavia, where the five modern nations of Denmark, Finland, Iceland, Norway, and Sweden were emerging during the early nineteenth century. The Scandinavian economy was still preindustrial in 1815, but structures of universal public education were already taking shape, and the transition to a modern society had begun. During the next half-century, the population of Scandinavia doubled, transportation networks were modernized, and crises of underproduction became increasingly rare. When they did occur, as in the famine years of 1849–1850 in Norway and 1866–1869 in Finland and Sweden, the result was a surge of emigration, not the demographic catastrophe of past centuries.[8]

The landowning peasantry was an important class in Scandinavia.[9] Literacy was high and rising, and the more prosperous peasants were increasingly assertive in politics. Class lines remained sharp, however, and the peasant elite rankled under the condescension of their social superiors. As the traditional order of Scandinavian society gradually collapsed, these upwardly mobile peasants helped to shape a more individualistic and dynamic world. The old customary and communal forces of social cohesion gave way to a welter of new voluntary associations, many of them religious. The all-encompassing Lutheran state church remained in place, but below its surface, revival movements led by literate peasants gave vigorous expression to the drive for a transformed religious and social order.[10]

Nineteenth-century Scandinavian emigration was led by this active, well-to-do, educated, and dissatisfied peasant elite. Numerous combinations of religious, political, and economic discontent pushed them to leave, so they were a varied and fragmented group from the beginning.[11] Some hoped to reestablish the vanishing world of their ancestors on the American frontier, while others dreamed of diverse new and better worlds. A few examples will illustrate how some of these groups developed their own particular community institutions and identity in America.

Nineteenth-century Scandinavian mass emigration began in the summer of 1825, when a party of fifty-two Quakers and Haugean Lutheran pietists purchased a single-masted sloop of thirty-nine tons, the *Restaurationen*, and set out from Stavanger, Norway, for America.[12] They had an English-speaking guide. Their contacts with American Quakers helped them to sell their ship and cargo in New York harbor and to find land near Rochester in western New York. The "Sloopers" were coastal people who were used to contacts with foreigners. Their small numbers, open-mindedness, and liberal religious views eased assimilation into the local English-speaking community. At the same time, their letters home began the pull process toward a specific Scandinavian settlement in America.

In 1836, two more ships containing a total of 167 immigrants arrived from Stavanger.[13] These people passed through the Slooper colony near the Erie Canal and, together with some of the Sloopers, followed the flow of Americans heading toward the prairies of northern Illinois. Most of their neighbors in the Fox River valley of Illinois were English speaking, but the Norwegian language remained alive because of a steady flow of new immigration. In general, however, the Fox River settlers assimilated to American ways with comparative ease. In particular, this settlement came to be characterized by a diversity of beliefs reflecting American religious pluralism and their own revivalist background. Some of the Norwegians attended Mormon river baptisms or Methodist tent meetings, while others remained Quakers, pietistic Haugean Lutherans, or even liturgical Lutherans.

Meanwhile, the pull was spreading into different parts of Norway. Two wandering sheep traders, Ole and Ansten Nattestad, came out of the mountains to buy stock in the coastal lowlands around Stavanger. There they heard for the first time about the land called America.[14] They took the news into the high valleys of Telemark, Numedal, and Setesdal. In 1837, a clan of over fifty mountain people left Telemark for America, and others followed in 1839. Economic stress was the main push, and the Fox River valley was their specific destination. When they arrived in Illinois, they were overwhelmed by the richness of the land and shocked by the religious variety. To them, the Fox River area was a hornet's nest of heresy. These mountain people may not have been overly pious, but they were innately conservative, suspicious of foreign ways, and therefore stubbornly loyal to the Church of Norway. Moreover, their Norwegian dialect was quite different from that of the Stavanger region.

These differing cultural values led to the fragmentation of the Norwegian immigrant community. The mountain clansmen headed north, toward the Wisconsin frontier, where they established settlements at places called Muskego, Jefferson Prairie, and Koshkonong. Their Scandinavian mountaineer background preadapted them to success on the American frontier. They were the ones who introduced skis to North America, moving with great speed across the winter snows, outrunning deer, and amazing others with their hunting skill.[15] By 1843–44, they were organizing Lutheran congregations as the central institution in each of their communities and even calling middle-class clergymen from Norway to duplicate the rituals and social hierarchies of the Old World.[16] Their settlements were close-knit, compact, conservative, and unified in religion. For a long time, they maintained their Norwegian mountaineer speech and values.

The Mormons were equally close-knit but far different in their religious beliefs. In 1839, the Latter-Day Saints, under their prophet, Joseph Smith, had settled in Nauvoo, Illinois. Mormon missionaries fanned across the prairies. Some Norwegians in the Fox River settlement attended Mormon meetings and became converts. In 1844, Joseph Smith was assassinated. Two years later, when the Mormons began their long trek to Utah Territory, Scandinavians were among them. The Scandinavians became active participants in the process of ethnogenesis that created the Mormon culture of Deseret. Their extensive kinship networks, predilection for organized community cooperation, and strong interests in education and the arts helped to shape emergent Mormon values and institutions. The primary identity of these Scandinavian American Mormons was always religious, and they were ostracized by other Scandinavians from the moment of conversion. The mixed communities of Danish, Norwegian, and Swedish Mormons in Utah lived in isolation from other Scandinavian Americans, recruiting new members directly from Scandinavia by means of missionary activity. Their institutions became those common to the Mormon empire, and they shifted rather quickly to the use of English. Religion, rather than regional background, gave them their particular identity and institutions. At the same time, by separating them from their fellow Scandinavian Americans, it led to further fragmentation of the Scandinavian American population. The same was true of the Janssonists. In the Swedish provinces of Uppland and Hiilsingland during the 1840s, popular religious fervor centered upon Erik Jansson, a lay preacher whose prophetic message was perfectionist and utopian. In 1846, fleeing prison and persecution, Erik Jansson came to America, and up to 1,500 of his disciples followed within a year. At Bishop Hill on the Illinois prairies, not far from Nauvoo and the Fox River settlement, they founded a communal utopia under the dictatorial leadership of the prophet and his successors. By 1858, the Janssonists held 14,000 acres in common, besides mills, factories, a plain house of worship, and handsome communal residences and dining halls built in the style of Swedish manor houses. The Janssonists worked in large communal crews, worshipped, sang, and conducted all their affairs in the Swedish language. Erik Jansson was assassinated in 1850. Within less than twenty years, the Bishop Hill colony had destroyed itself with acrimonious lawsuits. Most of the colonists moved away, vanishing into the mainstream of Swedish America. For as long as it survived, however, the Janssonist colony was a place with institutions and a collective identity quite unlike any other Scandinavian American community.

By 1850, Scandinavians were arriving in Minnesota. Here the old and new Scandinavian Americans crossed paths and discovered that they were strangers. Immigrants from Sweden arrived in the territory as early as 1850, where they soon organized their Swedish Lutheran congregations. William Thompson, who arrived around the same time, was of colonial Swedish descent.[17] He came with a group of Lutherans from Ohio who were descendants of Delaware Swedes and Pennsylvania Germans. They settled in Rice County, close to extensive settlements of Swedish and Norwegian immigrants in Goodhue County. Although both groups were Lutherans, the recent immigrants discovered that they had little in common with the Americanized Ohioans, and vice versa. Different times of arrival in America had turned them into different peoples.

Nineteenth-century Finnish emigration began in the early 1860s. The first Finns came by way of northern Norway, where the population was a mixture of

Norwegians, Finns, and Sami (Saami, Lapps). American recruiters in 1863–64 found both Finns and Norwegians who were willing to leave the declining copper mines at Kaafjord to work in American mines, but others went into farming on the Minnesota frontier. Some of the Finns settled in the mining community of Hancock, Michigan, but others went into farming on the Minnesota frontier.[18] Finns spoke a language completely different from the other Scandinavian tongues, and some of them adhered to the Laestadian revival, which more-orthodox Scandinavian Lutherans considered to be wildly emotional and fanatical. These differences strained relations with other Scandinavians and led Finns to establish their own communities and churches.[19]

On the eve of the Civil War, there were over 70,000 Scandinavians in America, and more of Scandinavian ancestry. Small islands of Scandinavians were scattered across the face of North America, from upstate New York, old New Sweden, the Moravian and Appalachian Midlands and South, to the Midwest, Texas, Utah Territory, and California. Some of these settlements were two centuries old and had lost their original ethnic character. In all areas, local variations in the patterns of cultural continuity and acculturation gave each settlement a character of its own, differentiating it from its non-Scandinavian neighbors, but also from other Scandinavian American settlements and from the Scandinavian homeland. Scandinavian America in 1860 was a fragmented world of isolated communities, each developing in its own direction.

The greatest density of Scandinavian settlement was in the upper Midwest in northern Illinois and Iowa, southern Wisconsin, and Minnesota. In Chicago, Milwaukee, Madison, the river towns of the upper Mississippi, and in many rural areas, small Scandinavian communities were scattered among a wide variety of other peoples and tongues. A Scandinavian American mainstream was taking shape in this region by 1860, composed of these numerous dispersed, local communities. Two studies illustrate the dynamics of transatlantic community formation in the region.

Jon Gjerde examined emigration from Balestrand on the Sognefjord in Norway, where the widening gap between landowning farmers and landless "cottagers" (crofters, dependent rural tenants) was widening in the nineteenth century, while an expanding rural economy led to earlier marriage and larger families.[20] Land fragmentation was avoided by giving one heir the right to work the whole farm. The farmers drew on a growing supply of cheap cottager labor to improve their holdings and shift toward market production, though the risk and costs were considerable. Emigration from Balestrand began as a movement of well-to-do farming families made to feel insecure by the rapidity of change, together with younger sons facing downward mobility into the cottager class. The early Balestrand immigrants settled at Spring Prairie, Wisconsin, in 1845. They reestablished their networks of family and friends and established a Lutheran church as the center of community life. On the Wisconsin frontier, however, the land-to-labor ratio was the reverse of Balestrand—labor was scarce, land abundant—so they had to shift from labor-intensive animals to grain production, and the family, not cottagers, became the source of farm labor, which soon resulted in immense flocks of children. In 1853, a religious revival divided the community between pietistic Haugean Lutherans and adherents of the more traditional Norwegian Lutheran Synod. Religious ideology then became the basis of community fragmentation and reformation. In 1854, Spring Prairie pietists sold out and moved to Minnesota, where they founded a rural community at Arendahl. They built new ties to other midwestern communities of Haugeans from the Sognefjord region, while the Spring Prairie people maintained links to other Norwegian Synod communities.

Robert Ostergren followed emigration from Riittvik in the Swedish province of Dalarna, where most inhabitants were landowning farmers.[21] Land reforms in the 1830s consolidated arable fields and parceled out the extensive common forests, where village farmers pastured their livestock in the summer and burned a cash crop of charcoal in winter. In this region, family holdings were customarily divided in each generational transfer, but strong cooperative ties were maintained within kinship networks. When crop failure brought hard times in the 1860s, some of the most prosperous and influential clans paid family members to emigrate in order to relieve pressure on the family lands.

Many of these Riittvik emigrants reached the American frontier in the mixed forest zone of Isanti County, Minnesota. They quickly established an "axis of information and migration" between this place and their home community. By 1880, four-fifths of Isanti County's inhabitants were Swedish immigrants, and every settlement contained clusters of old friends and relatives from the same villages in Sweden, mostly in and around Riittvik. However, their American farmsteads were scattered, not huddled in villages. New crops like wheat and maize replaced the rye and hay of Riittvik, and livestock was pastured on the farm, not on distant forest clearings, while mechanization shortened the harvest and threshing seasons. In these and other ways, life changed as Riittvik immigrants assimilated rapidly and easily into the American economy.

Socially, however, they retained familiar Swedish customs within remarkably homogeneous communities centered on Lutheran, Baptist, and Mission Covenant churches, even tending to marry people from the same district within their original home parish. In conservative Lutheran communities, where cultural values remained especially strong, the immigrants maintained Old World strategies of piecemeal land transfer before death, eventual division of the farm between all sons, and careful provision for the retirement of the older generation. Fertility rates in these communities remained high, and they expanded steadily. Meanwhile, modernization was transforming the traditional way of life back in Riittvik, but in the early twentieth century, the kinship networks that had once sent out emigrants were still better off than their neighbors. The strategy of migration had paid dividends on both sides of the Atlantic.

Similar forces to those in Spring Prairie and Isanti County were at work throughout the Midwestern mainstream of Scandinavian America on the eve of the Civil War. Local communities were linked and then differentiated in an endless dialectic. Groups left older settlements to establish daughter settlements farther west, but they brought along their ties of kinship and friendship and frequently also kept up their connections with the older settlement. Circuit riding Lutheran pastors and itinerant lay preachers shared in the leadership of five, six, or more communities. Larger networks of pastors and congregations met in annual Lutheran synods, from the low-church Augustana and Eielsen's Synods to the liturgical Norwegian Synod. Newspapers in the Dano-Norwegian and Swedish literary languages began to link the scattered Scandinavian American settlements in the 1850s. Immigrants became more avid readers and letter writers than the folks who stayed home. Many of the Scandinavian immigrants of this era were political activists who quickly became involved in local and county politics, mediating between their fellow countrymen and American society at large.

Around 1860, Midwestern Scandinavians made their first ventures into American higher education. In Chicago and Decorah, Iowa, they established bilingual Lutheran colleges to train their own community leaders. Though small, these institutions strove to maintain the academic rigor of the Old World. At Luther College in Decorah, for example, the curriculum went far beyond bilingualism: for over fifty years, Latin, Greek, Hebrew, and the three "American" languages, Norwegian, English, and German, were all required for the BA degree.[22] The goals of such an education were clearly cosmopolitan and pluralistic, not local and particular.

Within the Scandinavian American mainstream in the Midwest, there was still no dominant sense of ethnic identity on the eve of the Civil War. Elite groups like pastors and journalists had a cosmopolitan education and promoted a common, generally Scandinavian identity that reflected the pan-Scandinavian movement of mid-nineteenth-century Scandinavia. This coincided in a rough way with the perception of other Americans, who could not really see the difference between a Dane, a Norwegian, and a Swede. The average Scandinavian Americans of this era simply accepted their ethnic identity as a fact of life. They did not usually think of themselves in national terms as Norwegians or Swedes, but in terms of their dialect, social class, religion, or regional subculture. Their communities were organized the same way, not on national lines. They were Langelanders, Telemarkings, Janssonists, or Mormons, not Danes, Swedes, or Scandinavians. They also perceived their Anglo-American neighbors as a distinct people, called Americans or Yankees. To the Scandinavians, Americanization did not mean assimilation to the culture or structured communities of the Yankees. It simply meant learning enough about American institutions and the English language to participate in public life. In that sense, they were strongly in favor of it, and it did not disrupt their own sense of community.[23]

THE CIVIL WAR

The Civil War brought a slump in Scandinavian immigration. At the same time, the Dakota War in Minnesota stopped the westward movement of the frontier in the upper Midwest. During the war, substantial numbers of Scandinavians answered the call to arms, and some served in a Scandinavian ethnic regiment, the Fifteenth Wisconsin, which saw heavy action under Colonel Hans Christian Heg of Muskego.[24]

The war added two new dimensions to the meaning of Americanization: participation in a common American cause, and creation of Scandinavian American heroes. Ethnicity and patriotism remained quite compatible in this era. Scandinavian Americans could be loyal Americans while living in ethnic communities with a language, customs, social networks, and institutions of their own. In fact, the very battle cry of the Fifteenth Wisconsin Regiment was in Norwegian: *For Gud og vort Land* (For God and Our Country).

SCANDINAVIA FROM 1865 TO 1890

The population of Scandinavia doubled in the years 1815–1865. Large masses of young people were absorbed into rural economies through the explosive growth of the cottager class. By 1870, cottagers made up roughly 40 percent of the total population of Norway. They built cottages on land belonging to a farm or estate, paid their rent by working for their landlord without wages, and subsisted as farm laborers, lumberjacks, fishermen, rural artisans, and small-scale tenant farmers. Their conditions grew increasingly miserable as their numbers increased. To the peasant farmers, however, they were a source of cheap labor that allowed modernization and improved market production.[25]

Then came the flood of cheap foreign grain of the late 1860s, brought to Scandinavia by new global transportation networks. Small coastal towns with sailing fleets were devastated: Scandinavia was the most maritime region in Europe. At the same time, agricultural traditions were hammered by the foreign competition. Regional underproduction compounded the crisis of global overproduction. Crop failures in the years 1866, 1867, and 1868 drove Finnish and Swedish peasant families to emigrate in great numbers. The first parties of Icelanders came to America around the same time. Scandinavian mass emigration was under way.[26]

There was a growing political consciousness. Virtually all younger Scandinavians were literate, and they were the ones who emigrated. Women, cottagers, and workers struggled to enter the political arena. Parts of Scandinavia under foreign rule—Finland, Iceland, Norway, and North Schleswig after 1864—developed assertive, extremely resilient national identities as a form of resistance, and emigrants from these regions carried strong ethnic identities abroad.[27]

The early 1880s, when Scandinavian emigration peaked, was a time of rapid urban growth and early industrialization. All segments of the Scandinavian population were disrupted and dissatisfied. The emigration included cottagers, sailors, marginal fanners, and the politically oppressed, but also a "brain drain" of skilled artisans, machinists, engineers, clergymen, physicians, ship owners, and others who could not find opportunities in the constricted, slowly developing economies of Scandinavia.[28]

Many migrated by stages, moving first to an urban area and then overseas. Women could often find jobs in the Scandinavian cities, and the more highly urbanized areas like Denmark consequently sent out a preponderance of male emigrants. Cottager families frequently sent one member overseas to earn passage money for the others. One-third of the emigrants departing from Gothenburg in the early 1880s traveled on prepaid tickets sent from America. Young single men and women made up a larger percentage of Scandinavian immigrants, and remigration, permanent or temporary, became much more common.

By 1890, over 10 percent of all foreign-born people in America were Scandinavians. They numbered nearly a million, not counting their American-born descendants.

These boom years of Scandinavian immigration came to an abrupt end with the panic of 1893 and the hard times that followed. By 1903, however, the flow of Scandinavian immigration was renewed. It reached high levels again in the first decade of the twentieth century. Scandinavians were a part of the new immigration of that era, as they had been of the older transatlantic movements.[29]

SCANDINAVIANS IN AMERICA, 1865–1914

Such a varied group as the Scandinavian immigrants of the 1870s and 1880s could hardly be expected to have similar goals or similar patterns of acculturation. Engineers and other professionals pursued their careers in the cities, industrial towns, and mining areas of America. Some of them assimilated rapidly into the American middle classes, but there were so many of them in cities like New York, Chicago, and Minneapolis that they maintained their middle-class Scandinavian social patterns and even established Scandinavian American professional organizations.

Many social layers of Scandinavians came to American cities. Sometimes whole communities were reestablished in the New World. Sailors, skippers, shipwrights, ships' chandlers, and ship owners from the devastated Scandinavian coastal towns established durable waterfront colonies in Brooklyn, San Francisco, Milwaukee, Manitowoc, and other American port cities.[30] Skilled Scandinavian machinists and other artisans clustered in Boston, New York, Philadelphia, Chicago, Omaha, and many smaller industrial cities, including Hartford (Connecticut), Jamestown (New York), Moline (Illinois), Racine (Wisconsin), and Rockford (Illinois). Immigrant clergymen, journalists, physicians, pharmacists, merchants, and politicians pursued careers in urban Scandinavian communities among former cottagers, farmers, and townspeople now working as journalists, carpenters, masons, housemaids, and common laborers. In every city, there were diverse Scandinavian communities, not just one, by the end of the 1880s. The pan-Scandinavian communities of an earlier era became segregated along regional and social lines. For the masses, the process of Americanization was becoming a process of urbanization.

These new immigrants came from a Scandinavia far different from earlier times, and their America was different from that of the rural pioneers, who still lived their lives not far from the burgeoning cities. The community institutions of the urban settlements were saloons, clubs, theaters, mutual-aid associations, choral societies, marching societies, trade or professional organizations, orphanages, and deaconess hospitals. All of these, and even the pattern of urban church life, differentiated these new communities from the older rural settlements, augmenting the fragmentation of Scandinavian American life.

Assimilation into non-English communities was another process that fragmented the Scandinavians in America. Some assimilated into the large German Protestant communities that were scattered throughout urban and rural America. Lutheran culture, despite its many variations, gave Germans and Scandinavians so much in common that it was sometimes easier for Scandinavians to assimilate into German American than into Anglo-American life.[31] There was also a great deal of assimilation between different Scandinavian communities in America. Danes arrived later than Norwegians and assimilated in large numbers into the well-established Norwegian American communities, since they could understand the Norwegian language. By the 1890s, perhaps 10 percent of people referred to as Norwegian Americans were actually of Danish origin. As these Danes, who were generally more urbane and liberal, began to play their role in shaping some Norwegian American communities, those communities were differentiated from ones that lacked a Danish minority.[32]

Intermarriage frequently facilitated interethnic assimilation. There were many unmarried males among Danish and Finnish immigrants and among all Scandinavian immigrants on the West Coast. This led to higher rates of exogamy, especially with other Scandinavians and with Germans. It helps to explain why Danes—aside from the nationally conscious North Schleswigers and Grundtvigian Lutherans—assimilated more rapidly than other Scandinavians, though not always into the Anglo-American community. In general, Scandinavians in America were slow to marry outside their ethnic group and social class. When they did so, they usually moved to the margins of their ethnic community.

Rural areas still exerted a powerful attraction to Scandinavian immigrants of the 1870s and 1880s. Danes, Finns, and Icelanders established rural settlements of their own. Norwegians and Swedes established new settlements and continued to immigrate to well-established ethnic settlements in Illinois, Wisconsin, Iowa, and Minnesota. The newcomers worked as farm laborers, seasonal lumberjacks, railroad laborers, and tenant farmers. There were so many of them that the process of assimilation slowed down and backed up. Scandinavian American communities in the Midwest became more Scandinavian in the 1880s than they had been in the 1860s. At the same time, newcomers could learn the language and lore of America in the older ethnic settlements. It was a strange, unsettling experience, even among relatives and others from the same home area. The two patterns of change among the immigrants—rapid acculturation and its opposite, fossilization—both had the effect of differentiating the immigrant communities from the Old World. One Danish immigrant who arrived alone in central Iowa around Christmas of 1888 recalled,

> I was transplanted into an entirely new world where even the landscape was different. The people spoke a language I could not understand, and even when they spoke Danish, the trend of conversation was along lines of which I had no knowledge. The houses, the stores, and even the streets were different and un-familiar. The food we ate was entirely different; while much better food was served than I was used to, yet it was unfamiliar. The table manners and the ac-tions of people were all strange.[33]

Different times of arrival in America had transformed culture so that these im-migrants from the same Old World class and community found themselves to be strangers sitting at a common table.

After one to five years in the older settlements, the rural newcomers either went to the city to seek a job, or they loaded their possessions into prairie schooners or railroad boxcars and set off for the frontier. Each new settlement generally had a core of people from a single Scandinavian family, village, or re-gion, both newcomers and younger people who had grown up in America, but the pioneers of the 1870s and 1880s were not like those of earlier decades. Many of them were former cottagers or poor, marginal farmers, and many had lived for a time in the urban slums or in the older communities farther east. On the plains of Kansas, Nebraska, and the Dakotas they met a harsh environment suited to wheat ranching but generally not to traditional Scandinavian mixed farming. Railroads provided access to seemingly insatiable global markets, but at the price of a fluctuating market and economic dependence. The physical environment, economic situation, and social origins of the plains farmers all differentiated them from the older Scandinavian settlements.

Torben Grongaard Jeppesen described the role of leadership in building one such community, the Danish settlement of Dannebrog, Nebraska.[34] The history of this settlement began in the mother colony at Pine Lake, Wisconsin, where ed-ucated, middle-class Danes, Swedes, and Norwegians had begun settling in the 1840s, and where a cottager family named Hannibal arrived from Denmark in 1856. The Hannibals came from Nysted on the island of Lolland, an area domi-nated by the large landed estate of Count Raben Levetzau, where opportunities were limited for everybody except the count.[35] Lars Hannibal was handsome and talkative, with a quick mind and lively imagination but no fondness for physical labor. He bought some marginal land west of Pine Lake, served in the Union Army (1861–1862), and opened a tavern that quickly became a community cen-ter. In 1870, he and nine other Danes chartered a nonprofit company to estab-lish a county-sized colony where former cottagers like themselves could become landowners. That winter, a delegation including Hannibal traveled to Grand Is-land, Nebraska, and picked a site on the northern edge of the Union Pacific land grant, where settlers could choose eighty-acre plots of railroad land or 160-acre homesteads beyond. Hannibal plotted a town site and named it Dannebrog but lost the fight to make it the county seat. Within a year, the former cottager owned a nascent town and 1,802 acres of land, most of which he quickly sold to other Danish settlers. By 1875, there were 600 Danish settlers in the Dannebrog colony, many of whom arrived by way of Wisconsin. "Lars Hannibal created his colony as part of a new Midwestern American culture," wrote Grongaard Jeppesen, "but with values brought from his Danish upbringing."[36] He mastered American laws, regulations, politics, and economic and business structures in order to create opportunities for marginalized Danish cottagers and rural laborers.

These Scandinavian settlers on the plains seemed to be more progressive in their politics than the earlier farmers. Back in the 1930s, when the general tendency was to equate immigrants with bomb-throwing radicals, the Scandinavian American historian Marcus Lee Hansen asserted that immigrants were actually a conservative force in American politics.[37] Jon Wefald challenged this view in 1971, concluding on the basis of voting records and the editorial positions of Norwegian-language newspapers that Norwegian Americans of the late nineteenth century were "unrelentingly progressive, frequently radical," and consistently left of center in American politics.[38] Sten Carlsson found that Norwegians were exceptionally active in American politics and that Scandinavians in the upper Midwest region wielded political influence far beyond their numbers.[39] Meanwhile, Carl H. Chrislock was quick to challenge Wefald, arguing that regional differences among Norwegian American voters were shaped by American regional factors, and that they were not generally left of the center.[40] In 1991, after twenty years of scholarly debate, Lowell J. Soike reshaped thinking about Scandinavian American political attitudes by relating them to Scandinavian subcultural variations as well as American regional influences. He showed that political traditions brought from Scandinavia varied by class and regional origins as well as by time of arrival in America, and that the response to American conditions varied by region and rural or urban settlement, though some factors like the Prohibition issue and anti-Catholicism played a broadly unifying role in shaping Scandinavian American political attitudes.[41] Odd S. Lovoll found that Scandinavian Americans in the 1990s were still second only to Irish Catholics in their political activism and generally had reformist proclivities despite their moderate political outlook and social conservatism.[42]

In addition to politicians, there were many Scandinavian voices among the spokesmen for reform a century ago. The Industrial Workers of the World (IWW) songwriter and martyr, Joe Hill, was a Swedish immigrant. The New York journalist Jacob A. Riis and his Chicago friend, the urban planner Jens Jensen, were both natives of Denmark. Thorstein B. Veblen, the iconoclastic economist, was born in Wisconsin of Norwegian immigrant parents. All of them drew on their Scandinavian backgrounds in looking for solutions to broad American problems. They expressed an emerging Scandinavian American stance on public issues and social policy that was fragmented but generally community based and frequently at odds with the individualistic Anglo-American mainstream.

Despite the unifying institutions of politics, the press, the church, and personal ties between local communities, the fragmentation of Scandinavian America continued in the later years of the nineteenth century and beyond. Some of the rural immigrants of this era arrived with capital and skills. North Schleswig Danes, for example, fled for political, not economic reasons, and they came from one of the most modern agricultural areas in Scandinavia. One of them brought the first cream separator to America. Scandinavian immigrants of this type headed for the older settlements or for California and took the lead in establishing modern dairies, greenhouses, egg and poultry farms, fruit and vegetable operations, and various kinds of rural cooperatives. The misery and hardship of the plains was seldom their lot. At the same time, Mormon immigrants continued to head for Utah, and some Scandinavians went to the mining frontiers of the West and Alaska. Fishermen from western and northern Norway discovered the salmon, halibut, and black cod waters of the Columbia River, Puget Sound, and Alaska late in the century. People from the fishing regions of Norway had not emigrated previously, but now they flocked to the Pacific Northwest, where they formed communities apart from the Danish, Norwegian, and Swedish farmers and lumberjacks coming out from the Midwest. As ever new and more varied Scandinavian American communities came into existence, the process of fragmentation continued.

By the end of the nineteenth century, the total Scandinavian community in America was larger, more diverse, and more fragmented than ever before. The older communities of the Midwest had developed persistent local cultures combining American informality and technology with archaic Scandinavian customs, dialects, and mentalities. Newer communities reflected a more urbane, highly educated, and secularized Scandinavia. Scandinavian cooperative, socialist, and radical ideas flourished on the northern plains, in Chicago, and in the mines and mills of the North and West. Utopian and planned communities multiplied around the turn of the twentieth century. Finnish socialists started a utopia on an island in the Northwest. The Swedish Mission Covenant established successful, carefully planned suburban communities near Chicago and in California. The liberal, nationalistic Danish Lutheran Grundtvigians laid out farming communities, complete with churches and folk schools, in Minnesota, Texas, and California. Once established, these highly integrated communities were resistant to assimilation. So were the larger settlements with a wide range of social, religious, educational, political, and economic institutions. These large settlements were in urban, small town, and rural areas.

An example of the density of Scandinavian American institutions in this era can be found in the Norwegian settlements of northeastern Iowa and southern Minnesota. These settlements were established on the frontier around 1850, and Norwegian stock comprised from one-third to one-half of the total population in six contiguous counties by 1900. There were over eighty Norwegian Lutheran churches and a scattering of Norwegian Methodist congregations in these six counties. Worship services were mainly in Norwegian. Norwegian-language church schools supplemented the common school education. In one town, Decorah, Iowa, there was a Norwegian Lutheran elementary school, academy, and college that offered bilingual education in English and Norwegian from first grade through four years of college. Most of the county-seat towns of the region had Norwegian-speaking merchants, artisans, bankers, lawyers, physicians, and other professionals, and Norwegian specialty shops such as bookstores, groceries, and apothecaries. Norwegian-language newspapers were published in Decorah and nearby La Crosse, Wisconsin. Decorah was the seat of Winneshiek County, and all of the county officials were of Norwegian descent, as were the county's representatives in the state legislature and the U.S. Congress. In addition, there were innumerable Norwegian-language social circles, women's organizations, choral societies, mutual insurance companies, and other voluntary organizations in the region. Decorah had a large Norwegian-language library, two publishing houses specializing in Norwegian publications, and a nascent Norwegian American museum. Besides a newspaper and half a dozen journals in Norwegian, calendars, songbooks, poetry, stories, novels, and nonfiction in Norwegian were published in Decorah. In short, although the common schools were conducted in English and there were many other ethnic and linguistic groups living in the region, whole communities in this region were able to conduct virtually all the affairs of rural and small-town life in the Norwegian language. This was cradle-to-grave ethnicity.

Similar cultural environments were found in many parts of Scandinavian America around the year 1900: the Danish and Swedish settlements of western Iowa and Nebraska, the Finnish mining towns of northern Minnesota and Michigan, the Swedish side of Jamestown or Rockford, "Kringle Town" in Racine, Bay Ridge in Brooklyn, Humboldt Park in Chicago, Seven Corners in Minneapolis, Ballard in Seattle, Solvang in southern California, Sanpete County in Utah, and many other scattered places. Every place was different. Some of these communities were two or three generations old, and their ethnic life seemed to grow stronger and more firmly rooted in localized patterns with each passing year. There was no reason to think that it would not last forever. By 1910, there were over 3 million first- and second-generation Scandinavians in America.

National networks of contact between these communities were also growing stronger. For the first time, a sense of national Scandinavian American identity began to superimpose itself on the diversity of local identities. A few Scandinavian-language newspapers achieved national circulation. Rail transportation facilitated national gatherings of Scandinavian Americans. Church conventions, choral festivals, and Scandinavian American patriotic events turned into mass meetings, national in scope. Ski jumping meets and other athletic events, as well as conventions of ethnic professional and social organizations drew together Scandinavian Americans from many parts of America. Teachers and students in Scandinavian American colleges began to articulate highly sophisticated concepts of ethnic identity that merged cultural elements from America and Scandinavia.[43]

Overseas events helped to nationalize the Scandinavian American communities after 1900. National pride was strengthened by the exploits of Scandinavian explorers like Nordenskold, Nansen, and Amundsen. The dramatic separation of

Norway from Sweden in 1905 reverberated through the Swedish and Norwegian communities of America, just as North Schleswig's reunification with Denmark would galvanize Danish American communities in 1920. A patriotic national consciousness began to overpower the particular social, regional, and religious identities of earlier years. More and more, the Scandinavians in America began to identify with broader national ethnic communities and think of themselves as Danish Americans, Finnish Americans, Icelandic Americans, Norwegian Americans, or Swedish Americans.

On May 17, 1914, Norwegian Americans celebrated the centennial of the Norwegian constitution with parades, picnics, music, and mass meetings in many cities. Hundreds made steamship pilgrimages to Norway that spring and summer. Many were still in Europe when the World War I broke out in August.

SCANDINAVIAN AMERICANS AND WORLD WAR I

The outbreak of World War I led to intense attacks on immigrant communities in the United States. President Woodrow Wilson and former President Theodore Roosevelt were among those who condemned "hyphenism." At the same time, immigrants came to be associated with political radicalism. Scandinavians were among those who came under attack. Swedish Americans and Lutheran clergy were called disloyal.[44] Finnish Americans were branded as non-Nordic radicals and maligned for their role in the bitter Michigan copper strike of 1913–1914.

During the height of the war in 1917–1918, attacks on hyphenism approached collective hysteria. One Minnesota judge, John F. McGee, called for "firing squads" for German and Swedish Americans. Minnesota established a state Commission of Public Safety to ferret out disloyalty, with Judge McGee as a member. Similar campaigns took place in other states. Foreign-language newspapers were censored, and the editors of a Finnish-language socialist paper in Oregon were arrested. Under this extremist pressure, Scandinavian Americans did all they could to give public evidence of their patriotism. In 1918, without the support of legislation, Governor William L. Harding of Iowa issued a proclamation banning the public use of all languages other than English. This went too far. Strong protests arose from many ethnic communities in Iowa, not least from the North Schleswig Danes, who had fled similar persecution under Prussian rule.

Before things got better, however, they got worse. On the heels of the most virulent attacks on hyphenism came the "red scare," touched off by the outbreak of the Bolshevik Revolution in Russia. In Scandinavia, a socialist revolution was barely aborted in Norway, and civil war raged in Finland.[45] When the Finnish Reds were defeated, some fled to Russia, others to America. Their squabbles on the far left caused further ethnic fragmentation but had little effect on the Scandinavian American mainstream, which was loyally and doggedly struggling to survive the nativist and right-wing attacks.

A Scandinavian ethnic preponderance in many small towns and rural areas of the Midwest was able to cushion the worst effects of nativist attacks, but in a gen-

eral sense those attacks proved fatal. The cultural self-confidence and ethnic institutions of Scandinavian America never really recovered. Many Scandinavian
Americans bore the psychological scars of that era to the end of the twentieth
century. The dream of permanent subcultures speaking Scandinavian American
languages was shattered.

THE TRANSITION TO ENGLISH

Scandinavian America, however, survived. There was a postwar backlash
against nativist extremism. "We demand recognition as a part of the nation," wrote
a native-born Minnesotan of Scandinavian descent, "and we will not tolerate
being viewed as a flock of strange foreigners because we speak a language besides English."[46] The Scandinavian American press reached its highest circulation in the 1920s. Family and institutional use of Scandinavian languages seemed
to pick up, and the flow of immigration was renewed at moderately high levels
through the 1920s. Swedes, Finns, and Norwegians continued to maintain high
levels of endogamous marriage.

Scandinavian American literature reached a high point with writers like
Waldemar Ager, Enok Mortensen, and O. E. Rolvaag, whose *Giants in the Earth*
(1927) became an American bestseller. Immense ethnic festivals like the Norse
American Centennial of 1925 in Minneapolis and the New Sweden Tercentenary of 1938 in Philadelphia attracted the national attention associated with presidential attendance and commemorative postage stamps. All of the small, varied,
and scattered Scandinavian outposts of America seemed to be uniting into great
national ethnic communities. In Minneapolis in 1925, President Calvin
Coolidge even supported the effort to recognize the Scandinavian Leif Erikson
as the discoverer of America.

An inexorable change in language patterns was part of the shift toward a
broader Scandinavian American ethnic identity. The use of Scandinavian languages in schools and churches declined steadily during the 1920s and 1930s,
despite the resistance of nationally conscious groups like Finnish Lutherans,
Danish Grundtvigians, and the Swedish Mission Covenant. Many leading Scandinavian Americans now preferred to express themselves in English. Scandinavian American organizations were coming into existence with English as their
basis. Old loyalties had been reinforced by the innumerable cultural associations
of a common language or dialect. The shift to English laid those loyalties to rest
forever and allowed a new, broader Scandinavian American identity to emerge.[47]
It also allowed Scandinavian Americans like the poet Carl Sandburg, the composer Howard Hanson, the physicist E. O. Lawrence, and three Danish American cousins, the geneticist Roy E. Clausen, the economist J. Marvin Peterson,
and the entomologist Curtis P. Clausen, to make an impact on the American
mainstream. Until the shift to English occurred, a unified Scandinavian American ethnicity had been unthinkable. Now it seemed inevitable.

Against the background of these paradoxical developments, the Danish American historian Marcus Lee Hansen asserted his famous "law" that what the second generation wants to forget, the third generation remembers.[48] In retrospect, it is clear that the changes of the 1920s were shaped more by the developments of the era than by the passage of generations. The shift to English was due to nativist pressures, the decline of immigration, and the almost exclusive use of English in public education, rather than to a cultural generation gap. Some Scandinavian American families had maintained their language and ethnicity well beyond the two-generation limit only to switch to English in the face of the great, new obstacles to ethnicity that arose around the time of World War I.

Scandinavian Americans assimilated linguistically, but they remained apart socially and culturally.[49] Most of their churches retained an ethnic character. Individuals and communities remained conscious of their ethnic origins. Many Scandinavian Americans still preferred to socialize and marry within their own ethnic group. Certain habits of daily life continued to differentiate Scandinavian Americans from other Americans. An elaborate, solemn formality in personal relationships was so natural to many Scandinavian Americans that they did not realize it was an ethnic trait. Many Scandinavian Americans were unaware that the celebration of Christmas Eve was not a universal American practice or that some ethnic groups preferred to entertain guests "out" instead of at home, or that some well-mannered Americans left the dinner table without thanking the hostess. Scandinavian Americans, in other words, took their ethnic customs and values for granted without realizing that they were ethnic. This unacknowledged or "hidden" ethnicity was expressed in habits of Scandinavian American daily life and persisted long after the shift from bilingualism to English monolingualism.

By 1930, Scandinavian immigration was a thing of the past, which meant that the Scandinavian American communities were on their own. Through the hard times of the Great Depression and World War II, into the 1950s and beyond, the ethnic press in Scandinavian American languages slowly faded away while ethnic communities persisted around English-language churches and cultural organizations like the American-Scandinavian Foundation, the Society for the Advancement of Scandinavian Study, the Norwegian-American Historical Association, the Augustana Historical Society, and a variety of benevolent, choral, athletic, and social societies. Well-publicized visits of Scandinavian royalty on the eve of World War II gave a brief but exhilarating focus to ethnic celebration.[50] The war brought organized relief efforts and renewed feelings of solidarity with the Scandinavian countries. In general, Scandinavian Americans of these decades seemed to assume that their ethnicity was the remnant of a fading past, Though many continued to treasure it. Around 1960, Scandinavian American churches and cooperatives finally abandoned their ethnicity and merged with non-Scandinavian organizations.

THE NEW ETHNICITY

This attitude changed with what can be described as the new ethnicity of the 1970s. For many Scandinavian American leaders, the catalyst was ScanPresence in Minneapolis in the spring of 1973. This conference on the Scandinavian Presence in North America brought together a wide range of leaders from government, industry, cooperatives, the church, and the academic community, representing all five Scandinavian countries and innumerable Scandinavian American communities. The result was that ethnic pessimism soon gave way to optimism as Scandinavian America was reinvented one more time.[51]

Institutions like Vesterheim, the Norwegian-American Museum in Decorah, Iowa (the largest ethnic immigrant museum in America for a single group), the American-Swedish Historical Museum in Philadelphia, the American Swedish Institute in Minneapolis, the Bishop Hill restoration in Illinois, the Danish Immigrant Museum in Elk Horn, Iowa, and the Nordic Heritage Museum in Seattle, as well as the House of Emigrants in Viixjo, Sweden, came into existence or achieved new vitality in this era.

The new ethnicity was obviously far different from the old. Some 12 million Americans claimed Scandinavian ancestry in the United States census of 1980, but most of them no longer had a strong ethnic identity. Social and geographical mobility had dispersed most of the urban Scandinavian American communities to the suburbs, where some of their ethnic organizations were reestablished, but postwar immigrants in Los Angeles, Chicago, New York, and other cities had little in common with the ethnicity of largely assimilated Scandinavian Americans. Even in the dense rural and small-town settlements, most Scandinavian American ethnicity was now a combination of hidden ethnicity, ethnic hobby activities, and attendance at ethnic festivals.

By the 1980s, conscious Scandinavian American ethnicity was moving simultaneously along two tracks. One was the track of students and scholars who immersed themselves in academic studies of Scandinavia and spent extended periods in the Scandinavian countries. The other track was that of ethnicity as a leisure-time activity. Scandinavian American organizations had short courses in genealogy, cooking, music, folk dancing, and arts and crafts such as folk painting, woodcarving, embroidery, and weaving. They also sponsored group flights that brought Scandinavian Americans into brief but direct contact with modern Scandinavia.

Both tracks of the new ethnicity were voluntary, which meant that the participants were not necessarily of Scandinavian descent. Many were not. In Minneapolis during the 1970s, for example, a native of Pakistan taught Scandinavian languages, a native of Puerto Rico led a Danish folk-dancing group with at least one Chinese American dancer, and the leading exponent of Scandinavian American folk music was of east European Jewish background.

Regarding those who were of Scandinavian ancestry, a study of Norwegians Americans in the 1990s revealed that their ethnic identity remained remarkably strong into the fifth, sixth, and even seventh generation, though largely "privatized" into family traditions and ethnic festivals.[52] More significantly, Norwegian American cultural and ethical values remained distinct from the American mainstream, strongly egalitarian, socially compassionate, more inclined toward cooperation than competition, and leaning toward farming and service occupations more than hardball entrepreneurial activities. Over 4.5 million Americans claimed Norwegian ancestry in the 2000 census, which was slightly larger than the total population of Norway.[53]

The story of Scandinavian American acculturation is long and complex. Medieval Scandinavians established the first European communities in the New World. Colonial Scandinavians helped to shape the culture of America and especially of the American frontier. Nineteenth-century Scandinavian immigrants established innumerable, widely scattered communities with highly diverse ethnic institutions based on religion, social origins, regional dialect and culture that reflected diverse Scandinavian origins and varying experiences in the New World. Gradually, some of these diverse communities became linked into wider ethnic networks. During the first half of the twentieth century, immigration from Scandinavia virtually ceased and the Scandinavians in America shifted from bilingualism to English monolingualism. At the same time, they developed broad, clearly defined Scandinavian American national identities. English-speaking Scandinavian American communities persisted in a half-hidden state until the ethnic revival of the late twentieth century. By that time, ethnicity was voluntary, and Scandinavian American ethnic boundaries were no longer community based or impenetrable. At the start of the new millennium, Scandinavian American institutions were flourishing though sometimes anxious about the future, and Scandinavian American ethnic identity, expressed mainly in the English language, remained tenaciously strong in the sixth and seventh generation.

NOTES

1. William W. Fitzhugh and Elisabeth I. Ward, eds., *Vikings: The North Atlantic Saga* (Washington, DC: Smithsonian Institution Press, 2000), 189–349; Knud I. Krogh, *Viking Greenland* (Copenhagen: National Museum, 1967); Anne Stine Ingstad and Helga Ingstad, *The Norse Discovery of America*, 2 vols. (Oslo: Norwegian Univ. Press, 1985).

2. Thomas H. McGovern, "The Demise of Norse Greenland," in *Vikings* (see note 1), 327–339. Compares slightly differing views of other scholars in *Vikings*, 284, 292–294, 302–303, 316–317.

3. Terry G. Jordan and Matti Kaups, *The American Backwoods Frontier: An Ethnic and Ecological Interpretation* (Baltimore: Johns Hopkins Univ. Press, 1989).

4. Conrad Bergendoff, *The Church of Sweden on the Delaware, 1638–1831* (Rock Island, IL: Augustana Historical Society, 1988), *passim*.

5. Torstein Jahr, "Nordmrend i Nieuw-Nederland," *Symra* 5 (1909): 65–79; Torstein Jahr, "Nordmenn i Ny Nederland," *Symra* 9 (1913): 9–34. P. S. Vig, "Danske blandt hollrenderne i Ny Amsterdam (New York) i det 17. og 18. arhundrede," *Danske i Amerika* (Minneapolis) 1, no. 1 (1908): 39–45.

6. P. S. Vig, "Danske i bfodrekirken i Nordamerika fra 1742," *Danske i Amerika* 1, no. 1 (1908): 46–88.

7. On the 1768 society, see Johannes B. Wist, ed., *Norsk-Amerikanernes festskrift, 1914* (Decorah, IA: Symra, 1914), 268.

8. A model of mass emigration as a process that moves through four phases was proposed by Sune Akerman. The introductory phase consisted of upper-class adventurers, the growth phase of solid middle-class families with property, the saturation phase involved all social classes, and the regression phase saw a shift toward young, unmarried men and women. Akerman saw the growth phase in Scandinavia as lasting roughly from 1836 to 1865. See "Theories and Methods of Migration Research," in *From Sweden to America: A History of the Migration*, ed. Harald Runblom and Hans Norman (Minneapolis: Univ. of Minnesota Press, 1976), 25–32.

9. Oyvind Osterud, *Agrarian Structure and Peasant Politics in Scandinavia: A Comparative Study of Rural Response to Economic Change* (Oslo, Norway: Universitetsforlaget, 1978).

10. Hanne Sanders, "Peasant Revivalism and Secularization: Protestant Popular Culture in Denmark and Sweden 1820–1850," *The Bridge: the Journal of the Danish American Historical Society* 22, no. 1–2 (1999): 42–50.

11. See for example J. R. Christianson, "Danish Emigrants: Winners or Losers?" *The Bridge* 22, no. 1–2 (1999): 22–41.

12. Theodore C. Blegen, *Norwegian Migration to America, 1852–1860* (Northfield, MN: Norwegian-American Historical Association [hereafter cited as NAHA] NAHA, 1931), 24–80.

13. Henry J. Cadbury, "Four Immigrant Shiploads of 1836 and 1837," *Norwegian-American Studies* 2 (1927): 20–52.

14. C. A. Clausen, ed., *A Chronicler of Immigrant Life: Svein Nilsson's Articles in Billed-Magazin, 1868–1870* (Northfield, MN: NAHA, 1938), 50; see also Andres A. Svalestuen, "Emigration from the Community of Tinn, 1837–1907: Demographic, Economic, and Social Background," *Norwegian American Studies* 29 (1983): 43–88.

15. Clausen, *Chronicler of Immigrant Life*, 72. Olaus Fredrik Duus, *FrontierPastor: The Letters of Glaus Frdrik Duus, Norwegian Pastor in Wisconsin, 1855–1858*, ed. Theodore C. Blegen, trans. Verdandi Study Club (Northfield, MN: NAHA, 1947), 50. On Norwegian American skiing, see also John Weinstock, "Sondre Norheim: Folk Hero to Immigrant," *Norwegian American Studies* 29 (1983): 339–358; and Kenneth O. Bjork, *West of the Great Divide: Norwegian Migration to the Pacific Coast, 1847–1893* (Northfield, MN: NAHA, 1958), 274–299.

16. On a middle-class Scandinavian elite known as the "people of condition," which was transplanted to Scandinavian America, see J. R. Christianson, "Literary Traditions of Norwegian American Women," in *Makers of an American Immigrant Legacy*, ed. Odd S. Lovoll (Northfield, MN: NAHA, 1980), 92–110.

17. Dorris A. Flesner, "The Beginning of English Lutheranism in the Upper Midwest," *The Lutheran Historical Conference Essays and Reports*, 1984, 11 (St. Louis, 1986): 43–69.

18. Arnold R. Alanen, "The Norwegian Connection: The Background in Arctic Norway for Early Finnish Emigration to the American Midwest," *Finnish Americana* 6 (1983–1984): 23–33; Samuli Onnela, "Emigrationen fran Finland till Amerika over Nordnorge 1867–1892," *Beretning: Foredragogforhandlinger ved det nordiske historikermede i Kebenhavn* (Copenhagen: Fr. Bagge, 1971), 165–177.

19. Einer Niemi, "Niels Paul Xavier: Sami Teacher and Pastor on the American Frontier," *Norwegian-American Studies* 34 (1995): 245–270.

20. Jon Gjerde, *From Peasants to Farmers: The Migration from Balestrand, Norway, to the Upper MiddleWest* (Cambridge, England: Cambridge Univ. Press, 1985).

21. Robert C. Ostergren, *A Community Transplanted: The Trans-Atlantic Experience of a Swedish Immigrant Settlement in the Upper Middle West, 1835–1915* (Madison: Univ. of Wisconsin Press, 1988), 109–288.

22. Laur. Larsen, "Course of Instruction, Luther College, 1872," trans. John Robert Christianson, *Agora: A Journal for Interdisciplinary Discourse* (Fall 1996–Spring 1997) 96–101. Leigh D. Jordahl and Harris E. Kaasa, *Stability and Change: Luther College in Its Second Century* (Decorah, IA: Luther College Press, 1986), 9–10.

23. Peter A. Munch, "In Search of Identity: Ethnic Awareness and Ethnic Attitudes among Scandinavian Immigrants 1840–1860," in *Scandinavians in America: Literary Life*, ed. J. R. Christianson (Decorah, IA: Symra, 1985), 1–24.

24. Waldemar Ager, *Colonel Heg and His Boys: A Norwegian Regiment in the American Civil War*, trans. D. K. Catuna and C. A. Clausen, intro. Harry T. Cleven (Northfield, MN: NAHA, 2000).

25. Einar Hovdhaugen, *Husmannstida* (Oslo: Det norske samlaget, 1976); S. Skappel, *Om husmandsvcrsenet i Norge, dets oprindelse og utvikling*, "Videnskaps-selskapets skrifter, II. Hist.-filos. klasse 1922, no. 4" (Oslo, Norway: Jacob Dybwad, 1922).

26. Akerman saw this as the shift into the "saturation phase" (see note 8).

27. On North Schleswig, where Gottlieb Japsen linked the rise of national feeling with the emergence of a middle-class rural society, see Gerda Bonderup et al., "National udvikling og borgerliggorelse: Hovedlinier i Gottlieb Japsens forfatterskab," *Historie (Jyske Samlinger)*, new series, 13 (1979): 80–107.

28. One aspect of the brain drain is documented in Kenneth O. Bjork, *Saga in Steel and Concrete: Norwegian Engineers in America* (Northfield, MN: NAHA, 1947).

29. This corresponded to Akerman's "regression phase" (see note 8).

30. On the Norwegian maritime community in Brooklyn, see David C. Mauk, *The Colony That Rose from the Sea: Norwegian Maritime Migration and Community in Brooklyn, 1850–1910* (Northfield, MN: NAHA, 1997); see also Liv Irene Myhre, ed., *Norwegians in New York, 1825–2000: Builders of City, Community, and Culture* (Huntington, NY: The Norwegian Immigration Association, 2000).

31. John L. Davis, *The Danish Texans* (San Antonio: Institute of Texan Cultures, 1979), 40–42. Kristian Hvidt, *Flight to America: The Social Background of 300,000 Danish Emigrants* (New York: Academic Press, 1975), 168–169.

32. J. R. Christianson, "Danish Assimilation into the Norwegian-American Community" paper, Conference on Scandinavian Immigration, Settlement, and Acculturation, Univ. of Wisconsin, Madison, August 29, 1984.

33. J. R. Christianson, ed., "Becoming American: The Autobiography of C. P. Peterson, D.D.S. (1867–1958)," *The Bridge* 25, no. 2 (2002), 127.

34. Torben Grongaard Jeppesen, *Dannebrog on the American Prairie: A Danish Colony Project in the 1870s: Land Purchase and the Beginnings of a Town* (Odense, Denmark: Odense City Museums, 2000).

35. Pia Viscor, "Emigration from Jystrup and Valsolille," *The Bridge* 25, no. 1 (2002): 11–45, details the social situation and push factors in a similar Danish community.

36. Jeppesen, *Dannebrog on the American Prairie*, 256.

37. Marcus Lee Hansen, "Immigration and Democracy," in *The Immigrant in American History*, ed. Arthur M. Schlesinger (New York: Harper Torchbook, 1964), 77–96.

38. Jon Wefald, A Voice of Protest: Norwegians in American Politics, 1890–1917 (Northfield, MN: NAHA, 1971).

39. Sten Carlsson, "Scandinavian Politicians in Minnesota around the Turn of the Century: A Study of the Role of the Ethnic Factor in an Immigrant State," *Americana Norvegica* (Oslo) 3 (1971): 237–271.

40. Carl H. Chrislock, "The Norwegian-American Impact on Minnesota Politics: How Far 'Left-of Center'?" in *The Norwegian Influence on the Upper Midwest*, ed. Harald S. Naess (Duluth: Univ. of Minnesota Press, 1976), 106–116. In Worcester, Massachusetts, Swedish Americans were the mainstay of the local Ku Klux Klan during the 1920s; see C.W. Estus, K.I. Hickey, and K.J. Moynihan, "The Importance of Being Protestant: The Swedish Role in Worcester, Massachusetts, 1868–1930," in Ulf Beijbom, *Swedes in America*, (Vaxjo, Sweden: Swedish Emigrant Institute, 1993), 53–55.

41. Lowell J. Soike, *Norwegian Americans and the Politics of Dissent, 1880–1924* (Northfield, MI: NAHA, 1991). Compare Millard L. Gieske and Steven J. Keillor, *Norwegian Yankee: Knute Nelson and the Failure of American Politics, 1860–1923* (Northfield, MN: NAHA, 1995).

42. Odd S. Lovoll, *The Promise Fulfilled: A Portrait of Norwegian Americans Today* (Minneapolis: Univ. of Minnesota Press, 1998), 107–116.

43. See especially Dag Blanck, *Becoming Swedish-American: The Construction of an Ethnic Identity in the Augustana Synod, 1860–1917* (Uppsala, Sweden: Acta Universitatis Upsaliensis, 1997).

44. For the case of a Swedish Lutheran clergyman hounded out of Minnesota and the United States, see Nels T.A. Larson, "Life in Saskatchewan, 1918–1925: A Story of a Pioneering Missionary Family," *Swedish-American Historical Quarterly* 36, no. 1 (1985): 39–55.

45. The Finnish American left is discussed in Reino Kero, "The Background of Finnish-American Working Class Writers," in *Scandinavians in America* (see note 23), 176–187; and A. William Hoglund, "Finnish-American Humor and Satire: A Cultural Self-Portrait, 1890–1930s," *Scandinavians in America*, 160–175.

46. Quoted in Odd S. Lovoll, *The Promise of America: A History of The Norwegian-American People* (Minneapolis: Univ. of Minnesota Press, 1984), 195.

47. Einar Haugen, "Svensker og nordmenn i Amerika: en studie i nordisk etnisitet," *Saga och sed: Kungl. Gustav Adolfs akademiens arsbok* (1976): 38–55.

48. M.L. Hansen, "The Problem of the Third Generation Immigrant," in *American Immigrants and Their Generations: Studies and Commentaries on the Hansen Thesis after Fifty Years*, ed. Peter Kivisto and Dag Blanck (Urbana: Univ. of Illinois, 1990), 191–203.

49. Peter A. Munch, "Segregation and Assimilation of Norwegian Settlers in Wisconsin," *Norwegian-American Studies* 18 (1954): 102–140; and Rigmor Frimannslund, "Blantnorskamerikanere i Wisconsin," *By og bygd* 14 (196): 1–34.

50. On the visit of Swedish royalty to the New Sweden Tercentenary in 1938, see Allan Kastrup, *The Swedish Heritage in America* (New York: Swedish Council of America, 1975), 703–706. On the 1939 tour of Norwegian America by Norway's Crown Prince Olav and Crown Princess Martha, see Jens Schive and Hans Olav, *Med Kronprinsparet for Norge! 70 Dagers Ferd gjennem Stjernebannerets Land* (Oslo: H. Aschehoug, 1939).

51. Erik Friis, ed., *The Scandinavian Presence in North America* (New York: Harper's Magazine Press, 1976). See also J. R. Christianson, "Cooperation in Scandinavian-American Studies," *Swedish American Historical Quarterly* (October 1984): 380–384.

52. Lovon, *The Promise Fulfilled*. See also Birgit Flemming Larsen, "Impressions of Danishness in Chicago and Racine: Selected Results From a Questionnaire," *The Bridge:*

Journal of the Danish American Heritage Society 24, no. 1 (2001): 71–84; "On Being Swedish American Today," *Swenson Center News* 15 (2001): 4–5.

53. The 2000 U.S. census showed an estimated 11.7 million Americans of Scandinavian ancestry, while the 2001 population of the five Scandinavian countries was estimated by the Population Reference Bureau to be 24.3 million.

BIBLIOGRAPHICAL ESSAY

General surveys of Scandinavians in America do not exist, but a survey of each Scandinavian national group (Danes, Finns, Icelanders, Norwegians, and Swedes) is in Stephan Thernstrom et al. eds., *Harvard Encyclopedia of American Ethnic Groups* (Cambridge, MA: Harvard Univ. Press, 1980). See also the articles on the same groups in J. D. Holmquist, ed., *They Chose Minnesota: A Survey of the State's Ethnic Groups* (St. Paul: Minnesota State Historical Society, 1981).

Comparative studies include Bo Kronborg, Thomas Nilsson, and Andres A. Svalestuen, eds., *Nordic Population Mobility: Comparative Studies of Selected Parishes in the Nordic Countries, 1850–1900* (Oslo: Universitetsforlaget, 1977); Odd S. Lovon, ed., *Nordics in America: The Future of Their Past* (Northfield, MN: Norwegian-American Historical Association [hereafter cited as NAHA], 1993); Hans Norman and Harald Runblom, eds., *Transatlantic Connections: Nordic Migration to the New World after 1800* (Oslo: Norwegian Univ. Press, 1988); Ingrid Semmingsen and Per Seyersted, eds., *Scando-Americana: Papers on Scandinavian Emigration to the United States* (Oslo: American Institute University of Oslo, 1980); and J. R. Christianson, ed., *Scandinavians in America: Literary Life* (Decorah, IA: Symra, 1985).

For the Scandinavian background, see Byron Nordstrom, *Scandinavia since 1500* (Minneapolis: Univ. of Minnesota, 2000), and T. K. Derry, *A History of Modern Norvay, 1814–1972* (Oxford: Clarendon Press, 1973). See also Florence Edith Janson, *The Background of Swedish Immigration, 1840–1930* (Chicago: Univ. of Chicago Press, 1931); and Michael Drake, *Population and Society in Norway, 1735–1865* (Cambridge, England: Cambridge Univ. Press, 1969); as well as the transoceanic community studies done by Gjerde and Ostergren.

Scandinavian emigration is discussed in Kristian Hvidt, *Flight to America: The Social Background of 300,000 Danish Emigrants* (New York: Academic Press, 1975); Reino Kero, *Migration from Finland to North America* (Turku: Turun Yliopisto, 1974); Harald Runblom and Hans Norman, eds., *From Sweden to America: A History of the Migration* (Minneapolis: Univ. of Minnesota Press, 1976); and in eight articles on the regional background to Norwegian emigration in *Norvegian American Studies* 19 (1983). The persistence of transoceanic ties is investigated in H. Arnold Barton, *A Folk Divided: Homeland Swedes and Swedish Americans, 1840–1940* (Carbondale: Southern Illinois Univ. Press, 1994).

Colonial Scandinavians in America are the subject of Amandus Johnson, *The Swedish Settlements on the Delaware, 1638–1664*, 2 vol. (Philadelphia: Univ. of Pennsylvania Press, 1911); Stellan Dahlgren and Hans Norman, *The Rise and Fall of New Sweden: Governor Johan Risingh's Journal 1654–1655 in its Historical Context* (Stockholm and Uppsala, Sweden: Almqvist & Wiksell, 1988); Rune Ruhnbro, ed., *New Sweden in the New World, 1638–1655*, trans. Richard E. Fisher (Stockholm, Sweden: Wiken, 1988); and John O. Evjen, *Scandinavian Immigrants in New York, 1630–1674* (Minneapolis:

K. C. Holter, 1916). On New Sweden as the heart of Midland American frontier culture, see Terry G. Jordan, *American Log Buildings: An Old World Heritage* (Chapel Hill: Univ. of North Carolina Press, 1985); and Terry G. Jordan and Matti Kaups, *The American Backwoods Frontier: An Ethnic and Ecological Interpretation* (Baltimore: Johns Hopkins Univ. Press, 1989).

The business of trans-atlantic migration is summarized in Kristian Hvidt, *The Westward Journey* (Mankato, MN: Creative Education, 1982), and the American promotion of immigration in Lars Ljungmark, *For Sale-Minnesota: Organized Promotion of Scandinavian Immigration, 1873–1886* (Chicago: Swedish Pioneer Historical Society, 1973).

Surveys of individual Scandinavian American national groups include George R. Nielsen, *The Danish Americans* (Boston: Twayne, 1981), and Kristian Hvidt, *Danes Go West: A Book About the Emigration to America* (Copenhagen: Rebild Society, 1976). A. William Hoglund, *Finnish Immigrants in America, 1880–1920* (Madison: Univ. of Wisconsin Press, 1960) surveys the Finnish American transition from preindustrial to industrial life; see also Michael G. Karni, Olavi Koivukangas, and Edward W. Laine, eds., *Finns in North America: Proceedings of Finn Forum III* (Turku, Finland: Institute of Migration, 1988). Thorstina Jackson Walters, *Modern Sagas: The Story of the Icelanders in North America* (Fargo: North Dakota Institute for Regional Studies, 1953) treats Canada as well as the United States. Theodore C. Blegen, *Norwegian Migration to America*, 2 vols. (Northfield, MN: NAHA, 1931 and 1940); Ingrid Semmingsen, *Norway to America: A History of the Migration* (Minneapolis: Univ. of Minnesota Press, 1978); and Odd S. Lovoll, *The Promise of America: A History of the Norwegian-American People*, 2nd ed. (Minneapolis: Univ. of Minnesota Press, 1999), survey Norwegian-American life. Swedish immigration is described concisely by Lars Ljungmark, *Swedish Exodus* (Carbondale: Southern Illinois Univ. and Swedish Pioneer Historical Society, 1979); and in a thick one-volume reference work by a journalist, Allan Kastrup, *The Swedish Heritage in America* (New York: Swedish Council of America, 1975).

Immigrant letters arranged to survey the history of Scandinavian national groups include H. Arnold Barton, ed., *Letters from the Promised Land: Swedes in America, 1840–1914* (Minneapolis: Univ. of Minnesota Press, 1975); Theodore C. Blegen, ed., *Land of Their Choice* (Minneapolis: Univ. of Minnesota Press, 1955); Frederick Hale, ed., *Danes in North America* (Seattle: Univ. of Washington, 1984); Frederick Hale, ed., *Their Own Saga: Letters from the Norwegian Global Migration* (Minneapolis: Minnesota Press, 1986); Solveig Zempel, ed., *In Their Own Words: Letters from Norwegian Immigrants* (Minneapolis: Univ. of Minnesota Press, and NAHA, 1991); and Axel Friman, George M. Stephenson, and H. Arnold Barton, eds., *America, Reality and Dream: The Freeman Letters from America and Sweden, 1841–1862* (Rock Island, IL: Augustana Historical Society, 1996).

There are numerous other collections of primary sources in English translation, including Scandinavian immigrant guidebooks, letters, diaries, ballads, and oral interviews. Many primary sources were written by women, such as the letters of an Iowa farm wife in Pauline Farseth and Theodore C. Blegen, eds., *Frontier Mother: The Letters of Gro Svendsen* (Northfield, MI: NAHA, 1950); the diary of a pastor's wife in David T. Nelson, ed., *The Diary of Elisabeth Koren, 1853–1855* (Northfield, NAHA, 1955, numerous reprints); the letters of a pastor's wife in Peter A. Munch, ed., *The Strange American Way: Letters of Caja Munch from Wiota, Wisconsin, 1855–1859* (Carbondale: Southern Illinois Univ. Press, 1970); the letters of a governess in the antebellum South, Rosalie Roos,

Travels in America 1851–1855, ed. Carl L. Anderson (Carbondale: Southern Illinois Univ. Press, 1982); and the writings of a feminist in Texas in Clarence A. Clausen, ed., *The Lady with the Pen: Elise Waerenskjold* (Northfield, MN: NAHA, 1961).

Scandinavian American settlement is mapped in Carlton C. Qualey, *Norwegian Settlement in the United States* (Northfield, MN: NAHA, 1938), and Helge Nelson, *The Swedes and Swedish Settlements in North America*, 2 vols. (Lund S.: C.W.K. Gleerup, 1943; repr. New York: Arno Press, 1979).

A classic study of American bilingualism is Einar Haugen, *The Norwegian Language in America*, 2 vols. (Philadelphia: Univ. of Pennsylvania Press, 1953). Other studies of Scandinavian American languages include Reino Virtanen, "The Finnish Language in America," *Scandinavian Studies* 51 (1979): 146–161, and Nils Hasselmo, "The Language Question," in *Perspectives on Swedish Immigration*, ed. Nils Hasselmo (Duluth: Univ. of Minnesota Press, 1978), 225–243.

Community studies of Scandinavian Americans include urban, rural, and utopian communities. Among the best are Philip J. Anderson and Dag Blanck, eds., *Swedes in the Twin Cities: Immigrant Life and Minnesota's Urban Frontier* (St. Paul: Minnesota Historical Society, 2001); David C. Mauk, *The Colony That Rose from the Sea: Norwegian Maritime Migration and Community in Brooklyn, 1850–1910* (Northfield, MN: NAHA, 1997); Ulf Beijbom, *Swedes in Chicago: A Demographic and Social Study of the 1846–1880 Immigration* (Stockholm: Scandinavian Univ. Books, 1971); Odd S. Lovoll, *A Century of Urban Life: The Norwegians in Chicago before 1930* (Northfield, MN: NAHA, 1988); Jon Gjerde, *From Peasants to Farmers: The Migration from Balestrand, Norway, to the Upper Middle West* (Cambridge, England: Cambridge Univ. Press, 1985); Robert C. Ostergren, *A Community Transplanted: The Trans-Atlantic Experience of a Swedish Immigrant Settlement in the Upper Middle West, 1835–1915* (Madison: Univ. of Wisconsin Press, 1988); Paul Elmen, *Wheat Flour Messiah: Eric Jansson of Bishop Hill* (Carbondale: Southern Illinois Univ. Press, and Swedish Pioneer Historical Society, 1976); and Torben Grongaard Jeppesen, *Dannebrog on the American Prairie: A Danish Colony Project in the 1870s: Land Purchase and the Beginnings of a Town* (Odense, Denmark: Odense City Museums, 2000).

Churches were central institutions in many Scandinavian American communities. E. Clifford Nelson, ed., *The Lutherans in North America* (Philadelphia: Fortress, 1975), surveys Scandinavian and other Lutheran churches. Karl A. Olsson, *By One Spirit: A History of the Evangelical Covenant Church of America* (Chicago: Covenant Press, 1962), covers a Swedish American church with a strong sense of ethnicity. For Methodists, see Arlow W. Andersen, *The Salt of the Earth: A History of Norwegian-Danish Methodism in America* (Nashville: Norwegian-Danish Methodist Historical Society, 1962). Latter-Day Saints are discussed in William Mulder, *Homeward to Zion: Mormon Migration from Scandinavia* (Minneapolis: University of Minnesota Press, 2000). Paul Elmen, *Wheat Flour Messiah*, deals with Erik Jansson and his followers. See also Nicholas Tavuchis, *Pastors and Immigrants: The Role of a Religious Elite in the Absorption of Norwegian Immigrants* (The Hague: Martinus Nijhoff, 1963); and Todd W. Nichol, ed., *Vivacious Daughter: Seven Lectures on the Religious Situation among Norwegians in America by Herman Amberg Preus* (Northfield, MN: NAHA, 1990).

Education among Scandinavian Americans is the subject of articles by James S. Hamre, including "Norwegian Immigrants Respond to the Common School: A Case Study of American Values and the Lutheran Tradition," *Church History* (September

1981): 302–315. On higher education, see Richard W. Solberg, *Lutheran Higher Education in North America* (Minneapolis: Augsburg, 1985), and numerous biographies, including Karen Larsen, *Laur. Larsen: Pioneer College President* (Northfield, MN: NAHA, 1936); Lloyd Hustvedt, *Rasmus Bjorn Anderson: Pioneer Scholar* (Northfield, MN: NAHA, 1966); O. Fritiof Ander, *T. N. Hasselquist: The Career and Influence of a Swedish American Clergyman, Journalist and Educator* (Rock Island, IL: Augustana, 1931); James S. Hamre, *Georg Sverdrup: Educator, Theologian, Churchman* (Northfield, MN: NAHA, 1986); and Joseph M. Shaw, *Bernt Julius Muus: Founder of St. Olaf College* (Northfield, MN: NAHA, 1999). The Scandinavian American press is treated in Marion Tuttle Marzolf, *The Danish-Language Press in America* (New York: Arno Press, 1979). On editorial policy, see Arlow W. Andersen, *The Immigrant Takes His Stand: The Norwegian-American Press and Public Affairs, 1848–1872* (Northfield, MN: NAHA, 1953), and Finis Herbert Capps, *From Isolationism to Involvement: The Swedish Immigrant Press in America, 1914–1943* (Chicago: Swedish Pioneer Historical Society, 1966). On Scandinavian American comics, see Peter J. Rosendahl, *Han Ola og han Per: A Norwegian-American Comic Strip*, ed. Joan N. Buckley and Einar Haugen (Northfield, MN: NAHA, 1984); and Einar Haugen and Joan N. Buckley, eds., *More han Ola og han Per* (Iowa City: University of Iowa Press, 1988). On religious publishing, see Daniel Nystrom, *A Ministry of Printing: A History of the Publication House of the Augustana Lutheran Church* (Rock Island, IL: Augustana, 1962).

Novels dealing with Scandinavian American immigrants include O. E. Rolvaag, *Giants in The Earth* (New York: Harper, 1927); Vilhelm Moberg, *The Emigrants* (New York: Simon & Schuster, 1951); and Sophus Keith Winther, *Take All to Nebraska* (New York: Macmillan, 1936). On Scandinavian American literature as an historical source, see Dorothy Burton Skardal, *The Divided Heart: Scandinavian Immigrant Experience through Literary Sources* (Lincoln: Univ. of Nebraska Press, 1974). On American literature written in Norwegian, see arm Overland, *The Western Home: A Literary History of Norwegian America* (Northfield, MN: NAHA, 1996).

Music is discussed in Theodore C. Blegen; and Martin B. Ruud, *Norwegian Emigrant Songs and Ballads* (Minneapolis: Univ. of Minnesota Press, 1936); Robert L. Wright, *Swedish Immigrant Ballads* (Lincoln: Univ. of Nebraska Press, 1965); and Rochelle Wright and Robert L. Wright, *Danish Emigrant Ballads and Songs* (Carbondale: Southern Illinois Univ. Press, 1983).

Scandinavian American art is treated in Marion Nelson, ed., *Norwegian Folk Art: The Migration of a Tradition* (New York: Abbeville, 1995), and Marion John Nelson, ed., *Material Culture and People's Art among the Norwegians in America* (Northfield, MN: NAHA, 1994). See also Mary Towley Swanson, *The Divided Heart: Scandinavian Immigrant Artists, 1850–1950* (Minneapolis: University Gallery, Univ. of Minnesota, 1982); Marion John Nelson, *Painting by Minnesotans of Norwegian Background, 1870–1970* (Northfield, MN: NAHA, 2000); and the whole issue of *Swedish American Historical Quarterly* 37, no. 2 (April 1986). The impact of Scandinavian design on America is a theme of Robert Judson Clark et al., *Design in America: The Cranbrook Vision, 1925–1950* (New York: Harry N. Abrams, 1983). See also Robert E. Grese, *Jens Jensen: Maker of Natural Parks and Gardens* (Baltimore: Johns Hopkins Univ. Press, 1992), and Lea Rosson DeLong, *Christian Petersen: Sculptor* (Ames: Iowa State Univ. Press, 2000).

Scandinavian American voluntary organizations are described in Erik Friis, ed., *The Scandinavian Presence in North America* (New York: Harper's Magazine Press, 1976);

Odd S. Lovoll, *A Folk Epic: The Bygdelag in America* (Boston: Twayne for NAHA, 1975); and many other works on benevolent societies, temperance societies, choral societies, ski clubs, rifle clubs, gymnastic clubs, dramatic societies, literary societies, charitable institutions including hospitals, orphanages and missions, and professional organizations of Scandinavian American engineers, journalists, and musicians.

Studies of professional groups include Kenneth O. Bjork, *Saga in Steel and Concrete: Norwegian Engineers in America* (Northfield, MN: NAHA, 1947); and Knut Gjerset, *Norwegian Sailors in American Waters* (Northfield, MN: NAHA, 1933). Professional directories include Conrad Bergendoff, *The Augustana Ministerium* (Rock Island, IL: Augustana Historical Society, 1980), and Rasmus Malmin, O.M. Norlie, and O.A. Tingelstad, *Who's Who Among Pastors in All the Norwegian Lutheran Synods of America, 1843–1927* (Minneapolis: Augsburg, 1928). Many biographies of women and men are in John Andrew Hofstead, *American Educators of Norwegian Origin: A Biographical Dictionary* (Minneapolis: Augsburg, 1931), and Olaf M. Norlie, *School Calendar, 1824–1924: A Who's Who among Teachers in the Norwegian Lutheran Synods of America* (Minneapolis: Augsburg, 1924).

The nativist assault on Scandinavian American "hyphenism" during World War I has been studied by Carl Chrislock, *Ethnicity Challenged: The Upper Midwest Norwegian-American Experience in World War I* (Northfield, MN: NAHA, 1981). See also Peter L. Petersen, "Language and Loyalty: Governor Harding and Iowa's Danish-Americans During World War I," *Annals of Iowa*, 3rd series, 42 (1974): 405–417. A 1922 response to nativism is O.E. Rolvaag, *Concerning Our Heritage*, trans. and ed. Solveig Zempel (Northfield, MN: NAHA, 1998).

On the dynamics of ethnic identity, see April R. Schultz, *Ethnicity on Parade: Inventing the Norwegian American through Celebration* (Amherst: Univ. of Massachusetts Press, 1994), and Dag Blanck, *Becoming Swedish-American: The Construction of an Ethnic Identity in the Augustana Synod, 1860–1917* (Uppsala, Sweden: University of Uppsala, 1997). See also Jon Gjerde, *The Minds of the West: Ethnocultural Evolution in the Rural Middle West, 1830–1917* (Chapel Hill: Univ. of North Carolina Press, 1997), and Orm Overland, *Immigrant Minds, American Identities: Making the United States Home, 1870–1930* (Urbana: Univ. of Illinois Press, 2000). Ethnic persistence is examined in Odd S. Lovoll, *The Promise Fulfilled: A Portrait of Norwegian Americans Today* (Minneapolis: Univ. of Minnesota Press, 1998).

Biographical studies of Scandinavian American political figures range from successful politicians such as Hans Mattson, John A. Johnson, Charles A. Lindbergh, Sr., and Floyd B. Olson to reformers and social critics such as Jacob A. Riis, Thorstein B. Veblen, and the IWW martyr, Joe Hill. Recent examples include Millard One. Gieske and Steven J. Keillor, *Norwegian Yankee: Knute Nelson and the Failure of American Politics, 1860–1923* (Northfield, MN: NAHA, 1995), and two articles on Veblen in *Norwegian-American Studies* 34 (1995): 3–56. The founder of the Norwegian socialist movement who ended his days as a journalist in America is the subject of Terje I. Leiren, *Marcus Thrane: A Norwegian Radical in America* (Northfield, MN: NAHA, 1987).

Bibliographies on Scandinavians in America appear in each issue of *Norwegian-American Studies*, and reviews of books on Scandinavian America appear regularly in the *Swedish-American Historical Quarterly*. Additional serial publications devoted exclusively to Scandinavian Americans are *Finnish Americana* and *The Bridge: Journal of the Danish American Heritage Society*.

A directory of nearly a hundred North American scholars is H. Arnold Barton, "Scandinavian-Americanists in the United States and Canada: A Preliminary Directory of Academic Scholars," *Scandinavian Studies* 53 (1981): 320–341. See also Steven P. Sondrup, ed., SASS *Directory of Members* (Provo: Society for the Advancement of Scandinavian Study, 2000). Archival directories include Oivind M. Hovde and Martha E. Henzler, *Norwegian-American Newspapers in Luther College Library* (Decorah, IA: Luther College, 1975); Lloyd Hustvedt, *Guide to the Archives of The Norwegian-American Historical Association* (Northfield, MN: NAHA, 2001); Lilly Setterdahl, *Swedish-American Newspapers: A Guide to the Microfilms held by Swenson Swedish Immigration Research Center* (Rock Island, IL: Augustana College Library, 1981); Wesley M. Westerberg, *Guide to Swedish-American Archival and Manuscript Sources in the United States* (Chicago: Swedish-American Historical Society, 1983); and Nancy Ruth Bartlett, *A Guide to the North American Collections of The Danish Emigration Archives* (Aalborg, Denmark: The Danish Emigration Archives, 1997).

Archives, museums, and research centers in the field of Scandinavian American studies include the American-Swedish Historical Museum (1900 Pattison Avenue, Philadelphia, PA); the American-Swedish Institute (2600 Park Avenue, Minneapolis, MN 55407); archives of Suomi College (601 Quincy Street, Hancock, MI 49930); Augustana Historical Society (Augustana College, Rock Island, IL 61201); Bishop Hill Historical Restoration (Bishop Hill, IL 61419); Danish American Heritage Society (Grand View College, 1200 Grandview Avenue, Des Moines, IA 50316-1599); Danish Immigrant Archive–Grand View College, and Danish Immigrant Archive–Dana College (2848 College Drive, Blair, NE 68008); Danish Immigrant Museum (Elk Horn, IA 51531), Luther College Archives (700 College Drive, Decorah, IA 52101); Midwest Institute of Scandinavian Culture (Box 522, Eau Claire, WI 54702); Nordic Heritage Museum (3014 N.W. 67th Street, Seattle, WA 98117); Norwegian-American Historical Association (1510 St. Olaf Avenue, Northfield, MN 55057); Swedish-American Historical Society (5125 North Spaulding Avenue, Chicago, IL 60625); Swenson Swedish Immigration Research Center (Augustana College, 639 38th Street, Rock Island, IL 61201); and Vesterheim the Norwegian-American Museum (520 West Water Street, Decorah, IA 52101).

In addition, there are several research centers in Scandinavia, including the Danish Emigration Archives (P.O. Box 1731, DK-9100 Aalborg, Denmark); The Institute of Migration (Linnankatu 61, FIN-20100 Turku, Finland); The Icelandic Emigration Center (565 Hofsos, Iceland); The Norwegian Emigration Center (Strandkaien 31, N-4005 Stavanger, Norway); The Norwegian Emigrant Museum (Akershagan, N-2312 Ottestad, Norway); the Norwegian American Collection, National Library of Norway (Postboks 2674, Solli, N-0203 Oslo, Norway); and The Swedish Emigrant Institute (Box 201, S-351 04 Vaxjo I, Sweden).

VIETNAMESE AMERICANS

Hien Duc Do

HISTORICAL OVERVIEW

During the Annual Lunar New Year celebration, thousands of Asian Americans celebrate the coming of the New Year and all the possibilities that it offers. Across the country, from Falls Church, Virginia, to San Jose, California, there are hundreds of Vietnamese Tet (New Year) celebrations organized by Vietnamese Americans. Thousands of Vietnamese Americans and others participate in these cultural, social, political, commercial, athletic, and community activities. This is one of the occasions when the media's coverage of this community is rather extensive. According to the 2000 census, there are more than 1 million Vietnamese Americans living in the United States. Most Vietnamese immigrants live in urban and metropolitan areas. Within those areas they have also developed ethnic enclaves. However, the word *Vietnam* is still largely associated with the Vietnam War that the United States was involved in until 1975. This essay focuses on the historical development of the Vietnamese American community in the United States since their large influx in 1975.

Since there are many books and articles written on the Vietnam War, as well as films addressing this topic, this essay will only cursorily touch on the war itself. There are several critical events that have had an impact on the arrival of Vietnamese refugees in the United States. The triggering event that led to the collapse of South Vietnam was the Agreement on Ending the War and Restoring Peace in Vietnam signed in Paris, France, on January 28, 1973, by representatives of the United States government, the government of the Republic of Vietnam (South Vietnam), and the government of the Democratic Republic of Vietnam (North Vietnam). The main features of the agreement committed the United States and other signatories to respect the independence, sovereignty, unity, and territorial integrity of Vietnam. It called for prisoners of war to be exchanged and declared an immediate cease-fire. The agreement also required the United States to "stop all its military activities against the territory of the Democratic Republic of Vietnam by ground, air, and naval forces wherever they may be based; and end the mining of the territorial waters, ports, harbors, and waterways of the Democratic Republic of Vietnam." Furthermore, it required the United States to "not continue its military involvement or intervene in the internal affairs of South Vietnam." This agreement was enthusiastically approved by the North Vietnamese but reluctantly signed by the United States and South Vietnam's president Nguyen Van Thieu.

As a result of this agreement, the United States withdrew its military and economic support, which accelerated the deterioration and the downfall of the government of South Vietnam. The flight of the Vietnamese refugees began within the country, with the North Vietnamese military offensive of mid-March 1975 resulting in the defeats at Pleiku, Kontum, and Ban Me Thuot. As a result of this military offensive, about 1 million refugees poured out of these areas and headed for South Vietnam's capitol city, Saigon, and the coast. Most traveled by foot, but a few were fortunate enough to travel by car, truck, or motorbike. The coastal city of Da Nang was evacuated on the 27th and 28th of March 1975. Other coastal cities, such as Nha Trang and Cam Ranh, soon followed.[1] President Thieu resigned on April 21, 1975, and was succeeded by vice prime minister Tran Van Huong. As the political, economic, and military conditions continued to deteriorate even further, Vice Prime Minister Huong transferred the remaining government power to General "Big" Minh.[2] By the end of April 1975, South Vietnam, under the direction of General Minh surrendered to the North Vietnamese Communist government. On April 30, 1975, Saigon, the capital of South Vietnam, and thus South Vietnam, came under the control of the Provisional Revolutionary Government. This resulted in the plight of the newest Asian refugee group to the United States at the time.

THE VIETNAMESE REFUGEE IMMIGRATION EXPERIENCE

Social scientists have generally divided Vietnamese emigration history into two periods, each consisting of several waves.[3] The first period began in April 1975 and continued through 1977. This period included the first three waves of Vietnamese refugees to the United States.

The first wave of refugees, some 10,000–15,000 people, began at least a week to ten days before the collapse of the government. The second wave involved some 80,000 people who were evacuated by aircraft during the last days of April. The evacuation of American personnel, their dependents, and Vietnamese affiliated with them was achieved through giant helicopters under Operation Frequent Wind. According to *Newsweek* magazine, it was a "logistical success . . . the biggest helicopter lift of its kind in history."[4]

These individuals were relatively well educated, spoke some English, had some marketable skills, came from urban areas, and were westernized. Members of these two waves were primarily Vietnamese who worked for the U.S. government, American businesses and corporations, or the Vietnamese government. All were thought to be prepared for life in the United States on the basis of their contact with the U.S. government and association with Americans.[5]

Thu Hoai, a 37-year-old woman, recalled her experience of leaving Vietnam:

> We came in 1975. My father was an officer in the army. My father did not want to leave the country because he and his fellow officers didn't think we were going to lose. Somehow we got on a ship with my father's friends and were in the ocean watching the end of the war. When they finally realized that the war ended, we just stayed on the ship. A large ship eventually picked us up. After a few weeks, we were later processed at Wake Island.[6]

The final wave during this period involved 40,000–60,000 people who left on their own in small boats, ships, and commandeered aircraft during the first two weeks of May 1975. They were later transferred to Subic Bay and Clark Air Force base in the Philippines and Guam Island after having been picked up, in many cases, by the U.S. Navy and cargo ships standing off the coast of Vietnam. Kim-Phuong, a college student, recalled her family's narrow escape from Vietnam:

> We left during the summer. I remember my mom telling us to pack all our stuff and we were supposed to meet our father at the beach outside of Saigon. There were four of us kids and I was the youngest one. Our dad was going to meet us there and I guess he had access to a boat so he met us there. I was only five but I remember it took a long time to get to where we wanted to go. I think we walked for a day. . . . I just remember rushing, rushing, rushing. . . . We finally got on a boat and we just went out into the water, we didn't know where we were going, we were just going out toward the ocean. We were lucky because an American ship finally picked us up.

The second period of the Vietnamese refugees migration began in 1978 and continues even today. Since the fall of South Vietnam, many Vietnamese have tried to escape the political oppression and the major social, political, and economic reforms instituted by the authoritarian government of North Vietnam. Although the influx continues steadily, the numbers are no longer as massive as they once were. A significant characteristic of this period, especially from 1978 through 1980, is the large number of ethnic Chinese migrating out of Vietnam and Cambodia.[7] The following is an account of this migration process by Tommy, an ethnic Chinese:

> It cost us a lot of money and we had to go through the government and all these different agencies. Since paper money was unacceptable at the time, the way we had to pay the fees was in gold bars. I think you had to be Chinese or of Chinese descent before they let you go. We managed to get to Indonesia and then to San Francisco where my parents are still living.

In addition to the Vietnamese ethnic Chinese, there were many Vietnamese who also left during this period. These individuals have been called Vietnamese boat people because the majority of them escaped in homemade, poorly constructed boats and wooden vessels.[8] This escape route was very dangerous. In addition to the poor conditions of many of the boats, the danger was compounded by the escapees' scant knowledge of navigational skills, the limited amount of provisions they were able to bring, and finally, numerous attacks by Thai sea pirates. The death rate of the Vietnamese boat people was very high. Verbal testimony from some surviving refugees places the death rate as high as 50 percent, while Grant and Wain have placed it much lower, at 10 percent to 15 percent.[9] However, the percentage will never be accurately known, since there is no systematic way of knowing how many refugees actually left Vietnam, and only survivors are accounted for. Since 1979, many former receiving countries are turning away refugees because of the economic, political, and social strain that they are putting on their economies.[10] The following accounts are from two individuals who left Vietnam five years apart. The first account is from Thoa, a refugee who arrived in California in 1981. She was among the lucky ones, since her entire family was able to leave together:

> After 1975, life was pretty difficult because jobs were hard to find and you can only work if you had connections with the government. We didn't have anyone because we are all from the south so we did whatever we could to get by. My parents wanted to leave because they saw that there was no future in Vietnam for us. . . . The journey lasted more than a week. We went straight to Thailand. The boat was pretty small and very crowded. We were really lucky since we didn't have any major problems during our journey. We came to·Thailand and lived in the refugee camp there for three years and went to Indonesia.

The second account is from Hiep. He was not as fortunate, having left by himself in 1985, leaving behind his parents and his siblings:

> Our lives before 1975 were pretty normal. Both of my parents were into business and so they had a small shop. Once the communists came in, we were restricted a lot more in terms of our business activities. In fact, we tried to escape in 1975 but were caught at Phu Quoc and all of us spent two months in prison. Afterward, when we came out, we were left with nothing. . . . My father was then sent to re-education camp for nine years. My mother was left behind to take care of the eight of us. In 1978, when my two older brothers were threatened to be drafted, my uncle (who lived in the United States at the time) sent money for their journey out of Vietnam. They left in 1978. We heard they [made it to the U.S.] I left in 1984. . . . The journey was long and oftentimes frightening. I didn't know where we were going but we ended in Indonesia.

In sum, the exodus of Vietnamese refugees to the United States was a difficult process. Regardless of in which period they came, the journey to America left a long-lasting impression on all those involved. For some, the long journey was made easier because they were able to leave during the earlier period, or when they were younger. For others, the journey was more traumatic because of their circumstances and the uncertain journey across the ocean to a new and unknown destination.

THE UNITED STATES' RESPONSE

The Vietnamese exodus and their resettlement in the United States could not have come at a worse time in that period of American history. The Vietnam War, in which 57,692 American men and women died and 2,500 were listed as missing in action or as prisoners of war,[11] was an extremely unpopular war at home. The war deeply divided the nation.

Indeed, the general atmosphere of the American public at the end of the war was of hostility toward the Vietnamese refugees. A Gallup poll taken in May 1975 showed "54% of all Americans opposed to admitting Vietnamese refugees to live in the United States and only 36% were in favor with 12% undecided."[12] A common concern of the American public was one of economic self-interest—a fear of having jobs taken away as well as having too much public assistance and welfare given to the refugees. During this time, the United States was in a period of recession, with an unemployment rate of 8.3 percent.[13] Several early studies documented that a substantial number of Americans preferred the exclusion of the refugees from the United States.[14]

Apart from specific conditions resulting from the Vietnam War and the recession, this hostile reception given by the American public represented a continuation of the tradition of racism and hostility toward immigrant minority groups that has been prevalent and well-documented throughout U.S. history.[15] The Vietnamese refugees therefore arrived in the United States facing a legacy of hostility directed toward Asians. Most of the hostility was racially and economically based.[16] Despite this legacy, there were many Americans who extended humanitarian aid and sponsored families out of refugee camps.

THE UNITED STATES GOVERNMENT'S DISPERSAL POLICY

In order to minimize the social impact of the large influx of Vietnamese refugees, in 1975 President Ford adapted the Refugee Dispersion Policy. This policy served four purposes: (1) to relocate the Vietnamese refugees as quickly as possible so that they could achieve financial independence, (2) to ease the impact of a large group of refugees on a given community, which might otherwise increase the competition for local jobs, (3) to make it logistically easier to find sponsors, and (4) to prevent the development of an ethnic ghetto.[17] Given the political and social climate of the United States at the time, the influential factors leading to this Dispersion Policy were primarily political and financial, not social.[18] It was thought that if this policy were carried out successfully, the Vietnamese refugees would quickly assimilate into American society.

As a result, nine voluntary agencies (VOLAGs) were contracted by the government's Interagency Task Force to handle the resettlement of the refugees in the United States. The agencies were the United Hebrew Immigration and Assistance Service, the Lutheran Immigration and Refugee Service, the International Rescue Committee, Church World Service, the American Funds for Czechoslovak Refugees, the United States Catholic Conference, the Travelers Aid International Social Service, the World Relief Refugee Services, and the Council for Nationalities Service. While in refugee camps, each family was asked to choose a resettlement agency. If the family did not have a preference, one was assigned.[19]

The primary task of these voluntary agencies was to find sponsors who would have the ability to fulfill both financial and moral responsibilities and match them with refugees' families. The responsibilities included providing temporary food, clothing, and shelter, offering assistance in finding employment or job training for the head of the household, enrolling the children in school, and finally, arranging for ordinary medical care.[20] In other words, the sponsors would serve as a resource to introduce the Vietnamese refugees into the society while they become economically self-supporting.

THE RESETTLEMENT OF VIETNAMESE REFUGEES

There were four ways for the refugees to leave the four temporary refugee camps (Camp Pendleton in California, Fort Chaffee in Arkansas, Eglin Air Force Base in Florida, and Fort Indiantown Gap in Pennsylvania) and enter into American society: (1) resettle in a third country, (2) obtain repatriation to Vietnam, (3) demonstrate proof of being financially self-supportive, or (4) find a sponsor through the voluntary agencies.[21]

Although the United States government encouraged third-country resettlement, the Vietnamese refugees rarely chose this avenue. Very few other countries offered their assistance unless the refugees fulfilled at least one of the following criteria: (1) they were certified in needed professions, (2) they had relatives in that country, or (3) they could speak that country's language.[22] Since there was not a large group of Vietnamese living in different parts of the world, this option was not as viable for this group.

Only a small number of refugees chose to return to Vietnam. Darrel Montero, an anthropologist, reported, "By October 1975, repatriation had been granted to 1,546 refugees by the new government of Viet Nam."[23] The majority were military men who were forced to leave their families behind at the time of their evacuation.

The third method by which the refugees were allowed to leave the camps was to demonstrate their financial independence, but "the Task Force required a refugee family to show proof of cash reserves totaling at least $4,000 per household member."[24] However, due to their abrupt plight, very few refugees had resources that qualified them to follow this path. In addition, not many refugees would report their financial savings to the authorities, for fear of the unknown that awaited them in this new country. Thus, the first waves of Vietnamese refugees entered U.S. society primarily through the family-sponsorship method.

The sponsors recruited by voluntary agencies consisted of congregations, parishes or affiliates, individual families, corporations, and companies with former Vietnamese employees. In addition, if the refugees had relatives who could fulfill the same requirements, they could qualify as sponsors as well. However, one report indicates that only 15,000 Vietnamese lived in the United States prior to 1975, and most of these individuals were students staying temporarily on visas, former diplomats, or wives of American soldiers.[25] In essence, in 1975, the Vietnamese did not have an established ethnic community in the United States; therefore, this method hardly applied to the first waves of refugees.

The Vietnamese from the first waves, however, used the family-sponsorship method more frequently at a later time in order to sponsor family and relatives who were stranded in Vietnam after 1975. The primary ways in which this method was used was through the implementation of two federal government–sponsored programs that resulted from the Conference on Indochinese Refugees held in Geneva, Switzerland, on June 14, 1980: (1) the Orderly Departure Program and (2) the Humanitarian Operation Program.

The goal of these programs was to "provide Vietnamese a 'viable alternative' to dangerous clandestine departure by boat or over land."[26] However, this viable alternative was not as successful as originally anticipated, because many Vietnamese refugees continued to leave by boat. Currently, there are three categories under which people can participate in these programs: Category I–family reunification; category II–former U.S. government employees, U.S. firms or organizations, and so forth; category III–reeducation-center detainees. As a result of these avenues, many Vietnamese families who arrived during the first and second period and who now have citizenships or permanent-residence status, are using the first category to bring family members to the United States. Hoai has taken advantage of the Orderly Departure Program:

> My family has been trying to bring my mother's older sister over for a couple of years now. It has taken a lot of time and a lot of money because we have to bribe many of the government agencies in Vietnam in order for them to speed up the process and give her family the required papers. We've been waiting for the papers to clear. They have told us a few times that they were on the next flight out of Saigon but that's been going on for a few months. . . . I think we will probably receive two weeks' notice before they'll arrive. It's pretty hard on our family economically and emotionally for our family, but especially my mom.

There are also many others who arrived under the Humanitarian Operation Program. The majority of these individuals are older refugees who spent their adulthood as soldiers or civil servants in the South Vietnamese army and government. They would qualify under the Humanitarian Operation Program if they were imprisoned in Socialist Republic of Vietnam reeducation or labor camps for a number of years and can demonstrate this fact. All of these labor camps were located in remote and undeveloped areas. As a result of spending many years doing physical labor with limited nourishment in unbearable conditions, many of the people who came under this program were physically, psychologically, and emotionally spent when they arrived in the United States. They are a group within the Vietnamese American community that has faced many problems in adjusting to life in the United States.[27]

As a result of the U.S. federal government's Dispersal Policy, Vietnamese refugees were dispersed throughout the United States. The next section examines the adaptation processes by Vietnamese immigrants to the existing structural conditions since their arrival.

THE FORMATION OF VIETNAMESE AMERICAN COMMUNITIES

Vietnamese American communities have continued to form, develop, and expand over the past thirty years. Although the initial group of Vietnamese refugees was dispersed throughout the United States as a result of the Dispersal Policy, they have since congregated in several states. Although there are many reasons why these communities formed in specific states, these are some primary reasons. First, most communities were formed initially as a result of the geographical patterns of sponsorship. In other words, although they were dispersed throughout the United States, some cities and states received more refugees than others. This created both a critical mass and the opportunity for people to seek each other out for friendship in a strange and unfamiliar environment. From there, certain needs that were unfulfilled, including familiar foods, social services, religious services, and similar needs were developed and provided by the immigrants themselves. Family reunification is an important variable that compelled people to migrate. Those with extended families who were originally separated sought ways to live closer to their families in order to provide and to receive the support from this kinship network. Second, most refugees chose to migrate to states with job opportunities, especially those that required little English proficiency and specific skills. They sought jobs as assembly-line workers, low-level technicians, and quality-control staff in the hi-tech industry; low-end manufacturing positions; and work in the service sector, the garment industry, and similar industries. Third, they concentrated in areas where the cost of housing and overall cost of living was reasonable at the time, so that they could fulfill the dream of home ownership. Fourth, most of the communities have been formed in areas where the weather is milder than their original destinations and more like the weather in Vietnam. These and other variables played a significant role in the secondary migration process that led to continuing development of Vietnamese American communities throughout the United States but concentrated in a few states. Data from the 2000 census indicate that California is still the state most preferred by the total number of Vietnamese immigrants living in the United States, with 45.36 percent of the population. Texas is second at 11.27 percent, Washington, with 4.81 percent and Virginia, with 3.30 percent, have moved ahead of Louisiana, which has 2.85 percent. Florida is fifth, with 2.65 percent, while Pennsylvania is now sixth, with 2.57 percent. These seven states together have almost 73 percent of the Vietnamese immigrant population living in the United States.

In addition to the usual array of commercial enterprises that are present in Vietnamese American communities throughout the United States, many churches and temples have been built. Although only 10 percent of Vietnamese are Catholics, 30 percent of those who left in 1975 share that faith. This is not by accident. Rather, it reflects their previous experience as refugees in 1954, when they had to leave North Vietnam for fear of persecution by Vietnamese Communists. The rest of the community tends to be Buddhist because of the religious history of the region. There are also a small number of other Christians. However, regardless of what religion people identify with, there is also the strong influence of their national, cultural, and religious heritage; that is, of: Confucianism, Taoism, and Buddhism. These practices are carried out in their daily lives, and children are socialized with these values and norms through folk songs and stories, festival celebrations, family rituals, and cultural practices. In short, it is part of what it is to be Vietnamese.[28]

One of the benefits that Vietnamese Americans have enjoyed since their arrival in 1975 is a more tolerant climate in the United States as compared to other times in American history. America has gone through tremendous social, political, educational, and religious changes as a result of the civil rights movement, the antiwar movement, and the emergence of minorities of color as a social and political force. In addition, the 1965 Immigration Act had a tremendous impact on race relations in America.[29] This legislation opened the door to immigration, allowing many different immigrants to enter the United States. It also allowed them to bring their own culture, ethnic background, and more importantly, their religions. This created a multireligious America and was important for the development of the Vietnamese American religious community. In short, for Vietnamese refugees, although there was tremendous pressure to quickly assimilate economically, there was much less pressure to assimilate socially and religiously. Because of this, they were allowed to practice their religions without much interference and scrutiny and with much more freedom than at any other time in history.

For Vietnamese Buddhists, their religion was also not new in America. As a result of the Japanese American, Chinese American, and Tibetan American communities' practices of Buddhism, Americans were at least exposed to and familiar with some basic forms of this religion.[30] In addition, the Venerable Thich Nhat Hanh, an exiled Vietnamese Buddhist monk, is internationally known and has many followers throughout the world. He also holds annual retreats in Vermont and California that are well attended by Vietnamese and non-Vietnamese people alike. Vietnamese Catholics were able to practice their religion, since Catholic churches were already in place. In either case, religious institutions have played important roles in the development and maintenance of Vietnamese Americans communities. Currently, there are hundreds of Vietnamese American Catholic churches and Buddhist temples throughout the United States. Although the range size and makeup of their memberships and congregations vary widely, the large number indicates the importance of religion in their lives as well as their desires to practice their religion in their own language. In addition to providing the religious needs of its members, perhaps their most important role has been to serve as a way for the older and younger generations to adapt to life in America.

Although they support many activities, three celebrations in particular are noteworthy. For Vietnamese Catholics, Christmas is one of the most important religious celebrations. For Vietnamese Buddhists, Buddha's Birthday is the most important religious celebration. Thousands of members flock to their churches and temples to observe these religious celebrations. The Lunar New Year Celebration is another important community event. In the larger Vietnamese American communities, one can attend celebrations at either Buddhist Temples or Catholic churches on New Year's Eve.

Finally, both Catholic churches and Buddhist temples provide language courses on Sundays for children and young adults. The majority of the courses are taught by volunteers and are relatively inexpensive for the children. All of the courses are taught in Vietnamese, even though the majority of the teachers and some of the students are bilingual. Although these courses focus on some religious teachings, they are also a mechanism to maintain and preserve different aspects of the Vietnamese language, customs, and cultures. The activities are designed to create a strong bond between the students and their religion and culture, as well as to encourage their continued participation in other activities in the future. Additionally, ways for the children to cope with the many challenges in their daily lives and ways to interact with their parents and the older generation are included in the curriculum. Some churches and temples have also recently instituted courses for adults in which they help them deal with some of the different and sometimes conflicting cultural values that they encounter on a daily basis while raising their children and grandchildren in America. Although these religious institutions have been successful at identifying some of the problems faced by Vietnamese Americans and have provided ways to help maintain the language, customs, values, and traditions of the old country, what remains to be seen is how successful these institutions will be in the future as the next generation of Vietnamese Americans comes of age. Because the majority of the next generation of Vietnamese Americans have been born, raised, and socialized in the United States, it would be natural for them to identify more with American values, norms, and culture. However, with the majority of Vietnamese Americans also residing close to Vietnamese American communities, they are also likely to participate in many social and cultural activities available. As a result of these and other factors, there will be a continuing negotiation process for the new generation in developing, determining, and defining a new Vietnamese American identity and culture. For the time being, these religious institutions provide not only a place for worship but a place that reinforces ethnic solidarity.

SUMMARY

The end of the Vietnam War and the fear of the new Vietnamese communist government contributed to the large and sudden influx of Vietnamese refugees and immigrants to the United States. In this essay, I have argued that the social, political, and economic conditions in the United States during the time of their arrival greatly affected the ways in which the United States government designed and implemented its policies toward this immigrant group. That is, the Dispersal Policy was implemented with the intention of quickly assimilating Vietnamese refugees into the United States. However, despite the original intention of the federal government to disperse Vietnamese refugees throughout the United States, the Vietnamese refugees initiated a secondary migration by themselves, which has resulted in their concentration in seven states.

Moreover, as a result of the Orderly Departure Program, the Humanitarian Operation Program, and the Homecoming Act of 1987, many former refugees are now able to sponsor members of their immediate family for immigration to the United States. This has contributed to the continuing small influx of Vietnamese to the United States. As mentioned earlier, California has the largest number of Vietnamese among the fifty states. From all recent research reported, the geographic distribution of Vietnamese Americans in America has remained constant.

One of the major differences between the development of the Vietnamese American refugee communities throughout the United States and these of other recent immigrants is their original status as refugees from a war-torn country. Because of the long and controversial legacy of the Vietnam War, the initial reception of Vietnamese immigrants in America was mixed. Some Americans were against the refugees' resettlement because of their own negative views of the war, along with their fear of the possible negative economic and social impacts on the American society. Others welcomed refugees because they were fleeing a Communist country and because of their humanitarian beliefs. Vietnamese Americans also arrived at a time when the United States was going through tremendous social, political, civil, and religious transformations and actually benefited from these developments. Similarly to other immigrant communities who preceded them, they have come together to form cohesive communities in their various locations.

Although their initial focus was economic survival and adaptation to life in America, Vietnamese Americans have recently turned their attention to claiming a voice in America, as well as participating in all the available social, political, economic, and educational institutions. They originally focused on homeland politics and the overthrow of the Vietnamese Communist government, but with the coming of age of a new generation, they have expanded their participation into issues in the United States as well. That is, while Vietnamese Americans continue to bring Congress's and the public's attention to the issues of human-rights violations and religious persecution in Vietnam through demonstrations, petitions, and full-page advertising in newspapers, they have also focused on issues relating to their status in the United States. To this end, there is an increase in Vietnamese Americans engaged in the political process at the city, county, state, and national levels in recent years, with a number of Vietnamese Americans running for political office. There are also recent indications of Vietnamese Americans building coalitions and alliances with other groups, especially concerning the demands for more accountability from the local police and legal institutions.

NOTES

1. Gail Paradise Kelly, *From Vietnam to America: A Chronicle of the Vietnamese Immigration to the United States* (Boulder, CO: Westview Press, 1977), 11–12.

2. William T. Liu, Maryanne Lamanna, and Alice Murata, *Transition to Nowhere: Vietnamese Refugees in America* (Nashville, TN: Charter House Publishers Inc., 1979), 3–10.

3. Kelly, *From Vietnam to America*; Manh Hung Nguyen, "Vietnamese," in *Refugees in the United States: A Reference Handbook*, ed. David Haines (Westport, CT: Greenwood Press, 1985), 195–208.

4. *Newsweek*, May 12, 1975, 13–23.

5. Kelly, *From Vietnam to America*, 20–23.

6. The author did all the interviews. Names were changed to protect the interviewees' identities. Ages given are at the time of the interview, not at the time of immigration.

7. Keith St. Cartmail, *Exodus China* (Auckland, Exeter New Zealand: Heinemann, 1983); John K. Whitmore, "Chinese from Southeast Asia" in *Refugees in the United States: A Reference Handbook*, ed. David Haines (Westport, CT: Greenwood Press, 1985), 59–76.

8. Bruce Grant, *The Boat People: An "Age" Investigation* (Harmondsworth, Middlesex, England: Penguin Books, 1979); James Haskins, *The New Americans: Vietnamese Boat People* (Berkeley Heights, NJ: Enslow Publishers, 1980); Barry Wain, *The Refused: The Agony of the Indochina Refugees* (New York: Simon & Schuster, 1981).

9. Grant, *The Boat People*; Wain, *The Refused*.

10. Grant, *The Boat People*; *Los Angeles Times* 1989; *New York Times*, 1990.

11. Walter Capps, *The Unfinished War: Vietnam and the American Conscience*. (Boston: Beacon Press, 1982).

12. *Time*, May 19, 1975.

13. Kelly, *From Vietnam to America*, 17–19.

14. Richard T. Schaefer and Sandra L. Schaefer. "Reluctant Welcome: U.S. Responses to the South Vietnamese Refugees," *New Community* 4 (1975): 366–370; Liu et al., *Transition to Nowhere*; Paul Starr and Alden E. Roberts, "Attitudes toward New Americans: Perceptions of Indo-Chinese in Nine Cities," *Research in Race and Ethnic Rela-*

tions: 3 (1982): 165–186; *Rita Simon, Public Opinion and the Immigrant* (Lexington, MA: Heath & Company, 1985).

15. John Dollard, *Caste and Class in a Southern Town* (New Haven: Yale Univ. Press, 1937); Herbert J. Gans, *The Urban Villagers: Group and Class in the Life of Italian Americans* (New York: The Free Press of Glencoe, 1962); Thomas F. Gossett, *Race: The History of an Idea in America* (Dallas: Southern Methodist Univ. Press, 1963); Winthrop D. Jordan, *White over Black: American Attitudes toward the Negro 1550–1812* (Chapel Hill: The Univ. of North Carolina Press, 1968); Thomas, W. I. and J. Znanicki, *The Polish Peasant in Europe and America* (New York: Dover Publications, 1958); Louis L. Knowles and Kenneth Prewit, eds., *Institutional Racism in the United States* (Englewood Cliffs, NJ: Prentice Hall, 1969); Hilary Conroy and T. S. Miuyakawa, eds., *East Across the Pacific: History and Sociological Studies of Japanese Immigration and Assimilation* (Santa Barbara, CA: ABC-Clio, 1972).

16. Roger Daniels and Harry Kitano, *American Racism: Exploration of the Nature of Prejudice* (Englewood Cliffs, NJ: Prentice Hall, 1970); Violet Rabaya, "Filipino Immigration: The Creation of a New Social Problem." In *Roots: An Asian American Reader*, ed. A. Tacjhiki et al. (Los Angeles: UCLA Asian American Studies Center, 1971); Elmer Clarence Sandmeyer, *The Anti-Chinese Movement in California* (Urbana: Univ. of Illinois Press, 1971); Alexander Saxton, *The Indispensable Enemy: Labor and the Anti-Chinese Movement in California* (Berkeley: Univ. of California Press, 1971); Sue Stanley, and Harry Kitano. 1973. "Stereotypes as a Measure of Success," *Journal of Social Issues* 29(1973)L83-98; Sucheng Chan, *Asian American: An Interpretive History* (Boston: Twayne Publishers, 1990).

17. Liu et al., *Transition to Nowhere*, 15–19.

18. Kelly, *From Vietnam to America*, 129–136.

19. Liu et al., *Transition to Nowhere*, 20–23.

20. Ibid., 23–27.

21. Kelly, *From Vietnam to America*, 132–135.

22. Ibid., 135–151.

23. Darrel Montero, *Vietnamese Americans: Patterns of Resettlement and Socioeconomic Adaptation in the United States* (Boulder, CO: Westview Press, 1977).

24. Kelly, *From Vietnam to America*, 129; Montero, *Vietnamese Americans*, 27.

25. Kenneth A. Skinner, "Vietnamese American Diversity in Adaptation," *California Sociologist* 3 (1980): 103–124.

26. Manh Hung Nguyen, "Vietnamese" in Haines, *Refugees in the U.S.*, 195–208. See also Senate Subcommittee to Investigate Problems Connected with Refugees and Escapees, *Hearings, War-Related Civilian Problems in Indo-China. Part III—Vietnam*, 92nd Cong. 1st Sess., 22 April 1971.

27. Dac Thanh Tran, "The Vietnamese Elderly Refugees' Experience in America," Ph.D. dissertation, Univ. of Minnesota, 2000.

28. Hien Duc Do, *The Vietnamese Americans* (Westport, CT: Greenwood Press, 1999), 35–116.

29. Chan, *Asian American*; R. Stephen Warner, "Religion and New (Post-1965) Immigrants: Some Principles Drawn from Field Research," *American Studies* 41, no. 2–3 (Summer/Fall 2000): 267–286; L. Diana Eck, *A New Religious America: How a Religious Country Has Now Become the World's Most Religious Diverse Nation* (San Francisco: Harper, 2001).

30. Charles S. Prebish and Kenneth K. Tanaka, ed., *The Faces of Buddhism in America* (Berkeley: Univ. of California Press, 1998); Eck, *A New Religious America*.

BIBLIOGRAPHICAL ESSAY

Since there were very few Southeast Asians in the United States prior to the 1970s, it is not surprising that the body of literature concerning their immigration and adaptation is still relatively sparse as we enter the twenty-first century. It was not until 1992 that Joel Martin Halpern and Lucy Hing Nhiem edited *A Bibliography of Cambodian, Hmong, Lao, and Vietnamese Americans* (Amherst: Univ. of Massachusetts at Amherst), which brought together citations from a wide variety of sources and organized them between the covers of a 141-page book. Seven years later, anthropologist Hien Duc Do published *The Vietnamese Americans* (Westport, CT: Greenwood Press, 1999), as part of *The New Americans* series edited by Ronald H. Bayor, editor of the *Journal of American Ethnic History*. The book is divided into six sections, the first of which is an introduction to Vietnamese history and culture in their native habitat, as well as a brief history of U.S.–Vietnamese relations from World War II through the end of the Vietnam War. The second chapter discusses the immigration experience of Vietnamese, their refugee status, the ill-fated dispersal policy pursued by the United States, and the consequent voluntary resettlement process followed by Vietnamese once their initial period of sponsorship by voluntary American agencies (VOLAGS) was completed. The third section explores a variety of issues within developing Vietnamese American communities, including mental health and the problems inherent in resettlement. The fourth section examines Vietnamese American employment and educational trends, while the fifth assesses the impact of these newcomers on the host country, including holidays and festivals, food, enclaving, and political participation. The final section, titled "Conclusion and Future Prospects," covers such topics as economic survival, cultural preservation, intergenerational conflict, political agendas, and community involvement. Of special interest is the author's cogent discussion of how the Vietnamese American experience squares with "the myth of the model minority," which other Americans frequently apply to those of Asian ancestry. Readers will also benefit from the nine-page bibliography appended by the author that mixes books, articles in scholarly and popular journals, theses and dissertations, and newspaper accounts.

The process by which the Vietnamese became American immigrants is detailed by Gail Paradise Kelly in *From Vietnam to America: A Chronicle of the Vietnamese Immigration to the United States* (Boulder, CO: Westview Press, 1997). Particularly critical of that process are William T. Liu, Maryanne Lamanna, and Alice Murata, eds., *Transition to Nowhere: Vietnamese Refugees in the United States* (Nashville, TN: Charter House Publishers, Inc., 1979). Included in their book is a carefully detailed analysis of the "Southeast Asian Refugee Evacuation and Resettlement Program" by Norman Y. Mineta, Leslie Francis, Patricia Ginger, and Larry Low, originally written in 1975. To supplement these discussions, readers are also referred to two articles contained in David Haines, *Refugees in the United States: A Reference Handbook* (Westport, CT: Greenwood Press, 1985): "Vietnamese" by Manh Hung Nguyen and "Chinese from Southeast Asia" by John K. Whitmore. Additional insight can be gained from Paul Rutledge, *The Vietnamese Experience in America* (Bloomington: Indiana Univ. Press, 1992) and Darrel Montero, *Viet-*

namese Americans: Patterns of Resettlement and Socioeconomic Adaptation in the United States (Boulder, CO: Westview Press, 1979).

The ambivalent attitude of Americans toward the new arrivals is captured painstakingly by Barry Wain, *The Refused: The Agony of Indochina Refugees* (New York: Simon and Schuster, 1981). The particular plight of the "boat people" is the subject of James Haskins, *The New Americans: Vietnamese Boat People* (New Jersey: Enslow Publishers, 1980), as well as that of Bruce Grant, *The Boat People—An "Age" Investigation* (Harmondworth, Middlesex, England: Penguin Books, 1979); Nathan Caplan, John K. Whitmore, and Marcella H. Choy, *The Boat People and Achievement in America: A Study of Family Life, Hardwork, and Cultural Values* (Ann Arbor: University of Michigan Press, 1989); and Caplan, Choy, and Whitmore, *Children of the Boat People: A Study of Educational Success* (Ann Arbor: University of Michigan Press, 1991). Wain's analysis is largely paralleled by Richard T. Schaefer and Sandra L. Schaefer, "Reluctant Welcome: U.S. Responses to the South Vietnamese Refugees," *New Community* 4 (1975): 366–370. Florence E. Bayer, "'Give me . . . your huddled masses': Anti-Vietnamese Refugee Lore and the 'Image of the Limited Good'," *Western Folklore* 41 (1982): 275–291 examines the tension between America's self-image and its tendency to judge immigrants according to a cost-benefit analysis. This ambivalence is clearly reflected in Rita Simon, *Public Opinion and the Immigrant* (Lexington, MA: Heath and Company, 1985). Paul Starr and Alden E. Roberts, "Attitudes Toward New Americans: Perceptions of Indo-Chinese in Nine Cities," *Research in Race and Ethnic Relations* 3 (1982): 165–186, present a picture that is a little more complex, but still basically hostile. The particular trauma undergone by older refugees is the subject of Dac Thanh Tran, "The Vietnamese Elderly Refugees' Experience in America," masters' thesis, San Jose State University, 2000.

The impact of America on the Vietnamese is the subject of several scholarly studies: Robert and Jennifer B. Bach, "Employment Patterns of Southeast Asian Refugees," *Monthly Labor Review* 103 (1980): 10–14; Morton Beiser, "Influence of Time, Ethnicity, and Attachment on Depression in Southeast Asian Refugees," *American Journal of Psychiatry* 145 (1988): 36–51; Kenneth A. Skinner, "Vietnamese in America: Diversity in Adaptation," *California Sociologist* 3 (1980): 103–124; Barry N. Stein, "Occupational Adjustment of Refugees: The Vietnamese in America," *International Migration Review* 13 (1979): 25–45; and Paul J. Strand and Woodrow Jones, Jr., *Indochinese Refugees in America: Problems of Adaptation and Assimilation* (Chapel Hill: Univ. of North Carolina Press, 1985). Several other studies emphasize the negative results of the Vietnamese experience in the United States: Phuc Long Patrick Du and Laura Ricard, *The Dream Shattered: Vietnamese Gangs in America* (Boston: Northeastern Univ. Press, 1996); T. J. English, *Born to Kill: America's Most Notorious Gang, and the Changing Face of Organized Crime* (New York: William Morrow, 1995); James Freeman, *Hearts of Sorrow: Vietnamese American Lives* (Palo Alto, CA: Stanford Univ. Press, 1989); Steven J. Gold, "Mental health and Illness in Vietnamese Refugees," *The Western Journal of Medicine* 157 (1989): 290–294; and Alan B. Henkin and Nguyen Thanh Liem, *Between Two Cultures: The Vietnamese in America* (Saratoga, NY: Century Twenty One Publishing, 1981).

BIBLIOGRAPHICAL ESSAY

John D. Buenker, Joseph D. Buenker, and Lorman A. Ratner

Attempting to define the complex process by which myriad ethnic groups have adapted to mainstream American culture over the past two centuries has proven to be a protean task that has resisted the combined efforts of historians, anthropologists, sociologists, linguists, folklorists, geographers, political scientists, psychologists, and scholars of literature, religion, music, art, architecture, and drama. Great has been the temptation to eschew detailed, comparative analysis and to take refuge in metaphorical and rhetorical imagery, such as a melting pot, a salad bowl, a mosaic, or a kaleidoscope. So complex are the variables involved in the adaptive process that they inherently resist reduction to any formula, equation, or definition. Although the approach taken in this book provides an intensive and extensive introduction to the adaptation process as experienced by seventeen of America's myriad ethnic groups in a useful comparative framework, we do not claim to have produced anything more than a stimulus to further study. Even though most of the contributors to this volume are historians by academic training, the complex nature of immigration, ethnicity, and culture has forced us all to familiarize ourselves with much of the relevant literature from the social sciences and the humanities, as this bibliographical essay clearly demonstrates. Exploring these topics absolutely requires that all of us make a serious effort to break through the disciplinary boundaries that separate us and to develop an appreciation and understanding of the perspectives, insights, and contributions that we can make together toward understanding this issue that is so central to the character of the United States and that links Americans to the rest of the world.

Despite the number of sources discussed in the chapter bibliographies and in this bibliographical essay, it is important to remember that they constitute, in the apt phrase of Rudolph J. Vecoli, "a snapshot of an avalanche." The explosion of ethnic studies in every discipline over the past quarter century has produced a flood of literature, and the torrent is not likely to crest in the near future. One of the most difficult tasks faced by this book's contributors, and by all those who work in this field, is to provide the reader with reasonably coherent definitions of such slippery terms as *identity, ethnicity, race, accul-*

turation, assimilation, adaptation, integration, pluralism, diversity, and most vague and controversial of all, *Americanization.* In the end, each person will formulate his or her own working definitions and pick and choose among them for the concepts that best express his or her conceptualization of the adaptive process. In formulating the essays that comprise this volume, and in constructing the various bibliographical essays, the primary concern has been to provide each reader with the tools and concepts necessary to undertake this complicated, and frequently frustrating, task. Although the main focus is on culture and acculturation, there is no realistic way to avoid focusing on social structure and assimilation as well. Where that line should be drawn, if it can be drawn at all, is one of the many topics on which scholars of ethnicity generally agree to disagree.

Perhaps the most convenient beginning point for a study of ethnicity and adaptation are the various conceptual essays found in Stephan Thernstrom et al., *Harvard Encyclopedia of American Ethnic Groups* (Cambridge, MA: Belknap Press of Harvard Univ., 1980). The most relevant are: Philip Gleason, "American Identity and Americanization," 31–58; William Peterson, "Concepts of Ethnicity," 234–242; Harold J. Abramson, "Assimilation And Pluralism," 150–160; Michael R. Olneck and Marvin Logenson, "Education," 303–319; Tamara K. Hareven and John Modell, "Family Patterns," 345–354; Roger D. Abrahams, "Folklore," 370–379; Richard A. Easterlin, "Immigration: Economic and Social Characteristics," 476–486; David Ward, "Immigration: Settlement Patterns," 496–508; David M. Heer, "Intermarriage," 513–521; Joshua A. Fishman, "Language Maintenance," 629–638; John Higham, "Leadership," 642–667; Reed Ueda, "Naturalization and Citizenship," 734–748; Edward R. Kantowicz, "Politics," 803–813; George M. Frederickson and Dale T. Knobel, "Prejudice and Discrimination, History of," 829–847; and Harold J. Abramson, "Religion," 869–875. There can be little doubt that the *Harvard Encyclopedia* itself is the best single reference work on the topic of ethnicity, both for its conceptual essays and for its articles on virtually every ethnic group resident in the United States. Much briefer, but still informative, are the many relevant articles in Francesco Cordasco, ed., *Dictionary of American Immigration History* (Metuchen, NJ: Scarecrow Press, 1990).

Far less comprehensive, but valuable for specific ethnic groups, are several other reference works. Joan Morrison and Charlotte Fox Zabusky, *American Mosaic: The Immigrant Experience in the Words of Those Who Lived It* (Pittsburgh: Univ. of Pittsburgh Press, 1980) is extremely thought-provoking. *By Myself I'm a Book: An Oral History of the Immigrant Jewish Women* (Waltham, MA: National Council of Jewish Women, 1972) performs the same function for a more limited category of people. Irving J. Sloan, ed., *The Jews in America, 1621–1977: A Chronology and Fact Book* (Dobbs Ferry, NY: Oceana Publications, 1978) provides a wealth of data. Irving Howe and Kenneth Libo, eds., *How We Lived: A Documentary History of Immigrant Jews in America, 1880–1930* (New York: New American Library, 1979) contains much valuable information and ambience. Francis Bolek, ed., *Who's Who in Polish America* (New York: Harbinger House, 1970), originally published in 1943, is a valuable picture of intergenerational mobility. Hyung-Chan Kim, *Dictionary of Asian American History* (Westport, CT: Greenwood Press, 1986) contains many valuable insights into Chinese immigration and ethnicity. W. L. Tung, *The Chinese in America, 1820–1973: A Chronology and Fact Book* (Dobbs Ferry, NY: Oceana Publications, 1974) is a useful map through unfamiliar territory. Frank Chin et al., comps., *AIIIEEE! An Anthropology of Asian American Writers* (Washington, DC: Howard Univ. Press, 1974) presents an inside view, as does Victor G. and Brett de Bary Nee,

Longtime Californ': A Documentary Study of an American Chinatown (New York: Pantheon Books, 1973).

The availability of computer-aided search techniques has facilitated the proliferation of bibliographies on immigration and ethnicity during the past two decades. While many of these are extremely useful, all are limited by their dates of publication. John D. Buenker and Nicholas C. Burckel, eds., *Immigration and Ethnicity: A Guide to Information Sources* (Detroit: Gale Research Co., 1977) is the first such comprehensive work. A. William Hoglund, *Immigrants and Their Children in the United States: A Bibliography of Doctoral Dissertations, 1885–1982* (New York: Garland Pub., 1986) is a treasure trove of largely unpublished works. Paul Wasserman and Jean Morgan, eds., *Ethnic Information Sources of the United States* (Detroit: Gale Research Company, 1984) is especially helpful in locating nonacademic resources. Richard Kolm, *Bibliography of Ethnicity and Ethnic Groups* (Rockville, MD: National Institute of Mental Health, Center for Studies of Metropolitan Problems, 1973) is brief and general. Francesco Cordasco, ed., *A Bibliography of American Immigration History* (Fairfield, NJ: Fairfield-Dickinson University Press, 1978); and Perry L. Weed, *Ethnicity and American Group Life: A Bibliography* (New York: Praeger Publishers, 1972) nicely complement one another. Joseph J. Barton, ed., *An Annotated Guide to the Ethnic Experience in the United States* (Cambridge, MA: Harvard Univ. Press, 1976) is especially good on southern and eastern Europeans, while Francesco Cordasco, ed., *The Immigrant Woman in North America: An Annotated Bibliography of Selected References* (Metuchen, NJ: Scarecrow Press, 1985) provides a good introduction to the conjuncture of gender and ethnicity.

Other useful general bibliographies are Judith M. Herman, ed., *White Ethnic America: A Selected Bibliography* (New York: American Jewish Committee, 1969); Wayne C. Miller, ed., *Comprehensive Bibliography for the Study of American Minorities*, 3 vols. (New York: New York Univ. Press, 1976); William Ralph Janeway, ed., *Bibliography of Immigrants in the United States, 1900–1930* (San Francisco: R and E Research Associates, 1972); and Institute for Research in History, *Ethnic and Immigration Groups: The United States, Canada, and England* (New York: Haworth Press, 1983). Two bibliographies that especially focus on creative writing by and about ethnic Americans are Frank Deodene, comp., *The Origins of Ethnicity: Immigrants in America, Including the Immigrant in Fiction* (Chatham, NJ: The Chatham Bookseller, 1978); and Babette Inglehart and Anthony R. Mangione, comps., *The Image of Pluralism in American Literature: An Annotated Bibliography on the American Experience of European Ethnic Groups* (New York: Institute of Pluralism and Group Identity of the American Jewish Committee, 1974).

There are also a number of bibliographies that deal with the adaptation process through the prism of a single ethnic group. The University of California at Davis Asian American Studies program, for example, has issued *Asians in America: A Selected Annotated Bibliography* (Davis, CA: University of California, 1983). Works dealing with Jewish American ethnicity can be accessed through William W. Brickman, ed., *The Jewish Community in America: An Annotated and Classified Bibliographic Guide* (New York: B. Franklin, 1977), and through Jacob R. Marcus, ed., *An Index to Scientific Articles on American Jewish History* (Cincinnati, OH: American Jewish Archives, 1971). Entree to Polish American materials can be gained through Jan Wepsiec, ed., *Polish-American Serial Publications, 1842–1966* (Chicago: Polish Museum of America, 1968); Andrizey Brozek, "Historiography of Polish Immigration to North America," *Immigration History Newsletter* 18 (May 1986): 1–4; and Joseph W. Zurawski, *Polish-American History and*

Culture: A Classified Bibliography (Chicago: Polish Museum of America, 1975). For Norwegian ethnicity, consult John R. Jenswold, "The Missing Dimension: The Historiography of Urban Norwegian Immigration," *Immigration History Newsletter* 18 (May 1986): 4–7; for Finns, John I. Kolehmanien, ed., *The Finns in America: A Bibliographic Guide to Their History* (Hancock, MI, 1947); and for Danes, Enok Mortensen, *Danish-American Life and Letters: A Bibliography* (New York: Arno Press, 1979). The best guides to Swedish American adaptation are H. Arnold Barton, "Swedish-American Historiography," *Immigration History Newsletter* 15 (May 1983): 1–5, and Erik Erickson, ed., *Swedish American Periodicals: A Selective and Description Bibliography* (New York: Arno Press, 1979).

Especially valuable to understanding the adaptation process are a number of interpretive histories of immigration and ethnicity. The pioneer in this field was clearly Marcus Lee Hansen, whose *The Atlantic Migration, 1607–1860: A History of the Continuing Settlement of the United States* (Cambridge, MA: Harvard Univ. Press, 1940) and *The Immigrant in American History* (Cambridge, MA: Harvard Univ. Press, 1940) not only began the serious study of immigration history but also turned American historians outward in their search for the meaning of America, away from the frontier thesis of Frederick Jackson Turner and his followers. While Hansen focused his attention on immigration from northern and western Europe and stressed acculturation and assimilation, Oscar Handlin concentrated on immigration from southern and eastern Europe and found alienation in *The Uprooted: The Epic Story of the Great Migrations That Made the American People* (New York: Grosset & Dunlap, 1951). While the immigrants "made America," Handlin inferred strongly, they were repaid by the destruction of their culture and identities and the alienation of children from parents. Although he modified that pessimistic view somewhat in a revision of *The Uprooted*, Handlin continued to stress the negative impact of immigration on ethnic Americans, a view that largely dominated the field until the late 1960s. Curiously enough, Handlin predicted an optimistic outcome regarding the assimilation of African Americans and Puerto Ricans as "the last of the immigrants" in *The Newcomers: Negroes and Puerto Ricans in a Changing Metropolis* (Cambridge, MA: Harvard Univ. Press, 1959). Over the past quarter century, however, a new generation of immigration historians has departed from the emphasis on alienation and deprivation and built a new consensus around several key points: (1) Immigration was a purposeful and rational choice among viable alternatives, not an involuntary "uprooting"; (2) Most newcomers were part of migration chains of families and villages in which the earlier arrivals supplied their successors with information, money, housing, and employment; (3) Immigration was an ongoing process that featured a great deal of repatriation, both temporary and permanent; (4) Every ethnic group was divided internally by class, gender, religion, ideology, and pace, and degree of acculturation and assimilation; and (5) Some southern and eastern European immigrant groups shared more in common with earlier northern and western European arrivals than they did with their contemporaries.

This new consensus received a powerful boost from British historian Maldwyn A. Jones, *American Immigration* (Chicago: Univ. of Chicago Press, 1960), who virtually demolished the invidious distinction between the "old" (northern and western European) and "new" (southern and eastern European) immigration. Leonard Dinnerstern and David M. Reimers, *Ethnic Americans: A History of Immigration and Assimilation* (New York: Harper & Row, 1982), stress Handlin's traumatic view of the short-run plight of immigrants and Hansen's notion of long-term success. They and Roger L. Nichols, et al. *Natives and Strangers: Ethnic Groups and the Building of America* (New York: Oxford

Univ. Press, 1979), emphasize the great contributions made by ethnic groups to the growth of the United States despite or because of the hostility of nativists and racists. Maxine Schwartz Seller, *To Seek America: A History of Ethnic Life in the United States* (Englewood, NJ: J. S. Ozer, 1988), presents adaptation as an open-ended and ongoing process that is the meaning of America in itself. Alan M. Kraut, *The Huddled Masses: The Immigrant in the United States, 1880–1921* (Arlington Heights, IL: Harlan Davidson, 1982), concludes that southern and eastern European immigrants "were merely those who looked at what was being done to them, decided to leave their homelands, chose America, and, upon arrival, could not be stopped" (185). John Higham, *Send These to Me: Immigrants in Urban America* (Baltimore: Johns Hopkins Univ. Press, 1984) rejects all existing models of adaptation and substitutes his own concept of "pluralistic integration." And, deliberately choosing a metaphor to offset *The Uprooted*, John E. Bodnar, *The Transplanted: A History of Immigrants in Urban America* (Bloomington: Indiana Univ. Press, 1985), argues that while the lives of immigrants were not entirely of their own making, they made sure that they had something to say about them.

Also of great utility are various collections of eyewitness accounts or series of essays by a variety of scholars of immigration and ethnicity. The classic among the former is Oscar Handlin, ed., *Immigration as a Factor in American History* (Englewood Cliffs, NJ: Prentice-Hall, 1959), which focuses on the period from 1830 to 1953. Also interesting is Rhoda Hoff, ed., *America's Immigrants: Adventures in Eyewitness History* (New York: H. Z. Walck, 1967), which includes excerpts from people ranging from Benjamin Franklin (1784) to Rene Dubos (1966). Joan Morrison and Charlotte Fox Zabusky, *American Mosaic: The Immigrant Experience in the Words of Those Who Lived It* (New York: Dutton, 1980) includes interviews with nearly a hundred men and women. Thomas Kessner and Betty Boyd Caroli, eds., *Today's Immigrants, Their Stories: A New Look at the Newest Americans* (New York: Oxford Univ. Press, 1981), includes stories by an Irish woman, a Russian Jew, an Italian, and a Chinese and shows the continuity of experiences and issues. Moses Rischin, ed., *Immigration and the American Tradition* (Indianapolis, IN: Bobbs-Merrill, 1976) contains fifty-five excerpts that demonstrate the persisting ambivalence of America toward immigrants. O. Fritioj Ander, ed., *In the Trek of the Immigrants: Essays Presented to Carl Wittke* (Rock Island, IL: Augustana College Library, 1964) includes essays by sixteen scholars on the meaning of immigration for American history. Richard A. Easterlin, David Ward, William S. Bernard, and Reed Veda, *Immigration* (Cambridge, MA: Belknap Press, 1982), deals with economic and social characteristics, settlement patterns and spatial distribution, and naturalization and citizenship. In *The Immigrant Experience in America* (Boston: Twayne Publishers, 1976), editors Frank J. Coppa and Thomas J. Curran present nine essays on a variety of ethnic groups and the debate over immigration policy in the 1950s. Marjorie P. K. Weiser, ed., *Ethnic America* (New York: Wilson, 1978) is a collection of two dozen essays that focus on African Americans, American Indians, and the resurgence of Euro-American ethnicity. Virginia Yans McLaughlin, ed., *Immigration Reconsidered: History, Sociology, and Politics* (New York: Oxford Univ. Press, 1990) features eleven essays on migration patterns, ethnicity, and social structure, a new approach to the study of immigration, and the politics of immigration.

Perhaps the most perplexing question of all is trying to understand the nature of the adaptation process in the relationship between ethnicity and identity. Because both are relatively new and abstract concepts, it is difficult to achieve a consensus on much of anything, except to agree that ethnicity, however defined, is a vital component of identity, whatever we believe to be its essence. There can be little doubt that anyone hoping to grasp the meaning of the concept of identity must begin with the works of Erik Erikson. See especially his *Identity, Youth, and Crisis* (New York: W. W. Norton, 1968); *Identity and the Life Cycle* (New York: Norton, 1980); and *Life History and the Historical Moment* (New York: Norton, 1975). The serious psychological damage that can result from a failure to resolve an identity crisis rooted in the disparity between one's ethnic origins and the mainstream society and culture was first explored by Everett V. Stonequist, *The Marginal Man: A Study in Personality and Culture Conflict* (New York: Russell and Russell, 1961). See also Arnold Dashefsky, ed., *Ethnic Identity in Society* (Chicago: Rand McNally, 1976) and A. L. Epstein, *Ethos and Identity: Three Studies in Ethnicity* (Chicago: Aldine Pub. Co., 1978).

Arthur Mann, *The One and the Many: Reflections on the American Identity* (Chicago: Univ. of Chicago Press, 1979), argues that American national identity rests on a persistent faith that the "unum" and the "pluribus" in the national motto are not only mutually compatible but absolutely essential to the effective exercise of freedom. Perhaps among no ethnic group has this persisting paradox been more perplexing than among Jewish Americans, who have experienced the greatest sense of alienation because they have enjoyed the greatest degree of upward mobility. Allen Guttmann, *The Jewish Writer In America: Assimilation and the Crisis of Identity* (New York: Oxford Univ. Press, 1971), analyzes that phenomenon among nearly two dozen Jewish writers, ranging from Emma Lazarus to Saul Bellow. Charles Bezalel Sherman, *The Jew within American Society: A Study in Ethnic Individuality* (Detroit: Wayne State Univ. Press, 1961), argues that Jews have been virtually unique among American ethnic groups because they have fully integrated into society while retaining their "ethnic individuality." Milton Plesur, *Jewish Life in Twentieth-Century America: Challenge and Accommodation* (Chicago: Nelson-Hall, 1982), finds a complex mixture of anxiety, affluence, and affirmation. David Sidorsky, ed., *The Future of the Jewish Community in America: Essays Prepared for a Task Force on the Future of the Jewish Community in America of the American Jewish Committee* (New York: Institute of Human Relations Press, 1973) features eleven essays on perspectives, profiles, communal institutions, and issues.

Numerous other scholars have focused on establishing a clearer sense of the meaning of ethnicity as it has evolved over generations. William S. Bernard, ed., *Immigrants and Ethnicity: Ten Years of Changing Thought* (New York: American Immigration and Citizenship Conference, 1972) contains excerpts of papers given by seventeen sociologists and historians on the meaning of integration and on the position of ethnic groups within a pluralistic society. William Peterson et al., *Concepts of Ethnicity* (Cambridge, MA: Belknap Press, 1982) consists of essays on the title topic, on pluralism in a humanistic perspective, and on identity and Americanization. Basic to an understanding of the evolution of the concept of ethnicity are three articles by Rudolph J. Vecoli: "Contadini in Chicago: A Critique of *The Uprooted*," *Journal of American History* 51 (December 1964): 40417; "Ethnicity: A Neglected Dimension of American History," in *The State of American History*, ed. Herbert Bass (Chicago: Quadrangle Books, 1970); and "European Americans: From Immigrants to Ethnics," in *The Reinterpretation of American History and Culture*, ed. William H. Cartwright and Richard T. Watson (Washington, DC: National Council for the Social Studies, 1973), 87–112. Also instructive are two books by Frank J. Cavaioli and Salvatore J. La Gumina: *The Ethnic Dimension in American Soci-*

ety (Boston: Holbrook Press, 1974), which argues for the centrality of ethnicity to American history over three centuries, and *The Peripheral Americans* (Malabar, FL: R.E. Krieger Pub. Co., 1984), which focuses on the succession of "ethnic constellations" that have kept group interests, power, and aspirations at the center of American civilization.

Thomas C. Wheeler, ed., *The Immigrant Experience: The Anguish of Becoming American* (New York: Dial Press, 1971), echoes *The Uprooted* in its lament for the destruction of ethnic culture as explicated by writers of Irish, Italian, Norwegian, Puerto Rican, Chinese, African, Jewish, English, and Polish extraction. James S. Olson, *The Ethnic Dimension in American History*, 2 vols. (New York: St. Martin's Press, 1979), insists flatly that "ethnicity is the central theme of American history," that "the most powerful feelings of fidelity and security spring from the values and symbolic associations of the group itself," and that the United States will never become an ethnically homogeneous society, or at least not for many centuries. Leonard Dinnerstein and Frederic Cople Jaher, eds., *Uncertain Americans: Readings in Ethnic History* (New York: Oxford Univ. Press, 1977), contend that "all groups of non-English origin" are ethnic minorities who have had to undergo a complex and frequently painful process of acculturation. Andrew M. Greeley, *Ethnicity in the United States: A Preliminary Reconnaissance* (New York: Wiley, 1974), argues that the persistence of ethnic attitudes, values, and behaviors are largely subconscious but can be demonstrated empirically by survey research. See also Richard M. Juliani, *Immigration and Ethnicity* (Philadelphia: Bolch Institute, 1974).

Central to understanding the concept of ethnicity is the notion of race, a term that has frequently been used interchangeably with ethnicity, especially by nativists. Oscar Handlin, *Race and Nationality in American Life* (Boston: Little, Brown, 1957), presents racism as a series of "various divisive doctrines that have attempted to create different categories of men" and as a system of ideas fostered by certain personality types within particular social structures. Mark Haller, *Eugenics: Hereditarian Attitudes in American Thought* (New Brunswick, NJ: Rutgers Univ. Press, 1963), reaches optimistic conclusions by examining a checkered past. The perspective of British anthropologist Ashley Montagu, *Man's Most Dangerous Myth: The Fallacy of Race* (Cleveland: World Pub. Co., 1964), is apparent from the title. Thomas F. Gossett, *Race: The History of an Idea in America* (Dallas: Southern Methodist Univ. Press, 1963), reflects the optimism of the civil rights movement of the 1960s. Peter I. Rose, *The Subject Is Race: Traditional Ideologies and the Teaching of Race Relations* (New York: Oxford Univ. Press, 1968), calls for a critical, systematic, and objective assessment of this controversial concept. George W. Stocking, Jr., *Race, Culture, and Evolution: Essays in the History of Anthropology* (New York: Free Press, 1968), features addresses, essays, and lectures on ethnology. Ronald L. Takaki, *Iron Cages: Race and Culture in Nineteenth-Century America* (New York: Knopf, 1979), contrasts the lot of nonwhite peoples with the American Dream.

Numerous other scholars have written on the interrelationships between race and ethnicity. W. Lloyd Warner and Leo Srole, *The Social Systems of American Ethnic Groups* (New Haven, CT: Yale Univ. Press, 1945) is a pioneer work that focuses on the interplay among ethnic and racial groups with respect to residence and occupational patterns, family structure, religion, education, and associational life. Joseph B. Gittler, ed., *Understanding Minority Groups* (New York: Wiley, 1956) examines a variety of groups, including Indians, Jews, and African Americans, and discusses the philosophical and ethical dimensions of intergroup relations. James W. Vander Zanden, *American Minority Relations: The Sociology of Race and Ethnic Groups* (New York: Ronald Press Co., 1966) is a theoretical and descriptive analysis of the sociological foundations of race and minority relations, with sections on the sources of prejudice and discrimination, intergroup relations, and reactions to dominance and social change. Vincent N. Parillo, *Strangers to These Shores: Race and Ethnic Relations in the United States* (Boston: Houghton Mifflin, 1980), examines majority-minority relations, culture and social structure, and "the American mosaic." Bernard E. Segal, ed., *Racial and Ethnic Relations* (New York: Crowell, 1966) contains selections by a wide variety of scholars on such topics as ethic and racial subcultural variation, the scope and quality of social and ethnic attitudes, and prospects for the future in ethnic and racial relations. Norman R. Yetman and C. Hoy Steele, eds., *Majority and Minority: The Dynamics of Racial and Ethnic Relations* (Boston: Allyn and Bacon, 1971) is an anthology of nearly forty articles that attempts to analyze the dynamics of racial and ethnic relations within the broader field of majority-minority relations.

Peter I. Rose, ed., *Nation of Nations: The Ethnic Experience and the Racial Crisis* (New York: Random House, 1972) contains thirty essays by novelists, journalists, sociologists, and historians on the comparative and competitive experiences of ethnic and racial minorities. Rudolph Gomez, ed., *The Social Reality of Ethnic America* (Lexington, MA: D. C. Heath, 1974) concentrates on African Americans, Mexican Americans, and American Indians, examining their attitudes, grievances, activities, and leadership. Emerich K. Francis, *Interethnic Relations: An Essay in Sociological Theory* (New York: Elsevier, 1976) presents a worldwide perspective and outlines a theory of interethnic relations. Frank D. Bean and W. Parker Frisbie, *The Demography of Racial and Ethnic Groups* (New York: Academic Press, 1978) compares a variety of groups with respect to residential and school segregation, suburbanization, mental instability, labor force participation, fertility rates, family and household structure, and mortality. Ronald Takaki, ed., *From Different Shores: Perspectives on Race and Ethnicity in America* (New York: Oxford Univ. Press, 1987) features twenty-seven essays on ethnic patterns, culture, class, gender, and prospects for a more equal society. Lawrence H. Fuchs, *The American Kaleidoscope: Race, Ethnicity and the Civic Culture* (Hanover, NH: Wesleyan Univ. Press, 1990), and Alfred J. Wrobel and Michael J. Eula, eds., *American Ethnics and Minorities: Readings in Ethnic History* (Dubuque, IA: Kendall/Hunt Pub., 1990), are two important recent additions to the literature.

The debate over the nature, velocity, and eventual outcome, both desired and projected, of the adaptive process has been going on for at least two centuries. Probably the first statement of the melting pot concept was J. Hector St. John Crèvecoeur, *Letters From an American Farmer* (London: T. Davies, 1782). Even more well-known is that by Israel Zangwill, *The Melting Pot, Drama in Four Acts* (New York: Macmillan Co., 1909). See also Maurice Wohlgelernter, *Israel Zangwill: A Study* (New York: Columbia Univ. Press, 1964). The notion that all ethnic groups would and should eventually be amalgamated into the dominant Anglo-Protestant society and culture and disappear as identifiable entities, to some extent implied in the melting pot thesis, was made more explicit by the Chicago School of Sociology during the high point of immigration from southern and eastern Europe. See, especially, Robert E. Park and Ernest W. Burgess, *Introduction to the Science of Sociology* (Chicago: The Univ. of Chicago Press, 1921) and Fred H. Mathews, *Quest for an American Sociology* (Montreal: McGill-Queen's Univ. Press, 1977). But the assimilationist theory was quickly challenged by the "cultural pluralism" school led by Julius Drachsler, *Democracy and Assimilation: The Blending of Immigrant Heritages in America* (New York: The Macmillan Co., 1920), and Horace M. Kallen, *Culture and Democracy in the United States* (New York: Boni and Liveright, 1924), and *Cultural Pluralism and the American Idea: An Essay in Social Philosophy* (Philadelphia: Univ. of Pennsylvania Press, 1956).

All three models are carefully analyzed and compared in Milton M. Gordon, *Assimilation in American Life: The Role of Race, Religion, and National Origins* (New York: Oxford Univ. Press, 1964), in which he concludes that most ethnic groups eventually embrace "cultural assimilation" (acculturation) but that many are still denied "structural assimilation" (assimilation) years later. In *Human Nature, Class, and Ethnicity* (New York: Oxford Univ. Press, 1978), Gordon factors in class as an independent variable in the equation. In *"Why Can't They Be Like Us?" Facts and Fallacies about Ethnic Differences and Group Conflicts in America* (New York: Institute of Human Relations Press, 1969), Andrew M. Greeley posits a six-step process of "ethnogenesis" that runs from "cultural shock" to "emerging adjustment." Higham, as previously noted, discusses a model of "pluralistic integration" in *Send These To Me*. William M. Newman, *American Pluralism: A Study of Minority Groups and Social Theory* (New York: Harper & Row, 1973), finds a partial solution to the puzzle in the concept of "multiple realities." Focusing on Detroit, Edward O. Laumann, *Bonds of Pluralism: The Form and Substance of Urban Social Networks* (New York: J. Wiley, 1973) argues that religious affiliation and socioeconomic status most affect patterns of social integration. Will Herberg, *Protestant, Catholic, Jew: An Essay In American Religious Sociology* (Garden City, NY: Doubleday, 1955), concludes that all ethnic groups are being absorbed into a "triple melting pot" organized around three generic "civic religions." Neil C. Sandberg, *Ethnic Identity and Assimilation: The Polish-American Community* (New York: Praeger, 1974), concludes that the sense of ethnic identity varies with the length of residence, social class, degree of religious identification, and geographical mobility.

One of the most-debated issues involving the adaptation process is whether or not it proceeds in a straight line toward some expected outcome or whether it takes a less predictable course. Over half a century ago, Marcus Lee Hansen proposed that "what the son wishes to forget the grandson wishes to remember." Peter Kivisto and Dag Blanck, eds., *American Immigrants and Their Generations: Studies and Commentaries on the Hansen Thesis after Fifty Years* (Urbana: Univ. of Illinois Press, 1990) contains essays by ten modern scholars on the implications of Hansen's law of generations and on the switch in perception from process to structure over the past half century. As if to prove Hansen's contention, numerous writers in the 1970s proclaimed the emergence of a "new ethnicity," led by Michael Novak, *The Rise of the Unmeltable Ethnics: Politics and Culture in the Seventies* (New York: Macmillan, 1972). Novak definitely championed the cause of "Poles, Italians, Greeks, and Slavs," proposed their common cause with racial minorities, and chastised liberal intellectuals for their abandonment of the New Deal political alliance. Novak's perspective was reinforced in short order by Michael Wenk, Silvano Tomasi, and Gino Baroni, eds., *Pieces of A Dream: The Ethnic Workers Crisis with America* (New York: Center for Migration Studies, 1972), a collection of fifteen essays on the interplay of social class and ethnic pride; by Stanley Feldstein and Lawrence Costello, *The Ordeal of Assimilation: A Documentary History of the White Working Class, 1830s to the 1970s* (Garden City, NY: Anchor Press, 1974), a compilation of source materials organized around the theme of the ongoing struggling Euro-American laborers for assimilation; by Andrew Levison, *The Working-Class Majority* (New York: Coward, Mc-

Cann & Geoghegan, 1974), which tries to forge a white-black progressive economic and political alliance; by Joseph Ryan, ed., *White Ethnics: Their Life in Working Class America* (Englewood Cliffs, NJ: Prentice-Hall, 1973), which locates the persistence of Euro-American ethnicity in the family, church, and neighborhood and proposes action in the schools, the workplace, and the political arena; and by Richard J. Krickus, *Pursuing the American Dream: White Ethnics and the New Populism* (Garden City, NY: Anchor Press, 1976), which urges a new ethnic working-class movement to combat both the "cosmopolitan left" and the ethnic strategy of the (Richard) Nixon Republicans. In *Ethnic Dilemmas, 1964–1982* (Cambridge, MA: Harvard Univ. Press, 1983), Nathan Glazer proposes a plan to deal with bilingualism and affirmative action.

Not surprisingly, the "new ethnicity" quickly gave rise to a critique that regarded its tenets as romantic or reactionary. See, for example, Howard F. Stein and Robert F. Hill, *The Ethnic Imperative: Examining the White Ethnic Movement* (University Park: Pennsylvania State Univ. Press, 1977); Orlando Patterson, *Ethnic Chauvinism: The Reactionary Impulse* (New York: Stein and Day, 1977); Thomas Sowell, *Ethnic America: A History* (New York: Basic Books, 1981); and Stephen Steinberg, *The Ethnic Myth: Race, Ethnicity and Class in America* (New York: Atheneum, 1981). Two works that attempt to present all sides of the controversy over the resurgence of ethnicity in a developmental context are Richard J. Meister, ed., *Race and Ethnicity in Modern America* (Lexington, MA: Heath, 1974), a collection of twenty essays ranging from Crevecoeur through the 1970s; and David R. Colburn and George E. Pozetta, eds., *America and the New Ethnicity* (Port Washington, NY: Kennikat Press, 1979), an anthology of sixteen essays dealing with the emergence of ethnic awareness, the resurgence of ethnicity, and criticism of the new ethnicity. Robert N. Bellah et al., *Habits of the Heart: Individualism and Commitment in American Life* (Berkeley: Univ. of California Press, 1985) illustrates that ethnicity still provides many people with a "second language of community solidarity" with which to offset their "first language of the modern individual."

One of the factors that clearly influences the adaptive process is location of settlement. James P. Allen and Eugene J. Turner, eds., *We the People: An Atlas of America's Ethnic Diversity* (New York: Macmillan, 1988) contains a wealth of colored maps by both area and ethnic groups. Wilbur Zelinsky, *The Cultural Geography of the United States* (Englewood Cliffs, NJ: Prentice-Hall, 1973), and Raymond D. Gastil, *Cultural Regions of the United States* (Seattle: Univ. of Washington Press, 1975) are good introductions to the concept. Donald K. Fellows, in *A Mosaic of Americas' Ethnic Minorities* (New York: Wiley, 1972), plots the changing distribution of African-, Chinese-, and Mexican-Americans and of American Indians. Caroline Golab, *Immigrant Destinations* (Philadelphia: Temple Univ. Press, 1977), specifically interprets "immigrant adaptation as a function of spatial distribution." David Ward, *Cities and Immigrants: A Geography of Change in Nineteenth-Century America* (New York: Oxford Univ. Press, 1971), concentrates on "the spatial effects of selective urban growth and international differentiation." Dean R. Esslinger, *Immigrants and the City: Ethnicity and Mobility in a Nineteenth Century Midwestern Community* (Port Washington, NY: Kennikat Press, 1975), compares the geographical mobility of 10,000 immigrants of a variety of ethnic origins in South Bend, Indiana. Odd S. Lovoll, *Scandinavians and Other Immigrants in Urban America* (Northfield, MN: Saint Olaf College Press, 1985), demonstrates the significance of the urban environment on the adaptation of different immigrant groups.

The comparative experiences of two or more ethnic groups within a single locale provides a particularly valuable perspective on adaptation, as Esslinger's study of South Bend effectively demonstrates. Robert Ernst, *Immigrant Life in New York City, 1825–1863* (Port Washington, NY: I.J. Friedman, 1965), especially compares Irish and German newcomers, while Nathan Glazer and Daniel Patrick Moynihan, *Beyond the Melting Pot: The Negroes, Puerto Ricans, Jews, Italians, and Irish of New York City* (Cambridge, MA: M.I.T. Press, 1963), demonstrate the persistence of ethnicity in the country's largest metropolis. John E. Bodnar, ed., *The Ethnic Experience in Pennsylvania* (Lewisburg, PA: Bucknell Univ. Press, 1973) contains twelve essays, including those on Irish, Poles, Italians, Jews, and African Americans. In *Lives of Their Own: Blacks, Italians, and Poles in Pittsburgh, 1900–1960* (Urbana: Univ. of Illinois Press, 1982), Bodnar joins with Roger Simon and Michael P. Weber in a study with both comparative and chronological dimensions. Theodore Hershberg, ed., *Philadelphia: Work, Space, Family and Group Experience in the Nineteenth Century* (New York: Oxford Univ. Press, 1981), compares a variety of ethnic groups on those measures over a 120-year period. Donald B. Cole's *Immigrant City: Lawrence, Massachusetts, 1845–1921* (Chapel Hill: Univ. of North Carolina Press, 1963) traces occupational and residential patterns of two waves of immigrants to a New England mill town. Olivier Zunz, *The Changing Face of Inequality: Urbanization, Industrial Development, and Immigrants in Detroit, 1880–1920* (Chicago: Univ. of Chicago Press, 1982), demonstrates that the latest arrivals always inherit the lowest rung of the ladder. In *The Ethnic Frontier: Essays in the History of Group Survival in Chicago and the Midwest* (Grand Rapids, MI: Eerdmans, 1977), Melvin G. Holli and Peter d'A. Jones present essays on nine ethnic groups who took their place in "the cauldron of American values." Clyde and Sally Griffin, *Natives and Newcomers: The Ordering of Opportunity in Mid-Nineteenth Century Poughkeepsie* (Cambridge, MA: Harvard Univ. Press, 1978), and Tamara K. Hareven and Randolph Langenbach, *Amoskeag: Life and Work in an American Factory-City* (New York: Pantheon Books, 1978), demonstrate similar phenomena in smaller locales. And in *The Best Poor Man's Country: A Geographical Study of Early Southeastern Pennsylvania* (Baltimore: Johns Hopkins Press, 1972), James T. Lemon presents a regional case study of ethnic pluralism in southeastern Pennsylvania.

Another comparative perspective can be gained by matching studies of the same ethnic group in two or more locales. A comparative reading of Stanford M. Lyman, *The Asian in North America* (Santa Barbara, CA: ABC-Clio Books, 1977) and James W. Loewen, *The Mississippi Chinese: Between Black and White* (Cambridge, MA: Harvard Univ. Press, 1971) graphically illustrates the importance of locale. The bulk of the literature on Jewish Americans naturally has New York City as its locale. This includes Moses Rischin, *The Promised City: New York's Jews, 1870–1914* (Cambridge, MA: Harvard Univ. Press, 1962); Irving Howe, *World of Our Fathers* (New York: Simon and Schuster, 1976); Stephen Birmingham, *"Our Crowd:" The Great Jewish Families of New York* (New York: Harper & Row, 1967); Arthur A. Goren, *New York Jews and the Quest for Community* (New York: Columbia Univ. Press, 1970); and Ronald Sanders, *The Downtown Jews* (New York: Harper & Row, 1969). But these should be compared with a variety of other studies of Jewish Americans in other locales: Joseph Brandes, *Immigrants to Freedom: Jewish Communities in Rural New Jersey since 1882* (Philadelphia: Univ. of Pennsylvania Press, 1971); Stuart E. Rosenberg, *The Jewish Community in Rochester, 1843–1925* (New York: Columbia Univ. Press, 1954); Steven Hertzberg, *Strangers within the Gate City: The Jews of Atlanta, 1845–1915* (Philadelphia: Jewish Publication Society of America, 1978); Max Vorspan and Lloyd P. Gartner, *History of the Jews of Los Angeles* (San Marino, CA: Huntington Library, 1970); Marc Lee Raphael, *Jews and Judaism in a Midwestern Community: Columbus, Ohio, 1840–1875* (Columbus: Ohio Historical Society, 1979); Louis J. Swichkow and Lloyd P. Gartner, *The History of the Jews of Milwaukee* (Philadelphia: Jewish Publication Society of America, 1963); and Leonard Dinnerstein, *Jews in the South* (Baton Rouge: Louisiana State Univ. Press, 1973).

Comparative locational influences on Finnish Americans can be gained from reading Michael J. Karni et al., eds., *The Finnish Experience in the Western Great Lakes Region* (Minneapolis: Immigration History Research Center, 1975); John I. Kolehmainen and George W. Hill, *Haven in the Woods: The Story of the Finns in Wisconsin* (Madison: State Historical Society of Wisconsin, 1951); Hans R. Wasastjerna, ed., *History of the Finns in Minnesota* (Duluth, MN: Finnish American Historical Society, 1957); and John I. Kolehmainen, *A History of the Finns in Ohio, Western Pennsylvania, and West Virginia: From Lake Erie's Shores to the Mahoning and Monongahela Valleys* (Painesville: Ohio-Finnish American Historical Society, 1977). The same perspective on other Scandinavians can be gained from a comparative reading of Harold S. Naess, ed., *The Norwegian Influence in the Upper Midwest* (Duluth, MN: University of Minnesota, Duluth, 1976); Kenneth O. Bjork, *West of the Great Divide: Norwegian Migration to the Pacific Coast, 1847–1893* (Northfield, MN: Norwegian-American Historical Assoc., 1958); Sture Lindmark, *Swedish-America, 1914–1932: Studies in Ethnicity with Emphasis on Illinois and Minnesota* (Stockholm, Sweden: Läromedelsför laget, 1971); Byron Nordstrom, ed., *The Swedes in Minnesota* (Minneapolis: Denison, 1976); and John L. Davis, *The Danish Texans* (San Antonio: Univ. of Texas Institute of Texan Cultures at San Antonio, 1979).

Two of the most important concepts developed for comprehending the adaptation process are the realization that every ethnic group is divided internally by social class and a variety of other considerations and that each ethnic community eventually develops a cadre of leaders who serve as conduits or mediators between its members and mainstream society and culture. Gordon, *Human Nature, Class, and Ethnicity*, is an excellent introduction. Donald J. Noel, "A Theory of the Origins of Ethnic Stratification," *Social Problems* 16 (Summer 1968): 157–162, and James A. Henretta, "The Study of Social Mobility: Ideological Assumptions and Conceptual Bias," *Labor History* 18 (Spring 1977): 165–178 provide a good theoretical grounding. Lydio F. Tomasi, *The Ethnic Factor in the Future of Inequality* (Staten Island, NY: Center for Migration Studies, 1972), explores the tensions generated within individuals and ethnic groups by the interaction of the cultural bond and modernity. Richard Polenberg, *One Nation Divisible: Class, Race, and Ethnicity in the United States since 1938* (New York: Penguin Books, 1980), demonstrates how these three crosscutting realities have restructured society in the past half century. Michael J. Piore, *Birds of Passage: Migrant Labor and Industrial Societies* (New York: Cambridge Univ. Press, 1979) examines the lives of a class distinguished by its marginality, both to industrial society and to their own ethnic group. Simon Kuznets and Ernest Rubin, *Immigration and the Foreign Born* (New York: National Bureau of Economic Research, 1954), provide intensive statistical analysis of class differences, both within and among ethnic groups. Robert D. Parmet, *Labor and Immigration in Industrial America* (Boston: Twayne, 1981), illustrates how ethnicity provides many Americans with a sense of continuity and community denied them in the socioeconomic order. Gerald Rosenblum, *Immigrant Workers: Their Impact on American Labor Radicalism* (New York: Basic Books, Inc., 1973) finds that Old World expectations and fears were so powerful that only a small percentage were able to overcome them sufficiently to join unions and become militants. Sally M. Miller, *The Radical Immigrant* (New York: Twayne Publishers, 1974), explores those qualities that separated the relative handful of radicals from their more cautious compatriots. More intensively, Michael J. Karni and Douglas J. Ollila, eds., *For the Common Good: Finnish Immigrants and the Radical Response to Industrial America* (Superior, WI: Tyomies Society, 1977), provide many valuable insights into the qualities and characteristics that caused a relatively small ethnic group to produce a disproportionately large number of radicals.

At the opposite end of the spectrum, at least in some aspects, were the emerging leaders of most ethnic groups. John Higham, ed., *Ethnic Leadership in America* (Baltimore: Johns Hopkins Univ. Press, 1978) contains many indispensible insights into the crucial role played by leaders in the adaptation process. Victor R. Greene, *American Immigrant Leaders, 1800–1910: Marginality and Identity* (Baltimore: Johns Hopkins Univ. Press, 1987), interprets Irish, German, Scandinavian, Jewish, Polish, and Italian community leaders as "traditional progressives" because they urged integration and segregation at the same time. Yonathan Shapiro, *Leadership of the American Zionist Organization, 1897–1930* (Urbana: Univ. of Illinois Press, 1971), and Gary Dean Best, *To Free A People: American Jewish Leaders and the Jewish Problem in Eastern Europe, 1890–1914* (Westport, CT: Greenwood Press, 1982), both demonstrate the crucial relationship between New York leadership and Old World ties and issues.

Recent scholarship has also begun to focus more attention on the status and function of women in the ethnic experience. Cecyle S. Neidle, *America's Immigrant Women* (Boston: Twayne Publishers, 1975) surveys the broad range of pursuits engaged in by immigrant women from colonial times through the 1960s, ranging from housewives and mothers through clergy, teachers, industrial workers, political radicals, physicians, scientists, musicians, writers, and business leaders. Maxine Seller, ed., *Immigrant Women* (Philadelphia: Temple Univ. Press, 1981), generates the same impression through the testimony of nearly fifty participants. Joan Younger Dickinson, *The Role of the Immigrant Women in the U.S. Labor Force, 1890–1910* (New York: Arno Press, 1980), and Leslie Woodcock Tentler, *Wage-Earning Women: Industrial Work and Family Life in the United States, 1900–1930* (New York: Oxford Univ. Press, 1979), both explore the tensions felt and compromises made by millions of ethnic women who worked in one culture and lived in another, neither of which granted them full equality. Charlotte Baum et al., *The Jewish Woman in America* (New York: Dial Press, 1976), and Betty Boyd Caroli et al., eds., *The Italian Immigrant Women in North America* (Toronto: Multicultural History Society of Ontario, 1978), focus intensively on the impact of American life on two very different cultural perspectives regarding the status and value of women. Jade Snow Wong, *Fifth Chinese Daughter* (New York: Harper, 1950), and Maxine Hong Kingston, *The Woman Warrior: Memoirs of a Girlhood among Ghosts* (New York: Knopf, 1976), are both sensitive, first-person accounts of the peculiar difficulties faced by Chinese women in adapting to American life.

Changes in family structure and behavior and in marriage patterns have long been recognized as important indexes of acculturation, and the literature reflects that conviction. Tamara Hareven, *Family Time and Industrial Time: The Relationship between the Family and Work in a New England Community* (Cambridge, MA: Cambridge Univ. Press, 1982), explores the creative tension inherent in being caught between two culturally different concepts of the value and meaning of time. Charles H. Mindel and Robert W. Habenstein, eds., *Ethnic Families in America: Patterns and Variations* (New York:

Elsevier, 1976), provides a generally excellent synthesis regarding what is known and needs to be known about the varying patterns of ethnic group family life.

Few subjects have stirred up so much controversy in the past two decades as has the African American family. The conflict dates primarily from the publication of the Moynihan report, "The Negro Family: The Case for National Action" in 1965, which stated flatly that "at the heart of the deterioration of the fabric of Negro society is the deterioration of the Negro family." The reaction led to the publication of Herbert Gutman's *The Black Family in Slavery and Freedom, 1750–1925* (New York: Pantheon Books, 1976), which specifically contradicted Moynihan and argued that the African American family had proven to be amazingly resilient, at least until the impact of northern, urban, industrial life. Lee Rainwater and William L. Yancey, eds., *The Moynihan Report and the Politics of Controversy* (Cambridge, MA: M.I.T. Press, 1967) provides a balanced and enlightening discussion. Charles Vert Willie, *A New Look at Black Families* (Bayside, NY: General Hall, 1981) contains eighteen case studies and concludes with a theoretical explanation of family adaptation by race and social class, while his edited work, *The Family Life of Black People* (Columbus, OH: Merrill, 1970), includes essays by two dozen scholars on the general topics of social facts and family life, stability and instability in family life, family structure and interaction among the poor, and family circumstances and social consequences. Willie utilizes case studies of dozens of middle-class, working-class, and poor families, half of them "white" and the other half "black," and concludes that there is an "essential interdependency between all sorts and conditions of families by race and social class."

The general contours and significance of intermarriage as an index of acculturation are sketched briefly in Herr, "Intermarriage," in *Harvard Encyclopedia*, ed. Thernstrom et al., 513–521. Ruth Sharle Cavan's "Annotated Bibliography of Studies on Intermarriage in the United States, 1960–1970 Inclusive," *International Journal of Sociology of the Family* 1 (May 1971): 157–168 is a helpful guide to the literature. Milton L. Barron, ed., *The Blending American: Patterns of Intermarriage* (Chicago: Quadrangle Books, 1972) contains a wide variety of viewpoints on the attempts of ethnic institutions to regulate intermarriage and on its postmarital consequences. Hugh Carter and Paul C. Glick, *Marriage and Divorce: A Social and Economic Study* (Cambridge, MA: Harvard Univ. Press, 1970) contains some interesting data on ethnicity and religion as variables. Richard M. Bernard, *The Melting Pot and The Altar: Marital Assimilation in Early Twentieth Century Wisconsin* (Minneapolis: Univ. of Minnesota Press, 1980), finds that exogamy there did produce a veritable melting pot. Harold J. Abramson, *Ethnic Diversity in Catholic America* (New York: Wiley, 1973), asserts that 55 percent of American Catholics still practiced endogamy in the 1970s. Richard D. Alba, "Social Assimilation among American Catholic National Origin Groups," *American Sociological Review* 41 (December 1976): 103–148 modifies but does not completely overturn Abramson's findings.

Few conflicts have lent more anxiety to the adaptation process than has the clash between generations. Niles Carpenter, *Immigrants and Their Children, 1920: A Study Based on Census Statistics Relative to the Foreign Born and the Native White of Foreign or Mixed Parentage* (Washington, DC: Government Printing Office, 1927), compares the generations with respect to settlement patterns, length of residence, sex ratios, language retention, age, fecundity, vitality, marital status, marriage patterns, illegitimacy, citizenship, and occupation. Edward P. Hutchinson, *Immigrants and Their Children, 1850–1950* (New York: Wiley, 1956), focuses on the changing composition of immigration: geographical and occupational distribution, contributions to the American economy, and the effects of immigration restriction. Access to much of the best literature can be gained through A. William Hoglund, *Immigrants and Their Children in the United States: A Bibliography of Doctoral Dissertations, 1885–1982* (New York: Garland Publishers, 1986). June Namias, ed., *First Generation: In the Words of Twentieth-Century America Immigrants* (Boston: Beacon Press, 1978) presents the viewpoints of over two dozen newcomers, while Oscar Handlin, ed., *Children of The Uprooted* (New York: G. Braziller, 1966) contains nearly three dozen selections dealing with the second generation. Irene D. Jaworski, *Becoming American: The Problem of Immigrants and Their Children* (New York: Harper, 1950), compares the nature of the ethnic generation gap in a variety of cultures. Deborah Dash Moore, *At Home in America: Second Generation New York Jews* (New York: Columbia Univ. Press, 1981), finds a successful model of acculturation, while Judith R. Kramer and Seymour Leventman, *Children of The Gilded Ghetto: Conflict Resolution of Three Generations of American Jews* (New Haven, CT: Yale Univ. Press, 1961), argue that Jewish Americans in midwestern cities have moved from an ethnic to a status-oriented community due to occupational mobility.

Almost no other single index of acculturation has evoked so much heated controversy as has language retention. Nativists have long regarded the use of English as the ultimate test of loyalty, while traditionalists have insisted with equal fervor on retention as a mark of persisting ethnicity. The leading authority on the topic is certainly Joshua A. Fishman, author of the article "Language Maintenance" in Thernstrom et al., *Harvard Encyclopedia*, 629–638. Fishman's coedited *Language Loyalty in The United States: The Maintenance and Perpetuation of Non-English Mother Tongues by American Ethnic and Religious Groups* (The Hague: Mouton, 1966) is the standard work. See also his edited work, *Never Say Die! A Thousand Years of Yiddish in Jewish Life and Letters* (The Hague: Mouton, 1981). Also insightful into larger issues is Einar Haugen, *Language Conflict and Language Planning: The Case of Modern Norwegian* (Cambridge, MA: Harvard Univ. Press, 1966). Francesco Cordasco, ed., "Bilingual Education in American Schools: A Bibliographical Essay," *Immigration History Newsletter* 14 (May 1982): 1–8, is a useful guide to the literature on that thorny subject. The importance of language in the preservation of ethnic popular culture is evident from a reading of the article "Folklore," written by Roger D. Abrahams, in Thernstrom et al., eds., *Harvard Encyclopedia*, 370–379. Paradoxically, religion has been an element that has bound some ethnic groups, such as the Irish and the Poles, together, while generating faults lines among others, such as the Germans and American Indians. Edward R. Vollmar, comp., *The Catholic Church in America: An Historical Bibliography* (New York: Scarecrow Press, 1963) and Joseph M. White, "Historiography of Catholic Immigrants and Religion," *Immigration History Newsletter* 14 (November 1982): 5–11, provide entree to the literature on the most numerically significant religious group. Herberg's *Protestant, Catholic, Jew*, as already noted, sees civic religion as the ultimate melting pot. Gerhard Lenski, *The Religious Factor: A Sociologist's Inquiry* (Garden City, NY: Doubleday, 1963), provides a coherent conceptual framework, while John Wilson, *Religion in American Society: The Effective Presence* (Englewood Cliffs, NJ: Prentice-Hall, 1978), makes a strong case for religions importance. John Tracy Ellis, *American Catholicism* (Chicago: Univ. of Chicago Press, 1969); Nathan Glazer, *American Judaism* (Chicago: Univ. of Chicago Press, 1972); and Winthrop S. Hudson, *American Protestantism* (Chicago: Univ. of Chicago Press, 1961), are three cogent overviews. James G. Moseley, *A Cultural History of Religion in America* (Westport, CT:

Greenwood Press, 1981), surveys religion as an aspect of national culture. Sydney E. Ahlstrom, *A Religious History of the American People* (New Haven, CT: Yale Univ. Press, 1972), and Winthrop S. Hudson, *Religion in America* (New York: Scribner, 1965), are comprehensive overviews that focus on the changing character of American religious culture. Martin E. Marty, *Righteous Empire: The Protestant Experience in America* (New York: Dial Press, 1970), illuminates the evolution of the country's core denominations and their response to new religious traditions. Four books authored or coedited by Robert N. Bellah, *Religion in America* (Boston: Houghton Mifflin, 1968); *The New Religious Consciousness* (Berkeley and Los Angeles: Univ. of California Press, 1976); *Varieties of Civil Religion* (San Francisco: Harper & Row, 1980); and *The Broken Covenant: American Civil Religion in Time of Trial* (New York: Seabury Press, 1975) document the rise of civil religion in the United States.

Randall M. Miller and Thomas D. Marzik, eds., *Immigrants and Religion in Urban America* (Philadelphia: Temple Univ. Press, 1977) includes eight essays on various ethnic religious experiences. Besides Abramson, *Ethnic Diversity in Catholic America*, the Catholic experience has been examined thoroughly by Richard M. Linkh, *American Catholicism and European Immigrants, 1900–1924* (Staten Island, NY: Center for Migration Studies, 1975); Jay P. Dolan, *The Immigrant Church: New York's Irish and German Catholics, 1815–1865* (Baltimore: Johns Hopkins Univ. Press, 1975); and Aaron Abell, *American Catholicism and Social Action: A Search for Social Justice, 1865–1900* (Garden City, NY: Hanover House, 1960). The Scandinavian experience can be discovered in several works: Paul C. Nyholm, *The Americanization of the Danish Lutheran Churches in America* (Copenhagen: Institute for Danish Church History, 1963); Enok Mortensen, *The Danish Lutheran Church in America* (Philadelphia: Board of Publication, Lutheran Church in America, 1967); George W. Stephenson, *The Religious Aspects of Swedish Immigration: A Study of the Immigrant Churches* (New York: AMS Press, 1972); Ralph J. Jelkanen, ed., *The Faith of the Finns: Historical Perspectives on the Finnish Lutheran Church in America* (East Lansing: Michigan State Univ. Press, 1972); and Eugene L. Fevold, *The Lutheran Church among Norwegian-Americans: A History of the Evangelical Lutheran Church*, 2 vols. (Minneapolis: Augsburg Pub. House, 1960). The Polish religious experience is captured best in Daniel Buczek, *Immigrant Pastor* (Waterbury, CT: Heminway Corp., 1974) and Anthony J. Kuzniewski, *Faith and Fatherland: The Polish Church Wars in Wisconsin, 1896–1918* (Notre Dame, IN: Univ. of Notre Dame Press, 1980). The Jewish experience is also covered well in Marshall Sklare, *Conservative Judaism* (New York: Schocken Books, 1972) and Charles S. Liebman, *Aspects of the Religious Behavior of American Jews* (New York: Ktav Pub. House, 1974).

For most ethnic groups, the adaptation process has been accomplished largely through the mechanism of a variety of sociocultural institutions that have served as "compression chambers" between the traditional society and culture and that of the mainstream. Although frequently denounced by nativists and assimilationists as "un-American" and separatist, most of these institutions have actually facilitated the transition from immigrant or racial minority to ethnic American by allowing each individual to acculturate and assimilate at the pace and to the degree the person desired and that mainstream America permitted. Whether these institutions were Old World transplants, copies of those founded by earlier arrivals, or *de novo* creations, they generally passed through a process of evolution from regional through national to hyphenated-American orientation. Most weathered crises over such issues as the substitution of English for the mother tongue or the membership status of partners in an exogamous marriage, if they endured. Many disappeared with the first generation, while others persisted, in constantly evolving form, through several generations. As late as 1975, Lubomyr R. Wynar et al. eds., *Encyclopedic Directory of Ethnic Organizations in the United States* (Littleton, CO: Libraries Unlimited, 1975) still insisted that there were nearly 1,500 viable ethnic organizations representing over seventy distinct ethnic groups. If anything, the accelerated immigration of the past fifteen years has probably increased their number. Daniel J. Elazar, *Community and Polity: The Organizational Dynamics of American Jewry* (Philadelphia: Jewish Publication Society of America, 1976), analyzes the five spheres of Jewish community activity: religious-congregational, educational-cultural, community relations, communal-welfare, and Zionist, over time. Peter I. Rose, ed., *The Ghetto and Beyond: Essays On Jewish Life in America* (New York: Random House, 1969) contains twenty-seven scholarly essays on various institutions that define both the internal life of the American Jewish community and their relationship to other Americans. The significance of one long-standing ethnic organization is related in Naomi W. Cohen, *Not Free To Desist: The American Jewish Committee, 1906–1966* (Philadelphia: Jewish Publication Society of America, 1972). Thomas P. Christensen, *A History of the Danes in Iowa* (New York: Arno Press, 1979); O. Fritiof Ander, *The Cultural Heritage of the Swedish Immigrant: Selected References* (Rock Island, IL: Augustana College Library, 1956); and Ralph J. Jalkenen, ed., *The Finns in North America: A Social Symposium* (Hancock: Michigan State Univ. Press, 1969) provide a sense of the rich diversity of Scandinavian American institutional life. Ivan H. Light, *Ethnic Enterprise in America: Business and Welfare among Chinese, Japanese, and Blacks* (Berkeley: Univ. of California Press, 1972), examines credit associations, business leagues, church societies, and mutual aid and fraternal insurance organizations among those three groups. Maxine Schwartz Seller, ed., *Ethnic Theatre in the United States* (Westport, CT: Greenwood Press, 1983) includes many selections that document the variety and importance of that particular institution to various cultures. Perry R. Duis, *The Saloon: Public Drinking in Chicago and Boston, 1880–1920* (Urbana: Univ. of Illinois Press, 1983), amply demonstrates the social and cultural significance of that urban institution to a variety of ethnic groups. Nearly every general history of any ethnic group devotes at least a chapter to its institutions.

Few institutions have been more critical in the adaptation process than has the ethnic press. Frequently challenging the mainstream press for circulation in the heyday of migration, most ethnic newspapers and periodicals eventually fell victim to the loss of the language facility, the passage of generations, and the economics of publishing. However, Lubomyr R. and Anna T. Wynar, eds., *Encyclopedic Directory of Ethnic Newspapers and Periodicals in the United States* (Littleton, CO: Libraries Unlimited, 1975) estimate that there were still nearly 1,500 ethnic newspapers and periodicals in the mid-1970s. Their analysis should be compared to *The Ethnic Press in the United States: Lists of Foreign Language, Nationality and Ethnic Newspapers and Periodicals in the United States* (New York: Greenwood Press, 1974), published by the American Council for Nationalities Service. Sally M. Miller, ed., *The Ethnic Press in the United States: A Historical Analysis and Handbook* (New York: Greenwood Press, 1987) contains analytical essays on the publications of twenty-seven different ethnic groups. Rita J. Simon, *Public Opinion and the Immigrant: Print Media Coverage, 1880–1980* (Lexington, MA: Lexington Books, 1985), is concerned primarily with how the mainstream press viewed newcomers, while Robert F. Hueston, *The Catholic Press and Nativism, 1840–1860* (New

York: Arno Press, 1976), concentrates on how one segment of the ethnic press defended its constituents against prejudice and discrimination. Isaac Metzker, ed., *A Bintel Brief* (Garden City, NY: Doubleday, 1971) provides translations of scores of letters written by Jewish immigrants to the *New York Daily Forward* that express, eloquently, the myriad problems and frustrations of adaptation.

Equally central to the adaptation process has been the practice of ethnocultural politics. Given the existence of a decentralized political system with myraid loci of power, ethnic groups have been able to capture control of various locales and to utilize that leverage to gain much of what the socioeconomic order might otherwise have denied them. Given the reality of political parties without discipline and without program and of election contests that were largely nonideological struggles for power and office, selecting candidates or affiliating with a party because of its ethnocultural orientation or its positions on issues of ethnocultural salience made as much sense as did any other strategy. Ethnocultural conflict clearly galvanized nineteenth-century voters far more than did any other category of questions, while ethnocultural divisions defined the differences between the major political parties as well or better than any alternative explanation. Not surprisingly, then, the task of defining and evaluating the contours and meaning of American ethnic politics has engaged the talents and concerns of political scientists and historians.

The importance of ethnocultural identification and behavior in American political history was first stated explicitly by Lee Benson, *The Concept of Jacksonian Democracy: New York as a Test Case* (Princeton, NJ: Princeton Univ. Press, 1970), who challenged the prevailing views of Jacksonian era politics as a conflict among socioeconomic classes. Michael F. Holt, *Forging a Majority: The Formation of the Republican Party in Pittsburgh, 1848–1860* (New Haven, CT: Yale Univ. Press, 1969), and *The Political Crisis of the 1850s* (New York: Wiley, 1978) emphasizes the interaction between racial and ethnic politics. Ronald P. Formisano, *The Birth of Mass Political Parties, Michigan, 1827–1861* (Princeton, NJ: Princeton Univ. Press, 1971), makes the same point about a crucial northern state. Richard Jensen, *The Winning of the Midwest: Social and Political Conflict, 1888–1896* (Chicago: Univ. of Chicago Press, 1971), and Paul Kleppner, *The Cross of Culture: A Social Analysis of Midwestern Politics, 1850–1900* (New York: Free Press, 1970), both stress the importance of religious affiliation to political issues and alignments. Joel H. Silbey and Samuel T. McSeveney, eds., *Voters, Parties, and Elections: Quantitative Essays in the History of American Popular Voting Behavior* (Lexington, MA: Xerox College Pub, 1972) contains twenty-four essays, most of which focus on ethnocultural politics. For a cogent discussion of the strengths and weaknesses of ethnocultural interpretations of American political history, see Richard L. McCormick, *The Party Period and Public Policy: American Politics from the Age of Jackson to the Progressive Era* (New York: Oxford Univ. Press, 1986). Much of the theoretical analysis of ethnocultural conflict was provided by political scientists, beginning with the treatment by Robert Dahl, *Pluralist Democracy in the United States: Conflict and Consensus* (Chicago: Rand McNally, 1967), who sees ethnicity as one of the key "cross-cutting cleavages" that influence political choice. Edgar Litt, *Beyond Pluralism: Ethnic Politics in America* (Glenview, IL: Scott, Foresman, 1970), discusses the persistent, social, individual, and organizational base of ethnic politics, its patterns and varieties, and focuses on case studies of Irish, Jewish, and African Americans. Thomas J. Pavlak, *Ethnic Identification and Political Behavior* (San Francisco: R and E Research Associates, 1976), and Harold R. Isaacs, *Idols of the Tribe:*

Group Identity and Political Change (New York: Harper & Row, 1975), both examine the important role played by politics in the formation of individual and group identity. Michael Walzer, Edward R. Kantowicz, John Higham, and Mona Harrington, *The Politics of Ethnicity* (Cambridge, MA: Belknap Press, 1982), examine pluralism, loyalties, leadership, and voting behavior in the context of ethnic politics. Perry L. Weed, *The White Ethnic Movement and Ethnic Politics* (New York: Praeger Publishers, 1973), examines the role of resurgent ethnic community organizations in the reemergence of ethnic politics and analyzes the latter's impact on the two major political parties.

Numerous anthologies deal with the variety and importance of ethnic politics. Lawrence H. Fuchs, ed., *American Ethnic Politics* (New York: Harper & Row, 1968) includes a dozen essays on the operation of ethnocultural politics. Harry A. Bailey, Jr., and Ellis Katz, eds., *Ethnic Group Politics* (Columbus, OH: Merrill, 1969) contains over two dozen treaties on ethnic political behavior, its importance in urban politics, and its persistence. Brett W. Hawkins and Robert A. Lorinskas, eds., *The Ethnic Factor in American Politics* (Columbus, OH: Merrill, 1970) features ten essays on ethnicity as a durable social and political instrument, ethnic voting and policy attitudes, and ethnicity's impact on political forms and policy outputs. Mark R. Levy and Michael S. Kramer, *The Ethnic Factor: How America's Minorities Decide Elections* (New York: Simon and Schuster, 1972), examines the political behavior of African, Mexican, Jewish, Irish, Slavic, and Italian Americans. S. J. Makielski, Jr., *Beleaguered Minorities: Cultural Politics in America* (San Francisco: W. H. Freeman, 1973), focuses on the political status of African and Mexican Americans and American Indians.

Several other works focus on the ethnic politics of a particular locale or a specific group. Roger E. Wyman, *Voting Behavior in the Progressive Era: Wisconsin as a Case Study* (Ann Arbor, MI: Univ. of Michigan Press, 1975), argues convincingly that ethnocultural politics persisted during the ideological and socioeconomic furor of the reformist era in that critical state. Thomas W. Henderson, *Tammany Hall and the New Immigrants: The Progressive Years* (New York: Arno Press, 1976), gives a mixed review to the efforts of America's most formidable Democratic political machine. John M. Allswang, *A House for All Peoples: Ethnic Politics in Chicago, 1890–1936* (Lexington: Univ. Press of Kentucky, 1971), demonstrates why its midwestern counterpart was eventually much more successful. Angela T. Pienkos, ed., *Ethnic Politics in Urban America: The Polish Experience in Four Cities* (Chicago: Polish American Historical Association, 1978), evaluates the performance of Poles in the politics of Buffalo, Detroit, Milwaukee, and Chicago. See also Edward R. Kantowicz, *Polish-Americans Politics in Chicago, 1888–1940* (Chicago: Univ. of Chicago Press, 1975). Jon Wefald, *A Voice of Protest: Norwegians in American Politics* (Northfield, MN: Norwegian-American Historical Association, 1971), argues for the effectiveness and progressivism of that Scandinavian group. Lawrence H. Fuchs, *The Political Behavior of American Jews* (Glencoe, IL: Free Press, 1956), and Nathaniel Weyl, *The Jew In American Politics* (New Rochelle, NY: Arlington House, 1968), are both chronological surveys of that group's political odyssey. Henry L. Feingold's *The Politics of Rescue: The Roosevelt Administration and the Holocaust, 1938–1945* (New Brunswick, NJ: Rutgers Univ. Press, 1970) is a critical examination of the most important issue in Jewish American politics. For studies of Irish, German, African, Mexican, and Italian ethnic politics, see the bibliographical essay at the end of each relevant chapter.

Four important books deal with the salience of ethnocultural politics to the resurgence of the Democratic party in the New Deal coalition of the 1930s: Samuel Lubell, *The Fu-*

408 ■ Bibliographical Essay

ture of American Politics (New York: Harper & Row, 1965); J. Joseph Huthmacher, *Mass-achusetts People and Politics, 1914–1933* (Cambridge, MA: Belknap Press, 1959); David Burner, *The Politics of Provincialism: The Democratic Party in Transition, 1918–1932* (New York: Knopf, 1968); and Allen J. Lichtman, *Prejudice and the Old Politics: The Presidential Election of 1928* (Chapel Hill: Univ. of North Carolina Press, 1979). Louis Gerson, *The Hyphenate in Recent American Politics and Diplomacy* (Lawrence: Univ. of Kansas Press, 1964), stresses the persisting importance of Old World political issues in American politics. For a discussion of how American immigration policy activates ethnocultural politics, see Robert A. Divine, *American Immigration Policy, 1924–1952* (New York: Da Capo Press, 1972).

In no other arena has the adaptation process of ethnic minorities generated more bitter and prolonged conflict and produced more ambiguity and soul-searching than in the realm of formal education. "The school," according to two prominent historians of education, "is central to the immigrant epic." Immigrants and other ethnic minorities founded a series of parochial school systems running from kindergarten through graduate and professional school that sometimes educated one-fifth to one-fourth of the country's schoolchildren—and it reached a far higher percentage in many locales. While these parochial schools markedly eased the adaptive process for millions of children, they themselves became the objects of great controversy for ethnocultural, religious, political/financial, and ideological reasons. The majority of ethnic children were acculturated in the country's public schools, which were charged with a variety of tasks, from equipping them with the knowledge and skills to become productive and prosperous to inculcating the values of citizenship and social behavior. It was primarily in the public schools that ethnic youngsters daily confronted mainstream language, values, and culture and measured them against those of family, church, and neighborhood.

Prior to the 1960s, there was a prevailing consensus that the public schools had generally adjusted well to meeting the changing needs of a variety of ethnic groups (primarily European immigrants and their descendants) and that these groups, in turn, had utilized public education as a vehicle for significant social mobility. From that it followed, logically and ideologically, that schools would perform the same integrative function for racial minorities and for newer immigrants. The most complete expression of this credo is Ellwood P. Cubberley, *Public Education in the United States* (New York: Houghton Mifflin Company, 1919). This sanguine view was initially challenged by Bernard Bailyn, *Education in the Forming of American Society* (Chapel Hill: Univ. of North Carolina Press, 1960), in which he chastised the Cubberley school for producing "the parasitic *literature of* a powerful academic ecclesia." It was followed soon by Lawrence Cremin, *The Wonderful World of Ellwood Patterson Cubberley* (New York: Bureau of Publications, Teachers College, Columbia Univ., 1965), and by his three-volume *American Education* (New York: Harper Row, 1970, 1980, 1988). The relatively moderate revisionism of Bailyn and Cremin quickly gave rise to a thoroughgoing radical critique that viewed public education primarily as the instrument by which an economic, social, and cultural elite established and maintained hegemony over the rest of society, especially the ethnic working class, destroying its members' various cultures and condemning them to a position of virtual indentured servitude. The list of revisionist publications that espoused some variation of the radical revisionist critique is long and impressive: Colin Greer, *The Great School Legend: A Revisionist Interpretation of American Public Education* (New York: Basic Books, 1972); David Nasaw, *Schooled to Order: A Social History of Public School-*

ing in the United States (New York: Oxford Univ. Press, 1979); David B. Tyack, *The One Best System: A History of American Urban Education* (Cambridge, MA: Harvard Univ. Press, 1974); Robert Carlson, *The Quest for Conformity: Americanization through Education* (New York: Wiley, 1975); Michael Katz, *The Irony of Early School Reform* (Cambridge, MA: Harvard Univ. Press, 1968); and Stanley K. Schultz, *The Culture Factory: Boston Public Schools, 1789–1860* (New York: Oxford Univ. Press, 1973). Although their views have been severely challenged by Diane Ravitch, *The Revisionists Revised: A Critique of the Radical Attack on The Schools* (New York: Basic Books, 1978), the perception of the public schools as cultural battlegrounds and agents of social conformity remains widely held. Much additional literature may be located in Francesco Cordasco, ed., *Immigrant Children in American Schools: A Classified Annotated Bibliography with Selected Source Documents* (Fairfield, NJ: A. M. Kelly, 1976).

The persisting nature of cultural and class conflict in the schools is also conveyed in a number of other works. Bernard J. Weiss, ed., *American Education and the European Immigrant, 1840–1940* (Urbana: Univ. of Illinois Press, 1982) contains over a dozen essays that deal mostly with the impact of American schooling, at all levels, on various ethnic peoples. Lawrence Cremin, *The Transformation of the School: Progressivism in American Education, 1876–1975* (New York: Knopf, 1961), elucidates the strong nativist, acculturationist bias in progressive education. Meyer Weinberg, *A Chance to Learn: The History of Race and Education in the United States* (Cambridge, MA: Cambridge Univ. Press, 1977) makes implicit comparisons among ethnic groups with regard to educational access and payoff. Ronald K. Goodenow and Diane Ravitch, eds., *Schools in Cities: Consensus and Conflict in American Educational History* (New York: Holmes & Meier, 1983) contains eleven essays that explore similar topics in a variety of locales. And Ruth M. Elson, *Guardians of Tradition: American Schoolbooks of the 19th Century* (Lincoln: Univ. of Nebraska Press, 1964), examines one of the issues that generated fierce and protracted ethnocultural conflict in the school system.

Several other works, most of which incorporate many of the tenets of the revisionists, whether liberal or radical, concentrate on the educational experiences of a particular place or a specific ethnic group. Even Diane Ravitch adopts much of that viewpoint and terminology in her *The Great School Wars, New York City, 1805–1973: A History of the Public Schools as Battlefield of Social Change* (New York: Basic Books, 1974). Ronald D. Cohen, *Children of the Mill: School and Society in Gary, Indiana, 1906–1960* (Bloomington: Indiana Univ. Press, 1990), examines the long-term effects of the city's "work-study-play" system on various ethnic groups. Cohen and Raymond A. Mohl also collaboratively critique the Gary Plan in *The Paradox of Progressive Education: The Gary Plan of Urban Schooling* (Port Washington, NY: Kennikat Press, 1979). Focusing on another era of educational reform in a different setting is Marvin F. Lazerson, *Origins of the Urban School: Public Education in Massachusetts, 1870–1915* (Cambridge, MA: Harvard Univ. Press, 1971). Carl F. Kaestle, *The Evolution of an Urban School System: New York City, 1750–1850* (Cambridge, MA: Harvard Univ. Press, 1977), covers the fifty years prior to the scope of Ravitch's *Great School Wars*, while Sherry Gorelick, *City College and the Jewish Poor: Education in New York, 1880–1924* (New Brunswick, NJ: Rutgers Univ. Press, 1981), concentrates on that city's most enthusiastic consumers of public education. Alexander M. Dushkin, *Jewish Education in New York City* (New York: Bureau of Jewish Education, 1918) is a classic eyewitness account.

James W. Sanders, *The Education of an Urban Minority: Catholics in Chicago,*

1833–1965 (New York: Oxford Univ. Press, 1977), finds that the city's parochial schools, ironically enough, were more effective agents of "Americanization" than were its public schools. The passion of Scandinavians for education, especially under their own auspices, is apparent in Enok Mortensen, *Schools for Life: A Danish-American Experiment in Adult Education* (Askov, Denmark: Danish-American Heritage Society, 1977), a history of the Grundtvigian folk schools; William E. Christensen, *Saga of the Tower: A History of Dana College and Trinity Seminary* (Blair, NE: Lutheran Pub. House, 1959); Thorvald Hansen, *We Laid Foundations Here: The Early History of Grand View College* (Des Moines, IA: Grandview College, 1972); and Leigh D. Jordahl and Harris E. Kaasa, *Stability and Change: Luther College in Its Second Century* (Decorah, IA: Luther College Press, 1986). Information regarding the educational experiences of other specific ethnic groups can be gleaned from the sources included in the bibliographical essay at the end of each chapter. For brief general overviews, see Handlin, *The Uprooted*, 244–249; Bodnar, *The Transplanted*, 189–197; and Kraut, *Huddled Masses*, 133–141.

Regardless of origin or time and method of arrival, every single American ethnic group was, for a time at least, the victim of prejudice and discrimination that frequently culminated in paradoxical campaigns to forcibly acculturate them while seeking to send them "back to where they came from." Contrary to the intent of "Americanizers," forced acculturation drives generally retarded the adaptation process, as ethnic groups determined to resist such campaigns with all their might. And while most Euro-Americans found that partial assimilation, as least, was the reward for acculturation, racial minorities were generally held separate to a great degree, no matter how quickly and completely they attempted to acculturate. Philip Davis and Bertha Schwartz, eds., *Immigration and Americanization* (New York: Ginn and Company, 1920), is an anthology of works by various scholars and politicians on the effects of immigration of different groups and on the desirability of restriction and Americanization. Kate Holladay Claghorn, *The Immigrant's Day in Court* (New York: Arno Press, 1969), analyzes the difficulties encountered by newcomers in the legal and governmental system as a measurement of acculturation. Edward G. Hartmann's *The Movement to Americanize the Immigrant* (New York: Columbia Univ. Press, 1948) is a straightforward account of forced acculturation. Paul Boyer, *Urban Masses and Moral Order in America, 1820–1920* (Cambridge, MA: Harvard Univ. Press, 1978), contends that much of the urban reform movement of that century was motivated by an attempt to impose upon the unruly and diverse masses of the city the putative moral order of the American village. Barbara M. Solomon, *Ancestors and Immigrants: A Changing New England Tradition* (Cambridge, MA: Harvard Univ. Press, 1956), focuses on the efforts of the Immigration Restriction League to stop the influx of "undesirable" immigrants. Ray Allen Billington, *The Protestant Crusade, 1800–1860* (New York: Macmillan, 1938) is a richly detailed account of the Know-Nothing nativist movement against Catholic immigrants. John Higham, *Strangers in the Land: Patterns of American Nativism, 1860–1925* (New Brunswick, NJ: Rutgers Univ. Press, 2002), picks up the story where Billington leaves off and carries it through to the passage of the National Origins Quota Act. Gerd Korman, *Industrialization, Immigrants, and Americanizers: The View from Milwaukee* (Madison: State Historical Society of Wisconsin, 1967), examines the efforts of zenophobes, uplifters, and industrialists in the Cream City to acculturate their polyglot workforce in the name of efficiency and patriotism. Paul McBride, *Culture Clash: Immigrants and Reformers, 1880–1920* (San Francisco: R and E Research Associates, 1975), accuses both the Young Men's Christian Association and the social settlements of promoting forced acculturation. Allen F. Davis, *Spearheads for Reform: The Social Settlements and the Progressive Movement, 1890–1914* (New York: Oxford Univ. Press, 1967), argues strongly that some social settlements genuinely respected the ethnic heritage of their constituents and helped them retain a great deal of it. Stuart C. Miller, *The Unwelcome Immigrant: The American Image of the Chinese* (Berkeley: Univ. of California Press, 1969), attributes anti-Chinese hostility to a clash of extremely contrasting values and culture. Alexander Saxton, *The Indispensable Enemy: Labor and the Anti-Chinese Movement in California* (Berkeley: Univ. of California Press, 1971), argues that the experience of Chinese immigrant workers was more similar to that of African Americans than to that of European immigrants and that the United States has always had a racial definition of nationality. Robert J. Wechman and David M. Zielonka, *The Eager Immigrants: A Survey of the Life and Americanization of Jewish Immigrants to the United States* (Champaign, IL: Stipes Publishing Company, 1972), asserts that American Jews have retained their religiocultural identity while becoming "typically American" in appearance, language, dress, interests, occupations, attitudes, values, and names.

Even while striving to adapt to the pressures for forced acculturation coming from mainstream America, ethnic groups also have contended with one another for recognition, acceptance, and material benefits. Pitted against one another in a critical competition for housing, employment, education, and other necessities of life, ethnic groups have frequently developed strong negative stereotypes about one another. Some ethnic groups have also sought to deflect prejudice directed against them onto other peoples, a strategy that also sometimes curried favor with nativists and racists. Donald E. Gelfand and Russell D. Lee, *Ethnic Conflicts and Power: A Cross National Perspective* (New York: Wiley, 1973), demonstrate that this phenomenon is not limited to the United States. Arnold Rose and Caroline Rose, *America Divided: Minority Group Relations in the United States* (New York: A. A. Knopf, 1959), examines the legal, economic, and political status of ethnic minorities, their identification, morale, and organization, and the psychology of prejudice. Richard A. Schermerhorn, *Comparative Ethnic Relations: A Framework for Theory and Research* (New York: Random House, 1970), attempts to posit a sociology of intergroup relations. Robin M. Williams, *Strangers Next Door: Ethnic Relations in American Communities* (Englewood Cliffs, NJ: Prentice-Hall, 1964), analyzes the psychological and social bases of ethnocentrism, prejudice, and intergroup conflict. Peter I. Rose, *They and We: Racial and Ethnic Relations in the United States* (New York: Random House, 1964), discusses race, ethnicity and social status, the nature of prejudice, and varying reactions to discrimination. Milton L. Barron, ed., *Minorities in a Changing World* (New York: Knopf, 1967), looks at ethnic differentiation and inequality in American society and at various techniques for bettering ethnic relations. In *Ethnic Groups in Conflict*, Donald L. Horowitz (Berkeley: Univ. of California Press, 1985) posits a theory of ethnic conflict and strategies for reduction of that conflict, while John Slawson and Marc Vosk, *Unequal Americans: Practices and Politics of Intergroup Relations* (Westport, CT: Greenwood Press, 1979), examines the principles for treating problems in intergroup relations and analyzes the methods used in preventing them.

More concrete and focused are a number of studies that deal directly with the interaction among specific ethnic groups. Charles F. Marden and Gladys Meyer, *Minorities in American Society* (New York: American Book Co., 1968), deals primarily with African, Mexican, Chinese, Jewish, and Indian Americans. Charlotte Brooks, ed., *The Outnumbered: Stories, Essays, and Poems about Minority Groups by America's Leading Writers*

(New York: Delacorte Press, 1969) compares Americans of African, Irish, Jewish, and Indian descent. Bruce A. Glasrud and Alan M. Smith, eds., *Promises to Keep: A Portrayal of Non-Whites in the United States* (Chicago: Rand McNally, 1972), focuses on African, Mexican, Chinese, and Indian Americans. Stanley Lieberson's *A Piece of the Pie: Blacks and White Immigrants since 1880* (Berkeley: Univ. of California Press, 1980) is strong on the similarities and differences between the two. Everett C. and Helen M. Hughes, *Where Peoples Meet: Racial and Ethnic Frontiers* (Glencoe, IL: The Free Press, 1952) delineates the areas where both interaction and conflict frequently occur. Rudolf Glanz, *Jew and Italian: Historical Group Relations and The New Immigration, 1881–1924* (New York: KTAU Publishing House, 1972) concentrates on the interplay between the two largest segments of the turn-of-the-century immigration. Thomas Kessner, *The Golden Door: Italian and Jewish Immigrant Mobility in New York City, 1880–1915* (New York: Oxford Univ. Press, 1977), explores two different routes to "the good life." Ronald H. Bayor, *Neighbors in Conflict: The Irish, Germans, Jews, and Italians of New York City, 1919–1941* (Baltimore: Johns Hopkins Univ. Press, 1978), finds that the key element in initiating interethnic conflict is a perceived sense of threat. Carlos E. Cortes et al., *Three Perspectives on Ethnicity: Blacks, Chicanos, and Native Americans* (New York: Putnam, 1976) compares the adaptive strategies of these three groups. George Eaton Simpson and Milton J. Yinger, *Racial and Cultural Minorities: An Analysis of Prejudice and Discrimination* (New York: Harper & Row, 1965), examines prejudice and discrimination as weapons in group conflict. Edward C. McDonogh and Eugene S. Richards, *Ethnic Relations in the United States* (New York: Appleton Century-Crofts, 1953), compare the nature of African, Jewish, Mexican, Chinese, Indian, and Euro-Americans with respect to their social, educational, legal, and economic status. Brewton Berry, *Race and Ethnic Relations* (Boston: Houghton Mifflin, 1965), explores what happens when people who differ racially and culturally come into contact with one another. Ande Manners, *Poor Cousins* (New York: Coward, McCann & Geoghegan, 1972), portrays the initial intragroup conflict and eventual amalgamation of Germans and eastern European Jewish Americans. Finally, J. Anthony Lukas, *Common Ground: A Turbulent Decade in the Lives of Three American Families* (New York: Knopf, 1985), sensitively and perceptively portrays the conflict among Yankees, and African, and Irish Americans over the issue of busing for school integration in Boston.

ADDENDUM FOR THE SECOND EDITION

The vast outpouring of literature on ethnicity, acculturation, and assimilation that erupted during the 1970s has not abated during the twelve years since the publication of the first edition of *Multiculturalism in the United States* in 1992. Much of that literature is captured in the bibliographical essays at the end of each chapter in the second edition, some of which have been updated from the first edition and others of which appear for the first time. Since each of those bibliographical essays focuses on the literature pertaining to a specific ethnic group, however, we have felt it necessary to inform readers of additions to the literature since 1992 that have a wider focus and that deal with analysis, synthesis, interpretation, theory, methods, and processes.

Several of these more recent works present challenging reinterpretations and syntheses of America's multiethnic, multicultural experience: David Hollinger, *Postethnic America: Beyond Multiculturalism* (New York: Basic Books, 1995); Ronald Takaki, *A Different Mirror: A History of Multicultural America* (Boston: Little, Brown & Co., 1993); Silvia

Pedraza, *Origins and Destinies: Immigration, Race, and Ethnicity in America* (Belmont, CA: Wadsworth, 1996); David W. Haines, *Manifest Destinies: Americanizing Immigrants and Internationalizing Immigrants* (Westport, CT: Praeger, 2003); Ronald Bayor, *Race and Ethnicity in America: A Concise History* (New York: Columbia Univ. Press, 2003); and Ruben Rumbaut and Alejandro Portes, eds., *Immigrant America: A Portrait*, 2nd ed. (Berkeley: Univ. of California Press, 1996). Also thought-provoking are Joel Millman, *The Other Americans: How Immigrants Renew Our Country, Our Economy, and Our Values* (New York: Viking Press, 1993); Robert H. Tai, *Critical Ethnicity: Countering the Wave of Identity Politics* (Lanham, MD: Rowman & Littlefield, 1999); William C. Fisher, *Identity, Community, and Pluralism in American Life* (New York: Oxford Univ. Press, 1997); and David Levinson and Melvin Ember, *American Immigrant Cultures: Builders of a Nation* (New York: Macmillan Reference, 1997). Equally interesting in their approach are Timothy B. Powell, *Ruthless Democracy: A Multicultural Interpretation of the American Renaissance* (Princeton, NJ: Princeton Univ. Press, 2000); Nancy A. Denton and Stewart Emory Tolnay, *American Diversity: A Demographic Challenge for the Twentieth-First Century* (Albany: State Univ. of New York Press, 2002); Wendy Katkin and Ned Landsman, *Beyond Pluralism: The Conception of Groups and Group Identities in America* (Urbana: Univ. of Illinois Press, 1998); and Diane Shaver Clemens and Richard Allen, *The Forging of America: A Cultural Diversity Reader* (New York: McGraw-Hill, 1993). Particularly valuable for its historical perspective is the fourth edition of Leonard Dinnerstein and David M. Reimers, *Ethnic America: A History of Immigration* (New York: Basic Books, 1999).

Closely related to the above works are a number that focus on clarifying our understanding of the nature and meaning of those elusive terms *ethnicity* and *race*. Many of these books examine the essence of both concepts in some form of comparative analysis: Stephen Steinberg, ed., *Race and Ethnicity in the United States: Issues and Debates* (Malden, MA: Blackwell Publishers, 2000); Michael Hughey, *New Tribalisms: The Resurgence of Race and Ethnicity* (New York: New York Univ. Press, 1998); Michael P. Smith and Joe Feagin, *The Bubbling Cauldron: Race, Ethnicity, and the Urban Crisis* (Minneapolis: Univ. of Minnesota Press, 1995); Alma M. Garcia and Richard Garcia, *Race and Ethnicity* (San Diego, CA: Greenhaven Press, 2001); Georgia Anne Persons, *Race and Ethnicity in Comparative Perspective* (New Brunswick, NJ: Rutgers Univ. Press, 1999); Nancy Foner and George Fredrickson, *Not Just Black and White: Historical and Contemporary Perspectives on Immigration, Race, and Ethnicity in the United States* (New York: Russell Sage Foundation, 2004); Dvora Yanow, *Constructing "Race" and "Ethnicity" in America: Category-Making in Public Policy and Administration* (Armonk, NY: M. E. Sharpe, 2003); and Stephen H. Legomsky, *E Pluribus Unum: Immigration, Race, and Other Deep Divides* (St. Louis, MO: Washington University School of Law, 1996). Approaching the issue from a more top-down perspective is Eric P. Kramer, *The Rise and Fall of Anglo-America* (Cambridge, MA: Harvard Univ. Press, 2004).

Three other books reexamine the concept of race by itself: Eric Kramer, *Postmodernism and Race* (Westport, CT: Praeger, 1997); *New York Times, How Race is Lived in America: Pulling Together, Pulling Apart* (New York: Times Books/Henry Holt, 2002); and Howard Bodenhorn and Christopher Ruebeck, *The Economics of Identity and the Endogeneity of Race* (Cambridge, MA: National Bureau of Economic Research, 2004). Four other scholars perform the same service for the concept of ethnicity: Timothy Walch, *Immigrant America: European Ethnicity in the United States* (New York: Garland, 1994); William Peterson, *Ethnicity Counts* (New Brunswick, NJ: Transaction Publishers, 1997); Wilbur

Zelinsky, *The Enigma of Ethnicity: Another American Dilemma* (Iowa City, IA: Univ. of Iowa City Press, 2001); and Jeffrey G. Reitz and Raymond Breton, *The Illusion of Difference: Realities of Ethnicity in Canada and the United States* (Toronto: C. D. Howe Institute, 1994). Meanwhile, three other scholars have taken another look at the role that language differences play in the construction and persistence of ethnicity: Barry R. Chiswick, *Immigration, Language, and Ethnicity: Canada and the United States* (Lanham, MD: Univ. Press of America, 1992); Philip Gleason, *Speaking of Diversity: Language and Diversity in Twentieth Century America* (Baltimore: Johns Hopkins Univ. Press, 1992); and Werner Sollors, *Multilingual America: Transnationalism, Ethnicity, and the Languages of American Literature* (New York: New York Univ. Press, 1998).

Several other scholars have continued the ongoing debate over the nature, direction, and duration of the processes of acculturation and assimilation. Some of these newer works concentrate on the impact that the United States has had on individual immigrants: Vanessa Smith Castro, *Acculturation and Psychological Adaptation* (Westport, CT: Greenwood Press, 2003); Jaswinder Singh, *Americanization of New Immigrants: People Who Come to America, What They Need to Know* (Lanham, MD: Univ. Press of America, 2002); Gregory Rodriguez, *From Newcomers to New Americans: The Successful Integration of Immigrants into American Society* (Washington, DC: National Immigration Forum, 1999); Barry Edmonston and Jeffrey Passel, *Immigration and Ethnicity: The Integration of America's New Arrivals* (Lanham, MD: Univ. Press of America, 1994); and Lee D. Baker, *Life in America: Identity and Everyday Experience* (Malden, MA: Blackwell Pub., 2004). A particularly imaginative and entertaining approach to the interaction between immigrant and American cultures is Donna Gabaccia, *We Are What We Eat: Ethnic Food and the Making of Americans* (Cambridge, MA: Harvard Univ. Press, 1998).

Thanks to the introduction of Geographic Information Systems (GIS), choropleth mapping, and TIGER boundary files, geographers have shown an increasing interest in the settlement and spatial mobility patterns of ethnic groups over time. That activity was given additional impetus when the designers of the 1980 U.S. census decided to ask one out of every six households to self-identify their ancestry in descending order of salience, thus providing an enormous data sample on which to base not only the location of specific ethnic groups but also information concerning their demographic, social, and economic characteristics. The prototype for these studies was James P. Allen and Eugene J. Turner, *We the People: An Atlas of America's Ethnic Diversity* (New York: Macmillan, 1988). Utilizing data from the 1920 and 1990 censuses, Kazimierz J. Zaniewski and Carol J. Rosen, *The Atlas of Ethnic Diversity in Wisconsin* (Madison: Univ. of Wisconsin Press, 1998), produced a comparative/historical portrait of more than sixty ethnic groups in the state, providing analyses of data on their nativity, year of entry, age and sex ratios, household income, educational attainment, and employment. Other such works of note are Richard L. Nostrand, *Homelands: A Geography of Culture and Place across America* (Baltimore: Johns Hopkins Univ. Press, 2001) and Kate A. Berry, *Geographical Identities of New Immigrants: Race, Space, and Place* (Reno: Univ. of Nevada Press, 2002).

Another group of scholars have concentrated on letting immigrants and ethnic groups tell their stories in their own words. Recording the thoughts and feelings of earlier waves of immigrants is Matthew Frye Jacobson, *Special Sorrows: The Diasporic Imagination of Irish, Polish, and Jewish Immigrants in the United States* (Cambridge, MA: Harvard Univ. Press, 1995). Focusing directly on the viewpoints of more recent arrivals are Steve Farkas, Ann Duffet, and Jean Johnson, *Now That I Am Here: What America's Immigrants Have to Say about Life In The U.S. Today* (New York: Public Agenda, 2003); Meri Nana-Ama Danquah, *Becoming American: Personal Essays by First Generation Immigrant Women* (New York: Hyperion, 2000); and Dorothy MacNevin, *We The People: A Portrait of Diversity in America* (New York: Hyperion, 1998).

As the subtitle of Danquah's *Becoming American: Personal Essays by First Generation Immigrant Women* indicates, recent scholars have continued to investigate the role that gender has played in the adaptation of ethnic groups to life in the United States. Prominent among these studies are Catherine Tobin, *The American Experience: Race, Gender, and Ethnicity* (New York: American Heritage Custom Publishing Group, 1995); Joseph F. Healy, *Diversity and Society: Race, Ethnicity, and Gender* (Thousand Oaks, CA: Pine Forge Press, 2004) and Eileen O'Brien and Joseph F. Healy, *Race, Ethnicity, and Gender: Selected Readings* (Thousand Oaks, CA: Pine Forge Press, 2004).

Nor have present-day scholars neglected the topic of families and generations in the ethnic experience. Much of the recent literature on the subject has been the product of Alejandro Portes and Ruben Rumbaut, either individually or in tandem. While Portes is the sole author of record of *The New Second Generation* (New York: Russell Sage Foundation, 1996), he and Rumbaut have collaborated on three other works dealing with different aspects of the highly problematic and controversial experience of the children of immigrants: *Transformations: The Post-Immigration Generation in an Age of Diversity* (East Lansing, MI: Michigan State University Press, 1999); *Ethnicities: Children of Immigrants in America* (Berkeley: Univ. of California Press, 2001); and *Legacies: The Story of the Immigrant Second Generation* (Berkeley: Univ. of California Press, 2001). Taking a broader approach, psychologist Stephanie Coontz, a renowned expert on family dynamics, has edited *American Families: A Multicultural Reader* (New York: Routledge, 1999).

Looking at the situation from the perspective of the impact that large-scale immigration has, and is having, on the population and culture of the nation as a whole are Eric Mark Kramer, ed., *The Emerging Monoculture: Assimilation and the "Model Minority"* (Westport, CT: Praeger, 2003) and Michael D'Innocenzo and Josef Sirefman, *American Society: "Melting Pot" or "Salad Bowl"?* (Westport, CT: Greenwood Press, 1992). Examining the changing interaction between theory and practice (or rhetoric and reality) are Joan Ferrante-Wallace and Prince Brown, *The Social Construction of Race and Ethnicity in the United States* (Upper Saddle River, NJ: Prentice-Hall, 2001) and Bill Ong Hing, *To Be An American: Cultural Pluralism and the Rhetoric of Assimilation* (New York: New York Univ. Press, 1997). Several other works focus on various aspects of the adaptation process undergone by ethnic groups over time: Alejandro Portes, ed., *Economic Sociology of Immigration: Essays on Networks, Ethnicity, and Entrepreneurship* (New York: Russell Sage Foundation, 1995); Susan K. Wierzbicki, *Beyond the Immigrant Enclave: Network Change and Assimilation* (New York: LFB Scholarly Pub., 2004); Michael J. White and Ann E. Biddlecom, *Immigration, Naturalization, and Residential Assimilation among Asian Americans* (Providence, RI: Population Studies and Training Center, Brown University, 1994); Michael W. Hughey and Arthur Vidich, *The Ethnic Quest for Community: Searching for Roots in the Lonely Crowd* (Greenwich, CT: Manning Publishing Company, 1993); and Joel Perlmann, *Reflecting the Changing Face of America: Multiracials, Racial Classification, and American Intermarriage* (Annandale-on Hudson, NY: Jerome Levy Economic Institutute, 1997). Finally, Nancy Foner, Ruben Rumbaut, and Stephen J. Gold, eds., *Immigration Research for a New Century: Multidisciplinary Per-*

spectives (New York: Russell Sage Foundation, 2000) provides us with a blueprint for the future of immigration and ethnic studies.

It is almost axiomatic to state that roughly 90 percent of immigration to the United States over the past three decades has come from Latin America and Asia and that Latinos and Asians—aggregated into generic wholes—are the two fastest growing segments of the American population. While it is almost equally axiomatic to assert that there are differences among the various components of these two multiethnic categories, it is also true that outsiders have a distinct tendency to conflate the various ethnic groups within each category according to language, geography, or "race." It is also highly likely that such treatment increasingly motivates members of disparate Asian or Latino groups to emphasize their likenesses every bit as much as their distinctiveness. The possibilities inherent in that situation are examined by William Vincent Flores and Rina Benmayor, *Latino Cultural Citizenship: Claiming Identity, Space, and Rights* (Boston: Beacon Press, 1997); Roberto Suro, *Strangers among Us: How Latino Immigration Is Transforming America* (New York: Alfred A. Knopf, 1998); and Mia Tuan, *Forever Foreigners or Honorary Whites? The Asian American Experience Today* (New Brunswick, NJ: Rutgers Univ. Press, 1998). Immigration from Latin America and Asia is also the primary focus of Elliott Robert Barkan, *And Still They Come: Immigrants and American Society, 1920 to the 1990s* (Wheeling, IL: H. Davidson, 1996); Roger D. Waldinger, *Strangers at the Gates: New Immigrants in Urban America* (Berkeley: Univ. of California Press, 2001); Reed Ueda, *Postwar Immigrant America: A Social History* (Boston: Bedford Books, 1994); and David M. Reimers, *Still the Golden Door: The Third World Comes to America* (New York: Columbia Univ. Press, 1992). Two excellent studies of the impact of recent immigration on the nation's primary reception center are Frederick M. Binder and David M. Reimers, *All the Nations Under Heaven: An Ethnic and Racial History of New York City* (New York: Columbia Univ. Press, 1995) and Roger D. Waldinger, *Still the Promised City? New Immigrants and African Americans in New York City, 1940–1990* (Cambridge, MA: Harvard Univ. Press, 1996).

Several recent works have broadened and deepened our understanding of the nature of prejudice and discrimination suffered, to different degrees, by all ethnic groups. Particularly insightful on the experience of the newest wave of immigrants is James Stuart Olson, *Equality Deferred: Race, Ethnicity, and Immigration since 1945* (Belmont, CA: Wadsworth/Thomson Learning, 2003). Especially informative on the impact of discrimination are Adalberto Aguirre, *American Ethnicity: The Dynamics and Consequences of Discrimination* (Boston: McGraw-Hill, 2001) and John W. Frazier, *Race and Place: Equity Issues in Urban America* (Boulder, CO: Westview Press, 2003). The particular forms of discrimination faced by members of minority groups in the criminal justice system are explored by Samuel Walker, Cassia Spohn, and Miriam DeLone, *The Color of Justice: Race, Ethnicity, and Crime in America* (Belmont, CA: Wadsworth/Thomson Learning, 2000). Finally, Ronald Perlmutter, *Legacy of Hate: A Short History of Ethnic, Religious, and Racial Prejudice in America* (Armonk, NY: M. E. Sharpe, 1999) sees discrimination against newcomers and "others" as endemic to America's history.

One of the remarkable trends of the past decade has been the proliferation of studies explicating the concept of "whiteness" and its importance in understanding the pace and degree of acceptance experienced by various ethnic groups throughout U.S. history. The persistent themes of most of these works are the difficulties experienced by a succession of European and other groups in trying to establish their "whiteness," and the fact that joining in the persecution of nonwhites is one of the prerequisites to being accepted as white. One of the earliest pioneers of the movement is Noel Ignatiev, coeditor with John Garvey of *Race Traitor* (New York: Routledge, 1996) and author of *How the Irish Became White* (New York: Routledge, 1995). Labor historian David Roediger, whose editorship of *Black on White: Black Writers on What it Means to Be White* (New York: Schocken Books, 1988) helped inaugurate the movement, has produced three works on the subject over the several years: *Wages of Whiteness: Race and the Making of the American Working Class* (New York: Verso, 1991); *Towards the Abolition of Whiteness: Essays on Race, Politics, and Working Class Culture* (New York: Verso, 1994); and *Colored White: Transcending the Racial Past* (Berkeley: Univ. of California Press, 2002). Mike Hill has edited *Whiteness: A Critical Reader* (New York: New York Univ. Press, 1997) and authored *After Whiteness: Unmaking an American Majority* (New York: New York Univ. Press, 2004), while Tyler Stallings has edited *Uncontrollable Bodies: Testimonies of Identity and Culture* (Seattle, WA: Bay Press, 1994) and written *Whiteness: A Wayward Construction* (Laguna Beach, CA: Laguna Art Museum, 2003).

Several recent works have concentrated on the changing construction of whiteness over time: Matthew Frye Jacobson, *Whiteness of a Different Color: European Immigrants and the Alchemy of Race* (Cambridge, MA: Harvard Univ. Press, 1998); Todd Vogel, *Rewriting White: Race, Class, and Cultural Capital in Nineteenth-Century America* (New Brunswick, NJ: Rutgers Univ. Press, 2004); and Linda Joyce Brown, *The Literature of Immigration and Racial Formation: Becoming White, Becoming Other, Becoming American in the Late Progressive Era* (New York: Routledge, 2004). The importance of whiteness in the establishment of the Jim Crow South is analyzed by Grace Elizabeth Hale, *Making Whiteness: The Culture of Segregation in the South, 1890–1940* (New York: Pantheon Books, 1998). Particularly provocative is Mason Stokes, *The Color of Sex: Whiteness, Heterosexuality, and the Fiction of White Supremacy* (Durham, NC: Duke Univ. Press, 2001). Focusing directly on the present-day situation are George Yancey, *Who Is White? Latinos, Asians, and the New Black/Non-Black Divide* (Boulder, CO: L. Rienner, 2003) and Joe L. Kincheloe and Shirley S. Steinberg, *Changing Multiculturalism* (Philadelphia: Open Univ. Press, 1997). Kincheloe also presents a telling critique of whiteness in *White Reign: Deploring Whiteness in America* (New York: St. Martin's Press, 1998).

Closely related to efforts at exploring the meaning of whiteness are studies examining the boundaries or borderlands between and among whites and nonwhites. Particularly innovative in this endeavor are Johnella Butler, *Color-Line to Borderlands: The Matrix of American Ethnic Studies* (Seattle: Univ. of Washington Press, 2001); Scott Michaelson and David Johnson, *Border Theory: The Limits of Cultural Politics* (Minneapolis: Univ. of Minnesota Press, 1997); and Michele Lamont, *The Cultural Territories of Race: Black and White Boundaries* (Chicago: Univ. of Chicago Press, 1999).

INDEX

ABOUT THE CONTRIBUTORS

James M. Bergquist is professor emeritus at Villanova University, newsletter editor and board member of the Immigration History Society, and trustee of Balch Institute for Ethnic Studies.

John D. Buenker is professor emeritus of history and ethnic studies, University of Wisconsin, Parkside. His recent publications include *Wisconsin: The Progressive Era*; *Those United States: International Perspectives on American History*; *Sources of the American Tradition: The Gilded Age and Progressive Era*; and the *Encyclopedia of the Gilded Age and Progressive Era*.

Joseph D. Buenker is assistant librarian at Arizona State University at the West Campus. He is coeditor of the *Encyclopedia of the Gilded Age*, and contributor to Research Methods for Generalist Social Work (2005). He has created or contributed to several web projects including *Diversity Web*, a series of recommended resources for the study of various ethnic groups. He is currently compiling a book-length annotated bibliography on the works of contemporary Native American author Louise Erdrich.

Dominic Candeloro is director of the Division of Extended Learning at Governors State University in Illinois and president of the American Italian Historical Association. He is the author of *Italians in Chicago* (1999) and *Chicago Heights Revisited* (2000) and of two forthcoming books—*Italians in New Orleans* and *Chicago Heights: At the Crossroads of the Nation*. All are publications of Arcadia Publisher.

John Robert Christianson is research professor of history at Luther College, a director of the Vesterheim Norwegian-American Museum, and editor of *Scandinavians in America: Literary Life*.

Vine Deloria, Jr. is professor emeritus of history at the University of Colorado, professor emeritus of political science at the University of Arizona, and former executive director of the National Congress of American Indians. Some of his more recent books are *Evolution, Creationism, and Other Modern Myths*; *Spirit and Reason*; *Red Earth, White Lies: Native Americans and the Myth of Scientific Fact*; and *Power and Place: Indian Education in America*.

Hien Duc Do is professor of sociology and chair of the social studies department at San Jose University. He is the author of *The Vietnamese Americans* and was the Ohio State University's Distinguished Lecturer in Asian American History in 2002.

Augusto Espiritu is assistant professor of history at the University of Illinois at Urbana-Champaign, where he specializes in Asian American history, twentieth-century U.S. immigration history, postcolonial studies, and Philippine history. He has published in *Amerasia Journal*; *The Asian American Encyclopedia*; and *Winds of April*. He is currently completing a book manuscript entitled *Expatriate Affirmations: The Performance of Nationalism and Patronage in Filipino-American Intellectual Life*.

Cynthia Griggs Fleming is associate professor of history and African-American studies at the University of Tennessee and the author or coauthor of three books, including *In the Shadow of Selma: The Continuing Struggle for Civil Rights in the Rural South* and *Soon We Will Not Cry: The Liberation of Ruby Doris Smith Robinson*.

Edward R. Kantowicz is a public historian based in Chicago. His latest books are *Rage of Nations*; *Coming Apart, Coming Together*; and *Kids First, Primero lo Ninos: Chicago School Reform in the 1980s*.

Karen I. Leonard is professor of anthropology at the University of California at Irvine and is the author of *Making Ethnic Choices: California's Punjabi-Mexican-Americans*; *The South Asian Americans*; and *Muslims in the United States: The State of Research*.

Lawrence J. McCaffrey is professor emeritus at Loyola University of Chicago. His most recent books include *Textures of Irish America*; *The Irish Catholic Diaspora in American*; and *The Irish Question: Two Centuries of Conflict*.

Matt S. Meier was professor emeritus of history at Santa Clara University. Included among his works are *Encyclopedia of the Mexican American Civil Rights Movement*; *Notable Latino Americans*; *Mexican American Biographies*; *Bibliographies of Mexican American History*; and *Dictionary of Mexican American History*.

Gregory Orfalea is a journalist, author, and poet who is currently director of the Writing Center at Pitzer College. Included among his publications are *Before the Flames: A Quest for the History of Arab Americans*; *Grape Leaves: A Century of Arab American Poetry*; and *Messengers of the Lost Battalion: The Heroic 551st and the Turning of the Battle of the Bulge*. His father was part of that battalion.

Kyeyoung Park is assistant professor of anthropology and Asian American studies at the University of California at Los Angeles. She has published articles in *American Anthropologist*; *Urban Anthropology*; and *Amerasia Journal*. Her first book, *The Korean American Dream: Immigrants and Small Business in New York City* was the winner of the Outstanding Book Award in History and Social Science from the Association for Asian American Studies.

George Anthony Peffer is professor of history and political science at Lakeland College and author of *If They Don't Bring Women Here: Chinese Female Immigration before Exclusion*. He is also the editor of the *Journal of Asian American Studies* and was a visiting professor at the University of Chicago during the 2003–2004 academic year.

Marc Prou is director of Caribbean studies and a faculty member in Africana studies at the University of Massachusetts at Boston. He regularly takes study groups abroad to Haiti, Jamaica, and Cuba and teaches a summer institute in Haitian Creole language and culture.

Lorman A. Ratner is professor emeritus of history, University of Tennessee, and adjunct professor of History at the University of Illinois at Urbana-Champaign. His most recent books are *Andrew Jackson and His Tennessee Lieutenants: A Study in Political Culture* and *Fanatics and Fireeaters: Newspapers and the Coming of the Civil War*.

Edward S. Shapiro is professor emeritus at Seton Hall and has contributed reviews to *Book World*. He is currently working on a book about the Crown Heights (Brooklyn) riots of 1991.

Silvio Torres-Saillant is associate professor of English and director of the Latino-Latin American Studies Program at Syracuse University. He has contributed extensively to journals on Latin America and Latinos and is the author of *Caribbean Poetics: Toward an Aesthetic of West Indian Literature*; *Dominican Americans*; and *El Retorno de las Yolas: Ensayos Sobre Diaspora, Democracia y Dominicanidad*.